Vegetable Cookery

Vegetable Cookery

Terence Janericco

VNR VAN NOSTRAND REINHOLD
_____ New York

Copyright © 1992 by Van Nostrand Reinhold

Library of Congress Catalog Card Number 91-8750
ISBN 0-442-00534-2

Printed in the United States of America

Van Nostrand Reinhold
115 Fifth Avenue
New York, New York 10003

Chapman and Hall
2–6 Boundary Row
London, SE 1 8HN

Thomas Nelson Australia
102 Dodds Street
South Melbourne 3205
Victoria, Australia

Nelson Canada
1120 Birchmount Road
Scarborough, Ontario M1K 5G4, Canada

16 15 14 13 12 11 10 9 8 7 6 5 4 3 2 1

Library of Congress Cataloging-in-Publication Data

Janericco, Terence.
    Vegetable cookery / Terence Janericco.
        p. cm.
    Includes index.
    ISBN 0-442-00534-2
    1. Cookery (Vegetables). I. Title.
TX801.J36   1991
641.6'5—dc20   91-8750
                                                            CIP

My sincere thanks to Van Nostrand Reinhold, and the many people who work so hard to produce my books...

Especially to my editor Pamela Scott Chirls for her diligence, patience, and understanding.

Contents

Preface

On warm summer mornings, eight-year-old Louis Flerra would traipse the length of Windsor Avenue in Acton, Massachusetts, pulling a cart heaped with freshly picked corn and calling, "Corn, fresh corn," or chanting the glories of some other fresh vegetable from one of his father's gardens. Mother would send my brother or me out to buy the freshly picked ears for that evening's supper.

Further up the avenue, Mrs. Clemence would have been out since dawn, weeding, watering, picking, pruning, and otherwise tending to her sizable garden. She started her garden as soon as the last chance of frost had passed: hoeing, tilling and preparing the ground. She tended her pole beans, lima beans, peas, lettuces, radishes, carrots, turnips, parsnips, salsify, corn, potatoes, spinach, and other vegetables straight through until there was no possibility of producing any more for the season. Naturally, she left turnips and parsnips in the ground, to be pulled out after the first frost, and sometimes even later into the year.

Acton was still a farming community then. True, many people went to "business" and worked in the "office" in Boston, but most families did some gardening, if not actual farming. Some families, such as the Sweeneys, had a full-fledged farm with a dairy herd as well as a vegetable garden. Outside of the small downtown, people had homes with plots of land around them, and because it was during the Second World War, "victory gardens" were popular. Even after the war, many people continued to raise their own vegetables.

It was not until after the war that my father was able to plant his first garden, but he continues it to this day. Gardening usually meant vegetables rather than flowers. People did plant flowers, but the principal crop was good fresh vegetables. Neighbors spent hours discussing tomato varieties and the size of the zucchini. I often picked a sun-warmed tomato from the garden and ate it sprinkled with salt or sugar—a flavor memory that always makes me feel warm and happy.

When Mr. Strong first introduced frozen foods at his market, they were an oddity. Clarence Birdseye's peas were a treat to be sampled, but not to be eaten as part of a regular diet. Of course, considering the quality of canned peas, the frozen offerings were indeed a treat. In the dead of winter, frozen vegetables eventually worked their way into the menu to complement the limited selection of fresh vegetables—although it was not considered all that difficult (or boring, for that matter) to make do with cabbages, carrots, turnips, and parsnips. Lettuces were shipped from California and, because my parents did much of their food shopping in Boston's North End, we often had romaine and escarole in addition to the ubiquitous iceberg. As soon as dandelion started to appear in Mr. McAllister's field, Father would pick them. They served as a spring tonic and a harbinger of better things to come.

In my teens I worked for Leo White, a local caterer. I spent hours peeling, chopping, dicing, and mincing one vegetable or another. The standard jokes about Leo were that he could not cook enough potatoes for six (he always made enough for the week) nor could he make so much as a cup of coffee without at least a quart of finely minced celery as a security blanket—and I was elected to do the potato peeling and celery mincing. His catering business required us to hack quantities of large Blue Hubbard squashes into chunks before cooking them until tender and then pureeing the flesh. Carrots were peeled by the fifty-pound bag, and of course there were always the potatoes. The vegetables were always fresh.

When I finished college and started to work on my own, I bought fresh vegetables, and only occasionally served something frozen, or even more rarely, canned. Sometimes I would try a canned vegetable because it was so different from the fresh. At one time I found canned peas interesting because the flavor is so unlike real peas that they seem to be an entirely different vegetable—not necessarily one that I wish to know, however. Canned potatoes fascinated me because of their strange, occasionally appealing, texture. Frozen carrots, on the other hand, have always made me shudder because of their sponginess.

Over twenty years ago, when I started to teach cooking, I just assumed that people wanted to learn to cook fresh food. It is only in recent years that students have even raised the question of whether I would teach them to prepare fresh food. What did they think I would teach? How to open a package? It just makes no sense to use anything other than fresh food, whenever possible.

I am always amazed when people make comments similar to that of Marion Burros in the *New York Times* on April 25, 1990. She described the making of parsnip puree as labor-intensive. Did she mean that you needed to peel the parsnip? (She often recommends buying those precut vegetables at the market, so perhaps that *is* what she meant.) Parsnip puree is about as simple as you get in cooking. Peel some parsnips, cook them in boiling salted water, or if you prefer, steam them, and puree in a processor. Add some seasoning: a hint of nutmeg, a spoon of heaviest cream, a dab of butter, salt, and pepper. Would you then collapse into a state of exhaustion?

In recent years food writers seem to have become divided into two major groups: There are those, *à la* Alice Waters, who treat vegetables almost as objects of adoration, with the implication that no one ever ate a *fresh* vegetable until she/he (the food writer of the moment) came along. Then there are those, *àla* Marion Burros, who treats cooking as a chore just short of moving the world over two inches. There are millions of us who have always used fresh vegetables, and have only subjected ourselves or our guests to frozen or canned varieties under the most extreme conditions—such as the third week out of sight of land while sailing across the Pacific. Similarly, there are millions of us who consider cooking as a pleasure, and not as a duty or a chore. Peeling a potato is part of civilized living, like making your bed. You do it without necessarily thinking about it, but always with care. Chopping, dicing, and slicing are a joy, and the fact that one has learned to do them properly is every bit as pleasing as learning how to drive or to type.

Cooking is a skill that, like all skills, has to be learned. Until you learn it, it can be, like many other skills, terribly frustrating. Remember learning how to swim, or to dance? You have watched other people perform the skill for years, and think that they are able to do it automatically, and that you should be able to, also. However, the first time behind the knife can be as nerve-wracking as the first time behind the wheel of a car: You suddenly realize that there is more to cooking than eating. I have found that once my students (ninety-nine percent of my students are adults) realize that they need to learn the techniques of cooking (just as they needed to learn how to sew, do carpentry, or use a word processor) they relax and cooking becomes a pleasure.

In recent years writers have stressed *fresh* vegetables to the point where murder would seem a lesser crime than using frozen or canned vegetables. This is absurd. Under many circumstances canned or frozen vegetables are not only suitable, but are actually preferable. For instance, in mid-winter, when the tomatoes in the market have the flavor of cardboard, a quick tomato sauce is best made with good-quality canned tomatoes. For many preparations, canned corn is far more appealing than the tasteless ears shipped thousands of miles over several days.

Fresh vegetables need to be protected after picking. Corn on the cob that was picked in the early morning is less than wonderful after a full day in the sun at the farmstand. Farmers' markets, romantic as they may seem, are not always the source of the freshest vegetables. The care vegetables receive after picking is as important as the growing. Fresh green beans picked just as the sun rises are wonderful if eaten immediately, but after a trip on an unrefrigerated truck to a market, thirty, fifty or more miles away and several hours on display, they lose a lot of their appeal, and are no longer any better and possibly worse than some alternatives. The local supermarket, with its sophisticated delivery systems and refrigeration capabilities, may in fact present a far better product.

Select vegetables that look fresh, have good weight for their size, and that you know were recently picked. In Blue Hill, Maine, I shop at a local farmstand where the vegetables are picked throughout the day as needed. Depending on the time of day, I have waited while they picked corn or cut lettuce just for me (and for any other customers who might arrive after the last batch is sold). Admittedly we cannot have this luxury all of the time, but we can always use some common sense, and make choices based on what is available when we want it. Frozen peas offer a second-best, but still acceptable, substitute for use in a *risi e bisi* in November.

One of the thrills of dining is waiting for the pleasures it brings. We anticipate the meal before it arrives. We look forward to the flavors and textures of carefully prepared foods. If you use out-of-season vegetables this joy can be greatly diminished. Asparagus in December is nowhere near as good as those locally grown spears of May and June. In the past it was not uncommon to treat each new vegetable with a laudable respect. Dinners would be made up of heaps of fresh asparagus when they came into season. The peas of July are a treat that no canned or frozen version can match. After indulging fully during the peak of the season you were ready and even anxious to move on to a new vegetable and not notice the lapse of a year between seasons.

In an ideal world, eating only fresh vegetables in season would be perfect. However, considering our natures and our desire for variety, we should accept the fact that eating vegetables from other areas means perhaps a loss of some flavor, but at the same time provides variety to the menu. Also, sometimes frozen or canned vegetables can be used as a substitute for fresh vegetables, and can more than fill the bill. Some vegetables, such as beets, are as good canned as fresh and a lot easier to prepare. But do make those selections with enormous care. Take advantage of the season's offerings, and enjoy them to the fullest. If you do, you may well find that there is less need to serve the out-of-season alternatives.

Introduction

Mankind began by foraging for fruits, berries, roots and the like. Hunting provided a treat, but nuts, berries, and vegetables were the staples. When people settled into a more communal form of life, they realized that they had to rely on foods that could be harvested, because cultivating crops produced a larger, more stable food supply. Depending on the latitude, some vegetables were available year-round, and many could be stored for considerable periods to provide for times of scarcity. Today vegetables have returned to their proper place as one of the most important sources of nutrition and good health. Nutritionists, clinicians, cardiologists, and other health professionals constantly dwell on our need to consume more vegetables in relation to meats, and stress the health-giving qualities of vegetables.

Reaching this state has not been easy. For centuries, while many people considered vegetables to be the cure for all of humanity's ills, from gastric disorders to world wars, others considered them dangerous, not only as a source of food, but also and perhaps more important as a character-destroyer. The supporters of the so-called "lowly" vegetable have often presented their case with vehemence. They have often appeared to be cranks (and possibly, somewhat barmy) if not actually traitors to society. They have ascribed all sorts of horrors to meat, while extolling the virtuous vegetable. They have given vegetables powers well in excess of any that ever existed. In contrast, "meat eaters" have stressed the need for good red meat to make strong, stalwart people able to withstand the rigors of the world. And they have looked on vegetables as suspect, and any "new" vegetable as potentially, if not actually, poisonous. Potatoes, tomatoes, and eggplants have all at one time enjoyed this reputation. Fortunately, between these two factions there are the rest of us who know that both meat and vegetables are good, and that all-or-nothing approaches are usually ridiculous. A balanced diet allows for some of everything. We like our meat with potatoes and truly enjoy the broccoli. For many of us, vegetables and meat are equally important. We know that it is possible to enjoy them either together or separately, and that to be deprived of one or the other would be as unpleasant as having to do without the seasons.

Every year, it seems, another vegetable appears in the markets. We can expand our interest, trust, and faith in vegetables, and discover vegetables new to us that have long been a staple in other societies. As we learn more and more about nutrition, the importance of vegetables continues to grow. No matter how often they are maligned, no matter how often they are the brunt of jokes, they maintain their dignity and we realize their importance. Vegetables provide us with many valuable vitamins and minerals. In addition they provide us with the fiber that currently is touted as the solution to so many ills—from colon cancer to high cholesterol and heart disease.

Vegetables are not only readily available throughout the year, they are among the least expensive of foods. Vegetables provide enormous variety to the menu. Relatively speaking, there are few meats and fish from which to choose, but dozens if not hundreds of vegetables to enhance them and make a meal more exciting. Yes, some vegetables can carry a premium price and have a limited season. But most are inexpensive and constantly in season.

The very availability of some vegetables can dull our interest, while others, because they are are rare, unknown, or only available seasonally, make for excitement. Some vegetables are so common that they always have a place at the table, like the potato in its myriad preparations, while others appear to face a somewhat shortened life in the limelight, such as the spaghetti squash. Certain vegetables, such as the eggplant, enjoy enormous popularity in some cuisines while being virtually ignored in others. Of course with the influx of "new" vegetables, there are those that may earn a lasting place in the pantheon of foods, while others will always remain no more than a curiosity. The purple potato is an oddity that will appear on some restaurant menus, but it is highly unlikely that we will ever see it as a food staple. Quinoa, on the other hand, may become a major food staple and a solution to some of the food problems of the world.

For the cook, perhaps the most important point about vegetables is that they lend variety to every meal. The everyday diet of a limited selection of animals and fish is greatly enhanced because of the variety of vegetables. The clever chef soon realizes that vegetables are readily available and inexpensive answers to the need for variety and originality. In recent years vegetables have gone beyond being mere side dishes. We are more willing to consider a single vegetable or several vegetable dishes as a meal—an attitude that until recently was held by only a few vegetarians, and they were considered an oddity in themselves.

In many countries it has long been the custom to celebrate the seasons with menus based on particular vegetables. In France, as well as in many other countries, spring is heralded with the arrival of the first asparagus. Some areas make festivals around it and devote entire menus to it. Garlic, mushrooms, and corn are other vegetables that enjoy this treatment. Sometimes cooks do go a bit far by preparing such oddities as asparagus ice cream. These attempts are amusing, but not an example of fine cooking. There are so many options already that that sort of treatment seems a waste of creativity. That is not, of course, to say we that should not attempt new creations, but rather that a certain sensibility is in order. The very presence of a sauce can turn a plain dish into a dietary delight. A sauce used on one vegetable can seem different on another because of the difference in the vegetables. Similarly, the cut of a vegetable affects the flavor, some times dramatically. Sliced zucchini and grated zucchini taste like two entirely different vegetables, and pureed cauliflower tastes very much like mashed potatoes.

Over the years, much has been done to destroy the vegetable in the process of preserving it. In the past, it was common for almost every household to start canning vegetables at the peak of the growing season in order to have food for the cold months. In well-run households this provided truly superb quality food the year round. When commercial canners took over this job, the quality often diminished. The results were, and in many instances still are, disappointing. Very few vegetables survive the canning process with their fresh quality intact. Corn, beets, and some tomatoes survive, but generally green vegetables suffer disastrously, and root vegetables usually are mushy in texture. Frozen vegetables can be remarkably good, especially the green vegetables. Again, generally speaking, root vegetables do not fare well. However, the less perishable root vegetables are usually available year round and need only a cool, dark location to keep for a long time.

Today fresh food is available virtually year round. Perhaps vegetables that have been transported are not as wonderful as "just-picked," but very often they are markedly better than their canned or frozen counterparts. Fresh food can be flown in to supermarkets within hours of being picked, and often has a wonderful fresh quality to it. Sometimes, however, vegetables are picked when they are underripe, stored in cold storage warehouses for lengthy periods, and then shipped long distances. They are treated with chemicals to cause them to change color to give them the appearance of being ripe, although the flavor is clearly not wonderful. (A vine-ripened tomato is not green no matter what the sign in the market says. Describing a tomato as "vine-matured" is advertising at its worst. In both instances the result is tasteless pulp.) With the increased interest in nutrition and the quality of our food supply, many of these methods are being discontinued because consumers want fresh food that tastes good. They not only want it, but they are willing to pay for it. Many supermarkets have allotted considerable space to fresh produce grown without chemical additives. In addition, markets are stating clearly the source of the food, so that when the local corn is at its peak, you can know whether what the market is selling is local produce or is an import.

Today's interest in vegetables makes life for the cook that much more exciting. Parents who used to brag that their child did not eat vegetables now realize that such behavior is not only impolite, but also it can be dangerous for the child. Children who used to boast of the vegetables they did not eat now talk about the foods that they do eat. Needless to say, not every child, nor every adult, for that matter, will eat—never mind like— every vegetable in the market. However, with our vast variety of vegetables today, there is literally something for everybody. Over the last thirty years I have had students announce their loathing for certain vegetables. One would not eat any heavy-metal vegetable (which meant almost anything green). Another would not eat anything small and round, which cut out peas and most beans. Another student stated decisively in one class that he did not eat beets. (I would love to report that once I had prepared these foods I had converted all of these people for life, but that just is not true.) Because the dislike of vegetables often stems from a childhood experience (the overcooked cauliflower or cabbage, those frightful canned peas, or the "no dessert until you eat those over-vinegared beets" do leave lasting impressions). Current child development strategy is to say, "This is for dinner; if you do not want it, that is your loss." Making another vegetable is usually a mistake. Of course, remember to use variety; because you like cole slaw does not mean that you should make it for *every* meal. Be fair. Sometimes, when a person tries a vegetable as an adult his or her attitude changes dramatically. The man who would not eat beets came in the following week to say he had had them every night since the last class. On the other hand, the man who would not touch heavy metal vegetables, even after trying them again, stuck to his initial opinion.

The purpose of this book is to provide a compendium of vegetables, with ideas and suggestions for their preparation and presentation, as well as specific recipes. Many of these have been favorites in my classes and in my catering business over the last twenty years. I encourage you to attempt new combinations, and to realize that vegetables of similar types can be treated in much the same fashion. If you can prepare a carrot in a certain way almost any other root vegetable will work as well. There are certain preparations that are used with so many vegetables that it only makes sense to provide those ideas first. When you need a quick, easy flavor idea for carrots you can read the chapter on Basic Preparations for a hasty, but no less delicious, solution. The vegetables are separated into chapters that are listed in alphabetical order by principal ingredient, with one final chapter devoted to combinations of mixed vegetables in which no one vegetable predominates.

Vegetable Cookery

Basic Techniques and Preparations

Cooking is a learned experience that requires diligent study. There are few Mozarts of the kitchen who play culinary sonatas at the age of three. Most of us must practice the scales of cookery for many hours. Once we learn those scales, however, cooking becomes a joy as enchanting and as fulfilling as hitting high C. Basic techniques are vital to easy and efficient cooking. I have watched students labor over the simplest of food techniques, such as peeling, chopping, dicing, and the like, because they have not been taught, or have not taken the time to learn to perform these simple tasks correctly. Sometimes this ignorance has not only caused inconvenience and made more work, but has also been downright dangerous. Professional chefs spend the first years of their training learning the techniques for smooth kitchen operation and safety. The fact that your mother did something a certain way is not necessarily a good reason to continue. She was often wrong. My grandmother always cut bread by wrapping her arm around the whole loaf of Italian bread and clasping it to her bosom. With bread knife in hand, she cut towards her bosom in a sawing motion, lifting off the slice. One cousin has a scar across his chest as a result of copying Grandma.

When I was learning how to cook, Leo White, my mentor, insisted that the food be placed on a cutting board, and that the bottom of the vegetable be cut to make a steady base on the board. However, Marquerite, his wife, would cut an onion by holding it up in the air and cutting a cross hatch. She never cut herself—that I saw—but I always shuddered as I saw that knife descend toward her hand.

Do read and refer often to the techniques listed below in order to make your cooking easier and safer.

Read the Recipe!

This seems so elementary that most food writers dare not even mention it. Of course you will read the recipe before you start. Cooking teachers, however, know that many people, in their haste to get going,

1

jump directly into the middle of the recipe and end up in a mess. Or, they have to stop in the middle of an important step to mince an onion. The most important step in cooking is knowing what you are going to do. This means reading and understanding the recipe. Those who do not will get confused and find cooking difficult, too much work, or just plain frustrating.

The ingredient list tells you not only what to buy, but also what to do with it. One cup of chopped onion not only means that the onion is to be chopped before it is measured (1 cup of onion, chopped, is nigh impossible to measure) but also that the onion is to be chopped *before* you start to cook, so that it is ready to use when it is needed, in the condition in which it will be needed. The wise cook reads the recipe and assembles the ingredients before starting. How maddening it is to learn that you need a cup of milk and you only have 2 tablespoons. Yes, you can be clever and add water, or some cream, and even brag about how clever you are, but wisdom is having the ingredients in the first place. Although it is not necessary to make every measurement, chopping the onions and grating the cheese beforehand makes the assembly quicker and simpler. Then, and only then, do you start with the body of the recipe. In other words, do all that is instructed in the ingredient list, and then proceed with the recipe itself. Your cooking should go smoothly and pleasantly. Most food writers spend hours writing and rewriting recipes so that the work proceeds in a logical order. We do not always succeed and some do not even try, but most recipes are carefully written in logical order to make cooking fun and logical.

Washing

My belief is, if it is not dirty, do not bother. If the carrots were just pulled from the garden and are covered with soil, a thorough washing is required, but if they have just been removed from a cellophane bag and are clean, there is no need. Washing the carrots in cold, lukewarm, or even hot water is not going to destroy any bacteria—only several minutes of high heat will accomplish that. If you feel better washing the carrots, by all means do, but all this will do *is* to make you feel better. Of course, certain vegetables must be washed just before using because they can conceal and hold dirt. Spinach and leafy greens need to be washed in quantities of lukewarm water. Leeks need to be split and fanned open under cold running water, while mushrooms may need only a quick rinse or brush of the finger to remove some of the sterile growing-medium. See the chapters on the specific vegetables for information on washing.

Peeling

Some vegetables, the root vegetables in particular, need to be peeled; most other vegetables do not. There are exceptions, such as broccoli stems, and they are discussed under headings of the particular vegetable.

Peeling Round Vegetables Peel rutubagas, turnips, and other round vegetables (not potatoes) like an orange or grapefruit. Cut off the stem and root ends, and place one end on the cutting board. With a knife, cut

down the side to remove the outer skin, following the contour, to remove about a one-inch swath of peel. Continue around the vegetable to
remove all the peel.

Peeling Long Vegetables Peel long vegetables, such as carrots and parsnips, by holding the thicker end of the vegetable between the thumb and
fingers of one hand with the pointed end toward you. Hold the peeler in
the other hand, and scrape the entire length of the vegetable to remove a
slice of peel. With the fingers and thumb, rotate the vegetable to expose
more peel, and continue around the vegetable. Cut off the stem and root
ends. This method allows you to peel a carrot with half a dozen swipes.

Peeling Potatoes and Other Medium-Skinned Vegetables Plan to peel
russet, or Idaho potatoes, in the same fashion as a carrot, then peel the ends
separately with a few quick scrapes. Peel Maine or all-purpose potatoes
with a swivel-bladed peeler, stroking from the middle of the potato toward
one end, stroking away from you. Turn the potato and repeat.

Preparing Vegetables To Cut
Once it has been peeled, place the vegetable on a counter. If it is round,
such as a potato or carrot, cut a thin slice off one side so that it sits securely on the board. Onion, unless they are to be cut into rings, are always cut in half from stem to root end and the flat side placed on the
counter.

To Cut Logs, Strips, Juliennes, and Batons
These are different sizes of the same shape. Logs can be any size, but are
usually larger—over ½ inch thick. They can be any length, but are usually about 3 inches long. Strips or julienne are thinner, and can be as
fine as angel hair or as thick as ¼ of an inch. These can be any length,
but are usually about 3 inches long. Batons are sticks that are 3 inches
long and between ¼ inch and ½ inch in thickness. For most vegetables, cut into slices as thick as the julienne or baton is to be, then cut the
slices into juliennes or batons. If necessary, cut into shorter lengths.)
NOTE: If the vegetable is more than 6 inches long, cut into more manageable lengths before cutting into strips.

Leeks require special attention. Cut the leek in half lengthwise, clean
well, and remove about half of the center portion. Fold one section in
half, place the folded bundle on a counter, and cut into as fine a julienne
as possible. Fold the other portion of the leek, and cut in the same way.
NOTE: EQUIPMENT. A mandoline is the traditional piece of equipment
required to make batons and juliennes in quantity. A professional version is made of stainless steel, and has three cutting blades for slicing,
julienne, and batons. At last check it cost as much as a food processor.

Food processors fitted with the proper blades can make quick work
of juliennes. Batons, however, come out curved rather than straight,
and it takes some fiddling and precutting to achieve good results. However, if you do not wish to learn how to use a knife, a food processor is
an acceptable answer.

Chopping, Dicing, and Mincing

The difference among these is the size of the end result. Firm vegetables, such as carrots and onions, should be cut with a certain precision; leafy vegetables, such as spinach or parsley, can be chopped more haphazardly. To dice, cut vegetables into logs as described above and gather into groups. Cut across to make evenly sized dice.

Mincing Mincing is the same as dicing, just smaller. The end result depends on the vegetable. For instance, minced carrots, celery, and onions are cut into ¼ inch dice, but minced garlic is cut much finer, as are minced herbs.

Onions and shallots require special treatment because of their layers. To mince an onion or shallot, cut the vegetable in half from stem to root end, and peel off the outer layer of skin. Place cut side down on a cutting board. With a large sharp knife held horizontally, cut into the stem end to, but not through, the root end. Turn the knife vertically and cut again to, but not through, the root end. Holding the body of the onion, now cut vertically across the onion to produce the mince.

Three separate steps let you mince the entire onion in less than a minute, and provide evenly sized dice. People who hack and chop willy-nilly spend more time and have uneven pieces which cook unevenly.

Diagonal Cut and Roll Cut Diagonal cutting is used with reasonable frequency in Western cookery, but roll cutting is distinctly Asian in character. Both of these are attractive and effective ways of preparing vegetables that increase the surface area and hasten the cooking.

Diagonal cut: Use with long vegetables such as carrots, asparagus, or broccoli stems. Hold the vegetable on the board parallel to the edge of the counter. Hold the knife at a forty-five degree angle, and slice the vegetable into sections, from paper thin, to 1 to 2 inches thick.

Roll Cut: Use with long round vegetables such as carrots, parsnips, or asparagus.

Hold the vegetable on the board parallel to the counter. With the knife at a forty-five degree angle, make a cut across the very end of the vegetable. Roll the vegetable so that the cut is toward you, and make another cut, still holding the knife at a forty-five degree angle. The vegetable should look like a V, with the cuts the legs of the V, and the uncut portion the top of the V.

Shredding and Grating

With root vegetables such as carrots and turnips, shredding and julienne are the same, but with leafy vegetables, such as cabbage or spinach, shredding is slightly different. Grating is a finer version of shredding, and usually results in shorter pieces.

Shredding For cabbage, you can use a cabbage slicer, mandoline, processor, or a knife. Cut the head into a manageable size, and push over the blades of a cabbage slicer or mandoline, or into the funnel of a food processor with a fine slicing blade.

To shred with a knife, cut the cabbage in half, remove the core, and if very large, cut the half into quarters. Place the cut side down on a work surface and, using a large knife, cut across the head to make the finest possible slices.

Lettuces: Head lettuces are cut the same as cabbage. With some lettuces, Romaine and escarole for example, there is no need to remove the core.

Spinach: Place a pile of leaves on a board and grasp into a compact mass. Cut across the mass into fine shreds.

Grating The secret to grating is to relax. Take a four-sided grater and stand it on a cutting board. Place the side you wish to use away from you. Take a deep breath and exhale, relax, and think beautiful thoughts. Apply the lemon, orange, cheese, or whatever else must be grated and scrape it against the grater in a *circular* motion. Slowly rotate lemon or orange, after one or two scrapes. Do not exert a lot of pressure, or attack the grater, or it will attack your knuckles, but rythymic gentle raspings will do the job pain-free.

Pitting Olives

No one likes to pit olives, but often there is no choice. Canned, pitted olives are a good example of how canning neuters a wonderful food. The pulpy tasteless black olives sold in cans may look good, but cardboard has more flavor. Cured black olives have pits, and you must pit them.

Olive pitters (also called cherry pitters) come in two principal forms. One is rather like a set of tongs. At the end of one blade there is a bowl with a hole in the bottom. The other blade has a prong. Place the olive in the bowl, and press the prong into the olive, forcing the pit out through the hole in the bottom of the bowl.

The other type, and my preference, has a spring-loaded plunger with a holding pan that has a hole in the bottom. Place the olive in the holding pan, and press the plunger through the olive, forcing the pit out the hole. The advantage of this type is that if the pit is not exactly in the center, you can maneuver the plunger to get at the pit.

Basic Preparations

Certain basic preparations are suitable to many vegetables. Some are necessary to prevent vegetables from turning dark when exposed to the air, such as artichokes, or during cooking, such as cardoons or cauliflower. Other preparations enhance vegetables such as making simple boiled carrots into a treat by adding seasoned butter, or such as *alla Parmigiana*, which involves a quick toss in butter and a sprinkling of Parmesan, or turning them into *alla trifolati* with a toss in olive oil, minced garlic, and parsley. Other preparations may take a little more effort, such as coating vegetables for deep frying, or napping them with a luscious cheese sauce.

Each vegetable has a listing of recommended preparations, but if you think that a vegetable might work with one of these methods and it is not mentioned, try it, you might like it!

Cooking Methods

You can prepare vegetables using almost any cooking technique to great advantage. Boiled carrots are good, sautéing in butter enhances them, but so does roasting, deep-frying, broiling, or braising.

Use this section to review a specific technique or to learn a new method.

Acidulated Water

Many vegetables turn dark if exposed to the air for more than a few minutes. Some, such as potatoes, will remain white if kept in water, but others, such as artichokes or cardoons, quickly darken unless the water is acidulated with lemon juice or vinegar.

To Prepare: Add 1 tablespoon of lemon juice to each quart of water, and put the food into the water as soon as it is cut. With some vegetables it is necessary to rub a cut surface with pure lemon juice immediately after it is cut to prevent darkening. The individual chapters explain when acidulated water is required.

À Blanc

A *blanc* is used to keep vegetables from darkening during cooking. In classic French cooking *blancs* are used fairly often, but in home cookery they are only required on occasion. The recipes will tell when it is necessary to use a *blanc*.

Blanc

¼ cup flour	2 tablespoons lemon juice
1 quart cold water	salt to taste

In a saucepan, mix the flour with a couple of tablespoons of water to make a smooth paste, and then stir in the remaining water, lemon juice, and salt. Simmer 5 minutes, and then add the vegetable to be cooked *à blanc*.

Increase or decrease the quantities to suit your needs.

Yield: about 1 quart

Blanching

Many vegetables, as well as smoked or salted foods, need to be blanched to precook, or to remove strong flavors. Tomatoes are blanched about 20 seconds, and then dipped into cold water to make peeling easier. Cabbage is blanched for a couple of minutes to soften the flavor. It is drained and then reheated, usually with some other method such as sautéing or braising. Other vegetables, such as green beans or broccoli, are blanched until they are almost fully cooked. These are drained, dropped into very cold water to stop all cooking and set the color, and then drained again. They can then wait to be reheated and sauced just before serving. Using this method, the vegetables will have a fresh bright color without becoming over-cooked.

Boiling

In most recipes the vegetable is placed in boiling salted water to cover and simmered until tender. See the individual vegetables for specific instructions.

Steaming

Steaming takes longer than boiling, and although there is some saving of nutrients, the amount lost in boiling is not enough to be of concern. Place the vegetable in a steamer basket, and steam as directed with the individual recipe. Take care when removing the lid to let the steam escape before putting your hand over the pot, in order to avoid a serious burn.

Microwaving

Each vegetable has specific directions for cooking in a microwave, if that is appropriate.

Puréeing

Vegetables are puréed to remove tough fibers, to give a different texture, or to give variety to the menu. Puréed vegetables are cooked in water or stock until very tender, drained, and then puréed in a food mill, blender, or processor. The food mill is preferred because it removes the tougher fibers, while the machines chop them very finely and they remain as a texture in the purée. After puréeing, vegetables are treated differently according to type.

Starchy vegetables are stirred in a saucepan over medium heat until the excess liquid evaporates. Beat in a enough cream to bring to the desired consistency, and correct the seasoning with salt and pepper.

Watery vegetables require the addition of about ¼ cup of mashed potatoes, cooked rice, or thick béchamel sauce for each cup of purée, to give them body.

Sautéing

Most vegetables are precooked before they are sautéed. A few vegetables, such as potatoes and carrots, can be sautéed from the raw state.

Broiling

Most vegetables are precooked, and are only finished under the broiler. They may have been topped with grated cheese, a sauce, or just a brushing of butter or oil. There are exceptions, such as broiled eggplant or peppers.

Roasting

Roasting and broiling with vegetables are quite similar. The difference for roasting is that the oven heat is used rather than the broiler, and the time allowed is longer.

Baking

Some vegetables can be baked on their own, such as potatoes or certain squashes, but others are baked in a sauce after they have been precooked.

Deep-Frying

Deep-frying enhances many vegetables. Potatoes and turnips turn into crispy taste treats when cooked in oil without any coating, but most vegetables require a coating. The coating can be a dusting of flour, a batter, or egg and bread crumbs.

Some rules apply to all deep-frying: Use enough oil so the food will float, which means that if you are making french fries you can use a skillet, but in most instances you will want a deep, heavy saucepan or a casserole. Do not fill the casserole more than ½ full, because the moisture of the food will cause the oil to bubble up, and it could spill over and catch fire. Have a slotted spoon, or better still a Chinese brass wire and bamboo strainer to remove the food. Have a baking sheet lined with paper toweling to drain the food before putting it onto a heated platter. Make sure the food never gets cold, and always serve it on a warm platter. Deep-fried food is far less appealing when it has cooled.

Heat the oil to the specified temperature, which in most cases is 375°F, before adding the food. Do not crowd the pan, or the temperature will drop too low and the food will absorb too much fat. Let the oil reheat before cooking the next batch. Serve the food immediately, and let the guests wait, rather than the food.

If you must cook in advance, you can keep the food in a 250°F oven on paper-lined cake racks for up to 30 minutes, but it will not be as good.

Deep-Frying without a Coating Potatoes and turnips can be fried without a coating, but most other vegetables must be coated, because they are too moist and would absorb too much fat before they brown.

Deep-Frying with a Flour Coating Cut the vegetable into bite-sized pieces, and roll in flour seasoned with salt and pepper. If the vegetable is dry on the surface, such as green pepper, dip it in milk first to help the flour adhere.

Deep-Frying with a Batter Coating The lightest coating is made with a beer batter. You may substitute water or milk for the beer, if desired.

Pâté à Frire Pour Beignets (Beer Fritter Batter)

½ cup flour	1 egg
¼ teaspoon salt	½ cup beer
1 tablespoon melted butter	1 egg white, stiffly beaten

In a bowl or processor, combine the flour and salt, and add the butter and egg, and work to a stiff paste. Add a tablespoon of beer at a time, working the mixture until it becomes a thin paste, and finally a liquid about as thick as heavy cream. Let stand for 1 to 2 hours. Just before using, fold the beaten egg white into the mixture.

Yield: 6 servings

➤ Can be prepared the day before, but do not add the egg white until just before serving.

NOTE: If using a processor, add the flour, salt, butter, and egg. Turn on the machine, and add the beer in a slow, steady stream. Remove to a bowl, let rest, and fold in the egg white just before using. Add 1 to 2 tablespoons of minced fresh herbs to the batter, or ground spices to taste.

To Use Beer Batter Cut the vegetable into bite-sized pieces. Dip the pieces into the batter, and slip into the fat and cook until golden brown, about 1 to 2 minutes.

À l'Anglaise (Bread Coating for Deep-Frying) This creates a crisp, crunchy coating for many vegetables. It forms a shell within which the tender vegetable nestles until the diner bites into its crackling goodness.

Friture à l'Anglaise
(Bread-Crumb Coating for Deep-Fried Foods)

No one seems to know why the French call this after the English, but the result is great, no matter what the name.

1 cup flour	1 tablespoon cold water
2 eggs	2 cups bread crumbs
1 teaspoon salt	

Place the flour in a pie tin. In another tin, or a bowl, beat the eggs, salt, and water until fluid.

Place the bread crumbs in another pie tin.

Roll the bite-sized pieces of vegetable in the flour, coat with the egg, and roll in the bread crumbs to coat completely.

Arrange on a cake rack until ready to fry.

These benefit from being air-dried for several hours before cooking.

If desired, coat and store in the refrigerator uncovered overnight to help set the coating.

Yield: 6 servings

Braising

Braising is one of the finest methods of preparing vegetables, and a blessed relief from all of those barely cooked preparations. Braised dishes may need just a few minutes or up to several hours, but once ready to braise they need almost no attention and reward you with superb flavor. Blanch the vegetable, if instructed, and sauté in butter in a skillet until golden brown. Add some wine and/or stock, and season with an herb, salt, and pepper. Cover and simmer on top of the stove, or in the oven, until the vegetables are fork tender and permeated with flavor. If the liquid is too thin, remove the vegetable and reduce the braising liquid until lightly thickened, or even to a glaze, depending on the recipe.

À La Crème *(Finishing in Cream)*

Many ordinary vegetables are greatly enhanced by a brief simmer in cream. Place the blanched, tender, crisp vegetable in a skillet with a tablespoon of butter. Reheat and add ¼ to ½ cup cream, and cook over high heat until lightly thickened. Correct the seasoning with salt and pepper. If desired, add a favorite herb to vary the flavor.

À La Béchamel or Mornay

(Finishing in Cream or Cheese Sauce)

Butter a gratin pan or a baking dish large enough to hold the vegetable. Pour 1 to 2 cups of Béchamel or Mornay sauce (page 21–22) over the vegetable. If using Mornay, sprinkle the top with ½ cup grated Gruyere or Parmesan cheese. Bake in a 375°F oven until bubbling hot and golden brown on the top.

Italian Preparations

Italian cooks have two methods of preparing vegetables that enhance them quickly and easily: *Alla trifolati*, or with garlic and parsley, and *alla parmigiana*, or with butter and cheese. When the need arises to add interest to dinner, you can use either of these finishes for complete and quick success.

Alla Trifolati (Cooked Like Truffles)

1½ teaspoons minced garlic	if needed, salt and pepper to
½ cup olive oil	taste
1½ cups vegetables, blanched	3 tablespoons minced parsley

In a skillet, sauté the garlic in the oil until light golden. Do not burn.
Add the vegetable and cook until heated and just tender.
Season with salt, pepper, and parsley, and mix gently.
Serve.

Yield: 6 servings

➤ Prepare just before serving.

NOTE: Mushrooms will absorb all the oil and quickly release it. Most other vegetables need to be blanched until almost done before reheating in the garlic and oil.

Alla Parmigiana (With Butter and Cheese)

¼ cup butter	salt and pepper to taste
1½ pounds blanched vegetable	3 tablespoons grated Parmesan cheese

In a skillet, melt the butter, and toss the vegetable until heated and just done. Season with salt and pepper, and sprinkle with the cheese. Toss and stir until evenly coated, and serve.

Yield: 6 servings

➤ Prepare just before serving.

NOTE: Do not add too much cheese—it is supposed to accent the vegetable, not hide it.

Basic Sauces

Sauces ought to enhance the foods they accompany, instead of overwhelming them. This can be as simple as a butter: melt some butter, stir in a favorite herb, and pour over the vegetable. Others, however, are more involved to prepare and in effect become the clothes for the vegetable, such as a Mornay sauce: Cook the vegetable until almost done, arrange in a gratin, and coat with enough sauce to cover the vegetable without hiding it. Because this sort of preparation can become a meal in itself, it is often finished with an additional grating of cheese before the final reheating.

Choose sauces with care and thought, so that they enhance the food they accompany and bring out its special quality. Do not be hidebound by tradition. Green beans with savory-flavored butter is a classic, but you can use caraway seeds, poppy seeds, mustard, curry, and many other seasonings for variety and flavor. The wise cook is always careful to use seasonings with care. Adding several herbs can result in a dish that has a muddy flavor. Whenever you use a sauce, consider how it will work with another vegetable. You may create a taste treat.

Sauces are simpler to prepare than many writers would have us believe. If a sauce should "break," the repair is usually simple and quick. Have confidence in yourself and the recipes, and proceed apace. If there is a problem, try the suggested corrections.

Butter Sauces

Butter is the simplest sauce for any vegetable. Add a dot or two, season with salt and pepper, and the cooked vegetable is ready to go. With just-arrived, just-picked corn on the cob, what could be better? However, further into the season, after the initial delights have waned, or with corn that might not be perfectly fresh, using a butter flavored with minced herbs, such as chives, or summer savory, can create a new dimension of flavor and excitement. Try adding a bit of honey and a pinch of cloves to the butter, and use it on the corn or a sweet potato.

Butter sauces are made with melted butter, or with cold butter with the seasonings worked into it. Because they adhere to the vegetable differently, the same sauce ingredients produce different flavors. I suggest that the next time you are planning on baked potato, try this experiment: In a saucepan, melt 1 stick of butter with 1 tablespoon minced chives. In a processor, cream 1 stick of butter with 1 tablespoon of minced chives. Season both butters with salt and pepper to taste. Cut the cooked potatoes in half, and sauce each half separately. Serve each diner with one of each, and let them determine the difference.

Cold Butters

These are easy to prepare. In a processor, or mixer, beat cool, but not cold, butter until creamy and smooth, without letting it melt or soften to the point of becoming oily. Store in a cool area until ready to use. If it is necessary to refrigerate the butter, let it warm to room temperature before using so that it melts readily, providing the maximum flavor. For a pretty presentation, place the butter in a pastry bag, and pipe onto a sheet of foil or waxed paper, or shape into a log or butter balls before chilling.

Anchovy Butter

6 ounces butter	1 teaspoon lemon juice
2 tablespoons anchovy paste, or 4 anchovy fillets, minced	

In a processor, cream the butter until soft and smooth. Add the anchovy paste with the machine running, and add the lemon juice.

Remove from the processor and shape into a log, about 1½ inches in diameter.

Keep cool until ready to serve.

Yield: 6 servings

➤ Can be prepared 2 to 3 days before using.

Beurre Bercy (Bercy Butter)

Traditionally this is served on grilled meats, but you can use it on asparagus, broccoli, or cauliflower, for a change—or as a piquant counterpoint to sweet potatoes.

½ cup minced shallots	1 tablespoon minced parsley
¾ cup dry white wine	salt and pepper to taste
6 tablespoons butter	

In a saucepan, simmer the shallots in the wine until it is reduced to ¼ of the original quantity. Cool.

In a processor, cream the butter, and with the machine running, add the shallot mixture, parsley, salt, and pepper until fully incorporated.

Remove from the processor and shape into a log, about 1½ inches in diameter.

Keep cool until ready to serve.

Yield: 6 servings

➤ Can be prepared 2 to 3 days before using.

NOTE: The shallots should still have some texture.

Beurre Vert (Green Butter)

1 cup chopped spinach leaves	1 teaspoon minced tarragon
½ cup water	leaves
1 tablespoon minced parsley	6 tablespoons of butter
1 teaspoon minced chervil leaves	salt and pepper to taste

In a saucepan, simmer the spinach, water, parsley, chervil, and tarragon until the leaves are wilted—about 5 minutes.

Drain and press out the excess moisture.

In a processor, purée the greens, and add the butter and cream until smooth. Season with salt and pepper.

Remove from the processor and shape into a log about 1 ½ inches in diameter.

Keep cool until ready to serve.

Yield: 6 servings

➤ Can be prepared 2 to 3 days before using.

Garlic Butter

1 cup butter	1 tablespoon minced parsley
1 tablespoon minced shallots	salt and pepper to taste
2 cloves garlic, crushed	

In a processor, cream the butter. Add the shallots, garlic, parsley, and salt and pepper, and process until combined.

Remove from the processor and shape into a log, about 1½ inches in diameter.

Keep cool until ready to serve.

Yield: 6 servings

➤ Can be prepared 2 to 3 days before using.

Herb or Spice Butter

Use any herb of your choice—tarragon, chervil, coriander, rosemary, savory, dill, or marjoram—or select a spice such as cinnamon, cloves, nutmeg, cumin, or coriander seed.

2 tablespoons minced fresh	6 tablespoons butter
herbs	salt and pepper to taste

In a processor, cream the butter and herbs until fluffy.

Season with salt and pepper.

Remove from the processor and shape into a log, about 1½ inches in diameter.

Keep cool until ready to serve.

Yield: 6 servings

➤ Can be prepared 2 to 3 days before using.

Beurre de Marchand de Vins (Wine Sellers Butter)

This is the very same as Beurre Bercy, except that it calls for red wine instead of white wine.

Remove from the processor and shape into a log, about 1½ inches in diameter.

Keep cool until ready to serve.

Yield: 6 servings

➤ Can be prepared 2 to 3 days before using. Serve with baked potatoes, puréed cauliflower, or butter-nut squash.

Beurre à la Maître d'Hôtel
(Butter with Parsley and Lemon Juice)

6 tablespoons butter
1 tablespoon minced parsley

2 tablespoons lemon juice
salt and pepper to taste

In a processor or mixer, cream the butter, parsley, lemon juice, and salt and pepper.

Remove from the processor and shape into a log, about 1½ inches in diameter.

Keep cool until ready to serve.

Yield: 6 servings

➤ Can be prepared 2 to 3 days before using.

Serve with carrots, asparagus, broccoli, or green beans.

Nut-Flavored Butter

½ cup toasted ground
almonds, hazelnuts,
walnuts, or pecans

6 tablespoons butter
1 teaspoon lemon juice
salt and pepper to taste

In a processor, cream the nuts and butter until fluffy. Add the lemon juice, salt, and pepper.

Remove from the processor and shape into a log, about 1½ inches in diameter.

Keep cool until ready to serve.

Yield: 6 servings

➤ Can be prepared 2 to 3 days before using.

Paprika Butter

The flavor of paprika is brought out by cooking in a fat. If the paprika is added without cooking, it has a raw flavor.

½ cup minced onion
2 tablespoons butter
1 teaspoon paprika

4 tablespoons butter
salt and pepper to taste

In a small skillet or saucepan, sauté the onion in the 2 tablespoons of butter until it is golden. Add the paprika and mix well. Sauté 1 minute, and let the mixture cool to room temperature.

In a processor or mixer, cream the 4 tablespoons of butter, and add the paprika mixture and season with salt and pepper. Process until smooth.

Remove from the processor and shape into a log, about 1½ inches in diameter.

Keep cool until ready to serve.

Yield: 6 servings

➤ Can be prepared 2 to 3 days before using.

Hot Butters

Many of the cold butter recipes listed above can be made into hot butters by heating the ingredients until the butter is melted, but here are some butters that require heat to bring out their flavor. These should not be served cold.

Bagna Cauda I (Warm Anchovy Sauce I)

Bagna Cauda is the classic dip for raw vegetables in Italy. As with many old recipes, there are many variations on a theme as well as many uses. Serve the sauce with boiled or steamed vegetables.

2 cups heavy cream
¼ cup butter
8 anchovy fillets, minced

1 teaspoon minced garlic
1 small white truffle, minced
　(optional)

In a saucepan, simmer the cream until it is reduced by half. In a casserole, over low heat, melt the butter and stir in the anchovies and garlic. Cook, stirring over low heat until the anchovies dissolve. Add the truffle and bring to a simmer, stirring, and then stir in the cream.

Serve with vegetables.

Yield: 6 to 8 servings

NOTE: Truffles are expensive, but if there is room in the budget, they will add immeasurably to this recipe. Fortunately, the recipe is still delicious if the truffle must be omitted.

Bagna Cauda II *(Warm Anchovy Sauce II)*

1 cup butter	6 anchovy fillets, chopped
¼ cup olive oil	1 white truffle, minced
3 cloves garlic, minced	(optional)

In a shallow heavy pan, heat the butter and oil, and sauté the garlic until tender, without letting it brown. Remove from the heat, and stir in the anchovies until they dissolve. Season with salt, and add truffle slices, if desired.

Serve warm with vegetables.

Yield: 6 to 8 servings

Bagna Cauda III *(Warm Anchovy Sauce III)*

1 cup olive oil	½ tablespoon minced parsley
2 garlic cloves, crushed	1 tablespoon capers
8 anchovy fillets, mashed	2 tablespoons minced black
1 tablespoon minced mint leaves	olives

In a saucepan, cook the oil and garlic until the garlic turns golden, without burning. Discard the garlic. Add the anchovies, and cook until they dissolve. Remove from the heat, and stir in the mint, parsley, capers, and olives.

Serve warm with vegetables.

Yield: 6 to 8 servings

Beurre Noisette *(Brown Butter)*

Noisettes are hazelnuts, and the butter is to be cooked until it reaches the color of hazelnuts. Serve immediately.

6 tablespoons of butter

In a saucepan, melt the butter, and cook over medium heat until it smells nutty and is a hazelnut brown.

Pour over the vegetable and serve.

Yield: 6 servings

➤ Best if prepared just before serving. Serve with cauliflower, mashed potatoes, or celery root purée.

Caper Butter

6 tablespoons butter	salt and pepper to taste
1 tablespoon capers	

In a small saucepan, cook the butter until it starts to turn golden.

Add the capers, salt, and pepper, and serve with broccoli, cauliflower, asparagus, or the like.

Yield: 6 servings

➤ Cannot be prepared ahead.

Beurre à la Meunière *(Miller's Butter)*

Customarily this is served on sautéed fish, but you can use it on asparagus, carrots, turnips, and the like.

6 tablespoons butter	1 tablespoon minced parsley
1 tablespoon lemon juice	salt and pepper to taste

In a small skillet, melt the butter over medium heat, and cook until it is medium brown and smells nutty.

Add the lemon juice, parsley, salt, and pepper.

Serve immediately.

Yield: 6 servings

Beurre De Moutarde *(Mustard Butter)*

6 tablespoons melted butter	salt and pepper to taste
2 teaspoons Dijon mustard, or to taste	

In a saucepan, melt the butter, and whisk in the mustard, salt, and pepper.

Yield: 6 servings

➤ Can be prepared ahead and reheated.

NOTE: Serve with green beans, collard greens, cauliflower, or the like. You can add 2 to 3 times the amount of mustard to taste. Use flavored mustards, such as tarragon, chervil, or sweet mustards, for variety.

Sauce Polonaise *(Polonaise Sauce)*

A standard of French cooking, this may well have been introduced by the Polish king, Stanislaus Leszczynski, a noted gourmand who was also the father-in-law of Louis XV. Traditionally it is served with cauliflower, but it adds greatly to boiled or steamed potatoes, onions, or Brussels sprouts.

¼ pound butter	salt and pepper to taste
2 tablespoons fresh or dry white bread crumbs	1 hard cooked egg, chopped

In a small skillet, heat the butter until it starts to turn to light brown, add the bread crumbs, and cook until golden.

Season with salt and pepper, and immediately pour over the vegetable.

Sprinkle with the hard cooked egg and serve.

Yield: 6 servings

➤ Cannot be prepared ahead.

NOTE: I prefer fresh bread crumbs for a lighter finish. Pour the sauce over the vegetable while still foaming.

Hollandaise and Béarnaise Sauces

Perhaps the ultimate butter sauces are Hollandaise and its cousin—if not child—Béarnaise. These sauces are often described as fraught with problems. They are simple sauces to prepare, and a little attention will bring perfect results.

Sauce Hollandaise

3 egg yolks	salt to taste
1 tablespoon water	lemon juice to taste
½ cup butter, softened	

In a heavy saucepan, whisk the egg yolks and water over medium heat until light and fluffy. Beat in the butter in bits, whisking constantly until the butter is fully incorporated. If the sauce gets too hot and starts to look as if it is going too turn into scrambled eggs, remove from the heat and whisk in a bit of cold butter.

When all the butter has been incorporated, strain into a clean container and correct the seasoning with salt and lemon juice.

Yield: 6 servings

➤ Keeps 2 to 3 hours over warm water.

NOTE: Keep warm over warm water. Unsalted butter lets you control the amount of added salt. If the sauce starts to break, whisk in 1 tablespoon of boiling water. If that does not work, whisk in 1 ice cube. If the sauce does break, place 1 egg yolk in a warm bowl and whisk in the separated sauce, a teaspoon at a time until the mixture emulsifies. Continue adding the separated sauce until it is all incorporated.

Processor or Blender Hollandaise

4 egg yolks	dash of Tabasco (optional)
2 tablespoons lemon juice	½ cup hot melted butter
salt and pepper to taste	

In a processor, place the egg yolks, lemon juice, and Tabasco (if used). Turn the machine on and add the butter in a slow steady stream. When the butter is incorporated, taste for seasoning.

Remove the sauce to a double boiler and keep warm.

Yield: 1 cup

Sauce Maltaise
(Orange-Flavored Hollandaise Sauce)

The pinkish juice of blood oranges colors this sauce a rosy shade. If blood oranges are not available, adding the food coloring gives the color, if not the flavor, of these oranges.

1 cup Hollandaise sauce	½ teaspoon grated orange rind
3 tablespoons orange juice	red food coloring (optional)

Prepare the Hollandaise sauce and fold in the orange juice, orange rind, and just enough food coloring to tint the sauce a delicate pink.

Serve with steamed asparagus, broccoli or shellfish.

Yield: 1 cup

NOTE: If the sauce is to be held for any length of time, add the food color shortly before serving. Food color intensifies in the air, so beware, or a very delicate pink could turn into a rather bright orange.

Mustard Hollandaise

1 tablespoon Dijon mustard, or to taste	1 cup Hollandaise sauce

Fold the mustard into the Hollandaise sauce. Serve with brussel sprouts, cardoons, or artichokes.

Yield: 1 cup

Sauce Paloise (Minted Hollandaise Sauce)

1 cup Hollandaise sauce	1½ teaspoons minced mint
1 tablespoon mint infusion (see following)	

In a bowl, mix the Hollandaise and mint infusion, and let steep for 10 minutes. Fold in the fresh mint just before serving. Serve with beets, carrots, or cucumbers.

Yield: 1 cup

Mint Infusion

4 tablespoons water	2 tablespoons minced mint
2 tablespoons vinegar	

In a saucepan, simmer the water, vinegar, and mint until the liquid is reduced. Strain.

Yield: 1 tablespoon

➤ Keeps 2 days.

Sauce Béarnaise

1 tablespoon minced tarragon	1 tablespoon water
1 tablespoon minced chervil	½ cup butter
2 shallots, minced	salt to taste
¼ cup tarragon vinegar	Cayenne pepper to taste
¼ cup white wine	1 tablespoon minced tarragon
3 egg yolks	1 tablespoon minced chervil

In a small saucepan, simmer the tarragon, chervil, shallots, vinegar, and wine until reduced to a thick paste. Let cool slightly.

Place the tarragon paste into a saucepan, and add the egg yolks and water. Over medium heat, whisking constantly, beat the mixture until it starts to thicken. Whisk in the butter, bit by bit, until fully incorporated. Strain the sauce through a fine sieve.

Correct the seasoning with the salt and Cayenne, and fold in the remaining tarragon and chervil.

Yield: 1 cup

Sauce Choron (Tomato Flavored Béarnaise Sauce)

¼ cup hot tomato purée	1 cup Béarnaise

Stir the hot (but not boiling) tomato purée into the Béarnaise and serve.

Yield: 1¼ cups

➤ Can be prepared a couple of hours ahead and reheated carefully.

NOTE: Traditionally this is served with red meats, but it makes a luscious sauce for asparagus, artichokes, fiddleheads, and the like.

Béchamel Sauces

Often referred to as cream sauce, the French *béchamel* is cooked longer, starting with more liquid than its American counterpart, to create a silkier sauce that is worth the extra few minutes of cooking. Do not use prepared cream sauces or try substituting some form of cream soup. Béchamel is the base of the very popular Mornay sauce, which enhances almost every vegetable so well. At first it may seem time consuming, but you should realize that once prepared, it can go on simmering while you are preparing the vegetable itself. Double or triple the recipe and freeze the extra for a future occasion.

Sauce Béchamel (Cream Sauce)

2 tablespoons butter	¼ teaspoon salt
1 tablespoon minced onion	3 white peppercorns
4 tablespoons flour	sprig of parsley
3 cups milk, scalded	pinch of grated nutmeg

In a saucepan, melt the butter, and sweat the onion until soft. Stir in the flour, and cook the roux until it just starts to turn golden and is foamy. Add the milk, whisking constantly until the mixture is thick and smooth. Stir in the salt, peppercorns, parsley, and nutmeg. Simmer the sauce over low heat for about 30 minutes, or until reduced to ⅔ of the original quantity. Strain through a very fine sieve.

Yield: 2 cups

➤ Keeps 4 days refrigerated, and can be frozen.

Sauce Mornay (Cheese Sauce)

This is the most common use of béchamel sauce.

3 egg yolks	2 tablespoons butter
½ cup heavy cream	2 tablespoons grated Gruyère
2 cups hot béchamel	cheese

In a bowl, mix the egg yolks and cream. Add ¼ of the béchamel, whisking constantly to warm the mixture, then turn the egg yolk mixture into the remaining béchamel. Set over medium heat and cook, stirring, until the sauce just reaches the boiling point. Remove from the heat and stir in the butter and cheese.

Yield: 2 cups

➤ It can be reheated, but do not freeze it.

Béchamel for Croquettes

2 tablespoons butter	white pepper to taste
3 tablespoons flour	salt to taste
1 cup hot milk	2 eggs, lightly beaten

In a saucepan, melt the butter, stir in the flour, and cook until the roux is foamy and just starts to turn golden. Add the milk and cook, stirring until thickened and smooth. Simmer, stirring often, for 12 to 15 minutes or until very thick. Correct seasoning with salt and pepper.

Stir about ¼ of the hot sauce into the eggs to warm them. Return the egg mixture to the béchamel and cook, stirring until it just reaches the boil. Do not boil.

Yield: 1 cup

➤ Keeps 2 to 3 days, refrigerated. Can be frozen.

Curried Béchamel Sauce I

1 teaspoon butter	⅛ teaspoon turmeric
1 clove garlic, crushed	⅛ teaspoon ground cloves
1 teaspoon minced shallot	⅛ teaspoon cinnamon
1 teaspoon minced green pepper	2 cups béchamel sauce
1 teaspoon curry powder, or to taste	

In a skillet, melt the butter, and sauté the garlic, shallot, green pepper, curry powder, turmeric, cloves, and cinnamon for 2 to 3 minutes, until the vegetables are soft and the spices fragrant. Stir into the béchamel.

Yield: 2 cups

➤ Keeps 2 to 3 days, refrigerated. Can be frozen.

Curried Béchamel Sauce II

1 cup minced onion	pinch of saffron
3 tablespoons olive oil	salt and pepper to taste
2 tablespoons curry powder	1 cup béchamel sauce

In a saucepan, cook the onion in the olive oil over a low heat for 20 minutes, or until very soft. Stir in the curry powder, saffron, and salt and pepper, and cook 5 minutes longer until very fragrant. Stir in the béchamel sauce, and strain through a food mill. Return to the heat and correct the seasoning.

Yield: 1 cup

➤ Keeps 3 days refrigerated, and can be frozen.

Velouté Sauce

Velouté, which is never translated into English, is the same as béchamel, except that it is made with stock instead of milk. The flavor is rich and interesting, with fewer calories. Adding grated lemon or orange rind, and some lemon or orange juice, makes a delicious, low-calorie sauce for many vegetables. Even with the addition of cream, the caloric content is lower, because only a couple of tablespoons creates a rich, creamy sauce for 6 or more people. Thicker veloutés become the base for croquettes and certain sauces served with hors d'oeuvre. Take the time to let it simmer gently, and strain it for the right effect. Hastily made, it will be floury and heavy.

Velouté

2 tablespoons butter	3 white peppercorns
4 tablespoons flour	salt to taste
3 cups hot chicken, veal, or	sprig of parsley
fish stock	½ cup chopped mushrooms

In a saucepan, melt the butter, stir in the flour, and cook until the roux is foamy and just starts to turn golden. Gradually add the stock and cook, stirring, until it comes to a boil. Add the peppercorns, salt, parsley, and mushrooms.

Simmer, stirring often, until reduced by ⅓ to ⅔ of the original quantity. Strain through a fine sieve.

Yield: 2 cups

➤ Keeps 5 days in the refrigerator, and can be frozen.

Sauce Suprême (Supreme Sauce)

This is the penultimate cream sauce. Use it when you wish a full, rich flavor.

2 cups chicken stock	1 cup heavy cream
3 sliced mushrooms	salt to taste
1 cup velouté	cayenne pepper to taste

In a saucepan, cook the chicken stock with the mushrooms until it is reduced to ⅓ of the original quantity or ⅔ of a cup. Add the veloute and simmer until reduced to 1 cup. Stir in the heavy cream and correct the seasonings with salt and cayenne pepper. Strain.

Yield: 2 cups

➤ Can be prepared ahead or frozen.

Sauce Villeroi

This sauce is used as a base for croquettes.

1½ cups veloute sauce	1 egg yolk, lightly beaten

In a saucepan, reduce the veloute by ⅓. Add ¼ of the mixture to the egg yolks and mix well. Return the egg yolk mixture to the body of the sauce, and cook over medium heat, stirring until it just reaches a boil and strain through a fine sieve, immediately. Cool before using.

Yield: 1 cup

➤ Keeps 4 days refrigerated.

Tomato Sauce

There are many versions of tomato sauce, ranging from a simple, un-cooked, puréed fresh tomato with seasonings to a long-simmered, multi-ingredient *ragu Bolognese*. Select a light, freshly made sauce for most vegetable dishes. If a recipe calls for 1 or 2 tablespoons of tomato sauce, feel free to use a good, subtly flavored, canned sauce. If tomato sauce is the main ingredient, making your own is better, provided the tomatoes are fresh and flavorful. In many instances, canned tomatoes are to be preferred over pulpy, tasteless, out-of-season tomatoes.

Simple Tomato Sauce

1 tablespoon minced onion	¼ teaspoon dried oregano
¼ teaspoon crushed garlic	1 teaspoon minced basil
1 tablespoon butter	1 cup cream (optional)
2 cups tomato purée	

In a saucepan, sauté the onion and garlic in the butter until soft but not brown. Add the tomato purée, oregano, and basil. Simmer 15 minutes. Strain, and add the cream if desired.

Yield: 2 to 3 cups
➤ Keeps 3 days in the refrigerator, and can be frozen.

Fresh Tomato Sauce I

2 pounds ripe tomatoes
¼ pound butter
1 onion, peeled and halved

salt and pepper to taste
¼ teaspoon sugar

Cut the tomatoes in half and cook, covered, for 10 minutes over medium heat. Purée through a food mill into a saucepan. Add the butter, onion, salt, pepper, and sugar, and simmer, slowly, uncovered for 45 minutes. Correct the seasoning and discard the onion.

Yield: 2 cups
➤ Keeps 3 days in the refrigerator, and can be frozen.

Fresh Tomato Sauce II

3 tablespoons butter
1 cup minced onion
1 clove garlic, crushed
1½ pound tomatoes, peeled,
　seeded and chopped

½ bay leaf
½ teaspoon dried thyme
1 chili pepper
salt and pepper to taste

In a saucepan, melt ⅓ of the butter, and sauté the onions until soft but not brown. Add the garlic, tomatoes, bay leaf, thyme, chili, salt, and pepper. Simmer, stirring occasionally, for about 15 minutes. Stir in the remaining 2 tablespoons of butter, and cook until the tomatoes are soft but still have some shape.

Yield: 3 cups
➤ Keeps 2 to 3 days refrigerated, and can be frozen.

NOTE: For a smoother sauce, strain through a food mill.

Uncooked Tomato Sauce

1¼ pounds tomatoes, peeled,
　and seeded
1 teaspoon tomato paste
4 teaspoons red wine vinegar
¼ cup olive oil

½ teaspoon salt
½ teaspoon pepper
1 tablespoon minced tarragon
1 tablespoon minced parsley

Press the tomato pulp through a sieve. Just before serving, whisk in the tomato paste and vinegar. Beat in the oil, a little at a time and season with salt, pepper, tarragon, and parsley.

Yield: 2 cups
➤ Keeps 2 days in the refrigerator.

NOTE: Substitute fresh basil for the tarragon, if desired.

Salsa (Tomato Chili Sauce)

Salsa, a spicy tomato sauce from the Southwest, serves as a wonderful topping to vegetable pancakes such as corn cakes, or as a refreshing dip for raw vegetables.

2 large ripe tomatoes, diced
1 jalapeno chili, seeded and
   minced

1 tablespoon minced fresh
   coriander
salt and pepper to taste
2 ice cubes

In a bowl, mix the tomatoes, chilies, coriander, salt, pepper, and ice cubes. Stir until the ice cubes melt. Serve very cold with tortilla chips, broiled meats, or shellfish.

Yield: 1 cup

NOTE: People's tolerances for spicy foods vary greatly. A spicy dish to one person can seem mild to another. Take care in adding chilies to this dish that it is not *too* hot. However, there should be no question that the food is hot!

Sauce Vierge (Cold Tomato and Herb Sauce)

This is the French version of salsa.

1 cup tomatoes, peeled,
   seeded, and chopped
1 clove garlic, crushed
1 teaspoon minced chervil
1 teaspoon minced parsley
1 teaspoon minced tarragon

1 teaspoon coriander seed,
   crushed
3 tablespoons extra virgin
   olive oil
salt and pepper to taste

In a bowl, mix the tomatoes, garlic, chervil, parsley, tarragon, coriander, oil, salt, and pepper. Serve at room temperature.

Yield: 1¼ cups

➤ Keeps 2 days refrigerated.

NOTE: This sauce is best if freshly made and allowed to sit for 30 minutes. If you must refrigerate it, let it come to room temperature before serving.

Other Sauces

Pesto Sauce

In recent years this sauce has become abused by overuse. It has been put on or into every sort of dish. It was designed to complement pasta, and can be used successfully with vegetables, but do use it sparingly. It has a strong flavor that often hides the main ingredient.

1 cup firmly packed basil
   leaves
1 large clove garlic, chopped
½ cup pine nuts

½ cup grated Parmesan cheese
¼ cup olive oil
   (approximately)
salt to taste

    In a processor, purée the basil and garlic, stopping to push the mixture down several times. Add the pine nuts and cheese, and continue blending until almost smooth. With the motor running, add the oil in a steady stream until the pesto is the consistency of mayonnaise. Add salt to taste.
    Serve as a dip, to stuff vegetables, or as a flavoring ingredient.

Yield: 1 cup

➤ Keeps 2 days refrigerated, and can be frozen, but it is best fresh.

NOTE: A blender makes a smoother sauce than a processor.

Yogurt Garlic Mint Sauce

1 cup plain yogurt
2 tablespoons minced fresh
   mint

2 tablespoons lemon juice
1 teaspoon garlic

    In a bowl, mix the yogurt, mint, lemon juice, and garlic. Let mature in the refrigerator overnight.

Yield: 1 cup

➤ Can be prepared 2 or 3 days ahead.

Lemon Dill Sauce

3 egg yolks
1 tablespoon arrowroot
1 teaspoon salt
pinch of Cayenne pepper

1 cup chicken stock
1 tablespoon lemon juice
2 tablespoons minced dill

    In a saucepan, mix the egg yolks, arrowroot, salt, and Cayenne. Stir in the stock and cook over moderate heat, stirring until the mixture reaches 185°F and is thick enough to coat the back of a spoon. Do not let it boil. Stir in the lemon juice and dill. Correct the seasoning with lemon juice, salt, and pepper. It should have a tart lemon flavor.
    Serve with chicken, fish croquettes, or fish balls.

Yield: 1½ cups

Avgolemonou *(Egg Lemon Sauce)*

This sauce is the Greek version of Hollandaise sauce. It requires care to make, but it is so delicious that it is worth the effort.

2 eggs   ½ cup hot chicken or fish
3 tablespoons lemon juice   stock
                                          1 tablespoon butter, melted

In a saucepan, beat the eggs until light and foamy. Beat in the lemon juice and stock. Place the pan over medium heat and cook, beating constantly, adding the butter gradually until the sauce is thick enough to coat the back of a spoon. Serve warm with lamb, meatballs, or fish balls.

Yield: 1 cup

➤ Keep warm over hot, not simmering water.

Dipping Sauce for Fried Foods

¼ cup soy sauce   ½ teaspoon salt
2 tablespoons honey   pinch of pepper
2 tablespoons sherry   1 clove garlic, minced

In a saucepan, mix the soy sauce, honey, sherry, salt, pepper, and garlic. Bring just to a boil. Serve warm as a dip for deep-fried dim sum and other deep-fried foods.

Yield: ½ cup

Mayonnaise

Make your own mayonnaise! With the machinery available in every kitchen today, there is no reason why anyone cannot make his or her own mayonnaise. It takes but a few minutes, the cost is similar if not less than the cost to purchase, and you have control over the quality. You can select quality oil, preferably an equal mix of a good—not super-expensive—olive oil and a pleasant, unflavored vegetable oil such as cottonseed, soy bean, or corn oil. Fresh eggs are always available. You can control the acidity by the type and amount of vinegar, and of course the salt. Sugar *never* belongs in mayonnaise.

Mayonnaise

2 egg yolks   ½ teaspoon dry mustard
½ teaspoon salt   2 tablespoons vinegar
pinch of white pepper   1 cup oil

In a bowl, whisk the egg yolk, salt, pepper, mustard, and ¼ of the vinegar until the mixture starts to thicken. Slowly beat in the oil, drop by drop, until ¼ of the oil has been incorporated. Add another ¼ of the remaining vinegar, and continue to beat in the oil in a thin, steady stream. When ½ the oil has been added, add another ¼ of the remaining vinegar, and continue beating in the remaining oil. Taste for seasoning, and beat in as much additional vinegar as needed.

Yield: 1 cup

➤ Keeps 2 weeks or longer in the refrigerator.

NOTE: It will help, when making the sauce by hand, to have the ingredients at room temperature, and to use a warm bowl. However, with modern electric mixers this precaution is not necessary.

Use half olive oil and half vegetable oil for the best flavor.

The acidity of vinegar varies greatly, so add it sparingly to achieve a properly tart mayonnaise. You can substitute lemon juice or lime juice for the vinegar.

If the mayonnaise does not emulsify, or if it curdles, you probably added the oil too quickly. To correct the problem, put a fresh egg yolk in a clean warm bowl and beat in the broken sauce, a teaspoon at a time, until it begins to look like mayonnaise. Continue adding the broken sauce in a slow steady stream until it is fully incorporated.

If you wish to make the sauce in a blender or processor, use 1 whole egg for each 2 egg yolks. Place the eggs, salt, pepper, and mustard in the container with a small amount of vinegar, and turn on the machine. Add the oil in a slow, steady stream. Add the vinegar and oil as outlined above. Taste, and correct the seasoning.

Sauce Tartare (Tartar Sauce)

Traditionally served with deep-fried seafood, this adds excitement to many deep-fried vegetables, such as corn fritters, cauliflower, or eggplant.

1½ cups mayonnaise	1 tablespoon capers, minced
¼ cup cornichons, minced	2 teaspoons Dijon mustard
2 scallions, minced	1 tablespoon heavy cream
1 anchovy, minced	½ teaspoon lemon juice
1 teaspoon minced parsley	salt and pepper to taste

In a bowl, mix the mayonnaise, cornichon, scallions, anchovies, parsley, capers, mustard, cream, lemon juice, and salt and pepper.

Let the flavors meld for 2 hours before serving. Serve with fried foods, especially fish, seafood, mushrooms, or zucchini.

Yield: 2 cups

➤ Keeps 2 weeks.

Sauce Verte (Green Sauce)

Serve as a dip for raw vegetables, or as a salad dressing.

1 cup mayonnaise	1 tablespoon minced tarragon
1 tablespoon minced parsley	½ tablespoon cooked, sieved
1 tablespoon minced	spinach
watercress	lemon juice to taste
1 tablespoon minced chervil	salt and pepper to taste

In a bowl, mix the mayonnaise with the parsley, watercress, chervil, tarragon, and spinach. Mix well, and correct the seasoning with lemon juice, salt, and pepper. Serve with cold poached fish and vegetables.

Yield: 1¼ cups

➤ Keeps 3 to 5 days in the refrigerator.

Dill Mayonnaise

1 cup mayonnaise	½ cup minced dill

In a bowl, mix the mayonnaise and dill and let the flavors meld for at least 30 minutes before serving.

Yield: 1½ cups

➤ Keeps 1 week in the refrigerator.

Vinaigrette

Vinaigrette is made with oil, vinegar, salt, and pepper, whisked together rapidly to form an emulsion. It may include dry or prepared mustard, garlic, herbs, or possibly other ingredients. It is is used alone, or in combination with other ingredients, to marinate vegetables, fish, or meat. It is never the thick, creamy-red mixture sold as "French dressing." At the end of this section are the recipes for variations on salad dressings.

Vinaigrette

2 tablespoons vinegar or	¼ teaspoon salt
lemon juice	pinch of pepper
2 teaspoons Dijon mustard	6 tablespoons olive oil

In a bowl, mix the vinegar, mustard, salt, and pepper. Gradually whisk in the oil until the mixture thickens and emulsifies. Taste for seasoning.

Yield: ½ cup

NOTE: Depending on the acidity of the vinegar, you may need to add more or less oil. This can be made in a processor. If allowed to sit, it should be beaten to re-emulsify before using.

Variations:

Use olive oil, walnut oil, safflower, or any other flavored oil. So-called salad oil is usually flavorless, and is not recommended. Select from dozens of vinegars. Use herbed vinegars, fruit vinegars, aged wine vinegars such as Balsamic or Sherry, or just lemon juice. Add minced anchovies in place of salt. See the section on lettuces for further suggestions.

Herbed Vinaigrette

2 tablespoons vinegar	6 tablespoons olive oil
1/4 teaspoon salt	1 tablespoon minced parsley,
pinch of pepper	chives, chervil, basil,
1/4 teaspoon dry mustard	tarragon, and/or chives

In a bowl, mix together the vinegar, salt, pepper, and mustard. Gradually beat in the oil to create an emulsion, and fold in the herbs.

Yield: 1/2 cup

Sauce Ravigote

1/2 cup vinaigrette	1 teaspoon mixed minced
1 tablespoon minced onion	parsley, tarragon, chives,
1 tablespoon Dijon mustard	and chervil
1 hard cooked egg, minced	

In a bowl, mix the vinaigrette, onion, mustard, eggs, and herbs until emulsified. Taste for seasoning.

Yield: 3/4 cup

➤ Can be prepared ahead and rewhisked just before serving.

Creme Du Moutarde
(Mustard Cream Dressing for Salads)

1/2 cup heavy cream	lemon juice to taste
1 teaspoon or more of Dijon	salt and pepper to taste
mustard	

In a bowl, beat the cream to the soft peak stage, and fold in the mustard, lemon juice, salt, and pepper. Taste for seasoning, and add additional mustard if desired.

Yield: 1 cup

➤ Keeps 2 days in the refrigerator.

Roquefort Dressing

⅓ cup crumbled Roquefort cheese	1 teaspoon Cognac
½ cup heavy cream	pinch of cayenne pepper
	1 tablespoon wine vinegar

In a bowl, mix the cheese, cream, Cognac, cayenne, and vinegar. Let stand for 5 minutes before using.

Yield: 6 servings

➤ Can be prepared the day before.

Sauce Russe
(Russian Dressing or Thousand-Island Dressing)

1 cup mayonnaise	1 teaspoon minced pimiento
3 tablespoons chili sauce	1 teaspoon minced chives

In a bowl, mix the mayonnaise with the chili sauce, pimento, and chives.

Yield: 1¼ cups

Can be prepared several days before using.

Thousand-Island Dressing II

1 cup mayonnaise	1½ teaspoon minced chives
¼ cup peeled, seeded, and chopped tomato	¼ teaspoon Worcestershire sauce
1 tablespoon chili sauce	

In a bowl, mix the mayonnaise, tomato, chili sauce, chives, and Worcestershire sauce.

Yield: 1½ cups

➤ Can be prepared the day before.

Mayonnaise Tyrolienne

2 cups mayonnaise	1 teaspoon Dijon mustard
2 tablespoons tomato paste	1 teaspoon white wine vinegar

In a bowl, mix the mayonnaise, tomato paste, and mustard. If too thick, thin with vinegar. Serve with vegetables or seafood.

Yield: 2 cups

➤ Keeps 4 days, refrigerated.

Artichokes

French or Globe Artichokes

*A*rtichokes, relatives of the thistle, and hence the cardoon, are grown mostly in France, Italy, and the United States. The Jerusalem artichoke, a tuber unrelated to the globe artichoke, is described on page 246.

Artichokes are sold as tiny as a golf ball or as large as a grapefruit. The very smallest artichokes can be eaten raw with nothing but a little salt. However, these reach only a few markets, usually in Italian neighborhoods. The larger, more readily available artichokes must be cooked until tender. Artichokes are prepared whole, in hearts, or with the stem and outer leaves removed so that only the most tender bottom remains; and as *fonds*, bases, or bottoms.

Availability

Fresh

Year round, though March through June is the peak season. Look for heavy-feeling globes with tightly closed leaves. They should have a fresh, green look. In winter a few brown spots, caused by frost, on the outer leaves, are acceptable. Avoid artichokes with bruised, curled, or dried looking leaves, and those that are pale in color or that feel light for their size. The gray-green leaves have tiny sharp spines at the tips which can make handling uncomfortable.

Store in a tightly covered container or a plastic bag in the refrigerator to preserve moisture.

For a dried flower arrangement, let them stand in a warm, dry room for a few days, and the artichokes will dry to a bronzed brown and last for a month or more. A pile of them in a ceramic bowl makes an instant centerpiece.

Frozen

Hearts of small artichokes, quartered or halved, are suitable for cooked dishes.

Canned

Hearts Suitable for use in casseroles and mixed vegetable dishes. They are not as good as the fresh, but combined with other vegetables they can add a pleasant flavor, even though the texture is not as crisp.

Bottoms These tend to be mushy and should be avoided.

Marinated There are many producers of marinated artichoke hearts. These can be a delicious hors d'oeuvre or can be used as part of a salad or other cold plate. Try several brands, and choose the one with the best flavor and texture.

Preparation

Whole or for Stuffing

Cut the stem even with the base of the artichoke, and rub the bottom with the cut half of a lemon to prevent discoloring. (Some writers recommend bending the stem away from the artichoke to draw any tough fibers from the artichoke itself.)

Peel the stem and put into a pot of acidulated water. (Many cooks discard the stem, but if peeled, it is similar in texture to the bottom of the artichoke.) Cut off the upper third of the artichoke and discard. (The reason to remove the top third is to cut off any sharp spines and make it more comfortable for the diner. If the spines are not sharp, or you do not care, omit this step.) Rub the cut edges with half a lemon.

If the artichoke is to be stuffed, spread the leaves, pull out the purplish center leaves, and with a teaspoon scoop out the fuzzy choke. Fill the cavity with the stuffing. Press apart the outer leaves, and insert stuffing among the leaves, if desired.

Artichoke Hearts

Use only small artichokes; larger artichokes are too tough. Starting at the bottom of the artichoke, strip off the leaves until you are over the base and the tender paler leaves are exposed. Cut off the top third, and then cut the artichokes in half vertically through the stem and cut the halves to the desired thickness: halves, quarters, or slices. With a paring knife, cut out the fuzzy choke and immediately put the artichoke into acidulated water.

If the stem is tough, pare off the outer strings.

Poach, steam, deep-fry, or cook with other vegetables.

Artichoke Bottoms

In the past these were a favorite of *haute cuisine* as delicate containers for sauces, or other vegetables. Their delicate flavor is worth the effort involved in the preparation.

Cut off the stem even with the bottom. Starting with the outermost leaf, strip the leaves off the artichoke until the base of the leaves is above the bulge at the base. With a sharp knife, cut off the remaining leaves even with the top of the curve. You should have a pale-colored base, with the choke clearly visible. With a spoon, scoop out the choke, and dip the base into acidulated water. (The choke can be removed after cooking, if preferred.) With a paring knife, pare around the sides of the base to smooth the sides.

To Cook Artichoke Bottoms
Poach the bases in a *blanc* (page 6) until a knife can be inserted in the center easily—about 6 minutes. The bases should be fully cooked, but not overcooked. There should be a slight resistance. Artichoke bottoms are usually used as containers for saucers or vegetables, but they can be filled with a vegetable purée topped with bread crumbs or a cream sauce, and broiled until golden, to be served as a first course. The bottoms can also be used as a container for poached eggs for a brunch dish.

Methods of Cooking

Artichokes can be boiled, braised, fried, deep-fried, stuffed, or served in a gratin. They are suitable for appetizers, soups, vegetables, salads, or cooked with meat or fish.

When Is It Cooked?
Whole artichokes are cooked adequately when an outer leaf pulls away easily. A little overcooking is acceptable. The point of a sharp knife should be able to pierce a cooked bottom or heart with almost no resistance.

Sauces

Artichokes take well to sauces that have a slight acid edge, such as hollandaise, bearnaise, or vinaigrette. They also blend well with cream sauces, such as supreme, allemande, and Mornay. Diced artichoke bases are good tossed with herbed butters, especially if they have lemon juice. Cold artichokes marry well with strongly flavored mayonnaises such as aioli and mustard.

Stuffed artichokes are usually served without a sauce, but melted butter flavored with lemon juice or just butter alone can add tang.

Boiled or Steamed Artichokes with Various Sauces

6 artichokes	dipping sauces (see below)
1 lemon	

Prepare the artichokes as indicated above, rubbing the cut surfaces with the cut half of lemon. Slice the remaining half of the lemon thinly.

Place the artichokes in a noncorrosible sauce pan. Add 1 inch of water and the lemon slices. Cover tightly, and simmer over low heat until an outside leaf pulls away from the artichoke easily.

Or, place the artichokes in a steamer, and place a slice of lemon on top of each. Steam until tender enough so that an outside leaf pulls off easily. To serve, place each artichoke on a plate with a side dish of sauce.

Alternately—press open the center of the artichoke, remove the center leaves and choke and fill the center with the sauce. Serve hot or cold.

Yield: 6 servings

➤ Can be prepared one day ahead, if they are to be served cold.

Artichauts en Feuille Tiède
(Artichokes in Cream and Vinegar Sauce)

¼ cup cider vinegar	½ teaspoon sugar
1 teaspoon minced shallots	¾ cup heavy cream
½ teaspoon salt	6 warm boiled or steamed
pepper	artichokes

In a bowl, mix the vinegar, shallots, salt, pepper, and sugar together, and gradually whisk in the cream.

Serve the sauce in individual dishes.

Yield: 6 servings

➤ The sauce can be prepared the day before.

Purée d'Artichauts (Artichoke Purée)

12 cooked artichoke bottoms (see page 35)	1 to 2 tablespoons heavy cream
6 tablespoons butter	salt and pepper to taste

In a processor, purée the artichoke bottoms with 1 tablespoon butter, cream, salt, and pepper. In a saucepan, heat the remaining butter and cook the purée, stirring often until reheated.

Serve immediately.

Yield: 6 servings

➤ The purée can be made the day before and reheated, and can be frozen.

Artichoke Timbales with Tomato Coriander Sauce

1 large artichoke, cooked	6 eggs
4 cups chicken stock	⅔ cup heavy cream
10 ounce packages artichoke hearts	⅓ cup grated Parmesan
1 tablespoon butter	⅓ cup bread crumbs
2 tablespoons minced shallots	¼ teaspoon salt
1 teaspoon minced garlic	⅛ teaspoon pepper

Preheat the oven to 375°F. Butter 8½ cup timbale molds, and line the bottoms with waxed paper.

Remove leaves the from the cooked artichoke and reserve. Scoop out the choke and discard. Reserve the bottom. Bring stock to a simmer, and cook the artichoke hearts until soft, about 10 minutes. Drain.

In a processor, purée the artichoke hearts and the reserved artichoke bottom. In a skillet, melt the butter and sauté the shallots until soft, but not brown. Add to the processor and purée. Add the eggs, cream, Parmesan, breadcrumbs, salt, and pepper, and purée again.

Fill the prepared molds, place in a baking dish, and fill with 1 inch of boiling water. Bake until a knife inserted in the center comes out clean—about 30 minutes. Unmold onto plates, remove the waxed paper, and spoon the sauce over timbales.

Yield: 8 servings

Tomato Coriander Sauce

½ cup minced shallots	¼ teaspoon pepper
3 tablespoons olive oil	pinch of sugar
28 ounce can plum tomatoes, drained and chopped	½ cup heavy cream
	salt and pepper to taste
1 cup chicken stock	1 tablespoon minced coriander

In a 2 quart saucepan over medium heat, sauté the shallots in the oil until soft. Add the tomatoes, stock, pepper, and sugar, and simmer until the tomatoes are thickened, stirring occasionally—about 20 minutes. In a processor, purée the sauce and return to the saucepan. Add the cream, and cook over low heat until the sauce thickens slightly. Season with salt and pepper, and stir in the coriander.

Yield: 2½ cups

Artichaut a la Barigoule (Braised Artichokes)

12 tiny fresh artichokes, or 2 packages frozen hearts, thawed	4 garlic cloves, minced
	2 bay leaves
1 lemon, cut in half, if needed	1 teaspoon dried thyme
¼ pound bacon, ½ inch dice	1½ teaspoons salt
5 tablespoons olive oil	½ teaspoon pepper
1 cup diced onion	½ cup minced parsley
½ cup diced carrots	1 cup dry white wine
1 cup peeled, seeded, and chopped tomatoes	water, as needed

If using fresh artichokes, remove any dark outer leaves. If small, leave whole; if larger, cut into halves or quarters, and remove and discard the choke. Rub all cut surfaces with lemon halves.

If using frozen artichokes, thaw.

In a small saucepan of boiling water, blanch the bacon for 5 minutes, drain, repeat the blanching, and drain again.

In a casserole, heat 3 tablespoons of oil, and sauté the onions and carrots, stirring occasionally until softened. Add the tomatoes, garlic, and artichokes, and mix. Add the bay leaves, thyme, salt, and pepper. Stir in ¼ cup minced parsley. Add the wine, and bring to a boil and reduce by half. Add enough water to cover, and simmer 15 minutes.

Drain the vegetables, and reduce the cooking liquid to a glaze. Stir in the remaining 2 tablespoons of olive oil, and bring to a boil. Swirl in the remaining ¼ cup of parsley, and pour over the vegetables.

Serve immediately.

Yield: 6 servings

➤ Can be prepared the day before and reheated.

Variation:

Use whole artichokes; remove the center leaves and choke. Fill the center of each artichoke with ¼ cup duxelles (see page 304) mixed with 1 tablespoon minced bacon, 1 tablespoon minced ham, and 1 teaspoon minced parsley, and cook as above.

Braised Artichokes with Anchovy and Garlic Sauce

18 garlic cloves, unpeeled	1½ tablespoons lemon juice
⅔ cup olive oil	¾ teaspoon salt
3 garlic cloves, thinly sliced	¾ teaspoon pepper
6 anchovy fillets	6 artichokes
1½ cups water	3 tablespoons lemon juice
1½ cups chicken stock	

Cook the garlic cloves in boiling water until soft—about 5 minutes. Drain and press the flesh from the skins and mash.

In a skillet, heat ¼ cup oil, and sauté the sliced garlic until golden, but not burned. Add the anchovies, and stir until dissolved. Mix in the mashed garlic. Set the sauce aside.

In a large skillet heat the water, stock, lemon juice, salt, pepper, and ¼ cup olive oil. Prepare artichokes (page 34), cut in half, and scoop out the chokes. Place cut side down in skillet and simmer, covered, for 25 minutes. Uncover and boil until most of the liquid evaporates.

Arrange artichokes cut side up on serving plates, and spoon on sauce.

Yield: 6 servings

➤ Both the sauce and the artichokes can be prepared a day ahead and reheated.

Carciofi al Tegame (Braised Artichokes)

This recipe is best made with tiny, chokeless artichokes. If these are not available, use larger artichokes and prepare as hearts (see page 34).

12 small artichokes, or hearts	salt and pepper to taste
2 garlic cloves, minced	⅔ cup olive oil
2 tablespoons minced mint	

Prepare the artichokes, keeping only the tenderest part, and removing and discarding any choke. In a bowl, mix the garlic and mint, and rub over the artichokes. If using whole tiny artichokes, insert them into the center. Season with salt and pepper.

In a large non-corrosible skillet, place the artichokes, and drizzle on the oil and add 2 cups of water. Cover and simmer gently for 1 hour. Uncover and cook over high heat until the juices are almost evaporated. Serve hot or cold.

Yield: 6 servings

➤ Can be prepared 2 days ahead.

Fonds Des Artichauts Printanièrs
(Artichoke Bottoms Braised with Carrots, Onions, Turnips, and Mushrooms)

6 large artichokes	1 cup diced turnips
1 or 2 lemons	salt and pepper to taste
1 cup diced onions	2 tablespoons wine vinegar
3 tablespoons butter	½ cup dry white wine
2 garlic cloves, minced	1½ cups stock or water
1 cup diced mushrooms	bouquet of parsley, bay leaf,
12 small white onions, peeled	and thyme
1 cup diced carrots	2-3 tablespoons butter

Preheat the oven to 325°F.

Cut the artichoke bottoms into chunks, and cook in boiling salted water to cover for about 5 minutes, or until just barely tender. Drain.

In a casserole, sauté the diced onions in the butter until soft, but not brown. Stir in the garlic and mushrooms, and cook, stirring for 2 minutes. Add the whole onions, carrots, and turnips. Season with salt and pepper, and cook, stirring occasionally over moderate heat for about 10 minutes. Do not let brown.

Add the vinegar and wine, and reduce by half over high heat. Add the stock and herb bouquet, and bring to a simmer and cover.

Place in the oven bake for 30 to 45 minutes, or until tender. Discard the bouquet garni. If necessary, remove the vegetables and reduce the liquid to a glaze. Return the vegetables to the casserole and reheat.

Just before serving, taste for seasoning and swirl in the remaining butter.

Yield: 6 servings

➤ Can be made the day before and reheated.

Carciofi e Porri Stufato
(Braised Artichokes and Leeks)

3 large artichokes	¼ cup olive oil
½ lemon	salt and pepper to taste
4 large leeks	

With the stems still attached to the artichokes, peel them and pull off any coarse outer leaves. Cut the artichokes into wedges, 1 inch wide at the largest point. Immediately rub with lemon and put into acidulated water. Remove the green tops and roots from the leeks and clean (see page 263).

Lay the leeks in a casserole, pour on the oil, and add one inch of water. Cover and place over moderate heat for 10 minutes. Add the artichoke wedges, salt, and pepper, cover, and cook until the vegetables are tender—about 25 minutes.

Check after 10 minutes to see if more water is needed.

Yield: 6 servings

➤ Can be prepared ahead and reheated.

Carciofi Dorati e Fritti (Golden Sautéed Artichokes)

The egg batter turns these a lovely golden shade. This recipe is best made with tiny chokeless artichokes. If these are not available, use larger artichokes and prepare as artichoke hearts (see page 34).

12 small tender artichokes, or hearts	2 egg yolks
1 cup flour	2 cups olive oil
2 eggs	salt
	6 lemon wedges

Prepare the artichokes and cut into wedges. Keep in acidulated water for 15 minutes. Drain and pat dry. Dredge with the flour, and shake off the excess.

In a bowl, beat the eggs and egg yolks together.

In a skillet, heat the oil until hot, but not smoking. Dip the floured artichokes into the egg mixture, and fry until golden on both sides, over medium heat. Drain, sprinkle with salt, and serve with lemon wedges.

Yield: 6 servings

NOTE: It is important to keep the heat moderate so the artichoke cooks through before the egg coating becomes too dark. If you wish to prepare these with larger artichokes, blanch the prepared artichoke sections in boiling, salted, acidulated water until almost tender.

Fondi di Carciofi, Fritti (Deep-Fried Artichoke Hearts)

6 large, or 12 small artichokes
1 tablespoon lemon juice
3 tablespoons flour

oil for deep-frying
lemon wedges

Remove and discard the leaves from the artichokes. Cut into halves or quarters, and remove and discard the choke. Place the lemon juice in a bowl of water, add the prepared artichokes, and let stand for 2 hours. Just before serving, drain well and pat dry with paper towels.

Heat the oil to 375°F. Roll the artichokes in the flour and fry until golden—about 3 minutes. Drain and serve hot with lemon wedges.

Yield: 6 servings

➤ Cannot be prepared ahead.

Carciofi Fritti (Deep-Fried Artichokes in Batter)

8 medium artichokes
¼ cup flour
salt and pepper to taste
¼ cup olive oil

2 lemons
3 eggs
oil for deep-frying

Cut the artichokes as directed for hearts on page 34, leaving the stem attached. Cut each artichoke into 8 wedges and soak in water to cover with the juice of one lemon added.

In a bowl or processor, mix the flour, salt, and pepper with the oil, and add the eggs, one at a time, beating well after each addition. Let stand for 30 minutes before using. Heat the oil to 350°F.

Drain the artichokes, pat dry, and dip into the batter. deep-fry until golden. Serve sprinkled with salt, and garnish with lemon wedges.

Yield: 6 servings

Carciofi alla Giudia (Artichokes Jewish Style)

This dish is a speciality of Roman Jews. When cooked, the artichokes are particularly crisp and crunchy. Ideally the dish is prepared with tiny, chokeless artichokes. If these are not available, use the tiniest artichokes available, no larger than 2½ inches in diameter. Pull off any tough outer leaves to expose only the thinnest light green leaves. Press open the center leaves and scoop out any choke with a spoon.

12 tiny artichokes
juice of 2 lemons

salt and pepper to taste
2 cups olive oil

Leave at least 2 inch stems on the artichokes. Peel from the stems the tough outer layer. Soak in water acidulated with the lemon juice until ready to cook. Drain well.

With your hands, press the leaves from the center outward to shape into a flower. Place the opened artichoke top down on a counter, and press firmly to shape it into a flat flower. Season the inside with salt and pepper.

In a large skillet, heat the oil, and arrange the artichokes in the pan with the stem sticking upward. Cook until tender, pressing the stems occasionally, and turning in the pan to cook them evenly. When tender, press even more firmly to make large squat flowers, and continue cooking until the leaves are like bronzed flowers.

To make the outer leaves particularly crisp, dip your hand into cold water and shake the water over the boiling oil, taking care to avoid the splattering oil, and let cook another 2 minutes. Drain well, and serve very hot.

Yield: 6 to 12 servings

Artichauts Farcis à La Niçoise
(Stuffed Artichokes Niàoise)

Ideally these are made with artichokes that are so young they have not yet formed a choke. Since these are difficult to find, larger chokes are used here. Remove the choke before stuffing.

6 medium-sized artichokes	½ cup minced parsley
½ cup olive oil	4 garlic cloves, minced
4 slices stale bread	salt and pepper to taste

Preheat the oven to 375°F.

Prepare the artichokes for stuffing (see page 34). If there is a choke, spread the leaves, and with the aid of a teaspoon, scoop out the choke and discard it. In a bowl, toss the artichokes with the oil to cover all surfaces.

In another bowl, pour enough hot water over the bread slices to cover, and let stand for 5 minutes, or until the bread has swelled and become soggy. Drain and squeeze out the excess moisture. Return the bread to the bowl, and stir in the parsley, garlic, salt, and pepper, with a tablespoon or two of oil.

Turn each artichoke upside down to drain and then season the interior with salt. Place the stuffing on top and among the spread leaves. Arrange the artichokes in a gratin dish just large enough to hold them. Pour 1 tablespoon of olive oil over each artichoke and bake for 1 ¼ hours.

Serve hot or cold.

Yield: 6 servings

Variation:
Add ½ cup of grated Parmesan cheese to the bread mixture.

Carciofi Ripiene
(Neapolitan Artichokes Stuffed with Mozzarella)

6 artichokes	⅔ cup diced mozzarella
salt to taste	2-3 springs parsley, minced
1 egg	4 teaspoons bread crumbs
pepper to taste	2 anchovy fillets, slivered
4 teaspoons grated Parmesan	5 tablespoons olive oil

Preheat the oven to 350°F.

Prepare the artichokes for stuffing (see page 34). Scoop out the choke, pushing apart the leaves. Season with salt.

In a bowl, beat the egg, a pinch of salt, pepper, Parmesan, mozzarella, and parsley, and mix well. Stuff between leaves of chokes, and sprinkle with bread crumbs. Press the filling into the artichokes, and place a sliver of anchovy on top.

In a baking dish just large enough to hold the artichokes in one layer, arrange the artichokes upright, and sprinkle with oil and ¼ cup warm water. Cover and bake for 25 minutes. Uncover and bake 15 minutes longer, or until browned and tender.

Serve hot or cold.

Yield: 6 servings

Carciofi Ripiene Di Mortadella
(Stuffed Artichokes with Mortadella)

6 artichokes	½ cup Parmesan cheese
½ lemon	2 eggs
1 teaspoon minced garlic	pinch nutmeg
1½ tablespoons minced parsley	salt and pepper to taste
¾ cup chopped mortadella	2½ tablespoons bread crumbs
	½ cup olive oil

Prepare the artichokes for stuffing (see page 34). In a bowl, mix the garlic, parsley, mortadella, Parmesan, eggs, nutmeg, salt, and pepper with 1½ tablespoons bread crumbs. Stuff the artichokes and sprinkle with remaining crumbs.

In a casserole large enough to hold the artichokes in one layer, arrange the artichokes, drizzle with the olive oil, add about ½ inch of water, and cover. Simmer gently over low heat for about 30 minutes or until an outside leaf will pull off easily.

Cool and serve at room temperature.

Yield: 6 servings

Carciofi Ripiene alla Milanese
(Stuffed Artichokes Milan Style)

6 large artichokes, prepared for stuffing (page 34)	2 tablespoons water
5 tablespoons butter	½ teaspoon marjoram
½ cup minced onion	pinch of allspice
½ cup soft fresh bread crumbs	pinch of thyme
½ cup milk	salt and pepper to taste
¾ pound ground veal	¼ cup grated Parmesan
1 egg	¼ cup grated Gruyere
2 tablespoons minced parsley	2 cups fresh tomato sauce (see
2 garlic cloves, mashed	page 25)

Preheat the oven to 325°F.

Cook the artichokes in boiling salted and acidulated water for 10 minutes. In a skillet, melt the butter, and sauté the onion until soft, but not brown. In a bowl, soak the bread crumbs in the milk, and squeeze out the excess moisture. In a large bowl, mix the onions, bread, veal, egg, parsley, garlic, water, marjoram, allspice, and thyme. Season with salt and pepper.

Stuff the artichokes with the mixture, doming it over the top. In a flameproof baking dish, melt the remaining 3 tablespoons of butter, and arrange the artichokes in the dish. Sprinkle the artichokes with the Parmesan and Gruyere cheeses, and cover. Bake for 45 minutes, basting often. Uncover and bake 15 minutes longer, or until golden.

Serve hot or cold with the tomato sauce on the side.

Yield: 6 servings

➤ Can be prepared for the final baking the day before, or fully cooked and served at room temperature.

Baked Stuffed Artichokes

6 large artichokes, cooked	salt and pepper to taste
½ cup olive oil	1 tablespoon minced basil
1½ cups minced onion	grated zest of 2 lemons
4 garlic cloves, minced	juice of 1 lemon
½ pound ground veal	1½ cups fresh bread crumbs
½ pound ground pork	1 cup minced parsley

Preheat the oven to 375°F.

Spread the leaves of the artichokes, and remove and discard the choke. In a skillet, sauté the onion in half the oil until soft, but not brown. Add the celery and half the garlic, and cook, stirring for 5 minutes, or until tender. Add the veal, pork, salt, pepper, and basil.

Cook, stirring to break up any large clumps, until the meat loses its color. Remove from the heat, and stir in the lemon zest, lemon juice, bread crumbs, ¾ cup of the parsley, and the remaining garlic.

Stuff the artichokes, and arrange in a baking dish. Sprinkle with the remaining parsley. Drizzle with the remaining oil, and add ½ inch of boiling water. Cover and bake for 35 minutes. Remove the cover and bake for 10 minutes longer, or until the top is lightly browned.

Yield: 6 artichokes

➤ Can be prepared ahead and baked just before serving to serve hot, or baked and served at room temperature.

Tortino di Carciofi (Baked Artichokes)

This dish not only serves as a hearty vegetable with a light dinner, but also it makes a wonderful light lunch with a salad, or a main course for a brunch.

6 artichokes	6 eggs
1 lemon	4 tablespoons milk
flour	salt and pepper
1 cup olive oil	

Preheat the oven to 400°F.

Remove the outer leaves, saving only the tender inner leaves. Cut into thick slices, and remove any choke. Soak in acidulated water with lemon juice for 15 minutes. Drain dry and dust with flour.

In a skillet, heat ½ cup oil, and sauté the artichokes, in batches, until golden on both sides. This will take between 20 and 30 minutes. Sprinkle with salt, and arrange in one layer in a baking dish. Pour the remaining oil over the top.

In a bowl, beat the eggs, milk, salt, and pepper, and pour over the artichokes. Bake for 15 to 20 minutes, or until the eggs are set.

Yield: 6 servings

Artichoke and Potato Pancakes

2 potatoes, grated	1 egg
2 large artichoke bottoms, grated	2 tablespoons bread crumbs
1 teaspoon lemon juice	1 teaspoon salt
½ onion, grated	½ teaspoon pepper
	3 tablespoons oil

In a bowl, mix the potatoes and artichokes. Stir in the lemon juice, onions, egg, and bread crumbs. Season with salt and pepper.

Heat a large skillet and add the oil. When hot, drop into the pan 2 tablespoons batter for each pancake. Cook until browned and crisp on both sides. Drain on paper towels.

Serve immediately.

Yield: 6 servings

NOTE: If necessary, keep warm in a 250°F oven for 30 minutes, uncovered.

Artichokes and Rice

¼ cup butter	2½ cups boiling chicken stock
¼ cup minced onions	1 cup rice
1 garlic clove, minced	2 tablespoons minced parsley
1 10-inch package frozen	salt and pepper
artichoke hearts, thawed	

In a saucepan, melt the butter, and sauté the onions and garlic until soft, but not brown. Add the artichoke hearts, chicken stock, rice, parsley, and salt and pepper. Cover, and simmer for about 20 minutes, or until the rice is tender.

Serve immediately.

Yield: 6 servings

Artichoke and Pea Casserole

Both peas and artichokes freeze well, and make preparing this dish both quick and easy. You can use fresh peas and artichokes, but expect the cooking times to triple.

⅓ cup minced prosciutto	2 10-ounce packages frozen
¼ cup minced onion	artichoke hearts
¼ cup minced parsley	1 tablespoon minced basil
1 garlic clove, minced	salt and pepper to taste
¼ cup olive oil	½ cup chicken stock
	1 package frozen peas, thawed

On a board, mince the prosciutto, onion, parsley, and garlic together, very finely.

In a casserole, heat the oil, and cook the mixture until the onion is soft but not brown. Add the artichoke, basil, salt, pepper, and stock. Cover and simmer for 10 minutes, stirring occasionally. Add the peas, cover, and simmer for 3 to 5 minutes longer, or until the peas are just cooked.

Yield: 6 servings

Fonds d'Artichauts Archiduc (Artichoke Bottoms Stuffed with Spinach and Mushrooms)

Although these are usually a garnish for a meat platter, 2 bottoms make a sensational luncheon or brunch serving.

1 tablespoon butter	salt and pepper to taste
¼ pound thinly sliced	6 cooked artichoke bottoms
mushrooms	(see page 35)
¼ teaspoon nutmeg	1½ cups Mornay sauce
2 pounds spinach, stripped	6 teaspoons grated Parmesan
and wilted (see page 459)	cheese

Preheat the oven to 400°F.

In a skillet, heat the butter, and sauté the mushrooms until they are softened and all liquid has evaporated. Season with nutmeg. Squeeze any excess moisture from the spinach, add it to the skillet, and season with salt and pepper. Mix well. Drain the bottoms, and fill with the spinach mixture.

In an ovenproof serving dish, spread a thin layer of sauce, and top with the artichoke bottoms. Spoon more sauce over the top of the artichokes, and sprinkle with the cheese. Bake for 10 minutes, or until piping hot.

Yield: 6 servings

➤ Can be prepared for baking the day before.

Alcachofas Rellenos de Gamba y Jamón
(Artichoke Bottoms with Shrimp and Ham)

2 tablespoons butter	1½ tablespoons dry Sherry
1½ tablespoons minced shallot	¾ cup hollandaise sauce (see
½ pound raw shrimp, chopped	page 19)
⅓ cup minced ham	12 artichoke bottoms, cooked
2 tablespoons minced parsley	

Preheat the oven to 400°F.

In a skillet, melt the butter and sauté the shallot until soft, but not brown. Add the shrimp and ham and cook, stirring until the shrimp are just done. Stir in the parsley and sherry and cook until the liquid evaporates.

Remove from the heat and cool for 2 minutes. Stir in ½ cup hollandaise sauce and fill the bottoms with the mixture. Spoon a teaspoon of hollandaise over each artichoke and arrange in a baking dish. Bake for 10 minutes, or until just heated through and the top is golden.

Serve as a first course, or as an accompaniment to a roast.

Yield: 6 to 12 servings

➤ Can be prepared for baking the day before and kept refrigerated.

Alcachofas Rellenos de Loma y Champiñones
(Artichoke Bottoms Stuffed with Pork and Mushrooms)

3 tablespoons olive oil	¾ cup minced mushrooms
¼ cup minced onion	2 tablespoons minced parsley
3 garlic cloves, minced	3 tablespoons dry white wine
½ pound ground pork	¾ cup hollandaise sauce
salt and pepper to taste	12 cooked artichoke bottoms

Preheat the oven to 400°F.

In a skillet, heat the oil, and sauté the onion and garlic until soft, but not brown. Stir in the pork and cook, breaking up the meat until it loses its color. Season with salt and pepper, and add the mushrooms. Cook, stirring for 1 minute. Add the parsley and wine, and cook until the liquid evaporates.

Remove from the heat, and stir in ½ cup hollandaise sauce. Fill the artichoke bottoms with the meat mixture, and spoon a teaspoon of hollandaise over each artichoke.

Place in a baking pan, and bake for 10 minutes or until golden.

Yield: 6 to 12 servings

➤ Can be prepared for baking the day before.

Carciofi Marinati (*Marinated Artichoke Hearts*)

This recipe is best made with tiny, chokeless artichokes. If these are not available, use larger artichokes, and prepare as indicated on page 34. Canned or frozen (cooked) artichokes can be prepared in this fashion. The piquancy of the other ingredients makes up for the lack of texture.

12 small artichoke hearts	1 tablespoon minced pickled
2 cups wine vinegar	red pepper
2 teaspoons salt	2 tablespoons minced parsley
1 cup water	½ teaspoon black pepper
Juice of 1 lemon	1 cup olive oil
2 garlic cloves, minced	

Prepare the artichoke hearts: cut into slices about ½ inch thick, or quarter, removing any choke.

In a saucepan, simmer the artichoke slices in the vinegar, salt, and water until tender, about 20 to 30 minutes.

Drain well and put into a bowl. Toss with the lemon juice, garlic, red pepper, parsley, and black pepper. When well coated, pour on the olive oil, and refrigerate covered for about 2 hours before serving.

Serve as part of an antipasto, or use in salads.

Yield: 6 to 12 servings

➤ Can be prepared 2 to 3 days ahead.

Artichauts à la Grecque
(Artichoke Hearts, Greek Style)

This recipe is best made with tiny chokeless artichokes. If these are not available, use larger artichokes, and prepare as indicated on page 34.

1 cup finely diced carrot	1 cup water
1 cup finely diced onion	salt and pepper to taste
½ cup olive oil	1 teaspoon peppercorns,
12 raw artichoke hearts	crushed
bouquet garni of bay leaf,	6 coriander seeds
thyme, and parsley	1 lemon, peeled and sliced
2 cups dry white wine	

In a casserole, sauté the carrot and onion in 2 tablespoons of olive oil, over low heat until soft, but not browned. Add the artichoke hearts, bouquet garni, wine, water, salt, peppercorns, coriander seeds, and lemon slices. Cover and simmer for about 30 minutes, or until the hearts are tender-crisp.

Pour over the remaining olive oil, and let stand for 2 hours. Drain off the liquid, and reduce it to 1½ cups. Discard the bouquet garni, and pour the liquid over the vegetables. Cool.

Serve cold, or at room temperature as an hors d'oeuvre or as part of an antipasto.

Yield: 6 servings

➤ Can be prepared 2 or 3 days ahead.

Les Fonds d'Artichauts au Foie Gras
(Artichoke and Foie Gras Salad)

This is the sort of luxury salad that is reserved for the most special of occasions. Serve it on individual plates as a first course.

4 large cooked artichoke bottoms	6 slices foie gras, diced
½ cup Vinaigrette (see page 30)	6 slices truffle
3 cups shredded frisée lettuce,	
or Belgian endive	

In a small bowl, toss the artichokes with half the vinaigrette. In another bowl, toss the frisée with the remaining vinaigrette. Arrange some of the lettuce on each plate and top with a mound of artichoke. Scatter the foie gras over the top and garnish with the truffle slices.

Yield: 6 servings

➤ The artichokes can be marinated for several hours, but do not assemble more than 10 minutes before serving.

Mayonnaise of Artichoke, Celery Root, and Potatoes

A mayonnaise is an old fashioned type of salad that is finished with an "icing" of mayonnaise, which is then garnished to look something like a fancy cake. Do take care not to use too much mayonnaise in the basic mixture.

1 pound tiny new potatoes, peeled
1 pound celery root, peeled and cut into ¼ inch thick slices
6 large cooked artichoke bottoms (see page 35)
1½ cups mayonnaise
2 tablespoons heavy cream

1 tablespoon minced chervil or tarragon
3 tablespoons drained capers
3 tablespoons minced chives
2 bunches watercress, leaves removed
1 hard cooked egg, sieved
black olives and pimiento strips

In a pot of boiling salted water, cook the potatoes until just tender, about 10 minutes. Drain and chill. In another saucepan of boiling salted water, cook the celery root until just tender. Drain and cool.

Carefully slice the artichoke bottoms horizontally into ¼ inch thick disks. Cut the potatoes into ¼ inch thick slices. With a cookie cutter, cut the celery root slices to the same size as the artichoke slices. (Ideally, all three vegetables should be the same size. If you prefer, cut them all into a ¼ inch thick batons.)

In a small bowl, mix half the mayonnaise with the cream. In separate bowls, toss the vegetables with just enough mayonnaise to bind. In a 2 quart bowl, make a layer with half the potatoes, and sprinkle with half the chervil. Add a layer of celery root, and sprinkle half the capers. Top with a layer of artichoke, and sprinkle with half the chives. Repeat, and refrigerate for 6 hours.

Arrange the watercress leaves on a serving platter and unmold the salad. Spread the remaining mayonnaise over the surface and decorate with the egg, olives, and pimiento.

Yield: 6 servings

➤ Can be prepared the day before but do not decorate more than 2 hours before serving.

Shrimp Stuffed Artichokes Mimosa

6 large artichokes, boiled until tender
¾ cup vinaigrette, flavored with garlic and mustard
1 pound 21 to 25 count shrimp, cooked, peeled, and deveined

¼ cup minced onion
1 anchovy, minced
2 tablespoons minced pimientos
½ cup diced Greek olives
2 hard cooked eggs, separated
2 tablespoons minced parsley

Drain the artichokes, scoop out the chokes, and set them aside. In a bowl, combine the vinaigrette, and add 1 teaspoon to each artichoke. Set aside 6 shrimp, and dice the remainder.

Marinate the diced shrimp, onions, anchovy, pimientos, and olives with all but 2 tablespoons of the vinaigrette for 4 hours.

Force the whites and yolks of the eggs through a sieve separately and mix with the parsley.

Put the shrimp salad mixture into each artichoke, garnish with the egg-parsley mixture, spoon on 1 teaspoon of vinaigrette, and top with a reserved shrimp.

Yield: 6 servings

➤ Can be prepared the day before.

NOTE: It may seem precious to separate the yolk and white before sieving, but they will have a distinct white and yellow color if you do, while if they are sieved as a whole the color is pale yellow.

Asparagus

*A*sparagus is an exceptional member of the prolific and varied *liliaceae* family, which also includes onions and lilies. It appears in two major forms: white and green. The white, grown mostly in France, Belgium, and Germany, is highly prized by Europeans for its delicate flavor. To achieve the creamy white color, with just a hint of purple at the tip, the soil is mounded to cover each growing tip. This intense labor raises the cost, and in some three star restaurants it is comparable to caviar or foie gras. Although Europeans praise the white asparagus, personally I find it somewhat bland and overly fibrous. Green asparagus is more common in England and America, where it is prized for its more intense flavor and color. And, although the first asparagus of the season is expensive, and the price remains higher than that of most other vegetables, it is much less expensive than the white.

For many people, the first asparagus of the season is cause for celebration. They create parties with asparagus as the meal, serving heaping mounds of freshly boiled or steamed asparagus with a selection of sauces. Or they serve several different preparations at one time: cream of asparagus soup, steamed asparagus maltaise, gratin of asparagus with ham, a stir-fry of asparagus with scallops, and an asparagus vinaigrette.

Asparagus is one of the few foods that you can politely eat with your fingers. Grasp the stem end and dip the tip into the desired sauce, and eat toward the stem until it is too fibrous. If you are too finicky for this, you can purchase individual silver asparagus tongs, or just eat it with your fork.

Availability

Fresh
March, April, and May are the prime months for asparagus. However, fresh asparagus is available in many areas almost year round. It is imported from various countries, and the flavor and condition can be quite good.

Look for spears that have a fresh gray-green color with whitish ends. The tips may be touched with purple. The stalks should be firm, with no sign of shrinking or drying out. The tips should be tightly closed without any indication of sprouting.

Size is a matter of personal preference. Some insist that only the thinnest spears are suitable, while others prefer the fatter thicker spears. There does not seem to be much difference in the flavor between the two, except that the thinner spears often appear later in the season, and may be sightly bitter.

Frozen

Asparagus is available frozen either cut into sections or in whole spears. Frozen asparagus tends to be flabby in texture and is not a suitable substitute for fresh. Use it in soups or purées, if necessary.

Canned

Asparagus in cans or jars is to be avoided. The canning process changes the flavor drastically, and the texture is so limp and soggy that it has little relation to fresh.

Storage

To store fresh asparagus, cut a thin slice from the base and discard. Stand the stalks in about 1 inch of cold water, and store in the refrigerator for 3 to 5 days. If the bases are not kept wet, the asparagus has a tendency to dry out. If kept in water too long, the tips will start to open.

Preparation

The question is whether to peel or not. I find that the fibers of white asparagus are much tougher than the green and that they must be peeled, but that green asparagus is more tender and that peeling is not necessary if the asparagus is fresh.

Unpeeled

Break the tough stem from the tender edible stalk by holding the ends and bending until it snaps at the tender point. Trim the spears to the same length for a neater appearance. Use the tough ends in soups or purées.

Peeled

Cut off the tough base just as the stalk turns green. Hold the spear in one hand, and with a small sharp paring knife or vegetable peeler, peel from the stem toward the tip, lifting the knife or peeler just before you reach the immature buds near the tip.

Cooking Methods

Boil, steam, bake, sauté, deep-fry, gratin, and pudding. Asparagus is good hot, cold, or at room temperature. Serve it as a first course or vegetable course. Use it in soups, stir-fried dishes, casseroles, and salads.

Boiling

Bring a large kettle of salted water to the boil. (Many cooks prefer to use a large skillet for ease in adding and removing the asparagus.) You may tie the asparagus into bunches, but except for restaurant service where a quantity of individual servings are needed, I can see no reason to go to the trouble. Add the asparagus and cook over high heat until tender and crisp—about 10 minutes, depending on thickness. Cut off an end to test. It should be *slightly* crunchier than desired, because it will continue to cook during the draining and serving. Drain and serve at once. You can refresh it in ice water to stop the cooking, and reheat just before serving.

(A chef's secret is to blanch the asparagus several hours before and to keep it cool. When ready to serve, dip into boiling water, place over steam, or sauté quickly in butter just before serving. It takes the pressure off the cook who has trouble making all the parts of the meal come out at the same time.)

Steaming

Place the asparagus in the top of a steamer over boiling water, and steam until tender and crisp—about 10 minutes, depending on thickness.

Sautéeing

The asparagus is usually cut into small sections, either straight across, on the diagonal, or roll-cut (see page 4). Blanch the vegetable first by boiling or steaming, or sauté over direct heat.

Microwaving

Place the asparagus in a covered container, and cook until tender, turning the dish at least once. It takes about 8 minutes for a pound. If the asparagus is cut up, stir it once or twice during the cooking. Be careful not to overcook.

Quantity

A pound of asparagus will serve 2 to 6 people, depending on the accompaniments.

Sauces

Most butter, cream, and vinaigrette sauces are customary. Hot sauces: Maltaise, Hollandaise, mousseline, noisette, Bechamél, Mornay, Supreme, and Allemande. Prepare as alla trifolati and alla parmigiana (see pages 10–11).

Cold sauces: Vinaigrette, ravigote, remoulade.

Asparagus with Sesame

2 tablespoons butter	salt and pepper to taste
¼ cup sesame seeds	1½ pounds cooked hot
¼ cup lemon juice	asparagus

In a skillet, melt the butter and sauté the sesame seeds until golden. Add the lemon juice, salt, and pepper.

Pour over the asparagus.

Yield: 6 servings

➤ The asparagus can be blanched ahead and refreshed in cold water. Heat in the sauce just before serving.

Asparagi alla Zabaglione (Asparagus with Sabayon Sauce)

This is not a true zabaglione sauce, but the technique is the same.

2 egg yolks	¼ cup heavy cream
1 tablespoon water	¼ teaspoon white pepper
1 cup dry white wine	3 pound asparagus, trimmed
2 tablespoons unsalted butter,	and cooked until
softened	tender-crisp

In a heavy saucepan, or the top of a double boiler, whisk the egg yolks, water, and wine over low heat, or over hot (but not boiling) water, until the mixture is thick and creamy. Do not let it boil.

Beat in the butter, remove from the heat, and stir in the cream and pepper. Keep hot over hot (but not boiling) water until ready to use.

Arrange the asparagus on a platter and garnish with the sauce.

Yield: 6 servings

➤ The sauce should be prepared just before serving.

NOTE: This is a tricky but exquisite sauce. Plan to serve the asparagus as a first course, and set aside the time to prepare the sauce carefully. Once you get the feel for it, you will be able to prepare it with ease, but the first attempts may be frustrating.

Although most writers recommend using a double boiler, I have always found it easier to prepare it over direct heat. If it looks as if it is getting too hot, place the bottom of the pan in a pan of iced water to slow the cooking, and then return to the heat. If the sauce should curdle, place it in a processor or blender for a minute; this sometimes brings it back. If it does not, then you must remake the sauce with fresh ingredients.

Herbed Asparagus Sauté

¼ cup chicken stock	1-2 tablespoons minced fresh
2 teaspoons butter	rosemary, marjoram, savory,
1½ pounds asparagus,	tarragon, basil, chives, or
diagonally cut and	chervil
blanched	salt and pepper to taste

In a large skillet, heat the chicken stock and butter to a full rolling boil. Add the asparagus and herb of choice. Season with salt and pepper, and heat.

Yield: 6 servings

➤ Can be served at room temperature.

Asparagus and Mushrooms with Coriander

2 tablespoons olive oil	½ teaspoon salt
½ pound sliced mushrooms	pepper
1 pound asparagus, sliced	4 tablespoons minced
diagonally	coriander
2 tablespoons minced shallots	

In a large skillet, heat the oil, and sauté the mushrooms over high heat until lightly browned. Add the asparagus and cook, stirring for 2 minutes. Add the shallots, salt, and pepper, and cook for another minute, or until the asparagus is tender and crisp. Stir in the coriander and serve.

Yield: 4 to 6 servings

➤ Cook just before serving.

Potato and Asparagus Pancakes

As with most potato pancake recipes, you must grate the potatoes, and then cook the pancakes immediately. The potatoes will turn gray if required to stand for more than a few minutes.

1 onion, grated	2 eggs
3 potatoes, grated	2 tablespoons minced thyme
8 asparagus tips, cooked	salt and pepper to taste
¾ cup grated Parmesan cheese	vegetable oil

Squeeze the excess moisture from the onions and potatoes and place in a bowl. Stir in the asparagus, cheese, eggs, thyme, salt, and pepper.

In a large skillet, heat the oil and drop 2-4 tablespoons of the mixture into the fat to make small pancakes. Sauté the pancakes until golden on both sides.

Yield: 6 servings

➤ Can be kept warm in a 250°F oven for 20 minutes.

Variations:

For an hors d'oeuvre, make the pancakes about the size of a silver dollar, and top with a dollop of sour cream, and a few grains of salmon caviar or a thin slice of smoked salmon.

Asparagi Fritti (Semi–Deep-Fried Asparagus)

Serve these as a first course, or with broiled fish.

1½ pounds asparagus	1½ cups bread crumbs
1½ cups vegetable oil, approximately	1 egg, lightly beaten
	salt and pepper to taste

Break off the tough ends of the asparagus, and cut into 3 inch lengths. In a large skillet, heat ½ inch of oil to 375°F.

Place the bread crumbs in a pie plate. In a medium-sized bowl, mix the egg with salt and pepper.

Dip the asparagus in the egg, and then roll in the bread crumbs.

Fry the asparagus in the hot oil without crowding until golden on one side, then turn and fry the second side.

Drain on paper toweling, and sprinkle with salt.

Yield: 6 servings

➤ Can be prepared for frying the day before and kept on wire racks in the refrigerator. Fry just before serving.

Asperges à La Provençale (Asparagus Provence Style)

2 tomatoes, thickly sliced	1 garlic clove, minced
salt and pepper to taste	6 tablespoons melted butter, lightly browned
⅓ cup fresh bread crumbs	
2 tablespoons minced parsley	1½ pounds asparagus, cooked and refreshed
1 tablespoons minced shallots	

Preheat the broiler.

Salt the tomato slices, and let drain for 30 minutes. In a small bowl, mix the bread crumbs, parsley, shallots, and garlic.

Brush a baking dish with some of the butter, and arrange the asparagus at both ends of the dish. Place the tomatoes in overlapping rows in the center. Sprinkle tomatoes with bread crumb mixture and drizzle with the butter.

Broil for 5 to 6 minutes, or until heated and the crumbs are lightly browned.

Yield: 6 servings

➤ Can be prepared for cooking several hours ahead. If cold, bake at 350°F for 10 minutes before broiling.

Involtini di Prosciutto con Asparagi (Prosciutto-Wrapped Asparagus with Parmesan)

48 asparagus stalks, cooked	1 cup grated grated Parmesan cheese
12 thin slices prosciutto	
¾ cup butter, melted	

Preheat the oven to 350°F.

Drain the asparagus. Place 4 stalks of asparagus on each slice of prosciutto, and sprinkle with 1 teaspoon of melted butter and a pinch of grated Parmesan. Wrap and place seam side down in a baking dish.

Pour the remaining butter over the rolls, and sprinkle with the remaining Parmesan. Bake for 10 minutes or until the cheese is golden.

Yield: 6 servings

➤ Can be prepared for baking several hours ahead.

Asparagus Baked with Pecans

1½ pounds cooked asparagus   ½ cup finely chopped pecans
2-3 tablespoons butter   salt and pepper to taste

Preheat the oven to 350°F.

Butter a gratin or baking dish, and arrange the asparagus in the dish. Dot with butter, and sprinkle with pecans. Season with salt and pepper. Bake until heated, about 15 minutes.

Yield: 6 servings

➤ Can be prepared for baking several hours ahead.

Cassolettes of Morels, Fiddleheads, and Asparagus

Cassolettes are individual baking dishes. Use individual soufflé dishes, or if desired, arrange in one large baking dish or gratin pan.

4 cups fresh morels or other   6 ounces asparagus, cut into 1
  wild mushrooms   inch pieces
1 tablespoon butter   6 ounces fiddleheads, cleaned
3 tablespoons minced shallots   of brown leaves
1 teaspoon minced garlic   ½ cup bread crumbs
1 cup heavy cream   ⅓ cup grated Parmesan cheese
½ cup Madeira   ⅓ cup grated Gruyere cheese
salt and pepper to taste   1 tablespoon minced basil
                                      1 teaspoon minced thyme

Preheat the oven to 375°F.

Remove stems from mushrooms and reserve for another recipe.

In a medium skillet, melt the butter, and sauté the shallots and mushrooms for 8 minutes. Add the garlic and sauté 2 minutes longer. Add cream, Madeira, salt, and pepper, and cook for 5 minutes. Remove mushrooms, and reduce liquid until thick enough to coat the back of a spoon. Return the mushrooms to the pan.

In a saucepan of boiling salted water, blanch the asparagus and fiddleheads for 3 minutes. Drain, refresh under cold water, and drain again. In a small bowl, mix the bread crumbs, Parmesan, Gruyere, basil, and thyme.

Divide asparagus and fiddleheads among six cassolettes, and top with morels. Sprinkle with crumbs, and bake for 10 minutes until bubbling hot and browned on the top. If necessary, brown under a broiler.

Yield: 6 servings

➤ Can be prepared for the final baking the day before.

NOTE: If fresh morels are not available or are too expensive, substitute portobello or even shiitake mushrooms. The flavor will not be the same, but will not be less appealing.

Timbales d'Asperges aux Sauce d'Asperges
(Asparagus Molds with Asparagus Sauce)

These timbales are perfect as a first course for an elaborate dinner.

2 pounds asparagus, cooked
2 eggs
1 egg yolk
salt and pepper to taste
nutmeg to taste

asparagus sauce (see below)
2 tablespoons peeled, seeded,
  and minced tomatoes
1 tablespoon minced parsley

Preheat the oven to 400°F.

Butter the insides of 6 ¾-cup ramekins. Drain the asparagus, and reserve 12 perfect tips. In a processor, purée the remaining asparagus, and force through a fine sieve. Place the purée into a saucepan, and cook off any moisture. Cool.

In a bowl, beat the eggs, egg yolks, salt, pepper, and nutmeg. Beat in the asparagus purée. Fill the molds, and bake in a water bath until set—about 30 minutes. Reheat the asparagus tips in hot salted water.

Unmold the timbales onto serving plates. Arrange a ribbon of sauce around the bottom, and garnish the tops with the asparagus tips, minced tomato, and parsley.

Yield: 6 servings

➤ Can be prepared for baking the day before.

Sauce d'Asperges (Asparagus Sauce)

¾ pound asparagus
½ cup chicken stock
1 teaspoon salt

pinch of pepper
1 tablespoon heavy cream

Cook the asparagus in boiling salted water until tender. Purée in a processor, with the chicken stock, salt, pepper, and cream. Correct the seasoning.

Asperges en Casserole (Baked Asparagus)

This lovely casserole is the equivalent of a quiche without the crust. Serve it as a luncheon or brunch dish.

1½ pounds asparagus, cooked	salt and pepper to taste
6 slices ham	2 tablespoons grated Gruyere
2 eggs	cheese
2 egg yolks	2 tablespoons Parmesan cheese
1½ cups heavy cream	

Preheat the oven to 350°F.

Butter a 7 by 11 inch baking dish. Drain the asparagus, wrap 4 to 6 spears in a ham slice, and arrange in the baking dish. In a bowl, beat the eggs, egg yolks, cream, salt, and pepper until well mixed. Pour over the asparagus spears, and sprinkle with the Gruyere and Parmesan.

Bake until the top is browned, and a knife inserted halfway to the center comes out clean. Let stand for 5 minutes before serving.

Yield: 6 servings

➤ Can be prepared for baking several hours ahead.

Fettuccine with Asparagus and Prosciutto

This is a version of Fettuccine Alfredo with prosciutto and asparagus. It is a wonderful supper dish, to be served with a simple salad and a fruit dessert.

1 pound asparagus, sliced	2 cups heavy cream
2 tablespoons butter	2 egg yolks
½ cup chicken stock	½ cup grated Parmesan cheese
1 garlic clove, minced	salt and pepper to taste
¼ pound prosciutto, julienne	2 tablespoons minced parsley
1 pound fettuccine	

In a large skillet, sauté the asparagus in the oil for 1 minute. Add the stock, garlic, and prosciutto, and cook, stirring until the stock is almost evaporated and the asparagus is tender. Cook the fettuccine in boiling salted water until tender.

In a bowl, beat the cream, egg yolks, cheese, salt, and pepper, and add to the asparagus. Add the fettuccine and toss gently. Sprinkle with the parsley, and cook over medium heat until lightly thickened.

Serve immediately.

Yield: 6 servings

➤ Cannot be prepared ahead.

NOTE: The silky creaminess of this requires that you heat the pasta by lifting the strands with two forks to coat each piece with the sauce. Be careful not to let it boil.

Risotto Con Gli Asparagi (Risotto with Asparagus)

Many vegetables can be used as a flavor base for risotto. Use this recipe as a suggestion for other vegetables.

1 pound asparagus, cut into 1 inch sections.	2 cups Arborio rice
	salt and pepper to taste
1 cup chicken stock (see Note)	¼ cup grated Parmesan cheese
2 tablespoons minced onion	1 tablespoon minced parsley
5 tablespoons butter	

In a saucepan of boiling salted water, cook the asparagus until the tips are tender. Remove the tips, and refresh in cold water and drain. Cook the stems until just tender—another two to three minutes. Drain, reserving the cooking liquid.

Mix enough reserved liquid to the chicken stock to equal 5 cups, and set to barely simmer in a saucepan.

In another saucepan, sauté the onion in 2 tablespoons of butter until soft, but not brown. Add the rice, and cook until it is well coated with the butter and the grains start to turn white—about 2 minutes. Add ½ cup of hot stock, and cook over medium heat until it is absorbed, stirring constantly. Stir in another ½ cup of stock and simmer, stirring constantly until it is absorbed. Continue adding the stock ½ cup at a time until all of it has been added and the rice is tender, but still firm in the center.

Correct the seasoning with salt and pepper, and fold in the asparagus, Parmesan, remaining butter, and parsley.

Serve immediately.

Yield: 6 servings

➤ Cannot be prepared ahead.

NOTE: You can use 5 cups of chicken stock instead of the asparagus water. Some recipes recommend adding raw asparagus tips with the rice and cooking along with the rice. (See the following recipe.) Risotti are delicate dishes which when served should almost flow across the plate. However, as they start to cool, they absorb more liquid and become firmer. Make your guests wait for the treat, and serve it as quickly as possible.

Risotto with Asparagus and Pine Nuts

5 cups chicken stock	1 pound asparagus, in ½ inch slices
6 tablespoons butter	
¼ cup minced onion	½ cup toasted pine nuts
2 cups Arborio rice	½ cup grated Parmesan cheese
	salt and pepper to taste

In a saucepan, bring the chicken stock to a simmer, and keep over low heat.

In a 2 quart saucepan, melt two tablespoons of butter, and sauté the onion until soft, but not brown. Add the rice and cook, stirring until the grains start to turn white.

Add ½ cup chicken stock, and cook over high heat, stirring until evaporated. Add the asparagus stems, reserving the tips and another ½ cup chicken stock. Cook until stock evaporates, and then add another ½ cup. When this evaporates, add the asparagus tips, and continue adding chicken stock in ½ cup portions.

When all of the stock has been absorbed, fold in the remaining butter, pine nuts, and Parmesan cheese, and season to taste with salt and pepper.

Yield: 6 side dish servings, or 2 or 3 main course servings

➤ Must be prepared and served immediately.

Braised Asparagus with Black Mushrooms

This Chinese dish makes a delicious change of pace in a western meal.

4 Chinese mushrooms, soaked	1 teaspoon soy sauce
1 tablespoon oil	½ teaspoon salt
1½ pounds asparagus, 1½ inch lengths	¼ teaspoon sugar

Drain the mushrooms, reserving ¼ cup liquid. Cut off and discard the stems. Cut the caps into slivers.

In a wok, heat the oil until very hot, and stir-fry the asparagus and mushrooms for 1 minute. Add the mushroom liquid, soy sauce, salt, and sugar. Simmer about 2 minutes, or until the asparagus is tender but still crisp.

Yield: 6 servings

➤ Must be prepared and served.

Asparagus in Mustard Sauce

Almost any cold vegetable can be served with this sauce.

1 hard cooked egg, separated	1½ tablespoons white wine vinegar
1 egg yolk	
1½ teaspoons Dijon mustard, or to taste	1 teaspoon salt
½ cup olive oil	½ teaspoon white pepper
	1½ pounds asparagus, cooked and chilled

In a processor, purée the hard cooked egg yolk with the raw egg yolk and mustard. Gradually add the oil in a steady stream. Add the vinegar, salt, and pepper. Mince the hard cooked egg white. Arrange the asparagus on a serving platter, nappe with the sauce, and sprinkle with the egg white.

Yield: 6 servings

Asperges à La Vinaigrette de Framboises
(Asparagus with Raspberry Vinaigrette)

Towards the end of the asparagus season, when the clear fresh taste of the vegetable has lost some of its excitement, you might wish to try a more startling preparation.

10 ounce package frozen
  raspberries, thawed
6 tablespoons olive oil
¼ cup heavy cream
2 tablespoons sherry vinegar
salt and pepper to taste

30 spinach leaves, washed and
  chilled
30 asparagus spears, cooked
  and chilled
1 tablespoon minced chives
coarsely ground black pepper

In a processor, purée the raspberries, and strain through a fine sieve. Discard the seeds. In a bowl, whisk the olive oil, cream, vinegar, salt, and pepper, and stir in the raspberry purée. Correct the seasoning with salt and pepper.

Arrange the spinach leaves on salad plates, and top with the asparagus spears. Pour the dressing in a ribbon over the asparagus, and sprinkle with chives and pepper.

Yield: 6 servings

➤ Can be prepared two hours before serving. The sauce can be prepared the day before.

Asperges Tyrolienne (Cold Asparagus Tyrol Style)

2 pounds cooked asparagus,
  refreshed and drained
1 cup minced cooked beets

1 cup sauce Tyrolienne (see
  page 32)

Arrange the asparagus on a platter, and coat lightly with the sauce. Sprinkle with the beets. Pass the remaining sauce separately.

Yield: 6 servings

➤ Can be prepared several hours ahead.

Asparagus and Potato Salad

1 cup olive oil
¼ to ½ cup wine vinegar
½ cup red onion, minced
3 tablespoons minced dill
1 tablespoon Dijon mustard
salt and pepper to taste

2 pounds potatoes, boiled and
  sliced
2 pounds asparagus spears,
  cooked and refreshed
Dill sprigs (optional)

In a large bowl, whisk the oil, vinegar, onion, dill, mustard, salt, and pepper until emulsified. Fold in the potatoes, cover and refrigerate for several hours. Arrange the asparagus on a platter in a spoke pattern. Remove the potatoes from the dressing, letting it drain back into the bowl. Spoon the dressing over the asparagus spears and garnish with the dill, if desired.

Yield: 6 servings

➤ Can be prepared the day before.

NOTE: Tiny, unpeeled, red bliss potatoes that have been halved add another color to the salad, but any waxy potato works.

Salade d'Asperges (Asparagus Salad)

This salad demonstrates the wonderful simplicity of the finest of French cookery.

2 pounds asparagus spears,   2 bunches watercress
   cooked and refreshed   1½ cups vinaigrette
3 hard cooked eggs, separated

Arrange the asparagus on a serving platter. Cut the egg whites into thin strips, and sprinkle over the asparagus. Force the yolks through a sieve, and scatter over the top. Remove the leaves from the watercress, mince finely, and stir into the vinaigrette. Spoon the sauce over the top.

Yield: 6 servings

➤ Can be prepared several hours ahead.

NOTE: Asparagus, like many green vegetables, loses its color if left in a vinaigrette for too long. Do not plan to dress the salad too early.

For a different flavor, omit the watercress and add 1 tablespoon each of minced parsley, chervil, chives, and tarragon.

Beans

*T*here are three major types of beans: string or snap varieties, shell beans, and dried beans. Snap beans have long slender pods with under-developed beans. Older varieties had a tough, fibrous "string" that ran along the sides of the pod and had to be removed before cooking. Newer hybrids have eliminated the string, and are prepared by snapping off the stem end and if desired the tail end, although that is not necessary. The thinner the bean, the faster it cooks to a tender-crisp state. The truly string-like French *haricots verts* that appear in some markets cook within minutes to a bright green tender-crispness, but other varieties, such as Kentucky Wonders, are so thick that they turn grey in the time it takes to cook them. The wonder about Kentucky Wonders is that anyone would even try to cook them to the tender-crisp state. Their hearty meaty texture makes them perfect for the long slow cooking with the "pot likker" so ad-mired by Southerners and for dishes requiring long simmering. Asian markets sell "long" beans that are usually very thin and can be as long as 30 inches. Treat them in the same fashion as other snap beans. Their length makes them fun, especially for children (you only have to eat two). Snap beans include waxed beans, which are cooked in the same way.

Shell beans have well-developed beans in the long pods. The pod is opened to remove the bean and then the pod is discarded. They are not as common, and are only rarely found in supermarkets in most areas. Farmer's markets and green grocers carry fresh black-eyed peas, and cranberry, lima, and fava beans, seasonally. When you can get them, take advantage of these delectable vegetables.

Dried beans are dried shell beans. These are most often sold in 1 pound packages. They come in all sizes, shapes, and colors. Select pea beans, navy beans, pinto beans, kidney beans, or white beans, among the many options. Feel free to substitute one dried bean for another in a recipe.

Bean sprouts are the result of soaking and then keeping certain shell beans, or mung, soy, or alfalfa beans, as well as wheat berries, moist until they sprout tails. You can prepare your own, although most mar-kets sell one or more varieties.

NOTE: Beans and peas are both members of the *leguminosae* family, but fresh peas, in culinary terms, are such a large branch of the family I have given them a chapter unto themselves. Dried peas are treated in the same light as dried beans.

Availability

Fresh

Snap beans are sold as green or wax beans. The primary season for freshly grown beans is during the summer months of June through August, but they are available year round in most markets. Select firm fresh-looking, unblemished beans that snap easily and have barely visible pods. Try to select beans of the same size for even cooking. Some of the more common varieties are:

1. Haricot Verts or French beans, slender and very delicate.

2. Kentucky Wonder, also called Texas pole, and Old Homestead. These are liked for their meaty bean flavor.

3. Royal beans are a deep purple when mature, which turns green when cooked. They are particularly good raw, with a deep purple exterior and bright green interior.

4. Wax Beans are light yellow in color and taste similar to, but different from, green beans.

5. Chinese Long Beans are also called yard long beans and asparagus beans. They are pencil thin and 12 to 30 inches long with a slightly chewy texture.

6. Fresh shell beans are only available in limited quantities in a few markets, generally. Select fresh unblemished pods with full but not oversized beans, which indicates old age. Bean sprouts should be fresh, without signs of wilting or rot.

To Store

String beans, wax beans, and shell beans all should be stored in a plastic bag for no more than a few days. Bean sprouts are best if used immediately. They will keep a couple of days in a plastic bag, but begin to spoil quickly.

Frozen

Frozen string beans are sold whole, cut into lengths and "frenched," or sliced into slivers. They are blanched before freezing, and although acceptable as a vegetable, the flavor is rather different from and not equal to fresh. Plan to cook them only enough to heat them. French style beans in particular can become watery and lose a lot of flavor. Because true string beans take minutes to prepare and cook, there is little saving of time or effort to justify serving frozen beans.

I have not found frozen wax beans.

Black-eyed peas and lima beans are the two major shelled beans sold frozen. The flavor and texture is very close to fresh and make a much easier substitute.

Bean sprouts are not sold frozen.

Canned

Both green and wax beans are canned. The texture tends to be flabby and the flavor is poor.

A number of varieties of shelled beans are sold canned, including black eyed peas, cannellini beans, white beans, kidney beans, and chick peas. The flavor of canned shelled beans is close to fresh, but the consistency can be mushy. Select a brand with care.

Bean sprouts in cans are a poor substitute for the readily available fresh.

Dried

There are many different dried beans to be found in most markets. If the specific bean you want is not available, substitute another. Changing one for another will provide a delicious, albeit differently flavored, dish.

Preparation for Cooking

Snap or cut off the stem end and remove the tail if you prefer. Most varieties no longer have the tough "string." If there is a string, just draw it down the side of the pod as instructed for snow peas (page 361).

Shelled beans need a little more preparation. Press the bean pod, and run your thumbnail down the seam to open the pod.

Lima beans need only be slipped out into a bowl, but broad beans have a protective membrane that has to be removed. Split the membrane with your thumb nail to release the beans in a similar fashion to removing it from the pod.

Carefully pick over dried beans to remove any small stones or other foreign matter.

Cooking Methods

Fresh Beans

Boiling Bring a large kettle of salted water to a full rolling boil. Add the beans gradually so the water does not stop boiling, and boil until tender and crisp. Drain, and refresh under cold water to stop the cooking. For most preparations the beans should have a distinct texture but no raw taste. There are also memorable preparations that require extended periods of cooking to make the beans soft and almost mushy.

Steaming If preferred, steam the vegetables until just barely done and refresh under cold water. Steaming takes longer.

Microwaving Cook covered for 4 to 8 minutes with a small amount of water. Check frequently so you do not overcook, and turn the container and the beans during the cooking.

Other Methods Beans can also be sautéed, batter fried, deep-fried, and braised, and puréed (see Basic Techniques, page 1).

Shelled Beans

Boiling Cook in boiling salted water until tender. Depending on the variety, this can take from 5 to 20 minutes. They will hold their shape even after an extended period of slow cooking. Flavor the water with herbs of your choice if desired.

Dried Beans

Prepare for cooking in either of two ways: Soak them in water to cover overnight. Or, cover with cold water, bring to a boil and simmer for 5 minutes; turn off the heat and let stand for 1 hour. The choice is yours. There is no discernible difference in the result. Once soaked, the beans are simmered in at least twice the amount of boiling water. Flavor with bay leaf, savory, onions, or other aromatics. To tell if the beans are done, blow on a bean in a spoon. If the skin bursts they are cooked. Lentils can take as short a time as 30 minutes, but other dried beans can take several hours to be cooked. Check every 30 minutes if the package or the recipe does not specify a time.

Bean Sprouts

Serve raw in salads, as sandwich toppings, or a soup garnish. Sauté or stir-fry for just a few minutes. Longer cooking causes them to release a lot of water and to become limp.

Quantity

Plan on 1½ pounds of snap beans for 6 persons.

Shell beans have a lot of waste, and the number of beans in a pod vary from one variety to another. Generally, 3 pounds for 6 persons is sufficient.

Dried beans swell in cooking, and a pound will easily serve 6 persons.

Sauces

Simple preparations suit beans best. Butter flavored with an herb or spice, or the quickly prepared Italian trifolati and parmigiana preparations, are delightful with snap beans. Savory is called the bean herb, and it makes a delicious addition to the beans. Add the savory to the cooking liquid, or mince some and add it to plain butter before tossing the beans in it.

Poppy seeds are also excellent with snap beans. Sprinkle on just before serving.

Shell beans are sauced with butter, sprinkled with herbs such as chives or savory, or tossed with garlic and oil or with Parmesan. They are, however, often made into purées, or cooked with other vegetables, such as onions, garlic, or tomatoes.

Wax Beans

Wax beans are not as popular as the ever-present green bean. The flavor is less distinctive, but a wonderful change when the vegetable selection seems limited. Any preparation for green beans can be used with waxed beans, so most recipes are written for green beans without mentioning wax beans.

Green Bean and Basil Soup

2 leeks, thinly sliced	1 cup heavy cream
1 garlic clove, minced	1 tablespoon lemon juice
3 tablespoons butter	1 tablespoon minced savory
4 cups chicken stock	½ teaspoon salt
2 potatoes, peeled and diced	pinch of cayenne pepper
1 pound green beans, cut into	sliced raw mushrooms
1 inch lengths	½ cup blanched sliced green
½ cup basil leaves, chopped	beans

In a large saucepan, sauté the leeks and garlic in the butter until soft, but not brown. Add the chicken stock, potatoes, and green beans, and simmer until the vegetables are tender—about 20 minutes. Add the basil and simmer 5 minutes longer.

In a processor, purée the soup, and return it to the saucepan. Stir in the cream, lemon juice, savory, salt, and cayenne pepper.

Serve garnished with the mushrooms and beans.

Yield: 6 servings

➤ Can be prepared the day before and reheated.

NOTE: Serve this soup cold. If it is too thick, thin it with milk or chicken stock. Correct the seasoning with lemon juice, savory, salt, and pepper.

Haricots Verts d'Isigny (Green Beans Isigny Style)

1½ pounds green or wax	1 teaspoon minced shallot
beans, cooked until	4 tablespoons butter
tender-crisp and refreshed	salt and pepper to taste

Drain the beans. In a skillet, sauté the shallots in the butter until soft, and add the beans. Cook over medium heat, stirring until hot. Correct the seasoning with salt and pepper.

Yield: 6 servings

➤ The beans can be prepared for the final heating several hours ahead.

Green Beans with Shallots and Tarragon

1½ pounds green or wax   3 tablespoons minced shallots
  beans, cooked until   3 tablespoons minced tarragon
  tender-crisp, and refreshed pepper to taste
3 tablespoons butter

Drain the beans. In a skillet, melt the butter, and cook the shallots until soft, but not brown. Add the tarragon, salt, and pepper to taste. Stir in the beans and heat.

Yield: 6 servings

➤ The beans and sauce can be prepared ahead, combined, and heated just before serving.

Green Beans with Chervil or Savory

Chervil is a feathery herb with a delicate flavor. The more pungent savory has long been called the bean herb, because the flavors complement each other superbly.

1½ pounds green beans,   2 tablespoons minced chervil
  cooked until tender-crisp,   or savory
  and refreshed   salt and pepper to taste
2 teaspoons lemon juice

Drain the beans. In a saucepan, toss the beans with the lemon juice, chervil, salt, and pepper until coated and reheated.

Yield: 6 servings

➤ Can be prepared for reheating several hours ahead.

Haricots Verts à l'Hollandaise, Coquelicot
(Green Beans with Hollandaise and Poppy Seeds)

The tart buttery sauce is complemented by the crunch of the poppy seeds.

1½ pounds green or wax   1 tablespoon poppy seeds
  beans, cooked until   1 cup hollandaise (see page 19)
  tender-crisp, and drained

Drain the beans, and arrange on a heated serving platter. Stir the poppy seeds into the Hollandaise, and pour over the beans.
Serve immediately.

Yield: 6 servings

➤ The hollandaise can be prepared a few hours ahead and gently reheated.

Haricots Verts à la Crème (Green Beans in Cream)

1½ pounds green or wax beans, cooked until tender-crisp, and refreshed	3 tablespoons butter 2 tablespoons heavy cream salt and pepper to taste

Drain the beans. In a skillet, heat the butter, and reheat the beans over a low fire, stirring until the butter has been absorbed. Add the cream, salt, and pepper, stir to coat and serve.

Yield: 6 servings

➤ Can be prepared for reheating several hours ahead.

Fagiolini Fritti (Deep-Fried Green Bean Bundles)

This Italian recipe provides little bundles of beans that make an attractive garnish to a plate, and are especially good to eat.

1½ pounds green beans, cooked until tender-crisp, and refreshed 3 eggs, lightly beaten	1 cup flour oil for deep-frying salt

Preheat the oil to 375°F.
Drain the beans, and cut the beans into even lengths. Holding 3 or 4 beans together in a bundle, dip them into the eggs, and roll in the flour. deep-fry the bundles a couple at a time until golden. Drain on paper toweling, and season with salt.

Yield: 6 servings

➤ Cannot be prepared ahead.

NOTE: Do not be concerned if the ends of the beans you are holding do not get coated; there will be enough coating on the rest of the beans to hold the bundles together.

Haricots Verts Béarnais (Green Beans Béarn Style)

The Béarn in Southwest France is noted for the fineness of its cooking. The sauce, Béarnaise, was created in a restaurant just outside of Paris to honor one of Béarn's most famous sons, King Henri IV.

1½ pounds green or wax beans, cooked until tender-crisp, and refreshed 1 tablespoon butter	½ cup minced onion 4 slices bacon cut into ½ inch strips pepper to taste

Drain the beans. In a skillet, melt the butter, and cook the onion until tender, but not brown. Add the bacon, and increase the heat to medium high. Cook until the bacon is crisp and the onion is well browned.

Add the beans, and toss to coat and reheat. Correct the seasoning with pepper.

Yield: 6 servings

➤ Can be prepared ahead by several hours and reheated.

Kentucky String Beans

This is the way to cook Kentucky Wonders and other meaty snap beans.

4 slices lean bacon	2 tablespoons cold water
½ cup thinly sliced scallions	1 teaspoon salt
1½ pounds green beans,	¼ teaspoon pepper
trimmed and cut into 1 inch	1½ teaspoons red wine vinegar
lengths	2 tablespoons minced mint

In a skillet, sauté the bacon, turning often until brown and crisp. Remove the cracklings to paper toweling to drain.

To the fat in the skillet, add the scallions and cook until soft, but not brown. Add the beans, and stir to coat with the fat. Add the water and cover the pan. Cook over low heat for 5 minutes. Uncover and cook until tender, but still crisp.

Sprinkle with salt, pepper, and vinegar. Place in a serving dish and sprinkle with the bacon bits and mint.

Yield: 6 servings

➤ These can be reheated.

Fagiolini al Pomodoro (Green Beans with Tomatoes)

This is the Italian version of a recipe found in almost all the Mediterranean countries. The Provençal version, for instance, uses butter and 1 bay leaf, rather than the olive oil, basil, and oregano. The long slow cooking makes the beans very tender while instilling them with the other flavors. This and similar recipes prove that not every vegetable is at its best when just barely cooked.

1½ pounds green or wax	½ cup olive oil
beans, cut into 1 inch	1 tablespoon minced basil
sections, and cooked until	½ teaspoon oregano
tender-crisp, and refreshed	salt and pepper to taste
16 ounce can tomatoes or 4	½ teaspoon sugar, optional
large tomatoes, peeled	

Drain the beans. Drain the canned tomatoes and cut into wedges, if whole. Cut the fresh tomatoes into wedges, discarding the seeds.

In a skillet, cook the tomatoes in the oil, crushing lightly until softened. Add the beans and cook 2 minutes. Stir in the basil and oregano, and simmer for at least 30 minutes, or until the beans are very tender and most of the liquid has evaporated. Season with salt and sugar to taste.

Yield: 6 servings

➤ Can be prepared the day before and reheated.

NOTE: Some versions add 2 thickly sliced potatoes with the beans. During the cooking, some of the potato will disintegrate.

Fagiolini Verdi con Pepperoni e Pomodoro
(Green Beans with Peppers and Tomatoes)

You can add basil and oregano to this version.

4 tablespoons olive oil
1 large onion, ¼ inch slices
1 large green pepper, thinly
  sliced
1 cup canned tomatoes with
  juices

1½ pounds green or wax
  beans, trimmed
1½ teaspoons salt
pepper to taste

In a casserole or large skillet, heat the oil, and sauté the onion until translucent. Add the pepper and tomatoes, and cook over medium heat until the tomatoes separate from the oil and thicken into a sauce—about 25 minutes. Add the beans, stir to coat evenly with the sauce, and add ⅓ cup water. Season with salt and pepper, cover, and cook until tender—about 15 minutes.

Yield: 6 servings

➤ Can be prepared several hours ahead and reheated. Can be frozen.

NOTE: For a simpler version, leave out the peppers.

Vrasta Fasolakia Freska (Stewed Green Beans with Mint)

1 small onion, minced
¼ cup butter
1 pound green beans, cut into
  2 inch lengths
1 clove garlic, minced
1 tablespoon minced mint, or
  1 teaspoon dried

1 tablespoon minced parsley
1 teaspoon fennel seeds
½ cup tomato sauce
¼ cup water
salt and pepper to taste

In a skillet, sauté the onion in the butter until golden. Add the beans and sauté, stirring until they have turned bright green. Add the garlic, mint, parsley, fennel seeds, tomato sauce, water, salt, and pepper.

Simmer for 30 minutes, or until the sauce is thickened and the beans are very tender.

Yield: 6 servings

➤ Can be prepared the day before and reheated.

Green Beans with Sunflower Kernels

¼ cup butter
1 teaspoon minced marjoram
1 teaspoon minced basil
1 teaspoon minced chervil
1 teaspoon minced parsley
1 teaspoon minced chives
½ teaspoon minced savory

½ teaspoon minced thyme
1 small onion, chopped
1 clove garlic, minced
1 pound green beans, trimmed
¼ cup sunflower kernels
salt and pepper to taste

In a bowl, cream the butter, and stir in the marjoram, basil, chervil, parsley, chives, savory, and thyme.

In a saucepan of boiling salted water, place the onion and garlic, and return to a boil. Add the beans, and cook until tender—about 10 minutes. Drain, and add the herb butter and sunflower kernels. Swirl to melt the butter, and season with salt and pepper to taste.

Yield: 6 servings

Green Beans with Parsley and Garlic

1½ pounds green or wax
    beans, 2 inch lengths,
    cooked until tender-crisp,
    and refreshed
½ cup minced parsley

¼ cup olive oil
3 tablespoons white wine
    vinegar
2 garlic cloves, minced
salt and pepper

Drain the beans. In a skillet, heat the parsley, oil, vinegar, and garlic until hot and the garlic just starts to turn golden. Do not burn. Season with salt and pepper. Add the beans to the skillet and cook, stirring until hot.

Yield: 6 servings

➤ The beans can be cooked and the sauce prepared several hours ahead. Reheat the beans just before serving.

Green Beans with Pancetta and Pine Nuts

1½ pounds green or wax
    beans, cooked until
    tender-crisp, and refreshed
2 ounces thinly sliced pancetta
1 shallot, minced
¼ cup basil or raspberry
    vinegar

4 tablespoons butter
salt and pepper to taste
2 tablespoons minced parsley
½ cup toasted pine nuts

Drain the beans. In a skillet, fry the pancetta until crisp, and drain on paper toweling.

Add the shallot and vinegar to the skillet, and reduce the vinegar by half. Cut the butter into chunks, and whisk into the liquid. Add the beans to the skillet and cook, stirring over low heat until hot. Correct the seasoning with salt and pepper.

Turn into a serving dish, and sprinkle with the pine nuts, parsley, and the pancetta.

Yield: 6 servings

➤ The beans and sauce can be prepared several hours ahead and reheated just before serving.

Stir-Fried Green Beans with Garlic

1 pound green or wax beans, trimmed, and cut into 1½ inch pieces	½ teaspoon sugar
	3 tablespoons oil
	2-3 cloves garlic, crushed
2 tablespoons light soy sauce	salt to taste

In a kettle of boiling salted water, blanch the green beans for 3 minutes. Drain and rinse under cold water. In a bowl, mix the soy sauce and sugar.

Heat a wok and add the oil. Add the garlic, and cook until lightly browned. Add the beans, and stir-fry for 3 minutes. Add 1 to 2 tablespoons of water, cover, and let steam for 2 minutes. Add the soy mixture, and cook stirring for 1 minute. Season with salt and serve.

Yield: 6 servings

➤ Cannot be prepared in advance.

Chinese Green Beans in Ginger Sauce

1½ pounds long green beans or wax beans cooked until tender-crisp	1 tablespoon ginger juice (see Note)
½ teaspoon salt	1½ teaspoons minced ginger
7 teaspoons sesame oil	1 teaspoon sugar
3 tablespoons Chekiang vinegar (see glossary)	2 teaspoons chicken stock

Drain the beans, and put into a bowl. Toss with ½ teaspoon of salt and 4 teaspoons sesame oil. Let cool.

In a bowl, mix the remaining sesame oil, vinegar, ginger juice, ginger, sugar, and chicken broth. Pour over the beans, and toss to coat.

Serve at room temperature.

Yield: 6 servings

➤ Can be prepared the day before and refrigerated.

NOTE: Ginger juice is prepared by pressing pieces of ginger root through a garlic press to extract the juice.

Dry Fried Green Beans Hunan Yuan

1 pound green beans, trimmed	¼ teaspoon soy sauce
oil for deep-frying	¼ teaspoon vinegar
1 tablespoon chicken stock	¼ teaspoon salt
1 tablespoon minced scallion	pinch of sugar
1 teaspoon minced garlic	2 tablespoons minced
1 teaspoon minced ginger	preserved Szechwan
¼ teaspoon chili paste with	vegetable (see glossary)
garlic (see glossary)	2 tablespoons minced pork
¼ teaspoon sesame oil	

In a wok, heat the oil to 375°F. Fry the beans in batches until the skins are wrinkled. Drain on paper towels.

In a bowl, mix the stock, scallion, garlic, ginger, chili paste, sesame oil, soy sauce, vinegar, salt, and sugar. Pour off all but ½ teaspoon of oil from the wok, and heat. Stir-fry the Szechwan vegetable and pork, until the pork loses its color. Add the beans, and stir until heated. Add the sauce mixture, and stir until the beans are well coated—about 30 seconds.

Yield: 6 servings

➤ Best if prepared and served.

Green Bean Salad with Peanut Sauce

1 pound green beans, cut in	⅓ cup oyster sauce (see
julienne, steamed, and	glossary)
refreshed	⅓ cup rice vinegar
⅓ cup crushed roasted	2 garlic cloves, crushed
peanuts	

Drain the beans and dry on paper towels.
In a bowl, mix the peanuts, oyster sauce, vinegar, and garlic.
Add the beans and toss to coat evenly.
Arrange on a platter and serve.

Yield: 6 servings

➤ Can be prepared several hours ahead.

Szechuan Green Beans Vinaigrette

1½ pounds green or wax
  beans, cooked until
  tender-crisp, and refreshed
⅔ cups peanut oil
½ cup red wine vinegar
2 tablespoons light soy sauce
2 tablespoons dark soy sauce
2 tablespoons chili paste with
  garlic (see glossary)

1½ tablespoons sugar
1 tablespoon minced ginger
1 garlic clove, minced
2 teaspoons Asian sesame oil
salt to taste
2 tablespoons toasted sesame
  seeds

Place the beans in a bowl. In a small bowl, mix the peanut oil, vinegar, thin soy sauce, dark soy sauce, chili paste with garlic, sugar, ginger, garlic, sesame oil, and salt to taste. Toss with beans, and sprinkle with sesame seeds. Toss again.

Yield: 6 servings

➤ Can be prepared the day before and kept refrigerated.

Salade des Haricots Verts en Julienne
(Salad of Green Beans, Mushrooms, and Ham Cut into Julienne)

If your beans are larger than a string, "French cut" with a small sharp knife, or the special slicers sold in gourmet shops.

½ cup olive oil
2 tablespoons red wine vinegar
2 teaspoons Dijon mustard
1 large shallot, minced
1 garlic clove, minced
salt and pepper to taste
½ pound mushrooms cut into
  julienne

1½ pounds string beans,
  cooked and refreshed
¼ pound Westphalian or
  Prosciutto ham cut into
  julienne
2 tomatoes, peeled, seeded,
  and cut into julienne
1 hard cooked egg, minced
  (optional)

In a bowl, whisk the oil, vinegar, mustard, shallot, garlic, salt, and pepper together. Add the mushrooms, and marinate for 30 minutes. Add the beans and ham, and toss lightly. Taste for seasoning. Just before serving, fold in the tomatoes, toss gently, and arrange on a serving platter. Garnish with the hard cooked egg.

Yield: 6 servings

➤ Can be prepared 2 or 3 hours before serving.

Danish Green Bean, Mushroom, and Cheese Salad

1 tablespoon white wine
  vinegar
1 tablespoon olive oil
1 pound mushrooms, thinly
  sliced
1 pound green beans,
  trimmed, cooked until
  tender-crisp, and refreshed

1 cup mustard sauce (see page
  31)
1 pound Gruyere, julienne
dill sprigs
6 small radish roses

In a bowl, whisk the vinegar and oil together, and toss with the mushrooms. Let marinate at room temperature for 30 minutes. In a serving bowl, mix the beans and mushrooms with the mustard sauce, and toss gently to coat evenly. Garnish the top with cheese, dill, and radishes.

Yield: 6 servings

➤ Can be prepared several hours before serving.

Green Bean and Ham Salad

You can use any ham for this salad, but a smoked country ham gives it a special flavor.

½ cup walnut oil
3 tablespoons heavy cream
3 tablespoons minced chives
2 tablespoons sherry vinegar
salt and pepper to taste

1½ pounds green beans,
  cooked and refreshed
⅓ pound smoked ham, cut in
  julienne

In a large bowl, whisk the oil, cream, chives, and vinegar together.
Season with salt and pepper. Add the beans and ham, and toss gently to coat evenly with the sauce. Correct the seasoning with salt and pepper.

Yield: 6 Servings

Green Bean, Tomato, and Feta Salad

As with any dish with a number of ingredients, one or another may be left out. In this recipe, leaving out the potato makes a lighter salad, and allows you to use a starch elsewhere in the menu.

2 tablespoons red wine vinegar
3 tablespoons minced dill
salt and pepper
6 tablespoons olive oil
6 cups red leaf lettuce
1 pound green beans, cut into
  1 inch pieces, blanched

½ pound new potatoes,
  quartered and boiled
2 tomatoes, diced
12 pitted black olives
4 ounces feta cheese, crumbled

In a large bowl, whisk the vinegar, dill, salt, and pepper while gradually adding the oil. Add the lettuce, beans, potatoes, tomatoes, olives, and feta, and toss with the dressing.

Yield: 6 servings

➤ The ingredients can be prepared the day before, but do not mix the salad until shortly before serving.

Green Beans with Garlic and Coriander

2 large garlic cloves, minced
⅓ cup minced coriander
2 pounds green beans, boiled
   in salted water until
   tender-crisp

5 to 6 tablespoons olive oil
1 tablespoon lemon juice
2 to 3 tablespoons vinegar
½ teaspoon black pepper

In a large bowl, place the garlic and coriander. Drain the beans, and immediately place in the bowl and let stand for 10 minutes. The heat of the beans will bring out the flavors. Mix in 5 tablespoons of oil and cover. Chill for 3 to 4 hours.

About 45 minutes before serving, let warm to room temperature. Add the lemon juice and 2 tablespoons of vinegar. Season with pepper, toss well, and correct seasoning with vinegar and olive oil if needed.

Yield: 6 servings

➤ Can be prepared the day before.

Shaker Salad

This is an example of the Shakers' skill with herbs.

3 tablespoons tarragon vinegar
1 tablespoon minced onions
½ teaspoon crumbled dried
   thyme
½ teaspoon crumbled dried
   savory
½ teaspoon dry mustard
1 teaspoon salt
pepper

½ cup olive or vegetable oil
1½ pounds green beans, cut
   into 1½ inch lengths,
   cooked, drained, and
   refreshed
2 heads Boston or bibb lettuce,
   cut up
2 tablespoons minced scallions

In a large bowl, whisk the vinegar, onions, thyme, savory, mustard, salt, and pepper with the oil to make a vinaigrette. Add the beans to the bowl with the lettuce and scallions, and toss gently.

Yield: 6 servings

➤ The beans can be prepared the day before but do not toss the salad until shortly before serving.

Green Bean Salad with Feta, Walnuts, and Mimosa

Arrange this attractively, and leave the beans whole for the prettiest appearance.

1½ pounds green beans,
  cooked and refreshed
4 teaspoons white wine
  vinegar
¼ cup walnut or vegetable oil
salt and pepper

1 scallion, minced
2½ ounces feta, crumbled
⅓ cup walnut halves, toasted
2 eggs, hard cooked, yolks and
  whites separated
½ cup minced parsley

Arrange the beans on a serving platter in even rows. In a small bowl, whisk the vinegar, oil, salt, pepper, and scallions together, and spoon over the beans. Crumble the feta, and arrange on top. Sprinkle the walnuts in a separate row next to the feta. Press the yolks and whites of the egg through a sieve separately, and make rows on the beans next to the walnuts. Sprinkle the parsley in a final row.

Yield: 6 servings

➤ Can be prepared about 2 hours before serving. Keep covered, at room temperature.

NOTE: If you press the whole egg through a sieve you will get a pale yellow color, but if you press the white and egg separately you get white and bright yellow. The white and yellow of the egg with the minced parsley resembles the mimosa flower.

Salade Des Haricots Verts
(Green Bean Salad with Walnut and Tarragon)

1½ pounds green beans,
  cooked and refreshed
Boston or bibb lettuce leaves
Radicchio, shredded
strips of pimiento, optional
½ cup chopped walnuts

¼ cup walnut oil
⅓ cup vegetable oil
juice of 1 lime or ½ lemon
½ teaspoon dry mustard
1 tablespoon minced tarragon
salt and pepper to taste

Spread the beans on a towel to dry. On a salad plate or platter, arrange lettuce leaves, and top with radicchio and beans. You may "tie" the beans in bundles with the pimiento. Sprinkle with the walnuts.

In a bowl, whisk the walnut oil, vegetable oil, lime juice, mustard, tarragon, and salt and pepper together. Sprinkle over salad.

Yield: 6 servings

➤ Prepare the salad no more than 2 hours before serving.

Flageolets

Flageolets are a dwarf green kidney bean popular in France as a traditional accompaniment to roast lamb, but their subtle flavor is complimentary to other meats and poultry. They are usually sold dried in gourmet shops and some health food stores, but if you cannot locate them, you can substitute any other dried bean for the recipes below.

Flageolets (Baby Green Kidney Beans)

The juices from roast lamb are often mixed into the beans instead of the butter.

2 cups dried flageolets
¼ cup minced onion
2 tablespoons butter

¼ cup melted butter, or meat juices, or to taste
1 tablespoon minced parsley

Soak the flageolets in water to cover for at least 2 hours. Drain. In a heavy casserole, combine the flageolets and 2 quarts of salted water, and simmer for 1 to 2 hours or until tender. Drain.

In a skillet, sauté the onion in the butter until soft, but not brown. Stir into the hot beans with the melted butter or meat juices, and sprinkle with the parsley.

Yield: 6 servings

➤ The beans can be cooked ahead. Reheat in the skillet with the onions just before serving.

Flageolets à la Gascogne
(Baby Green Kidney Beans Gascony Style)

1 pound flageolets
½ pound fresh pork rind cut into small dice
salt to taste

¼ cup garlic butter (see page 14)
¼ cup minced parsley or chives

Preheat the oven to 350°F.

Soak the beans in water to cover by 2 inches for at least 8 hours. Strain off the water, and place the beans in a casserole. Add the pork rind, 1 tablespoon salt, and water to cover. Cover the casserole and bake for 3 hours, or until the beans are quite tender.

In a small saucepan, melt the garlic butter, and pour it into a heated serving dish. With a slotted spoon, lift the beans into the serving dish, and stir gently. Sprinkle with the minced parsley or chives.

Yield: 6 servings

➤ The beans can be prepared ahead. Heat in a skillet in the garlic
butter just before serving.

Flageolets à la Crème
(Baby Green Kidney Beans in Cream)

2 cups flageolets	¼ teaspoon dried thyme
2 quarts cold water	salt and pepper to taste
1 carrot, chopped	2 tablespoons butter
1 onion stuck with 2 whole	1 teaspoon minced garlic
cloves	1 tablespoon minced shallot
2 stalks celery	¼ cup minced parsley
3 parsley sprigs	1 cup heavy cream
1 bay leaf	

Soak the beans overnight in water to cover by 2 inches.

Drain the beans, and put into a casserole with the water, carrot,
onion, celery, parsley, bay leaf, thyme, 1 tablespoon salt, and ¼ teaspoon pepper.

Cover, and simmer for 2 hours, or until the flageolets are almost
cooked, but still slightly underdone.

Remove and discard the onion, celery, parsley, and bay leaf.

Remove the carrot, dice, and set aside.

Drain the beans, reserving ½ cup of cooking liquid.

In a skillet, melt the butter, and sauté the garlic and shallots until
soft, but not brown.

Add the beans, minced parsley, diced carrot, and the cream.

Simmer 5 minutes, or until tender.

Yield: 6 servings

➤ Can be prepared, to the point of adding the cream, several hours
ahead.

Flageolets, Corn, and Green Beans with Scallion Butter

1 cup dried flageolets or pea	½ cup butter
beans	salt and pepper to taste
3 cups cold water	1 garlic clove, minced
1 quart water	2 cups cooked corn kernels,
1 bay leaf	drained
¼ teaspoon dried thyme	½ pound green or wax beans,
2 scallions, 1 inch pieces	1 inch pieces, cooked

Soak the flageolets in 3 cups of water for 8 hours or overnight. Drain.
In a saucepan, combine 1 quart water, flageolets, bay leaf, and thyme,
and simmer until tender—about 1½ hours. Drain well, reserving ¼
cup cooking liquid. Discard the bay leaf.

In a processor, mince the scallions, and add the butter. Process until
smooth. Season with salt and pepper.

In a saucepan, heat the reserved liquid, flageolets, garlic, salt, pepper, and corn until hot. Add the green beans and all but 1 tablespoon of scallion butter. Heat just until the butter is absorbed. Turn into a serving dish and top with remaining butter.

Yield: 6 servings

Warm Bean Salad with Tomatoes and Basil

Although this is supposed to be warm, it can be prepared ahead and served at room temperature. If the beans sit in the dressing too long they will absorb it, making the salad dry. If you choose to serve it cold, prepare twice as much dressing, and add it to taste.

½ cup dried chick peas, rinsed and sorted	2 tablespoons lemon juice
	¼ teaspoon salt
½ cup Great Northern beans, rinsed and sorted	pepper to taste
	½ pound tomatoes, diced
4 cups water	½ cup black olives, halved and pitted
1 bay leaf	
salt to taste	3 tablespoons chopped basil
8 tablespoons olive oil	½ pound 1 inch pieces green or wax beans, cooked
1 onion, thinly sliced	

In separate bowls, soak the chick peas and Great Northern beans in water to cover for 8 hours. Drain the beans separately.

In one saucepan, simmer the chick peas and 2 cups of water about 45 minutes. In another saucepan, simmer the Great Northern beans, 2 cups of water, and the bay leaf about 45 minutes. Add a pinch of salt to both beans, and simmer 30 to 45 minutes longer or until tender. Cover and keep warm.

In a skillet, heat 3 tablespoons of oil, and sauté the onion until soft, but not brown. Drain the cooked dried beans, and discard the bay leaf. In a bowl, whisk the lemon juice, salt, pepper, and remaining olive oil. Add the beans, onion, tomatoes, olives, and basil. Correct the seasoning with salt and pepper. Fold in the green beans just before serving.

Yield: 6 servings

➤ Best when prepared and served.

Lima Beans

My teaching has taught me that many people detest certain foods, often without reason. Lima beans are high on the list. People become incensed at the idea of being fed the lowly lima. Possibly they will eat a lima purée because they cannot identify the culprit. But more often they will announce loudly and clearly their true feelings about lima beans. Since to many of us lima beans are delicious, I can only hope that the interesting recipes below will lead those who are reluctant to eat lima beans to give them another chance.

Lima beans benefit from a sharp, tangy flavor. Horseradish and mustard accent the bean nicely. Some of the recipes below call for horseradish, but try a mustard sauce (see page 31) with cooked lima beans for a change.

Lima Bean Purée

Try this first to see if you can obtain minimal acceptance from lima-bean haters.

2 10-ounce packages frozen
   lima beans, or 1½ pounds
   shelled fresh lima beans
1 medium onion, thinly sliced
½ teaspoon salt

¾ cup heavy cream
3 tablespoons butter
2 tablespoons grated
   horseradish, or to taste
salt and pepper to taste

In a 1 quart saucepan, simmer the beans, onion, and salt until the beans are tender—about 10 minutes. Drain.

In a processor, purée the beans, adding the cream in a slow, steady stream. You can leave the purée coarse, or strain it through a fine sieve. Return the purée to the saucepan and stir in the butter, horseradish, salt, and pepper. Heat, stirring over medium heat until hot. Add more cream if the purée is too thick.

Yield: 6 servings

➤ Can be prepared the day before and reheated.

Lima Beans with Horseradish and Tomato

2 10-ounce packages frozen
   lima beans, or 1½ pounds
   shelled fresh lima beans,
   cooked until tender
1 tablespoon olive oil
1 cup peeled, seeded, and
   diced tomato

1 tablespoon horseradish, or to
   taste
½ teaspoon salt, or to taste
pepper to taste
2 tablespoons minced
   coriander

Drain the beans. In a skillet, heat the oil and reheat the beans, stirring for about 2 minutes. When hot, add the tomato, horseradish, salt, and pepper, and cook, stirring gently for 1 minute or until the tomato is warmed. Sprinkle with coriander, stir to combine, and serve.

Yield: 6 servings

➤ The beans can be cooked ready for reheating several hours ahead.

Lima Beans and Corn in Custard Sauce

1½ cups shelled baby lima
   beans, or frozen
1½ cups corn kernels
2 tablespoons butter
2 tablespoons minced onion

¼ cup diced green pepper
¼ cup diced red pepper
salt and pepper to taste
3 eggs, beaten
1 cup heavy cream

Cook the lima beans in boiling water until just tender—about 15 to 20 minutes for fresh, or 6 minutes for frozen. Drain. If corn kernels are fresh, blanch them in boiling water for 3 minutes. Drain.

In a skillet, melt the butter, and sauté the onion and the green and red peppers, stirring until the vegetables are soft, but not browned. Stir in the lima beans, corn, salt, and pepper, and cook until heated. Lower the heat under the skillet. In a bowl, whisk the eggs and cream together, and pour over the vegetable mixture. Cook, stirring constantly until it thickens. Correct seasoning and serve immediately.

Yield: 6 servings

➤ Prepare the vegetable several hours ahead. Do not add the egg mixture until just before serving.

Lima Bean and Corn Salad with Basil Dressing

¾ cup olive oil
¼ cup balsamic vinegar
2 garlic cloves, crushed
¼ cup thinly sliced scallions
¼ cup minced basil
salt and pepper to taste

3 cups cooked lima beans
3 cups cooked corn kernels
½ cup minced onion
½ cup diced red pepper
½ cup diced green pepper
3 scallions, thinly sliced

In a bowl, whisk the olive oil, vinegar, garlic, ¼ cup scallions, basil, salt, and pepper to taste. In a large bowl, mix the lima beans, corn, onion, red pepper, green pepper, and scallions. Fold in the dressing, and let stand for at least 30 minutes before serving.

Yield: 6 servings

➤ Can be prepared the day before.

Country Style Lima Beans

2 10-ounce packages frozen
   lima beans, or 3 cups
   shelled fresh lima beans
¼ cup butter

1 garlic clove, minced
salt and pepper to taste
2 tablespoons corn meal
⅓ cup minced parsley

Cook lima beans in salted water until tender—about 5 minutes for frozen and 20 minutes for fresh. Drain.

In a skillet, heat the butter until it turns nutty brown. Add the beans and garlic, season with salt and pepper, and cook, stirring until hot. Add the cornmeal and parsley, and toss to coat.

Yield: 6 servings

➤ Can be prepared the day before, and can be frozen.

Fava alla Campagnola (Lima Beans Country Style)

2 packages frozen lima beans, or 1½ pounds fresh lima beans	olive oil
	salt and pepper to taste
	1 or 2 scallions, minced

Cook the beans until tender, drain, and turn into a bowl. Dress while still hot with the olive oil, salt, and pepper. Stir in the minced scallion, and let cool to room temperature.

Yield: 6 servings

➤ Can be prepared several hours ahead.

NOTE: 1 or 2 cloves of minced garlic adds piquancy to the dish.

Ensalada de Habas a la Cataloña
(Lima Bean Salad with Fresh Mint)

1¼ pounds shelled lima beans, or frozen	salt and pepper to taste
2 sprigs mint	2 teaspoons mint leaves, minced
½ cup water	2 ounces serrano ham or prosciutto in julienne
1 teaspoon Dijon mustard	
1 tablespoon Sherry vinegar	½ Boston lettuce, shredded
2 tablespoons olive oil	fresh mint leaves

In a covered saucepan, cook the lima beans and mint in the water until just tender. (If cooking fresh lima beans, use enough water to cover the beans.) Cool in the liquid.

In a bowl, whisk the mustard, vinegar, oil, salt, pepper, and minced mint. Discard the mint sprigs from the beans, and toss the drained beans with the sauce until well-coated. Fold in the ham and lettuce, and serve garnished with mint leaves.

Yield: 6 servings

➤ If preparing ahead, fold in lettuce just before serving.

Fagioli all 'Uccelletto
(White Beans Cooked Like Small Birds)

1 pound shelled fresh white beans	1 sprig sage
salt to taste	14 ounce can Italian tomatoes,
¼ cup olive oil	chopped
2 cloves garlic, crushed	pepper

If fresh white beans are not available, substitute dried beans, and soak overnight, or cover with water, bring to a boil, and simmer 5 minutes. Let stand for an hour, and then proceed. Cook the fresh beans in salted water for 30 minutes or until tender.

In a large skillet, heat the oil, and sauté the garlic until brown. Discard the garlic, and add the beans, sage, and tomatoes. Season with salt and pepper, and simmer for 20 minutes or until thickened.

Yield: 6 servings

➤ Can be prepared ahead and reheated.

Spicy White Beans with Tomatoes

¼ cup olive oil	¼ pound piece prosciutto, diced
1 onion, minced	2 cups canned cannellini
4 garlic cloves, minced	beans, rinsed and drained
½ teaspoon dried red pepper	4 small tomatoes, peeled,
flakes	cored, and quartered
1 pound Swiss chard,	¼ cup minced parsley
stemmed (see page 492)	salt and pepper to taste

In a skillet, heat the oil, and sauté the onion and garlic until soft.

Add red pepper flakes, and stir 1 minute. Add the chard and prosciutto, and cook, stirring until the chard is wilted. Add the beans, tomatoes, and parsley.

Season with salt and pepper, and simmer covered for 5 minutes. Uncover, and simmer 5 minutes longer, stirring occasionally.

Taste for seasoning, and correct with salt, pepper, and pepper flakes.

Yield: 6 servings

➤ Can be prepared the day before and reheated.

NOTE: This recipe calls for the leaves of the chard; use the stems for one of recipes in the chapter on chard.

White Beans with Marjoram

Select from the many white beans available in the market.

1 pound dried white beans	1 teaspoon minced garlic
8 cups cold water	6 sprigs parsley
¾ pound salt pork	salt and pepper to taste
1 onion stuck with 4 cloves	2 tablespoons butter
2 teaspoons dried marjoram	¼ cup minced parsley
1 carrot, peeled	

Soak the beans in cold water to cover by 2 inches for at least 8 hours. Drain.

In a casserole, combine the beans, 8 cups water, salt pork, onion, marjoram, carrot, garlic, parsley, 1 tablespoon salt, and ¼ teaspoon pepper. Cover and simmer 1½ hours, or until the beans are tender. Remove the salt pork, onion, carrot, and parsley sprigs. Discard the parsley sprigs and the cloves stuck into the onion.

Dice both the onion and the carrot, and (if you wish to serve it) the salt pork. Return the diced pork, carrot, and onion to the beans, and stir in the butter and minced parsley. Let stand for 30 minutes.

Reheat, put into a serving dish, and sprinkle with additional marjoram if desired.

Yield: 6 to 8 servings

➤ Can be prepared several hours ahead for a final reheating.

Cabbage and Beans

3 tablespoons olive oil	2 cups cooked or canned
4 ounces prosciutto, julienned	cannellini or Great
3 garlic cloves, minced	Northern beans, rinsed and
1 onion, chopped	drained
½ teaspoon red pepper flakes	¼ cup plus 1 tablespoon
1½ pounds Savoy cabbage,	minced parsley
shredded	salt and pepper to taste
2 tablespoons tomato paste	

In a skillet, heat the oil, and sauté the prosciutto, garlic, and onion until soft—about 3 to 5 minutes. Add the hot pepper, and stir 30 seconds. Add the cabbage and mix well. Add the tomato paste and 1 cup of water, and stir into the cabbage.

Cover and simmer, stirring until almost tender—about 20 minutes. Add the beans and ¼ cup parsley. Cook covered until the beans are hot—about 5 minutes. Correct seasoning with salt and pepper.

Yield: 6 servings

➤ Can be cooked ahead and reheated.

Black Eyed Peas and Bacon

4 thick slices bacon, diced	1½ teaspoons honey
⅓ cup minced onion	½ cup olive oil
1 garlic clove, minced	2½ cups cooked black eyed
½ teaspoon celery seed	peas, kept warm
½ teaspoon dill seed	salt and pepper
6 tablespoons red wine vinegar	1 red onion, thinly sliced

In a skillet, fry the bacon until crisp, and drain on paper towels. Add onion to the bacon drippings, and cook over medium heat until soft, stirring often. Add the garlic, celery, and dill seeds, and stir 1 minute.

Stir in the vinegar and honey, and simmer 2 minutes, stirring. Whisk in the olive oil, and remove from the heat. Pour over the peas, and season with salt and pepper. Add the onion slices and toss gently.

Serve sprinkled with bacon.

Yield: 6 servings

➤ Can be prepared ahead, and served at room temperature or cold.

Hoppin' John

There are a number of variations of beans and rice. This is one example. Feel free to substitute any other type of bean for the black eyed peas. Use water instead of chicken stock, and omit the salt pork if you wish. Many cooks prefer to liven the dish with red pepper flakes, minced jalapeno peppers, or generous dashes of hot pepper sauces, such as Tabasco, or hot green pepper sauce.

¼ pound salt pork, diced and	1 pound cooked black eyed
rinsed under cold water	peas, or other fresh shell
1 cup minced onion	bean or dried bean
1 cup long grain rice	salt and pepper
2 cups chicken stock	

In a 2 quart saucepan, fry the salt pork over low heat until crisp. Remove the cracklings and drain on paper toweling.

Add the onion to the pan and cook, stirring, until soft but not brown.

Add the rice, and stir until well coated.

Add the chicken stock, and cook, covered, over high heat until it reaches a boil. Lower the heat and cook 15 minutes.

Add the peas and cook, covered, 5 minutes longer.

Correct the seasoning with salt and pepper.

Stir the ingredients together gently, and put into a serving dish. Sprinkle with the pork cracklings.

Yield: 6 servings

➤ Can be prepared ahead and reheated in a casserole in a 350°F oven for about 20 minutes. You may want to add another ¼ cup chicken stock for moisture.

Texas Pinto Beans

1 pound dried pinto beans	2 teaspoons chili powder
½ pound smoked bacon, cut into 1-inch pieces	2 garlic cloves minced
	1 jalapeno pepper minced
1 tomato, diced	salt to taste
2 teaspoons cumin	

In a large saucepan, cover the beans with water, and bring to a boil. Let sit 1 hour and drain.

Return beans to the pan, add enough water to cover by 2 inches.

Add the bacon, tomato, cumin, chili powder, garlic, and jalapeno pepper, and simmer until tender, about 3½ hours, adding more water as needed.

Season with salt, and cook 15 minutes longer.

Yield: 6 servings

➤ Can be prepared ahead and reheated.

Black Beans with Rum

Serve this as a side dish, or for a complete meal. Accompany it with bowls of chopped onion, green and or red pepper, celery, garlic, and grated Monterey Jack.

2 cups black beans	salt and pepper to taste
2 stalks celery, diced	½ cup dark rum
1 onion, chopped	¼ cup butter
1 garlic clove, chopped	sour cream
1 carrot, chopped	

Soak the beans in 2 inches of water to cover overnight. Drain the beans. Place the beans in a casserole and add the celery, onion, garlic, carrot, 1 tablespoon salt, and ¼ teaspoon pepper. Add water to cover by 2 inches.

Simmer for 2 hours, or until the skins burst. Most of the liquid should have been absorbed. If there is liquid on top of the beans, spoon it off and discard.

Preheat the oven to 350°F. Add the rum to the casserole, dot with the butter. Cover and bake until the beans are tender.

Serve with sour cream on the side.

Yield: 6 servings

➤ Can be prepared ahead and reheated.

Lentil Salad

2 cups dried lentils
1 small onion stuck with 3 cloves
2 garlic cloves, sliced
1 bay leaf
salt to taste
⅔ cup vegetable oil
2 tablespoons Asian sesame oil

2 tablespoons cider vinegar
salt and pepper to taste
1 large red onion, thinly sliced
1 small bunch radishes, thinly
  sliced
¼ cup capers
¼ cup minced parsley

In a kettle, cook the lentils with water to cover, along with the onion, garlic, and bay leaf, for 25 to 60 minutes. They should not be too soft. Drain.

Discard the onion, garlic, and bay leaves. Cool.

In a bowl, mix the lentils, vegetable oil, sesame oil, and vinegar. Correct the seasoning with salt and pepper. Add the onions, radishes, capers, and parsley.

Yield: 6 servings

➤ Can be prepared the day before.

Lentil and Walnut Salad

2 cups lentils
1 bay leaf
⅓ cup olive oil
3 tablespoons wine vinegar
3 tablespoons sour cream
¼ teaspoon dry mustard

salt and pepper to taste
⅔ cup chopped walnuts
¼ cup thinly sliced scallions
tomato wedges
black olives
minced parsley

Rinse and pick over the lentils. In a large saucepan, simmer the lentils in water to cover by 2 inches, along with 1 teaspoon of salt and the bay leaf until just tender—25 to 60 minutes. Drain, and discard the bay leaf.

In a bowl, whisk the oil, vinegar, sour cream, mustard, salt, and pepper. Fold in the lentils with the walnuts and scallions.

Serve garnished with the tomato wedges, olives, and parsley.

Yield: 6 servings

➤ Can be prepared the day before.

Pois Chiches aux Moutarde (Chick Peas with Mustard)

Serve this as part of an hors d'oeuvre platter with other salad mixtures
and slices of saucisson and pâtés for a luscious lunch or supper.

1 cup mayonnaise	salt and pepper to taste
2 tablespoons Dijon mustard, or to taste	2 cups cooked or canned chick peas, drained
1 tablespoon minced chives	

In a bowl, mix the mayonnaise, mustard, chives, salt, and pepper.
Fold in the chick peas, and let marinate for at least 30 minutes.

Yield: 6 servings

➤ Can be prepared the day before.

Chick Pea and Shrimp Salad

2 cups cooked or canned chick peas	½ cup lemon juice
2 pounds shrimp, cooked, peeled, and deveined	½ cup olive oil
	2 garlic cloves
1 small red onion, thinly sliced	1 tablespoon dry mustard
½ cup Niçoise olives, pitted	salt and pepper to taste
3 tablespoons roasted red pepper, cut in julienne	Cayenne pepper to taste

In a bowl, mix the chick peas, shrimp, onion, olives, and red peppers.
In a processor, combine the lemon juice, olive oil, garlic, mustard, salt
and pepper, and Cayenne pepper, and purée. Pour over the salad, toss
gently, and let marinate for 2 hours.

Yield: 6 servings

➤ Can be prepared the day before.

Hummus (Chick Pea Spread)

1 cup drained chick peas (garbanzos)	pepper to taste
	¼ to ½ cup olive oil
2 tablespoons lemon juice	minced mint or parsley
2 cloves garlic, crushed	olive oil
½ teaspoon salt	paprika

Rinse the chick peas in cold water and drain again. Dry on paper
toweling.

In a processor, purée the peas, lemon juice, garlic, salt, pepper, and ½
of the olive oil, adding additional oil until the mixture is slightly thicker
than mayonnaise. Correct the seasoning with salt and lemon juice. Place
in a bowl, and sprinkle with mint or parsley around the edge, a drizzle of
oil over the top, and a sprinkling of paprika, if desired.

Yield: 1¼ cup

➤ Keeps 2 weeks, refrigerated.

Hummus Bi Tahini
(Chick Pea Spread with Sesame Paste)

Stir ¾ cup tahini into the chick pea spread.

NOTE: Tahini is sold in Middle Eastern Markets. Do not mistake Asian sesame seed paste for this product (see glossary).

Falafel (Chick Pea Croquettes)

2 cups canned chick peas	2 tablespoons fresh bread
1 teaspoon salt	crumbs
¼ teaspoon white pepper	1 egg, beaten
¼ teaspoon Cayenne pepper	1 tablespoon olive oil
¼ teaspoon dried basil,	flour
marjoram, or thyme	oil for frying

Drain the chick peas, and purée in a processor with the salt, white pepper, cayenne pepper, basil, and bread crumbs. With the machine running, add the egg and oil. Shape into croquettes and roll in the flour. Heat the oil to 370°F, and fry until golden.

Yield: 24 croquettes

➤ Can be prepared for frying the day before.

Bean Sprouts

Bean sprouts do not have much flavor of their own, but add a texture to various dishes. They are usually used in Asian dishes, and few recipes have appeared with solely western characteristics. Fortunately, the Asian dishes are superb in their own right. Many cooks use the sprouts raw in salads and sandwiches. The truly meticulous cook will carefully remove the hull of the bean and use just the tail. The rest of us rinse the bean sprouts and discard any shriveled sprouts before proceeding with the recipe.

Chinese New Year Bean Sprouts

3 cups bean sprouts	½ cup chicken stock
10 dried black mushrooms,	1 tablespoon dry sherry
soaked	1½ teaspoons salt
1-2 pieces bamboo shoot	1 teaspoon sugar
10 teaspoons peanut oil	½ teaspoon dark soy sauce

Rinse the bean sprouts and drain. Drain the mushrooms, squeeze dry, and remove and discard the stems. Cut bamboo shoots into triangles, rinse, and drain.

In a wok, heat 3 tablespoons oil and stir-fry the bean sprouts for 30 seconds. Add the mushrooms, and stir-fry for 20 seconds. Add the bamboo shoots, chicken stock, sherry, salt, sugar, and soy sauce. Cook, stirring, over high heat for about 5 minutes.

Arrange the bean sprouts and bamboo shoots on a platter, leaving the mushrooms in the wok. Add the remaining teaspoon of oil and cook for 45 seconds. Arrange on top of the sprouts.

Yield: 6 servings

➤ Cannot be prepared ahead.

Shanghai Bean Sprout Salad

1½ pounds bean sprouts	3 tablespoons white vinegar
1½ tablespoons peanut oil	1½ to 2 tablespoons sugar
1 red pepper, thinly sliced	½ to 1 tablespoon salt
4 scallions, cut into 1 inch julienne	1 teaspoon sesame oil

Wash and drain the bean sprouts.

In a wok, heat the peanut oil, and stir-fry the sprouts for 30 to 45 seconds. Add the pepper and stir-fry for 1 minute. Add the scallions and stir-fry 30 seconds longer.

Drain in a sieve.

Place vegetables in a bowl, and toss with vinegar, sugar, salt, and sesame oil, and chill.

Yield: 6 servings

➤ Can be prepared the day before and kept refrigerated.

Beets

Beets are grown in enormous quantity, but relatively few reach the table as a vegetable, because most beets are grown for other uses. Acres are devoted to produce beets for animal fodder, for a base for distilling liquor, and perhaps most of all for sugar. In the United States, most sugar is from sugar cane, but much of the rest of the world relies on the sugar beet. In addition, although very popular in northern European countries, beets have a limited appeal in other cultures. I have learned that students have a distrust, if not actual dislike, of beets. There is no reason for the lack of interest, because beets provide a delicious flavor and satisfying texture. They are easy to cook, although they do take longer than many other vegetables. I suspect their lack of popularity is due to the color. Bright and appealing as it may look, it gets all over everything, coloring any food mixed with it, and staining the cook's hands.

Vegetable beets are often sold with the tops, providing you with a dividend, because the greens are similar to spinach, and as tasty in their own right as the roots.

Availability

Fresh
June through September is the principal growing season, but fresh beets appear in the markets throughout the year. Look for small to medium deep red smooth skinned beets with crisp, green-to-red leaves and stems. If the leaves have been removed, 2 inches of stem should remain to prevent bleeding. If the stems are much shorter, the beet can lose moisture and become leathery. Avoid beets with scaly, shriveled, or bruised skin, or with wilted tops. Beet greens should have fresh, clean leaves with tender ribs. If you buy them with the tops, remove the greens 2 inches from the root, and use or discard according to your needs. Ideally, the beets should be no more than 2½ inches in diameter. Try to select beets of a similar size for even cooking. If there is no choice, remove the smaller beets as they are cooked.

To Store Beets store well kept in cool areas, once the tops are removed. Store the beets in a plastic bag in the vegetable drawer in the refrigerator for up to two weeks without washing.

Store the greens in a tightly closed bag for no more than 1 or 2 days.

Frozen

Freezing changes the texture, and the freezing of dishes containing beets is not recommended.

Canned

Canned beets are almost as good as fresh. Use them when you need beets for a salad, grate them for a quick sauté, or cook them in a sauce. Try several brands to determine which has the best quality.

Cooking Methods

Boiling

Rub the beet under cool running water with your hands rather than a brush, to avoid scratching the surface. Add 1 tablespoon of vinegar each quart of water to help retain the color. Place the beets with stem attached in a large pot of cold water and simmer until they are done— about 25 to 30 minutes. To test (after at least 20 minutes), pierce with the point of a paring knife. If you start testing too early, the beets will bleed into the water and lose their color. When cooked, run the beet under cold water and slip off the skins. If the beet has not cooked evenly, it is sometimes necessary to use a knife to pare off a stubborn section. If the beet is to be served cold, cool before peeling.

Removing Beet Stains Few foods stain as readily as beets. They can stain the cutting board, and particularly your hands. Rub the surface with lemon juice and salt, then wash with soap and water.

Steaming

Place the beets in a steamer over an inch or so of boiling water and steam for about 40 minutes.

Baking

Baking is the preferred method of cooking beets. Wrap the washed and trimmed beets in aluminum foil (to make clean-up easier) and place on a pie plate. Bake at 325°F for about 1 hour. To test for doneness, press the beets with your fingertips. They should feel as if they are sliding around in their skin. Or when they are almost done, pierce with the point of a paring knife. Larger beets can require another 30 minutes or longer.

Braising

Peel and slice before braising.

Microwaving

Place the beets in a covered dish with with ¼ cup liquid and cook for 10-11 minutes, turning the dish occasionally.

Quantity

1½ pounds will serve 6 persons. Toss leftover beets with vinaigrette or mayonnaise to serve as a salad.

Sauces

Beets are wonderful with butter sauces, especially those with a citrus or fruit flavor (see Orange Baked Beets, page 99). Serve with a sprinkling of poppy seeds, dill seeds, caraway seeds, or toasted sesame seeds. Minced dill, tarragon, and chervil enhance the flavor. Vinaigrette and sour cream sauces are also particularly suitable. Yogurt and mint make a wonderful topping for cold beets, and mayonnaise flavored with mustard and dill is another favorite.

Russian Borscht

There are many recipes for borscht; here are two quick, easy versions to serve hot or cold.

2 bunches of beets, or 1 pound of canned beets with juices	2 tablespoons cider vinegar
½ cup tomato purée	2 tablespoons brown sugar, or to taste
1 small cabbage	2 bay leaves
½ cup diced carrots	salt and pepper to taste
¾ cup chopped onion	sour cream
1 quart beef stock	

Cut off all but 2 inches of the beet stalks, and boil in water to cover until tender. Drain, reserving the cooking liquid. Peel and grate the beets. If using canned beets, grate, reserving the liquid. Mix the liquid with the tomato paste.

In a 4 quart saucepan, simmer the cabbage, carrots, onion, stock, vinegar, sugar, bay leaves, salt, and pepper. Simmer uncovered for 20 minutes, or until the vegetables are tender. Add the beets and beet juice, and heat. Taste for seasoning, and adjust with vinegar and sugar to achieve a sweet-sour taste. Discard the bay leaves.

Serve hot or cold, and pass the sour cream.

Yield: 6 servings

➤ Can be prepared ahead and frozen.

Simple Summer Borscht

Cold borscht makes a pretty, flavorful, and refreshing summer soup.

1-pound can of beets	1 bay leaf
3 cups beef stock	juice of 1 lemon
2 teaspoons meat extract	salt and pepper to taste
Bovril (optional)	1 pint sour cream
1 tablespoon sugar	

Into a 2 quart saucepan, drain the beet liquid, and mix with the stock and beef extract. Stir in the sugar and bay leaf, and bring to a boil.

Grate the beets and stir into the soup. Simmer 5 minutes. Add more sugar and lemon juice to achieve a sweet sour taste. Remove and discard the bay leaf. Chill. Correct the seasoning with salt and pepper.

Serve with the sour cream on the side.

➤ Keeps 3 to 4 days, refrigerated.

Yield: 6 servings

Roasted Beets with Sherry Vinegar and Walnut Oil

1½ pounds beets, cooked, and skins removed	2 tablespoons olive oil
3 tablespoons walnut oil	2 tablespoons sherry vinegar
	salt and pepper to taste

Cut beets into ½ inch cubes, and toss with the walnut oil, olive oil, and vinegar. Season with salt and pepper.

Serve hot or cold.

Yield: 6 servings

➤ Can be prepared the day before. Reheat in a skillet over medium heat.

Purée de Betteraves (Beet Purée)

Traditionally, the purée is bound with a thick brown or béchamel sauce. However, simply puréeing the beets in a processor and heating the mixture in a saucepan to remove excess moisture works beautifully.

1½ pounds beets	salt and pepper to taste
1½ cups thick béchamel sauce	1 tablespoon butter

Bake the beets, run under cold water, and slip off the skins. Chop the beets coarsely, and purée in a processor. Add the béchamel sauce and purée again.

Return to the saucepan, and correct the seasoning with salt and pepper. Stir in the butter and heat.

Yield: 6 servings

➤ Can be prepared ahead and can be frozen.

Purée of Baked Beets and Garlic

3 tablespoons vegetable oil
1½ pounds beets, trimmed
  and washed
12 unpeeled garlic cloves
¼ cup butter

3 tablespoons raspberry
  vinegar
2 tablespoons sugar
1½ teaspoons salt
½ teaspoon pepper

Preheat the oven to 400°F.

In a casserole, place the vegetable oil, beets, and garlic, turning to coat. Cover, and bake until tender—about one hour. Cool under cold water, and slip the skins from the beets. Cut the beets into ½ inch dice. Cut off the ends of the garlic cloves, and press the garlic out of the skin.

In a processor, purée the beets, garlic, butter, vinegar, sugar, salt, and pepper. Reheat in a saucepan, and correct the seasoning with salt and pepper.

Yield: 6 servings

➤ Can be prepared the day before or frozen. Line the casserole with foil for easier cleaning.

Betteraves À la Poitevine (Braised Beets Poitou Style)

1½ pounds beets, peeled and
  sliced
2 tablespoons butter
1 cup minced onions
1 garlic clove, minced

1 tablespoon flour
1 tablespoon vinegar
1¼ cups chicken or beef stock
salt and pepper to taste

In a casserole, heat the butter, and sauté the onions and garlic until soft, but not brown. Add the beets, and cook until they start to soften. Stir in the flour, and cook for 2 minutes. Stir in the vinegar and stock, and correct the seasoning with salt and pepper.

Cover, and cook over low heat until tender—about 25 minutes.

Yield: 6 servings

NOTE: The casserole can be baked in a 350°F oven for about the same time.

Orange Baked Beets

The sweetness of beets combines well with citrus flavors. Try substituting lemon, lime, or grapefruit for a change.

1½ pounds beets, baked with
  skins removed
¼ cup butter

finely slivered peel of an
  orange
⅓ cup orange juice

If the beets are large, slice, cut into julienne, or cut into ½ inch dice. Leave baby beets whole. In a skillet, melt the butter, and cook the orange peel for 1 minute. Add the orange juice and simmer 2 minutes. Add the beets and heat until hot.

Yield: 6 servings

➤ Can be prepared the day before and reheated.

Sweet and Sour Beets

1½ pounds cooked beets, peeled, and cut into julienne	2 tablespoons red wine vinegar
	1 tablespoon sugar
2 tablespoons butter	½ teaspoon salt

In a skillet, melt the butter, and heat the beets until hot. Add the vinegar, sugar, and salt, and heat until hot. Correct the seasoning with salt and pepper.

Yield: 6 servings

➤ Can be prepared the day before and reheated.

Braised Grated Beets

This typical Middle-European dish should have a sweet-sour quality.
Add the lemon juice a little at a time for the sour, and let the beet provide the sweet. For further excitement, add a teaspoon of caraway or dill seeds with the flour.

1½ pounds raw beets, peeled and grated	1½ teaspoons salt
	¼ teaspoon pepper
2 tablespoons butter	1 tablespoon flour
3-4 tablespoons lemon juice, or to taste	½ cup water or chicken stock

In a large skillet, melt the butter, stir in the beets, 3 tablespoons lemon juice, salt, and pepper. Cover and cook, stirring occasionally for 25 minutes, or until the beets are tender-crisp. Sprinkle the flour on the top and stir.
Stir in the water and bring to a boil. Correct the seasoning with lemon juice, salt, and pepper.

Yield: 6 servings

➤ Can be prepared the day before and reheated.

NOTE: The easiest and least messy way of grating the beets is in a food processor, but if you do it by hand, grate the beets into a bowl, rather than onto the cutting board to make cleaning up easier.

Beets Glazed with Raspberry Vinegar

1½ pounds small cooked
  beets, skins removed
⅔ cup chicken stock

½ cup raspberry vinegar
3 tablespoons butter
salt and pepper

In a saucepan, simmer the stock, vinegar, and butter until slightly thickened. Add the beets and cook, stirring until it is heated and the sauce is thick and shiny.
    Correct the seasoning with salt and pepper.
    Serve hot or cold.

Yield: 6 servings

➤ Can be prepared ahead and reheated.

Betteravesà la Crème
(Cold Beets with Mustard Cream Sauce)

1½ pounds cooked beets,
  skins removed and sliced
3 tablespoons Dijon mustard
½ cup heavy cream
juice of 1 lemon

salt and pepper to taste
2 hard cooked eggs, chopped
  (optional)
1 teaspoon freshly grated
  horseradish (see Note)

Arrange the beet slices in a long, flat serving dish or platter. Chill.
    In a bowl, mix the mustard and cream with the lemon juice, and salt and pepper to taste.
    Pour the sauce over the beets, and decorate with the chopped hard cooked eggs and a sprinkling of freshly grated horseradish.

Yield: 6 servings

➤ The beets and sauce can be prepared the day before.

NOTE: If you use bottled horseradish, add it to taste to the sauce before putting it on the beets.

Syltede Rødbeder (Danish Pickled Beets)

½ cup white vinegar
½ cup water
½ cup sugar
1 teaspoon salt

⅛ teaspoon black pepper
3 cups thinly sliced cooked
  beets

In a saucepan, simmer the vinegar, water, sugar, salt, and pepper for 2 minutes. Place the beets in a heat-proof bowl, and pour over the vinegar mixture. Cover, and refrigerate until cold.

Yield: 6 servings

➤ Can be prepared several days before.

Beet Salads

This is more a concept than a recipe. Prepare the salad based on what is on hand, and arrange the ingredients like a painting.

1½ pounds cooked, peeled beets	hard cooked eggs
½ cup vinaigrette, or to taste	minced pickles
assorted greens	capers
Belgian endive	anchovies

Cut the beets into slices, cubes, julienne, batons, or grate them from coarse to medium. Each method of cutting changes the flavor and the way the vegetable absorbs the dressing.

Arrange on individual plates, one large platter, or use as part of an arrangement of cold appetizer or main course salads. Surround the beets, or place them on a bed of assorted greens, such as lettuce, shredded cabbage, watercress, or parsley sprigs. Use the Belgian endive and other distinctive vegetables, such as asparagus, around the edges.

Slice, chop, or separate and sieve the hard cooked eggs. Scatter over the beets, or present separately. Garnish with pickles, capers, and anchovies. Sprinkle additional dressing over the salad.

Yield: 6 servings

Beet and Romaine Salad

1½ teaspoons Dijon mustard	salt and pepper to taste
2 tablespoons wine vinegar	½ pound cooked beets, grated
¼ cup olive oil	1 head romaine

In a bowl, mix the mustard, vinegar, olive oil, salt, and pepper. Stir in the beets, and coat evenly with the sauce. Shred the lettuce and arrange on plates. Place the beets in the center, and spoon the sauce in the bowl over the greens.

Yield: 6 servings

➤ Marinate the beets for up to 2 days.

Beet and Vidalia Onion Salad

The particularly mild, sweet flavor of the onions brings out the flavor of the beets.

1 pound cooked beets, sliced	½ cup vinaigrette
1 large Vidalia onion, thinly sliced	¼ cup minced parsley

Arrange the beet and onion slices on a large platter and sprinkle with vinaigrette. Sprinkle with the parsley.

Yield: 6 servings

➤ Can be prepared several hours before serving. Serve at room temperature.

Beet and Potato Salad

2 tablespoons vinegar
1 tablespoon sugar
1½ teaspoons dry mustard
salt and pepper to taste
1 tablespoon grated
   horseradish, or to taste
¼ cup heavy cream

1 pound new potatoes, cooked
   until tender, and diced
1 pound beets, cooked and
   diced
6 scallions, minced
6 hard cooked eggs, peeled
   and halved
1 cup mayonnaise

In a large bowl, mix the vinegar, sugar, mustard, salt, and pepper until the sugar is dissolved. Stir in the horseradish and the cream. Fold in the potatoes, beets, and scallions with as few strokes as necessary. Place the salad on a serving platter, surround with eggs, and coat the eggs with the mayonnaise.

Yield: 6 servings

➤ Can be prepared several hours ahead.

NOTE: If serving meat or fish omit the eggs. Stir the salad as little as possible, to keep the separate colors.

Käsesalat (Beet and Cheese Salad)

2 cups chopped celery
2 cups chopped beets
1 cup mayonnaise
salt and pepper to taste

Radicchio leaves
1½ cups grated Gruyere cheese
2 hard cooked eggs
12 rolled, stuffed anchovies

In a bowl, mix the celery and beets with ½ cup mayonnaise. Season with salt and pepper. In a bowl, make cups of the Radicchio around the edges and put the salad in the center. Sprinkle the salad with the cheese. Cut the eggs into 12 slices, and arrange around the edge of the salad. Place an anchovy on each egg slice. Serve the remaining mayonnaise on the side.

Yield: 6 servings

➤ Can be prepared several hours ahead. Do not let stand more than 6 hours, or the celery will make the salad watery.

Beet Greens

Treat beet greens the same as spinach. It is not necessary to strip off the stem, if it is tender, but with larger leaves and stouter stalks, stripping the leaves (as described on page 460) is advised. You need about 3 pounds of beet greens for 6 people.

Wash the leaves well. Place in a saucepan with only the water on the leaves, cover, and cook over medium heat for 3 minutes. Stir and cook until the leaves are tender—about 2 more minutes. Drain and squeeze out the excess moisture.

Reheat in a tablespoon or so of butter, and season with salt and pepper.

Caraway Flavored Beets and Greens

1½ pounds beets with greens	¼ teaspoon caraway seeds, or
¼ cup balsamic vinegar	to taste
1 garlic clove, minced	salt and pepper to taste
1 tablespoon Dijon mustard	

Remove the greens from the beets, leaving 2 inches of stem attached. Wash the beets, wrap in foil, and bake in a 325°F oven until tender—about 1 hour. Wash the beet greens in lukewarm water and drain.

With the water on the leaves, cook the greens in a covered pot until wilted—about 5 minutes—stirring once. Drain. Cool the cooked beets under cold water, slip off the skins, and cut into cubes or slices.

In the skillet, heat the vinegar, garlic, mustard, caraway seeds, and salt until reduced by half. Add the greens and beets, and cook, stirring, until heated.

Yield: 6 servings

➤ Can be prepared the day before and reheated.

Broccoli

*B*roccoli is one of the most loved of vegetables. The crispy texture, fresh flavor, and bright green color appeal to almost everyone. Unlike many members of the cabbage family, the flavor is not too strong, the crunch of it when undercooked is appealing, and it looks attractive unless truly overcooked. And—it is good for you! It is so full of vitamins and minerals that it is considered one of the perfect diet foods. Although it can be sauced and garnished elaborately, it is one vegetable that can be eaten with relish hot or cold without any dressing at all.

Broccoli has been mistreated over recent years. Poor cooks have used the excuse that overcooked vegetables are unacceptable to save themselves from cooking foods properly. Virtually raw broccoli is served in restaurants and homes with the comment that they did not want to overcook it. Cooking broccoli and most other vegetables requires care and attention. The vegetable should be cooked until tender, but still crisp. When eaten there should not be an audible crunch, but rather a resistant texture. Hot raw broccoli is as unacceptable as mushy overcooked broccoli.

Availability

Broccoli is in the market year round.

Fresh
Look for bright green heads with tightly closed buds and no sign of yellowing. The ends of the stalk can look dried where it was cut from the plant, but just above the cut the stalk should look fresh, and the stalks should be firm, not limp.

Store the broccoli, unwashed, in the vegetable drawer for 3 to 5 days. Wash, if it needs it, just before using.

Frozen
Broccoli is sold frozen in whole spears, or chopped. In either case the blanching and freezing process changes the texture considerably, and there is a great loss of quality.

Canned
Broccoli is not sold in cans.

Preparation

Cut the florets from the broccoli, leaving only a small section of stem attached. Cut the florets into bite sized sections. If the the florets are too large, separate into smaller sections. Cut off the dried end of the stem, and peel the deep green color to expose the pale green tender core. Cut the core into slices, dice, or julienne.

If preparing ahead, store in cold water to cover for 1 or 2 hours, or in a plastic bag in the refrigerator for up to 12 hours.

Cooking Methods

Boiling
Cook the broccoli in boiling salted water until tender-crisp—about 6 to 8 minutes. Broccoli goes from just barely done to overdone very quickly. Pay close attention as it nears the tender-crisp point. Drain the broccoli, run under cold water and drain again. Because the stems take longer, either put them into the water 1 or 2 minutes before the florets, or cook them separately.

Blanching
In most recipes broccoli needs to be blanched before it receives its final heating and sauce. Cook it in boiling salted water, or steam it until tender but still crisp. Drain, run under cold water, and drain again. It will finish cooking when it is reheated.

Steaming
Place the stems in the steamer, steam 1 or 2 minutes, add the florets and steam until done—about 6 to 8 minutes.

Microwaving
Cook in a covered container with ½ cup water for 5 to 7 minutes. Turn the broccoli in the dish and turn the dish at least once during the cooking.

Quantity

Plan on 1 large bunch of broccoli (about 2 pounds) for every 6 persons.

Sauces

Treat broccoli and cauliflower the same. Interchange the sauces as you wish. Principal sauces include butter sauces, (especially with a citrus flavoring), Hollandaise, Maltaise, mustard sauces, and anchovy sauces. Serve it tossed alla trifolati, Parmigiana (pages 10–11), or serve in cream and cheese sauces.

Crostini con Broccoli *(Croutons with Broccoli Purée)*

For a low calorie hors d'oeuvre, toast the bread in the oven until golden. You can use just the peeled stems and save the florets for another use.

½ pound peeled broccoli
  stems
1 garlic clove
2½ tablespoons olive oil

salt and pepper to taste
12 slices French bread
olive oil

Cook the broccoli stems in boiling salted water until tender. Drain. In a processor, purée the stems with the garlic until smooth. Add the 2½ tablespoons olive oil in a slow steady stream. Correct the seasoning with salt and pepper. Place in a saucepan and reheat.

In a large skillet, sauté the bread slices in the olive oil until golden on both sides. Drain on paper toweling. Spread with warm purée just before serving.

Yield: 6 servings

➤ The purée can be prepared the day before.

Fiori di Broccoli Fritti *(Fried Broccoli Florets)*

1 bunch broccoli, blanched
  and cut into florets
1 egg

salt and pepper to taste
1 cup bread crumbs
oil for deep-frying

Dry the broccoli on paper towels. In a bowl, beat the egg, and season with salt and pepper. Place the bread crumbs in a pie plate. Heat the oil to 375°F. Dip the broccoli into the egg, roll in the bread crumbs, and fry until golden. Serve immediately.

Yield: 6 servings

➤ Can be prepared for frying two hours before.

Shredded Broccoli Stems with Pecans and Prosciutto

Here is a delicious way to use leftover broccoli stems. Shredding the stems give them a slightly different flavor.

⅓ cup butter
⅓ cup chopped pecans
2½ cups shredded broccoli
  stems

6 slices prosciutto, shredded
salt and pepper to taste

In a small skillet, melt 1 tablespoon of butter, and sauté the pecans until lightly toasted. Cook the stems in a steamer, or in boiling salted water, until tender-crisp—about 2 minutes. Drain well. Toss the hot stems with the remaining butter, pecans, salt, pepper and ham slices.

Broccoli a Crudo
(Broccoli Sautéed with Wine and Garlic)

1 bunch broccoli	salt and pepper to taste
5 tablespoons olive oil	2 cups dry white wine
2 garlic cloves, minced	

Cut the broccoli into florets, peel the stems, and cut into ½ inch slices.

In a skillet, heat the oil, and sauté the garlic until it starts to turn golden.

Add the broccoli, and season with salt and pepper.

Sauté, stirring often over medium heat until almost tender.

Add the wine, and cook until the broccoli is very tender.

Yield: 6 servings

➤ Can be prepared ahead and reheated.

Broccoli with Orange Veloute

This seemingly elaborate sauce is a low-calorie method of adding flavor. Use lemon juice instead of orange.

1 orange	salt and pepper to taste
1 tablespoon butter	1 large bunch broccoli, cut up
2 tablespoons flour	and cooked until
½ cup chicken stock	tender-crisp

With a zester, remove the rind of the orange in julienne, or grate the orange rind. Squeeze the juice from the orange and reserve. In a small pan of boiling water, blanch the orange julienne for 2 minutes, drain, and set aside. If using grated rind, just set aside.

In a small saucepan, melt the butter, whisk in the flour, and cook until foamy. Stir in the chicken stock, and cook until thickened and smooth. Stir in the orange juice, and correct the seasoning with salt and pepper to taste.

Serve over the broccoli.

Yield: 6 servings

➤ The sauce can be prepared the day before and reheated.

NOTE: You can add ¼ cup heavy cream to further enrich the sauce, or use a low calorie sour cream to keep the calories down.

Broccoli Parisienne (*Broccoli and Carrots*)

3 cups water
2 tablespoons white wine
 vinegar
1 bay leaf
1 parsley sprig
1 celery stalk
1 carrot, peeled and thinly
 sliced

1 onion, thinly sliced
salt and pepper to taste
4 peppercorns
1 large bunch of broccoli, cut
 up for cooking
Beurre Manié (see glossary)
6 tablespoons butter

In a saucepan, simmer the water, vinegar, bay leaf, parsley, celery, carrot, onion, salt, and peppercorns for 20 minutes, or until the vegetables are tender. Add the broccoli, and cook until just tender. Drain, reserving the cooking liquid. Refresh the vegetables under cold water, and drain again. Discard the bay leaf, parsley, and celery.

In the saucepan, reduce the cooking liquid to 1 cup, and whisk in enough *Beurre Manié* to thicken the sauce to the consistency of medium cream. Whisk in the butter a tablespoon at a time. Correct the seasoning with salt and pepper.

Reheat the broccoli, carrots, and onion in a pan of boiling water or in a steamer. Drain and put into a serving dish. Pour over the sauce.

Yield: 6 servings

➤ The sauce can be made an hour ahead, but reheat it very gently to prevent separating.

Broccoli Savoyarde

1 large bunch of broccoli,
 cooked and refreshed
butter
4 eggs

2 cups milk
pinch of nutmeg
salt and pepper to taste
1 cup grated Gruyere cheese

Preheat the oven to 400°F.
Drain the broccoli. Butter a 2 quart casserole, and add the broccoli.
In a bowl, beat the eggs, milk, nutmeg, salt, and pepper. Stir in the Gruyere, and pour over the broccoli. Bake for 20 minutes, or until the custard is set and the top is a little puffy.

Yield: 6 servings

➤ Can be prepared for baking 2 hours ahead.

Broccoli Stufati al Vino Rosso
(Stewed Broccoli with Red Wine)

2 cups thinly sliced onion	4 anchovy fillets, chopped
1 bunch broccoli, cut into florets and stems into ¼ inch slices	½ cup Parmesan, cut into slivers
	salt and pepper to taste
½ cup black olives, pitted and halved	⅓ cup olive oil
	1 cup red wine

In a large sauté pan, cover the bottom with half the onions, the broccoli stems, and half the olives, anchovies, and Parmesan. Season lightly with salt and pepper, and add half the olive oil.

Repeat using the remaining ingredients. Add the wine, and simmer for 1 hour, or until the wine has evaporated. Do not stir.

Yield: 6 servings

➤ Can be prepared ahead and served at room temperature.

Rigatoni Con Broccoli

Any tubular pasta is suitable, as long as it is roughly the size of the broccoli. Long pastas are not as successful.

1 bunch broccoli, cooked, drained, and refreshed	¼ teaspoon hot red pepper flakes
6 tablespoons olive oil	⅓ cup chicken stock
2 teaspoons minced garlic	salt and pepper to taste
	1 pound rigatoni

Drain the broccoli on paper towels. In a skillet, heat the oil, and sauté the garlic until golden, without browning. Add the broccoli and heat. Add the pepper flakes, stock, salt, and pepper.

Cook the rigatoni in boiling salted water until tender. Drain, and toss with the broccoli mixture.

Yield: 6 servings

➤ Best if prepared and served.

Noodles with Broccoli and Chicken

A few years ago many chefs experimented with mixing ingredients from different cultures to give East-West accents to their food. This is a particularly successful combination.

1 pound noodles (see Note)	3 cups broccoli florets
¼ cup vegetable oil	½ cup dry sherry
¼ cup Asian sesame oil	½ cup soy sauce
1 cup diced raw chicken breast	3 tablespoons butter
2 teaspoon minced garlic	½ cup grated Parmesan cheese
2 teaspoons minced ginger	½ cup toasted almond slices

Cook the noodles until al dente.

In a wok, heat the oil, and stir-fry the chicken until it loses its color. Add the garlic, ginger, and broccoli, and stir-fry one minute. Add the sherry and soy sauce, and simmer 1 minute.

Drain the noodles, and add to the wok with the butter. Toss to coat evenly. Add the cheese and toss again.

Serve sprinkled with the almonds.

Yield: 6 servings

➤ Cannot be prepared ahead.

NOTE: Use fettuccine, Chinese egg noodles, or even rice sticks.

Mousseline de Broccoli au Sauce Morille
(Broccoli Custards with Morel Sauce)

This elegant preparation makes a superb first course or luncheon.

1 large bunch broccoli florets, cooked and refreshed	1 cup butter
½ cup heavy cream	16 dried morel mushrooms, soaked and halved
1 teaspoon salt	1 shallot, minced
pinch of pepper	½ cup dry white wine
pinch of nutmeg	1 cup heavy cream
1½ tablespoons lemon juice	salt and pepper to taste
4 eggs	lemon juice to taste

Preheat the oven to 375°F. Butter 10 ½-cup ramekins.

In a saucepan, bring the cream to a boil, and add the broccoli, salt, pepper, nutmeg, and lemon juice. Cook, stirring until the cream is absorbed. In a processor, purée the broccoli, and add the eggs. Process until smooth.

Pour the custard into the molds, and place them in a baking pan filled with 1 inch of boiling water. Cover the molds with buttered foil, and bake for 30 to 35 minutes, or until just set.

In a skillet, melt 2 tablespoons of the butter, and sauté the mushrooms and shallots until the liquid evaporates. Cut the remaining butter into small pieces. Add the wine to the skillet and reduce by half. Add the cream, and cook until the sauce is slightly thickened. Whisk in the butter pieces, one piece at a time.

Correct the seasoning with salt, pepper, and lemon juice. Unmold the custards, and surround with the sauce.

Yield: 10 servings

➤ Can be prepared ahead and held in a warm area in the water bath for up to 1 hour.

NOTE: For easier serving and less fuss, pour the mixture into a 10 inch round cake tin, and bake for about 1 hour, or until it tests done. Unmold and put onto a serving platter, pour the sauce over the top, and serve cut into wedges.

Broccoli and Carrots with Garlic and Curry

The spiciness of this dish will depend on the curry powder. Serve with roasted chicken or grilled fish.

1¾ pounds broccoli, trimmed
   and cut into long spears,
   leaving florets attached
2 carrots, cut into batons
2 teaspoons curry powder

¼ cup vegetable oil
10 large garlic cloves
½ teaspoon sugar
1 small lime

In a large kettle of boiling salted water, cook the broccoli and carrots until tender-crisp—about 3 minutes. Drain, refresh under cold water, and drain again. Shake off the excess water, and sprinkle the vegetables with curry powder.

In a large skillet, heat the oil, and sauté the garlic cloves over medium heat until golden, but not burned. Remove and reserve the garlic. Add the broccoli and carrots to the skillet, and cook, stirring until softened. Sprinkle with sugar, and cook until lightly browned.

Arrange a bouquet of broccoli and carrots on a serving platter, and sprinkle with garlic and lime juice.

Yield: 6 servings

➤ The broccoli and carrots can be blanched and the garlic sautéed the day before.

Broccoli with Straw Mushrooms

This is a classic dish of Chinese cookery, providing color, taste, and texture in one dish.

1 tablespoon vegetable oil
1 can straw mushrooms, or 6
   large Chinese mushrooms,
   soaked (see glossary)

1 teaspoon oyster sauce
1 teaspoon soy sauce
1 bunch broccoli, cut into florets
   and cooked until tender-crisp

In a wok, heat the oil, and stir-fry the mushrooms for 1 minute. Add the oyster sauce and soy sauce, and stir until well coated.

Arrange the broccoli florets facing out on a platter so they resemble the original head. Place the mushrooms in the center.

Yield: 6 servings

➤ Cannot be prepared ahead. Serve within 3 hours or the vegetables will lose their color.

Chow Gai Laan (Stir-Fried Broccoli)

1 head broccoli
1 teaspoon sugar
1 tablespoon cornstarch
2 tablespoons soy sauce
½ cup water or chicken stock

¼ cup oil
1 clove garlic, minced
2 tablespoons sherry
salt to taste

Remove the tough ends from broccoli, peel the stems, and cut into ⅛-inch thick diagonal slices. Separate the heads into florets. In a bowl, mix the sugar, cornstarch, soy sauce, and chicken stock.

Heat a wok, add the oil and then the salt. Add the garlic, and when golden, add the broccoli. Stir-fry for 2-3 minutes. Add the sherry, cover, and cook 2 minutes. Add the cornstarch mixture and cook, stirring until thickened.

Yield: 4 to 6 servings

➤ Cannot be prepared ahead.

Broccoli in Oyster Sauce

¾ cup chicken stock
1 ½ pounds broccoli, cut into
  florets, stems peeled and
  cut into 1 inch chunks
2 tablespoons peanut oil
1 tablespoon minced ginger

1 scallion, minced
1 garlic clove, minced
1 ½ tablespoons oyster sauce
½ teaspoon sugar
1 teaspoon cornstarch

In a saucepan, bring the stock to a boil, add the broccoli, and boil 3 minutes. Drain, reserving ½ cup plus 2 teaspoons stock.

In a wok, heat the oil, and stir-fry the ginger, scallion, and garlic until fragrant—about 30 seconds. Add the broccoli, and stir-fry 2 minutes. Add the oyster sauce, sugar, and ½ cup of reserved stock. Stir-fry for 2 minutes.

Mix the cornstarch and remaining 2 teaspoons of stock, and stir into the wok. Cook until lightly thickened.

Yield: 6 servings

➤ Cannot be prepared ahead.

Shallow Fried Noodles with Shrimp and Broccoli

Cook the noodles while you prepare the shrimp and broccoli, and keep warm in a 250°F oven if necessary.

½ pound Chinese egg noodles
½ cup oil
1 bunch broccoli
¼ pound shrimp, shelled and
  deveined
1 tablespoon soy sauce
1 tablespoon sherry
3½ teaspoons cornstarch

¾ cup chicken stock
1 teaspoon sugar
¼ teaspoon salt
1 tablespoon minced ginger
1 garlic clove, chopped
2 tablespoons fermented black
  beans, rinsed and chopped
  (see glossary)

In a large kettle of boiling water, cook noodles until tender, drain, refresh under cold water, and drain again. In a large skillet, heat 3 tablespoons oil, spread the noodles evenly over the bottom, and cook without stirring until golden and crisp on bottom. Turn noodles over, add 1 tablespoon oil to the skillet, and fry until crisp on second side.

Meanwhile, separate broccoli into florets. Peel and cut the stems into thin slices. In boiling salted water, blanch the stems 30 seconds and the florets 15 seconds, refresh, and drain. With a sharp paring knife, cut ¾ of the way through the shrimp lengthwise and spread them open to butterfly them. In a bowl, mix the soy sauce, sherry, 2 teaspoons cornstarch, and shrimp, and mix well. In another small bowl, mix 1½ teaspoons cornstarch, chicken stock, sugar, and salt.

Heat a wok, add ¼ cup oil, and stir-fry ginger and garlic 15 seconds. Add the shrimp and stir until just opaque. Add broccoli and black beans, and stir-fry 30 seconds. Add the chicken stock, and simmer until broccoli is tender, but firm—about 2 minutes. Remove from heat. Slide onto a platter, and place shrimp and broccoli on top.

Yield: 4 to 6 servings

➤ Cannot be made ahead.

Broccoli di Rape

Periodically it appears that a new vegetable is in the market. In most instances it is a vegetable that has been well known by one ethnic group, but not others. Why it surfaces when it does is unclear, although the current interest in vegetables is reason enough to add to the already large list. *Broccoli di rape*, or broccoli rabe (actually turnip tops) has long been familiar to Italians and the Chinese, but other cultures have generally ignored it.

Treat it the same way you do broccoli or spinach. It responds particularly well to quick sautéing and stir-frying.

Broccoli di Rape con Prosciutto
(Broccoli Rabe with Prosciutto)

2 pounds broccoli di rape, stems peeled	2 small red or green chilies, thinly sliced
6 ounces prosciutto, thinly sliced	salt and pepper
¼ cup olive oil	olive oil
	lemon wedges

Cut the broccoli di rape into 3-inch pieces. Blanch in boiling salted water for 2 minutes, rinse, and drain. Separate the meat from fat of the prosciutto and mince both.

In a skillet, sauté ¼ cup olive oil and prosciutto fat until the prosciutto fat is crisp and brown. Remove and reserve. Add the broccoli di rape, prosciutto meat, chilies, and salt. Cover, and cook until tender—about 10 minutes. If the mixture seems dry, add 1 or 2 tablespoons of water as needed. Add the prosciutto cracklings and toss well. Serve hot or at room temperature, with the olive oil and lemon on the side.

Yield: 6 servings

➤ Can be prepared several hours ahead and reheated.

Cantonese Chinese Broccoli
(Broccoli Rabe) in Crabmeat Sauce

4¾ cups chicken stock
1½ pounds Chinese broccoli
(broccoli rabe)
2 teaspoons cornstarch
¼ teaspoon salt

⅛ teaspoon five-spice powder
(see glossary)
1½ tablespoons vegetable oil
½ pound crabmeat, picked over
2 tablespoons minced red
pepper

In a large saucepan, bring 3 cups of stock to a boil. Cut the broccoli into 3-inch pieces, and blanch in the chicken stock until tender-crisp. Drain. Arrange on a warm serving platter.

In a bowl, mix the cornstarch with 2 tablespoons of cold chicken stock. In another saucepan, bring the remaining chicken stock, salt, and five-spice powder to a boil. Stir in the cornstarch mixture, and cook until thickened and clear.

In a wok, heat the oil, and stir-fry the crabmeat and pepper until hot. Stir into the sauce, and pour the sauce over the broccoli.

Yield: 6 servings

➤ Cannot be prepared ahead.

Broccoli Salads

Broccoli is as good cold as it is hot. Add it raw, or blanch it so that it is cooked but still crunchy, or use it fully cooked. Take care not to add the dressing until shortly before serving or the broccoli will turn gray. If you are planning on a broccoli salad for a crowd, prepare the broccoli the day before and keep it in a sealed container. Combine the other ingredients of the salad and refrigerate overnight. An hour or two before serving, add the broccoli to the salad, and let the mixture come to room temperature for the best flavor.

Broccoli Valencienne

This dish is best when served at room temperature.

1 large bunch of broccoli,
cooked until tender-crisp
2 shallots, minced
1 red onion, thinly sliced
1 orange
1 teaspoon Dijon mustard

¼ cup tarragon vinegar
1 tablespoon dry sherry
salt and pepper to taste
1 cup olive oil
¼ cup toasted slivered
almonds

Drain the broccoli, refresh under cold water, and drain again. Add the shallots and onion to the broccoli. With an orange zester, remove the zest in julienne, and add to the broccoli.

In a bowl, whisk the mustard, vinegar, sherry, salt, and pepper until smooth. Whisk in the oil, and pour over the broccoli. Toss gently to coat evenly, and arrange in a serving dish. Sprinkle with the almonds.

Yield: 6 servings

➤ Because broccoli loses its color and crisp texture if left in a dressing for too long, do not make more than 3 hours ahead.

Spicy Broccoli Salad

1½ pounds broccoli, cooked and refreshed	1 tablespoon Dijon mustard
salt and pepper to taste	½ cup olive oil
⅓ cup sherry wine vinegar	1 small hot green chili, minced
1½ tablespoons soy sauce	¼ teaspoon red pepper flakes

Season the broccoli with salt and pepper. In a small bowl, whisk the vinegar, soy sauce, mustard, and olive oil together, and add the chili and red pepper flakes. Toss with broccoli just before serving.

Yield: 6 servings

Broccoli and Avocado Salad

1 bunch broccoli, blanched until tender-crisp, and refreshed	3 tablespoons olive oil
	2 tablespoons grapefruit or lemon juice
1 large ripe avocado	1 teaspoon Dijon mustard
juice of ½ lemon	salt and pepper to taste

Chill the broccoli. Cut the avocado in half, remove the seed, and peel. Cut the avocado meat into strips, and put into a bowl. Add the lemon juice and toss gently, coating all sides. Arrange the broccoli and avocado slices on a platter.

In a bowl, whisk the oil, grapefruit juice, and mustard until combined. Correct the seasoning with salt and pepper. Pour over the salad and serve.

Yield: 6 servings

➤ The broccoli and the dressing can be prepared the day before, but the avocado should not be peeled and the salad assembled more than an hour before. The broccoli can be cooked and the sauce prepared the day before, but do not mix them until just before serving because the broccoli quickly turns grey and loses its texture.

Broccoli with Snow Peas and Sesame Oil

1 bunch broccoli florets	2 tablespoons sesame seeds
½ pound snow peas, stringed	2 tablespoons soy sauce
4 tablespoons sesame oil	2 tablespoons rice vinegar

In a pot of boiling salted water, cook the broccoli until tender-crisp—about 4 minutes. Remove with a slotted spoon, refresh, and drain. Add the snow peas to the pot, and cook about 1 minute, drain, and refresh. Drain again. Put the broccoli and snow peas into a bowl.

In a small skillet, heat 1 tablespoon sesame oil, and sauté sesame seeds until golden. Set aside.

In a bowl, whisk the soy sauce, vinegar, and remaining sesame oil together. Pour over the vegetables and toss gently. Pour over the sesame seeds and toss again.

Yield: 6 servings

Brussels Sprouts

Many members of the cabbage family are viewed with derision, and one of the least appreciated members is the Brussels sprout. This lovely little vegetable gets poor treatment indeed. People become incensed at the thought of it, and many cooks attempt to cook it to an early death. The longer Brussels sprouts hang around before and after they are cooked, the stronger and the less appealing the vegetable becomes. If you garden, cook them immediately after harvesting; if you must purchase them in a market, cook them the same or the next day, because prolonged storage makes the flavor less agreeable.

Growing Brussels sprouts have an exotic appearance. The stalk grows straight up from the ground, with the sprouts spiraling around the stalk to the top. Interspersed among the sprouts are large fanlike leaves. In most markets Brussels sprouts are sold loose in bins or pint containers, but in some areas you can buy them on the stalk. Even if you will never eat Brussels sprouts, you may well want a stalk for a table decoration.

Brussels sprouts, like broccoli and many other vegetables, and especially those in the cabbage family, turn from undercooked to overcooked rapidly. As they approach being done, test them often so that they are just done. Undercooked, near-raw vegetables in a delicate sauce ruin the dish. Overdone vegetables are just as bad, and taste worse.

Availability

Fresh
Domestic Brussels sprouts arrive in October and last through March, with imports arriving year round. Look for small sprouts with firm, bright leaves, and avoid those with wilted or pale leaves, or with holes, which can indicate insect infestation. If you should get sprouts with insects, remove them and discard.

Frozen
Brussels sprouts freeze better than most leafy vegetables, and if cooked briefly, they are an acceptable substitute for fresh.

Canned
Brussels sprouts become mushy and stronger in flavor during the canning process, and so canned Brussels sprouts are not recommended.

Preparation

Cut a slice from the base of each sprout and peel off any tough leaves. With the point of a knife cut a deep cross into the base of each sprout to prevent them from falling apart while cooking.

Cooking Methods

Most recipes call for blanching and refreshing in a cold water to stop the cooking. When Brussels sprouts are ready to serve, reheat them in the sauce, or drop into boiling water until just reheated to prevent them from over-cooking.

Boiling
Cook the sprouts in boiling salted water until tender-crisp—about 8 minutes, depending on the size. It is most important not to overcook, or the flavor becomes stronger and the texture becomes mushy.

Steaming
Place the sprouts in a steamer over an inch of boiling water and cook until just barely done, about 8 minutes, depending on size.

Microwaving
Cook the sprouts in a covered dish with ¼ to ½ cup of water for 2 to 8 minutes, depending on the size. Check often, and turn the sprouts in the dish and the dish itself several times during the cooking.

Quantity

Plan on 1½ pounds for six persons.

Sauces

Brussels sprouts take well to a number of sauces. Serve with butter sauces, curry sauce, cream sauce, and Mornay, and cook them with pork products, such as bacon, ham, or sausage. They are suited to both the trifolati and parmigiana methods of Italian cooking (see pages 10–11). They are delicious served cold as part of a crudite, either raw or blanched. Blanch and use in salads.

Brussels Sprouts with Poppy Seeds

1½ pounds Brussels sprouts, cooked until tender-crisp, drained, and refreshed	3 tablespoons butter 2 teaspoons poppy seeds salt and pepper to taste

In a large skillet, reheat the Brussels sprouts in the butter until hot, and sprinkle with the poppy seeds. Season with salt and pepper to taste.

Yield: 6 servings

➤ Can be prepared for the final heating a couple of hours before.

Brussels Sprouts with Hazlenut Butter

¼ cup hazelnuts, peeled 6 tablespoons butter 1 tablespoon minced shallot	1½ pounds Brussels sprouts, cooked until tender-crisp, and refreshed salt and pepper to taste

Coarsely chop 8 to 10 hazelnuts, and set aside. In a processor, grind the remaining nuts to a powder.

In a skillet, heat 1 tablespoon of butter, and sauté the shallot until soft, but not brown. Remove, and let cool to room temperature. In the processor, cream the butter, hazelnuts, and shallots. Chill.

When ready to serve, reheat the sprouts by putting into boiling water for 2 to 3 minutes, or steaming until hot. Drain, and put into a serving dish.

In a saucepan, heat the butter over low heat, swirling the pan until the butter is melted to a creamy mass. Pour over the sprouts, and sprinkle with the chopped hazelnuts.

Yield: 6 servings

Choux de Bruxelles Frites (Deep-Fried Brussels Sprouts)

Although these are intended as a vegetable course, they make a wonderful hors d'oeuvre, especially when served with a mayonnaise made with lemon juice, or with a tomato salsa (see page 26).

1 cup flour salt and pepper to taste 1 egg, lightly beaten 1½ cups fresh bread crumbs (see glossary)	1½ pounds Brussels sprouts, cooked until tender-crisp, and refreshed oil for deep-frying

In a bowl, mix the flour with salt and pepper. Place the beaten egg in another bowl. Spread the crumbs on a baking sheet or pie plate. Roll the drained sprouts in the flour, egg, and finally the bread crumbs.

Place on a sheet of waxed paper or a baking rack, and let stand for 20 minutes or longer to set the coating. Just before serving, heat the oil to 375°F, and fry until golden. Drain and serve.

Yield: 6 servings

➤ Can be prepared for frying 6 hours ahead, and kept uncovered in the refrigerator.

Choux de Bruxelles Ménagère
(Brussels Sprouts with Bacon and Onion)

½ cup finely diced fatback	1½ pounds Brussels sprouts,
2 tablespoons minced onion	cooked until tender-crisp,
1 tablespoon butter	and refreshed
	salt and pepper to taste
	minced parsley

In a skillet, sauté the fatback and onion in the butter until the pieces are golden. Add the sprouts, and cook, stirring until heated. Correct the seasoning with salt and pepper.
Serve sprinkled with the parsley.

Yield: 6 servings

➤ Do the final cooking just before serving.

NOTE: Fatback is quite salty, so taste the dish before adding salt.

Choux de Bruxelles Aux Noix
(Brussels Sprouts with Walnuts)

4 tablespoons butter	1 cup chopped walnuts
½ cup bread crumbs	1½ pounds Brussels sprouts,
1 tablespoon flour	cooked until tender-crisp,
¾ cup chicken stock	and refreshed
salt and pepper	

In a small skillet, melt 2 tablespoons of butter, and sauté the bread crumbs, stirring until golden brown—about 3 minutes. Set aside.
In a saucepan, melt 2 tablespoons of butter, stir in the flour, and cook until it is foamy and starts to turn golden. Stir in the chicken stock, and bring to a boil, stirring with a wire whisk until slightly thickened and smooth. Season with salt and pepper.
Stir in the walnuts and Brussels sprouts, and cook until heated. Turn into a serving dish, and sprinkle with the bread crumbs.

Yield: 6 servings

➤ The bread crumbs can be prepared the day before. The sprouts can be prepared several hours ahead. The sauce can be prepared the day before. Do not combine and reheat until just before serving.

Braised Brussels Sprouts and Chestnuts

If you are making a pork roast, with which these are particularly good, plan to do the braising during the last half hour of the roasting.

1 pound chestnuts, unpeeled, or ½ pound dried chestnuts	1 pound Brussels sprouts, cooked until tender-crisp, and refreshed
1 cup chicken stock	¼ cup butter (optional)
2 tablespoons butter	salt and pepper to taste

If using unpeeled chestnuts, cut a cross in the flat side of each chestnut, cutting through the shell and piercing the inner skin. In a large kettle of boiling salted water, boil the chestnuts for 6 to 10 minutes. Drain, and keep in a pot of warm water. Peel off the shell and any skin that does not come off with it. If using dried chestnuts, soak overnight in cold water. Drain, and cook in boiling salted water until tender—about 30 to 45 minutes. Drain.

In a saucepan combine the chestnuts, chicken stock, and 2 tablespoons of butter, and simmer 20 to 30 minutes, or until the chestnuts are tender. Drain.

In a saucepan or skillet, sauté the Brussels sprouts and chestnuts in the remaining butter until hot. Season with salt and pepper.

Yield: 6 servings

➤ The chestnuts can be prepared the day before. Cook the Brussels sprouts only a few hours ahead, and do the final heating just before serving.

NOTE: If you wish to cook with the roast, add them to the fat in the pan about 30 minutes before the roast is done, instead of heating them in the butter.

Sweet and Sour Brussels Sprouts

1½ pounds Brussels sprouts, trimmed	¼ cup lemon juice
6 tablespoons chicken stock	2 tablespoons finely diced pimentos
2 teaspoons sugar	pepper to taste

In a saucepan, simmer the brussels sprouts in the chicken stock, sugar, and lemon juice until tender-crisp—about 8 to 10 minutes. Stir in the pimentos and season with pepper.

Yield: 6 servings

➤ If desired, undercook slightly, cool, and serve at room temperature.

Brussels Sprouts with Mustard Cream

1 tablespoon butter	1 cup heavy cream
½ cup minced onion	3 tablespoons Dijon mustard
¼ cup water	pinch of pepper
2 tablespoons white wine	1½ pounds Brussels sprouts,
vinegar	cooked until tender-crisp,
salt to taste	and refreshed

In a saucepan, sauté the onion in the butter until soft. Add the water, vinegar, and salt. Increase heat to medium, and reduce the liquid to 2 tablespoons. Add the cream, and cook until the sauce thickens enough to coat the back of a spoon.

Whisk the mustard and pepper into the hot sauce, fold in the Brussels sprouts, and season with pepper. Heat until hot.

Yield: 6 servings

➤ The sauce can be prepared the day before. Cook the sprouts and refresh them no more than a couple of hours ahead. Reheat them just before serving.

Brussels Sprouts with Cream and Garlic

2 tablespoons butter	1½ pounds Brussels sprouts,
2 garlic cloves, minced	cooked until tender-crisp,
⅔ cup heavy cream	drained, and refreshed
salt and pepper to taste	

In a skillet, sauté the garlic in the butter over medium heat until soft, but not brown.

Add the cream, salt, and pepper, and bring to a boil. Add the sprouts and boil until the cream coats the Brussels sprouts—about 6 minutes.

Yield: 6 servings

➤ Brussels sprouts can be prepared for final cooking a couple of hours ahead.

Shredded Brussels Sprouts with Parmesan Sauce

1½ pounds Brussels sprouts	1 tablespoon lemon juice
¼ cup butter	1¼ cups grated Parmesan
¼ cup olive oil	cheese
1 cup beef or chicken stock	salt and pepper
1½ cups heavy cream	

In a processor, or on a hand grater, shred the Brussels sprouts. In a skillet, melt the butter in the oil. Stir in the Brussels sprouts until well-coated. Add the stock, and cook over medium heat until the stock has been absorbed. Stir in the cream and lemon juice, and simmer until the sprouts are tender-crisp. Stir in 1 cup of grated Parmesan, and correct the seasoning with salt and pepper. Turn into a serving plate, and sprinkle with the remaining cheese.

Yield: 6 servings

➤ Best if prepared and served. If desired, prepare ahead and turn into a baking dish. Sprinkle with the cheese, and reheat under a broiler until golden.

Cabbage

Cabbage heads one of the largest vegetable families, with the direct descendants of green, red, and Savoy, and aunts, uncles, and cousins of broccoli, broccoli di rape, Brussels sprouts, cauliflower, rutabaga, and kohlrabi, to name a few Western favorites. In Asia, the list swells with the addition of celery cabbage, Nappa, and Bok Choy. They all have flavors that are reminiscent of one another, but usually quite different. The textures vary from delicate leaf varieties to quite firm roots. They also share the fact that over-cooking brings out the worst. They become soft and soggy, and the flavor strengthens to an unappealing level. Fortunately, with a little care they rank as one of the best vegetables there is.

In the not too distant past, cabbage was cooked for hours, and homes reeking of cabbage indicated poverty. Today we know that cooking cabbage quickly allows the retention of nutrients and avoids the tell-tale aroma. We also know that cabbage is delicious, and that financial status has nothing to do with its appeal.

Availability

Fresh
The head cabbages that are the focus of this chapter are at their peak in the late fall. Savoy becomes "old" by midwinter and, unless it is going to be braised or stuffed, should be avoided. Other cabbages store well, and are available year round. Summer coleslaw is as wonderful as any other green salad.

Green Cabbage Select light-green heads that feel heavy for their size, with smooth, tight leaves, and no indication of splitting. Avoid cabbages with white heads, which indicate overmaturity, or bright green heads, which are immature.

Cabbages are usually shipped with their outer leaves still attached. Some markets trim them to present very smooth shiny heads, while others leave the outer leaves as a petalled collar around the base. If you are planning a party, select those with the petals, which gives a giant rose-like appearance. Hollow the center of the cabbage, and fill it with a dip or spread, so that it can serve as a container and centerpiece at the same time.

Store in the vegetable drawer in the refrigerator, or if too large, in a plastic bag in the refrigerator, for a week.

Savoy Cabbage This green, crinkly, loose-leafed cabbage should have firm heads that are heavy in relation to their weight, with intact outer leaves. Lightweight heads, or those with yellow, wilted, or blemished leaves, should be avoided.

Store in the vegetable drawer, or a plastic bag, for up to a week.

Red Cabbage Look for bright red or purplish heads that feel heavy for their size, with unblemished outer leaves. Avoid blemished leaves or lightweight heads.

Store in the vegetable drawer, or a plastic bag, for up to a week.

Celery Cabbage This is also called Chinese cabbage in confusion with Nappa. They can be interchanged in recipes. Some writers, however, also confuse Chinese Cabbage with Bok Choy, which is a Chinese chard, and though they can be interchanged in some recipes, they cannot in all.

Select compact heads with pale stalks and bright-green, crisp leaves, and avoid heads with yellowing or wilted leaves.

Store in the vegetable drawer, or in a plastic bag, for up to a week.

Nappa Cabbage Look for firm, smooth, white stems with crisp green to pale yellow or greenish white leaves. Avoid stems that are not firm, and avoid wilted leaves.

Store in the vegetable drawer, or in a plastic bag, for up to a week.

Frozen
Cabbage is not sold frozen.

Canned
Cabbage is not canned, except as sauerkraut.

Preparation

Wedges
Cabbage needs little advance preparation prior to cooking. Cut large heads in half, quarters, or eights, and remove part of the core, leaving a section of core to hold the leaves together.

Shreds
Cut the cabbage into halves or quarters, and remove the core completely. Finely shred the cabbage by slicing across the leaves. The tender cores of celery and nappa cabbages are chopped or shredded.

Stuffed
Cabbage can be stuffed as individual leaves or as a whole head.

To Stuff Cabbage Leaves

Place the whole head in a pot of boiling water and cook for 2 to 3 minutes, until the outside leaves soften. With a knife cut at the base of the stem of each leaf, slip the leaf off, and remove to a colander. Continue cooking and removing the leaves as they soften, until the inside leaves are so crinkled that you cannot remove any more. Simmer the center of the cabbage about 10 minutes until it is tender-crisp. Remove from the water, and when cool enough to handle, chop, or shred, and use as part of the filling, or as a bed for the stuffed leaves.

Take a tablespoon or more of filling and put in the center of each leaf. Roll the bottom over the filling, fold in the sides, and then roll into a compact package. If the stem of the leaf is particularly thick or tough, either shave it from the back until it is about as thick as the leaf, or cut it out with a paring knife and overlap the cut area slightly before wrapping the filling.

To Stuff a Whole Cabbage

Using the Whole Cabbage A loose-leafed cabbage, such as a Savoy, is easiest to work with, but green or red cabbages can be used successfully. Place the whole head into a kettle of boiling water and boil until the outer leaves are quite tender. Drain the cabbage, and remove to a pan. Carefully peel back as many outer leaves as you can. At the center, when the leaves no longer pull away without tearing, cut out the center without slicing through the bottom. Chop the center to use as part of the filling, for another purpose, or as bed for the stuffed cabbage. Arrange a large piece of cheesecloth on the counter, and place the cabbage in the center and put one large leaf over the center section. Top with the filling, and bring the leaves up around the filling to reshape into a whole cabbage. Use the corners of the cheesecloth to tie it into a round ball. Twist the top of the cheesecloth to make as compact a package as possible. Place the cheesecloth-wrapped cabbage into a casserole, add enough stock barely to cover, and simmer for about 1 hour. Drain in a colander for 5 minutes, open the cheesecloth, and place a plate on top of the colander. Invert the whole cabbage onto the plate, and remove the cheesecloth. Let stand 5 minutes longer, and drain off any accumulated liquid. Cut into wedges to serve.

Using the Leaves Many people find this method easier. Blanch and remove the leaves from the head as directed for stuffing the individual leaves. In a large bowl, place the leaves top down and stem up so they overlap each other and extend up the sides of the bowl. Reserve one or two leaves. Spoon the filling into the bowl, wrap the overlapping leaves over the filling and press firmly, cover with the reserved leaves, press again, and pour the stock into the bowl. Bake at 375°F for 1½ hours. Drain off the liquid, and leave the rest in the bowl for 5 minutes. Drain again, unmold onto a platter, and let stand with the bowl on top for 5 minutes longer. Drain off any liquid, remove the bowl, and serve, cut into wedges.

Cooking Methods

Overcooking cabbage creates a strong flavor and mushy texture. Make sure that the cabbage is just tender-crisp for most preparations. However, stuffed cabbages, either whole or as individual leaves, and other braised dishes do withstand longer, slower cooking.

Boiling

Cook the cabbage in boiling salted water until tender, about 8 to 10 minutes. Drain well, and use in recipes, or serve with melted butter. Flavor the butter with dill seed, caraway seed, minced dill weed, savory, or even a hint of cinnamon.

Steaming

Steam the cabbage for 6 to 8 minutes until tender-crisp.

Microwaving

Green cabbage cut into small wedges will cook in about 6 minutes in a covered dish. Celery and Nappa cabbages can be cooked in the same way, but take about 4 to 5 minutes. Red cabbage should be cooked with 1 tablespoon of vinegar in the dish to help preserve the color, and will take about 10 minutes.

Quantity

1½ pounds of cabbage will serve 6 people as a vegetable. Larger cabbages weighing as much as several pounds are used in stuffed recipes.

Sauces

Cabbage is not usually served with the traditional sauces, such as Hollandaise or Mornay sauce. However, creamed shredded cabbage with Mornay is wonderful. The composed butters flavored with herbs, anchovies, and the like, are also subtle ways of giving cabbage dishes a distinctive note.

Cabbage Soups

When I started the research for this book, I assumed that I would have difficulty limiting the cabbage soup recipes. In fact, what I found was that there were few real cabbage soup recipes, but many soups that call for cabbage. I can only wonder whether this poor man's staple is considered so obvious that few have bothered to write down recipes for it.

Scandinavian Brown Cabbage Soup

¼ cup butter	1½ quarts hot beef stock
1 large white cabbage,	1 teaspoon salt
shredded	½ teaspoon pepper
2 tablespoons sugar	⅛ teaspoon allspice

In a large kettle, melt the butter, and sauté the cabbage, stirring occasionally, until it is very tender and the edges start to brown—about 30 minutes. Add the sugar, and cook until lightly caramelized, about 10 minutes longer. Stir in the stock, salt, pepper, and allspice, and simmer for 1 hour, partially covered.

Yield: 6 servings

➤ Can be prepared ahead and frozen.

Soupe aux Choux (French Cabbage Soup)

3 tablespoons butter	½ cup tomato purée
1 garlic clove, crushed	salt and pepper to taste
2 pounds cabbage, shredded	3 tablespoons bacon fat
1 onion, thinly sliced	6 thick slices french bread
1 quart beef stock	grated Parmesan cheese

In a large kettle, melt the butter, and sauté the garlic until golden. Discard the garlic. Add the cabbage and onion, and cook until golden brown, stirring often. Stir in the broth, tomato purée, salt, and pepper, and simmer for 30 minutes.

Meanwhile, in a skillet, melt the bacon fat, and lightly brown the bread slices on both sides. Serve the soup with a bread slice in each bowl. Pass the cheese separately.

Yield: 6 servings

➤ Can be prepared ahead and reheated.

Sautéed Cabbage

When cabbage is sautéed, the natural sugar will caramelize, giving the dish a golden brown color with a sweet aftertaste.

1 cup minced onion	salt, pepper, and nutmeg to
¼ cup olive oil	taste
1½ pounds cabbage, shredded	3 hard cooked eggs, sliced,
½ cup minced parsley	optional
2 tablespoons tarragon vinegar	1 tomato, sliced

In a large skillet, sauté the onion in the oil until soft, but not brown. Add the cabbage, parsley, vinegar, salt, and nutmeg. Cover, and cook over medium heat for 30 minutes, stirring occasionally. If the mixture starts to stick, add a little stock or water.

Arrange the cabbage on a platter, and surround with egg and tomato slices.

Yield: 6 servings

➤ The cabbage can be cooked the day before and reheated.

NOTE: Many European recipes call for hard cooked eggs. If you plan to serve this as a complete meal, then add them, but they are not required.

Sautéed Cabbage with Caraway

3 tablespoons butter	⅓ cup red wine vinegar
3 cups shredded cabbage, cooked until tender-crisp, and drained	1½ tablespoons caraway seeds
	1 teaspoon sugar, or to taste
	salt and pepper to taste

In a large skillet, melt the butter, and cook the cabbage, stirring until coated. Add the vinegar, caraway seeds, sugar, salt, and pepper, and cook, stirring, until heated.

Yield: 6 servings

➤ Can be prepared ahead and reheated.

Pepper Sautéed Cabbage and Noodles

This is a hearty, delicious family supper dish. Accompany it with ham steak, or stir in cooked sliced Italian sausage or kielbasa while the cabbage is browning, for a complete meal.

½ cup butter	salt and pepper to taste
6 cups shredded cabbage	12 ounces thin egg noodles, cooked
2 tablespoons sugar	

In a skillet, melt the butter, and sauté the cabbage until lightly browned—about 8 minutes. Mix in the sugar, salt, and pepper, and add the noodles. Toss to combine. Cook stirring until heated.

Yield: 6 servings

➤ The cabbage can be prepared ahead. Add the noodles and reheat just before serving.

Timbale de Chou Liegeoise *(Cabbage Custard Ring)*

Serve this easily prepared elaborate vegetable hot or cold.

6 slices bacon	4½ cups finely shredded
2½ cups scalded milk	cabbage, cooked until
3 eggs	tender-crisp, and drained
salt and pepper to taste	1 cup fine dry bread crumbs
dash of nutmeg	creamed peas, or carrots
	(optional)

Preheat the oven to 350°F. Butter a 2 quart ring mold, and line with waxed paper.

In a skillet, fry the bacon until crisp. Reserve the fat, and drain the bacon on paper towels. Crumble the bacon.

In a large bowl, whisk the milk, eggs, salt, pepper, and nutmeg. Add the cabbage, bread crumbs, bacon, and bacon fat. Mix well and turn into the mold. Place the mold in a baking pan, and fill with ½ inch of water. Bake for 40 to 45 minutes, or until a knife inserted in the center of the custard comes out clean. Let stand for 15 minutes. Unmold and peel off the waxed paper. Fill the center with the creamed peas or carrots, if desired.

Yield: 8 servings

➤ Can be prepared for baking several hours ahead.

NOTE: If serving cold, garnish with a lemon-flavored mayonnaise.

Stuffed Cabbage

Almost any stuffing will work wrapped inside of cabbage leaves. Apart from a few specific recipes for stuffing cabbages, I have listed several other stuffings that you can use. You decide whether to stuff the individual leaves, or stuff a whole cabbage. The individual leaves take more time to roll, but are easier to serve. Whole cabbages are a stunning presentation suitable for family or company.

Cheese Stuffed Cabbage Leaves

1 cup fresh bread crumbs	salt and pepper to taste
5 tablespoons butter	12 cabbage leaves
1 cup grated Parmesan cheese	¼ cup butter
4 eggs, lightly beaten	1 cup chopped onions

In a skillet, brown the bread crumbs in the 5 tablespoons of butter. Stir in the cheese and eggs, and season with salt and pepper. Stuff the cabbage leaves with the mixture, and roll as directed on page 127.

In the skillet, melt the remaining butter, and sauté the onions until soft, but not brown. Add the cabbage rolls, and sauté until golden on both sides. Add ¼ cup of water to the pan, cover, and simmer 10 minutes.

Yield: 6 servings

➤ Can be prepared ahead and reheated.

Polish Stuffed Cabbage

These are rolled individually, but you can prepare this recipe as a whole cabbage.

1 large head of cabbage	salt and pepper to taste
½ pound ground pork	3 cups beef or chicken stock
½ pound ground beef	1 cup tomato purée
½ pound ground veal	½ cup raisins
3 cups cooked rice	1 cup sour cream

Preheat the oven to 325°F.

Prepare the cabbage for stuffing as individual leaves (see page 127) or as a whole cabbage (see page 127). In a bowl, mix the pork, beef, veal, rice, salt, and pepper. Fill the cabbage.

For individual rolls: In a large baking pan, place the rolls, seam side down, in one layer. Add the stock—there should be just enough to cover—and bake for 1½ hours. Add more stock if necessary.

For a whole cabbage: Poach in stock to cover for 1½ hours. When ready to serve, remove the cabbage from the stock to a platter and keep warm.

Add the tomato purée and raisins to the stock and boil until lightly thickened. Remove from the heat, stir in the sour cream, and correct the seasoning with salt and pepper to taste. Reheat, if necessary, but do not boil. Pour the sauce over the rolls and serve.

Yield: 6 to 8 servings

➤ Can be prepared the day before or frozen, but do not add the sour cream until just before serving.

Chou Farci à la Provençale
(Stuffed Cabbage Provence Style)

1 large head cabbage, blanched for stuffing whole (see page 127)	2 tomatoes, peeled, seeded and chopped
½ pound beet greens, blanched and drained	⅔ cup cooked rice
1 cup minced onion, sautéed in 2 tablespoons butter until soft	1 cup raw or thawed peas
	1½ pounds sausage meat mixed with 1 tablespoon minced garlic
	chicken, beef, or lamb stock

Place the cabbage leaves on a large sheet of cheesecloth. Chop the center of the cabbage, arrange on top, and add the beet greens, onion, tomatoes, rice, peas, and sausage meat in layers on top of the cabbage. Bring the leaves up around the filling and, using the cheesecloth ends, form into a ball and tie securely.

Place in a large casserole, and add stock barely to cover. Simmer for 2½ hours. In a colander, drain the cabbage for 5 minutes. Degrease the stock and reduce by half.

Unwrap the cabbage, turn onto a serving platter, and let stand 5 minutes longer. Remove the colander and cheesecloth, and pour off any accumulated liquid.

Serve with the reduced stock.

Yield: 6 to 8 servings

➤ Can be prepared the day before. To reheat, place the cabbage in a colander over a pot with simmering stock, and steam until heated through.

NOTE: Mutton stock is used in Provence, but I find that a rich chicken stock provides a lighter flavor. If desired, after degreasing the stock, serve it as a soup, with slices of French bread that have been sautéed in olive oil until golden, and grated Gruyere, as a first course, and the cabbage as the main course. Serve a fresh tomato sauce with the cabbage, if desired.

Chou en Farce (Casserole of Cabbage, Ground Meat, and Apples with Cream)

The cabbage is not stuffed, but some of the leaves are used to line a casserole.

1 head of cabbage, quartered	2 eggs
salt and pepper to taste	½ teaspoon allspice
2 teaspoons ground cumin	½ teaspoon paprika
¾ cup chopped onion	1¼ pounds apples, peeled,
2½ tablespoons vegetable oil	cored, and diced
pinch of saffron	1 tablespoon oil
1 pound ground pork	8 thin slices prosciutto
¾ pound ground ham	1¼ cups cream
3-4 slices prosciutto, chopped	

Preheat the oven to 375°F.

In a kettle of boiling water, cook the cabbage and 1 tablespoon of salt for 10 minutes, or until tender. Drain, refresh under cold water, and drain again. Spread on paper toweling to dry. Season with salt, pepper, and 1 teaspoon cumin. Set aside.

In a skillet, sauté the onions in the oil until soft, and stir in the salt, pepper, and saffron. Continue cooking until the onions are slightly browned. Remove and set aside. In the same skillet, cook the ground pork until it loses its color, stirring to break up any clumps. Drain off any fat.

In a bowl, mix the pork, ham, prosciutto, onions, eggs, allspice, paprika, and remaining cumin.

Brush a 4½ quart casserole with the oil, and line the bottom and sides with some cabbage leaves. Spoon in a little cream, and make a layer of apples, cabbage leaves, half the meat mixture, and half the prosciutto, spooning some of the cream between each layer.

Repeat with the remaining ingredients, and finish with a layer of apples and a layer of cabbage. Cover, and bake for 30 minutes, lower the heat to 350°F, and bake for 1¼ to 1½ hours longer.

Yield: 6 servings

➤ Can be prepared for baking the day before.

Whole Stuffed Savoy Cabbage with Jambalaya Stuffing

1 large Savoy cabbage	½ teaspoon white pepper
2 tablespoons olive oil	1 teaspoon filé powder
1 pound andouille, or kielbasa	⅛ teaspoon cayenne pepper
1 cup chopped red peppers	1½ cups chicken stock
½ cup chopped onion	16 ounce can plum tomatoes,
⅟1 cup chopped celery	drained and crushed
2 garlic cloves, minced	1 teaspoon salt
2 teaspoons thyme, crumbled	1¼ cups rice
1 bay leaf	½ cup thinly sliced scallions
½ teaspoon pepper	2 cups chicken stock

Prepare the cabbage for stuffing whole (see page 127).

In a heavy 3-quart casserole, heat the oil, and sauté the andouille until crisp and brown. With a slotted spoon, transfer it to a bowl.

To the skillet, add the peppers, onion, celery, garlic, thyme, bay leaf, pepper, white pepper, filé, and cayenne pepper, and cook over low heat until tender. Add the stock, tomatoes, and salt, and bring to a boil. Add the rice and cook, covered, until the rice has absorbed the liquid. Transfer the rice to the bowl with the andouille and scallions. Cool.

Preheat the oven to 375°F.

Fill the cabbage and put into the casserole. Cover with the stock and bake, covered, for 1 hour. Let stand for 5 minutes. Pour off the stock and reserve. Remove the cheesecloth, or invert the bowl onto the platter and let stand 5 minutes longer. Pour off any liquid, and add to the reserved stock. Reduce the stock by half.

Serve the cabbage in wedges, and pass the stock separately.

Yield: 6 servings

➤ Can be prepared for baking the day before.

Spicy Sausage Stuffing

For an unspicy version, substitute sweet sausage and omit the chilies.

¾ pound hot Italian sausage, skins removed	4 garlic cloves, minced
7 tablespoons butter	1 tablespoon cumin
1 cup chopped celery	1 teaspoon turmeric
1 cup chopped onion	¼ cup minced parsley
2 serrano chilies, minced	3 tablespoons minced scallions
salt and pepper to taste	2 tablespoons chicken stock
2 tablespoons minced ginger	3 cups cooked rice
	chicken or beef stock

Preheat the oven to 375°F.

In a skillet, cook the sausage until the color changes. While cooking, break up the meat. Drain in a sieve, reserving 1 tablespoon drippings in the skillet. Add 5 tablespoons butter to the skillet, and cook the celery, onions, chilies, salt, and pepper until soft, but not brown—about 10 minutes. Add the ginger, and cook 2 minutes longer. Add the sausage, garlic, cumin, and turmeric, and stir 1 minute. Mix in remaining 2 tablespoons butter. Add the sausage mixture, parsley, and scallions to the rice, and use to stuff whole or individual cabbage leaves.

Add enough chicken or beef stock barely to cover, and bake for 1 hour and 30 minutes.

Yield: enough for one large cabbage

Sweet Pepper and Rice Stuffing

6 tablespoons olive oil	6 tablespoons butter
2 red peppers, ½ inch squares	2 cups rice, cooked until barely tender
2 green peppers, ½ inch squares	¼ teaspoon black pepper
2 yellow peppers, ½ inch squares	1 cup onion, chopped
½ teaspoon crushed red pepper	1 garlic clove, minced
	¾ pound chicken livers, diced
	chicken stock

In a skillet, heat 3 tablespoons of the oil, and sauté the peppers and pepper flakes for 2 minutes. Lower the heat to moderate, add 2 tablespoons of butter, and cook until the peppers are tender-crisp. Season with salt and pepper.

In a bowl, mix the rice and the peppers.

In the same skillet, heat 1 tablespoon of butter and 1 tablespoon of oil over high heat, and sauté the onion and garlic until soft, but not brown. Add to the rice.

In the skillet, heat the remaining 3 tablespoons of butter and 2 tablespoons of oil, and sauté the livers until medium. Season with salt and pepper, and add to the rice.

Yield: enough stuffing for one large cabbage

Coleslaw

No picnic or barbecue is complete without coleslaw. Its crisp, cool crunch appeals to everyone. Additionally, some versions are low in calories, and a great boon to the dieter. After chomping through a cup or more of this there is not strength left to eat more fattening foods. Even the vegetable-hating child will often succumb to the lure of coleslaw.

Recipes for coleslaw range from as simple as shredded cabbage mixed with a bottled dressing to elaborate versions with numerous other ingredients.

Colesaw

1½ pounds shredded green cabbage	¾ cup Mayonnaise or to taste
1 cup chopped onion	salt and pepper to taste

In a bowl, mix the cabbage, onion, enough mayonnaise to bind and season with salt and pepper. Let marinate for at least 1 hour.

Yield: 6 servings

➤ Can be prepared the day before. The longer the cabbage marinates, the tenderer it becomes.

Variations:

Use part or all red cabbage for the green. The red cabbage needs to marinate longer than the green, but it will become tender within a couple of hours.

Add 2 tablespoons caraway seeds.

Add 2 tablespoons dill seed.

Use half or all sour cream for the mayonnaise.

Add orange segments.

Add grated carrot, shredded, green, red, or yellow pepper—about 1 cup of any or each.

Add grated pineapple about ½ to 1 cup.

Add some sugar to taste if you like a sweeter version.

For a dietetic version, omit the mayonnaise and add ½ cup of cider vinegar, and sugar or a sugar substitute to taste to the basic slaw. Expand its quantity and its flavor by adding some of the variations listed above.

Sautéed Red Cabbage

1½ pounds red cabbage, shredded	2 tablespoons brown sugar
5 tablespoons lemon juice	1 tablespoon cider vinegar
5 tablespoons butter	½ teaspoon salt
1 apple, peeled, cored, and diced	¼ teaspoon pepper
	¼ teaspoon ground cloves

In a large pot of boiling salted water, cook the cabbage with 4 tablespoons lemon juice for 6 minutes. Drain well. In a large skillet, melt the butter, and sauté the apple until it begins to soften. Add the remaining lemon juice, sugar, vinegar, salt, pepper, cloves, and drained cabbage.
Cook until tender-crisp.

Yield: 6 servings

➤ Can be blanched several hours ahead.

Chou Rouge à la Limousine
(Red Cabbage Limousine Style)

1½ pounds shredded red cabbage	½ teaspoon salt
2 cups peeled, chopped, fresh, or dried chestnuts (see glossary)	pinch of black pepper
	½ teaspoon sugar
	1 cup beef stock

Preheat the oven to 350°F.
Butter a 2-quart casserole, and make layers of cabbage and chestnuts, beginning and ending with the cabbage.
In a bowl, mix the salt, pepper, and sugar with the beef stock, and pour over the cabbage. Cover and bake for 40 minutes, or until the cabbage and chestnuts are tender.

Yield: 6 servings

➤ Can be prepared the day before and reheated.

Sweet and Sour Celery or Nappa Cabbage I

4 tablespoons oil	1 teaspoon salt
1 large carrot, shredded	1½ tablespoons brown sugar
3 tomatoes, chopped	2½ tablespoons vinegar
1¼ tablespoons cornstarch	1 celery or nappa cabbage, shredded
⅔ cup stock	
2½ tablespoons soy sauce	2½ tablespoons sherry

Heat 1½ tablespoons oil in a sauce pan, and cook the carrots and tomatoes until the tomato is soft—about 2 to 3 minutes.
In a bowl, mix the cornstarch, stock, soy sauce, salt, sugar, and vin-

egar. Add to the tomato mixture, and bring to a boil. When thickened and cleared, let it simmer while preparing the cabbage. In a wok, heat the remaining oil, and stir-fry the cabbage until it starts to wilt—about 3 minutes.

Add the sherry and mix well. Cook 2 minutes longer.

Pile the cabbage in a serving dish, and pour the sauce over all.

Yield: 6 servings

➤ Cannot be prepared ahead.

Fried Sweet and Sour Cabbage II

2 tablespoons brown sugar	½ teaspoon salt
3 tablespoons dark soy sauce	1 head nappa cabbage,
2 tablespoons vinegar	shredded
2 tablespoons water	¾ cup dry sherry
3 tablespoons vegetable oil	

In a bowl, mix the brown sugar, soy sauce, vinegar, and water.

Heat a wok, and add the oil and salt. Add the cabbage, and stir-fry for 1 minute. Add the brown sugar mixture, cover, and cook over high heat for 1 minute. Remove the cover, and add the sherry. Stir to mix well, and serve.

Yield: 6 servings

➤ Cannot be prepared ahead.

Braised Chinese Cabbage with Mushrooms

1 head of Nappa or Celery	2 tablespoons soy sauce
cabbage	1 tablespoon sugar
2 cups salted water	6 Chinese mushrooms, soaked
2 ounces dried shrimp, soaked	and cut into julienne
2 tablespoons vegetable oil	2 chile peppers, sliced

Cut the cabbage into 8 wedges, and boil in the salted water for 10 minutes.

Drain, reserving ½ cup of the liquid.

Drain the shrimp.

In a wok, heat the oil, and sauté the shrimp for 2 minutes. Add the cabbage, and cook 2 minutes longer.

Add the reserved liquid, and simmer 15 minutes.

Add the soy sauce, sugar, mushrooms, and chili peppers, and simmer 10 minutes, or until most of the liquid has evaporated.

Yield: 4 to 6 servings

➤ Can be prepared ahead and reheated.

Chinese Cabbage with Mushrooms and Bamboo Shoots

6 Chinese mushrooms, soaked   ½ cup sliced bamboo shoots
   (see glossary)   1¼ teaspoons salt
3 tablespoons oil   ½ teaspoon sugar
1 pound head cabbage, cured
   and cubed

Drain the mushrooms, reserving ¼ cup of the liquid. Cut off and discard the stems, and cut the caps in half.

In a wok, heat the oil, and stir-fry the cabbage and bamboo shoots for 2 minutes.

Add the mushrooms, and stir-fry for 1 minute.

Add the salt and sugar, and mix well.

Add the reserved mushroom liquid and cover.

Cook over high heat for 2 minutes.

Stir and serve.

Yield: 6 servings

➤ Can be prepared ahead and reheated.

Cardoons

Cardoons have long, off-white, coarse-ribbed stalks that are coated with fine fibers. Like artichokes, they are members of the thistle family and consequently appear slightly forbidding. Hardly a well-known vegetable, only recently have they appeared in supermarkets, although they have long been favored by Italians, who seem to have a fondness for foods with a slightly bitter aftertaste.

My first encounter with cardoons, after years of reading about them, was in Madison, Wisconsin, about 10 years ago. I could not wait to get them home. Unfortunately, none of my hostess's cookbooks listed them, but I recalled that they were similar to artichokes and that Italians loved them. With that knowledge, I shaved the coarser ribs, cut them into sections, and cooked them in boiling salted water with the juice of a lemon until tender. Once they were drained, I sautéed them in a little butter with a generous sprinkle of grated Parmesan cheese and freshly ground black pepper. They were a new taste treat.

In Italy, cardoons are served raw as part of a vegetable platter with *Bagna Cauda*, a warm anchovy and garlic dip. They are a tender, sweet dwarf version of the cardoon available in the United States. The cardoons grown here are often quite bitter, although the tender heart can sometimes be eaten raw. Fortunately, the Bagna Cauda is equally good with a variety of other vegetables.

Availability

Cardoons are only available fresh and in the early winter months. You will find them from November through January. Look for fresh-looking stalks with a minimum of brown on the ribs. Do not buy limp or soft stalks.

Preparation

With a vegetable peeler, remove the stringy outer fibers. With your hand, break about ½ inch from the bottom towards the inside of the stalk, and pull the fibrous membrane up the stalk to remove. Rub the cut areas with half a lemon to prevent discoloring. Cut them into sections and keep in acidulated water (see page 6) until ready to cook.

Cooking Methods

Before finishing in a sauce, precook cardoons in a blanc (to keep them light in color) until tender—about 50 minutes. Carbon steel knives also darken them.

I have found that cooking them in a water acidulated with the juice of a lemon works as well.

Other Methods

Once precooked, turn cardoons into purées, or deep-fry after dipping into a batter or coating with bread crumbs. Coat with Mornay sauce and grated Gruyere for a substantial vegetable course.

Quantity

Plan on 1½ pounds of cardoon for 6 persons.

Sauces

Like artichokes, cardoons can be sauced with a number of sauces, such as butter, cream, hollandaise, and vinaigrette.

Raw Cardoons with Bagna Cauda

Use the youngest, freshest cardoons for this, because older vegetables are too bitter.

1½ pounds raw cardoons, prepared as above and cut into bite sized pieces	Juice of 1 lemon Bagna Cauda (see page 16)

When ready to serve, prepare the sauce, drain the cardoon, and serve alone or with other vegetables.

Yield: 6 servings

➤ The cardoons can be prepared the day before, so long as they are immersed in the acidulated water, but it is safer to prepare them just before serving.

Cardoons in Cream

1½ pounds cardoons, cooked and drained ½ cup butter	⅓ cup heavy cream ⅓ cup grated Parmesan cheese salt and pepper

In a skillet, sauté the cardoons in the butter for 5 minutes. Stir in the cream and cheese, and cook 2 minutes. Season with salt and pepper.

Yield: 6 servings

➤ Can be prepared for the final heating in the butter the day before.

Carrots

*W*hen in doubt, serve carrots. They are as safe to serve as lima beans or kohlrabi are risky. When truly in doubt, serve boiled carrots with butter: no raves, no complaints. Children coming? Pull out the carrots. Unfortunately, the very fact that they are so safe makes them seem dull, although they can be extraordinarily appealing.

Carrots have a history of abuse. One era insists that they be cooked to mush, and then the next era decrees that they be served so undercooked that every bite resounds across the dining room. For many years I worked with Katherine Shaftoe and Virginia Carchia Parsons demonstrating various food products. For one product, we needed carrots. I would cook the carrots to the tender-crisp stage and then ask Katherine if they were cooked. She would raise her index finger high over the carrot and slowly lower it to the carrot.

"No," she would say.

I would drain and serve the carrots. After many months of this charade, I asked her when the carrot was cooked. She gave me her "only a clod could even pose such a question" smile and announced, "When you place your finger on the carrot and it sinks to the spoon without any pressure." After letting me gasp in horror for a minute or two she said, "Of course, I would never eat them that way, but that is how *I* was taught to cook them."

Today many restaurants, perhaps in fear of reaching Katherine's goal, serve warm, raw carrots, and insist they are cooked. The goal should be a vegetable that is fully cooked and that still has texture. If you can hear it, it ain't cooked!

Carrots are not only a perfect vegetable on their own, they bring out and enhance the flavors of many other foods. They are the basis of minced aromatics such as *mirepoix, brunoise, or soffrito*, which in turn are the flavoring bases of so many stews and brown sauces. Carrots are added to *court bouillons* and stocks to provide a certain sweetness. Many cooks add sliced or shredded carrots to tomato sauce to counteract the acidity of the tomatoes.

Ideally, all carrots used in cooking (they are also used for animal fodder) are young and tender. In the late winter months, in some areas, the ideal is hard to find, but even then you can split old, huge carrots and remove the woody core, leaving the sweeter, more tender, outer layer to use in your favorite carrot dishes (see page 144). But most of the time all you need to do is scrub and eat, or if desired, cook first. Carrots are a reliable, much-loved, delicious vegetable that need not be hackneyed. It is up to the cook to make them ever more appealing, with different methods of preparation and different sauces.

Availability

Fresh
In the spring, search for the tiny carrots about the size of your little finger. As the year progresses, expect the carrots to get larger. There are growers who specialize in the baby carrots, and if they are available do take advantage of them, but remember that for many preparations the larger carrots are not only suitable, but preferable.

Look for firm, smooth, bright-orange carrots with crisp greens, if attached. Avoid carrots with wilted tops, pale-orange color, cracks, green tops, or hairy roots.

Frozen
Freezing carrots changes their texture so that they are no longer crisp and inviting. Because fresh carrots are available year round and take only minutes to prepare, there is no reason to purchase frozen carrots.

Canned
Canned carrots have a mushy texture and are unacceptable. As with frozen carrots, there is no reason to buy canned, unless you are trekking in the wilderness or at sea for months at a time.

Preparation

Peeling
To peel or not—that is the question. Unless the carrots are going into the stock pot, or they are so young and tender that a vegetable brush will remove the outer layer, peel. Older carrots have a skin that can be tough, and once cooked looks unattractive at best. The amount of nutrients you might loose are insignificant compared to the pleasure you will attain. Remember that although many of the nutrients are in the skin, there are still a lot in the vegetable itself.

Chefs spend the early days of their training peeling mountains of vegetables, especially carrots. Over the years, they have developed the most efficient way of peeling carrots. While most amateurs take the vegetable peeler and scrape toward each end of the carrot, starting from the middle, the chef approaches the problem so that each stroke covers the whole carrot, and completes the job in half the time (see page 3 for details).

Cutting

Carrots are sliced, cut into batons, diced, roll cut, cut into olives, cubed, chopped, julienned, shredded, grated, ground, or puréed. These methods are outlined in detail in Basic Techniques (see page 1). Whatever cut you select, it is most important that they all be of the same size to allow for even cooking.

Old Carrots

Occasionally, the market may get a shipment of very large carrots that seem more like logs than fresh garden produce. (A student once told me that the California growers shipped these east because no one in California would think of eating them.) As a child we called them horse carrots and fed them to the horses. But they do appear, and if you should get some, realize that it is not necessarily a disaster. Use them for stock, if possible, but if you do need to use them, then remove the hard center core. Peel them and with a large knife, and then cut the carrot in half lengthwise. With the point of a sharp paring knife, cut into the lighter-colored center core, starting at the large end, and pry the core out the length of the carrot. Discard the woody core. Cut the outer layer, and use as usual.

Cooking Methods

Boiling

Simmer in boiling salted water until tender-crisp. This is not as easy as it sounds. Tender means that there is no crunch when it is bitten, and crisp that it is not soggy. Arriving at the point when they are just done requires attention and care. Test the carrots as they cook.

Steaming

Place the prepared carrots in a steamer over an inch or so of boiling water and steam until just done, taking care not to over- or under-cook.

Microwaving

Place the carrots in a covered dish with 2 to 4 tablespoons of water for 4 to 6 minutes. Whole carrots take longer.

Sautéeing

Prepare the carrots for cooking, put into a skillet with a 2 or 3 tablespoons of butter, and cook over low heat until tender. You can use olive oil, or another oil, if you prefer. When they are tender, raise the heat to brown them if necessary.

Grilling

Blanch the carrots until barely tender, brush with oil, and place over a grill until cooked and nicely browned.

Roasting

Carrots can be a luscious, easy garnish for almost any roast. Cut the peeled carrots into large chunks, or if small, leave whole, add to the fat in the roasting pan about an hour before the roast is done, and cook until golden and tender. (If the carrots should be cooked before the roast, remove and let cool. Return them to the pan juices and reheat a few minutes before serving.)

Braising

For the simplest version, brown carrot chunks in butter or oil over high heat for 2 to 3 minutes. Place in a casserole with 2 to 4 tablespoons white or red wine and 2 to 4 tablespoons chicken or beef stock. Season with salt and pepper. Add an herb of choice, if desired—bay leaf, tarragon, thyme, savory, or the like—and bake at 325°F until tender and most of the liquid is absorbed—about 25 to 50 minutes.

Quantity

Plan on 1½ pounds for six persons.

Sauces

Carrots can take almost any sauce. Fresh chervil is the herb of choice. (Interestingly, chervil leaves look like delicate carrot leaves.) Butter sauces, perhaps flavored with various herbs, cream sauces, and mornay sauce all enhance carrots. Hollandaise is not usually used, but if flavored with lime or mustard instead of—or in addition to—lemon, it is an excellent accompaniment. Cold carrots are delicious with vinaigrette and mayonnaise.

Carrottes à la Vichy (Carrots Vichy Style)

In classic cooking parlance, Crécy, a town noted for the quality of its carrots, also indicates the presence of carrots. Because the spa whose waters are considered most favorable to conditions of the liver and, carrots also are considered to be good for liver condition, the name "Vichy" is given to many carrot recipes. There is no relation between the Vichy used in regard to carrots and vichysoisse, a potato soup created in New York.

1½ pounds carrots, cut into olives	1 tablespoon sugar
½ cup water	¼ teaspoon salt
2 tablespoons butter	2 tablespoons minced parsley

In a saucepan, simmer the carrots, water, butter, sugar, and salt, covered, until the water evaporates. Continue to cook, uncovered, tossing the carrots occasionally, until the sugar caramelizes and coats the carrots.

Sprinkle with parsley and serve.

Yield: 6 servings

➤ Can be prepared to the point where the water evaporates several hours ahead.

NOTE: Be careful when cooking in the butter and sugar that the sugar does not burn.

Timbales à La Vichy (Carrot Timbales)

This is an elegant first course or separate vegetable that works well for a light luncheon or brunch.

2 shallots, minced
1 tablespoon butter
1/4 cup dry white wine
1/4 cup Madeira
1 cup heavy cream
salt and pepper, to taste

1½ pounds carrots, chopped
  and cooked à la Vichy (see
  immediately preceding)
3 eggs
½ cup milk
chervil or parsley sprigs

Preheat the oven to 400°F. Butter 6 timbales.

In a saucepan, sauté the shallots in the butter until soft, but not brown. Add the white wine, and reduce to 2 tablespoons. Add the Madeira, and bring to a boil. Add the cream and simmer, until thick enough to coat the back of a spoon. Season with salt and pepper. Set aside.

In a processor, purée the carrots Vichy. If the purée is too wet, dry over medium heat, stirring until the excess liquid evaporates. Season with salt and pepper.

In a bowl, whisk the eggs and milk with the carrot purée, and season with salt and pepper to taste. Fill the ramekins, and top with small squares of waxed or parchment paper. Place the ramekins into a baking pan, add 1 inch of boiling water, and bake for about 30 minutes, or until a knife inserted in the center comes out clean.

Peel off the waxed paper and the skin on top of the timbales. Unmold the timbales onto individual plates, surround with sauce, and garnish with chervil or parsley sprigs.

Yield: 6 servings

➤ The sauce can be made the day before. The ramekins can be filled and readied for baking, except for adding the boiling water the day before. Keep refrigerated.

Carottes Glacées au Miel *(Honey-Glazed Carrots)*

This preparation calls for baby carrots, but if they are not available, take larger carrots and trim them into small olives.

1½ pounds baby carrots,
  scrubbed
6 tablespoons butter
salt and pepper to taste

⅓ cup honey
1 teaspoon lemon juice
⅓ cup sugar

Place the carrots in a saucepan of cold water, bring to a boil, and drain.

In a sauté pan, over medium heat, cook the carrots, butter, and salt and pepper to taste until the carrots are almost tender-crisp. Add the honey and lemon juice, and simmer until the carrots are still crisp.

Sprinkle with the sugar, raise the heat, and cook until the carrots are glazed to a golden brown.

Yield: 6 servings

➤ Can be prepared up to the final glazing and set aside. They will reheat during the final glazing.

Carrots with Lime Butter

1½ pounds carrots, thinly
  sliced
3 tablespoons sugar
salt and pepper to taste

4 tablespoons butter
grated rind of 1 lime, or cut
  into julienne
2 tablespoons lime juice

In a saucepan, place the carrots and 6 cups of cold water, and bring to a boil. Boil 3 minutes, and drain. Return the carrots to the pan, add 1 cup of water, the sugar, and salt to taste.

Boil over moderate heat until the carrots are just tender and the liquid has reduced to 1 or 2 tablespoons. Add the lime rind, and stir in the butter and lime juice.

Yield: 6 servings

➤ Can be cooked until the carrots are tender, allowed to cool, and then reheated as the sauce is made.

Carottes à La Provençale *(Carrots Provence Style)*

The large amount of garlic, found in many Provençale dishes, becomes mild and delicate through the slow cooking.

2 tablespoons olive oil
1½ pounds carrots, sliced
1 whole head of garlic cloves,
  peeled and halved

½ cup chopped black olives
salt and pepper to taste

In a large skillet, heat the oil, and cook the carrots, stirring occasionally, over moderate heat for 20 minutes. Add the garlic, season with salt, and cook over low heat until the carrots are almost caramelized and the garlic is tender—about 15 minutes longer. Sprinkle with olives, and correct the seasoning with the salt and pepper.

Yield: 6 servings

➤ Can be prepared and reheated.

NOTE: Tasteless canned black olives are unacceptable. Tiny, difficult to pit, Niçoise olives are preferred, but large Greek black olives, which are easier to pit, have a full olive flavor.

Cassis Glazed Carrots

1½ pounds whole baby carrots, or larger carrots trimmed to size, cooked until tender-crisp	3 tablespoons sugar ¾ cup crème de cassis 3 tablespoons red wine vinegar 4 scallions, cut in julienne

In a saucepan, bring the sugar, cassis, and vinegar to a boil. Add the carrots and cook, stirring, until the sauce caramelizes. Put into a serving dish, and sprinkle with the scallions.

Yield: 6 servings

➤ Can be prepared for caramelizing several hours ahead.

Carrots with Almonds and Raisins

The relatively strong seasonings of Asian cookery complement carrots as well as the subtler flavors of Western cooking.

1½ pounds carrots, sliced 6 tablespoons butter ¼ cup blanched almonds or unsalted cashews 1½ tablespoons minced ginger	½ cup raisins 2 tablespoons minced basil 1 tablespoon minced coriander ⅛ teaspoon red pepper flakes salt and pepper to taste

In boiling salted water, cook the carrots until tender-crisp, drain, and set aside.

In a skillet, melt the butter, and sauté the almonds and ginger until the almonds are golden. Add the carrots, and stir to coat evenly. Add the raisins, basil, coriander, and red pepper flakes, and cook until heated. Correct the seasoning with salt and pepper.

Yield: 6 servings

➤ Can be prepared ahead and reheated.

Carrots and Grapes

1½ pounds carrots, cut into
  batons
2 tablespoons butter
pinch of sugar

boiling water
1 cup of red or green grapes
2 tablespoons minced mint
1 tablespoon butter

In a saucepan, simmer the carrots, butter, sugar, and enough water to cover, until tender-crisp. Drain. Peel, halve, and seed the grapes. In a skillet, sauté the carrots, grapes, and mint in the remaining butter until heated.

Yield: 6 servings

➤ Can be prepared for the final heating several hours ahead.

NOTE: Peeling grapes is an arduous job, so I often use seedless red and green grapes, and if small, leave them whole.

Carrots with Fennel

Fennel is also called anise.

1½ pounds baby carrots,
  scrubbed
1 head fennel, finely chopped

1 teaspoon fennel seeds
  (optional)
¼ cup butter
1 or 2 tablespoons lemon juice

Cook the carrots in boiling salted water for 2 minutes. Add the fennel, and cook until tender-crisp.

Place the carrots in a serving dish, and arrange the fennel in a band around the edge.

Sprinkle with the fennel seeds, if desired.

In a saucepan, melt the butter, and add the lemon juice to taste.

Pour over the vegetables.

Yield: 6 servings

➤ Best if cooked and served.

Carottes Râpés (Grated Carrots)

Cutting vegetables differently changes the way they taste. Grated carrots is a wonderful example. Shred them as finely as possible on the julienne blade of a food processor for this dish.

1½ pounds carrots, shredded
3 tablespoons butter

salt and pepper to taste

In a 3-quart saucepan, bring 1½ quarts of water to a full rolling boil, and season with salt. Place the carrots in the water, and cook for 45 seconds. Drain. In a skillet, melt the butter, and stir-fry the carrots until well coated.

Correct the seasoning with salt and pepper.

Yield: 6 servings

➤ The blanching can be done a few hours ahead, but the final cooking in the butter should be done at the last moment for the shortest possible period.

Variations:

Cream Add ½ cup cream to the skillet with the carrots and cook, stirring, until well coated.

Herbed Add 1 to 2 tablespoons of a favorite fresh herb to the carrots in the skillet. Chervil, savory, parsley, or chives are all good.

Grated Carrots and Mushrooms

I created this dish for a demonstration to a cardiac study group at the School of Public Health, Harvard University. The idea was to show that heart-healthy food need not be dull.

1 pound carrots, julienne	2 tablespoons corn oil
½ pound mushrooms, julienne	margarine
	salt and pepper to taste

Place the carrots and mushrooms in a steamer over 1 inch of boiling water, or preferably chicken stock, and steam for 2 or 3 minutes, until the carrots are tender-crisp. Place in a bowl, and toss with the margarine, salt, and pepper.

Yield: 6 servings

➤ To serve cold, toss with a vinaigrette made with 2 tablespoons extra virgin olive oil, 2 to 4 teaspoons lemon juice to taste, and 2 teaspoons Dijon mustard. Season with pepper to taste.

Carrot Pancakes

Serve these small pancakes as a vegetable course, or as an hors d'oeuvre (see the note).

½ pound grated carrots	2 eggs
4 scallions, minced	2 to 4 tablespoons butter
salt and pepper to taste	

In a bowl, mix the carrots, scallions, salt, pepper, and eggs. In a skillet or on a griddle, heat enough butter to moisten the surface and prevent sticking. Drop tablespoons of the carrot mixture onto the griddle and flatten slightly. Brown on both sides. Drain on paper towels.

Yield: about 24 small cakes, or 12 vegetable portions

➤ Best if cooked and served, but can be kept warm in a 250°F oven for 30 minutes.

NOTE: To serve as an hors d'oeuvre, top with a teaspoon of sour cream and a demitasse spoon of the best caviar you can afford.

Sprinkle with minced chives if you wish.

Sprinkle with grated Gruyere, or Parmesan, and brown under a broiler.

Sprinkle with grated Cheddar mixed with minced jalapeno and fresh coriander.

Carrots with Sherry Sauce

This sauce is a cross between a Hollandaise and a custard. Take care not to curdle it by overheating.

3 tablespoons butter
1½ pounds carrots, ½ inch slices
1 cup chicken stock

½ cup dry sherry
salt and pepper to taste
2 egg yolks

In a skillet, melt 2 tablespoons of butter, and sauté the carrots until golden, stirring often so they do not scorch. Add the chicken stock and sherry. Cover, and simmer until the carrots are tender. Remove the carrots to a serving dish.

In a small saucepan, melt the remaining butter, remove from the heat, whisk in the eggs, and then pour the mixture into the slightly cooled cooking liquid. Place over low heat and heat gently, until thickened. Do not boil. Correct the seasoning with salt and pepper. Pour over the carrots.

Yield: 6 servings

➤ The carrots can be cooked ahead, and reheated in the liquid just before finishing the sauce.

NOTE: This is a tricky sauce to prepare. Both the butter and stock should be below 185°F when added to the eggs.

Carottes Braisés au Madère *(Carrots Braised in Madeira)*

1½ pounds carrots, 2 inch pieces
4 tablespoons butter
3 tablespoons minced onions
2 cups chicken or beef stock

bouquet garni of thyme, parsley, and bay leaf (see glossary)
pinch of allspice
salt and pepper to taste
¼ cup Madeira

Preheat the oven to 350°F. In a skillet, sauté the carrots and onion in the butter until light brown. Add the stock, bouquet garni, allspice, and a pinch of pepper. Cover, and simmer over low heat for 10 minutes. Add the Madeira, and bake for 10 to 20 minutes longer, or until the carrots are tender.

Remove the carrots to a serving dish, discard the bouquet garni, and reduce the liquid by half. Taste for seasoning and strain over the carrots.

Yield: 6 servings

➤ Can be prepared ahead. When the carrots are tender, set aside. Reheat the carrots, remove from the skillet, and finish the sauce.

NOTE: Allspice is a potent spice; use it prudently.

Carottes à La Paysanne
(Carrots Braised with Parsley and Garlic)

1½ pounds carrots, ½ inch slices	1 cup water
5 tablespoons olive oil	2 teaspoons sugar
2 garlic cloves, crushed	salt and pepper to taste
	2 tablespoons minced parsley

In a covered skillet, over low heat, cook the carrots in the olive oil for 10 minutes, shaking the pan occasionally. Remove the cover, add the garlic, water, sugar, salt, and pepper, and cook 20 minutes. Add the parsley, and toss gently. Correct the seasoning with salt and pepper.

Yield: 6 servings

➤ Can be reheated.

Carottes au Lard (Carrots with Bacon)

¾ pound bacon, sliced	1 tablespoon minced parsley
2 pounds carrots, 2 inch pieces	1 tablespoon minced chives
2 cups chicken stock	salt and pepper to taste

In a saucepan, render the fat from the bacon for 5 minutes over medium heat, and pour off the fat. Add the carrots, and cook 5 minutes longer, stirring occasionally. Add the stock, cover, and simmer until the carrots are very tender—about 25 minutes. Sprinkle with the parsley and chives, and correct the seasoning with the salt and pepper.

Yield: 6 servings

➤ Can be prepared and reheated.

Étouffade des Carottes *(Carrots with Mustard and Butter)*

1½ pounds carrots, thinly sliced	4 slices bread, cut in triangles
½ cup plus 2 tablespoons butter	2 tablespoons flour
salt	2 tablespoons Dijon mustard
1 teaspoon sugar	⅓ cup chicken or beef stock
	3 tablespoons minced parsley

In a saucepan, blanch the carrots in boiling salted water for 5 minutes, and drain.

In a heavy skillet over low heat, cook the carrots in the butter with salt to taste and the sugar for 20 minutes, stirring occasionally. Add ⅓ cup water, and cook, uncovered, until the water has been absorbed.

In another skillet, sauté the bread triangles in 1 tablespoon of butter until golden, and set aside. Add the remaining tablespoon of butter to the carrots, sprinkle with flour, and cook, stirring, for 2 minutes. Stir in the mustard and the stock, and cook, stirring, for 3 minutes or until lightly thickened. Turn into a serving dish, surround with the toast triangles, and sprinkle with the parsley.

Yield: 6 servings

➤ Can be prepared ahead and reheated. If necessary, reheat the toast triangles in a 350°F oven.

NOTE: Although the toast triangles can easily be omitted, they add a finishing touch.

Carrot Fritters

Make these small for hors d'oeuvre, or larger as a vegetable for grilled meat or chicken.

2¾ cup flour	1½ teaspoons dried thyme, crumbled
2 tablespoons baking powder	6 cups grated carrots
2 teaspoons salt	oil for deep-frying
2 teaspoons ground pepper	Tartar sauce, Bearnaise, or salsa
1½ cups milk	
6 tablespoons minced shallots	
2 tablespoons minced parsley	

In a bowl, mix the flour, baking powder, salt, and pepper. Gradually stir in the milk, and fold in the shallots, parsley, thyme, and carrots. Cover, and let stand for 1 to 3 hours.

Heat the oil to 375°F. Fry the batter by spoonfuls until golden. Drain.

Serve plain, or with the sauce of your choice.

Yield: 70 or more fritters

➤ Do not prepare the batter more than three hours ahead.

Carrot Pudding Fines Herbes

1½ pounds carrots, sliced	1 tablespoon minced chervil
1 cup chopped scallions	1 tablespoon minced tarragon
3 eggs	1 tablespoon minced parsley
1½ cups milk	salt and pepper to taste

Preheat the oven to 350°F. Butter a 1½ quart baking dish.

In a saucepan, boil the carrots with water to cover until very tender, and drain. In a processor, purée the carrots and scallions.

In a bowl, beat the eggs, milk, chervil, tarragon, parsley, salt, and pepper. Stir in the carrots, and turn the mixture into the baking dish. Bake for 25 minutes, or until a knife inserted halfway between the edge and center comes out clean. Let it sit for 5 minutes before serving.

Yield: 6 servings

➤ Can be prepared for baking the day before.

Gratin des Carottes en Julienne (Grated Carrot Pudding)

1 pound carrots, grated	salt and pepper to taste
⅓ cup butter	water
juice of ½ lemon	1½ cups heavy cream
1 teaspoon sugar	3 eggs

Preheat the oven to 350°F. Butter a 1½ quart baking dish.

In a covered saucepan, simmer the carrots, butter, lemon juice, sugar, salt, and pepper for 20 minutes. Remove the cover, and boil at high heat until the liquid evaporates, stirring constantly. Cool for 10 minutes.

In a bowl, mix the cream and eggs, and salt and pepper to taste. Stir in the carrots, and turn into the prepared baking dish. Bake about 35 minutes, or until the surface is golden brown, and a knife inserted halfway between the edge and the center comes out clean. The center may still be undercooked, but it will finish cooking while it stands. Let it rest 5 minutes.

Yield: 6 servings

➤ Can be prepared for baking the day before.

NOTE: This recipe is supposed to have very tender carrots. For a different texture, cook the carrots, uncovered, over high heat until the liquid evaporates.

Carottes en Chevaux d'Ange
(Carrots with Angel Hair and Lemon)

½ pound carrots, julienne	1 cup heavy cream
2 tablespoons butter	salt to taste
2 teaspoons grated lemon rind	1 pound angel hair pasta
½ cup dry white wine	1 cup grated Parmesan cheese
¼ cup lemon juice	freshly ground pepper to taste

In a saucepan, stir the carrots, butter, and lemon rind for 2 minutes. Add the wine and lemon juice, and cook, stirring occasionally, for 3 minutes, or until tender-crisp. Add the cream, and bring to a boil.

In a large kettle of boiling salted water, cook the angel hair until just done—about 3 minutes for fresh and 8 minutes for dried. Drain, and return to the kettle. Add the carrot mixture, and toss with ½ cup grated Parmesan and a generous grating of pepper. Pass the remaining cheese.

Yield: 6 servings

➤ The sauce can be prepared a few hours ahead, but do not cook the pasta until you are ready to serve it.

Indian Rice Pilaf with Carrots and Raisins

Basmati rice, with its aromatic flavoring, is perfect for this dish. If it is not available, any good brand of long grain rice is suitable. Converted rice will work, but the grains are a little too separate.

¼ cup sugar	1½ cups Basmati, or other
2 tablespoons water	long-grain rice
3 cups hot chicken stock	½ teaspoon salt
1¼ cups of ¼ inch dice	¼ teaspoon ground cardamom
carrots	¼ teaspoon ground cinnamon
2 tablespoons golden raisins	¼ teaspoon ground nutmeg
3 tablespoons butter	grated nutmeg to taste

In a 2 quart saucepan, heat the sugar and water to a boil, covered. Uncovered, boil until the mixture turns golden. Remove from the heat, and carefully pour in the hot stock, stirring until the sugar dissolves. Return to the heat, and bring to a boil.

In another 2 quart covered saucepan, sweat the carrots and raisins in the butter for 10 minutes. Add the rice, and stir until well-coated. Stir in the chicken stock, salt, cardamom, cinnamon, and ground nutmeg. Cover, and simmer until the liquid is absorbed—about 20 to 25 minutes. Transfer to a serving dish, and sprinkle with freshly grated nutmeg.

Yield: 6 servings

➤ Once prepared, the rice can stand for another 30 minutes, but it is best when freshly prepared.

NOTE: Grated nutmeg loses its potency very quickly. If you have ground nutmeg, smell it, and if it has little or no smell, discard it.

Grated Carrot Salads

The first-time visitor to France can easily believe that the French only eat grated carrot salads. It seems as if every charcuterie and food stall has a neon-like mound of grated carrot salad in the window. Europeans prepare grated carrot and other vegetable salads more often than the leafy salads of America. The possibilities are endless. Make them sweet, sour, or somewhere in between. Make them unctuous and luscious with mayonnaise and sour cream dressings, or virtually Spartan with a squeeze of lemon juice. If you love raw carrots, here is a wonderful way of serving them often, and always with interest.

In the past, the carrots were always sliced into the finest shreds on a mandolin, but today many food processors have a julienne blade to turn out shreds as small as fine string. If you do not have this available, you can use the largest holes of a four-sided grater. The shreds will not be as long, but the salad will still be delicious.

Carottes Râpées (French Grated Carrot Salad)

1½ pounds shredded carrots   ½ cup vinaigrette, or to taste

Place the carrots in a large bowl, and toss with the vinaigrette. Let stand for several hours before serving.

Yield: 6 servings

➤ Can be made the day before.

Variations:

Curry   Add 1 or more tablespoons of curry powder to the vinaigrette, or better still, a mayonnaise. If desired, add grated pineapple, raisins, and/or toasted cashews. If adding nuts, it is best to add them just before serving. (The amount of curry powder depends on how spicy you want the salad, and how spicy the brand you are using is. Asian markets sell a curry paste that has a marvelous zing.)

Garlic   Add 1 or 2 cloves crushed garlic to the vinaigrette.

Herb   Add 1 to 4 tablespoons minced fresh herbs to the vinaigrette. Use as much herb as needed to flavor the salad, but not overpower it.

Try using basil, chervil, coriander, dill, mint, savory, or tarragon. Add a small amount, and after 30 minutes, taste the salad and add more as needed. Caraway, dill, or poppy seeds are tasty.

Horseradish Add 2 tablespoons grated horseradish, or to taste, to the carrots, and toss with a vinaigrette mixed with an equal quantity of sour cream.

Mustard Add 2 to 4 tablespoons of Dijon mustard to the vinaigrette.

Orange Add 4½ tablespoons orange flower water, 4½ tablespoons lemon juice, 1½ tablespoons sugar, and salt to taste to the carrots, and marinate for 2 to 12 hours. Serve garnished with orange wedges.

Onion Cut a red onion in half and thinly slice each half. Separate into pieces, and toss with carrots and any vinaigrette.

Pineapple Add ½ cup shredded pineapple to the carrots and toss with the vinaigrette. Add sugar for a sweeter flavor.

Raisin Add ½ cup or more of raisins to taste. Sweeten the salad with 2 or 3 tablespoons of honey, if desired.

Vegetable Once you have the carrot base, you can vary it by adding other grated vegetables—whatever is available—shredded green, red, or yellow peppers, cabbage, celery, cucumbers, parsnips, or turnips. Grated broccoli stems are colorful and flavorful.

Prepare any of the above salads with vinaigrette, or substitute ½ cup or more of mayonnaise. Mix the mayonnaise with sour cream, or use it on its own.

Herbed Carrots Vinaigrette

1½ pounds carrots, sliced on the diagonal	salt and pepper to taste
4 tablespoons butter	3 tablespoons minced parsley
⅓ cup chicken stock	3 tablespoons minced chervil
pinch of sugar	½ cup vinaigrette

In a saucepan, simmer the carrots in the butter, chicken stock, sugar, salt, and pepper for 20 minutes, or until just tender. Cool. Just before serving, toss with the parsley, chervil, and vinaigrette.

Yield: 6 servings

➤ Can be prepared the day before.

Pickled Baby Carrots

1 cup white vinegar	1 teaspoon pickling spices
½ cup chopped onion	1 pound, baby carrots,
1 teaspoon sugar	trimmed and scrubbed
1 teaspoon salt	

In a saucepan, bring the vinegar, onion, sugar, salt, and spices to a boil. Add the carrots, and simmer until tender-crisp. Cool in the liquid and chill.

Yield: 1 quart

➤ Keeps 2 weeks, refrigerated.

NOTE: Substitute green or wax beans, cauliflower, or zucchini for the carrots.

Marinated Carrots

1 pound carrots, cut into	2 garlic cloves, split
batons	1 teaspoon dried basil
½ cup olive oil	1 teaspoon salt
¼ cup white wine vinegar	½ teaspoon pepper
1 small onion, sliced	2 tablespoons lemon juice

In a saucepan of boiling water, simmer the carrots until just tender—about 3 to 5 minutes. Drain.

In a bowl, mix the oil, vinegar, onion, garlic, basil, salt, and pepper. Add the carrots, and toss. Refrigerate for 12 hours. Remove, and discard the onion and garlic. When ready to serve, drain, and sprinkle with lemon juice.

Yield: 6 servings

➤ Keeps 6 days, refrigerated.

Serve on lettuce leaves as part of an hors d'oeuvre platter, or mix with other ingredients for a salad. Cut the carrots into sections and serve with wooden skewers as an hors d'oeuvre.

NOTE: You can substitute beans, beets, broccoli, cauliflower, or zucchini for the carrots.

Shaker Carrot Marmalade

While researching the recipes for this book, I spent a lot of time with *Larousse Gastronomique*. In my 1961 edition (it is left out of the the most recent edition), M. Montagné states, "This preparation with a carrot base is hardly ever used today. It was popular about 80 years ago in the south-west of France." The man never knew my aunt, Harriet Hargrove, of Contoocook, New Hampshire. She made this marmalade for years, gave it to friends, and supplied every bake sale for miles around. She thought it was Shaker in origin, but it is possible that it came from the French-Canadians, who may well have emigrated from south-west France.

It is a wonderful way of preserving a bounty of carrots, and a delicious treat for breakfast or afternoon tea.

4 pounds of shredded carrots	6 lemons, thinly sliced and
7 cups of sugar	seeds discarded

In a heavy covered saucepan, simmer the carrots, sugar, lemon, and enough water to cover, until it is reduced by two-thirds. Towards the end of the cooking, it is important to watch it carefully and stir often to prevent scorching on the bottom of the pan.

Turn the boiling carrot mixture into sterilized jelly jars, and let cool. Seal.

Yield: 6 cups

➤ Can be kept in a cool area for a year, or longer.

NOTE: Aunt Harriet's recipe called for cooking it for 7 to 8 hours on the back of a wood-burning stove. I have found that 2 to 3 hours is usually sufficient. Test it by putting a tablespoon of it onto a saucer and letting it cool. If it gels, it is done. Do keep the heat low, and stir often, because the mixture burns easily.

Aunt Harriet was a nurse who had ideas of her own. "Sterilized to me means washed and then rinsed in good hot water—I always thought sterilization could be overdone."

Cauliflower

*A*nother prestigious member of the cabbage family, Cauliflower appears with its green ruff and snowy white heads in the best of markets, and minus the ruff on the best of tables. It is a vegetable of great elegance. However, when old or overcooked, it gives off a disagreeable odor, making it unacceptable almost everywhere. Treat cauliflower with respect and care and you will be rewarded with a culinary treasure, but mistreat it and you will pay the consequences.

The white head is called a curd, and the individual sections are called flowerets or florets. The curd can be cooked whole or broken into florets, depending on how you wish to serve it. Some recipes call for breaking the curd into florets, cooking them, and then placing them in a bowl, flower side out, to reshape the head. Once firmly placed, the bowl is inverted onto a platter. For color, broccoli florets are often interspersed to present horizontal, vertical, or marbled patterns. If the pieces are firmly placed, they will hold their shape. If you wish to add some security to this arrangement, make a fairly firm purée of potatoes or carrots, and pack that into the center.

Availability

Fresh
Cauliflower appears in the markets year round, but especially in October and November. Look for heads with compact white curds and bright green leaves. Avoid heads with brown or discolored spots, heads where the curd is loosely packed, or where there is an indication that the greengrocer cut off some of the curd. This usually indicates age, which means that it will have a strong flavor. Store the head in its wrapper, if it has some air holes, or if you are buying it loose, wrap it loosely in plastic wrap, allowing in air. Keep refrigerated for 2 to 3 days. Once cooked, cauliflower should be eaten immediately. The flavor becomes stronger the longer it stands. Leftover cauliflower can become too potent.

Frozen
Although the flavor of frozen cauliflower is not bad, the freezing af-

fects the fibers, and it becomes watery and unappealing. If necessary, frozen cauliflower can be used in a purée.

Canned
Cauliflower is not usually sold in cans.

Preparation

From the bottom of the head, cut straight down into the greens around the outer edge of the core. This exposes the base of the stem, which can then be cut off even with the bottom of the curd. If the cauliflower is to be cooked whole, use a small sharp paring knife to cut a cone-shaped piece from the center of the stem.

For florets, cut around the stem, and let the florets fall off. Cut off the topknot of florets at the end of the stem, and then cut the florets into smaller sections. Some writers suggest cutting a cross in the stem of each floret for even cooking. I have not found this necessary.

The stems and leaves are edible. Peel the stem as you would a broccoli stem, and slice. Cook with the florets, or save for another purpose. Because these pieces are not as tender as the florets, even after peeling, I prefer to save them for purées or soups, or use the stem sliced on a crudité platter.

For Stuffing
You can prepare a cauliflower for stuffing from the stem end or the curd side.

From the curd side: Cut a cone starting about one third of the way down the curd. Usually, the removed cauliflower is used in the filling.

From the stem side: Cut into the stem, removing as much as possible without cutting off the florets. With this method, extra stuffing can be pressed into the bottom, and become a bed for any florets that may have become detached.

After making the hole for the stuffing, the cauliflower is cooked until tender, and then the stuffing is added.

Cooking Methods

Á Blanc
Some writers suggest cooking the cauliflower in boiling water with milk or lemon juice added. The intent is to whiten the curd rather than present it in its natural creamy color. If the cauliflower is truly fresh, this is unnecessary.

Cauliflower goes from underdone to overdone very quickly. You must pay close attention as it cooks, or it will overcook and become unappealing. Most recipes call for a precooking by boiling, steaming, or microwaving before being finished.

Once cooked and refreshed, the cauliflower needs to be reheated. Place it in boiling water, in a steamer, or in a microwave until just heated without further cooking.

Boiling

Cook the cauliflower whole or in florets in boiling water to cover until just tender—about 8 to 10 minutes. Drain, refresh under cold water to stop the cooking, and drain again.

Steaming

Cook the curd or the florets in a steamer over boiling water until just tender-crisp—about 8 to 10 minutes.

Microwaving

Place in a covered container with ¼ cup of water, and cook for 6 to 8 minutes for florets or 8 to 10 minutes for a whole head.

Batter Frying

Cauliflower, once blanched, can be dipped into a beer batter or a bread coating, and deep-fried. It makes a wonderful hors d'oeuvre, or a vegetable course.

Quantity

Generally you can plan on 4 ounces per person, or 1½ pounds for 6 people. But half the weight or more of a cauliflower can be stem and leaves. The best you can do is to look at the curd, and try to figure if it will provide the quantity you need. Because the flavor becomes stronger if cooked cauliflower is stored, attempt to cook just enough for a particular meal and not leave any leftovers.

Sauces

Presentation: Cauliflower in most instances can be served as a whole curd, or in individual florets. It is up to the cook to decide how to present it.

Cauliflower and broccoli can be sauced the same, although sauce polonaise is the classic sauce for cauliflower. For hot sauces, plan on composed butters, noisette, cream, Hollandaise, or cheese sauces. Adding anchovies, capers, and other piquant foods gives the vegetable zest. Use cold sauces such as mayonnaise, vinaigrette, aioli, mustard, curry, or green mayonnaise.

Cauliflower can also be treated by alla trifolati, or alla parmagiana.

Choufleur aux Herbes (Cauliflower with Herbs)

¼ cup butter	salt and pepper to taste
2 tablespoons finely minced	1 head cauliflower, cooked
and mixed parsley, chives,	and refreshed
and tarragon	

In a saucepan, melt the butter, stir in the herbs, and season with salt and pepper. Heat until fragrant.
Heat the cauliflower, and pour the sauce over all.

Yield: about 6 servings

➤ The butter and cauliflower can be prepared an hour or two before, and reheated just before serving.

Choufleur au Cari (Curried Cauliflower)

Cauliflower and curry are a delicious combination.

1 head cauliflower, cooked	1 teaspoon curry powder, or to
and refreshed	taste
½ cup heavy cream	salt and pepper to taste
1 tablespoon minced shallots	1 tablespoon butter

Place the cauliflower into a skillet, and chop with a metal spoon into coarse pieces. Add the cream, shallots, and curry, and cook until hot. Season with salt and pepper. Stir in the butter.

Yield: about 6 servings

➤ Can be prepared an hour ahead and reheated.

Indian Cauliflower and Peas

1½ cups sliced mushrooms	¼ teaspoon pepper
5 tablespoons clarified butter	¼ teaspoon salt
1 tablespoon black mustard	2 cups of chopped raw
seeds	cauliflower
1 tablespoon cumin seeds	1 cup frozen or fresh peas

In a large covered skillet, sauté the mushrooms in 2 tablespoons of butter until browned. Set aside.

In the same skillet, over medium heat, melt the remaining butter, and cook the mustard and cumin seeds, covered, until the mustard seeds stop popping. Add the pepper and salt. Add the cauliflower, and stir until well coated with the spices and the butter.

Lower the heat and cook, stirring occasionally, for 10 minutes. Add the peas and mushrooms, and cook 5 minutes longer, or until the cauliflower and peas are tender.

Yield: 6 servings

➤ Can be prepared ahead by several hours and reheated.

Cauliflower with Tomato Curry Sauce

1 head cauliflower in florets, cooked and refreshed	½ teaspoon minced chili pepper
2 tablespoons butter	¼ teaspoon grated nutmeg
2 tomatoes, peeled, seeded, and chopped	salt and pepper to taste
1 teaspoon curry powder, or to taste	½ cup fresh or frozen peas

Prepare cauliflower and set aside.

In a large saucepan, cook the butter, tomatoes, curry powder, chili pepper, and nutmeg, until the tomatoes are very soft. Correct the seasoning with salt and pepper. Add the cauliflower and peas, and cook until heated.

Yield: 6 servings

➤ Can be prepared several hours ahead and reheated.

Iranian Cauliflower Fritters

These serve as a wonderful hors d'oeuvre as well as a vegetable.

1 large cauliflower, in florets, cooked and refreshed	1 tablespoon water
½ cup flour	1 tomato, peeled, seeded, and chopped
½ teaspoon baking powder	3 tablespoons minced parsley
½ teaspoon salt	½ cup minced onion
2 eggs	oil for frying
⅓ cup light cream	

In a processor, mix the flour, baking powder, and salt. With the machine running, add the eggs, cream, and water to make a smooth batter. Add the tomato, parsley, and onion with on-off turns.

Heat the oil to 375°F. Dip the cauliflower into the batter, and fry until golden.

Yield: 6 vegetable, or up to 18 hors d'oeuvre servings

➤ Do not prepare the batter more than 30 minutes before serving.

Deep-Fried Cauliflower

1 large cauliflower, in florets, cooked and refreshed	¼ teaspoon curry powder
½ cup flour	2 eggs, well beaten
1 teaspoon salt	fresh bread crumbs
1 teaspoon minced dill	oil for frying
¼ teaspoon pepper	tartar sauce (see page 29)

Prepare the cauliflower and set aside.

In a bowl mix, mix the flour, salt, dill, pepper, and curry powder. Dredge the florets in the flour, dip into the eggs, and roll in the bread crumbs. Place on a wire rack and let the coating set for 30 minutes.

Heat the oil to 375°F. Fry the florets until golden—about 2 minutes—drain, and serve with the rémoulade sauce.

Yield: 6 servings

➤ The florets can be coated the day before and kept refrigerated, uncovered.

Purée de Choufleur Simple (Simple Cauliflower Purée)

This is a dieter's delight. Puréed cauliflower has the taste and texture of mashed potatoes. It is a pleasant way of eating a lot of a remarkably low-calorie vegetable without the feeling of dieting.

1 head cauliflower, in florets   salt and pepper to taste
½ cup low-fat sour cream

In a kettle of boiling salted water, cook the cauliflower until very tender. Drain. In a processor, purée the cauliflower, and season with the cream, salt, and pepper.

Yield: 6 servings

➤ Can be prepared ahead and reheated.

Purée Barfleur (Cauliflower Purée)

Because cauliflower has such a high water content, it is common to thicken the purée. This recipe uses potatoes, but you can use puréed carrots, or a thick béchamel sauce. Barfleur is a town in France noted for its cauliflower.

1½ pounds cauliflower curd   1 cup heavy cream
1 pound potatoes, peeled and   salt and pepper to taste
  quartered

In a saucepan, simmer the cauliflower and potatoes until very tender, and drain.

In a processor or a food mill, purée the vegetables. Return to the saucepan, and add the cream, salt, and pepper. Reheat.

Yield: 6 to 8 servings

➤ Can be prepared several hours ahead and reheated.

Mousse au Choufleur (Cauliflower Mousse)

1 large head cauliflower	salt and pepper to taste
2 cups Bechamél sauce	1 or 2 tablespoons minced
5 eggs	parsley
1 tablespoon minced savory	

Preheat the oven to 375°F. Butter a 2 quart soufflé dish or charlotte mold.

Cook the cauliflower in boiling salted water until very tender. Drain, and purée in a processor or a food mill.

In a bowl, beat the purée, 1 cup béchamel, and eggs. Season with savory, salt, and pepper. Turn into the prepared baking dish, and bake for about 1 hour, or until a knife inserted in the center comes out clean. Let stand 5 minutes. Unmold onto a heatproof serving platter.

Pour the remaining cup of béchamel over the top, and sprinkle with the parsley.

Yield: 8 servings

➤ Can be prepared for baking several hours ahead.

NOTE: For a different finish, preheat the broiler. After the béchamel has been poured over the mousse, put it under the broiler and brown the top.

Soufflé of Cauliflower

You can bake this in a 1½ quart soufflé dish if preferred.

1 head cauliflower, trimmed and cooked until very tender	salt and pepper to taste
8 anchovy fillets, minced	2½ tablespoons butter
2 tablespoons grated Parmesan cheese	3 tablespoons flour
1 tablespoon grated onion	1¼ cups milk
	6 eggs, separated
	Sauce Polonaise (see page 18)

Preheat the oven to 375°F. Butter an 11- by 16-inch jelly-roll pan, line with waxed paper, and butter the paper. Sprinkle with flour or dry bread crumbs and shake out the excess.

In a processor, purée the cauliflower with the anchovies, Parmesan, onion, salt, and pepper. Set aside.

In a saucepan, melt the butter, add the flour, and cook until the mixture starts to turn golden. Stir in the milk, and cook, stirring, until thickened and smooth. Over high heat, reduce to 1 cup, stirring constantly.

In a small bowl, beat the egg yolks, and beat into the hot sauce. Fold in the cauliflower purée.

Beat the egg whites until stiff, but not dry, and fold ¼ into the cauliflower mixture to lighten it. Fold in the remaining egg whites, and turn into the prepared pan. Smooth the top and bake for 10 to 12 min-

utes, or until just cooked. Line a counter with waxed paper and unmold the soufflé onto the paper and peel off the waxed paper on top of
the soufflé. Using the ends of the paper on the counter, roll the soufflé
and turn onto a warm platter. Pour on the Sauce Polonaise, and serve
immediately.

Yield: 6 to 8 servings

➤ Cannot be prepared ahead.

NOTE: The rolled soufflé is slightly firmer than a regular soufflé, and
will not collapse as quickly.
   If baked in a soufflé dish, bake for 30 to 35 minutes.

Bucatini al Cavolfiore (Bucatini with Cauliflower Sauce)

Bucatini is a pasta, like a large macaroni; substitute rigatoni or penne
if necessary.

2½ pounds ripe tomatoes, peeled and seeded	salt and pepper to taste
½ cup olive oil	2 tablespoons minced parsley
1 garlic clove, minced	1 pound bucatini
1 head cauliflower in florets	grated Caciocavalo or Romano cheese

   In a processor, purée the tomatoes. In a saucepan, heat the oil, and
sauté the garlic until golden. Discard the garlic, and add the tomatoes.
Bring to a boil, and add the cauliflower and ⅔ cup of hot water. Season
with salt and pepper, cover, and simmer for 40 minutes, or until the
cauliflower has disintegrated and the sauce has thickened. Correct the
seasoning with salt and pepper.
   Cook the pasta until al dente, drain, and stir into the sauce. Serve
with the cheese.

Yield: 6 servings

➤ The sauce can be prepared ahead.

Swedish Stuffed Cauliflower

You can prepare a cauliflower for stuffing from the top of the curd, or
the stem end (see page 161). The choice is yours. The Swedes usually
do it from the stem end.

1 cauliflower, hollowed for stuffing	½ teaspoon pepper
½ pound ground meat (see below)	dash Tabasco sauce
	⅓ cup butter
¼ cup fine dry bread crumbs	1 cup thinly sliced mushrooms
¼ cup minced parsley	2 tablespoons butter
1 egg	1 cup heavy cream
1½ teaspoons salt	1 tablespoon Cognac
	salt and pepper to taste

Preheat the oven to 350°F. Place a large sheet of foil in a baking pan or in a 9-inch cake tin.

Cook the prepared cauliflower in boiling salted water until just tender.

In a bowl, mix the meat, bread crumbs, parsley, egg, salt, pepper, and Tabasco sauce. Fill the cauliflower. Butter the sheet of foil, and place the cauliflower, meat side down, on the foil. Dot with remaining butter. Wrap foil around cauliflower and bake for 30 minutes, or until the meat is cooked.

Meanwhile, in a saucepan, sauté the mushrooms in the butter until soft. Add the cream and Cognac, and bring to a boil. Season with salt and pepper.

Serve the cauliflower cut into wedges, with the sauce on the side.

Yield: 6 servings

➤ Can be prepared for the final baking several hours ahead.

NOTE: Ground lamb is the meat most commonly used in Scandinavia, but you may use beef, pork, turkey, or chicken.

Sausage-Stuffed Cauliflower

This is an example of stuffing the cauliflower from the top (see page 161).

1 large head cauliflower, hollowed from the top	¼ teaspoon fennel seeds salt and pepper to taste
½ pound sweet Italian sausage	fresh tomato sauce (see page 25)
½ cup fresh bread crumbs	

Preheat the oven to 375°F. Cut a large piece of foil, and put it into a baking pan or a 9-inch cake pan.

In a kettle of boiling salted water, cook the cauliflower, along with the florets removed from the top, until tender. Drain the cauliflower, and set aside.

Chop the florets. Peel the skin from the sausage, and sauté the meat in a small skillet, until it loses its color. Stir in the chopped cauliflower, bread crumbs, fennel seeds, salt, and pepper.

Place the cauliflower on the foil, and fill with the stuffing. Bake uncovered until it is heated and the top is golden—about 30 minutes.

Serve with the tomato sauce on the side.

Yield: 6 servings

➤ Can be prepared for the final baking several hours ahead.

Marinated Cauliflower

If the curd is left whole, this makes a pretty presentation, but the marinade does not get to all of the cauliflower.

1 large cauliflower, in florets, cooked and refreshed	2 tablespoons white wine
2 garlic cloves, minced	1 tablespoon lemon juice
6 tablespoons olive oil	salt and pepper to taste
	paprika (optional)

Prepare the cauliflower and set aside.

In a saucepan, sauté the garlic in the oil until golden, but not burned. Pour over the cauliflower, and sprinkle with the wine and lemon juice. Season with salt and pepper, and mix gently. Let marinate for at least 1 hour.

Serve dusted with paprika, if desired.

Yield: 6 servings

➤ Can be prepared several hours or even the day before, but the longer it stands, the stronger the flavor becomes.

NOTE: Substitute, broccoli, beets, carrots, or zucchini, if you prefer.

Choufleur à la Pimprenelle *(Cauliflower with Mustard Cream Dressing)*

1 head cauliflower, cooked and refreshed	2 tablespoons heavy cream, whipped until stiff
½ cup vinaigrette (see page 30)	2 tablespoons minced mixed tarragon, chervil, chives, and parsley
1 cup mustard cream sauce	

Place the cauliflower in a bowl, and toss with the vinaigrette. Let marinate for 2 hours.

In a bowl, mix the mustard cream dressing with the cream. Drain the cauliflower, and arrange in a serving dish. Coat with the sauce, and sprinkle with the herbs.

Yield: 6 servings

➤ Can be prepared several hours ahead.

Salade de Choufleur Landaise *(Cauliflower Salad from Lande)*

The Landé is an area below Bordeaux in Southwestern France.

1 head cauliflower, trimmed, and left whole	1 medium beet, boiled, peeled, and sliced
1 green pepper, cut in julienne	½ cup vinaigrette
2 tablespoons butter	

In a saucepan, cook the cauliflower in boiling salted water until just tender, but still crisp. Drain. In a skillet, sauté the pepper slices in the butter until soft, but not brown. Drain.

In a bowl, combine the pepper slices and beets, sprinkle with some of the vinaigrette, and let marinate for 10 minutes. Arrange the warm cauliflower on a serving platter, and pour over half the vinaigrette. Arrange the beet slices around the base, and garnish with the pepper slices.

Serve at room temperature.

Yield: 6 servings

➤ Can be prepared several hours ahead.

Celery and Celery Root

*F*or many cooks, celery has two uses: raw as a snack or salad ingredi-ent, or cooked in stock as a flavoring agent. Cooked celery is rarely served in America, whereas in Europe and Asia it is far more common. Europeans braise it and serve it with pride, and Asians use it often in stir-fried dishes—sometimes to excess. The truly awful egg rolls sold in many supermarkets and some less-than-wonderful restaurants are filled with shreds of celery as a filler. In this chapter you will find a number of suggestions for cooking celery that can make it delicious and interesting.

It is only in the last few years that celery root, also called celery knob or celeriac, has appeared in anything but the most esoteric of greengroceries. This standard of French and German hors d'oeuvre platters is most often used in salads, but it also is wonderful when cooked.

I suspect that the reason cooked celery and celery root have such a limited audience is that older cookbooks required that they be cooked to submission. Today we prefer vegetables to have some tex-ture, and avoid cooking them until they are limp and unappealingly soggy. A little care in the cooking of celery and you will be de-lighted not only with the result, but that such a low-calorie vegeta-ble can stand the enhancement of a sauce without turning into a caloric nightmare.

Definitions

A head of celery is a collection of stalks and is also called a bunch. A stalk is one single rib, and on rare occasions that is called a stem.

Availability

Both celery and celery root are available year round, with October through March being the prime season.

Fresh
Celery should have compact, tight bunches of stalks without blemishes or cracks. The color should be light green, with the leaves a

171

crisp deeper green with no sign of browning. Avoid bunches with flabby stalks or wilted leaves. Store in the refrigerator in the vegetable drawer, or in a plastic bag, for up to 2 weeks.

Celery root should have firm, round bulbs, preferably no larger than 4 inches, without soft spots. Ideally, there should be a little tuft of leaves at the top of the bulb. The bulbs themselves are ugly. They have a coarse skin and much tangled root growth at the bottom. Fortunately, once peeled they become far more attractive.

Store the roots in a plastic bag, or the vegetable drawer, for up to a week.

Frozen

Freezing destroys the texture of both celery and celery root. However, you can freeze celery purée, if necessary.

Canned

Celery and celery root lose their texture when canned. They are sometimes canned in combination with other vegetables. Canning is not recommended.

Preparation

Celery can be quite dirty, because soil is packed around the stalks to blanch them. Separate the stalks until you get to the heart, washing each stalk carefully. If the ribs are older and tougher, the strings may be too fibrous and unpleasant to eat. There are two methods of removing the strings: Use a vegetable peeler to peel the length of the stalk, removing the layer of strings. Or, break the stalk about ¼ inch from the bottom, and pull the strings along the length of the stalk toward the leaves.

The stalks can be cut on the diagonal, sliced, chopped, minced, or cut into batons or julienne. The heart, with the tough outer stalks removed, is braised.

Celery root has a thick, tough outer skin that has to be removed. The easiest method is to cut stem and root ends off the celery root. Stand it on one end on a counter and cut down the sides, removing all of the coarse brown covering (see page 2 for round vegetables). Once the covering has been removed, immerse the root in acidulated water. Remove, and cut into the desired shape. Celery root is cut into slices, julienne, or batons. As soon as it is cut, it should be put into acidulated water to prevent it from darkening.

Cooking Methods

Boiling

Blanch both celery and celery root before using either in other methods of cooking. Blanch celery in boiling salted water for 5 minutes, drain, and refresh. Longer cooking leeches out too much flavor. Blanch celery root in a *blanc* (see page 6) for 5 minutes before preceding with the final cooking. Do not plan to serve celery that has been boiled until tender. It will be tasteless.

Steaming
Steaming takes so long to cook celery and celery root that they lose their texture.

Microwaving
Both can be microwaved in a covered container with ¼ cup of liquid for 8 to 10 minutes. Turn the cooking dish and take care not to over-cook.

Quantity

One and one-half pounds of celery will serve 6 persons. Because of the amount of waste, you need 2 pounds of celery root to serve 6 persons.

Sauces

Treat celery and celery root interchangeably. Celery should be blanched, and then braised in butter before it is served with any of the sauces suited to asparagus: butter sauces, Hollandaise, cream, Mornay, and the like. Celery root can be cooked until tender in the *blanc*, and then sauced in the same manner.

Minestra di Sedano e Riso *(Rice and Celery Soup)*

This is a delicious light soup suitable for luncheon or as a first course for dinner.

2 cups diced celery stalks	2 cups meat broth, or 1 cup
⅓ cup olive oil	canned beef broth, mixed
1 teaspoon salt	with 1 cup water
2 tablespoons minced onion	3 tablespoons grated Parmesan
2 tablespoons butter	cheese
1 cup raw rice	2 tablespoons minced parsley

In a saucepan, simmer the celery, olive oil, and salt with enough water to cover, covered, until tender but not mushy.

In another saucepan, sauté the onion in the butter until soft, but not brown. Add half the celery, using a slotted spoon, and sauté for 2 or 3 minutes. Add the rice, and stir until well-coated with oil. Add the broth.

Purée the rest of the celery and its cooking liquid, and add to the pan. Simmer, covered, until the rice is tender—about 15 to 20 minutes. Sprinkle with the cheese and parsley, and serve. Pass additional cheese, if desired.

Yield: 6 servings

➤ Can be prepared a little before serving, but the longer it sits the soggier the rice will become.

Butter-Braised Celery

1½ pounds celery, blanched and refreshed	2 tablespoons butter salt and pepper to taste

In a covered saucepan, finish cooking the celery in the butter until tender-crisp—about 10 to 15 minutes longer.

Yield: 6 servings

➤ Can be prepared the day before and reheated.

Céleri Étuvée (Stock-Braised Celery)

1½ pounds celery, blanched ½ cup minced onion ½ cup minced carrot 2 tablespoons butter 1 cup chicken or beef stock	salt and pepper to taste a bouquet garni of parsley, thyme, and bay leaf (see glossary)

Preheat the oven to 325°F. Split the celery into quarters, or use cut up celery.

In a casserole or baking dish, large enough to hold the celery in a single layer, sweat the onion and carrot in the butter, covered, until soft, but not brown. Place the celery on top, and pour in the stock. Season with salt and pepper, and place the bouquet garni in the center. Cover, and braise for 1 to 1½ hours, or until tender.

The cooking liquid should be reduced to a glaze. If it is too thin, remove the vegetables, discard the bouquet garni, and reduce the liquid to a glaze.

Yield: 6 servings

➤ Can be prepared the day before and reheated.

Céleri à la Ménagère (Celery Braised with Tomatoes)

2 cups diced onions 1 cup sliced carrots 2 tablespoons butter 1½ pounds celery, cut into 2 inch pieces, and blanched	2 tomatoes, peeled, seeded, and quartered salt and pepper to taste pinch of sugar ½ cup chicken stock

In a gratin, brown the onions and carrots in the butter. Place the celery on top, and arrange the tomatoes on the celery. Season with salt and pepper, and sprinkle with the sugar. Add the stock, and cover. Simmer over low heat for about 40 minutes, or until tender.

Yield: 6 servings

➤ Can be prepared the day before and reheated.

Celery Slaw

Try this delicious variation on coleslaw.

1 pound celery	⅔ cup vegetable oil
¼ cup wine vinegar	½ cup sour cream
1 tablespoon sugar	1 onion, thinly sliced and
¼ teaspoon paprika	separated into rings
2 teaspoons salt	1 pimiento, cut into strips
black pepper	

Discard the leaves from the celery, and separate into stalks. Wash carefully, and scrape off the heavy strings. Cut diagonally into thin slices, and place in a bowl.

In a small bowl, whisk the vinegar, sugar, paprika, salt, and pepper, until the sugar dissolves. Whisk in the vegetable oil until the sauce thickens. Add the sour cream, and taste for seasoning. Pour over the celery, and fold in the onions. Refrigerate for 3 hours. Before serving, correct the seasoning, and fold in the pimiento strips.

Yield: 6 servings

Salade Neuchâtel *(Celery, Gruyère, and Mushroom Salad)*

4 ribs celery, cut into julienne	1 bunch watercress
½ pound Gruyère, cut into	½ cup vinaigrette
julienne	1 tablespoon minced parsley
½ pound mushrooms, thinly	
sliced	

In a bowl, mix the celery, cheese, mushrooms, watercress, and the vinaigrette until evenly coated. Let marinate for 20 minutes. Arrange on a serving platter, and sprinkle with the parsley.

Yield: 6 servings

Gratin de Pommes de Terre et Céeleri-Rave
(Potato and Celery Root Casserole)

4 baking potatoes	salt and pepper
1 pound celery root	2 tablespoons minced basil
2 tablespoons lemon juice	¾ cup heavy cream
1 tablespoon olive oil	pinch grated nutmeg
1 teaspoon minced garlic	¼ pound grated Gruyère
4 tomatoes, peeled, seeded,	cheese
and chopped	

Preheat the oven to 375°F. Butter an 8 by 10 by 2½ oval gratin.

In a saucepan, cook the potatoes in boiling salted water for 15 minutes. Drain, and run under cold water. Peel, and cut into half-inch slices. Peel the celery root, cut it into ¼-inch slices, and put into a saucepan with water to cover, lemon juice, and salt.

Simmer 10 minutes. Drain, and reserve half a cup of cooking liquid. In a skillet, heat the oil, and sauté the garlic, tomatoes, salt, pepper, and basil, stirring for 1 minute. Add the cream, reserved cooking liquid, nutmeg, salt, and pepper, and simmer 2 minutes.

In the gratin pan, arrange the potatoes in one layer. Sprinkle with half the cheese, cover with the celery root, and pour the tomato mixture over all. Sprinkle with the remaining cheese, and bake for 40 minutes, or until nicely browned.

Yield: 6 servings

➤ Can be prepared for baking the day before.

Scalloped Celery Root in Cream

1 garlic clove, halved	salt and pepper
4 garlic cloves, minced	1½ cups heavy cream
5 tablespoons butter	1 teaspoon cornstarch
2 pounds celery root, cut into ½ inch thick slices, and blanched *a blanc* (see page 6)	⅓ pound grated Gruyère or Parmesan cheese

Preheat the oven to 325°F. Rub a 1½ quart baking dish with the garlic halves.

In a skillet, sauté the minced garlic in the butter until soft, but not brown. Add the celery root, and toss to coat. Season with salt and pepper.

In a saucepan, mix the cream and cornstarch, and scald (bubbles will form around the edges). Layer the celery root and cheese in the casserole, and slowly pour the cream over the top. Bake until golden, celery root is very tender, and the top is browned—about 1½ hours.

Yield: 6 servings

➤ Can be prepared for baking the day before.

Celery Root Salads

Celery root salads must be made of thin shreds of root so that the dressing will tenderize the vegetable much the same way as it does cabbage for coleslaw. The flavor of celery root can stand up to other flavors, so be assertive in seasoning the sauces.

2 pounds celery root, peeled and cut into julienne	1 cup dressing (see Note)

In a bowl, toss the celery root with the dressing, and let marinate for at least 2 hours before serving.

Yield: 6 servings

➤ Can be prepared 2 days ahead.

NOTE: The classic dressing for celery root is rèmoulade (see below), however, any vinaigrette or mustard based dressing will do. I like to add as many minced anchovies as I think my guests can stand.

Sauce Remoulade *(Remoulade Sauce)*

2 teaspoons dry mustard	½ teaspoon minced garlic
2 teaspoons lemon juice	1 hard cooked egg, minced
1 teaspoon capers	2 cups mayonnaise
2 tablespoons minced dill	salt and pepper to taste
1 tablespoon minced parsley	

In a bowl, mix the mustard and lemon juice to a paste. Stir in the capers, dill, parsley, garlic, and egg. Fold in the mayonnaise and correct the seasoning with salt and pepper.

Yield: 2½ cups

➤ Keeps 1 week or longer.

Corn

Corn has been grown in Peru for centuries, but it was not until the sixteenth century that it appeared in Europe, where it is still used mostly as animal fodder. Europeans, especially the French, find the American love of chomping on an ear of corn as nearly barbaric. Too bad for them! Americans know that there are few culinary delights equal to eating a freshly-picked, freshly-cooked ear of corn. Corn has enormous appeal and tremendous acceptance; almost everyone likes corn even if they do not love it. Children seem to adore it, perhaps because when eating it they can get messy without fear of correction.

Corn on the cob has to be freshly picked. Many years ago, Craig Claiborne wrote that ideally you would haul a cart with boiling water with you as you went through the cornfield—picking, cooking, and eating as you went. The very trip to the house from the field was too long. Corn does convert its sugar into starch rapidly, and though the cart idea may be extreme, it is a good reminder that freshest is best. Even farm stands that seem to have fresh corn should be looked at warily. If the ears are picked in the early morning and left in the sun until you buy them, they are not going to be at their best. Supermarkets that keep the corn well-chilled may well provide you with a better product.

Availability

Fresh
Corn is available throughout the year, but its peak season is May through September. Look for ears with fresh-green husks, pale-green stems, and compact kernels of a medium yellow color. Avoid ears that have dried or wilted husks, dried-out looking stems, and kernels that are immature, separated, or very bright yellow, which indicate over-maturity. The tassels should be silky, and not a matted brown. Obviously, any ear with corn borers in evidence should be avoided. If you split a kernel with your finger nail, the juice of a ripe ear will spurt forth as a creamy liquid. If it is underripe, the juice will be watery, while overripe ears have a starchy or doughy consistency. If the ears are not at the peak of perfection, you do not have to forget them; just plan to use the corn for puddings, chowders, soups, or other preparations. Save eating off the cob for the perfect ears.

Store the corn in its husks in a refrigerator until shortly before eating. If you must husk, keep in a plastic bag, refrigerated.

Frozen
Corn freezes well, and all of the preparations here work very well with frozen corn.

Canned
Corn also cans well, and again can be used for the preparations here.
   Creamed corn is also sold canned, but often has fillers and particles of the cob that make it unacceptable.

Preparation

Peel the husks from the cob, break off at the stem, and brush or rub the silky hairs from each ear. If you wish to grill the corn, pull the husk from the ear, leaving it attached at the stem. Brush or rub off the silky hairs and discard. Rewrap the husk around the ear, and if necessary, tie in place.

Cut Kernels
In a large bowl, hold the end of a husked ear against the bottom of a bowl, and with a sharp knife, cut the kernels off the ear about ⅛ inch from the cob. Turn the ear slightly, and make the next cut. Continue until all the kernels are removed. Placing it in a bowl saves the kernels from flying all over the room. Use the cut kernels in all recipes calling for corn kernels.

Scraped Kernels
Scraping the corn from the ear brings out the cream in the center, leaving the outside of the kernel on the cob. This is best used in puddings and soups.
   With a sharp knife, cut through the center of the kernels along each row. Place the ear in a bowl and, holding one end, scrape along the kernels, forcing out the creamy interior.

Cooking Methods

Many cooks believe that salt helps turn the sugar in corn to starch more rapidly, and therefore add a teaspoon of sugar to the corn instead. I have never found any noticeable difference, but tend to use the sugar anyway.

Boiling
Place corn in a large kettle of boiling water, and simmer for 6 to 10 minutes, depending on the size and age of the corn. Another method is to place 1 inch of boiling water in a skillet large enough to hold the corn

in one layer. Add a teaspoon of sugar and the corn. Cover, and bring to a boil. Turn off the heat, and let stand for 8 to 10 minutes. This method allows you to hold the corn for up to 30 minutes without overcooking.

Steaming
Place the corn in a steamer over boiling water, and steam for 8 to 10 minutes.

Microwaving
Place whole ears in a covered dish with 2 or 3 tablespoons of water, and cook 5 to 7 minutes, turning at least once. Place 2 cups of corn kernels in 2 tablespoons of butter in a covered dish, and microwave for 3 to 5 minutes, depending on the age of the corn. Taste to see if it is done.

Roasting and Grilling
Prepare the corn ears with the husks on and soak in water for 10 minutes. Place the ears in a 375°F oven for about 20 minutes, or over a grill for 10 to 15 minutes, turning often. Some chefs prefer to blanch the husked ears in boiling salted water for 6 minutes, and then place the buttered ears over an open fire for about 5 minutes to char the kernels slightly.

Quantity

Six ears will produce about 3 cups of kernels—enough for 6 persons in most preparations, but there are people who love the vegetable so much that they will feel happier with half again as much, or even twice as much.

One or two whole ears are enough for most people, but children may feel that any fewer than three is an insult!

Sauces

Corn can be made into a gratin with kernels and a coating of Mornay sauce, but corn is not usually combined with other classic sauces. Cold corn does mix well with vinaigrette and with mayonnaise.

For a change during the fresh corn season, serve the corn with flavored butters, such as mint, tarragon, mace, or garlic. Corn marries well with peppers of all types. Mix them together with red, green, or yellow sweet peppers, or add chilies from mild to fiery hot. Black pepper complements corn particularly well.

Corn Cakes

Corn cakes make a delicious vegetable and a fabulous hors d'oeuvre. Serve them plain, or with various toppings.

2 cups kernel corn	3 tablespoons minced chives
⅓ cup milk	or scallions
⅓ cup flour	salt and pepper to taste
⅓ cup cornmeal	butter for frying
¼ cup butter	various toppings (optional, see
2 eggs	below)
1 egg yolk	

In a food processor, mix the corn, milk, flour, cornmeal, and butter for 30 seconds. Add the eggs, egg yolks, chives, salt, and pepper, and process until well-blended. It should not be smooth.

In a large skillet, heat a thin film of butter, and drop the batter in by spoonfuls to make cakes about 2 to 3 inches in diameter. Fry until golden on both sides. Drain on paper toweling.

Yield: about 32 cakes

➤ The batter can be prepared several hours ahead. The cooked cakes can be kept warm in a 250°F oven for about 30 minutes, but they are best if served immediately.

Toppings

Caviar Place a dollop of sour cream and the most generous portion of the best caviar you can afford. Salmon caviar, which is less expensive, is wonderful, and becomes a budget stretcher.

Cheese Sprinkle some of your favorite grated cheese, such as Parmesan, Gruyere, Cheddar, or chèvre, on top, and heat in a 350°F oven until the cheese melts. You can go further with this topping by adding a fresh herb—such as minced basil, mint, or savory—to the cheese. Monterey Jack, salsa (see page 26), and chilies make an exciting topping.

Herbs Cream 3 ounces of cream cheese with about 2 tablespoons of a favorite herb—such as basil, coriander, savory, dill, or tarragon—and season with salt and pepper. Pipe a dab on each cake before serving.

Salsa Place a dollop of sour cream on top, and then top this with a spoonful of salsa.

Galettes de Maïs (Corn Cakes)

This recipe makes a denser corn cake that is better as a vegetable course rather than as a base for an hors d'oeuvre.

2 cups corn kernels	salt and pepper to taste
⅓ cup flour	oil for cooking
3 eggs	

In a processor, purée the corn, flour, eggs, salt, and pepper. In a skillet, heat a thin film of oil, and pour tablespoonfuls of the mixture to make small cakes. Press flat with a fork, if needed. Brown on both sides, and drain on paper toweling.

Yield: 6 servings

➤ Can be prepared for frying several hours ahead. Keep warm in a 250°F oven for 30 minutes, if needed.

New England Corn Chowder

It would seem that everyone has a favorite version of corn chowder. This is perhaps the simplest version with the best flavor.

¼ pound salt pork, diced	2 cups scraped corn kernels,
1 cup chopped onion	or canned creamed corn
2 cups water	1 quart milk
2 cups diced potatoes	salt and pepper to taste

In a saucepan, render the salt pork over medium heat, until the fat has been removed and the cracklings are crisp. Strain the fat into a small bowl, and drain the cracklings on paper toweling.

Clean the saucepan, and pour 2 tablespoons of fat into the saucepan, leaving the residue in the bottom of the bowl. Discard the remaining fat. In the saucepan, sauté the onion until soft, but not brown. Add the water and potatoes, and cook until the potatoes are tender—about 15 minutes. Add the corn, and bring to a simmer. Add the milk, and heat. Correct the seasoning with salt and pepper.

Serve the soup sprinkled with the cracklings.

Yield: 6 servings

➤ Can be prepared ahead and reheated.

Variations:

If desired, omit the salt pork, and use 2 tablespoons of butter to cook the corn. Add a dollop of butter to each serving, if desired.

Substitute light cream for the milk for a richer version.

Add 1 cup corn kernels to the soup.

Use 2 minced leeks in place of the onion.

Add ½ cup diced red and or green pepper with the onion.

Serve with sliced Kielbasa, or chorizo.

Add ¼ cup minced dill.

Corn Soup with Corn Relish

The corn relish in this recipe can be multiplied and served as a corn salad for another occasion.

¾ cup corn kernels cut from ear, not scraped
1 tomato, peeled, seeded, and diced
2 tablespoons minced basil
salt and pepper to taste

4 tablespoons butter
3 cups scraped corn with liquid
3 cups chicken stock, or water
½ cup heavy cream

In a bowl, mix the cut corn, tomato, and basil with salt and pepper, and let the relish stand.

In a saucepan, cook the butter, corn, and its liquid for 3 minutes. Add the chicken stock and simmer, stirring occasionally for 15 minutes (if using canned corn, 5 minutes).

In a processor, purée the soup, and strain through a fine sieve. Return to the saucepan, add the cream, and heat. Correct the seasoning with salt and pepper.

Serve topped with corn-tomato relish.

Yield: 6 servings

Corn Soup with Red-Pepper Purée

You can present this soup as imaginatively as you wish. Place the red-pepper purée in a plastic squeeze bottle with a small nozzle and drizzle it onto the hot soup. Swirl it from the center around the bowl or tureen. Drop dots of the purée over the soup, and run a knife through them to give the dots tails. Draw lines as cross hatching. Another idea is to whip ½ cup heavy cream until stiff, season with salt, and drop in the center of the soup. Draw spokes of purée from the cream, or run concentric circles and draw a knife tip through that alternately.

2 red peppers, peeled
1 cup chopped onions
2 tablespoons butter
3 cups corn kernels

2 cups chicken stock
1 cup heavy cream
½ teaspoon salt
¼ teaspoon pepper

In a processor, purée the peppers, and set aside.

In a saucepan, sauté the onions in the butter until soft, but not brown. Add the corn, and cook for 5 minutes. Add the stock, and simmer, covered, for 15 minutes.

In a processor, purée the soup, and strain through a fine sieve. Return to the saucepan, add the cream, and heat. Correct the seasoning with salt and pepper. Pour the soup into bowls, and drizzle the red pepper purée into each bowl and swirl decoratively.

Yield: 6 servings

➤ The soup can be prepared ahead and reheated.

Curried Corn and Tomato Chowder

1 cup minced onion	¼ cup rice
½ cup minced celery	3 cups tomatoes, cut into ¾
1 teaspoon minced garlic	inch cubes
¼ cup butter	1 bay leaf
2 tablespoons curry powder	salt and pepper
1 teaspoon ground coriander	3½ cups corn kernels
¼ teaspoon cumin	2 cups yogurt
4 cups chicken stock	1 tablespoon minced mint

In a saucepan, sauté the onions, celery, and garlic until soft, but not brown. Stir in the curry powder, coriander, and cumin, and stir for 2 minutes to bring out the flavors. Stir in the chicken stock, rice, tomatoes, bay leaf, salt, and pepper. Simmer for 25 minutes.

In a processor, purée the soup, and strain through a sieve. Return to the pan, and correct the seasoning with salt and pepper. Add the corn, and heat. Remove from the heat, and stir in the yogurt.

Serve sprinkled with the minced mint.

Yield: 6 servings

➤ Can be prepared the day before, but add the yogurt just before serving. Do not boil with the yogurt; it will make the soup curdle.

NOTE: To serve cold, add the corn, and simmer 2 minutes. Chill, and stir in the yogurt and mint.

Corn Chowder with Seafood

1½ cups diced onion	¼ teaspoon ground mace
1 cup diced celery	salt and pepper to taste
⅓ cup diced carrot	1 pound small shrimp, or 1
2 tablespoons butter	pound bay scallops, or 3
4 cups corn kernels	pounds mussels or steamed
2 cups heavy cream	clams, shelled, or 1 pound
1½ cups milk	soft-shell crabs, cleaned and
1 cup chicken stock	cut into 1-inch pieces
1 cup dry white wine	2 tablespoons minced parsley.
1 tablespoon paprika	

In a saucepan, sauté the onion, celery, and carrot in the butter until soft, but not brown. Stir in the corn, cream, milk, stock, wine, paprika, mace, salt, and pepper. Simmer until the corn is tender—about 10 minutes. Add the shrimp or scallops, and cook about 2 minutes.

Cook the mussels and clams until heated. The soft-shell crabs take about 5 minutes.

Serve sprinkled with minced parsley.

Yield: 6 servings

Corn Pudding

2 cups corn kernels
2 cups medium cream
⅓ cup sugar
2 eggs, beaten

2 tablespoons melted butter
1 teaspoon salt
½ teaspoon grated nutmeg

Preheat the oven to 325°F. Butter a 1½ quart casserole.
In a bowl, mix the corn, cream, sugar, eggs, butter, and salt. Pour into the casserole, and sprinkle the nutmeg over the top.

Place the casserole in a baking pan with 1 inch of boiling water, and bake until a knife inserted half-way between the edge and the center comes out clean.

It will take 45 minutes to 1 hour, depending on the shape of the casserole. Remove from the water bath, and let stand 5 minutes before serving.

Yield: 6 servings

➤ Can be prepared for baking several hours ahead.

Elote Con Queso *(Mexican Corn Custard)*

2½ cups corn kernels
9 eggs
3 cups heavy cream
½ pound Monterey Jack,
   chopped
½ pound Cheddar, chopped

1 cup canned mild chilies,
   chopped
3 tablespoons sugar
1 tablespoon baking powder
1 tablespoon salt

Preheat the oven to 350°F. Butter an ovenproof 3 quart baking dish. In a processor, chop the corn until it is just broken. In a bowl, whisk eggs and cream until well mixed. Add the corn, Monterey Jack, Cheddar, chilies, sugar, baking powder, and salt. Pour into the baking dish, and bake until a knife inserted halfway between the center and the edge comes out clean—about 45 to 55 minutes. Let stand 5 minutes before serving.

Yield: 6 servings

➤ Can be prepared for baking several hours ahead.

Corn and Tomato Casserole

2 cups corn
5 tomatoes, peeled, seeded,
   and chopped
1 egg, lightly beaten
1 teaspoon light brown sugar

1½ teaspoons salt
black pepper
1 cup soft bread crumbs
4 tablespoons butter

Preheat the oven to 325°F. Butter a 1½ quart baking dish.
In a bowl, mix the corn, tomatoes, egg, sugar, salt, and black pepper

to taste. Turn into the baking dish, sprinkle with the bread crumbs, and dot with the butter. Bake for 1 hour, or until crumbs are golden. •

Yield: 6 servings

➤ Can be prepared for baking several hours ahead.

Corn and Zucchini Casserole

1 cup diced yellow pepper	2 cups diced zucchini
¾ cup minced onion	¼ cup cream
2 tablespoons butter	salt and pepper to taste
2 cups corn kernels	⅓ cup minced basil

In a saucepan, sauté the pepper and onion in the butter until soft, but not brown. Add the corn and zucchini, and cook, stirring, for 1 minute. Add the cream, salt and pepper. Cover, and cook 3 minutes. Stir in the basil.

Yield: 6 servings

➤ Can be reheated.

Corn and Barley Casserole

1 pound sliced bacon	1 jalapeño, minced
1 cup barley	1 teaspoon ground cumin
3 cups corn kernels, freshly cooked, frozen, or canned	3 cups heavy cream
	½ teaspoon salt
2 red peppers, peeled and chopped	pepper

Preheat the oven to 350°F. Butter a 1½ quart casserole.

In a skillet, fry the bacon until crisp. Drain on paper towels, break into little pieces, and set aside.

In a saucepan, cook the barley in 1 quart of boiling salted water for 30 minutes. Drain, rinse under cold water, and drain again. Transfer to a bowl. Add the corn and the pepper to the barley. Add half the bacon, jalapeño, and cumin to the corn mixture, and set aside.

In a saucepan, boil the cream with the remaining bacon, jalapeño, and cumin with the cream until reduced by half. Correct the seasoning with salt and pepper, and fold into the corn. Turn into the casserole, cover, and bake for 25 minutes.

Yield: 6 servings

➤ Can be prepared for baking several hours ahead.

Maquechou

In creole cookery there are many versions of a corn casserole called Maquechou. Here are three versions.

Maquechou I

¼ cup bacon drippings	1 pound 12 ounce can
1 cup chopped onion	tomatoes, drained and
1 teaspoon minced garlic	chopped, with liquid
4 cups fresh or frozen corn	reserved
kernels	½ teaspoon Cayenne pepper
½ cup chopped green pepper	1½ teaspoons salt

In a saucepan, melt the bacon drippings, and sauté the onion and garlic until soft, but not brown. Add the corn, green pepper, tomatoes, tomato liquid, cayenne, and salt. Simmer 10 minutes, or until the corn is tender. Correct the seasoning with salt and pepper.

Yield: 6 servings

Maquechou II

6 tablespoons butter	¼ teaspoon salt
4 cups corn kernels	¼ teaspoon Cayenne pepper
½ cup minced onion	1¼ cups chicken stock
2 tablespoons sugar	½ cup evaporated milk
½ teaspoon white pepper	1 egg

In a skillet, over high heat, melt 4 tablespoons of butter, and cook the corn, onions, sugar, white pepper, salt, and Cayenne until they start to form a crust on the bottom of the pan—about 12 minutes. Gradually add ½ cup of stock, scraping up the crust, and cook 5 minutes longer, stirring occasionally. Add the remaining butter and stock, and cook another 15 minutes, stirring often. Stir in ¼ cup evaporated milk, and cook until most of the liquid is absorbed.

In a bowl, beat the egg and remaining milk, and stir into the corn. Heat until lightly thickened.

Yield: 6 servings

➤ Can be prepared to the point of adding the egg, several hours in advance.

Maquechou III

4 cups corn kernels	Cayenne pepper to taste
¼ pound butter	1 egg
1 medium onion, thinly sliced	1 cup milk
½ cup minced green pepper	1 tablespoon sugar
salt and pepper to taste	

In a skillet, sauté the corn in the butter for 2 minutes. Add the onion and pepper, and cook over medium heat until the onion is soft. Add the salt, pepper, and cayenne.

In a bowl, beat the egg, milk, and sugar, and stir into the corn mixture. Heat gently until lightly thickened.

Yield: 6 servings

➤ Can be prepared, to the point of adding the egg mixture, several hours ahead.

Baby Corn

Baby corn is popular in parts of China and in other areas of Asia, but is not often found fresh in the United States. The baby ears are so tender that the entire ear is edible. They are particularly good in stir-fry dishes, where they add texture as well as taste.

Baby Corn with Chinese Mushrooms

3 cups chicken stock	1 teaspoon sugar
1 cup Chinese mushrooms,	1 tablespoon soy sauce
soaked (see glossary)	½ teaspoon sesame oil
15 ounce can baby corn	1 tablespoon cornstarch
2 tablespoons peanut oil	dissolved in 1 tablespoon
1 tablespoon dry sherry	cold water

Remove and discard the mushroom stems. In a saucepan, simmer the chicken stock, mushrooms, and corn for 15 minutes. Drain, reserving 1 cup of the cooking liquid.

In a wok, heat the oil, and stir-fry the mushrooms and corn until well coated. Add the reserved stock, sherry, sugar, soy sauce, and sesame oil. Stir in the cornstarch mixture, and cook until thickened and clear.

Yield: 6 servings

➤ Can be prepared ahead, except for the final thickening.

Corn, Salami, and Cheese Salad

⅓ cup balsamic vinegar	2½ cups corn kernels
1 tablespoon yellow mustard	2 red peppers, ¼ inch dice
seeds	4 scallions, thinly sliced
¾ cup olive oil	salt and pepper to taste
1 pound salami, ½ inch cubes	1 head Romaine
¾ pound Gruyere, ½ inch	
cubes	

In a small bowl, marinate the vinegar and mustard seeds for 30 minutes, then whisk in the oil. In a bowl, toss the salami, cheese, corn, peppers, scallions, and dressing together. Correct the seasoning with salt and pepper.

Serve on a bed of Romaine.

Yield: 6 servings

➤ Can be prepared the day before. Do not add the Romaine until just before serving.

NOTE: The romaine can be left as whole leaves, or shredded to make a bed. Or, if you prefer, just before serving you can fold the shreds into the salad itself.

Cucumbers

Cucumbers mean cool and crisp. Scandinavians may immediately think of cucumber salad, and the English may envision lazy summer afternoons with cucumber sandwiches. But more likely the association is the "tossed" salad found in every eatery across the land, from local steak house to school cafeteria—a bowl of iceberg lettuce topped with a wedge of underripe tomato and a slice of cucumber: the green slice that so many people set aside. A few people may think of pickles, but I question how many make the connection between pickles and cucumbers. The point is that few people think of *cooking* a cucumber.

Cooked cucumbers are a taste treat. When all the other vegetables in the market seem ordinary and you want something different, try cooking a cucumber. Blanch or salt them to remove any bitterness and excess water. Sauté quickly in butter, perhaps with a favorite herb, until tender-crisp. Serve these with sautéed or grilled fish for a great taste treat. Cucumbers accompany chicken nicely, and are delicious stir-fried with pork. In other words, when other vegetables pall, or whenever you want a change, try cooking cucumbers.

Availability

Fresh
Cucumbers come in a variety of sizes. The common cucumber is 6 to 8 inches long, but there are also Asian varieties that are twice as long, and the European burpless variety grown in green house and packed in plastic sheaths. In many markets, smaller, unwaxed pickling varieties of cucumbers with smaller seeds are available.

The season for fresh cucumbers is May, June, and July. However, they are shipped into markets fresh year round. They are often wax coated to retain the moisture and to give the cucumber longer shelf life. Unwaxed pickling cucumbers are also available year round in many areas.

Frozen
Cucumbers do not freeze well.

Canned
Cucumbers are not canned for use as a substitute for fresh, but rather are cured in brine to make dozens of different pickles.

Preparation

Cucumbers come ready to eat. Rinse, if necessary, and start chewing. For salads and other cold dishes, cut into slices, or sections, and use. For a decorative look, score the cucumber with the tines of a fork to make decorative lines the length of the cucumber, before slicing. For a greater contrast, cut the skin off in alternating strips, or peel completely.

To seed cucumbers: Peel, cut in half lengthwise, support the cucumber in one hand, and with the spoon held in the other hand, scrape out the seeds.

To remove any bitterness and excess water, blanch the cucumbers in boiling salted water for 5 minutes, or sprinkle with salt and let drain in a colander for 30 minutes.

Cooking Methods

Boiling
Place the peeled and seeded cucumber in boiling salted water, and boil until tender-crisp—about 5 minutes. Drain, refresh under cold water, and drain again. Proceed with the final cooking.

Steaming
Place the cucumber in a steamer over boiling water and steam until tender-crisp—about 8 minutes. Drain, refresh under cold water, and drain again. Proceed with the final cooking.

Microwaving
Place the cucumbers in a covered dish, and cook for 4 to 6 minutes, depending on the size, turning once or twice. Water or stock is not needed, because of the moisture in the cucumber.

Sautéeing
After blanching the cucumber, sauté quickly in butter, with a minced herb, if desired. Add lemon juice to taste.

Braising
Blanched cucumbers are braised in a little chicken or beef stock until tender. Cucumber shells can be stuffed.

Quantity

Serve half a cucumber a person for most preparations. Cucumber salads, as opposed to salads with cucumbers as one ingredient, may need
as much as a cucumber a person, because salting reduces the bulk.

Sauces

Once blanched or sautéed, cucumbers are dressed with a number of
sauces—herbed butters, Hollandaise, cream, Mornay, and the like.
Cold cucumbers take well to vinaigrette, mayonnaise, and sauces
based on these.

Cucumber and Spinach Soup

3 cucumbers, peeled, seeded,
  and chopped
1 leek, split lengthwise
4 cups chicken stock
1 cup spinach leaves
1 teaspoon minced dill
1 teaspoon minced chervil

salt and pepper, to taste
½ cup yogurt, *crème fraîche,*
  or sour cream
1 cucumber, scored and thinly
  sliced
minced dill for garnish

Cut the cucumbers into 2-inch lengths. In a saucepan, simmer the
cucumbers, leeks, and chicken stock for 30 minutes.

In a processor, purée the soup and spinach leaves. Return the soup
to the saucepan, and season with dill, chervil, salt, and pepper.

Serve hot or cold, with the yogurt, cucumber slices, and a sprinkling of dill.

Yield: 6 servings

➤ Can be made the day before, and reheated or served cold.

Green Jade and Red Ruby Soup

5 cups chicken stock
2 cucumbers, peeled, seeded,
  and cut into ¼ inch slices

½ teaspoon salt
2 tablespoons chopped
  Virginia ham

In a saucepan, bring the stock to a boil, add the cucumber and salt,
and simmer 4 minutes. Pour into a tureen and sprinkle with the ham.

Yield: 6 servings

➤ Best if prepared and served.

Chinese Stuffed Cucumber Soup

6 Chinese mushrooms, soaked
  and minced
¾ pound ground pork
1 tablespoon minced scallion
1 egg, lightly beaten
½ teaspoon sesame oil
2 teaspoons dry Sherry
parsley
¼ teaspoon sugar
pinch of white pepper

3 large cucumbers, cut into
  1½ inch lengths and
  hollowed with an apple
  corer
6 cups boiling chicken stock
3 scallions, shredded
2 tablespoons minced
  coriander

In a bowl, combine the mushrooms, pork, scallion, egg, sesame oil, sherry, parsley, coriander, salt, sugar, and pepper. Mix well. Generously stuff the cucumbers with the mixture. Arrange on a plate in a steamer and steam for 15 minutes.

In a large, preferably shallow, soup tureen, arrange the cucumbers and pour over them the boiling stock. Sprinkle with the scallions and coriander, and serve.

Yield: 6 servings

➤ Can be prepared they day before. Reheat the cucumbers in the steamer.

Cold Cucumber Soup

Cucumbers are a natural for cold soups. Their crisp, clean flavor is often accented with the tartness of yogurt or sour cream.

2 cucumbers, peeled, seeded,
  and chopped
4 cups chicken stock
1 cup yogurt

1 teaspoon grated lemon rind
1 teaspoon minced dill
salt and pepper to taste
dill sprigs

In a saucepan, simmer the cucumbers in the stock until tender.

In a food processor or blender, purée the soup, and add the yogurt, lemon rind, and minced dill. Correct the seasoning with salt and pepper to taste. Turn the soup into a bowl, and chill.

Serve garnished with the dill sprigs.

Yield: 6 servings

➤ Can be prepared the day before.

NOTE: Vary the flavor of the soup by adding 2 cups of yogurt, ¼ cup raisins, and 1½ teaspoons curry powder, or to taste.

Yayla Corbasi (Turkish Cold Cucumber Yogurt Soup)

½ cup raisins	2 teaspoons salt
3 cups yogurt	½ teaspoon white pepper
½ cup light cream	6 ice cubes
1 cucumber, peeled, seeded,	1 cup ice water
and chopped	1 tablespoon minced parsley
¼ cup minced scallion	1 tablespoon minced dill
1 hard cooked egg, chopped	

Soak the raisins in water to cover while preparing the soup. In a large bowl, mix the yogurt, light cream, cucumber, scallion, egg, salt, pepper, and ice cubes. Chill 3 to 4 hours. Just before serving, stir in the ice water, raisins, parsley, and dill.

Yield: 6 servings

➤ Can be prepared 2 to 3 days before serving.

Sopa Del Sol (Spanish Cucumber Soup)

3 cucumbers, peeled, seeded,	2 cups sour cream
and chopped	3 tablespoons white vinegar
½ cup chopped onion	salt and pepper to taste
1 garlic clove, minced	1 cup peeled, seeded, and
2 cups chicken stock	chopped tomato

In a processor, purée the cucumbers, onion, and garlic in the chicken stock. Strain into a bowl. Stir in the sour cream, vinegar, salt, and pepper, and chill.

Serve garnished with the tomato.

Yield: 6 servings

➤ Can be prepared 2 to 3 days before serving.

NOTE: Substitute medium cream or yogurt for the sour cream, if desired.

Concombres Sautés (Sautéed Cucumbers)

This a refreshingly different vegetable. It is particularly pleasant served with poached, grilled, or sautéed fish.

4 tablespoons clarified butter	½ to 1 tablespoon sugar
3 large cucumbers, peeled,	salt and pepper to taste
seeded, cut into 1 inch	minced parsley
pieces, and blanched	

In a large skillet, heat enough oil to film the bottom of the pan. Sauté the cucumbers over high heat, and sprinkle with the sugar to help them turn light golden. Cook until tender-crisp. Season with salt and pepper, and sprinkle with the parsley.

Yield: 6 servings

➤ Best if sautéed and served.

NOTE: In the cooking, the sugar should caramelize and turn golden, so that the dish does not taste sweet.

Cucumbers in Orange Sauce

3 cucumbers, seeded, and thinly sliced on the diagonal	1½ cups orange juice salt and pepper to taste
3 tablespoons butter	2 tablespoons grated orange rind
2 tablespoons cornstarch	

In a skillet, sauté the cucumbers in the butter until tender-crisp. In a bowl, mix the orange juice into the cornstarch and stir into the cucumbers.

Simmer until thickened and clear. Remove from the heat and season with salt and pepper. Stir in the orange rind.

Yield: 6 servings

➤ Best if made and served.

Concombres à La Napolitaine
(Braised Cucumbers with Tomatoes)

½ cup minced onion	½ cup chicken stock
3 tablespoons butter	1 tablespoon minced mint
4 cucumbers, peeled, seeded, and cut into ½ inch slices	salt and pepper to taste
1½ tablespoons flour	2 cups tomatoes, peeled, seeded, and quartered

In a large skillet or casserole, sauté the onions in the butter until soft, but not brown. Add the cucumbers, and simmer over low heat for 5 minutes.

Sprinkle the flour over the cucumbers, and cook, stirring, for 2 minutes. Add the chicken stock and mint. Add salt and pepper to taste.

Cover and simmer 15 minutes. Add the tomatoes and heat until hot, about 2 minutes.

Yield: 6 servings

➤ Can be prepared to the point of adding the tomatoes, several hours ahead.

Baked Stuffed Cucumbers

6 large cucumbers, peeled, scored, and seeded	¾ cup barely cooked rice
salt	1 egg
½ cup minced onion	¾ cup minced spinach
4 tablespoons butter	¼ cup minced dill
1 pound salmon, cut into ¼ inch dice	salt and pepper to taste
	1 cup chicken stock
	¼ cup dry white wine.

Preheat the oven to 350°F. Salt the cucumber shells, and let drain for 30 minutes.

In a skillet, sauté the onion in 2 tablespoons of the butter until soft, but not brown. In a bowl, mix the onions, salmon, rice, egg, spinach, and dill. Season with salt and pepper.

Stuff the cucumber shells. Place the shells in the baking dish with the remaining butter, chicken stock, and wine. Cover and bake for 30 minutes, or until the shells are tender, basting often.

Yield: 6 servings

➤ Can be prepared the day before and reheated.

Concombres Farcis *(Stuffed Cucumbers)*

6 tablespoons olive oil	3 tablespoons minced basil
6 cucumbers peeled, halved, and seeded	1 tablespoon minced thyme
3 tablespoons salt	1 tablespoon minced parsley
¼ cup chopped shallots	1 tablespoon tomato paste
1½ pounds ground lean beef	salt and pepper to taste
pinch of black pepper	¼ cup grated Parmesan cheese
1½ cups peeled, seeded, and chopped tomato	2 tablespoons bread crumbs
	¾ cup dry white wine

Preheat the oven to 400°F. With 3 tablespoons of oil, oil a large, shallow baking dish large enough to hold the cucumbers in one layer.

In a bowl large enough to hold the cucumbers, place the cucumber, sprinkle with 2 tablespoons of salt, and cover with cold water. Let stand for 20 minutes.

In a skillet, heat the remaining 3 tablespoons of oil, and sauté the shallots until soft, but not brown. Add the beef and the remaining salt and pepper, and cook until the beef loses its color, breaking up any lumps. Add the tomatoes, basil, thyme, parsley, and tomato paste, and simmer for 5 minutes. Correct the seasoning with salt and pepper. Stir in the Parmesan cheese.

Drain the cucumbers, rinse under cold water, and pat dry. Fill each cucumber with the meat mixture, and sprinkle with the bread crumbs.

Place in the baking dish, and bake for 15 minutes. Add the wine, and bake for 25 minutes longer, basting often.

Serve hot, or at room temperature.

Yield: 6 servings

➤ Can be prepared the day before and served cold.

Cucumbers in Lemon Sauce

Vary this basic method of cooking the cucumbers in cream by substituting Dijon Mustard for the lemon juice.

4 cucumbers, peeled, seeded, and cut into ¾ inch slices	1 large lemon thinly sliced
1 teaspoon salt	1 cup heavy cream
3 tablespoons butter	1 teaspoon *beurre manié* (see glossary)
salt and pepper to taste	3 tablespoons minced chives

Place the cucumber slices in a colander, and sprinkle with the salt. Let stand for 1 to 2 hours.

In a skillet, heat the butter, and sauté the cucumbers over high heat, stirring often, until light golden. Season with salt and pepper. Add the lemon slices and cream, and cook until lightly thickened. Add the *beurre manie* in pea-sized bits, stirring constantly, until thickened. Stir in the chives. Remove and discard the lemon slices.

Yield: 6 servings

➤ Can be prepared several hours ahead and reheated.

Mousse de Concombres (Cucumber Mousse)

Vibrantly colored gelatin salads with canned fruits, marshmallows, and the like, have long been denigrated by serious cooks, but quality food can be prepared with gelatin. This mousse is a perfect example.

6 thin cucumbers	4 egg whites
¼ cup water	3 cups heavy cream
1 loosely packed cup of dill sprigs	1 egg white
salt and pepper to taste	1 cup mayonnaise
2 tablespoons unflavored gelatin	½ cup heavy cream
1 teaspoon lemon juice and 2 teaspoons cold water	1 smile cucumber, peeled, seeded, and minced
	1 cucumber
	dill sprigs

Peel three of the cucumbers, and then cut all 6 cucumbers into chunks. In a saucepan, simmer the cucumber chunks with the water, cup of dill, salt, and pepper, covered, over low heat until very soft. Strain, discarding the liquid.

In a processor, purée the cucumber and dill, and strain through a fine sieve, discarding the seeds. Let cool. In a small saucepan, dissolve the gelatin in the lemon juice and water, and heat over very low heat until melted. Stir into the cucumber purée. Whip the egg whites to the soft peak stage, and fold into the cucumber mixture. Beat the cream until it holds semi-firm peaks, and fold into the mousse. Turn into a 2-quart mold, and chill for at least 4 hours.

Meanwhile, beat the remaining egg white to soft peaks, and fold into the mayonnaise. Beat the remaining cream to the soft peak stage, and fold into the mayonnaise with the minced cucumber.

Peel the remaining cucumber, and with a vegetable peeler, shave off thin lengthwise slices. Shape the slices into cornucopias. When ready to serve, unmold the mousse onto a platter, and garnish with the cucumber cornucopias and dill sprigs, and pass the sauce separately.

Yield: 6 to 8 servings

➤ Can be prepared the day before. The sauce should not be made more than 6 hours ahead. If preparing the cornucopias ahead, use a wooden skewer to hold together, and store in ice water.

Coupes de Concombres Raifort
(Cucumber Cups with Horseradish Cream)

This garnish is a wonderful hors d'oeuvre, or an accompaniment to cold poached fish or grilled meats.

3 cucumbers, scored, and cut
   into 1 inch sections
½ cup heavy cream, whipped
   until stiff

¼ cup grated horseradish
   (fresh preferred)
salt and pepper to taste
2 tablespoons ground toasted
   almonds

With a melon-baller, scoop out most of the center of the cucumber sections to make small cups. In a bowl, fold the cream, horseradish, and salt together. Mound in the cups, and sprinkle with the almonds.

Yield: 6 servings

➤ Can be prepared several hours ahead and kept refrigerated.

Concombres au Jambon (Cucumbers Stuffed with Ham)

This is another garnish to serve as a luncheon dish or an hors d'oeuvre.

3 cucumbers, peeled and cut
   into 1 inch lengths
½ cup vinaigrette (see page 30)
2 cups finely diced smoked
   ham

heavy cream
salt and pepper to taste
grated horseradish

With a melon-baller, scoop out most of the center of the cucumber sections to make small cups. Marinate the cucumbers in the vinaigrette for 1 hour, and drain.

In a bowl, mix the ham with enough cream to bind. Season with salt and pepper. Spoon into the cucumber cups, and sprinkle with the horseradish.

Yield: 6 servings

➤ Can be prepared 3 to 4 hours ahead and kept refrigerated.

Concombres aux Duxelles
(Cucumbers Stuffed with Mushrooms)

3 cucumbers, peeled, and cut into 1 inch lengths	1 tablespoon lemon juice
1 pound mushrooms, minced	salt and pepper to taste
⅓ cup butter	3 tablespoons minced dill

With a melon-baller, scoop out some of the seed section of each cucumber section, and reserve the base and the seed section.

In a skillet, sauté the mushrooms in the butter with the lemon juice, salt, and pepper, until the liquid evaporates. Stir in the dill, and cook until quite dry.

Chill the mushroom mixture. Stuff the cucumber sections with the mushrooms, and top with a crown of seed section.

Yield: 6 servings

➤ Can be prepared the day before and kept refrigerated.

Barquettes de Concombres aux Roquefort
(Cucumber Boats with Roquefort)

3 to 6 small cucumbers, peeled and seeded	¾ cup minced parsley
salt	½ cup minced pimiento
4 ounces cream cheese	½ cup minced green pepper
1 ounce Roquefort cheese	2 tablespoons capers
1 cup sour cream	2 tablespoons minced scallion
¼ cup lemon juice	2 garlic cloves, crushed

Sprinkle the cucumber boats with salt, and drain, cut side down, on paper toweling for 30 minutes.

In a processor or a bowl, cream the cream cheese and Roquefort until smooth. Add the sour cream and lemon juice, and process until smooth. Stir in ½ cup parsley, pimiento, green pepper, capers, scallion, and garlic.

Correct the seasoning with salt and pepper. Wipe the boats dry, and sprinkle with the Roquefort mixture. Sprinkle with the remaining parsley.

Yield: 6 servings

➤ Can be prepared several hours before serving.

Concombres Farcis á la Printaniére
(Cucumbers Stuffed with Mixed Vegetables)

3 large cucumbers, peeled	2 tablespoons olive oil
1 cup cooked, mixed, and	2 teaspoons vinegar
diced vegetables (see Note)	salt and pepper to taste
2 or 3 tablespoons mayonnaise	

Cut the cucumbers into 3 inch pieces. In a saucepan of boiling salted water, blanch the cucumbers for 2 minutes. Drain and cool. With a melon-baller, scoop out a deep well from each cucumber section.

In a bowl, fold the mixed vegetables with just enough mayonnaise to bind. Fill the cucumber cups, and arrange standing up on a platter.

In a small bowl, whisk the olive oil, vinegar, salt, and pepper, and drizzle over the cucumber cups.

Yield: 6 servings

➤ Can be prepared several hours in advance.

NOTE: This is a charming way of using leftover vegetables. Use diced green beans, beets, zucchini, summer squash, potatoes, carrots, turnips, parsnips, and the like.

Cucumber Salads

The most common use of cucumbers is a slice or two on top of iceberg lettuce, accompanied by an underripe tomato wedge and an overload of a thick, overpowering, "French," Roquefort, or Russian dressing. Fortunately, this not the only possible treatment. In much of Middle Europe and Scandinavia, cucumber salads are standard fare.

Slice, dice, grate, or cut the cucumbers into julienne. Salt the cucumbers, using about 1 teaspoon for each 4 cups of cucumber, and let drain for at least 30 minutes. Rinse the cucumber under cold running water to remove the salt, and then press dry.

Agurkesalat (Danish Cucumber Salad)

This is a dieter's delight: few calories and a luscious, refreshing flavor.

3 cucumbers, scored and	1 tablespoon sugar
thinly sliced	1 teaspoon salt
1 tablespoon salt	¼ teaspoon white pepper
¾ cup white vinegar	2 tablespoons minced dill

Arrange the cucumber slices in a thin layer in a shallow china or glass bowl, and sprinkle with the tablespoon of salt. Let stand for several hours, weighted with 2 or 3 plates.

Remove plates, drain off the liquid, and spread the cucumbers on toweling.

In a bowl, mix the vinegar, sugar, salt, and pepper together. Add the cucumbers, and sprinkle with the minced dill.

Chill.

Yield: 6 servings

➤ Can be prepared the day before.

NOTE: This salad preparation shrinks as the cucumbers lose moisture. If you prepare enough for 6, the next day you may find that it seems there is only enough for 5, or even 4.

Variations on Cucumber Salad:
Once the cucumbers have been salted and drained, mix them with any of a variety of dressings.

Cream Add heavy cream to taste, and season with minced dill and/or Dijon mustard. Add sugar to taste, if desired.

Sour cream Substitute sour cream for the heavy cream. Add horseradish for a different flavor.

Mayonnaise Fold in enough mayonnaise to moisten, without making the salad too wet. It is best to add the mayonnaise just before serving.

Vinaigrette Add vinaigrette flavored with mustard, garlic, and fresh herbs.

Concombres en Salade de Martinique
(Martinique Cucumber Salad)

3 cucumbers, peeled, seeded, and chopped	1½ tablespoons lime juice
1½ teaspoons salt	1 or 2 tablespoons minced hot pepper
2 garlic cloves, crushed	

In a bowl, mix the cucumbers with the salt, and turn into a colander. Drain for 30 minutes. Press gently, and stir in the garlic, lime juice, and hot peppers.

Yield: 6 servings

➤ Can be prepared several hours ahead.

Gingered Cucumber Salad

½ pound snow peas, stringed
1 pound cucumbers, peeled,
  seeded, and cut in ¼ inch
  slices
½ pound thinly sliced water
  chestnuts

½ cup scallions
2 tablespoons minced ginger
2 tablespoons safflower oil
¼ cup rice vinegar
¼ teaspoon white pepper
salt to taste

In boiling salted water, blanch the snow peas 1 minute, drain, refresh under cold water, and drain again. In a bowl, combine the snow peas, cucumbers, water chestnuts, scallion, and ginger. In a small bowl, mix the oil, vinegar, pepper, and salt. Toss with salad.

Yield: 6 servings

➤ Do not mix the dressing into the salad ingredients more than 30 minutes before serving, because the snow peas will lose their fresh color.

Insalata di Citrioli (Cucumber Salad)

3 large cucumbers, peeled and
  thinly sliced
salt

½ cup olive oil
paprika

Arrange the cucumbers in a deep dish, sprinkle each layer liberally with salt, and cover with another dish and wait for at least 1 hour. Drain off the water. In a bowl, toss the cucumbers with the oil, and sprinkle with the paprika.

Yield: 6 servings

➤ Can be prepared the day before.

Kheera Ka Raita (Cucumber with Tomato and Yogurt)

Raitas, cold relishes, serve as an accompaniment to curries, and also make delicious salads on their own.

2 cucumbers, peeled, seeded
  and chopped
2 tablespoons minced onions
2 tablespoons salt
2 tomatoes, peeled, seeded,
  and diced

2 cups unflavored yogurt
2 tablespoons minced
  coriander
2 teaspoons ground cumin,
  toasted in an ungreased
  skillet for 30 seconds

In a bowl, mix the cucumbers, onions, and salt and let stand for 10 minutes. Drain, and squeeze gently to remove the excess moisture.

In a larger bowl, combine the cucumber mixture with the tomatoes, yogurt, coriander, and cumin, and marinate in the refrigerator for 1 hour.

Yield: 6 servings

➤ Can be prepared the day before.

Pan Huang Kua *(Cucumber Salad)*

2 cucumbers, peeled, seeded, and cut into ¼ inch slices	2 teaspoons sesame oil
1 tablespoon soy sauce	1 teaspoon sugar
1 tablespoon wine vinegar	½ teaspoon salt

In a bowl, mix the cucumbers, soy sauce, vinegar, sesame oil, sugar, and salt, and mix gently. Let marinate for at least 30 minutes.

Yield: 6 servings

➤ Can be prepared the day before.

Cucumber Fans

There is a trick to making these fans.
Use two chop sticks placed on the board on either side of the cucumber, to prevent you from cutting all the way through the slices. With a little practice, it is quite simple.

2 Japanese or burpless cucumbers, cut into 2 inch sections	1½ teaspoons shredded ginger
	½ teaspoon dried red pepper flakes
2 teaspoons salt	3 tablespoons sugar
1 tablespoon vegetable oil	2 tablespoons rice vinegar
½ teaspoon sesame oil	1 tablespoon soy sauce
1 tablespoon minced garlic	

Place 2 chop sticks side by side on a counter. Place a cucumber section between the chop sticks. With a thin-bladed sharp knife, cut through the cucumber to the top of the chop sticks at ⅛ inch intervals.

Place the cucumber sections in a bowl of water seasoned with the salt. Let stand for 30 minutes. Drain, rinse under cold water, and pat dry.

In a wok, heat the vegetable oil and sesame oil. Lower the heat, and add the garlic, ginger, and pepper flakes, and stir until fragrant. Add the cucumbers, sugar, vinegar, and soy sauce, and stir for 2 minutes. Turn into a shallow dish, and cool, stirring occasionally, for 6 to 24 hours.

Serve slightly chilled.

Yield: 6 servings

➤ Can be prepared the day before.

Hot and Spicy Cucumber Salad

2 large cucumbers, peeled,   3 tablespoons soy sauce
  seeded, and cut on diagonal   1 tablespoon rice vinegar
  into ½ inch slices   2 teaspoons chili paste with garlic
1½ teaspoons salt   1 teaspoon sesame oil

In a bowl, toss the cucumber slices with the salt, and let stand for 10 minutes. Drain well.

In another bowl, whisk the soy sauce, vinegar, chili paste, and sesame oil. Fold in the cucumbers and chill.

Yield: 6 servings

➤ Can be prepared the day before.

Eggplant

*E*ggplant ranks as one of the favorite vegetables of the Mediterranean. Every country in the region has its own specialties, with as many variations as there are cooks, and the "right" version is always in dispute. Fortunately, this gives us an enormous variety from which to choose. Eggplants are also used often and well in the cuisines of Asia, including China, Japan, and India.

The full, rich, meaty quality of eggplant marries well with many other vegetables, and you can use almost any method to cook eggplant. Prepare it with or without its skin, and serve it as the simplest casserole of baked eggplant, garlic, and tomatoes, or turn it into a sophisticated mold for the most elegant buffet.

Few vegetables absorb oil with the thirst of eggplant. It is truly astonishing. To prevent this, many cooks recommend broiling or baking eggplants brushed with oil (see page 207). These methods work, and are recommended for those who wish to avoid the oil. However, the results are less authentic. Many of the recipes come from regions where poverty prevails, and using quantities of oil is a necessary part of the diet. I recommend enjoying the dishes as presented, but not eating them daily. Also, plan to serve these richer, fuller dishes as main courses instead of as side courses.

Because eggplant marries so well with so many other vegetables, I have chosen to place some recipes that might be considered as eggplant recipes in the Mixed Vegetable Chapter (see page 524). Please look in both areas to make sure that you have not missed an old (or a new) favorite.

Availability

Fresh
Available year round, eggplants are sold in various sizes and shapes. For the most common varieties, look for smooth, dark-purplish skins, and fruit that feels heavy in relation to its size. Small-to-medium eggplants are a good choice, but pressing the skin is a better method of telling ripeness than size.

When you press the flesh with your finger, it should give and bounce back. If it does not give to pressure, it is under-ripe, and if the imprint does not bounce back, it is overripe.

205

Avoid eggplants with soft or hard skins that have brown spots on the skin. The green topknot should look fresh. Store eggplants at room temperature 2 to 3 days, or if necessary, refrigerate for 3 to 4 days. (Refrigeration can cause bitterness.) Happily, most eggplant dishes can be held for a day or more before serving, because the vegetable must be cooked until very tender, rather than tender-crisp, and reheating often gives the flavors of the other ingredients a chance to mingle.

Frozen

Eggplant is not sold frozen, and although some prepared dishes can be frozen, they are seldom as good as when freshly prepared.

Canned

Eggplant is not canned, except as eggplant pickle.

Preparation

There is a lot of conjecture about removing the bitterness from eggplant, and each method has its adherents. Choosing ripe eggplants that bounce back after giving to finger pressure, and keeping them out of the refrigerator, is the best way to avoid bitterness.

Peeling

Unless the skin is to be used as a container, some cooks insist on peeling, while others insist that peeling causes loss of nutrients. Sometimes I like to eat the skin and other times not. Generally, I follow the recipe as presented and do not worry. Because I like the color, I tend to leave it on if it is my option, or peel alternating strips for contrast. I have not found a difference in bitterness because of the skin.

Salting

Salting removes the excess moisture and, according to many, bitterness. My experience is that it does not remove the bitterness, but does remove the moisture. Here are several methods of salting.

To Salt Eggplant

Slices   Sprinkle with salt, place in a colander, and let drain for at least 30 minutes. Press out the excess moisture. If you think the eggplant is salty, rinse under cold water, press, and pat dry.

Halves   Cut the eggplant in half, and with a sharp knife cut a crosshatch design deep into the cut side without piercing the skin. Sprinkle with salt, and let drain, cut side down, for at least 30 minutes. Press out excess moisture. If it is too salty, rinse under cold water, press, and pat dry.

Soaking

Soak the eggplant in a container of salted water for 30 minutes and drain. Press and pat dry.

Blanching

Blanch in boiling salted water for 5 minutes. I find that this method leeches flavor, but other writers recommend it.

Excess Oil

Eggplant slices, cubes, and even halves are often browned in hot oil. The problem is that the eggplant absorbs so much oil that it makes the dish heavy with oil. Salting by one of the methods above removes the excess moisture, and the eggplant absorbs less oil.

If it has absorbed quantities of oil, the oil surfaces after a while, and the dish will have a thick, unappealing oily layer. Therefore, in the interest of saving oil and having a less greasy dish, I prefer to salt when sautéing or frying.

Sautéing

If you are going to sauté the eggplant in oil, salt, drain, and press and pat dry. Heat the oil until very hot, brown the slices a few at a time on both sides, and drain on paper toweling. To keep the eggplant from absorbing too much oil, be sure that the oil is hot before adding the next batch of eggplant and keep the oil about ¼ inch deep. Make sure any added oil is up to temperature before adding cold eggplant.

Broiling and Baking

To use less oil and get a different flavor, brush the slices with a little oil, and arrange them on baking sheets. Broil or bake at 375°F until brown on both sides.

Cooking Methods

Eggplant can be treated by every cooking method—boiling, steaming, microwaving, sautéing, broiling, baking, grilling, stewing, deep-frying, and making into gratins and purées. In addition, it can be served as an hors d'oeuvre, appetizer, part of a fish or meat course, or as a vegetable. I have not yet found (nor do I wish to find) it used as a dessert.

Boiling

This is the least desirable way to prepare eggplant, but is suitable when a purée is needed.

Steaming

Place the eggplant in a steamer over boiling water, and steam until tender. This can replace the sautéing called for in many recipes, but with a resulting loss of flavor, from the lack of oil and browning.

Microwaving

A one-pound eggplant cooks medium to soft in 6 to 8 minutes in a covered container. When shells to stuff are needed, this is a quick method.

A pound of eggplant cubes cooks in 3 to 4 minutes.

Sautéing

Salt the slices, pat dry, and sauté in hot oil until golden on both sides. Do not add cold oil to the pan until the eggplant has been removed, and do not add more eggplant to the oil until the oil is hot.

Broiling or Grilling

Brush the slices with oil, and broil or grill until golden on both sides.

Bake

Usually the eggplant is stuffed, or combined with other ingredients. Follow the recipe.

Deep-Frying

Dredge the eggplant slices or batons in seasoned flour, and fry in oil at 375°F. Eggplant can be coated with bread crumbs or a batter before deep-frying.

Quantity

Plan on about 1½ pounds of eggplant for 6 persons. There is little waste in preparing eggplant.

Sauces

Eggplant is not usually boiled, steamed, or sautéed in butter, and then sauced, as are so many vegetables. However, fried eggplant takes well to tomato- and mayonnaise-based sauces. Bechamél and Mornay are used in many preparations.

Eggplant Spread

1 eggplant	1 tablespoon mayonnaise
1 tablespoon peanut oil	1 garlic clove, crushed
1 tablespoon wine vinegar	salt and pepper to taste

Preheat the oven to 400°F.

Remove and discard the eggplant stem. Place the eggplant in a shallow baking pan, and bake for 40 minutes, or until tender. Peel and discard the skin. Place the pulp in a bowl, and mash with a fork.

When cool, mix in the oil, vinegar, mayonnaise, and garlic, and season with salt and pepper. Chill at least 2 hours.

Serve with crackers or melba toast.

Yield: about 1 cup

➤ Can be prepared several days ahead.

Eggplant Caviar

I think it takes a stretch of the imagination to think of this as caviar, but whatever it is called, it is a wonderful low-calorie spread.

1 medium eggplant	1½ tablespoons minced
½ cup minced onion	parsley or dill
1 tomato, peeled, seeded, and	1 tablespoon lemon juice
chopped	1 garlic clove, crushed
2 tablespoons olive oil	½ teaspoon sugar
	salt and pepper to taste

Preheat the oven to 400°F.

Remove and discard the eggplant stem. Place the eggplant in a shallow baking dish, and bake for 40 minutes, or until tender. Peel and discard the skin. Place the pulp in a sieve and let drain for 10 minutes. Press gently.

In a processor, purée the pulp. Add the onion, tomato, olive oil, parsley, lemon juice, garlic, sugar, salt, and pepper, and process into a coarse pulp. Chill.

Serve with buttered toast.

Yield: about 1 cup

➤ Can be prepared several days ahead.

Baba Ghanouj

This Middle Eastern eggplant spread is flavored with Tahini, a sesame seed paste (see below).

1 eggplant	1 garlic clove, minced
3 tablespoons tahini	salt and pepper to taste
3 tablespoons lemon juice	

Preheat the oven to 400°F.

Remove and discard the eggplant stem. Place the eggplant in a small baking dish, and bake for 40 minutes, or until tender. Peel.

In a food processor, purée the pulp with the tahini, lemon juice, garlic, salt, and pepper.

Serve with sesame crackers or toasted pita.

Yield: about 1 cup

➤ Can be prepared several days ahead.

Tahini (Sesame Seed Paste)

1 cup sesame seeds	1 teaspoon salt
1 cup water	dash of cayenne pepper
2 garlic cloves, chopped	few drops of vinegar
juice of 2 lemons	

In a food processor or blender, purée the sesame seeds, water, garlic, and lemon juice. Add a little more water, if needed, to reach the consistency of mayonnaise. Season with salt, cayenne, and vinegar. Serve with toasted pita bread, vegetables, or broiled meats.

Yield: 2 cups

➤ Keeps 3 weeks, refrigerated.

NOTE: A blender seems to do a better job than a food processor. If the oil separates, whisk it back into the paste.

Melanzane alla Liguria (Eggplant Stew with Eggs)

Serve this with hot, crusty bread for brunch, and add tossed green salad at lunch or supper.

3 pounds eggplant, thickly
  sliced
salt and pepper to taste
1 cup olive oil

1 onion, thinly sliced
3 large tomatoes, peeled,
  seeded, and quartered
4 to 6 eggs

Salt the eggplant, and drain in a colander for 1 hour. In a skillet, heat the oil, and sauté the onion until golden.

Rinse the eggplant slices, pat dry, and add to the onions. Simmer 10 minutes. Add the tomatoes, and season with salt and pepper. Cover and simmer 30 minutes, or until the eggplant is soft and amalgamated with the tomatoes. Uncover the pan.

Beat the eggs with salt and pepper, and pour over the contents of the pan. Cook, uncovered and without stirring, until the eggs are set—about 6 minutes.

Serve.

Yield: 6 servings

➤ The eggplant mixture can be prepared ahead and reheated.

NOTE: You can provide as many as 1 egg per person, or add just enough to give an egg flavor.

Melanzane a Fungetelli
(Eggplant Cooked Like Mushrooms I)

Another version of alla Trifolati.

3 pounds eggplant, peeled,
  and cut into 1-inch cubes
salt
6 tablespoons olive oil
4 large tomatoes, peeled,
  seeded, and chopped

8 large black olives, pitted and
  chopped
4 teaspoons capers
1 tablespoon minced basil
1 teaspoon minced oregano
1 garlic clove, minced

Sprinkle the eggplant with salt, and let drain in a colander for 1 hour. Wipe dry.

Heat the oil in a casserole, and sauté the eggplant over high heat, stirring often, for 15 minutes. Add the tomatoes, olives, and capers, and lower the heat. Cook 15 minutes longer, or until the eggplant is soft. Add the basil, oregano, and garlic, and stir to combine. Correct the seasoning with salt and pepper.

Serve hot or cold.

Yield: 6 servings

➤ Can be prepared the day before.

Melanzane al Funghetto
(Eggplant Cooked Like Mushrooms II)

The difference between funghietelli and funghetti is that funghetti are larger.

2 medium eggplants, peeled and cut into 1 inch cubes	5 tablespoons olive oil
salt	2 tablespoons parsley
1 teaspoon minced garlic	pepper to taste

In a colander, toss the eggplant cubes and salt, and let drain for 30 minutes. Rinse under cold water, and pat dry.

In a large skillet, sauté the garlic with 4 tablespoons of olive oil, until it turns golden. Add the eggplant, and toss in the oil to coat evenly. Cook, turning the eggplant in the pan, even though it absorbs all the oil, for 5 minutes. Add the remaining tablespoon of oil and cook, stirring occasionally, for 10 minutes longer. It should have released the oil. Add the parsley, and stir to combine. Cook over low heat until the eggplant is tender—about 30 minutes.

Correct the seasoning with salt and pepper.

Yield: 6 servings

➤ Can be prepared ahead and reheated.

Melanzane alla Foggiana (Eggplant Foggia Style)

Usually, each person gets a single eggplant, so use tiny Italian or Japanese eggplants. If only very large eggplants are available, prepare one large one and serve in sections.

6 small eggplants	pinch of sugar
salt and pepper to taste	2 tablespoons minced basil
5 tablespoons olive oil	2 tablespoons minced parsley
1 garlic clove, crushed	¼ cup bread crumbs
1 pound tomatoes, peeled, seeded, and chopped	½ pound sliced ripe tomatoes
	½ cup olive oil

Cut the stem from the eggplants and reserve.

With a melon baller, scoop out the inside, removing as much pulp as possible but still leaving a firm shell. Reserve the pulp and the shells. Sprinkle the inside of the shells with salt, and drain upside down for 1 to 2 hours.

In a large skillet, heat the 5 tablespoons of olive oil, sauté the garlic until brown, and then discard the garlic. Add the eggplant pulp and chopped tomatoes, and season with salt, pepper, and a pinch of sugar. Cover, and cook over high heat for 20 minutes, stirring occasionally. Stir in the basil, parsley, and bread crumbs.

Rinse out the eggplant shells, and dry carefully. Stuff with the egg-plant-tomato mixture, and put on the lids.

Place the eggplants upright in a casserole, and scatter over them the tomato slices. Drizzle with the remaining olive oil. Add ½ cup water, cover, and cook over low heat, shaking the pan occasionally, for about 1 hour, or until the shells are very soft. Add more water if needed.

Serve hot or cold.

Yield: 6 servings

➤ Can be prepared the day before.

Roasted Eggplant

6 small eggplants, cut in half lengthwise	¼ cup olive
	¼ teaspoon dried oregano

Preheat the broiler or grill.

Arrange the eggplants cut side down in a broiling pan, or skin side down on a grill, and broil for 3 to 4 minutes, or until softened.

In a small bowl, mix the olive oil and oregano together. Turn the egg-plant, and brush with olive oil and oregano mixture, and broil or grill until brown on the cut side. If you are using large eggplants, it may be necessary to cut them.

Yield: 6 servings

➤ Can be prepared ahead and served at room temperature.

NOTE: The success of this dish depends upon the eggplants being small. If you can only purchase large eggplants, cut them into thin slices. If the eggplants are young and tender, they should cook in a short period of time, but if older, you may need to let them cook longer.

Aubergine Frites or Melanzani Fritti (Fried Eggplant)

Every Mediterranean country claims this method as its own. Serve it with grilled meat or chickens. For a first course, serve with fresh to-mato sauce.

1 small eggplant cut into batons	salt and pepper
flour	milk
	oil for frying

Cut the eggplant into batons, about the size of your small finger. In a pie tin, mix the flour, salt, and pepper.

Heat the oil to 375°F. Dip the batons into the milk, roll in the flour, and fry until golden—about 2 minutes. Drain on paper toweling, and serve hot.

Yield: 6 servings

➤ Coat the eggplant just before frying for a crisp crust. Do not cover, and serve as soon as possible.

NOTE: As with most fried foods, these become soggy if not served immediately. It is better to let your guests wait the few minutes required to give them perfect fried eggplant.

Stuffed Fried Eggplant Slices

Thick slices of eggplant are stuffed with a variety of fillings, coated with bread crumbs, and then fried for a delicious luncheon dish. Slices from the much smaller, almost finger-sized eggplant can turn these into hors d'oeuvre.

6 1-inch-thick slices eggplant
salt and pepper to taste
6 tablespoons minced, cooked
   spinach
6 tablespoons Gorgonzola
   cheese
flour

1 egg beaten
2 cups fresh bread crumbs
oil for frying
Tomato sauce (see page 24) or
   Bagna Cauda sauce (see
   page 16)

With the point of a small, sharp knife, cut a large slit into the side of each eggplant slice to make a pocket. Season the pocket with salt and pepper. Stuff the pockets with a tablespoon of spinach and a tablespoon of Gorgonzola. Press to close.

Place the flour in a bowl, and season with salt and pepper. Place the egg in another bowl, and the bread crumbs on a plate. Dredge the eggplant slices in the flour, coat with the egg, and roll in the bread crumbs to coat on all sides. Set on a cake rack to dry for about 20 minutes.

Heat the oil to 375°F. Fry the eggplant slices until golden on both sides.

Serve immediately, and pass the sauce separately.

Yield: 6 servings

➤ Can be prepared for frying the day before.

NOTE: For hors d'oeuvre, or just tinier portions, select the tiny Japanese or Italian varieties, and cut into ¼-inch thick slices. Place the filling on one slice, press another slice on top, and coat the eggs and bread crumbs. Instead of deep-frying, cook in ½ inch of oil in a skillet, and fry until golden on both sides.

Variations:

Chèvre and Walnuts Stuff 1 tablespoon of crumbled chevre and 1 teaspoon chopped walnuts into each slice.

Fontina and sun-dried tomatoes Stuff 1 tablespoon of finely diced fontina cheese and 1 tablespoon minced sun-dried tomatoes into each slice.

Mozzarella and basil Stuff 1 tablespoon of diced Mozzarella mixed with 1 tablespoon minced basil into each slice.

Mozzarella and Parmesan Mix 3 egg yolks with ¼ cup grated Parmesan and ½ cup diced mozzarella, and stuff each slice.

Provolone and anchovy Stuff 1 tablespoon finely diced provolone and 1 teaspoon minced anchovies into each slice.

Shrimp, Chèvre, and Rosemary Stuff 1 tablespoon of chopped shrimp mixed with ¼ teaspoon minced rosemary and 1 tablespoon crumbled chèvre into each slice.

Baked Eggplant Sandwiches

2 small eggplants, cut into ¼ inch thick slices, salted, and drained	2 tablespoons minced parsley
salt and pepper to taste	¼ pound provolone, thinly sliced
1 cup fine dry bread crumbs	¼ pound mortadella, thinly sliced
2 tablespoons grated Parmesan cheese	1 egg, lightly beaten
	2 tablespoons olive oil

Preheat the oven to 350°F.

Rinse the eggplant slices under cold water, drain, and pat dry. In a bowl, mix the bread crumbs, cheese, and parsley, and set aside. Cut the provolone and mortadella into circles slightly smaller than the eggplant slices.

Make sandwiches of 1 slice of provolone, 1 slice of mortadella, and 2 slices of eggplant. Dip each sandwich in the egg, and then roll in the bread crumbs. Place on a cake rack, and let stand for 20 minutes.

Pour the olive oil on a baking sheet, and heat in the oven for 4 minutes. Place the eggplant sandwiches on the baking sheet, and bake for 15 minutes, or until golden, turning once. Cut into bite sized pieces, and serve hot or at room temperature.

Yield: 6 servings

Aubergine Menagère (Stewed Eggplant)

1½ pounds eggplant, peeled
and cut into 1 inch cubes
flour
salt and pepper to taste
⅓ cup hot olive oil
2 tablespoons minced onion

3 tomatoes, peeled, seeded,
and chopped
a faggot of celery, parsley, bay
leaf, and thyme
minced parsley

Dredge the eggplant in the flour seasoned with salt and pepper. Sauté
in the hot oil until golden—about 5 minutes. Add the onion, tomatoes,
and the faggot, and simmer until the tomatoes are sauce-like and the
eggplant is tender—about 20 minutes. Discard the faggot, and correct the
seasoning with salt and pepper.
Serve sprinkled with the minced parsley.

Yield: 6 servings

➤ Can be prepared ahead and reheated.

NOTE: To make a faggot or bundle of herbs, break a stalk of celery in
half and place the herbs in the bottom half and cover with the top half
of the celery and tie into a bundle.

Variation:
Prepare the eggplant as above, but omit the faggot and substitute 2
cloves garlic, crushed.

Sardinian Baked Eggplant

3 small eggplants, about 1½
pounds altogether
salt and pepper to taste
½ cup olive oil
¾ cup fresh bread crumbs
2 tablespoons minced parsley

3 garlic cloves, crushed
5 anchovy fillets, minced
1 teaspoon dried oregano or
marjoram
minced roasted red pepper
2 tablespoons capers

Preheat the oven to 350°F. Cut the eggplant into half lengthwise,
and make slits ½ inch apart the length of the halves, without piercing
the skin.
Sprinkle the cut areas with salt, and let drain for 1 hour, cut side
down. Drain, rinse under cold water, and drain again. Pat dry. In a
large skillet, heat 6 tablespoons of olive oil, and sauté the eggplant, cut
side down, until tender and nicely browned.
When cool enough to handle, scoop out the flesh without breaking
the skins. Place the skins in a well oiled baking dish, cut side up.
Mince the pulp, and put into a bowl with the bread crumbs, parsley,
garlic, anchovies, and oregano. Stir, and correct the seasoning with
salt and pepper. Stuff the eggplant shells, and drizzle with the remaining olive oil. Bake for 20 minutes, or until golden on top.
Garnish with the peppers and capers, and serve at room temperature.

Yield: 6 servings

➤ Can be prepared ahead. If refrigerated, let warm to room temperature before serving.

Aubergines Farcies
(Eggplant Stuffed with Chicken and Rice)

Serve with a green salad and freshly baked bread for luncheon or supper.

1 large eggplant, about 1½ pounds	3 shallots, minced
olive oil	1 bay leaf
2 cups minced cooked chicken	1 tablespoon minced thyme
1 cup cooked rice	1 tablespoon minced parsley
1 cup crushed tomatoes	salt and pepper to taste

Preheat the oven to 350°F.

Cut the eggplant in half lengthwise, and score the surface, without cutting through the skin, in a criss-cross pattern. In a large skillet, heat ½ inch of oil, and fry the eggplant halves until tender—about 10 minutes. Remove the flesh and chop coarsely. Place the shells in an oiled baking dish.

In a bowl, mix the chopped eggplant, chicken, rice, ½ cup tomatoes, shallots, bay leaf, thyme, and parsley. Season with salt and pepper. Stuff the eggplant shells, and spread the remaining tomatoes over the top. Bake until hot—about 25 minutes.

Yield: 6 servings

➤ Can be prepared for baking the day before.

Melanzane alla Genoese
(Baked Eggplant Genoa Style)

2 medium-sized eggplants, about 2 pounds altogether	½ tablespoon minced oregano
salt and pepper to taste	2 tablespoons water
⅓ cup minced basil	½ cup olive oil (approximately)
¼ cup fresh bread crumbs	2 tomatoes, cut into ¼ inch slices
2 tablespoons minced parsley	
2 or 3 cloves garlic, minced	

Preheat the oven to 375°F.

Cut the eggplants in half lengthwise, and make slits ¼ inch apart the length of each half. Sprinkle with salt, and let drain, cut side down, for 1 hour. Rinse under cold water, drain, and pat dry.

In a bowl, mix the basil, bread crumbs, parsley, garlic, oregano, salt, and pepper to taste. Press the crumb mixture into the slits of the eggplant.

Place the eggplant in a baking dish, and add ¼ cup olive oil and the water. Arrange the overlapping slices of tomato on the eggplant, and drizzle with the remaining olive oil. Bake for 45 minutes, basting often with the oil in the pan.

Cool to room temperature, and drizzle with any remaining oil.

Yield: 6 servings

➤ Can be prepared ahead.

Melanzane alla Sarda (Sardinian Baked Eggplant)

3 medium eggplants, cut in half
salt and pepper to taste
¼ cup bread crumbs
1 garlic clove, minced
1 tablespoon minced basil

2 tablespoons minced parsley
3 large tomatoes, peeled and
  thinly sliced
½ cup olive oil

Preheat the oven to 375°F.

Sprinkle the cut side of the eggplant with salt, and drain in a colander for 1 hour. Wipe the surface dry.

Cut deep slits in the cut surface. In a bowl, mix the bread crumbs, garlic, basil, parsley, salt, and pepper. Sprinkle over the eggplant, pressing into the slits.

Arrange the eggplant in a baking dish, cut side up, and cover with tomato slices. Drizzle the oil over the top. Bake for 45 minutes, or until tender, basting often with the juices in the pan.

Yield: 6 servings

➤ Can be prepared ahead and served at room temperature.

Eggplant Stuffed with Shrimp and Crab

1 large eggplant, about 1½
  pounds
¼ cup butter
¼ cup minced scallions
2 tablespoons parsley

salt and pepper to taste
¼ pound cooked crab meat
¼ pound cooked tiny shrimp
¼ cup grated Parmesan cheese

Preheat the oven to 350°F.

Cut the eggplant in half, lengthwise, and make deep criss-cross incisions in the surface, without cutting through the skin. Place in a baking dish and bake for 20 minutes, or until the pulp is tender. Remove the pulp from the skins and chop. Save the shells.

In a skillet, melt the butter, and sauté the scallions and parsley until the scallions are soft, but not brown—about 3 minutes. Stir in the eggplant pulp, crab, and shrimp, and heat. Correct the seasoning with salt and pepper to taste. Fill the shells, and sprinkle with the grated Parmesan. Bake for 25 minutes or until golden.

Yield: 6 servings

➤ Can be prepared for baking the day before.

Eggplant with Red Peppers and Capers

1 large eggplant, halved and
   cut into ½ inch batons,
   salted and drained
salt and pepper to taste
5 tablespoons olive oil
2 onions, quartered

2 garlic cloves, minced
3 red peppers, julienne
1 pound canned plum
   tomatoes, crushed
1 tablespoon red wine vinegar
2 tablespoons capers

Preheat the oven to 400°F.

On a rimmed baking sheet, pour 3 tablespoons of olive oil. Dip the eggplant into the oil, coating each side, and arrange neatly. Bake for 15 minutes, or until lightly browned and tender.

In a skillet, heat the remaining oil, and sauté the onion until it starts to turn golden. Add the garlic, and sauté for about 1 minute. Add the peppers, and sauté until soft, but not brown. Stir in the eggplant, tomatoes, and vinegar, and simmer, covered, until the eggplant is tender and the liquid has evaporated—about 45 minutes. Stir in the capers, and correct the seasoning with salt and pepper.

Yield: 6 servings

➤ Can be prepared the day before and reheated.

Melanzane di Lecce
(Baked Eggplant with Tomato and Romano)

This is a delicious main-course casserole that can be served in smaller portions as a vegetable. Serve any leftovers at room temperature as an antipasto, or chop the mixture finely and serve with crackers or red and green pepper slices as an hors d'oeuvre.

1 cup minced onion
2 tablespoons olive oil
¼ cup minced basil
1 garlic clove, minced
28 ounce can crushed
   tomatoes with purée
salt and pepper to taste

2 pounds eggplant, ¼ inch
   slices, salted and drained
flour
olive oil
2 tablespoons olive oil
1 large onion, thinly sliced
¾ cup shredded basil leaves
2 cups grated Romano

Preheat the oven to 375°F.

In a saucepan, over very low heat, stew the onions in 2 tablespoons of olive oil until very tender and just turning golden. Add the basil and garlic, raise the heat to medium, and cook 3 minutes. Add the tomatoes, and simmer until thickened. Season with salt and pepper, and set aside. Pat the eggplant slices dry.

In a bowl, season the flour with salt and pepper. Dredge the eggplant in flour, and shake off the excess.

In a skillet, heat ¼ inch olive oil, and fry the eggplant, in batches, until golden on both sides. Drain on paper towels. Pour off all but 2 tablespoons of oil in the skillet, or add oil to make 2 tablespoons, and sauté the onion until golden. Spread ¼ of the sauce in an 8 inch baking dish, and top with a layer of eggplant, ⅓ of the onion, another ¼ of sauce, and ⅓ of the basil and ⅓ of the Romano. Repeat twice, ending with the Romano. Bake 30 minutes, or until bubbling and lightly browned. Let stand 10 minutes before serving.

Yield: 6 generous servings

➤ Can be prepared the day before and served at room temperature.

NOTE: The leftover possibilities of a dish of this sort seem to be endless. Use it as a filling for an omelet, or a bed for poached eggs. Stuff tomatoes, zucchini, or peppers with the mixture for a different vegetable course.

Aubergines Niçoises (Baked Eggplant Niçoise Style)

1½ pounds eggplant, peeled, cut into ¼ inch thick slices, salted, and drained.
olive oil
salt and pepper to taste
1 cup grated Parmesan cheese

⅔ cup heavy cream
4 to 6 tomatoes, peeled and sliced
½ cup fresh bread crumbs
2 tablespoons butter

Preheat the oven to 375°F. Pat the eggplant slices dry.
In a large skillet, heat ¼ inch of oil until very hot, and brown the eggplant on both sides. Drain the slices in a colander.
Place a layer of slices in the bottom of a deep casserole (a soufflé dish will do), and season with salt and pepper. Sprinkle with the cheese and some cream. Add a layer of tomatoes, season with pepper, and sprinkle with cheese and cream. Continue filling the casserole, ending with the cream. Sprinkle the bread crumbs over the top, and dot with butter. Bake for 45 minutes, or until bubbling hot and golden.

Yield: 6 servings

➤ Can be prepared for baking the day before. Serve hot or at room temperature.

Timballo di Melanzane (Eggplant Timbale)

There are many versions of layers of eggplant baked with various ingredients. This is a particularly fine main course for brunch, lunch, or supper.

3 pounds eggplant, sliced
salt and pepper to taste
flour
olive oil
¼ pound prosciutto, thinly sliced

½ pound Scamorza, thinly sliced
4 tablespoons butter
4 to 6 eggs

Preheat the oven to 375°F. Butter a 2 quart baking dish.

Sprinkle the eggplant slices with salt, and let drain in a colander for 1 hour. Rinse under cold water, and wipe dry. Dust the slices with flour, and fry in 1 inch of olive oil until golden on both sides. Drain on paper toweling.

Arrange a layer of eggplant in the bottom of the baking dish, and top with a layer of ham and another layer of cheese. Continue filling the dish, finishing with eggplant. Melt the butter, and pour over the eggplant. Bake for 14 minutes.

In a bowl, beat the eggs, and season with salt and pepper. Pour the eggs over the eggplant, and bake for 15 minutes longer, or until the eggs are set.

Yield: 6 servings

➤ Can be prepared for baking several hours ahead.

Charlotte d'Aubergines (Eggplant Mold)

1½ pounds eggplant, cut into ½ inch slices, salted, and drained	2 pounds tomatoes, peeled, seeded, and chopped
½ cup olive oil	salt and pepper to taste
¾ cup minced onion	1 cup yogurt
1 garlic clove, crushed	½ cup chicken stock

Preheat the oven to 350°F. Rinse the eggplant under cold water, drain, and pat dry.

In a saucepan, heat 2 tablespoons of oil, and sauté the onion until golden. Add the garlic, tomatoes, salt, and pepper, and simmer, stirring, until the mixture is thick and pulpy—about 20 to 25 minutes. In a skillet, heat the remaining oil until very hot, and sauté the eggplant slices until golden on both sides.

Arrange a layer of eggplant in the bottom of a charlotte mold, or a soufflé dish. Spread with a little tomato and yogurt. Continue making layers, ending with eggplant. Add the chicken stock to the remaining tomato mixture, and set aside.

Cover the mold, and bake for 40 to 50 minutes, or until bubbling hot and tender. Let cool in the mold for 10 minutes, and unmold. Reheat the sauce, and spoon over the mold.

Yield: 6 servings

➤ Can be prepared for baking the day before.

Papeton d'Aubergines (Eggplant Custards)

This dish was prepared originally for one of the Avignon popes in the fourteenth century.

2 pounds eggplant, peeled, cut into ½ inch slices, salted, and drained
¾ to 1 cup olive oil
2 garlic cloves, minced
6 eggs
1 cup heavy cream

1 cup minced onion
3 garlic cloves, minced
1½ pounds tomatoes, cut into chunks
pinch of sugar
3 tablespoons minced basil
1 tablespoon of butter

Preheat the oven to 375°F. Butter a 2½ quart mold, or 8 individual ramekins. Save a few strips of eggplant skin for garnish, if desired.

Drain the eggplant, rinse under cold water, drain again, and pat dry. In a large skillet, heat ¼ inch of the oil until very hot, and sauté the eggplant until brown on both sides. Drain the slices in a colander. Add fresh oil, as needed.

If you wish to use the eggplant skin for a garnish, blanch in boiling water until tender—about 3 minutes. Drain, rinse under cold water, and drain again. Cut the skin into fine strips, flowers, or other patterns, and place skin side down in the bottom and up the sides of the mold.

In a food processor, purée the eggplant and garlic. Add the eggs and cream, and mix well. Season with salt and pepper. Pour into the mold, and cover with a sheet of buttered foil or parchment paper. Place the mold in a cake tin, and add 1 inch of boiling water. Bake for 40 to 50 minutes, or until a knife inserted halfway between the center and the edge comes out clean. Let stand for 15 minutes before unmolding. Unmold onto a heated platter, and serve coated with the sauce.

In a saucepan, sauté the onion in 3 tablespoons of olive oil for 2 minutes. Add the garlic, and cook 1 minute. Add the tomatoes, cover, and cook 10 minutes. Correct the seasoning with salt and pepper.

In a processor, purée the sauce, and strain into the saucepan. Add the basil and butter, and reheat.

Yield: 6 to 8 servings

➤ The mold can be prepared for baking hours ahead. The sauce can be prepared the day before.

Pork and Eggplant Garlic Sauce

¾ pound pork loin, cut in
  julienne
1 tablespoon dry sherry
½ egg white
pinch of salt
1 tablespoon cornstarch
5 tablespoons chicken stock
2½ tablespoons soy sauce
1½ tablespoons vinegar
1½ tablespoons sugar
1 tablespoon cornstarch
1 tablespoon water
1 tablespoon chili paste with
  garlic

1 tablespoon dry sherry
4 cups vegetable oil
¾ pound eggplant, peeled and
  cut into batons
1 tablespoon vegetable oil
½ cup julienned green pepper
½ cup julienned red pepper
1 tablespoon minced ginger
1 teaspoon minced garlic
⅓ cup sliced scallion
½ teaspoon sesame oil

In a bowl, mix the pork, sherry, egg white, and salt until foamy. Stir in the tablespoon of cornstarch, and mix until smooth. Cover, and refrigerate for 1 hour. In another bowl, mix the chicken stock, soy sauce, vinegar, sugar, cornstarch, water, chili paste with garlic, and sherry.

In a wok, heat the 4 cups of peanut oil to 375°F, and fry the eggplant until lightly colored. Drain. Let the oil cool to 280°F. Add the pork, and stir constantly until the pieces separate. Cook 1 minute longer. Drain. Drain off all but 1 tablespoon of oil from the wok. Heat the wok, and stir-fry the green pepper, red pepper, ginger, and garlic for 30 seconds. Add the eggplant and pork. Stir the sauce mixture, and add to the wok. Cook, stirring, until thickened—about 1 minute. Stir in the scallion, and then the sesame oil.

Yield: 6 servings

➤ The pork, sauce, and eggplant can be prepared several hours ahead. Do not finish until ready to serve.

NOTE: To measure half an egg white, pour white into a bowl and whisk until foamy, and discard half or save for another use.

Spicy Lamb with Eggplant Szechuan

1 tablespoon cornstarch
2 tablespoons cold water
½ pound eggplant, peeled and
  cut into ¼ inch cubes
½ cup oil
½ pound ground lamb, beef,
  or pork
1 tablespoon chili paste with
  garlic
1 tablespoon soy sauce

1 teaspoon sugar
2 tablespoons minced ginger
2 tablespoons minced garlic
½ cup chicken stock
⅓ cup minced scallions
1 tablespoon powdered
  Szechuan pepper
1 tablespoons sesame oil
¼ cup minced coriander

In a small bowl, mix the cornstarch with the water, and add to the dish. In a wok, heat ¼ cup oil, and heat until almost smoking. Add the eggplant, and stir-fry until golden. Drain.

In a bowl, mix the lamb, chili paste with garlic, soy sauce, and sugar. In the wok, heat the remaining oil, and stir-fry the lamb, breaking it up until it loses its color. Add the ginger and garlic, and cook 30 seconds. Add the stock, and cook, stirring, for 1 minute. Add the eggplant, scallions, and peppercorn powder. Stir in the cornstarch mixture, and when thickened, stir in the sesame oil. Arrange on a platter, and sprinkle with the coriander.

Yield: 4 to 6 servings

➤ Cannot be prepared ahead.

Hot Garlic Eggplant

This is another version of spicy eggplant Chinese style.

⅓ pound ground pork
2 teaspoons dark soy sauce
1½ pounds eggplant, trimmed
1 onion, ½ inch cubes
¼ cup sherry
3 tablespoons oyster sauce
1 tablespoon dark soy sauce
2 teaspoons sesame oil

1 teaspoon sugar
3 tablespoon peanut oil
10 garlic cloves, minced
1 tablespoon chili paste with garlic
½ teaspoon minced ginger
chicken stock (optional)

In a bowl, mix the pork and 2 teaspoons dark soy sauce together, and set aside.

Quarter each eggplant lengthwise, and cut into ⅓-inch-thick slices. Transfer to a bowl, and mix in the onion.

In another bowl, mix the sherry, oyster sauce, remaining tablespoon of soy, sesame oil, and sugar, and set aside.

In a wok, heat the oil, and stir-fry the garlic, chili paste, and ginger for 30 seconds. Add the pork, and stir-fry until pork loses its raw color. Add the eggplant mixture, and stir in the sauce. The liquid should half cover the ingredients; if necessary, add more sherry. Cover, and cook over high heat until the eggplant softens—about 3 minutes. If the mixture is dry, add chicken stock. Cook uncovered until most of the sauce evaporates.

Yield: 4 to 6 servings

➤ Cannot be prepared ahead.

Cold Eggplant Provençale

As with so many dishes from Provence, this requires long, slow cooking for the flavors to meld, but the real work is a matter of moments, and once it is set to bake, you can do other things.

1½ pounds eggplant, cut into
   ½ inch slices, salted, and
   drained
1 cup minced parsley
2 large onions, thinly sliced
5 tomatoes, peeled and sliced
2 garlic cloves, minced
2 celery hearts, minced

2 teaspoons currants
1 tablespoon minced basil
1 teaspoon crushed
   peppercorns
1 teaspoon minced capers
salt and pepper to taste
1 cup olive oil
lemon wedges

Preheat the oven to 300°F.

Rinse the eggplant slices under cold water, drain, and pat dry. In an 11 by 15 inch baking dish, arrange half the eggplant slices, and sprinkle with half the parsley.

Spread the onions, tomatoes, garlic, celery, currants, basil, peppercorns, capers, and salt and pepper on top. Sprinkle with the remaining parsley, and cover with the remaining eggplant. Drizzle the olive oil over the top. Cover, and bake for 4 hours. Remove the cover, stir, and bake 1 hour longer. Cool.

Serve with the lemon wedges.

Yield: 6 servings

➤ Can be prepared a day ahead.

Grilled Eggplant Salad

This is a recipe where the quality of the olive oil is important. Plan to use an extra virgin oil in the dressing and on the bread. A less expensive oil will do for the eggplant.

2 shallots, minced
1 tablespoon balsamic vinegar
1 tablespoon red wine vinegar
⅔ cup olive oil
salt and pepper
2 pounds eggplant, ¼ inch
   slices

4 slices crusty bread
1 red pepper, peeled and
   chopped
24 black olives
¼ cup shredded basil leaves
1 clove garlic, halved

In a bowl, marinate the shallots in the balsamic vinegar and red wine vinegar for 10 minutes. Whisk in half the olive oil, salt, and pepper, and set vinaigrette aside.

Brush the eggplant and bread slices with the olive oil. Grill the eggplant over a hot fire until browned. Arrange the eggplant on a platter, and drizzle with vinaigrette. Garnish the eggplant with the pepper, olives, and basil.

Grill the bread until golden and crisp. Rub the bread with the garlic halves, and serve with the salad.

Yield: 6 servings

➤ Can be prepared several hours ahead, but it is best if not refrigerated.

Roasted Eggplant, Pepper, and Goat Cheese Salad

Clearly the secret to this salad is the roasted flavors. To peel the peppers, roast them (see page 373).

6 small Japanese eggplants, cut into ½ inch slices lengthwise
olive oil
1 red pepper, peeled and cut into strips
1 yellow pepper, peeled and cut into strips

4 thin slices red onion, separated into rings
¼ pound Chèvre, crumbled
2 tablespoons sherry vinegar
6 tablespoons extra virgin olive oil
1 tablespoon minced thyme
salt and pepper to taste
2 tablespoons minced parsley

Heat the grill. Brush the eggplants with olive oil, and grill until tender and lightly browned, turning once. Cool.

In a bowl, or on a platter, arrange the eggplant, peppers, and onions. Crumble the cheese over the top.

In another bowl, whisk the vinegar, olive oil, thyme, salt, and pepper until they emulsify, and pour over the vegetables. Sprinkle with the parsley.

Yield: 6 servings

➤ Can be prepared early in the day. Best if not refrigerated.

NOTE: The small, pale-purple Japanese eggplants are preferred, but use any eggplant, cut into ½-inch-thick slices, if necessary.

Melanzane alla Siciliana (Sicilian Eggplant Salad)

3 medium eggplants
½ cup olive oil
¼ cup red wine vinegar
3 tablespoons minced parsley

3 garlic cloves, minced
½ teaspoon dried oregano
salt and pepper to taste

Preheat the oven to 450°F.

Pierce the eggplants with the tines of a fork all over. Place in a lightly oiled baking pan, and bake for 14 minutes, turning often, until they feel tender. Remove from the oven, and peel.

Wrap each eggplant in clean toweling, and squeeze out as much moisture as possible. Cut the eggplant into cubes, and place in a bowl.

In a small bowl, whisk the oil, vinegar, parsley, garlic, oregano, and salt and pepper. Pour over the eggplant cubes, toss to coat evenly, and let marinate for at least 1 hour.

Yield: 6 servings

➤ Can be prepared the day before.

Chinese Eggplant Salad

1½ pounds small eggplants, halved	¼ cup sesame oil
3 tablespoons soy sauce	1 tablespoon shredded scallion
½ teaspoon salt	1 tablespoon shredded gingeroot

Oil a heatproof plate, and place in the top of a steamer. Place the eggplants, cut side down, on the plates, and steam for 30 minutes, or until tender. Cool, and discard the skin. Tear into shreds, lengthwise. In a bowl, mix the soy sauce, salt, and eggplant.

In a skillet, over high heat, heat the sesame oil, and stir-fry the scallion and ginger for 10 seconds. Pour the hot oil over the eggplant, stir, and let cool.

Serve at room temperature.

Yield: 6 servings

➤ Can be prepared the day before.

Variation:

Instead of the sauce above, steam the eggplant, and toss with a sauce of 1 tablespoon soy sauce, 1 tablespoon sesame oil, 2 teaspoons rice vinegar, 1 teaspoon sugar, and a pinch of cayenne pepper.

Melanzane con Prosciutto e Bel Paese
(Eggplant with Prosciutto and Bel Paese)

2 pounds eggplant, peeled and cut into ¾ inch thick slices lengthwise	4 ounces thinly sliced prosciutto
¼ cup butter, melted	1 pound Bel Paese
pepper to taste	chicory or escarole leaves

Preheat the oven to 375°F.

Brush with butter a baking dish large enough to hold the eggplant slices in one layer, and brush the slices with the remaining butter. Sprinkle generously with pepper, and cover each slice with prosciutto and then cheese slices. Bake until the eggplant is tender—about 15 to 20 minutes. Arrange on a platter, and garnish with the chicory or escarole.

Yield: 6 servings

➤ Can be prepared several hours ahead. Best if not refrigerated.

Eggplant and Feta Salad

1 eggplant unpeeled, cut in 1 inch cubes

1 yellow squash cut into 1 inch cubes

1 zucchini cut into 1 inch cubes

1 red pepper, cut into 1 inch cubes

1 green pepper, cut into 1 inch cubes

1 yellow pepper, cut into 1 inch cubes

1 large onion, cut into 1 inch cubes

½ cup olive oil

black pepper

2 tablespoons minced basil

2 tablespoons minced oregano

¾ pound feta cheese, ½ inch cubes

Preheat the oven to 350°F.

In a large roasting pan, toss the eggplant, squash, zucchini, red pepper, green pepper, yellow pepper, and onion with the olive oil. Season with salt and pepper. Bake for 30 minutes, or until the vegetables are tender, stirring every 5 minutes.

Cool, stir in the basil and oregano, and correct the seasoning with the salt and pepper. Top with the feta, and mix in if desired. If the salad seems dry, drizzle with a little more of the best olive oil you can buy.

Yield: 6 servings

➤ Can be prepared the day before, but best if served at room temperature.

Endive

Belgian endive, also called endive, chicory, or witloof, should not be confused with the other greens called endive or chicory. Endive is the shoot of the witloof root, which is grown in darkness to produce compact heads with almost pure white leaves with just a tinge of pale yellowish-green around the edges. The heads are 3 to 4 inches long and 1 to 1½ inches in diameter. Chicory and endive are larger curly-leafed greens that look much more like a lettuce and have a deeper green color, although the stalks are white. Belgian Endive is pronounced "on deeve," and endive is pronounced "end dive."

Cultivating endive requires a lot of labor. Seeds are used to grow a large leafy green that is discarded, and the resulting root is then grown in a dark cool area to produce the compact heads that we buy. To keep the endive white, they are grown under cover and some times with soil piled up around them similar to the cultivation of white asparagus. Because of the work involved, few farms in the United States grow it. Most of it is still imported from Belgium; therefore, endive is expensive. Serving braised endive as a vegetable can cost more than most vegetables, but still is affordable. Happily, the leaves separate easily to add to salads, and a disassembled head makes an attractive display for a crudites platter.

The slightly bitter taste is a luscious counterpoint to rich sauces and meats, and a foil to the sweet tartness of citrus fruits in salads.

Availabilty

Fresh
Endive is found in the markets year round, but is best from October through May. Look for crisp, firm, compact heads with creamy white leaves, with only a touch of pale green. Avoid loose heads or those with more than a few brown spots or streaks.

Store the endive in a plastic bag in the refrigerator for 2 to 3 days.

Frozen
Fresh Endive does not freeze well. Can be frozen after cooking.

Canned

Endive used to be found in fancy food shops in cans, but the canning process makes the endives watery, limp, and soggy. They should be avoided.

Preparation

In most instances endive needs no preparation. Some writers recommend cutting a conical section from the core, but I have never found this to be necessary, although it can make separating into leaves easier.

Cooking Methods

Boiling; Steaming; Microwaving

Although you can use any of these methods, they turn the endive gray, and it becomes limp and soggy.

Braising

Braising the endive in butter with a little lemon juice is the best method of cooking endive. Once it has been braised, it can be served as is, or coated with a sauce.

Quantity

Plan on one average or two small heads of endive per person. If using in a salad, one medium to large head can serve 6 or more in combination with other greens.

Sauces

The slightly bitter quality of endive is enhanced when coated with cream sauces or sprinkled with Parmesan cheese. Serve endive salads with vinaigrette or mayonnaise-based sauces.

Endives Braisées (Braised Endive)

6 to 12 Belgian endives	1 teaspoon sugar
5 tablespoons butter	salt and pepper to taste
1 tablespoon lemon juice	

In a large skillet, arrange the endive in one or two layers, dotting each layer with butter. Sprinkle with lemon juice, sugar, salt, and pepper.

Put over low heat, cover, and simmer for 45 minutes, or until tender. Reduce the juices to a glaze, and pour over the endive. If serving with a sauce, just drain and coat with the sauce.

Yield: 6 servings

➤ Can be prepared ahead and reheated.

Endives à la Créme (Braised Endives with Cream)

6 to 12 braised endives (see page 229)	1 cup heavy cream salt and pepper to taste

About 5 minutes before the braising is finished, add the cream, and simmer until lightly thickened. Correct the seasoning with salt and pepper.

Yield: 6 servings

➤ Can be prepared ahead and reheated.

Endives au Gratin

6 to 12 braised endives (see page 229)	⅓ cup grated Gruyère cheese 2 tablespoons melted butter

Preheat the broiler.
Drain the endives, and press to remove excess moisture. Arrange in a buttered baking dish in one layer, sprinkle with the cheese, and drizzle with the butter. Broil until golden.

Yield: 6 servings

➤ Can be prepared for the final browning several hours ahead.

Endives en Vinaigrette (Endive Salad)

6 Belgian Endives, braised (see above)	1 tablespoon minced scallions
½ cup olive oil	½ teaspoon Dijon mustard
⅓ cup minced parsley	¼ teaspoon dry mustard
1½ tablespoons tarragon vinegar	2-3 cooked beets, diced
	2 tablespoons minced chives

Cool the endives, cut in half, and arrange on a platter. In a bowl, whisk the olive oil, parsley, vinegar, scallions, Dijon mustard, and dry mustard. Pour over the endive, and garnish with the beets and chives.

Yield: 6 servings

➤ Can be prepared several hours ahead.

Endive à la Vinaigrette Lyonnaise
(Belgian Endive with Lyonnaise Vinaigrette)

3 tablespoons heavy cream	salt and pepper to taste
3 tablespoons white wine vinegar	½ cup walnut oil
1½ tablespoons Dijon mustard	6 Belgian endives, thinly sliced lengthwise
½ teaspoon dry mustard	3 tablespoons minced scallions

In a bowl, whisk the cream, vinegar, Dijon mustard, dry mustard, salt, and pepper, and let stand for 30 minutes. Whisk the oil into the mustard sauce.

Arrange the slivers of endive on a platter, and drizzle with the dressing. Sprinkle with the scallions.

Yield: 6 servings

➤ The dressing can be prepared the day before.

Endive, Watercress, and Beet Salad

5 heads of Belgian endive, separated into leaves
1 bunch of watercress
2 large beets, cooked, peeled, and shredded
¼ cup olive oil

2 tablespoons Dijon mustard
2 tablespoons white wine vinegar
2 garlic cloves, minced
salt and pepper to taste

Arrange the endive leaves around the edge of a platter.

Pick the leaves from the watercress, and arrange in the center of the platter.

Place the beet shreds on top of the watercress.

In a bowl, whisk the oil, mustard, vinegar, garlic, salt, and pepper until emulsified, and pour over the salad.

Yield: 6 servings

➤ Do not prepare more than 1 hour before serving.

Salade de Jambon et Endive Ravigote
(Ham and Endive Salad with Ravigote Sauce)

1¼ pounds thinly sliced ham, cut into ½ inch squares
4 large heads of Belgian endive, cut into ½ inch sections and separated
½ cup olive oil
1 tablespoon red wine vinegar

2 teaspoons Dijon mustard
salt and pepper to taste
2 tablespoons minced parsley
2 tablespoons minced onion
1 tablespoon capers
1 tablespoon minced chives
1 tablespoon minced tarragon

In a bowl, toss the ham and endive together. In a small bowl, whisk the oil, vinegar, mustard, and salt and pepper to taste. Stir in the parsley, onion, capers, chives, and tarragon. Pour over the salad, and toss gently.

Yield: 6 servings

➤ Can be prepared 1 hour before serving.

Fennel

*F*or many people fennel is a new vegetable. Until recently, unless you grew up in or lived near an Italian neighborhood you never saw or heard of fresh fennel. I first discovered it when I was a student at Columbia. I rented a room in a large apartment, and another roomer, a Florentine professor of Italian, would prepare it for her supper. One night she gave me a taste, and I was enchanted. Licorice or anise had never been a favorite flavor, but the delicate sweetness of the fennel bulb was so much better that my dislike of the flavor was dispelled.

Also called anise, fennel bulbs have become common in many markets in recent years. Fennel being originally from Italy, many of the preparations have at least an Italian accent, although the French have created recipes and use sauces that make the bulb their own. Its peak season is brief, so in the late fall, when it is in season, plan to enjoy it with all the gusto you reserve for the arrival of asparagus in the spring.

Availability

Fresh
Fennel arrives in the markets in October, and is prime through Christmas. Look for firm, white bulbs with feathery green leaves. Try to purchase the whole bulb with all the leaves attached (use the leaves as a garnish or in soups). Unfortunately, many greengrocers remove the stems to give the bulb longer shelf life and to take up less space. Avoid bulbs with brown spots, wilted leaves, or those that feel spongy rather than firm.

Frozen
Fennel does not freeze well, except as a purée.

Canned
Fennel does not can well; when canned the texture is soft and the flavor is insipid.

Preparation

Fennel requires little preparation for cooking. Cut off the stalks as close to the top of the bulb as possible. Remove all but 1/8 inch of the base, and pull off any damaged outer leaves. Cut the bulb into halves, quarters, or slices for the various preparations. If the heads are small, serve one per person.

For crudités or salads, serve raw, separated into sections and cut to the desired size.

Cooking Methods

The best method of preparing fennel is to braise or stew it in butter to concentrate its delicate flavor.

Boiling
Boiling removes much of the delicate flavor, and should be avoided.

Steaming
Fennel can be steamed over boiling water for about 15 to 20 minutes, or until tender-crisp, but it will not have as much flavor as braised fennel.

Microwaving
Cook the bulbs in a covered dish with about ¼ cup of water for 8 to 10 minutes, turning once.

Quantity

One small head per person, if served whole. If the heads are large, allow 1½ pounds for 6 people.

Sauces

Butter-braised fennel goes well with cream and Mornay sauces. Season it with its own feathery leaves, or sauté with mushrooms. Citrus-flavored sauces bring out the sweetness of the fennel, as long as they are used in moderation. Tomatoes and garlic are natural partners, as they are with so many Italian dishes. Or, serve with a tablespoon or two of Hollandaise or Maltaise. Use fennel in salads with vinaigrette, especially those flavored with Dijon mustard, or orange or lemon juice.

The delicate flavor of fennel is particularly suited to fish and chicken. Chop braised fennel, season with salt and pepper, and use as a quick, easy stuffing for either.

Finocchi a la Crema *(Cream of Fennel Soup)*

2 tablespoons butter	2 cups heavy cream
1 cup minced onion	salt and pepper to taste
2 large fennel bulbs, chopped, with fronds reserved	1 tablespoon Anise-flavored liqueur (approximately)
4 cups chicken stock	

In a saucepan, melt the butter, and sauté the onion until soft, but not brown. Add the fennel, and cook, stirring, until tender—about 20 minutes. Add the chicken stock and cream, and simmer 15 minutes.

In a processor or blender, purée the soup, and strain through a fine sieve. Return to the saucepan. Correct the seasoning with the salt, pepper, and just enough liqueur to enhance the flavor without overpowering it.

Serve garnished with the reserved fronds.

Yield: 6 servings

➤ Can be prepared in advance and reheated.

Fenouil Etuvé au Beurre (Fennel Braised in Butter)

This simple method gives fennel a luscious flavor.

6 small fennel heads, trimmed
6 tablespoons butter
salt and pepper to taste

3 tablespoons minced mixed
tarragon, chervil, chives,
and parsley (optional)

In a large, covered skillet, sauté the fennel in the butter until it begins to soften. For a more intense flavor, you can brown the fennel. Season with salt and pepper, and cover.

Simmer, over low heat, until the fennel is tender, but still a little firm. Sprinkle with the herbs before serving.

Yield: 6 servings

➤ Can be prepared ahead and reheated.

NOTE: If the heads are large, quarter, halve, or slice them, and cook in the same manner.

Finocchio all'olio (Fennel Braised in Olive Oil)

6 small or 3 large heads
  fennel, cut into
  ½-inch-thick slices

⅓ cup olive oil
salt and pepper to taste

In a large skillet, arrange the slices in one or two layers. Add the oil and enough water barely to cover the fennel. Simmer uncovered for 20 to 25 minutes; or until tender. Add more water if the fennel starts to brown.

When cooked, the fennel should have absorbed all of the liquid and be a glossy pale-gold color. Correct the seasoning with salt and pepper.

Yield: 6 servings

➤ Can be prepared ahead and reheated.

Braised Fennel with Garlic

1½ pounds fennel	salt and pepper to taste
¼ cup butter	½ cup dry white wine
1 head garlic, separated into cloves, unpeeled	

Remove any tough outer stalks from the fennel, and cut into halves or quarters. Do not remove the core.

In a skillet, melt the butter, and add the fennel in a single layer with the garlic. Season with salt, and cook, uncovered, until the fennel is lightly browned, turning often—about 20 minutes. Add the wine, and simmer, covered, until the fennel is very soft and the liquid is syrupy.

Serve the fennel with the garlic, letting the guests press the garlic from the skins with their forks.

Yield: 6 servings

➤ Can be prepared ahead and reheated.

Finocchi al Forno
(Baked Fennel with Tomatoes and Garlic)

½ cup olive oil	salt and pepper to taste
1 onion, thinly sliced	¾ cup fresh bread crumbs
2 garlic cloves, chopped	½ cup grated Parmesan cheese
6 fennel, halved and cut into julienne	2 tablespoons minced parsley
	2 teaspoons grated lemon rind
¾ pound tomatoes, peeled, seeded, and chopped	1 garlic clove, minced

Preheat the oven to 425°F.

In a skillet, sauté the onion and garlic in the oil until soft, but not brown. Add the fennel, and cook, stirring occasionally, until the fennel begins to brown. Add the tomatoes, salt, and pepper, and simmer for 5 minutes longer. Transfer to a gratin or baking dish.

In a bowl, mix the bread crumbs, cheese, parsley, lemon rind, and minced garlic. Sprinkle over the fennel.

Bake for 15 minutes, or until bubbling hot and the topping is golden.

Yield: 6 servings

➤ Can be prepared for baking the day before.

Fennel in Salads

Fennel is a delicious salad ingredient. Use it wherever you would use celery and you will have a new treat. Serve fennel in its own right in much the way that you would use celery root. Cut it into fine julienne and toss with vinaigrette, rémoulade, or mayonnaise. Add julienne of fennel to coleslaw for a change. Fennel mixes well with radicchio, arugula, and mozzarella with a simple lemon-flavored vinaigrette.

Fennel and Escarole Salad

1 head escarole cut into bite-sized pieces	2 tomatoes, peeled, seeded, and cut into wedges
2 heads fennel, cut into paper-thin slices	¾ cup vinaigrette with basil

In a salad bowl, toss the escarole, fennel, and tomatoes. Pour on the vinaigrette, and toss again.

Yield: 6 servings

➤ Serve within 10 minutes of adding the vinaigrette.

Fennel and Walnut Salad

1½ pounds fennel	1 tablespoon Dijon mustard
¾ cup chopped walnuts	salt and pepper to taste
¼ cup heavy cream	1 tablespoon minced basil or tarragon
2 tablespoons lemon juice	

If there are any fennel leaves, mince enough to make ¼ cup, and set aside. Cut the bulbs into paper-thin slices, and put into a salad bowl with the walnuts.

In a small bowl, whisk the cream, lemon juice, mustard, salt, and pepper. Pour over the salad, and toss to coat evenly. Sprinkle the reserved fennel leaves and basil over the top.

Yield: 6 servings

➤ Serve within 1 hour of adding the sauce.

Fiddlehead Ferns

You do not have to be a native of Aroostook County, Maine, to know about fiddleheads, but it helps. It is only recently that this spring treasure has made its way beyond those borders into other parts of the country. The fiddleheads are the new sprouts of one of the swamp-grown ferns. The ostrich fern is the variety usually found in the markets, but locally the cinnamon fern, and the brake fern or bracken, are also eaten. The fern is picked just as the fiddle headed top appears, and before it starts to unfurl. It is usually coated with a brown or gray scale, which must be removed before eating.

To the knowledgeable, the appearance of fiddleheads is as exciting as the arrival of the first asparagus. And (as is the case with asparagus) there are others who do not understand all the fuss. The flavor of fiddleheads has been compared to asparagus, green beans, mushrooms, and artichokes. I think fiddleheads taste like fiddleheads, with a woodsy green flavor and a slightly bitter aftertaste.

Availability

Fresh
The fiddleheads appear in the market in late April and early May, and are in season for a few weeks. Look for ferns with jade-green leaves without any sign of yellowing. They should be firm, and the brown husk should be loose, if not absent. Store in a plastic bag in the refrigerator for no more than 2 days.

Frozen
Frozen fiddle heads are never as crisply tender as fresh, but can be used, especially if prepared as a gratin with a Mornay topping.

Canned
The ferns are quite popular in Canada, where they are sold in cans, but the result is soggy and unappealing.

Preparation

Trim the ends, and rub off the fuzzy brown covering, if necessary. Rinsing the ferns in a sink of cold water helps the brown covering to float to the surface for easy removal.

Cooking Methods

Boiling
Boil the ferns in boiling salted water until tender-crisp—about 15 minutes. Do not undercook.

Steaming
Steam over boiling water for about 20 to 25 minutes.

Microwaving
Place in a covered dish with ¼ cup water and cook for 5 to 8 minutes, turning occasionally.

Quantity

Allow 1½ pounds of fiddleheads for 6 persons.

Sauces

Ferns are treated like asparagus. Serve them with the same sauces: Hollandaise for hot fiddleheads, and a mustard vinaigrette are two favorites. Fiddleheads can be cooked alla Trifolati, or alla Parmigiana.

Gratin of Fiddleheads

¼ cup bread crumbs	½ cup grated Parmesan cheese
1½ pounds fiddleheads, blanched until tender-crisp and drained	salt and pepper to taste
	1 tablespoon olive oil
	2 tablespoons minced parsley
1 cup light cream	2 garlic cloves, minced
3 eggs	1 tablespoon minced shallot
1 egg yolk	

Preheat the oven to 350°F. Butter a 2 quart oval gratin dish, and sprinkle with 2 tablespoons bread crumbs. Dry the fiddleheads on paper toweling, and place in the gratin.

In a bowl, mix the cream, eggs, egg yolk, ¼ cup Parmesan, salt, and pepper. Pour over the fiddleheads, and bake for 14 to 18 minutes, or until almost set.

In a small skillet, heat the olive oil, and sauté the remaining bread crumbs, parsley, garlic, and shallots until fragrant—about 1 minute. Sprinkle over the gratin, and bake 5 minutes longer. Sprinkle the remaining Parmesan over the top, and brown under a broiler.

Yield: 6 servings

➤ Can be prepared for baking several hours ahead.

Sautéed Fiddleheads and Mushrooms in Cream

¼ cup butter
2 tablespoons minced shallots
1 pound fiddleheads,
  blanched and refreshed

½ pound thickly sliced
  mushrooms
½ cup heavy cream
salt and pepper to taste

In a skillet, melt the butter and sauté the shallots until soft, but not brown. Add the fiddleheads, and cook for 3 minutes. Add the mushrooms, and cook, stirring often, until the liquid evaporates. Add the cream, and simmer until lightly thickened. Correct the seasoning with salt and pepper.

Yield: 6 servings

➤ Best if cooked just before serving.

Variations:

Add ¼ pound smoked ham, cut into julienne, with the cream.
Omit the cream, and add ½ cup grated Romano cheese.

Fiddlehead and Ramp Salad

Ramps are a form of wild garlic grown principally in Western Virginia, but are found as far north as Maine.

1 pound fiddleheads,
  blanched until tender, and
  refreshed
½ pound ramps, sliced and
  blanched for 1 minute
¼ cup heavy cream

¼ cup olive oil
3 tablespoons white-wine
  vinegar
2 tablespoons Dijon mustard
salt and pepper to taste

In a salad bowl, toss the fiddle heads and ramps. In a small bowl, whisk the cream, olive oil, vinegar, mustard, salt, and pepper. Pour over the salad, and toss gently.

Yield: 6 servings

➤ Can be prepared 1 hour before serving.

Greens

Greens is a grouping of leafy vegetables that includes dandelion, collards, mustard, and turnip greens. Some writers include beet greens, broccoli di rabe, kale, spinach, and Swiss chard as well. However, their flavor is less assertive, and I have chosen to write of them separately. Greens may not be part of your regular diet, but do consider them as a luscious, full-flavored option to the potato and carrot regimen.

When I was a child, my father would happily dig the dandelions from the neighbors' lawns so he could boil them to eat with olive oil and a lot of vinegar. He claimed it was a tonic. I found the sharp flavor disagreeable. A number of years later, while in Paris one January, I had the salad, *Pissenlit au lard*, and finally understood what father meant. In January or February, while in the midst of winter doldrums, I search the markets for the earliest dandelions in order to prepare that salad and dream of spring and summer. The blizzard may rage, but I know that there is hope for the future.

It is very possible that you have never tasted these greens. Many of us go for years without enjoying the delicious flavors of dandelion, collard, mustard, or turnip greens. To many Northerners, the mention of collard, mustard, or turnip greens brings vague recollections of poor Southerners who eat greens with "pot likker." However, those with more cooking knowledge or greater familiarity with Eastern cultures know that they are common to Asian home cooking, though not often found on restaurant menus. I live near the Asian community in Boston, and at one time there was a city block available for neighborhood gardens. My neighbors would plant in early spring, and within weeks, it seemed, they would reap the results with the first greens. All summer and through the fall they would harvest huge arm loads to feed their families. The incredibly healthy collards, mustard, kale, and turnip greens were high on the list.

Availability

Fresh
Dandelion greens are available in the early spring through May, and then disappear from the market. The later dandelion becomes too bitter. Select fresh-looking, deep-green leaves with white or cream colored stems. Avoid wilted or yellowed leaves.

Collard greens are available year round, but are most prevalent in the late fall. They have large flat leaves with a thick stem. Look for leaves that are firm and not wilted or limp. Avoid yellowish or wilted leaves.

Mustard leaves are available year round but mostly in the late fall. Look for leaves with a bright, yellow-green color with a crisp, crinkly texture. Avoid yellowed wilted leaves.

Turnip greens are also available year round, with the largest amount coming to the market in early winter. The leaves should be firm, with grayish-green leaves, without yellowing or wilted stalks.

Frozen
In some areas of the country, frozen collard, mustard, and turnip greens are readily available. Because greens freeze well, they can readily be substituted for fresh.

Canned
Canning turns the crisp, firm texture of greens into a limp watery vegetable that is not appealing.

Preparation

Greens, especially mustard greens, need to be washed in lukewarm water to relax the leaves in order to release any grit caught in the folds.

Dandelions are tender enough to use, but the other greens need to have the tough stalks removed: fold the leaf so the insides are together and the back of the stalk is exposed. Grasping the stalk, lift it toward the top of the leaf.

Before adding the greens to other ingredients, it is wise to blanch them in boiling salted water to remove some of the bitterness, or they can "bitter" an entire dish.

Cooking Methods

Greens are cooked in many of the same ways as beet greens, broccoli di rabe, spinach, and Swiss chard. Check those recipes for ideas to give greater variety.

Boiling
You can boil the greens in boiling salted water until tender (especially dandelion greens), but the others are best if cooked in a bouillon. The exception to this is soup. The greens make a wonderful addition to soups with multiple ingredients. Use one or another in place of kale in Portuguese Kale Soup, for instance, or add to any soup with a variety of greens. Because greens take longer to cook, if adding to lettuce soups, add the greens first, and when almost tender, add the lettuce, to avoid overcooking it.

Bouillon *(Pot Likker)*

In a large kettle, bring 2 ham hocks and 3 quarts of water to a full roll-ing boil. Add the greens, and cook until tender but not overcooked—about 10 to 25 minutes, depending on the green. Taste every few minutes. To enhance the flavor of the bouillon, add a sliced onion and/or red pepper flakes to taste. Drain the greens, saving the broth for soups, if desired, and serve, or finish cooking by sautéing.

Steaming

Greens can be steamed over boiling water until tender, but their flavor is truly enhanced by cooking in the bouillon.

Microwaving

Cook the greens in ½ cup water in a covered dish for 6 to 10 minutes. Again the flavor of the bouillon is missing.

Braising

After draining the bouillon, put the greens into a skillet with some but-ter or olive oil and a clove of garlic, and cook, covered, for about 10 minutes, until most of the liquid has evaporated and the greens are permeated with the flavors.

Quantity

Greens lose about 50% of their weight when the stems are removed, and then the leaves shrink by at least 50% when they are cooked. Plan on at least 3 to 4 quarts for 6 persons, before trimming and cooking.

Sauces

Greens and traditional sauces are not usually thought of together, but because greens can be treated in the same ways as spinach, you can coat them with cream or Mornay sauce and serve as a gratin, or coat with garlic or shallot butter. These greens, with the exception of young dandelion leaves, are not eaten raw, and therefore vinaigrette is not appropriate.

Decorative

Over the years I have treasured the leaves of greens not just as edibles, but also as floral decorations. The leaves make attractive replacements for the usual paper doily on serving platters for deep-fried foods, and curly mustard leaves make an attractive ruching around a roast.

Spring Green Soup

2 tablespoons butter
1 cup chopped onion
¾ pound potatoes, thinly sliced
1 tablespoon flour
12 cups chopped dandelion
½ medium head romaine,
   chopped
3 cups shredded sorrel or
   spinach leaves

1 tablespoon lemon juice
1 garlic clove, halved
1 teaspoon salt
5 cups water
1 or 2 teaspoons sugar
   (optional)
½ cup heavy cream
4 scallions, thinly sliced

In a large pot, melt the butter, and sauté the onions and potatoes until they start to turn golden—about 15 minutes. Sprinkle with the flour, and stir. In batches, stir in the dandelion, romaine, and sorrel or spinach. Stir in the lemon juice, garlic, salt, and water. Simmer until tender—about 45 minutes. Strain the soup, reserving the solids and the liquid. In a processor, purée the solids, and return to the pot with the liquid. Reheat, and correct the seasoning with salt and pepper, and pinch of sugar, if too bitter. Whip the cream to stiff peaks, and serve each portion with a dollop of cream and a sprinkling of scallions.

Yield: 6 servings

➤ Can be prepared ahead and frozen.

Pissenlit au Lard (Dandelion Salad with Bacon)

This is my favorite spring salad. A large bowl makes a perfect lunch. The long, thin loaf called a ficelle, with a crisp crust, is best for the crust, but any crusty bread can be used.

1 clove garlic, halved
1 12 inch section thin French
   bread
½ cup olive oil
6 cups dandelion greens, cut
   into bite-sized pieces

¼ pound thick-sliced bacon,
   diced
¼ cup white wine vinegar
salt and pepper to taste

Preheat the oven to 375°F.
Rub the crust of bread with the halves of garlic. Cut the bread into 1 inch cubes. In a bowl, toss the bread cubes with the olive oil to coat evenly.
Place the cubes in one layer on a baking sheet, and bake until golden—about 10 minutes. In a large salad bowl, combine the dandelions and the croutons.
In a small skillet, sauté the bacon until crisp. Remove the cracklings from the pan. Add the vinegar to the hot fat, and pour over the dandelion. Put a lid on the salad, and let it sit for 2 minutes. Remove the lid, and add the cracklings, salt, and pepper. Toss gently.

Yield: 6 servings

➤ The bread can be prepared ahead and the bacon fried. Reheat the fat just before adding to the salad.

Salade de Mouraillons *(Hot Dandelion Salad)*

Only in very recent years have warm salads met with any acceptance in America. Although in France and Germany these have long been popular, in America the feeling was and often is, unfortunately, that salads must be frigid. Warming the ingredients brings out the flavor.

2 teaspoons olive oil	½ cup heavy cream
¼ pound thick-sliced bacon, diced	salt and pepper to taste
1 tablespoon vinegar	6 cups dandelions, cut into bite-sized pieces

In a skillet, heat the oil, and fry the bacon until crisp. Add the vinegar to the skillet, and remove from the heat. Stir in the cream, and season with salt and pepper. Pour over the dandelions, and serve.

Yield: 6 servings

➤ The dressing can be prepared ahead and reheated.

Salade de Nevers *(Dandelion Salad)*

2 tablespoons oil	salt and pepper to taste
3 garlic cloves	6 cups dandelion greens,
3 slices bread, ½ inch cubes	cleaned and dried
1 cup salt pork, ¼ inch dice	2 tablespoons minced parsley
3 tablespoons wine vinegar	or chives
1 tablespoon Dijon mustard	4 hard cooked eggs, quartered
2 tablespoons Roquefort cheese	

In a skillet, heat 1 tablespoon of oil, and sauté the garlic cloves until golden, but not burned. Remove and discard. Add the bread cubes to the oil, and sauté until golden on all sides. Set aside on paper toweling.

In the skillet, heat the remaining tablespoon of oil, and sauté the pork until crisp and dark brown. Leave in the pan.

In a salad bowl, mix the vinegar, mustard, and Roquefort cheese to a paste, and season with salt and pepper. Add the dandelion, warm pork cracklings with its fat, and the bread cubes, and toss gently. Sprinkle with the chives, and serve garnished with the hard-cooked eggs.

Serve immediately.

Yield: 6 servings

➤ The bread cubes can be prepared the day before and reheated in a warm oven. The pork can be rendered ahead and reheated. Do not toss the salad until just before serving.

NOTE: The ubiquitous hard-cooked eggs can be omitted, unless the salad is a main course.

Collard Greens with Smoked Pork Chops

If smoked pork chops are not available, substitute Canadian bacon or a ham slice.

2 tablespoons olive oil
1 onion, thinly sliced
4 pounds collard greens, stems
   removed and chopped

1 cup chicken stock
½ pound smoked pork chop,
   cut into julienne
salt and pepper to taste

In a saucepan, heat the oil, and sauté the onion until soft, but not brown. Add the collard greens, and stir until coated with the oil. Add the stock, and simmer until the collards are very tender and no longer taste bitter—about 25 minutes. Stir in the pork chop, and simmer 5 minutes. Correct the seasoning with salt and pepper.

Yield: 6 servings

➤ Can be prepared ahead and reheated.

Creamed Mustard Greens

¼ cup minced shallots
2 garlic cloves, minced
¼ cup butter
4 pounds mustard greens,
   stems removed and chopped

salt and pepper to taste
2 cups heavy cream
nutmeg to taste

In a large saucepan, sauté the shallots and garlic in the butter until soft, but not brown. Stir in the mustard greens, and cook, stirring, until wilted. Cover, and simmer until most of the liquid has evaporated—about 15 minutes. Season with salt and pepper, and stir in the cream. Simmer another 10 minutes, or until the cream is thickened. Correct the seasoning with salt, pepper, and nutmeg.

Yield: 6 servings

➤ Can be prepared ahead and reheated.

Jerusalem Artichokes

*J*erusalem artichokes, tubers of the sunflower family, are unrelated to globe artichokes. The name derives from the Italian name for sunflower, *girasole*, meaning turn to the sun. It is one of the many truly American vegetables. It was cultivated by the Indians of North and South America. In the seventeenth century this curious vegetable arrived in France at the same time as members of an Indian tribe called Topinambour, and thus got its French name. The vegetable has also been called Canadian potatoes. The French sometimes call it Canadian artichokes, or even "pears of the earth."

Whatever you call them, Jerusalem artichokes are a delicately flavored tuber with a texture akin to water chestnuts. They have a delicate light brown skin and a tendency to turn dark when left in the air. Have a bowl of acidulated water on hand to hold them as soon as they are peeled or sliced. Fortunately, the thin skin is edible and does not always need to be peeled. The Jerusalem artichokes that appear in the markets are often very knobby, and peeling is tedious.

Availability

Fresh

The prime season is November and December. The artichokes appear in the market through the spring. Look for large, smooth, round tubers with as few protrusions as possible, to make peeling easier. They should be firm, with no soft spots or bruises, and feel heavy for their size.

Store Jerusalem artichokes in the vegetable drawer, or a perforated plastic bag, for no more than 2 or 3 days. They do not store well.

Frozen

Because freezing turns the artichokes black, they should not be frozen.

Canned

Canning destroys the texture, and makes them mushy and unappealing.

Preparation

For many recipes, all that is needed is a good scrubbing with a vegetable brush to remove any soil. The skins are edible and can be left on. In those preparations where the skin needs to be removed, use a vegetable peeler to peel off the thin layer of skin, and immediately put the artichokes into acidulated water until ready to cook.

Cooking Methods

Jerusalem artichokes, if peeled, should be cooked *a blanc* (see page 6) to keep them white.

Boiling
Cook in boiling salted water, peeled or unpeeled, until tender-crisp—anywhere from 10 to 30 minutes, depending on the size. Take care to test them as they cook, and remove as soon as done. Jerusalem artichokes turn from under-cooked to over-cooked rapidly. Attempt to get artichokes that are roughly the same size. If they are different sizes, peel, cut to a uniform size, and cook them *a blanc*. If boiled with the skins on, run under cold water, and slip off the skins like beets.

Steaming
Place in a steamer over boiling water, and steam until just tender-crisp. Remove from the steamer when just underdone so that they do not overcook.

Microwaving
Place in a covered dish and cook for 5 to 6 minutes.

Roasting
Place whole, unpeeled Jerusalem artichokes in a casserole with a film of olive oil, 1 or 2 cloves of garlic, and salt and pepper to taste, and bake, covered, for 30 minutes at 350°F. Or, scatter around a roast beef, pork, or lamb, and let them cook in the pan juices for the same amount of time. Place the larger chokes in early and add smaller ones about 10 minutes later. If the roast is done and some of the artichokes are not, remove the roast and the cooked chokes, and let the others cook a few minutes longer, or until done.

Quantity

If the artichokes are knobby, peeling can result in a lot of waste. Plan on at least 1½ pounds of raw Jerusalem artichokes for 6 persons; if they are particularly knobby, allow 2 pounds.

Sauces

Jerusalem artichokes are called artichokes with some reason. The flavor is similar to that of globe artichokes, and thus the sauces suggested for those are suitable. Hollandaise is a particular favorite. They can also be simmered in cream and coated with Mornay. Once cooked and cooled, they can be mixed with vinaigrette in salads.

Jerusalem Artichoke and Tomato Soup

2 tablespoons butter	4 cups chicken stock
1 cup minced onion	4 garlic cloves, chopped
2 pounds Jerusalem artichokes, thinly sliced	rind of 1 small orange
1 tablespoon flour	1 tablespoon minced thyme
8 ounces canned tomatoes and their liquid	1 bay leaf
	salt and pepper to taste

In a saucepan, melt the butter, and sweat the onion and artichokes, covered, for 10 minutes. Stir in the flour, tomatoes and their liquid, chicken stock, and garlic.

In a small square of cheesecloth, tie the orange peel, thyme, and bay leaf. Add to the soup, and simmer 20 minutes, or until the artichokes are soft. Remove and discard the cheesecloth bag.

In a processor or blender, purée the soup, and return it to the saucepan. Correct the seasoning with salt and pepper, and reheat.

Yield: 6 servings

➤ Can be prepared ahead and reheated.

NOTE: If the thyme is left on its stem, the thyme, bay leaf, and orange rind can be added without the bag, and removed with a slotted spoon before the soup is puréed.

Les Topinambours à la Provençale
(Sautéed Jerusalem Artichokes Provence Style)

2 pounds Jerusalem artichokes, peeled or unpeeled, ¼-inch-thick slices	1 tablespoon minced garlic
	3 tomatoes, peeled, seeded, and chopped
3 tablespoons olive oil	2 tablespoons minced parsley
	salt and pepper to taste

In a skillet, sauté the artichokes in the oil until they start to turn golden. Add the garlic, and cook until fragrant—about 30 seconds. Add the tomatoes, parsley, salt, and pepper, and simmer over medium heat until the artichokes are tender and the tomatoes are lightly thickened. Correct the seasoning with salt and pepper.

Yield: 6 servings

➤ Can be prepared ahead and reheated, if the artichokes are not overcooked.

Les Topinambours au Cari
(Curried Jerusalem Artichokes)

2 pounds Jerusalem
  artichokes, peeled and cut
  into 1 inch dice
2 tablespoons butter
½ cup minced onion
2 tablespoons curry powder

salt and pepper to taste
½ cup milk
½ cup heavy cream
½ cup golden raisins
2 tablespoons chopped
  chutney

In a saucepan, sauté the artichokes in the butter for 2 minutes. Add the onion, and sauté until the onion is soft, but not brown. Stir in the artichokes, curry powder, salt, and pepper. Cook, stirring, for 1 minute. Add the milk, cream, raisins, and chutney. Simmer until tender-crisp—about 10 minutes longer.

Yield: 6 servings

➤ Can be prepared ahead and reheated, if undercooked, after adding the cream.

Topinambours au Beurre
(Jerusalem Artichokes in Butter)

Try to get small roundish artichokes, about the size of a walnut. If you have larger artichokes, cut them to uniform size.

2 pounds Jerusalem
  artichokes, peeled and cut
  into small balls

¼ cup butter
salt and pepper to taste

In a skillet, sauté the artichokes in the butter, shaking the pan often, until they are golden-brown on all sides and tender-crisp. Season with salt and pepper.

Yield: 6 servings

➤ Cannot be prepared ahead.

Stir-Fry of Jerusalem Artichokes

2 tablespoons vegetable oil
1 tablespoon minced ginger
1 tablespoon minced garlic
1½ pounds Jerusalem
  artichokes, peeled or
  unpeeled, thinly sliced, and
  kept in acidulated water

½ cup diced onion
½ cup diced red pepper
½ cup diced green pepper
3 tablespoons thin soy sauce
1 teaspoon sesame oil

In a wok, heat the oil, and stir-fry the ginger and garlic until fragrant—about 30 seconds. Drain the artichokes, add to the wok, and stir-fry for 2 minutes. Add the onion, and the green and red pepper, and stir-fry for another minute. Add the soy sauce, and stir for 2 minutes longer, or until the vegetables are tender-crisp. Drizzle over the sesame oil.

Yield: 6 servings

➤ Cannot be prepared ahead.

Jerusalem Artichokes Avgolemonou

2 pounds Jerusalem artichokes, peeled and cut to uniform size	1 cup water
	3 egg yolks
	3 tablespoons lemon juice
3 tablespoons butter	2 tablespoons vegetable stock

In a saucepan, sauté the artichokes in the butter until lightly browned. Add water, and simmer 15 minutes or until tender. Drain, and reserve 2 tablespoons of cooking liquid.

In a bowl, beat the egg yolks until light, and gradually beat in lemon juice and stock. Turn into the saucepan with the artichokes, and cook over low heat, stirring constantly, until lightly thickened.

Yield: 6 servings

➤ Do not prepare the sauce until just before serving.

Deep-Fried Jerusalem Artichokes

1½ pounds Jerusalem artichokes	oil for deep-frying
	salt

Pare the artichokes, and cut into very thin slices. Wash in several changes of cold water, and pat dry.

Heat the oil to 375°F and fry the artichoke slices, a handful at a time, until golden brown. Drain on paper toweling. Sprinkle with salt and serve.

Yield: 6 servings

➤ Cannot be prepared ahead.

Jerusalem Artichoke Salads

Jerusalem artichokes are good raw as well as cooked. Serve them as a salad of their own tossed in vinaigrette, or as part of a mixed salad.

Jerusalem Artichokes Vinaigrette

1½ pounds Jerusalem
   artichokes, peeled or well
   scrubbed, and cut into thin
   slices

1 cup vinaigrette
½ cup thinly sliced scallions
½ cup diced Gruyè cheese

In a bowl, toss the artichokes with the vinaigrette as soon as they
are sliced, and marinate for 3 hours. Stir in the scallions and cheese
just before serving.

Yield: 6 servings

➤ Can be prepared the day before.

Jerusalem Artichoke, Cucumber, and Radish Salad

1½ pounds Jerusalem
   artichokes, peeled or well
   scrubbed, and cut into thin
   slices

1 cup vinaigrette flavored with
   1 tablespoon minced dill
1 small cucumber, seeded and
   thinly sliced

In a bowl, marinate the artichokes and vinaigrette with the dill for
at least 2 hours. Shortly before serving, fold in the cucumbers and
radishes.

Yield: 6 servings

➤ Can be prepared the day before.

Jerusalem Artichoke and Carrot Salad

Blanch the vegetables until just tender-crisp without over- or under-
cooking, refresh under cold water, and drain again.

1 pound Jerusalem artichokes,
   peeled, thinly sliced, and
   blanched *a blanc* (see page
   6)
½ pound carrots, thinly sliced
   and blanched

1 cup vinaigrette
1 cup thinly sliced scallions
1 clove garlic, finely minced
1 tablespoon minced basil
½ to 1 cup mayonnaise

In a bowl, marinate the warm artichokes and carrots in the vinaigrette for 1 hour. Drain, fold in the scallions, garlic, basil, and enough
mayonnaise to bind.

Yield: 6 servings

➤ Can be prepared the day before.

Jicama

*R*ecently the interest in native American cookery has brought about a search for local products. Consequently, jicama, a tuber widely used in Mexican and Southwestern cookery, has gained in popularity and acceptance. Jicama, like water chestnuts and to some extent bean curd, is an interesting foil to other flavors. Its delicate flavor and crisp texture act as a counterbalance to the fire of hot chilies and the tartness of citrus fruits.

Availability

Fresh
The light-tan tubers are found in markets year round. Look for tubers that are about 2 to 3 inches in diameter; the larger versions tend to be woody. Avoid shriveled or bruised jicamas. They keep a week or longer, unwrapped, in the vegetable drawer.

Frozen
Jicama are not sold frozen.

Canned
Jicama are not canned.

Preparation

Peel the skin from the jicama, and then cut it into the desired shape.

Cooking Methods

Boiling
Cook in boiling salted water until tender-crisp, drain, and serve with a spicy tomato sauce.

Steaming
Steam over boiling water for 5 to 10 minutes, depending on the size of the pieces.

Microwaving
Cook in a covered dish for 4 to 8 minutes, depending on the size of the pieces.

Quantity

Plan on 1 pound of jicama for 6 persons.

Sauces

Jicama is usually cooked with other vegetables, rather than sauced separately.

Stir-Fried Jicama

2 tablespoons vegetable oil
1 tablespoon minced ginger
1 garlic clove, minced
1 pound jicama, peeled and
  cut into batons

¼ teaspoon red pepper flakes
4 tomatoes, peeled, seeded,
  and chopped
1 tablespoon minced coriander

In a wok, heat the oil, and stir-fry the ginger and garlic for 30 seconds. Add the jicama and pepper flakes, and stir-fry for 2 minutes. Add the tomatoes, and stir for 2 minutes longer, or until the tomatoes have wilted but still have some of their shape.

Serve sprinkled with the coriander.

Yield: 6 servings

➤ Cannot be prepared ahead.

Jicama and Orange Salad

1 pound jicama, peeled and
  thinly sliced
2 oranges
½ cup vinaigrette flavored
  with 1½ teaspoons minced
  rosemary

salt and pepper to taste
1 small head romaine lettuce,
  shredded
2 tablespoons minced
  coriander

In a bowl, place the jicama. With a zester, remove the rind from one orange, or use a vegetable peeler to remove the zest, and then cut into fine julienne, and add to the jicama.

With a sharp knife, cut the pith and rind from both oranges. With a sharp knife, cut on either side of the membrane of each orange segment, and add the segments to the jicama. Fold in the vinaigrette, and let marinate for 1 hour.

Arrange the romaine on a platter, put the jicama salad on top, and sprinkle with the coriander.

Yield: 6 servings

➤ The jicama and orange can be prepared the day before.

Kale

*K*ale, like parsnips, tastes best after it has been through a frost. If you grow it on your own, leave it in the garden and pick the outer leaves throughout the winter. The slightly bitter flavor provides a pleasant counterpoint to other winter vegetables, such as carrots, parsnips, and turnips.

Kale is also a wonderful platter decoration. Its crinkly texture and blue-green color complements many other foods. For a grand centerpiece, cover a chicken wire or styrofoam form with kale, using wooden skewers to hold the leaves in place. Skewer other vegetables and flowers on this lovely backdrop. Use hollowed cabbages as bowls to hold dips, and create a centerpiece and a crudité arrangement all in one. To prevent the kale from wilting, wrap the construction in wet paper towels until just before the guests arrive. For variety, use collard and mustard greens along with the kale.

Availability

Fresh
Found in markets from late September through May, and in some areas the year round. Look for crisp, dark, bluish-green leaves. Avoid any soft or yellowed leaves.

Store in a perforated plastic bag, or the vegetable drawer, for 2 to 3 days.

Frozen
Frozen kale is a suitable substitute for fresh.

Canned
Canned kale tends to be soggy and limp.

Preparation

Unless the leaves are very young and tender, it is best to strip the stems. Fold the inside of the leaves toward each other, exposing the stem on the back. Lift the stem toward the top of the leaf, and discard.

Kale has a strong flavor that is best removed by blanching, as with mustard or collard greens. Sauté or braise after the blanching. Kale is not as bitter as mustard greens, and can be put directly into soups without blanching.

Cooking Methods

Boiling
Boil blanched kale in boiling salted water until tender—about 15 minutes.

Steaming
Place the blanched kale on a rack over boiling water for 15 to 20 minutes, or until tender-crisp.

Microwaving
Cook the blanched kale in a covered dish for about 4 minutes.

Sautéing
Cook the blanched kale in butter or olive oil until tender.

Braising
Blanch the kale, and proceed with the recipe.

Quantity

Plan on 2 to 3 pounds of kale for 6 persons. It will seem like a lot, but it will shrink.

Sauces

Kale is cooked and sauced in the same manner as beet greens, broccoli di rabe, collards, mustard greens, spinach, and Swiss chard. Refer to those chapters for other ideas.

Portuguese Kale Soup

There are dozens of different versions of this soup. This is the simplest. Variations are listed after the recipe.

1 pound linguica, sliced	2 pounds kale, chopped
1 cup chopped onion	1 pound potatoes, sliced
2 tablespoons olive oil	salt and pepper to taste
2 quarts chicken stock	

In a kettle, sauté the linguica and onion in the oil until golden. Add the chicken stock and kale, and simmer 20 minutes. Add the potatoes, and cook until tender. Correct the seasoning with salt and pepper.

Yield: 6 servings

➤ Can be prepared ahead and reheated.

Variations:
The additions to this basic recipe are almost endless. You must have kale and you must have linguica; other than that, you can add almost anything.

Sauté 1 tablespoon minced garlic with the linguica and the onion.
Sauté ½ cup diced carrot and/or celery with the onion and linguica.
Use beef stock instead of chicken stock.
Add 1 pound of stripped spinach with the kale.
Add 3 large tomatoes, peeled, seeded, and chopped, or a 1-pound can of tomatoes and their juices with the stock.
Add 1½ cups of cooked kidney or cannellini beans with the potato.

Kale with Vinaigrette

Kale is not usually served cold, but it can be served warm with a vinaigrette.

3 pounds kale   1 hard cooked egg
½ cup vinaigrette with
   mustard

In a large kettle of boiling salted water, cook the kale until tender-crisp—about 8 minutes. Drain and chop finely.

In a bowl, toss the kale with the vinaigrette, and turn into a serving dish. Separate the yolk and the white of the egg, and sieve separately. Sprinkle the kale with the egg, and serve at room temperature.

Yield: 6 servings

➤ Can be prepared a couple of hours ahead.

NOTE: If the egg is separated before sieving, the colors will be white and yellow, if it is not it will be a pale yellow.

Ginger Kale

1 pound kale, stems removed,   1½ tablespoons minced ginger
   and blanched   2 garlic cloves, minced
2 tablespoons butter   salt and pepper to taste
1 tablespoon vegetable oil

In a large skillet, melt the butter with the oil, and sauté the ginger and garlic until fragrant—about 30 seconds. Add the kale, and cook, covered, for 10 minutes, or until tender-crisp. Correct the seasoning with salt and pepper.

Yield: 6 servings

➤ Can be prepared ahead and reheated.

Kale with Mushrooms and Mustard

1 onion, thinly sliced	1 large bunch of kale, stripped
3 tablespoons olive oil	of heavy stalks, finely
½ pound thinly sliced	chopped
mushrooms	3 tablespoons Dijon mustard
1 garlic clove, crushed	salt and pepper to taste

In a large skillet, sauté the onion in the oil until soft, but not brown. Add the mushrooms and garlic, and sauté until the mushrooms release their liquid. Add the kale, lower the heat to low, cover, and cook until the kale is tender—about 15 minutes—stirring often.

If the kale starts to stick, add a tablespoon of water. When the kale is tender, stir in the mustard, and season with salt and pepper.

Yield: 6 servings

➤ Can be prepared ahead and reheated.

Kale with Ham Hocks

¾ pound ham hocks	1 cup thinly sliced onion
(approximately)	2 tablespoons vegetable oil
3 pounds kale, stems removed	salt and pepper to taste
and chopped	

In a large kettle, simmer the ham hocks for 1 hour. Add the kale, and simmer 20 minutes, or until tender-crisp.

In a small skillet, sauté the onion in the oil until it starts to turn golden and is very soft.

Drain the kale and ham hocks. Return the kale to the pan. Remove the meat from the ham hocks, and shred. Stir in the onions, and correct the seasoning with salt and pepper.

Yield: 6 servings

➤ Can be prepared ahead and reheated.

Kale with Potatoes and Bacon

4 slices bacon, diced	salt to taste
2 tablespoons olive oil	red pepper flakes to taste
1 cup chopped onion	1 pound kale, stems removed,
2 cups potatoes cut into ½	chopped, and blanched
inch cubes	until tender-crisp, and
½ cup water	refreshed

In a skillet, render the bacon until crisp. Remove the cracklings and set aside. Drain off the fat, reserving 1 tablespoon. Rinse out the skillet, to remove the excess salt from the bacon and return it to the heat. Add the reserved fat and the olive oil.

Sauté the onion until soft, but not brown. Add the potatoes, water, salt, and red pepper flakes. Simmer until the potatoes are tender about 10 to 15 minutes. Stir in the kale and reheat. Correct the seasoning with the salt and pepper.

Serve sprinkled with the bacon cracklings.

Yield: 6 servings

➤ Can be prepared ahead and reheated.

Kohlrabi

*T*he literal translation of Kohlrabi is cabbage turnip, which is a good description of its flavor. The French name *choux rave*, cabbage root, gives a vague description of the vegetable itself. In the garden, kohlrabi looks like a visitor from outer space. A round base close to the ground with long arms supporting great fan-like leaves. It is really quite beautiful. The bulb of the kohlrabi is the swollen stem of the plant. The leaves are also edible, but they seldom appear in the markets. If there is a farm stand nearby, you may well be able to enjoy all of the plant instead of just the stem.

Kohlrabi is white, actually a pale green, or purple. The purple skin has a white interior. The vegetable is very popular in Central Europe and parts of Asia, but little known in most areas of America. Its delicate radish-like flavor when raw and subtle turnip-like flavor when cooked are worth the search.

Availability

Fresh
Look for kohlrabi from mid summer to late fall. Select small heads, no more than 2½ inches, without cracks or tough skins. Older kohlrabi is disagreeable, with more fibers than edible flesh, and a flavor reminiscent of old cabbage. If the greens are available, they should be young, and not large and yellow and tough.

Frozen
Freezing destroys the texture and darkens the color.

Canned
Canning ruins the texture of kohlrabi.

Preparation

Cut off the stem and root ends, and cook the kohlrabi with the skin on to protect the flavor. Once it is cooked, peel from the root end to remove the skin and fibrous matter under it. If serving the kohlrabi raw, peel with a small, sharp knife to remove the fibers. Because the fiber is tough and unpleasant to eat, it is necessary to remove all of it.

Cooking Methods

Treat kohlrabi leaves as you would kale or other greens. Strip out the vein, and blanch before finishing the recipe. Select from recipes for greens, including spinach and Swiss chard.

Boiling
Cook unpeeled kohlrabi in boiling salted water for about 30 minutes or until tender. Peel, and use in the recipes.

Steaming
Steam the unpeeled kohlrabi over boiling water for 30 to 35 minutes, or until tender. Peel, and use in the recipes.

Microwaving
In a covered dish with 2 tablespoons of water, cook whole unpeeled kohlrabi for 6 to 9 minutes, depending on their size. Peel, and use in the recipes.

Sautéing
If grated and salted for 30 minutes, like grated zucchini (see page 000), the kohlrabi can be sautéed without further cooking.

Quantity

Because the skin is so thick, you need 2 pounds for 6 persons to account for the waste, or select one or two bulbs per person.

Sauces

Serve kohlrabi with the same sauces you would use for carrots, turnips, and other root vegetables. Serve it raw, sliced, or grated, with vinaigrette or mayonnaise. Serve it hot with butter flavored with a favorite herb such as tarragon or dill; or in cream, whether fresh cream, sour cream, or cream sauce. Serve it with cheese sauce, or tossed with cheese, or mixed with garlic. Remember that the flavor of kohlrabi is delicate, so avoid sauces with too much character.

Choux-Raves Braisés (Braised Kohlrabi)

¼ cup butter	1½ pounds kohlrabi, peeled
¼ cup minced celery	and sliced
¼ cup minced carrot	1 cup chicken stock
¼ cup minced onion	salt and pepper to taste

In a saucepan, melt the butter, and sauté the celery, carrot, and onion until they start to turn golden. Add the kohlrabi, and cook, stirring occasionally, for 5 minutes. Add the chicken stock, cover, and simmer for 20 minutes, or until the kohlrabi are tender. Remove the cover, raise the heat to high, and reduce the liquid to a glaze.

Yield: 6 servings

➤ Can be prepared ahead and reheated.

Choux-Raves Farcis (Stuffed Kohlrabi)

6 kohlrabi, unpeeled	salt and pepper to taste
1 tablespoon olive oil	1 cup fresh bread crumbs
½ cup minced onion	1 cup sour cream
¼ cup minced celery	¼ cup minced dill
½ pound ground turkey	

Preheat the oven to 350°F.

In a lightly oiled baking dish, bake the kohlrabi until tender—about 20 to 25 minutes.

In a skillet, heat the olive oil, and sauté the onion and celery until soft, but not brown. Stir in the turkey, and cook, breaking up the lumps until the turkey loses its color. Season with salt and pepper to taste. Stir in the bread crumbs, sour cream, and dill. Correct the seasoning with salt and pepper.

When the kohlrabi are cool enough to handle, cut off the woody tops, and carefully hollow each kohlrabi, leaving a ¼-inch-thick wall. Chop the flesh, and stir into the turkey mixture. Fill the shells with the turkey, and bake for 10 to 15 minutes to reheat.

Yield: 6 servings

➤ Can be prepared for the final heating the day before.

Kohlrabi and Carrot Salad

1 pound kohlrabi, peeled and cut into ½ inch cubes	mustard cream sauce (see page 31)
1 pound carrots, pared and cut into ½ inch cubes	minced mint

In a bowl, mix the kohlrabi and carrots. Fold in the mustard cream sauce, and turn into a serving platter. Garnish with the mint.

Yield: 6 servings

➤ Can be prepared the day before.

Leeks and Ramps

*W*hen I was first learning to cook, I desperately wanted to prepare vichysoisse—I was 14—but leeks were not only not available in the local markets, I did not even have a hint as to what they looked like. Leo White, my employer, would shrug me off, saying they were like onions. Some years later, I finally found them and learned that they are like onions in the same way that lilies are: members of the same family, but hardly close. The flavor is sublime! It permeates foods, especially those with cream, to create magic.

Leeks are the national vegetable of Wales, and men sport them in their hat bands on St. David's day. David, of course, is the patron saint of Wales. Leeks are so common in Europe that they are referred to as "poor man's asparagus." Yet in the United States they are almost as expensive as asparagus. I asked a favorite green grocer several years ago why leeks were so scarce and expensive, and he blamed it on the length of the growing season, but many other vegetables have long growing seasons and still appear more regularly and less expensively.

Perhaps the problem lies with the leeks themselves. Leeks are grown in gritty soil that is hilled up around the stalks as they grow, in order to blanch the bulb in much the same way as white asparagus or Belgian endive. Consequently, the gritty sand works its way between the leaves and must be removed. The inexperienced cook who chops a clean-looking stalk of leek and tosses it into the the pot soon realizes the error. The grit is ruinous. One ruined dish, and the cook may decide to substitute an onion the next time. What a pity.

No matter that leeks are not always available or as cheap as one would like, they are worth the expense and the trouble. When they are plentiful, use them generously as a vegetable in their own right, but when scarce or more costly, use them to flavor other dishes.

Ramps

Ramps, also called wild leeks, are slimmer than a scallion, and have a violet streak and leaves that look similar to those of lily of the valley. (Unlike lily of the valley, they are not toxic!) They are reputed to have a ferocious onion-garlic flavor that causes grown men to weep. My experience has been that though well-flavored, they are no more so than a full-flavored clove of garlic. The flavor is different and quite pleasant.

Availability: Leeks

Fresh

Leeks are available the year round from markets across the country, but their prime period is the summer months. Because leeks can be wintered over, be most cautious when buying leeks in the early spring. If the leeks have not been picked soon enough, they will attempt to set seed, and in the process they develop a woody stem inside the softer outer leaves. This stem is hard, flavorless, and of no use. You can still use the outer leaves, but you have paid for more than you received. When buying leeks, I take the precaution of bending the leek partway down. If it gives easily, I am sure there is no stem, but if it is stiff, I set the leek aside. Considering the cost of this vegetable, returning a bunch or more with woody stems can convince the produce manager to correct his supplier.

Look for leeks with delicate blue-green to bright-green leaves and compact, smooth bulbs. Choose leeks that are no more than 1½ inches in diameter; larger leeks can be too strong. Avoid leeks with bruised bulbs or wilted, yellow, or dried leaves.

Store leeks in a plastic bag, roots and leaves attached, for up to 2 weeks in the refrigerator. If the leaves start to get limp, or are a space problem, cut off the green and discard, if you cannot use it immediately in a stock.

Frozen

Leeks tend to turn bitter if frozen, so do not freeze them—except in soups, where they are only a small part of the whole.

Canned

Canning destroys the texture of leeks, so canned leeks are not recommended.

Availability: Ramps

Available late March to mid May. Choose firm, springy, bright-green bunches without yellowing, and with the dirt still on the roots. Once the roots are removed the ramps lose their fresh flavor. Store wrapped in plastic for about a week, refrigerated.

Clean the ramps by slipping off the first layer of skin like a scallion, and cutting off the roots. Use in place of onions or leeks in any recipe.

NOTE: Although the flavor of scallions is quite different and they are not a substitute for leeks, they are a first cousin and can be prepared in many of the same ways. Scallion recipes are in the onion chapter.

Preparation

Care is required in washing leeks, and if you do not give it, you will regret it.

Cut off the green tops where the white begins. Use the leaves to flavor stock, or blanch them and use as wrappers for other foods, such as poached fish. They are not usually eaten on their own. Cut off and discard the roots.

Starting about 1½ inches from the root end, cut the leek in two, and fan the leaves under lukewarm running water to remove any grit. Many recipes require leeks cut in julienne (see page 3).

Cooking Methods

Boiling
Cook whole, cleaned leeks in boiling salted water until tender—about 12 minutes.

Steaming
In a steamer, over boiling water, steam whole leeks for 15 to 18 minutes, or until tender.

Microwaving
Not recommended for whole leeks, because the outside becomes chewy and the interior is mushy. You can braise chopped leeks in the microwave.

Braising
This is perhaps the best method for bringing out the subtle flavor of leeks.

Other Methods
Leeks can be roasted with meats the same way as roasted onions, sautéed, or stir-fried with other ingredients.

Quantity

If serving leeks whole, plan on 1 to 2 leeks per person, depending on their size. If the leeks are chopped, 3 pounds of untrimmed leeks should be enough for 6, unless the white bulb area is very small. If they are long enough, sometimes they arrive in the market with only 2 inches of white, and other times with 6 or more inches of white. Consider an average leek as 4 to 5 inches of white.

Sauces

Serve leeks with the same sauces and in the same manner as asparagus. Leeks also blend particularly well with tomato and garlic flavors. Once blanched, they can be prepared alla trifolati or alla Parmigiana. Serve raw leeks in place of onion, or boiled, or steamed and dressed with a vinaigrette.

Potage Bonne Femme (Leek and Potato Soup)

6 leeks, thinly sliced	1 garlic clove, minced
3 tablespoons butter	2 quarts chicken stock
4 boiling potatoes, peeled and	¾ cup milk
cut into ½ inch cubes	salt and pepper
½ cup chopped onion	2 tablespoons minced parsley

In a kettle, sweat the leeks in the butter until soft, but not brown. Add the potatoes, onion, and garlic, and cook, stirring, 1 minute. Add the chicken stock, and simmer covered for 20 minutes. Add the milk, salt, and pepper, and taste for seasoning. Heat and serve sprinkled with parsley.

Yield: 6 servings

➤ Can be prepared ahead and reheated.

Poireaux Sautés à l'Arlesienne
(Sautéed Leeks Arles Style)

2 eggs, lightly beaten	12 whole leeks, cleaned and
1 cup flour	blanched until barely tender
salt and pepper to taste	juice of 1 lemon
½ cup olive oil	¼ cup minced parsley
1 bay leaf	1 garlic clove, minced
	¼ teaspoon dried thyme

Place the eggs in a pie plate. In another pie plate, mix the flour with salt and pepper.

In a skillet, heat the oil and bay leaf. Dip the leeks into the eggs, and dredge in the seasoned flour. Cook over low heat until nicely browned on both sides. Add the lemon juice, 2 tablespoons of parsley, garlic, and thyme, and cook 1 minute longer. Remove from the heat, and arrange the leeks in a serving dish. Spoon on the cooking juices, and sprinkle with the remaining parsley. Serve at room temperature.

Yield: 6 servings

➤ Can be prepared several hours ahead.

Leeks with Red Wine

6 to 12 leeks, cleaned	½ cup red wine
4 tablespoons olive oil	3 tablespoons beef stock
¼ teaspoon salt	

In a skillet, sauté the leeks in the olive oil and salt until lightly browned. Add the wine and stock, cover, and simmer 10 minutes, or until tender.

Place the leeks in shallow dish. Reduce sauce to a glaze, if necessary, and pour over the leeks.

Yield: 6 servings

➤ Can be prepared ahead and reheated.

Leeks in Armagnac

6 to 12 leeks	⅓ cup consommé
3 tablespoons olive oil	¼ cup Armagnac
1 teaspoon salt	juice of ½ lemon
¼ teaspoon thyme	chopped parsley

In a skillet, brown the leeks in the oil, season with salt, thyme, stock, and Armagnac, and cook briskly for 10 minutes. Lower heat, and simmer until tender. Add lemon juice, and correct the seasoning. Sprinkle with minced parsley.

Serve hot or cold, with a drizzle of oil and lemon juice.

Yield: 6 servings

➤ Can be prepared ahead.

Sautéed Leeks and Romaine

1 large Romaine, cut into ½ inch pieces	¼ cup butter
	salt and pepper to taste
4 large leeks, trimmed, cleaned, and cut into ¼ inch slices	

In a kettle of boiling salted water, blanch the Romaine for 2 minutes, drain, refresh under cold water, and drain again. Set aside. In a large covered skillet, sweat the leeks in the butter until soft, but not brown—about 10 minutes.

Remove the cover, raise the heat, and add the Romaine. Cook, stirring, until it has heated, and the water has evaporated. Correct the seasoning with salt and pepper to taste.

Yield: 6 servings

➤ Can be prepared ahead and reheated.

Variations:

Add ½ cup of heavy cream, when the water has evaporated, and simmer until thickened.

Add ½ pound thickly sliced mushrooms to the leeks, and sauté until softened, before adding the Romaine.

Poireaux Niçoise (Leeks Nice Style)

3 tomatoes, peeled and quartered	2 tablespoons mince basil
salt and pepper to taste	1 tablespoon minced oregano
6 to 12 leeks, cleaned	juice of 1 lemon
½ cup olive oil	8 pitted black olives, halved
1 bay leaf	½ cup crumbled chèvre cheese
2 garlic cloves, peeled	minced parsley

Sprinkle the tomatoes with salt, and let drain in a colander for 30 minutes.

In a skillet, combine the leeks, olive oil, bay leaf, and garlic, and simmer, covered, over low heat for 10 to 15 minutes, or until the leeks are tender, but not browned. Add the tomatoes, basil, oregano, lemon juice, and olives. Season with salt and pepper. Simmer 3 to 4 minutes, or until the tomatoes are hot.

Serve hot, or pour into a bowl and serve at room temperature. Sprinkle with the cheese and parsley just before serving.

Yield: 6 servings

➤ Can be prepared ahead.

Poireaux à la Basquaise (Grilled Leeks Basque Style)

These are best grilled over a wood fire with hickory chips, but they are delicious cooked over grill, and still quite good if cooked under a broiler.

12 leeks, trimmed, cleaned, and blanched until barely tender	2 tablespoons olive oil
	salt and pepper to taste

Preheat a charcoal or gas grill, or a broiler.

Brush the leeks with the olive oil, and grill over high heat until lightly charred. Turn, and char the second side. Season with salt and pepper.

Serve hot or at room temperature.

Yield: 6 servings

➤ Can be prepared several hours ahead.

NOTE: Serve alone, or as part of a mixed vegetable grill, with eggplant, zucchini, thick onion slices, and green and red peppers, all cooked in the same manner. Blanching is not necessary.

Variation:
Enhance the flavor by adding garlic, minced thyme, savory, or marjoram to the olive oil.

Porri al Burro e Formaggio
(Braised Leeks with Parmesan)

6 to 12 leeks, cleaned	3 tablespoons grated Parmesan
3 tablespoons butter	cheese
salt and pepper to taste	

In a gratin pan, place the leeks in one or two layers, and add the butter and just enough water to cover. Cover the pan and simmer 25 minutes, or until almost tender. Remove the cover, and cook over moderate heat until the liquid evaporates and the leeks start to turn brown.

Sprinkle with the cheese, and serve hot or at room temperature.

Yield: 6 servings

➤ Can be prepared and reheated.

Poireaux à la Braise (Braised Leeks)

3 pounds leeks, trimmed,	1 garlic clove, minced
cleaned, and sliced	¼ cup butter
¼ cup minced celery	1 sprig of thyme
¼ cup minced onion	1 cup chicken stock
¼ cup minced carrot	salt and pepper to taste

In a large covered skillet or casserole, sauté the leeks, celery, onion, carrot, and garlic in the butter until soft, but not brown. Add the thyme and chicken stock. Cover, and simmer until very tender—about 20 minutes. Remove the cover, and reduce the liquid over high heat to a glaze. Correct the seasoning with salt and pepper.

Yield: 6 servings

➤ Can be prepared ahead and reheated.

Braised Leeks and Tomatoes

1 cup chopped onions	1 cup peeled, seeded, and
¼ cup olive oil	chopped tomatoes
2 pounds leeks, trimmed and	1 teaspoon minced garlic
cut into 2 inch lengths	salt and pepper to taste
1 cup sliced carrots	

In a skillet, sauté the onions in the olive oil until golden. Add the leeks, carrots, tomatoes, garlic, salt, and pepper, and cook, stirring, for 5 minutes, or until the tomatoes start to release their moisture. Add 1 cup hot water, and simmer 1 hour.

With a slotted spoon, remove the vegetables, and reduce the liquid to ½ cup. Return the vegetables to the pan and reheat. Correct the seasoning with salt and pepper.

Yield: 6 servings

➤ Can be prepared ahead and reheated.

Orange Braised Leeks

12 whole leeks, trimmed, blanched, and refreshed	¾ teaspoon grated nutmeg
2 cups chicken stock	salt and pepper to taste
1 cup orange juice	1 orange, peeled and thinly sliced, seeds removed
9 strips orange rind	

In a skillet, arrange the leeks in 1 or 2 layers. Pour on the chicken stock and orange juice. Sprinkle with the orange rind, nutmeg, salt, and pepper. Cover, and simmer for 15 minutes, or until the leeks are tender. Remove the leeks to a serving platter, and boil the juices until lightly thickened. Spoon the juices over the leeks, and garnish with the orange slices.

Yield: 6 servings

➤ Can be prepared ahead and reheated.

Braised Leek Gratin

½ cup sliced carrot	½ cup chicken stock
½ cup sliced celery	salt and pepper to taste
¼ cup butter	¼ cup fresh bread crumbs
12 whole leeks, trimmed and cleaned	¼ cup grated Parmesan cheese

Preheat the oven to 325°F.

In a large gratin pan or heat-proof baking dish, sweat the carrots and celery over low heat until soft, but not brown. Arrange the leeks on top, add the chicken stock, and season with salt and pepper. Cover, and bake for 40 to 55 minutes, until the leeks are tender.

Preheat the broiler. Drain off the liquid.

In a bowl, mix the bread crumbs and Parmesan cheese, and sprinkle over the leeks. Brown under the broiler.

Yield: 6 servings

➤ Can be prepared for the final browning several hours ahead. If they have been refrigerated, heat in a 350°F oven until bubbling, and then brown under the broiler.

Leek Tarts

Braised leeks, combined with other ingredients, create magnificent tarts or quiches. The flavor melds particularly well with cream and eggs, as well as a variety of cheeses and mushrooms, and in addition, various pork products, such as ham of various types and bacon. Here is a basic tart recipe, followed by a number of variations. Use your imagination and whatever is in the fridge to create your own specialty.

Leek Tart

1 10 inch tart shell, partially baked (see variations below)	4 eggs
	1½ cups heavy cream
2 cups of braised leeks (see page 269)	salt and pepper to taste

Preheat the oven to 375°F.

Fill the tart shell with the leeks. In a bowl, whisk the eggs, cream, salt, and pepper.

Pour into the tart shell, and bake for 35 to 40 minutes, or until a knife inserted halfway between the edge and the center comes out clean. Let rest for 10 minutes before serving.

Yield: 6 servings

➤ Can be prepared ahead and served at room temperature.

Variations:

Doughs Use pâté feuilleté, puff pastry, phyllo, or even a yeast dough. Do not prebake the puff pastry, phyllo, or the yeast dough. Bake the filled pastry at 425°F for 30 minutes, and then lower the temperature until the filling is cooked.

Doughless For a crustless tart, put the filling into a buttered quiche dish and bake in a baking pan filled with 1 inch of boiling water for about the same length of time. This results in a savory custard.

Bacon In a skillet, fry 8 slices bacon until crisp, drain well, and crumble the bacon. Add to the leeks before adding the eggs.

Carrot Add 1 cup of shredded carrots to the leeks when braising.

Cheese Spread ¼ cup of Mornay sauce on the bottom of the pastry and arrange the leeks on top. Pour over another 1½ of Mornay sauce. Sprinkle with grated Gruyère or Parmesan.

Chèvre Add ¼ pound crumbled chèvre to the leeks. For even more interest, add ½ cup chopped sun-dried tomatoes and 1 tablespoon minced rosemary.

Garlic and Tomato   Add 2 tablespoons minced garlic and 2 peeled, seeded, and chopped tomatoes to the leeks when braising. Reduce any liquid to a glaze.

Ham   Add ½ cup chopped or julienne cut ham to the leeks. Add a cheese of choice to the mixture—Edam and ½ teaspoon caraway seeds, or use Muenster and 1 tablespoon minced dill, or Cheddar and 1 medium hot jalapeno, minced.

In Savoie they add 2 tablespoons kirsch to the liquid and sprinkle ¼ pound diced boiled ham in the pie shell.

Mushroom   Add ¼ pound sautéed mushrooms to the leeks with bacon, ham, or pancetta, and possibly a cheese. Use Shiitake, oyster, or other wild mushrooms for a more interesting flavor.

Pancetta   Sauté ¼ pound of this Italian bacon until crisp. Use the rendered fat instead of butter to braise the leeks. Combine with a cheese of choice—chèvre is particularly good, especially with a ¼ teaspoon of dried oregano.

St. David's Salad

12 leeks, cleaned	1 tablespoon minced chervil
¾ cup olive oil	1 tablespoon minced parsley
¼ cup cider vinegar	1 teaspoon chives
1 tablespoon minced onion	salt and pepper to taste

In a kettle of boiling salted water, cook the leeks until tender. Drain, pat dry, and chill.

In a saucepan, over medium heat, cook the oil, vinegar, onion, chervil, parsley, chives, salt, and pepper until hot but not boiling. Pour over the leeks, and marinate for 2 hours.

Yield: 6 servings

➤ Can be prepared ahead.

Poireaux Froids à la Moutarde
(Cold Leeks with Mustard Sauce)

6 to 8 leeks, cleaned, trimmed, and boiled until tender	1½ tablespoons wine vinegar
	2 teaspoons capers
1 hard-cooked egg, separated	salt and pepper to taste
1 egg yolk	1 tablespoon minced pimiento
1½ tablespoon Dijon mustard	2 tablespoons minced parsley
½ cup olive oil	

Pat the leeks dry with paper toweling, and arrange on a serving platter. In a processor, purée the hard-cooked egg yolk, egg yolk, and mustard.

With the machine running, slowly add the oil, and then the vinegar.

Add the capers, and correct the seasoning with salt and pepper. Spread the sauce over the leeks.

Mince the hard cooked egg white, and sprinkle over the sauce, with the pimiento and the parsley.

Yield: 6 servings

➤ Can be prepared several hours ahead.

Leeks Wrapped in Ham with Green Sauce

12 leeks, cleaned, boiled until tender, and cooled	1 tablespoon minced chives
	1 tablespoon minced parsley
12 thin slices boiled ham	1 tablespoon minced tarragon
1½ cups mayonnaise	1 tablespoon minced
1 cup cooked spinach, minced and squeezed dry	hard-cooked egg
	salt and pepper to taste

Wrap each leek in a slice of ham, and place on a serving platter. In a bowl, mix the mayonnaise, spinach, chives, parsley, tarragon, egg, salt, and pepper. Spoon some of the sauce over the leeks, and pass the remaining sauce.

Yield: 6 servings

➤ Can be prepared the day before.

NOTE: If you make fresh mayonnaise in a processor, add the spinach, chives, parsley, and tarragon to the processor at the end and purée. Remove from the processor, fold in the egg, and correct the seasoning with salt and pepper.

Salade de Poireaux et Crevettes
(Leek and Shrimp Salad)

6 leeks, cleaned and cut into bite-sized pieces	1 cup sauce verte (see page 30)
	1 small head radicchio
salt and pepper to taste	2 hard-cooked eggs, separated
1 pound medium shrimp, peeled and deveined	3 tablespoons minced parsley

In a saucepan of boiling salted water, blanch the leeks for 4 minutes. Drain, refresh under cold water, and drain again.

In another saucepan, cook the shrimp in boiling salted water until they turn pink—about 1 minute. Drain, refresh under cold water, and drain again. In a bowl, toss the leeks and shrimp together. Add enough sauce to moisten the mixture.

Separate the leaves form the radicchio, and arrange on a platter. Spoon the leeks onto the radicchio. Force the egg whites and egg yolks through a sieve separately, and mix with the parsley. Sprinkle the egg mixture over the salad.

Serve remaining sauce separately.

Yield: 6 servings

➤ Can be prepared several hours ahead.

Ramps and Seafood Timbales with Lime Sabayon

2 bunches ramps (about ¾ pound)	½ teaspoon salt
1½ tablespoons butter	3 eggs
¾ pounds shrimp, in shells	½ cup heavy cream
1½ teaspoons tomato paste	1 egg yolk
½ pound scallops	1½ tablespoons lime juice
	1 tablespoon minced mint

Trim roots from ramps, and cut apart leaves and stems, leaving no stem on the leaves. Wash well. In a skillet of simmering water, simmer leaves for 2 minutes, drain, refresh under cold water, and spread flat on a towel. Peel bulbs, and select 8 of the prettiest. Blanch in boiling salted water until just tender. Drain and refresh. Slice remaining bulbs.

In a skillet, melt the butter, and sweat the ramps with 1 tablespoon water, uncovered, until very tender. Cool and chill.

Peel the shrimp, place the shells in a saucepan with 2 cups water, and simmer, partially covered, 20 minutes. Uncover, and reduce liquid to ⅓ cup. Strain out shells, add the tomato paste, and reduce to ¼ cup. Let cool.

Butter 8 custard cups, and line with ramp leaves, overlapping slightly. Preheat the oven to 350°F.

In a processor, combine shrimp, scallops, and ¼ teaspoons salt, and purée. Add 1 egg and egg white, process 10 seconds, scrape down sides, add the cooked ramps, and process. Pour in the cream. Divide the mousse among the custard cups and even the tops. Fold over leaves.

Bake in a bain marie water bath, uncovered for 14 minutes, or until they test done. In a double boiler, beat the remaining egg and egg yolks with lime juice and salt until light and fluffy. Beat reserved shrimp stock and beat into the sauce. Correct the seasoning with lime juice and mint.

Yield: 8 servings

Lettuces and Salad Greens

*L*ettuce means salad. For most Americans, salad means iceberg lettuce. And for most food mavens, iceberg lettuce means bad salad. All of these generalizations are regrettable. Lettuce *is* primarily served as salad, iceberg lettuce is used in salads, and often those salads are not very good. There are many other greens to select for salads, including Boston or Bibb lettuce, butterheads, escarole, chicory-endive, Belgian endive, dandelion, radicchio, rocket, romaine, sorrel, spinach, mâche or corn, and watercress. There are red leafs, oak leafs, large heads, and small heads. Almost any green is suitable for salad and its taste will be brought out beautifully when mixed with a light, fresh oil and vinegar dressing.

Many food writers denigrate iceberg lettuce, calling it tasteless, common, useless, and the like. It does have flavor, and it has definite uses, but not in every salad. Iceberg developed when refrigeration was rare and shipping lettuce to the East in winter months was impossible. Iceberg would stand up to long refrigerated train trips and provide a fresh green in January. It is not the same as butter lettuces or romaine, but it is not supposed to be. It does have a crisp clean texture with a mild, but refreshing, flavor. It is very good with heavy salad dressings, such as creamy Roquefort and Russian, where other lettuces cannot stand up to those sauces. It is also very good as the wrapper for fish to keep in the flavors. It is particularly good to add moisture, crunch, and flavor to sandwiches, where the more subtle lettuces quickly become limp and unappealing. In other words, iceberg has a well-deserved place in the pantheon of lettuces.

Lettuces have other culinary uses besides in salads. They are superb sautéed, boiled, stir-fried, and poached. Use the leaves to wrap fish for braising to keep in the moisture, or for stuffing. Cold iceberg makes a wonderful wrapper for certain stir-fried dishes. In other words, lettuce is as versatile in cookery as many other vegetables.

This chapter deals with the principal salad lettuces used both in salads and for cooking. Belgian endive, dandelion, spinach, and the like, are subjects of other chapters.

As I noted under Belgian endive, the names for some greens are confusing. Curly endive is often called chicory, but then again so is escarole. Curly endive is also called chicory, or escarole, or in some cases *frisée*. Fortunately, they are all delicious and interchangeable. To add further information, if not confusion, some Italian members of the chicory family are called radicchio, chioggia, or treviso. These are colored white and deep maroon, sometimes with tinges of green. They taste much the same, and the difference is more in shape. Radicchio and chioggia are round, and treviso is elongated. Belgian endive, frisée, and radicchio are all expensive greens, but escarole and curly endive (or chicory) are usually quite inexpensive. Buy and use what you can afford, and do not worry about the names.

Arugula

Arugula, also called rugula, roquette, rocket, and (in England at least) rocket cress, is a current favorite green. It has a slightly bitter, peppery quality. Dark-green leaves with narrow lobes no more than 3 inches are preferred; chop larger leaves.

Belgian Endive

Witloof, or chicory. Cream colored, with tightly formed narrow leaves. Slightly bitter, especially the larger heads.

Bibb

Butterhead, or limestone. Developed in Frankfort, Kentucky by John J. Bibb in 1856. Select round heads with crinkly dark leaves around paler leaves. Crunchier than Boston, with mild buttery flavor.

Boston

Butterhead, or cabbagehead. Select dark-to-medium green leaves, loosely rounded shape, silky texture. Has a mild buttery flavor.

Buttercrunch

Butterhead. Crunchy textured leaves range from dark to pale green. More tightly formed than other butterheads. Crisp texture, sweet flavor that resembles Tom Thumbs.

Curly Endive

Chicory, frisée, or sometimes escarole. Select curly leaves with frizzy ends, dark green to yellow. The yellow is less bitter.

Dandelion

From *dent de lion*, or lions tooth, also called pissenlit, or stain in the bed, for the color of the flowers. Select dark green leaves. They have a somewhat bitter taste, and are better if picked before blooms appear. Cultivated leaves are much milder.

Escarole
Chicory, or endive. This has large broad dark-green outer leaves with a pale yellow inner core and flattened heads. Yellow heart is more tender, not as bitter as curly endive.

Iceberg
Crisphead. Its name was changed in the 1930's after it was shipped on beds of ice from California. Accused of having less flavor; preferred for its crisp quality. Can be cut or broken.

Leaf Lettuce
Loose leaf, or bunching. Developed by U.S.D.A. to withstand hot weather. The green and red leaf salad bowl are most common. The flavor is sweet with a crisp texture.

Mâche
Corn, field, or lamb's lettuce. Look for medium- to dark-green small round leaves. It has a sweet nutty flavor, with a soft creamy texture.

Radicchio
Red leaf chicory. Early summer growth is dark green tinted with bright red. Later it becomes white with deep maroon. Select small tightly furled heads from golf ball to grapefruit sized. It has a strong flavor with a bitter aftertaste.

Romaine
Cos. Discovered by Romans on the Greek island of Kos, this lettuce has large, crunchy leaves from dark green to pale yellow. Can be moderately flavorful to mild and sweet.

Spinach
Dark green leaves, flat or crinkly, large or small leaves, and strong texture and flavor.

Treviso
Radicchio. This a variety of radicchio. The heads are elongated with white ribs with deep maroon leaves.

Watercress
Sprigs have tender dark-green leaves attached to crisp succulent stems. Flavor varies from moderately spicy to peppery and pungent.

Availability

Lettuces are available year round, and for the most part there is a large selection of lovely salad greens available in most markets. Even in the worst of times there is the much-maligned iceberg. Look for crisp, firm, bright lettuces with no sign of wilting or decay. Head lettuces such as iceberg, butter, and Boston should feel heavy for their size. The weight indicates a more compact head and a better buy. Light airy heads may mean that you get as few as half the servings.

Frozen
Freezing destroys lettuce.

Canned
Canning destroys the texture of lettuce.

Preparation

There has been much folderol written about preparing lettuces. I recommend that you not wash lettuce until shortly before using. If you wash it as soon as you get it home and try to store it in plastic bags, it starts to decay quickly. Store the unwashed heads in the refrigerator, and remove the leaves you need as you need them.

Wash lettuce, either whole or in single leaves, in a large sink of lukewarm water. The lukewarm water relaxes the leaves and opens those tightly crinkled areas where grit hides, and it will fall to the bottom of the sink. Give the lettuce a good sloshing to force water into those tiny places and float out the grit. Lift it straight up and let it drain back into the sink. Place in a colander to drain. To dry lettuce, ideally put it into a lettuce dryer and spin off the water. If you do not have one, place the drained leaves in single layers on paper toweling.

Wrap the lettuce in paper toweling, and recrisp in the refrigerator. Within an hour the leaves will be snappy crisp. If you wish to do this the day before, put them into an unsealed plastic bag. If the greens are truly fresh they will keep 2 or 3 days in this wrapping. Frost-free refrigerators can dry the toweling, and you may need to sprinkle them with a little water at the end of the second day. Other types of refrigerators may require that you rewrap the lettuce in dry paper toweling to prevent decay.

Many writers insist that you tear lettuce for salads because a knife can bruise the leaves. Apparently they have dull knifes!

If you are willing to pick up each leaf and gently pull it apart into bite-sized pieces, then do indeed tear the lettuce. But if you grab handfuls at a time and wrench the leaves into chunks, *please* use a sharp knife. A sharp knife will cut quickly and neatly through the leaves without damage. Dull knives are useless.

Clearly, chiffonades (shreds) of lettuce used as a base for salads must be cut with a knife.

Cooking Methods

Blanching
Cook lettuce in boiling salted water to cover until softened—1 to 4 minutes, depending on the type of lettuce.

Boiling
Lettuce is not usually boiled and served as a vegetable. The flavor is better developed by sautéing or braising.

Sautéing
Cut the lettuce into a chiffonade, thin shreds, and sauté in butter or olive oil until tender—about 5 to 10 minutes, depending on the quantity. Season with salt and pepper. If desired, add ½ cup of cream, and reduce by half after the lettuce is fully wilted.

Steaming
Steaming is not recommended, because the lettuce turns gray and loses its bright-green color. If you feel you must, steam for about 8 minutes. Drain and serve with lemon juice, salt, and pepper.

Microwaving
This method destroys the color of the lettuce and seems to bring out the bitterness. It is not recommended.

Braising
This is the preferred method of cooking lettuce. Once the lettuce is braised, it can be coated with various sauces.

Quantity

The amount of lettuce required depends on the way it is being served. For salad, plan on 1 cup of salad greens per person. For chiffonades, ¾ cup will do. However, if you are cooking, plan on at least twice that quantity. Braised lettuces are easier to plan. Use 1 head per person, unless they are very small.

Sauces

Vinaigrette is the sauce of choice for uncooked lettuce. A simple olive oil, vinegar, salt, and pepper preparation is the beginning, but you can add countless ingredients to vary the flavor (see vinaigrette, page 30). Cooked lettuce is sauced with Hollandaise, Mornay, and cream sauces.

Mixed Greens Soup

2 tablespoons olive oil	3 cups milk, or chicken stock
1 onion, chopped	2 tablespoons flour
2 garlic cloves, chopped	salt and pepper
5 cups mixed shredded	grated rind of 1 lemon or
romaine, spinach, red leaf,	orange
or Boston lettuce	¼ cup minced basil or
¼ cup chicken stock, or water	coriander

In a saucepan, heat the oil, and sauté the onion and garlic until soft, but not brown. Add the greens, and stir to combine with the onion mixture. Sprinkle with chicken stock or water, cover, and cook over low heat until wilted. Add 2¾ cups milk or chicken stock. Remove from heat, and purée, 2 cups at a time. Return to the pan.

In a bowl, mix the flour and ¼ cup milk or chicken stock to make a slurry, and stir into the simmering soup. Season with salt and pepper, and simmer for 5 minutes.

Serve garnished with grated lemon or orange rind, and basil or coriander.

Yield: 6 servings

Chicken Soup with Escarole and Tiny Pasta

This light, clean-tasting soup is ideal for the dieter, because it does not seem dietetic.

1½ quarts chicken stock	¾ cup minced cooked chicken
3 carrots, thinly sliced	3 tablespoons minced parsley
3 leeks, thinly sliced	salt and pepper to taste
⅓ cup small pasta	⅓ cup grated Parmesan cheese
¾ pound escarole, shredded	

In a large saucepan, bring the stock to a boil, and add the carrots, leeks, and pasta. Cook until the pasta is tender. Add the escarole, and return to the simmer. Add the chicken, parsley, salt, and pepper.

Serve with grated cheese.

Yield: 6 servings

➤ If prepared too far ahead, the pasta becomes soggy.

NOTE: Omit the carrots and leeks, if desired.

Sautéed Lettuce

12 cups shredded lettuce	salt and pepper to taste
¼ cup butter, or olive oil	

In a large skillet, sauté the lettuce in the olive oil until wilted and the water evaporates—about 10 minutes. Season with salt and pepper.

Yield: 6 servings

➤ Can be prepared ahead and reheated.

Variations:

Add ½ to ¾ cup heavy cream, and cook until lightly thickened.

Add ½ cup minced onion and/or 1 clove of minced garlic to the butter, and sauté until soft, but not brown, before adding the lettuce. Finish as above, or add the cream.

Just before serving, stir in ¼ to ½ cup grated Parmesan cheese.

Sautéed Escarole

3 pounds escarole or romaine, thickly sliced, blanched, and refreshed	½ cup minced shallots
	3 tablespoons olive oil
	salt and pepper
1 teaspoon minced sage	grated Parmesan cheese

Squeeze the excess moisture from the escarole.

In a skillet, sauté the sage and shallot in the oil until soft, but not brown. Add the escarole and cook, stirring, to separate the strands until the liquid evaporates—about 5 minutes. Correct the seasoning with salt and pepper.

Pass the Parmesan cheese.

Yield: 6 servings

➤ Can be prepared ahead and reheated.

Romaine au Gratin

This is a particularly simple gratin.

3 heads romaine	2 tablespoons heavy cream
⅓ cup minced onion	salt and pepper to taste
2 tablespoons butter	½ cup grated Gruyère cheese

Preheat the oven to 375°F.

Cut off the base of the romaine and discard. Shred the leaves and blanch in boiling salted water for 8 minutes, or until tender. Drain, rinse under cold water, and drain again, pressing out any excess liquid.

In a saucepan, sauté the onion in the butter until soft, but not brown. Add the romaine and heat. Stir in the cream, salt, and pepper, and heat until hot.

Turn into a baking dish or gratin pan, and sprinkle with the Gruyère. Bake for 10 minutes, or until bubbling hot and the top is browned. If the gratin is hot and not browned, brown under the broiler for 2 or 3 minutes.

Yield: 6 servings

➤ Can be prepared the day before, and baked just before serving.

NOTE: Substitute any of the stronger lettuces, such as escarole or chicory (curly endive), or if your budget can afford it, radicchio.

Stir-Fried Greens

2 tablespoons oil
1 inch gingeroot, shredded
4 garlic cloves, minced
2 heads Belgian endive, ½ inch slices

1 bunch watercress, stems attached, 2 inch lengths
2 cups shredded Escarole or Romaine
1 tablespoon sesame oil
1 tablespoon soy sauce

In a wok, heat the oil, and stir-fry the ginger and garlic until aromatic. Add the greens, and stir-fry for about 2 minutes. Add the sesame oil, and stir for another minute.

Add the soy sauce, and turn into a serving dish.

Yield: 6 servings

Cuore di Lattuga al Gratinata (Heart of Lettuce Gratin)

6 hearts of lettuce (see Note)
6 thin slices prosciutto ham
5 tablespoons butter
2 tablespoons flour
1 cup milk

nutmeg to taste
salt to taste
4 tablespoons grated Parmesan cheese

Preheat the oven to 350°F.

In a sink of lukewarm water, wash the heads of lettuce without breaking off any leaves. Drain well, and blanch in boiling salted water for 5 minutes. Drain, and press out the moisture. With your hands, shape each lettuce into a compact package, and place in a buttered casserole. Wrap each lettuce in a slice of prosciutto.

In a saucepan, melt 3 tablespoons of butter, stir in the flour, and cook until it starts to turn golden. Stir in the milk, and cook until thickened and smooth. Season with salt and nutmeg.

Pour over the lettuces, and sprinkle with the Parmesan. Dot with the remaining butter. Bake for 20 minutes, or until golden.

Yield: 6 servings

➤ Can be prepared for the final baking the day before.

NOTE: Select whatever lettuce is available and plentiful. If the budget can stand it, this is a delicious method of preparing radicchio.

If you must use large heads of lettuce, such as romaine, blanch them, then cut in half, and fold the halves for individual portions.

Grilled Radicchio

Grill radicchio over a wood, charcoal, or gas fire for the best flavor. Broilers are not worth the effort.

3 heads radicchio
½ cup olive oil

salt and pepper to taste

Trim the stem from the radicchio, and cut through the core into 2 inch wedges. The core is needed to hold the wedges together.

Brush with olive oil, and grill over a charcoal fire for about 1 minute on each side until heated through and slightly charred. Season with salt and pepper.

Yield: 6 servings

➤ Can be prepared ahead and served at room temperature.

Braised Lettuce

6 Boston lettuces, blanched,
　drained, and refreshed
juice of 1 lemon

salt and pepper to taste
2 cups beef or chicken stock

Preheat the oven to 375°F.

Lightly butter a baking dish or gratin pan large enough to hold the blanched lettuces in one layer. Season with lemon juice, salt, and pepper. Pour on just enough stock to cover. Cover with a lid or foil, and bake for 45 minutes, or until tender.

Remove the lettuces to a platter, and press out the moisture. Return the liquid to the gratin pan, and boil over high heat until reduced to a glaze. Pour over the lettuces.

Yield: 6 servings

➤ Can be prepared ahead and reheated.

Variations:

Add ¼ cup minced onion and ¼ cup minced carrot to the casserole before adding the lettuces.

Line the bottom of the casserole with 4 slices of bacon, and add the carrot and onion as in previous variation before adding the lettuces.

Add a pinch of thyme and 1 bay leaf to the liquid before braising.

When the liquid has been reduced to a glaze, whisk in 2 to 4 tablespoons of butter to enrich the sauce.

Add blanched leeks to the lettuce, and braise together.

In a skillet, sauté 1 pound whole button mushrooms, stems removed, until they turn golden. Add to the lettuce—particularly romaine—in the casserole. Add ¼ cup cream sherry to the stock and braise as above.

Scarola Ripiene (Stuffed Lettuce)

Serve these as a first course, part of a mixed hors d'oeuvre platter, or as a main course for a light supper or picnic.

24 large unbroken escarole leaves, blanched for 10 minutes, drained, and refreshed
1 cup minced onion
1/3 cup olive oil
6 ounces ground beef, lean
6 ounces sweet Italian sausage, broken up

6 ounces lean veal
1 1/2 cups dry white wine
1/2 teaspoon anise seeds, crushed
2 eggs, well beaten
1/4 cup grated Parmesan cheese
salt and pepper to taste
6 tablespoons oil and vinegar dressing

Preheat the oven to 350°F.

Pat the leaves dry on paper toweling, taking care not to tear them. In a deep skillet, sauté the onions in the oil until soft, but not brown. Add the beef, sausage, and veal, and cook over moderate heat until lightly browned.

Add the stock, wine, and anise seeds, and simmer, uncovered, 30 minutes or until liquid is almost evaporated. Remove from heat, and allow to cool. Blend in the eggs and cheese, and season with salt and pepper to taste.

Lay 6 of the leaves on a flat surface, smooth sides up, and separated from each other. Cover each with a second leaf. The remaining leaves are intended as replacements for any torn leaves. If not needed or torn, stack and roll together, and cut into chiffonade. Set aside.

Place 1/6 of the meat mixture on each pair of leaves, and fold the leaves envelope fashion, to enclose the filling. Arrange seam side down in an oiled baking pan, and bake for 20 minutes. Remove and cool.

Shape the shredded escarole leaves in 6 nests on a platter, and place a stuffed leaf on top. Dress with the oil and vinegar dressing.

Yield: 6 servings

➤ Can be prepared the day before. Serve at room temperature.

NOTE: For the dressing, mix 4 tablespoons of extra virgin olive oil with 2 tablespoons of balsamic vinegar, and season with salt and pepper.

Pain de Laitues *(Lettuce Molds)*

Bake in custard cups for individual servings, or in a loaf pan, and slice after baking.

6 Boston lettuces, blanched for 10 minutes, drained, refreshed, and drained again	1 cup cold milk
	4 eggs
	½ cup grated Parmesan cheese
¼ cup minced shallots	⅓ cup heavy cream
¼ cup butter	salt and pepper to taste
1¾ cups dry bread crumbs	nutmeg to taste

Preheat the oven to 350°F.

Butter 6 custard cups or timbale molds, or a 9" by 5" loaf pan. Line the bottoms of the molds with buttered waxed or parchment paper. Squeeze the extra water from the lettuces, and chop coarsely. In a skillet, sauté the shallots in the butter until soft, but not brown. Add the lettuce, and cook gently until the moisture evaporates.

In a bowl, soak the bread crumbs in the milk, and mash with a fork until all of the milk is absorbed. Beat in the eggs, lettuce, cheese, and cream. Correct the seasoning with salt, pepper, and nutmeg. Turn into the prepared molds, and place in a baking pan. Add 1 inch of boiling water, and bake 15 minutes for the custard cups or 30 to 35 minutes for the loaf pan.

They are done when a knife inserted in the center comes out clean. Let stand for 5 minutes before unmolding.

Yield: 6 servings

➤ Can be prepared for baking the day before.

Summer Rice

2 tablespoons oil	½ cup chicken stock
4 garlic cloves, minced	2 cups shredded lettuce, escarole, or spinach
1 cup sliced scallions	
¼ cup sesame seeds	2 cups cooked rice or noodles
¼ cup chopped celery leaves	2 tomatoes, cut into wedges

In a wok, heat the oil and stir-fry the garlic, scallions, and sesame seeds for 2 minutes. Add the celery leaves, and cook 1 minute. Add the chicken stock and shredded greens, and stir for 2 minutes. Stir in the rice and tomatoes, cover, and steam for 5 minutes.

Yield: 6 servings

Laitues Farcis a la Bourbonnaise
(Braised Stuffed Lettuces)

6 Boston lettuce, blanched, refreshed, and drained	3 eggs
4 cups cubed crustless bread	¼ cup butter
⅓ cup heavy cream	½ cup thinly sliced carrot
2 cups diced poached chicken	½ cup thinly sliced onion
2 tablespoons minced chives	3 tablespoons white wine
2 tablespoons minced parsley	2 cups chicken stock
salt and pepper to taste	bouquet garni of thyme, parsley, and bay leaf

Press out the excess moisture from the lettuces, and set them aside.

In a bowl, combine the bread and cream. Add the chicken, chives, parsley, salt, and pepper. Beat in the eggs until combined. Pat the lettuces dry, and cut the leaves, down to, but not through, the core.

Open the lettuces, and put in the stuffing, using the outer leaves to wrap around the filling. Tie each head gently with cotton string.

In a large deep skillet, melt 2 tablespoons of butter, and sauté the carrots and onions over until soft, but not brown. Add the wine. Arrange the lettuces on the vegetables and pour on the chicken stock. Push the bouquet into the center of the lettuces and season with salt and pepper. Bring to a simmer, cover and simmer 1 hour. Remove the lettuces to a serving platter, and remove the strings.

Pour any accumulated liquid into the skillet. Over high heat, reduce the liquid to 6 tablespoons, and whisk in the remaining butter. Spoon over the lettuces and serve.

Yield: 6 servings

➤ Can be braised and reheated before finishing the sauce.

Paupiettes de Sole en Laitue (Filets of Sole in Lettuce)

Wrap any fish in lettuce to maintain moisture and give it a subtle flavor. After it is poached, serve the fish plain, with lemon juice, melted butter, Hollandaise, or the sauce in this recipe.

12 Boston lettuce leaves	¾ cup dry white wine
6 fillets of sole	¼ cup butter
salt and pepper to taste	½ cup heavy cream
3 tablespoons minced shallots	lemon juice

Preheat the oven to 400°F. Butter a gratin pan.

In a kettle of boiling salted water, blanch the lettuce for 1 minute to soften. Drain the leaves, put into a bowl of cold water to stop the cooking, and carefully unfold each leaf and spread it onto paper toweling to dry.

Season the sole on both sides with salt and pepper. With the skin side up, roll the sole, place each roll onto two lettuce leaves, and wrap.

Sprinkle the shallots in the gratin pan, place the fish on top, and pour on the wine. Dot the fish with 2 tablespoons of butter.

Cover the pan with parchment or waxed paper, and bring to a simmer on top of the stove. Bake for 10 to 15 minutes (cook 10 minutes per inch of thickness of the roll, starting after the liquid reaches a simmer). Remove the fish to a warm platter, and cover loosely with foil.

Strain the juices from the gratin into a saucepan, and reduce by half. Add the cream, and reduce over high heat until thick enough to coat the back of a spoon. Remove the pan from the heat, and whisk in the remaining 2 tablespoons of butter. Correct the seasoning with salt, pepper, and lemon juice.

Serve over the fish.

Yield: 6 servings

➤ Can be prepared for baking several hours ahead and kept refrigerated.

Variations:

If lily-gilding is your forte, here is a chance to elaborate. You can fill the sole rolls with almost anything, and you can substitute thin fillets of other fish, such as salmon, bass, or trout. Obviously, the fillet must be skinless and boneless.

Place a slice of smoked salmon, shrimp, scallop, or whitefish on the sole before rolling.

Place a large scallop on the sole before rolling.

Place shrimp, or a minced shrimp stuffing, on the sole before folding.

Place blanched sticks of carrots and leeks on the sole before folding.

Tossed Salad

Tossed green salad, *salade verte, insalata verde,* or greens with a dressing, is popular in most European countries and countries influenced by Europeans. The salads reflect the culinary traditions of each country. For many, the American version is iceberg lettuce and some thick reddish liquid poured from a bottle. The French is delicate buttery lettuces, with a few sprigs of rocquette (arugula), watercress, or mâche for accent, with a dressing with more oil than vinegar and a mustard accent. Italians serve heartier lettuces such as chicory, romaine, and escarole, and the dressing is heavy on the vinegar. The Greeks add tomatoes, cucumbers, olives, or cheese, and serve it with lemon-flavored dressings accented with mint or oregano.

How do you decide what to serve for a salad? Americans who have graduated from the iceberg lettuce stage toss any green into a bowl and serve almost anything for a dressing with the attitude that it is green, low-calorie, and good for you—so eat. In fact, salads should be works of art, with thought given to taste, color, composition, and the type of meal they are accompanying. Greek salads, with all of their wonderful parts, are terrific for luncheon or a light meal anytime, but are unsuitable after a formal dinner. The Italian coarser salad, with the stronger lettuces and vinegary dressing, works well after pasta and high-starch meals, but following a delicate dinner they are too much. The more subtle (subtle, not better) salad is perfect following a multi-course dinner with several wines, but cannot stand up at a picnic.

Once you have selected the occasion for serving the salad, prepare a salad to suit the menu. Steak and potatoes? A wedge of iceberg with a thick, creamy Roquefort is terrific, although I prefer to precede the steak with a Caesar salad. Picnic, or simple pasta dinner? Serve an assortment of lettuces, such as romaine, chicory, escarole, arugula, and radicchio, mixing the shades of greens, and serving with a dressing of ⅔ oil, ⅓ red-wine vinegar, salt, and pepper. Crush a clove of garlic and add it to the dressing, and perhaps toss in a few chunks of toasted (or frankly stale) French or Italian bread. A more elaborate dinner with a first course, perhaps a fish course and meat main course, is best followed by a light, but refreshing salad. Use Bibb or Boston lettuces, red leaf, and arugula, and Belgian endive or radicchio for sharpness, with a dressing that is ¾ oil and ¼ white-wine vinegar. Add some Dijon mustard, and perhaps some minced tarragon, chervil, or chives. For picnic fare, luncheon, or a barbecue, go for the Greek version of tomatoes, cucumbers, olives, and the like.

The dressing is vital to the success of any salad. It should have balance. Too much vinegar can make a salad harsh, and too much oil makes it bland. One herb can bring out the flavor, while several can turn the flavors muddy and uninteresting. Enough salt to enhance the salad is important, and without it the finest of dressings will seem bland and unappealing.

There are three ways of dressing a salad: Place the dressing ingredients in a bowl, blend, and toss in the greens and blend. Prepare the dressing in a jar or bowl and pour over the greens and toss. Or, place the greens in a bowl, and sprinkle the ingredients over the top and toss. They give three different flavors. I prefer the first method. Whichever method you choose, prepare the salad dressing fresh for every salad. It takes seconds, and is far better than anything from a bottle. A decent wire whisk and a bowl are the only equipment required. Put some mustard, salt, and pepper into a bowl, add the vinegar, and whisk in the oil until the dressing emulsifies. Toss.

Storing dressing in a jar for several days takes away the fresh quality, and if the dressing has garlic and herbs they quickly become tired. Avoid mincing garlic and storing it in oil for more than a day; it can become rancid.

Oils

You can select from all types of oils. Using different oils changes the flavor dramatically. Olive oil is usually preferred, but there are many options, from the varying grades of olive oil, to nut flavored oils and safflower oil.

Olive Oil

This is the place to spend money on a truly superb extra virgin olive oil. Take care, though, that the money goes for the oil and not for a fancy container. Olive oil is graded depending on how the oil was extracted from the olives. Simple pressure, without any heat, produces extra virgin. As the oil loses quality, harsher means are used, until finally the pulp is cooked in hot water to remove the last and least desirable oil.

For every day use I recommend using an average oil from any of the major producers, as long as it is pure olive oil. Do read the label carefully. Sometimes the large print saying olive oil has a subscript, in much smaller print, stating a percentage with the remainder from another source. Simple salads show extra virgin oil best. Serve it with a pleasant mixture of greens, salt, pepper, and perhaps some mustard and a complementary vinegar.

You can select oils from France, Greece, Italy, or Spain, and compare the flavors.

Store the oil in a cool, dark area for no more than 6 months, because it can turn rancid. Refrigerating the oil will give it longer life, but it thickens and is difficult to use until warmed to room temperature.

Walnut Oil

Imported from France, this oil has a wonderful walnut flavor. Do not substitute the health store variety that is virtually flavorless. Because it is expensive, some cooks mix it with half olive oil.

Hazelnut Oil

Another imported product that, though expensive, is worth it. The flavor is delightful and is a welcome change. It also can be cut with olive oil to make it less costly.

Safflower Oil

This lends a delicious flavor to salads and is low in saturated fat.

Salad Oil

So-called salad oil is made from soy beans, corn, peanuts, canola, or cotton seed. These are all relatively tasteless, and add nothing more than lubrication to a salad. If those are the options, consider just sprinkling the salad with lemon juice and pepper.

Vinegars

Like oils, there are many vinegars to use in salads.

Wine Vinegar

Vinegar can be prepared from almost any wine. Use white wine, red wine, or sherry vinegars for variety in flavors.

Balsamic Vinegar

Balsamic vinegar is an aged wine vinegar from Italy that can be costly. It has a milder, slightly sweeter taste that is perfect when mixed with extra virgin olive oil.

Cider Vinegar

Cider vinegar made from apples is too strong for most salads; however, it works well with heartier vegetables, such as cabbage and celery root. Use this to acidulate water and in marinades, unless another vinegar is recommended.

Distilled Vinegar

Many vinegars are distilled. This is a white vinegar that has a sharp edge, and is used with cucumber and cabbage salads. Use it to acidulate water as well.

Flavored Vinegars

Vinegar is flavored with herbs such as tarragon, rosemary, and the like. Or, it is flavored or distilled from fruits, such as raspberries, strawberries, or currants. I recommend that you prepare a small amount of dressing and sample it before you proceed with some of these. They can be somewhat startling.

Mustards

Mustard is the third component of salad dressing, but it is not always necessary. Use a Dijon mustard for everyday use, and sample some of the herbed flavors for special occasions. The mustard should accent the salad and not overpower it. Sample the mustard first in small quantities; some are much stronger than others.

Sweet mustards, which are delicious on a slice of ham, may be less appealing on a delicate salad. Whole-grain mustards can be fun occasionally. Dry mustard can add a fiery spark to a dressing.

Seasonings

Salt and pepper are necessary to balance the flavors, of course. Unsalted salads are lifeless. Coarse ground pepper accents the greens nicely.

Use herbs with care. One herb can give a definite flavor to a salad, but using all those on the shelf usually results in a murky, muddy flavor. Select one or two herbs with care, and accent those. Also remember that the herb must compliment the lettuces. The standard *fines herbes* grouping of tarragon, chervil, chives, and parsley is delicious on buttery lettuces, but gets lost on escarole and chicory.

Garlic

The best way of adding garlic to a salad is to cut the clove in half and rub it over the bowl, or over the *outer* crust of a French or Italian loaf. Toss the crust with the salad and dressing until the greens are evenly coated. The cook then eats the crust of bread—heavenly!

Cheese

For added excitement, serve a salad with cheese in one form or another. Crumble feta or Chèvre over the top, or sprinkle with grated Parmesan. Use a cheese slicer to shave paper-thin sheets of Parmesan, and then cover the top of the salad. Warm slices of Chèvre in the oven to bring out the flavor, or toast French bread on one side, spread with Chèvre on the other, sprinkle with minced rosemary or savory, and grill until melted. Serve a cheese pastry such as cheese palmiers, or cheese straws. These, of course, are changes from the traditional cheese tray, which can seem too heavy after a full menu.

Serving

Salad is served before, during, or after the main course. In the Western United States it is common to serve salad as a first course, or just following appetizers and before the main course. This is a restaurant convenience. Restaurants need to keep the customers occupied while they are preparing the main course. If the guest does not order a first course, there could be a reasonable but lengthy wait for dinner. With nothing to do, customers feel neglected and get irritated. If they are eating salad, they do not notice the wait. On the East Coast, where there is a greater European influence, people understand that wine and salad often compete, and are more likely to eat salad after the main course, once the wine is finished. Although I eat salad after the main course, I let the server bring it at the beginning of the meal, because so many restaurants serve it too cold. If it has a chance to warm to room temperature, the flavor is far better.

Iceberg Lettuce with Roquefort or Russian Dressing

1 head iceberg lettuce cut into   1½ cups Roquefort or Russian
  6 wedges   dressing (see page 32)

Place the wedges on a serving plate, and pour over the dressing over the wedges.

Yield: 6 servings

➤ Do not prepare ahead.

Caesar Salad

Writers for years have been chasing down the source of this salad and the rumors are rife. Julia Child, after extensive investigation, decided that it was created by Caesar Cardini in Tijuana, Mexico. Whoever may have created it, properly made, it is outstanding. Serve it as a first course to give it its due.

1 or 2 large heads romaine,   8 anchovy fillets
  cleaned   ½ cup olive oil
1 egg   juice of 1 lemon
1 garlic clove, minced   ½ cup grated Parmesan cheese
salt and pepper to taste   1 cup croutons (see Note)

Remove the large outer leaves of the lettuce, and save for another use. Break or cut the inner leaves into fairly large chunks. Wrap the lettuce in paper toweling, and refrigerate until ready to serve.

In a small saucepan, place enough water to cover the egg, and bring to a boil. Boil the egg for 1 minute. Remove from the water.

In a salad bowl, mash the garlic with 1 teaspoon of salt and 4 anchovy fillets. Whisk in the olive oil. Add the romaine to the bowl, and toss to coat. Break the egg over the top, and toss again, coating evenly. Pour over the lemon juice and Parmesan, and toss again. Add the croutons, and toss for the final time.

Serve on plates with a knife and fork.

Yield: 6 servings

➤ Cannot be prepared ahead.

NOTE: The salad is supposed to be eaten with a knife and fork. For the croutons, rub the crust of a loaf of French or Italian bread with half a clove of garlic, and cut into ½ inch cubes. Toast the cubes in a 375°F oven, or sauté in olive oil until golden. The croutons can be prepared the day before.

Greek Salad

When I was a child, the Athens-Olympia Restaurant in Boston was a favorite source for Greek salad. Theirs included beets but, as with so many ethnic recipes, you use what you have.

6 cups mixed salad greens:
  romaine, escarole, chicory,
  and the like
1 large cucumber, scored, and
  cut into ¼ inch thick slices
3 tomatoes, cut into wedges
½ red onion, thinly sliced
6 to 12 pepperoncini (optional)

16 Alfonso olives
1½ cups Feta cheese
Vinaigrette made with lemon
  (see page 30)
2 tablespoons minced mint or
  oregano
salt and pepper to taste
1 cup sliced cooked beets

In a large salad bowl, place the greens, cucumber, tomatoes, onion, pepperoncini (if using), olives, and feta.

In a bowl, mix the vinaigrette, mint, and salt and pepper to taste. Pour the sauce over the salad, and toss to coat evenly. Add the beets, and toss gently until lightly coated. Serve.

Yield: 6 servings

➤ Can be prepared up to adding the dressing several hours ahead. Do not add the dressing until shortly before serving.

NOTE: This is the sort of salad to use on a buffet where you want it to look picture pretty as the guests enter. Toss it in front of them. Another presentation is to toss each ingredient with some of the dressing separately, and then arrange them attractively on individual plates or in a large bowl. Make a layer of lettuce, surround with overlapping slices of cucumber, arrange wedges of tomato in the center, place the pepperoncini and olives around the edges, and sprinkle with the cheese. Arrange the beets at one edge of the plate. Pepperoncini are pickled peppers sold in many markets. Drain them before using.

Salade Chiffonade (Shredded Salad)

1 head romaine, shredded
1 head Boston lettuce,
  shredded
1 head chicory, shredded
4 stalks celery, cut into fine
  julienne
3 tomatoes, peeled and
  quartered

2 hard cooked eggs, chopped
1 bunch of watercress, stems
  removed
1 cup cooked diced beets
¼ cup minced chives
½ to ¾ cup vinaigrette

In a salad bowl, place the romaine, Boston lettuce, and chicory, and toss to combine. Arrange concentric circles of celery, tomatoes, eggs, watercress, and beets on top of the greens. Sprinkle the chives over all. When ready to serve, toss with the vinaigrette.

Yield: 6 servings

➤ Can be prepared for the dressing several hours ahead. Cover with damp towels in the refrigerator.

Salade de Gascogne *(Gascony Salad)*

In Gascony, they serve the garlic croûte (chapon) to the guests, instead of letting the cook have it.

1 large head or chicory or escarole	½ to ¾ cup vinaigrette
1 garlic clove, halved	salt and pepper to taste
1 4 inch section of French bread	

Wash the lettuce, tear or cut into bite size pieces, wrap in paper toweling, and refrigerate until ready to use. Rub the inside of a salad bowl with the garlic.

Rub the bread section with the garlic, and pour on 2 tablespoons of vinaigrette. Place the chapon in the bottom of the bowl, put the lettuce on top, and toss with the dressing. Correct the seasoning with salt and pepper.

Yield: 6 servings

➤ The lettuce and the dressing can be prepared several hours ahead.

Salade à l'Huile de Noix *(Salad with Walnut Oil)*

¼ cup blanched, oven-dried walnut halves	2 tablespoons white wine vinegar
2 heads Boston or other soft lettuce	½ teaspoon salt
⅓ cup walnut oil	white pepper to taste

Preheat the oven to 400°F.

In a small saucepan, boil the walnuts in 1 cup of water for 2 minutes, drain, place in a towel, and rub off the skins. Put the walnuts on a pie plate and bake for 10 minutes, or until dried and crisp.

Wash the lettuce, and cut or tear into bite-size pieces. Wrap the lettuce in paper towels, and refrigerate until ready to serve.

In a small bowl, combine the walnut oil, vinegar, salt, and pepper. When ready to serve, put the lettuce and walnuts in a bowl. Whisk the dressing until emulsified, and toss with the salad.

Yield: 6 servings

➤ Do not dress the salad until just before serving.

NOTE: Use raspberry or currant vinegar instead of the white wine vinegar for a change, or use hazelnut oil instead of the walnut oil.

Sautéed Chèvre with Romaine Chiffonade

½ pound cold Montrachet
  cheese, cut into 6 slices
1 cup olive oil
1 cup bread crumbs

¼ cup dry red wine
salt and pepper to taste
1 head romaine, cleaned and
  shredded

Dip the cheese slices in the oil, roll in the bread crumbs, and place on a rack and chill for 1 hour. Dredge again in the bread crumbs, and chill for 30 minutes, or until ready to serve the salad. In a large bowl, combine ¼ cup of the oil with the wine, salt, and pepper.

In a skillet, heat the remaining oil, and sauté the cheese rounds until golden on both sides. Place the rounds on individual plates. Whisk the dressing, and fold in the lettuce. Toss to coat evenly, and arrange around the cheese on the plates.

Yield: 6 servings

➤ The cheese can be prepared for sautéing the day before. The dressing can be prepared the day before. Do not sauté the cheese, or toss the salad until ready to serve.

Romaine Salad with Mustard Cream Dressing and Walnuts

½ cup heavy cream
1 tablespoon Dijon mustard
1 teaspoon dried chervil
salt and pepper to taste

1 head romaine, bite-sized
  pieces
¾ cup toasted walnut halves

In a bowl, whisk the cream, mustard, chervil, salt, and pepper.

In a salad bowl, toss the romaine and walnuts. Add the dressing, and toss to coat evenly.

Yield: 6 servings

➤ Do not toss with the dressing until ready to serve.

Watercress and Water-Chestnut Salad with Walnut Oil

3 bunches watercress, stems
  removed
1 cup sliced waterchestnuts
½ cup walnut oil
1 teaspoon Dijon mustard

1 tablespoon lemon juice
3 tablespoons white wine
  vinegar
salt and pepper to taste

In a bowl, toss the watercress and water chestnuts. In a bowl, whisk the walnut oil, mustard, lemon juice, vinegar, salt, and pepper. Toss with the salad, and serve.

Yield: 6 servings

➤ Do not toss with the dressing until ready to serve.

Watercress, Pepper, and Mushroom Salad

2 bunches watercress, stems
  removed
½ pound spinach, stripped
  and torn or cut into
  bite-sized pieces
½ pound mushrooms, thinly
  sliced

1 red pepper, cut in julienne
⅔ cup olive oil
⅓ cup white wine vinegar
1 teaspoon Dijon mustard
½ teaspoon sugar
salt and pepper to taste

In a salad bowl, toss the watercress, spinach, mushrooms, and pepper.

In another bowl, whisk the olive oil, vinegar, mustard, sugar, salt, and pepper until emulsified.

Pour over the greens, and toss gently.

Yield: 6 servings

➤ Do not add the dressing until ready to serve.

Mushrooms

Mushrooms remind me of a dictionary definition of caviar I read when I was a child: "a delicacy unappreciated by the ignorant." I was insulted until I looked up ignorant and learned that it meant lacking in knowledge, uninformed. Mushrooms are prized by connoisseurs of fine foods everywhere, but those who have not developed their palates often find them less than appealing.

There are many species of mushrooms, mostly edible (although not all of the edible varieties are worth eating), and a few poisonous and even fewer deadly varieties. However, the deadly varieties cause prolonged painful deaths that can take from a few hours to as much as ten days. And there is a good possibility that your doctor may not diagnose the cause of your illness. Fortunately, only those who pick wild mushrooms are at risk. Unless you have been trained by a mycologist, *never* pick a wild mushroom, and if you do pick one, *do not eat it.* Many of the wild mushrooms have little or no flavor, and you risk illness or death for nothing. The only way to determine which mushrooms are poisonous is to know biology. Old wives tales about knifes darkening and such are just that—tales of old wives. Poisonous mushrooms are poisonous no matter what; cooking does not make them safe. Even as I write this I can look out the window and see a number of mushrooms sprouting around the cottage. I shall enjoy the view, but buy my mushrooms.

By the same token, the common white mushrooms are not dangerous raw! Several years ago a woman at a party became hysterical when her husband ate a raw mushroom on a crudité platter because she was convinced he was going to die. We were finally able to convince her that he would live, but her fear was palpable.

Safe, edible mushrooms are available year round, reasonably priced in almost every market. In addition, there are dried mushrooms, which are more expensive but have an unlimited shelf life. Only a few years ago the only mushrooms available were the *Champignons de couche* or *Champignons de Paris*, the cultivated white mushroom grown in cellars. Years ago, three-fourths of the American production was grown in a small Pennsylvania town. Recently, large corporations have started mushroom farms in other areas. Not only are white mushrooms grown in sheds in sterilized soil, but also brown, shiitake, enokitake, and oyster mushrooms.

In some areas wild mushrooms, such as morels, cèpes, porcini, and Portobello mushrooms are grown. Although more expensive than cultivated mushrooms, these are still within reason, especially compared to prices in the past.

Europeans, especially those from the Slavic countries, and Asians have long appreciated dried mushrooms and made them a staple. Once dried, the mushrooms keep for years. The drying intensifies the flavor. Some writers have suggested replacing the dried mushrooms with fresh shiitake mushrooms, but the flavor is not at all the same. An ounce of dried porcini has as much flavor impact as a pound of fresh. Needless to say, you pay for this. Dried mushrooms can be hideously expensive, ranging from a few cents to more than $10.00 an ounce! Fortunately, you do not need a lot for a full flavor, and the Chinese mushrooms that you use in larger amounts are in the lower price range.

Availability

Fresh

White mushrooms are available year round in almost every market. Wild mushrooms and cultivated special types are not as available, but usually one variety or another can be found throughout the year. The best time for the mushrooms is early spring and late summer and fall. Select mushrooms with no sign of shrinkage or slime. White mushrooms should have tightly closed caps so the gills do not show. If the gills show they are older and will be drier, but also more flavorful. There are occasions when the opened caps are desirable. Shiitakes, brown mushrooms, and Portobellos should have a dry-appearing, medium-brown cap. Portobellos are large—as much as 5 inches in diameter—and the gills fully exposed. Brown and shiitake mushrooms should have closed caps. Oyster mushrooms have a pale oyster color with fully exposed gills. Make sure they are not slimy. Morels should feel dry without any sign of sliminess.

Frozen

Freezing changes the texture of mushrooms, and they are not sold frozen. However, you can freeze preparations with cooked mushrooms (cooking changes the texture as well).

Canned

In most instances canned mushrooms are to be avoided. The canning process generally removes much of the flavor and changes the texture. In fact the only canned mushroom I recommend is the Chinese straw mushroom, which I have yet to find fresh.

Dried

Dried mushrooms have to be rehydrated before you can use them in a recipe. Soak them in warm water for 10 to 30 minutes until softened. Morels may need a diligent washing under running water to remove any grit from the crevices. After soaking, drain, squeeze out any excess moisture, and pat dry. The stem of the shiitake mushroom is very tough, and once dried even more so, so cut it off and discard. It never softens enough to serve. If porcini, cèpes, morels, or others still have a hard part, cut it off and discard it. Some frugal cooks will save the stems to flavor broths or sauces, and discard them before serving. I have not found them to have enough flavor to bother.

Preparation

Mushrooms, if dirty, should be cleaned carefully and quickly. (If they are not dirty do not bother to clean them. They are grown in a sterile soil, and if the caps are white, dry, and clean, further cleaning is unnecessary. If the stem has some of the soil attached, cut it off and proceed with the recipe.) Clean cultivated mushrooms by placing in a colander and shaking under running cold water. Do not let them sit in the water or soak up any more than absolutely necessary. Mushroom brushes, soft cloths, and the like are all very nice if you are cleaning a couple, but if you are cleaning a pound or more, it is not only tedious but unnecessary. It is important not to *soak* mushrooms in water, but you can rinse them quickly. Even tossing several pounds in a sink of cold water, swishing them around quickly, and draining immediately does not harm them. Letting them stand in a bowl of water for 10 minutes or longer will cause them to absorb too much water.

Wild mushrooms, especially morels, are quite gritty, and the *only* way of cleaning them is to put them into a large container of cold water and slosh diligently. Drain and pat dry.

Peeling

Hardly anyone peels mushrooms anymore. In the past it was common to peel them to keep them as white as possible, but this is no longer necessary. To peel mushrooms, peel the loose material just under the edge of the cap up and over the top with your thumb and index finger. It will come off in strips. Peeled mushrooms are soaked in acidulated water to keep them white, and often cooked in a *blanc* to keep them white.

Turning

Turned mushrooms are also becoming a lost art, except in the largest hotels and a few of the most serious restaurants. To peel a mushroom, hold the cape in your left hand, place the blade of a sharp paring knife against the top of the cap, and turn the cap against the edge of the blade to remove a thin wedge of mushroom. Turn the cape about ¼ inch, and repeat until you have circled the cap. You should have a cap that looks something like a turban when finished. To give the cap a finished appearance, press the point of the blade into the center of the cap in 5 or 6 places to make a star in the center. Toss the caps in lemon juice to keep them white until ready to use. Sauté the capes in a little butter, or simmer in boiling acidulated water, or a *blanc* until just tender.

Cooking Methods

Boiling
Boiling is the least recommended method of cooking mushrooms. Except when cooking in a *blanc*, this should be avoided.

Steaming
This method also drains the flavor from the mushroom.

Microwaving
Cook in 2 tablespoons of butter for 2 to 4 minutes. This is satisfactory, but you can cook them as quickly and have them taste better in a skillet.

Sautéing
This is the preferred method of cooking mushrooms. It brings out the flavor and allows for some browning.

Braising
This method also enhances the flavor of mushrooms, and allows them to marry with other ingredients.

Grilling
Brush mushrooms with butter or garlic oil and grill over charcoal. This works well for large, beefy mushrooms that take long enough to cook to absorb some of the charcoal flavor.

Quantity

Mushrooms shrink in cooking, so allow at least 1½ pounds for 6 persons, and 2 pound will not be too much.

Sauces

Mushrooms in cream is as perfect a marriage as peaches and cream. Mushrooms mix well with many herbs, and herbed butters are a perfect combination. Serve them cold, mixed with vinaigrette alone or flavored with herbs, and if raw, toss with mayonnaise. Mushrooms marry well with other vegetables, in particular, garlic, onions, and tomatoes.

Two Mushroom Consommé

The onion skins, which are strained out later, give color as well as flavor.

1 quart chicken stock	14 ounce can Italian tomatoes,
2 pounds minced mushrooms	drained and chopped
1½ ounces dried porcini,	12 parsley stems
soaked	3 garlic cloves, crushed
1 pound unpeeled onions,	2 sprigs thyme
chopped	salt and pepper to taste
5 carrots, chopped	½ cup thinly sliced
	mushrooms

In a saucepan, simmer the chicken stock, mushrooms, porcini, onions, carrots, tomatoes, parsley, garlic, thyme, pepper, and 5 cups of water for one hour.

Line a sieve with several layers of cheesecloth, and pour in the soup. Press on the solids to extract as much liquid as possible. Return the soup to the pan and taste for seasoning. If necessary, reduce over high heat to 8 cups. Correct the seasoning with salt and pepper.

Serve boiling hot, garnished with mushroom slices.

Yield: 6 servings

➤ Can be prepared ahead and frozen.

Zuppa di Funghi alla Siciliana (Sicilian Mushroom Soup)

¾ ounce dried Porcini	1 quart chicken or beef stock
mushrooms	16 ounce can Italian tomatoes,
1 cup hot water	drained and chopped
1½ tablespoons olive oil	salt and pepper to taste
1½ tablespoons butter	1 tablespoon minced parsley
½ cup minced onion	2 eggs
1 garlic clove, crushed	6 slices toasted Italian bread
½ pound thinly sliced	¾ cup grated Parmesan cheese
mushrooms	

In a bowl, soak the porcini in the hot water for 30 minutes, or until softened. Drain, reserving the liquid. Rinse the porcini to remove the grit, squeeze dry, and chop coarsely.

In a large casserole, heat the oil and butter, and sauté the onion and garlic until soft, but not brown. Add the mushrooms, and cook until the liquid evaporates. Add the porcini, the soaking liquid, stock, tomatoes, salt, and pepper. Simmer for 20 minutes. Just before serving, stir in the parsley.

In a bowl, beat the eggs until fluffy. Hold the bowl about 15 inches from the simmering soup, and pour in the egg in a thin, steady stream, stirring constantly. Immediately remove from the heat.

Place a slice of bread in each bowl, and ladle on the soup. Pass the cheese separately.

Yield: 6 servings

➤ Can be prepared, to the point of adding the parsley, the day before.

Minestra di Funghi Friulana (Friulian Mushroom Soup)

Friuli is a mountainous region in Northern Italy near the Swiss and German borders.

1 ounce dried porcini mushrooms	½ cup dry white wine
1½ cups hot water	1 tablespoon flour
2 tablespoons butter	5 cups beef or chicken stock
1 garlic clove, minced	salt and pepper to taste
¾ cup chopped onion	6 slices Italian bread, toasted
¾ pound mushrooms, thinly sliced	¾ cup grated Parmesan cheese

Soak the porcini in the hot water for 30 minutes. Drain the porcini in a sieve lined with a coffee filter or a double thickness of the finest cheesecloth. Reserve 1 cup of the soaking liquid. Rinse the porcini to remove any grit, squeeze dry, and chop.

In a saucepan, melt the butter, sauté the garlic until golden, and discard. Sauté the onion until soft, but not brown. Add the mushrooms, and cook, stirring occasionally, until the liquid evaporates. Add the porcini and reserved soaking liquid, and bring to a boil.

In a small bowl, stir the wine into the flour until smooth, pour into the soup, and simmer until the liquid is reduced by half. Stir in the stock, salt, and pepper. Simmer 15 minutes.

Place a slice of toast in the bottom of each soup bowl, and ladle the hot soup over the top. Sprinkle with cheese.

Yield: 6 servings

Marlborough Soup

1 pound mushrooms, minced
3 tablespoons butter
6 cups veal or chicken stock
1½ cups hot cream

½ teaspoon curry powder
salt and pepper to taste
croutons or tiny cream puffs

In a saucepan, sauté the mushrooms in the butter until soft. Stir in the chicken stock, cream, and curry powder, and simmer 5 minutes. Correct the seasoning with salt and pepper.

Serve with croutons or tiny unfilled cream puffs.

Yield: 6 servings

➤ Can be prepared the day before, or frozen.

Mushroom Bisque

⅓ cup butter
⅓ cup minced onion
¼ cup minced celery
6 tablespoons flour
½ teaspoon dried thyme
¼ teaspoon dried basil
4½ cups chicken stock
½ cup Sherry
3 bay leaves

1¼ pounds mushrooms, sliced
1 cup heavy cream
1 tablespoon lemon juice
1¼ teaspoons salt
¼ teaspoon ground white
  pepper
¼ teaspoon Worcestershire
  sauce
dash Tabasco

In a saucepan, melt the butter, and sauté the onion and celery until soft, but not browned. Add the flour, thyme, and basil, and stir for 5 minutes. Whisk in the stock and sherry, and bring to a boil, stirring. Add the bay leaves and mushrooms, and simmer 20 minutes, stirring occasionally.

Remove and discard the bay leaves, and if desired, purée the solids in a blender. Add the cream, lemon juice, salt, pepper, Worcestershire sauce, and Tabasco sauce.

Yield: 6 servings

➤ Can be prepared ahead and frozen.

Mushroom Filling I

Use this to fill small cream puffs, phyllo dough, or fresh vegetables, to serve as an hors d'oeuvre.

1½ pounds mushrooms,
  minced
¼ cup butter

salt and pepper to taste
2 tablespoons lemon juice
1 cup sour cream

In a large skillet, sauté the mushrooms in the butter until they start to give off their liquid. Add the salt, pepper, and lemon juice, and cook until almost dry. Remove from the heat, and stir in the sour cream.

Yield: about 1½ cups

➤ Can be prepared several days ahead.

NOTE: Many writers suggest squeezing the mushrooms in toweling, before sautéing, to remove the excess liquid. I think that discards much of the flavor, and prefer to concentrate the flavor by cooking over high heat until reduced. For flavor variations, add 1 or 2 tablespoons of herbs, such as tarragon, dill, summer savory, parsley, and the like.

Duxelles (Mushroom Filling II)

This is the classic French mushroom filling with a variation.

6 tablespoons of butter	1½ pounds mushrooms,
¼ cup minced shallots	minced
	salt and pepper to taste

In a skillet, melt the butter, and sauté the shallot until soft but not brown. Add the mushrooms, and sauté until the liquid evaporates and the mixture is quite dry. Season with salt and pepper.

Use to stuff tomatoes and other vegetables, as a paste to spread on meats before wrapping in pastry (as used in beef Wellington), or as a stuffing for fish, for example.

Yield: about 1½ cups

➤ Can be prepared ahead and frozen.

NOTE: You can flavor the duxelles with tarragon or parsley, if desired.

Some chefs will add 1 cup of thick cream sauce, or add 1 cup of heavy cream, and reduce it until most of the liquid has evaporated.

You can provide a richer and more intense flavor by substituting some wild mushrooms for some of the cultivated white mushrooms usually used in this recipe.

Funghi Trippati (Stewed Mushrooms with Tomato)

2 garlic cloves, minced	4 teaspoons tomato paste
5 tablespoons olive oil	salt and pepper to taste
1½ pounds mushrooms,	1 teaspoon dried oregano
thickly sliced	

In a skillet, sauté the garlic in the oil until golden, and discard. Add the mushrooms, and sauté until the moisture evaporates.

In a small bowl, mix the tomato paste with 1 tablespoon of hot water, and add to the pan with the salt, pepper, and oregano. Simmer over low heat for 15 minutes.

Yield: 6 servings

➤ Can be prepared ahead and reheated.

Wild Mushrooms Russian Style

The greater the variety of mushrooms, the more interesting this dish will be. If necessary, add some cultivated mushrooms to stretch the budget.

1½ pounds assorted wild mushrooms, sliced	2 tablespoons minced chives
3 tablespoons butter	2 tablespoons minced parsley
salt and pepper to taste	1 tablespoon minced dill
	½ cup sour cream

In a large skillet, sauté the mushrooms in the butter until the liquid evaporates. Season with salt and pepper, and stir in the chives, parsley, and dill. Cook 1 minute. Remove from the heat, and fold in the sour cream.

Yield: 6 servings

➤ Best if made and served.

Variations:

A Czech version of this replaces the herbs with ½ teaspoon of caraway seeds, and leaves the sour cream as an option.

Champignons aux Herbs (Mushrooms with Herbs)

10 tablespoons butter	3 tablespoons minced dill
½ cup thinly sliced shallots	¼ cup minced chervil
3 garlic cloves, left whole	1½ pounds mushrooms,
½ cup minced chives	thinly sliced
½ cup minced parsley	salt and pepper to taste
½ cup minced coriander	

In a skillet, heat 4 tablespoons of butter, and sauté the shallots and garlic until they are soft, and just start to turn brown. Add the chives, parsley, coriander, dill, and chervil, and cook 1 minute, stirring. Remove from the heat.

In a large skillet, melt the remaining butter, and sauté the mushrooms until the liquid evaporates, stirring to cook evenly. Season with salt and pepper. Remove the garlic from the herbs and discard, stir the herbs into the mushrooms, and heat.

Yield: 6 servings

➤ Can be prepared ahead and reheated.

Cèpes à la Bigourdane (Sautéed Cèpes)

2 pounds cèpes	1 bunch parsley, minced
3 tablespoons olive oil	2 tablespoons fresh bread
4 or 5 cloves garlic, minced	crumbs
2 shallots, minced	salt and pepper to taste

Wash the mushrooms well and dry.
In a skillet, sauté the mushrooms in the oil until tender. When almost done, stir in the garlic, shallots, parsley, bread crumbs, salt, and pepper.
Serve.

Yield: 6 servings

➤ Cannot be prepared ahead.

NOTE: If cèpes are not available, you can prepare the dish with cultivated mushrooms. To give a wild flavor, soak some porcini or other dried mushroom in hot water for 30 minutes, drain, saving the liquid, and add to the mushrooms. Sauté until the liquid evaporates, add the soaking liquid, and reduce until almost evaporated, before adding the remaining ingredients.

Funghi Trifolati
(Sautéed Mushrooms with Parsley and Garlic)

This is the basic recipe for all dishes called trifolati, "cooked liked truffles."
It is a simple, easy, quick method of enhancing almost any vegetable.

1½ teaspoons minced garlic	salt and pepper to taste
½ cup olive oil	3 tablespoons minced parsley
1½ pounds mushrooms, ¼	
inch thick slices	

In a skillet, sauté the garlic in the olive oil until it colors lightly, but does not brown. Turn the heat to high and add the mushrooms. When the mushrooms have absorbed the oil, lower the heat, and season with salt and pepper.
When the mushroom juices appear, raise the heat, and cook 4 to 5 minutes, stirring often, until the liquid evaporates. Correct the seasoning with salt and pepper, and sprinkle with parsley.
Serve immediately.

Yield: 6 servings

➤ Can be prepared ahead and reheated, but best if prepared and served.

Champignons Roses aux Herbs
(Mushrooms Sautéed with Shallots, Garlic, and Herbs)

Not to be outdone, here is a similar French version of sautéed mushrooms. The rose refers to a particular type of wild mushroom with a white cap and slightly pink undergills, but cultivated mushrooms do nicely.

1 tablespoon minced shallots	1½ pounds mushrooms,
6 tablespoons butter	quartered
1 teaspoon minced chives	2 teaspoons minced parsley
1 teaspoon minced chervil	1 clove garlic, minced
	salt and pepper to taste

In a skillet, sauté the shallots in the butter until soft, but not brown. Add the mushrooms, and sauté over medium heat for 5 minutes, stirring occasionally. Add the parsley, chives, chervil, and garlic, and sauté 2 minutes longer. Correct the seasoning with salt and pepper.

Yield: 6 servings

➤ Best if cooked and served, but can be reheated.

Champignons Provençale
(Mushrooms Provence Style)

This is a perfect dish for the garlic and mushroom lover. The bread adds flavor and texture. It is a good way to use not quite fresh bread.

2 pounds button mushrooms	12 ½ inch cubes of French bread
olive oil	½ cup minced parsley
1 garlic clove, chopped	2 tablespoons minced garlic
salt and pepper to taste	lemon juice to taste

Cut the mushroom stems evenly with the bottom of the cap. In a bowl, toss the caps with just enough olive oil to coat evenly. Add the garlic, and season with salt and pepper. Marinate for 1 hour.

When ready to serve, place the mushrooms in a hot skillet, and sauté over high heat until any water evaporates. Add the bread cubes, sauté until the bread browns, and sprinkle with the minced parsley, garlic, and lemon juice.

Serve hot.

Yield: 6 or more servings

➤ The mushrooms can be marinated for several hours, but cook just before serving.

Champignons Frites aux Herbes
(Breaded, Herbed Mushroom Fritters)

1 pound mushrooms	¼ teaspoon minced oregano
½ cup flour	¼ teaspoon minced marjoram
2 eggs	pinch of Cayenne pepper
¼ cup water	½ teaspoon minced thyme
1 tablespoon olive oil	oil for frying
salt and pepper to taste	anchovy mayonnaise (see
2 cups fresh bread crumbs	Note)

Rinse the mushrooms, drain well, and dredge in the flour.

In a bowl, mix the eggs, water, olive oil, salt, and pepper. In another bowl, mix the bread crumbs, oregano, marjoram, Cayenne pepper, and thyme.

Heat the oil to 360°F. Dip the mushrooms in the eggs, and then in the crumbs. Fry until golden.

Serve immediately with anchovy mayonnaise as a dip.

Yield: about 24 fritters

➤ The mushrooms can be coated several hours ahead.

NOTE: For anchovy mayonnaise, add anchovy paste to lemon-flavored mayonnaise to taste.

Grilled Mushrooms with Marrow and Herbs

If marrow is not available, these will be almost as good (see Note).

¼ cup olive oil	½ teaspoon rosemary leaves
¼ cup lemon juice	salt and pepper to taste
1 scallion, chopped	36 mushroom caps
1 garlic clove, halved	3 ounces marrow, sliced
2 tablespoons parsley sprigs	(optional)
1 teaspoon thyme leaves	parsley sprigs

In a processor, process the olive oil, lemon juice, scallion, garlic, parsley, thyme, rosemary, salt, and pepper until finely minced. Brush the mixture over the mushroom caps, and arrange on a baking sheet. Place a slice of marrow on each cap, and broil until the marrow is melted. Decorate with parsley sprigs.

Yield: 6 servings

➤ Can be prepared for broiling several hours ahead.

NOTE: For marrow, buy "dog" bones at the market and simmer in water for a few minutes until you can extract it. Chill and then cut into slices. Or, with a narrow bladed knife, scoop out the marrow in one piece.

If desired, skewer the basted mushrooms and cook over charcoal, basting with any remaining liquid until browned and tender.

Rôties au Comte (Morels and Comte Cheese on Toast)

Serve these as a first course, or even as a supper with sliced smoked turkey and a tossed green salad.

1 ounce dried morels	½ pound grated Comte or
4 tablespoons butter	Gruyère cheese
½ pound thinly sliced	salt and pepper to taste
mushrooms	6 slices whole wheat French
1 cup crème fraîche, or heavy	bread, toasted
cream	¼ cup minced chives

Preheat the broiler.

In a bowl of hot water, soak the morels for 30 minutes, or until softened. Drain, rinse under cold water, and cut in half lengthwise. Rinse again to remove any grit, and drain well.

In a skillet, melt the butter, and cook the morels and mushrooms until they have absorbed the butter and are wilted. Add the crème fraîche to the mushrooms, and reduce by half over high heat. Lower the heat, add the cheese, and cook, stirring, until melted and incorporated. Correct the seasoning with salt and pepper.

Place a generous tablespoon on each piece of toast, and sprinkle with chives. Broil until hot and bubbling.

Yield: 6 servings

➤ The mushroom mixture can be prepared the day before and reheated.

Champignons en Ramekins
(Mushrooms in Small Cups)

3 tablespoons butter	1½ cups heavy cream, scalded
1½ pounds mushrooms,	nutmeg to taste
thinly sliced	

Preheat the oven to 350°F.

In a large skillet, melt the butter, and sauté the mushrooms until the liquid evaporates. Divide the mushrooms among 6 ramekins (custard cups), and spoon the cream over them. Sprinkle with the nutmeg. Bake for 10 minutes or until bubbling hot.

Yield: 6 servings

➤ Can be prepared for the final baking several hours ahead.

Mushrooms Gratin

⅓ cup fresh bread crumbs	3 tablespoons medium-dry
⅓ cup grated Gruyère cheese	sherry
¼ cup grated Parmesan cheese	1¼ cups heavy cream
2 tablespoons minced parsley	salt and pepper to taste
1½ tablespoons minced basil	¾ pound mushrooms,
2 teaspoons minced thyme	quartered
¼ cup butter	¾ pound assorted wild
¼ cup minced shallots	mushrooms, quartered
2 garlic cloves, minced	parsley
3 tablespoons dry Madeira	

Preheat the broiler.

In a small bowl, mix the bread crumbs, Gruyère, Parmesan, parsley, basil, and thyme. Set aside.

In a skillet, heat the butter, and sauté the shallots and garlic until soft, but not brown. Add the mushrooms, and cook, stirring, until the liquid evaporates, and turn into a bowl. Add the Madeira, sherry, cream, salt, and pepper to the skillet, and reduce to ½ cup. Add the mushrooms to the sauce, and blend.

Turn into a heat-proof serving dish, and sprinkle with the crumb mixture. Brown under the broiler, and garnish with the parsley.

Yield: 6 servings

➤ Can be prepared for broiling several hours ahead.

Cèpes en Papillote (Wild Mushrooms in Paper)

Sealing various foods in paper concentrates the flavors in and around the food, so that when it is first served, the diner is enveloped in all of the aromas before tasting.

1½ pounds fresh cèpes,	3 garlic cloves, minced
shiitakes, or morels	salt and pepper to taste
¾ cup crème fraîche	1 or 2 tablespoons butter,
⅓ cup olive oil	melted
¼ cup minced tarragon	

Preheat the oven to 400°F.

Rinse the mushrooms and dry well. Quarter if large, or leave whole.

In a bowl, whisk the cream, oil, tarragon, garlic, salt, and pepper. Add the morels, and toss to coat.

With a single sheet of parchment, or 6 smaller pieces, cut into heart shapes. Fold the paper in half, and cut into half a heart so that it opens to a heart.

Place the mushroom mixture on one side of the paper, fold over, and crimp the edges, starting at one end, folding the cut edge into small pleats. If necessary, seal the final fold with a paper clip.

Place the hearts on a baking sheet. Brush the heart with melted butter. Bake for 20 minutes until puffed and golden.

Serve at once, opening envelope at table.

Yield: 6 servings

➤ Can be prepared for baking up to 24 hours before.

NOTE: If desired, make the heart from foil.

Mushrooms Cooked in Vine Leaves

12 grape leaves, rinsed and
  drained
3 tablespoons olive oil
1 pound cleaned button
  mushrooms

3 or 4 whole garlic cloves,
  peeled
salt and pepper to taste

Preheat the oven to 325°F.

In a large casserole, with a tight fitting cover, arrange half of the vine leaves. Pour 2 tablespoons of oil over the leaves, and add the mushrooms. Sprinkle the mushrooms with garlic, salt, pepper, and the remaining oil.

Cover with the remaining vine leaves and the casserole cover. Bake for 45 minutes. Remove the top layer of vine leaves when serving.

Yield: 6 servings

➤ Can be prepared for the final baking several hours ahead.

Roasted Garlic Mushrooms

Serve these as a first course, or with grilled veal chops and garlic roasted potatoes.

2 pounds mushrooms,
  preferably wild
12 tablespoons butter
1 teaspoon minced thyme
10 sprigs thyme, parsley, or
  tarragon

¼ cup red wine vinegar
salt and pepper to taste
1 cup whole, unpeeled,
  roasted garlic cloves (see
  page 334)

Preheat the oven to 450.

Remove the mushroom stems, and use in soups. Arrange the caps in a double layer in a gratin pan.

In a bowl, cream the butter and minced thyme. Dot over the mushrooms. Push the herb in and around the mushrooms. Sprinkle with vinegar, salt, and pepper.

Bake 15 minutes, sprinkle with garlic cloves, and stir the mushrooms, basting with the butter. Bake 10 minutes longer, basting twice more.

Yield: 6 servings

➤ Can be prepared for baking several hours ahead.

Braised Mushrooms with Pancetta and Pine Nuts

1 ounce dried porcini	1½ pounds mushrooms,
¼ pound pancetta, diced	thinly sliced
2 to 4 tablespoons olive oil	¼ cup dry Madeira
¼ cup pine nuts	½ cup heavy cream
1 garlic clove, minced	¼ cup minced parsley
½ cup minced onion	salt and pepper

In a small bowl, soak the porcini in warm water for an hour. Remove mushrooms, and strain the liquid through several layers of damp cheese cloth. Rinse the porcini, squeeze dry, and chop.

In a skillet, cook the pancetta in 2 tablespoons olive oil over low heat until golden. Remove with a slotted spoon. Add enough olive oil to measure 3 tablespoons, and sauté the pine nuts until golden. Remove, and add to pancetta.

Sauté the garlic and onion until soft, but not brown. Increase the heat, add the porcini and fresh mushrooms, and cook, tossing, until the mushrooms begin to give up their juices. Add the Madeira and mushroom liquid, and cook until reduced to 2 tablespoons. Add the cream, and simmer until the sauce thickens slightly. Stir in the parsley, pancetta, and pine nuts. Season with salt and pepper.

Yield: 6 servings

Rolled Mushroom Soufflé with Spinach Filling

This soufflé is baked in a jelly-roll pan, so it can be filled and rolled. It is a wonderful brunch, luncheon, or supper main course.

oil	1 cup sour cream
2 pound spinach, washed and	4-5 mushroom caps (optional)
stripped	1½ pounds mushrooms,
6 tablespoons butter	minced
pinch grated nutmeg	2 tablespoons lemon juice
salt and pepper to taste	6 eggs, separated

Preheat the oven to 350°F. Brush an 11 by 15 inch jelly-roll pan, line with waxed paper, and brush with oil again.

In a large covered kettle, cook the spinach in the water on its leaves until wilted, stirring often. Drain, squeezing out the excess moisture. Chop the spinach finely.

In a skillet, sauté the spinach in the tablespoon of butter until heated, and stir in ¾ cup sour cream. Season with nutmeg, salt, and pepper. Set aside. In a small saucepan, warm the remaining sour cream, and set aside.

Sauté the mushrooms in another tablespoon of butter until golden, and set aside. In a large skillet, sauté the minced mushrooms in the remaining 4 tablespoons of butter and lemon juice until the liquid evaporates.

In a bowl, beat the egg yolks until light and fluffy, and stir into the mushrooms. In another bowl, beat the egg whites until almost stiff, and carefully fold into the mushroom mixture.

Pour into the prepared baking sheet and bake in the middle of the oven for 15 minutes, or until it springs back when touched and just starts to turn golden.

Place two sheets of waxed paper on the counter, and unmold the soufflé onto the paper. Carefully peel the paper from the soufflé, spread with the spinach mixture and, using the waxed paper on the counter to help, roll along the long side and turn onto a heated serving platter.

Garnish with the reserved sour cream and the sautéed mushroom caps.

Yield: 6 servings

➤ The spinach filling, sautéed mushrooms, and the minced mushrooms can all be prepared several hours ahead. The soufflé will stand for 30 minutes before baking.

Stuffed Mushrooms

Stuffed mushrooms are a perfect accompaniment to a main course, and make a delicious first course, served with a knife and fork. However, as an hors d'oeuvre at a cocktail party they are unsuitable. They are slippery and difficult to pick up when perfectly cooked, and are very juicy and therefore messy, which can easily soil the guests. If you must have them, place the mushrooms on slices of toast to act as blotters for the juices, and to make it easier to lift them. Of course, they must be no more than 2 bites big.

Funghi Ripiene (*Stuffed Mushrooms*)

12 large mushroom caps	3 tablespoons white bread
½ cup melted butter	crumbs
salt and pepper to taste	½ cup grated Gruyère cheese
1 tablespoon olive oil	¼ cup grated Parmesan cheese
3 tablespoons minced onion	¼ cup minced parsley
¼ cup dry Marsala	2 or 3 tablespoons cream

Preheat the oven to 375°F.

Remove the mushroom stems and mince. Brush the caps inside and out with 3 tablespoons melted butter. Place hollow sides up in lightly buttered gratin. Season with salt and pepper.

Heat 2 tablespoons butter with oil in sauté pan, and sauté onion until soft, but not brown. Add the mushroom stems, and cook over high heat for 6 to 8 minutes. Add the Marsala, and cook until liquid is almost evaporated.

In a bowl, mix the bread crumbs, ¼ cup grated Gruyère and the Parmesan, with the parsley, and salt and pepper. Stir in the cooked mushrooms and the cream. Fill the caps with the stuffing, and top with remaining Gruyère.

Baste with remaining 3 tablespoons of butter, and bake until tender and lightly browned—about 15 to 20 minutes.

Yield: 6 servings

➤ Can be prepared for the final baking the day before.

Baked Stuffed Mushrooms with Chestnuts

24 large mushrooms	1½ cups boiled, or
¼ cup minced onion	unsweetened, canned
6 tablespoons butter	chestnuts, crumbled
1 tablespoon minced chives	1 egg
1 tablespoon minced parsley	2 tablespoons Madeira
½ cup dry bread crumbs	salt and pepper to taste

Preheat the oven to 450°F.

Remove the stems from the mushrooms, and mince.

In a skillet, sauté the mushroom stems and onions in 4 tablespoons of butter until the liquid evaporates. Add the chives and parsley, and stir to incorporate. Add the crumbs, and cook until the crumbs are browned. Stir in the chestnuts, egg, Madeira, salt, and pepper.

In a saucepan, melt the remaining butter, and brush the caps on all sides. Place the caps in a baking dish, stuff with the filling, and brush with any remaining butter. Bake for 8 to 10 minutes, or until tender.

Yield: 6 servings

➤ Can be prepared for baking several hours ahead.

NOTE: These have a substantial filling; plan on 8 to 12 servings if the menu is large.

Champignons Farcis aux Palourdes
(Mushrooms Stuffed with Clams)

18 to 24 hard-shelled clams,	1 teaspoon arrowroot
shucked and juices reserved	1 egg yolk
24 large mushrooms	2 tablespoons minced chives
1 tablespoon butter	2 tablespoons minced basil
2 tablespoons minced shallots	1 tablespoon Pernod
½ cup dry white wine	1 teaspoon minced tarragon
¾ cup heavy cream	

Chop the clams and set aside. Remove the stems from the mushrooms, and save for another use.

In a skillet, sauté the mushrooms in the butter, stemmed side up, until golden on the bottom. Turn, and cook 1 minute longer.

In a small saucepan, boil the shallots and wine until almost evaporated. Add the cream and all but 1 tablespoon of reserved clam juice, and reduce to 1 cup.

In a small bowl, mix the tablespoon of clam juice, arrowroot, and egg yolk. Stir into sauce, and simmer until just thickened. Remove from the heat, and stir in the chives, basil, Pernod, and tarragon. Fold in the chopped clams.

Place the hot caps on a serving platter, fill with the clam mixture, and serve immediately.

Yield: 6 servings

➤ Both the caps and the sauce can be prepared ahead, reheated, and combined just before serving.

Stuffed Mushrooms with Ham

Use this simple version to garnish roasted tenderloin.

12 large mushrooms	juice of ½ a lemon
1 cup cooked minced ham	pepper to taste
2 egg yolks	

Preheat the oven to 350°F.

Remove the mushroom stems and mince finely. In a bowl, mix the stems, ham, egg yolks, lemon juice, and pepper. Fill the caps with the mixture, letting it mound over the top.

Place the caps in a baking dish, and bake for 15 minutes, or until tender.

Yield: 6 servings

➤ Can be prepared several hours ahead and baked just before serving.

Chinese Mushrooms Stuffed with Shrimp

¾ pound raw shrimp, chopped	1 head iceberg lettuce, leaves separated
¼ pound Smithfield or Prosciutto, minced	1½ teaspoons waterchestnut flour, or cornstarch
salt and pepper to taste	¾ cup chicken stock
⅛ teaspoon Asian sesame oil	1 teaspoon dry sherry
24 Chinese mushrooms, soaked, drained, and stems discarded	salt to taste
	½ teaspoon sesame oil

In a small bowl, mix the shrimp, ham, salt, pepper, and sesame oil, and marinate, refrigerated, for 30 minutes. Stuff the mushrooms with the mixture, and place in a steamer basket.

Bring 2 quarts of water to a boil, and blanch the lettuce until limp. Drain and pat dry. Arrange the lettuce on a serving platter, and top with the mushrooms.

In a small bowl, mix the waterchestnut flour with 1 tablespoon of stock. In a small saucepan, bring the remaining stock, sherry, salt, and sesame oil to a boil, and add the waterchestnut flour mixture. Cook until clear, and pour over the mushrooms.

Yield: 6 servings

➤ Can be prepared ahead and reheated.

NOTE: You can use any steamer (see page 7).

Funghi a Funghetto Genovese
(Mushrooms with Eggplant and Zucchini Genoa Style)

3⁄4 ounce porcini	2 zucchini, peeled, 1⁄2 inch
1 cup hot water	slices
1⁄2 pound mushrooms, thinly	1 tablespoon minced parsley
sliced	1⁄2 teaspoon dried oregano
1 eggplant, peeled, 1⁄2 inch dice	1 garlic clove, minced
salt and pepper to taste	salt and pepper to taste
4 tablespoons olive oil	lemon juice to taste

Soak the porcini in the hot water for 30 minutes and drain, reserving 1⁄2 cup liquid. Rinse the mushrooms under cold water, and squeeze dry. Chop coarsely, and set aside.

Sprinkle the eggplant with salt, let drain for 30 minutes, rinse, and pat dry. In a skillet, sauté the eggplant in 2 tablespoons oil until browned on all sides. Add the zucchini, and sauté, adding more oil if needed.

In a small bowl, mix the parsley, oregano, and garlic together, and set aside. In another skillet, heat 2 tablespoons of oil, and sauté the mushrooms until the liquid has evaporated. Add the porcini and soaking liquid, and cook uncovered until the liquid is absorbed. Add to the eggplant mixture, and correct the seasoning with salt and pepper.

Just before serving, sprinkle with the garlic mixture and lemon juice.

Yield: 6 servings

➤ Can be cooked ahead and reheated. Do not add the garlic mixture until just before serving, for a fresher taste.

Wild Mushroom Potatoes Anna

There is a special heavy copper pan for making this preparation, but you can improvise with a 9 inch cake pan, or even use two baking sheets (see the note below).

3⁄4 pound shiitake mushrooms,	1 tablespoon minced basil
sliced	4 baking potatoes, thinly sliced
2 tablespoons butter	salt and pepper
1⁄3 cup grated Parmesan cheese	

Preheat the oven to 425°F. Butter a potatoes Anna mold, or a 9 inch cake pan.

In a skillet, sauté the mushrooms in the butter until they are tender and the liquid evaporates. Stir in the Parmesan and basil.

Arrange half the potato slices in overlapping circles in the mold. Cover with the mushroom mixture, pressing as flat as possible, and season with salt and pepper.

Top with overlapping circles of the remaining potatoes. Butter the cover of the mold, or butter a sheet of foil and place on the potatoes. (The potatoes should be mounded above the top of the pan.) If using a cake pan, place an 8 inch cake tin on top of the foil, and a brick or other heavy, ovenproof weight on top of that.

Bake until the potatoes are tender—about 1 hour and 10 minutes. The potatoes should be browned and crisp. If they have not, carefully unmold onto a baking sheet, and broil until golden brown on the top.

Yield: 6 servings

➤ Because the potatoes will darken if left too long, it is best to assemble and bake it immediately. If desired, you can bake it, let it cool, and then crisp it in a hot oven.

NOTE: If you wish to do it on a baking sheet: Butter the sheet, make a round circle of potato slices, top with the mushrooms, and cover with the remaining potato slices. Cover with a sheet of buttered foil, another baking sheet, and a heavy weight. Bake until tender. Cool, remove the weight, and brown under the broiler just before serving.

Fettuccine with Sun-Dried Tomatoes and Wild Mushrooms

¼ cup butter	2 cups heavy cream
¼ cup minced shallots	salt and pepper to taste
½ pound wild mushrooms, quartered	1 pound fettuccine
6 sun-dried tomatoes, julienne	2 or 3 scallions, sliced

In a skillet, melt the butter, and cook the shallots until soft, but not brown. Add the mushrooms and tomatoes, and cook, stirring, over high heat for 3 minutes. Add the cream, and season with salt and pepper. Simmer until thick enough to coat the back of a spoon.

In a large kettle of boiling salted water, cook the fettuccine until al dente. Drain, put into a bowl, and toss with sauce. Garnish with scallions.

Yield: 6 servings

➤ The sauce can be prepared the day before and reheated. It can be frozen.

Risotto ai Funghi *(Rice with Mushrooms)*

In many restaurants, risotti have become a double-digit fad.

½ cup butter	1 cup dry white wine
½ cup onion, thinly sliced	3 cups Arborio rice
¾ pound wild mushrooms,	7 cups boiling meat stock
thinly sliced	¾ cup grated Parmesan cheese

In a saucepan, melt half the butter, and sauté the onion until soft, but not brown. Add the mushrooms, and stir to coat with the butter. Add the wine, and cook until almost evaporated. Add the rice, and cook, stirring, until the grains start to turn opaque.

Add ½ cup stock, and cook until it has been absorbed. Add another ½ cup stock, and cook until it is absorbed. Continue adding the stock, ½ cup at a time, stirring constantly, until all the stock has been absorbed. Add the remaining butter and the cheese, cover, and let rest 2 to 3 minutes before serving.

Yield: 6 servings

➤ Cannot be prepared ahead (see Note).

NOTE: Risotto is one of the few dishes that requires constant attention and has to be prepared just before it is served. The rice must absorb the liquid slowly, so it is added slowly and stirred steadily. When it is done, the rice should be creamy and smooth, with a little bite in the center of each grain.

The time and patience required is worth the wait. Do as many restaurants do: serve the risotto as a first course (it deserves that much attention) rather than as the accompaniment to a meat course. Serve the meat with a simple vegetable to accentuate the specialness of the rice.

Wild Rice with Mushrooms and Almonds

Wild rice and mushrooms are a perfect combination. The woodsy earthy tones and flavors complement each other.

5 tablespoons butter	½ pound mushrooms, thinly
4 tablespoons minced onion	sliced
1 cup wild rice	¼ cup slivered almonds,
3 cups chicken stock	toasted
salt and pepper to taste	

Preheat the oven to 350°F.

In a 2 quart casserole, melt 2 tablespoons butter. Add 2 tablespoons of onion and cook, stirring, until soft, but not brown. Add the wild rice, and stir to coat with the butter. Add the chicken stock and ½ teaspoon salt, and stir until it reaches a boil. Cover, and bake for 1 hour.

Add the remaining butter to a skillet, and sauté the onion until soft, but not brown. Add the mushrooms, and cook until the liquid evaporates. Season with salt and pepper. Fold the almonds and mushrooms into the cooked rice.

Yield: 6 servings

➤ Can be prepared ahead and reheated, but best if freshly prepared.

Variations:
Add pecans, walnuts, or cashews instead of almonds.
  Sauté 1 diced red pepper with the mushrooms.
  Fold in 1 cup of cooked corn kernels.
  Add 1 to 2 cups of white rice if you want a less earthy flavor.

Barley and Mushroom Casserole

Barley is one of the more neglected grains. Its deep, rich, earthy flavor goes particularly well with rich, meaty, wine-flavored stews and braised dishes. It is also good with baked ham.

3 tablespoons butter	2½ cups chicken stock
½ cup minced onions	1/2 cup unsalted roasted
½ pound shiitake mushrooms,	cashew nuts
sliced	3 tablespoons minced parsley
salt and pepper to taste	2 scallions, thinly sliced
1 cup barley	

Preheat the oven to 350°F.

In a 1 quart casserole, heat the butter, and sauté the onion until soft, but not brown. Add the mushrooms, salt, and pepper, and sauté for 5 minutes. Add the barley, and cook, stirring, until it starts to turn golden. Add the stock, bring to a boil, and bake for 30 minutes. Stir in the cashews, parsley, and scallions.

Yield: 6 servings

➤ Can be prepared for baking several hours ahead.

Variations:
Use of any mushroom of choice instead of shiitake.
  Use beef or veal stock in place of chicken stock.
  Use almonds or pecans instead of cashews.
  Add sautéed minced red pepper for color and flavor.
  Add 1 clove minced garlic to the onion.

Bulgur with Mushrooms and Almonds

Bulgur, or cracked wheat, is a favorite starch in the Middle East. It makes a delicious change from the usual potato, rice, or pasta.

1 quart chicken stock	5 tablespoons olive oil
2½ cups bulgur	salt and pepper

| 12 ounces mushrooms, thinly sliced | ½ cup slivered almonds, toasted |

In a saucepan, bring the stock to a boil, and add bulgur in a slow, steady stream, without stirring. Cover, and simmer until tender—about 45 minutes.

In a saucepan, heat three tablespoons of oil until almost smoking, and pour over the cooked bulgur. Cook over medium heat for another 7 minutes, or until the bulgur is tender. Season with salt and pepper.

Meanwhile, in a skillet, sauté the mushrooms in the remaining 2 tablespoons of oil until browned. Add the mushrooms and almonds to the bulgur.

Yield: 6 servings

➤ Cannot be prepared ahead.

Escargots with Wild Mushrooms

2 cloves garlic, minced	¼ cup vermouth
1 shallot, minced	2 tablespoons almond liqueur
3 tablespoons butter	2 cups heavy cream
1 cup sliced wild mushrooms	salt and pepper
juice of 1 lemon	36 snails, drained and rinsed
¼ cup minced fresh herbs:	under cold water
thyme, basil, and parsley	

Preheat the oven to 350°F.

In a large skillet, sauté the garlic and shallot in the butter until soft, but not brown. Add the mushrooms, and cook over high heat until the juices start to flow. Add the lemon juice, herbs, vermouth, and liqueur, and reduce by ¼. Add the cream, and reduce, stirring, until it is thick enough to coat the back of a spoon. Correct the seasoning with salt and pepper.

In shallow gratins, place 6 snails, and coat the with the sauce. Bake for 8 to 10 minutes, or until bubbling hot.

Yield: 6 servings

➤ Can be prepared for the final baking the day before.

NOTE: If desired, place the snails on a bed of semolina gnocchi or toasted french bread.

Crêpes

Mushrooms are a delicious filling for crêpes. You can fill the crêpes with any of the sautéed mushroom mixtures on previous pages, or even those that have been baked in cream. Crêpes do wonders for leftovers. Use any extra mushroom mixtures as a filling, and drizzle with a little melted butter if there is no leftover sauce. To help you, here are a few specific recipes.

Crêpes aux Champignons Mornay
(Mushroom-filled Crêpes with Mornay Sauce)

This is the classic mushroom preparation for crêpes. You can change as you wish.

1½ pounds thinly sliced
  mushrooms
¼ cup butter
1 cup heavy cream
salt and pepper to taste

12 crêpes
1 cup Mornay sauce (see page
  22)
½ cup grated Gruyère cheese

Preheat the oven to 375°F.

In a large skillet, sauté the mushrooms in the butter until the liquid evaporates and the mushrooms start to brown. Add the cream, and simmer until thick enough to coat the back of a spoon. Season with salt and pepper.

Fill the crêpes, roll into tubes, and place in a single layer in a gratin pan. Coat the crêpes with the Mornay sauce, and sprinkle with the Gruyère.

Bake for 15 minutes, or until bubbling hot and the cheese starts to brown.

Yield: 6 servings

➤ Can be prepared for baking the day before.

Variations:

Season the mushrooms with an herb such as tarragon, dill, chervil, chives, savory, or rosemary.

Omit the cream, and use only the Mornay sauce on top.

Substitute a variety of wild mushrooms for the cultivated ones.

Use one of the garlic-flavored sautéed mushroom recipes, and coat with a fresh tomato sauce and a sprinkling of grated Parmesan or Romano.

Use only 1 pound of mushrooms, and fold in 1 cup of cooked, chopped shrimp, crab, lobster, scallops, or white fish, or use a combination of fish.

Add ½ cup minced ham to the mushrooms before adding the sauce.

Mixed Mushrooms over Fried Noodles

5 dried black mushrooms, soaked	1 tablespoon oyster sauce
3 medium bok choy stalks,	1¼ teaspoons cornstarch
halved lengthwise	¾ cup drained straw
½ carrot, thinly sliced	mushrooms, rinsed
9 ounces chow mein noodles	½ cup button mushrooms
¼ cup plus 2 tablespoons oil	¼ teaspoon salt
5 dried shrimp soaked in water	⅛ teaspoon white pepper
1 tablespoon plus 1 teaspoon	¼ cup red-wine vinegar
soy sauce	

Drain the black mushrooms, and cut off and discard stems. Cut the caps into halves.

In a large pot of water, blanch the bok choy and carrots. Remove from the pot with slotted spoon, and drain. Add noodles, and cook 4 or 5 minutes. Drain.

Heat a wok and ¼ cup oil until hot, and arrange the noodles into a large pancake. Cook until the bottom is crisp and golden—about 7 minutes. Turn in one piece, and cook second side until crisp. Transfer to a plate.

In a small bowl, mix the soy sauce, oyster sauce, and cornstarch.

Heat the wok with 2 tablespoons oil, and stir-fry black mushrooms until evenly coated. Add the straw mushrooms and button mushrooms, and stir-fry 45 seconds. Add Bok Choy cabbage, salt, and pepper, and stir-fry 30 seconds. Add soaked and drained shrimp, stir the soy mixture, and stir into the wok until the sauce boils and thickens. Pour over the noodles.

Serve with vinegar and additional soy sauce as condiments.

Yield: 6 servings

➤ This is best if made and served.

Raw Mushroom Salad

1½ pounds mushrooms,	¼ cup minced chives
thinly sliced	1 tablespoon caraway seeds
¾ cup sour cream	salt and pepper to taste

In a bowl, mix the mushrooms, sour cream, chives, caraway, salt, and pepper. Let marinate for 2 hours. Correct the seasoning with salt and pepper.

Yield: 6 servings

➤ Can be prepared the day before.

Champignons Vinaigrette *(Mushrooms Vinaigrette)*

1½ pounds button mushrooms   lettuce leaves
1 cup vinaigrette   minced parsley

Cut the mushroom stems evenly with the caps, and save for another use. In a covered container, combine the mushrooms and vinaigrette, and shake to coat evenly. Refrigerate for a couple of hours, shaking periodically.

Line serving plates with lettuce leaves, mound mushrooms in the center, and sprinkle with the parsley.

Yield: 6 servings

➤ Can be prepared the day before.

Mushroom and Water Chestnut Salad

¾ pound thinly sliced   3 tablespoons minced parsley
  mushrooms   ¼ cup lemon juice
¾ pound water chestnuts,   ⅓ cup olive oil
  peeled and thinly sliced   salt and pepper to taste
3 tablespoons minced scallions

In a bowl, toss the mushrooms, water chestnuts, scallions, parsley, lemon juice, olive oil, salt, and pepper until evenly coated.

Yield: 6 servings

➤ Can be prepared up to 2 hours before serving.

NOTE: This recipe calls for fresh water chestnuts. If they are not available, canned will do.

Okra

*I*t is not necessary to be born in the South to love okra, but it does help. Generally, those not born to it find the flavor uninteresting and the *texture* decidedly unpleasant. The juices of okra become slimy if boiled. This is wonderful if you need a slight thickening agent for other ingredients, as in a gumbo. To many of us a bowl of boiled okra is about as appealing as a bowl of warm glue; however, fried okra is a delight. Those who hate the vegetable often find the deep-fried versions delicious.

Okra is a favorite food and is highly prized in the cooking of South America, Africa, and India, but other cultures seem to have left it alone. The plant grows in Northern climes, and is most decorative with relatively large yellow flowers with red centers. It might do to just grow it as a flower and forget the eating. The advantage to growing your own is that you know how fresh and how young it is—the younger the better. Mature pods are woody and fibrous, and should be avoided.

Availability

July and August are the prime times for fresh okra, though it is found in the markets year-round shipped from other areas.

Fresh
Look for bright green pods, with flexible tips, about 2 to 3 inches long. Avoid larger pods, those with a dull color, or those that are hard or shriveled. Store no more than two days in the refrigerator uncovered. They will soften and will be even slimier when cooked.

Frozen
Okra does freeze well, and frozen okra is suitable for most recipes.

Canned
Canned okra can be used in soups or stews where other ingredients will diminish the slimy quality.

Preparation

Wash the fresh pods with a scrub brush, or scrape the fuzz off the pod with a paring knife. Take care not to pierce the pod. To avoid sliminess, use the pods whole, whenever possible. With a paring knife, cut around the top of each pod to remove the stem without exposing the inside. If the pods are so large they must be sliced, none of these precautions will work.

Cooking Methods

Boiling
There are people who like okra boiled until tender and served with butter and some lemon juice, but for most people this is the least acceptable method of cooking the vegetable.

Steaming
Steam okra over an inch of boiling water for 5 to 6 minutes, or until tender. If the pods have not been cut, the okra will be tender, and not very slimy.

Microwaving
Place the okra in a covered container with the water from washing on the surface, and cook for about 6 minutes.

Stewing
This is one of the best methods of cooking okra. Tomatoes are the usual accompaniment, but any eggplant stew can be made with okra instead.

Deep-Frying
Okra is fried in a bread coating to produce a crunchy-tender vegetable.

Quantity

Plan on 1½ pounds of okra for 6 persons.

Sauces

Okra is not usually served with sauces, but steamed or microwaved okra is enhanced by flavored butter sauces and Hollandaise, and makes a delicious gratin if blanched and coated with Mornay and sprinkled with Gruyère.

Fried Okra

1½ pounds okra	2 cups fresh bread or cracker
3 eggs	crumbs
¾ cup milk	oil for deep-frying
salt and pepper to taste	

Carefully trim the top of each okra to remove the stem without cutting into the flesh.

In a bowl, mix the eggs, milk, salt, and pepper.

Dip the okra into the eggs, roll in the crumbs, and set on a rack until ready to fry.

Heat the oil to 375°F, and fry the okra until golden.

Drain on paper towels, and serve immediately.

Yield: 6 servings

➤ Can be prepared for frying several hours ahead.

NOTE: Use fresh bread crumbs, crusts removed (see glossary), or commercial cracker crumbs, or crush saltines. If using saltines, adjust the salt used in the egg accordingly.

For spice, add up to ¼ teaspoon Cayenne pepper to the egg mixture.

For additional flavor, add ¼ to 1 teaspoon of curry powder to the egg mixture.

Stewed Okra and Tomatoes

1 pound okra, stems trimmed	1 pound tomatoes, peeled,
2 tablespoons butter	seeded, and chopped
½ cup minced green pepper	salt and pepper to taste
½ cup minced onion	1 tablespoon minced parsley

If small, leave the okra whole; if large, cut into ½ inch slices.

In a skillet, melt the butter, and sauté the okra for 2 minutes. Add the pepper and onion, and sauté, stirring occasionally, for 6 minutes. Add the tomatoes, and season with salt and pepper. Simmer 20 minutes.

Serve sprinkled with the parsley.

Yield: 6 servings

➤ Can be prepared ahead and reheated.

Variations:

Render ¼ pound bacon until crisp, remove the cracklings, and drain on paper towels. Drain off the fat, rinse out the skillet to remove any excess salt, and then use two tablespoons of bacon fat instead of the butter.

Add 1 clove minced garlic with the peppers and onions.

Add ½ cup cream to the stew when it is cooked, and simmer until lightly thickened.

Onions and Garlic

*O*nions are a leading member of the Liliaceae family. They are the prize and pride of almost every kitchen in almost every country in the world. Pity the poor Eskimo who has to do without. How does one survive without the various family members, such as chives, scallions, leeks, red onions, white onions, Bermuda onions, Spanish onions, yellow onions, garlic, or shallots? Less happily, I am sure.

Onions have a remarkable history unmet by almost any other vegetable. The ancient Egyptians thought them worthy of worship, and many people today feel much the same. Especially those addicts of the Vidalia onion. Onions add flavor and spice to our lives. People have often given onions powers beyond that of nourishment. One old wives tale is "the more layers the harder the winter," although it probably has more to do with variety than weather. Garlic is given all sorts of propensities. Wearing it is supposed to ward off the "evil eye," keep away vampires, and prevent sore throats. Recent scientific research indicates that onions and garlic do indeed aid in reducing the risk of heart disease—proving that everything good is not bad for you.

Onions come in all strengths, from the truly mild, pleasantly-flavored chive to the full flavored, tear-making yellow onion, or the luscious exuberance of garlic. Cooking can tame the tiger, as it were, turning the strongest clove of garlic into a subtle perfume, and turning an onion-hater into a lover. Many people consider the family members too strong and therefore unpleasant, but once they have tried a dish with garlic cooked long, slowly, and with great love, they realize—one hopes—what they have been missing.

Onions fit almost everywhere in a menu. Many years ago I jokingly suggested to a friend that we prepare an onion ice. He took me seriously, but since then I have come across a recipe for a garlic sorbet! (I did not find the result worth sharing.) Onions make exquisite hors d'oeuvre, soups, vegetables, main courses, and salads on their own, and bring out the flavor and enhance many other vegetables and meats. No serious kitchen is ever without several varieties on hand.

Availability

Fresh

Chives Available in the spring and early summer, they usually disappear from the markets until the following spring. Chives, once cut, do not store well. Many stores sell plants to keep on a sunny window sill.

Look for firm, crisp, straight leaves that have not begun to turn yellow. If you have a fresh plant, cut them from the plant as needed.

Garlic Available year round, garlic grows in heads composed of a number of cloves. Usually a recipe uses 1 or more cloves, but do not be surprised at recipes calling for whole heads of garlic.

Look for firm, white, or purple-tinged heads with dry, smooth skins that feel heavy for the size. Avoid those with shrunken or shriveled cloves, or indications of sprouting. (If your garlic starts to sprout, use it as quickly as possible. Some writers allege that the green sprout is bitter and must be discarded. I have not found any problem with a small sprout. If it is large, I discard the entire clove.) If at all possible, buy garlic loose rather than packaged, so you can select the best heads, preferably with the largest cloves to make peeling easier.

Store the garlic in an airy dry location out of direct light. I keep mine in a small basket next to the stove for months at a time. It should keep at least 3 to 4 weeks, if not much longer.

Elephant Garlic Why bother? This has become a cooking rage in recent years for no known reason. Elephant garlic is very expensive. A single head can cost 2 or 3 times as much as a pound of garlic, and it has far less flavor. For general cooking, I do not think it is worth the expense. The only time I find it interesting is when I roast the heads, and then serve the buttery soft pulp as a spread for crusty French bread with a glass of red wine, but standard heads have more flavor.

Onions Virtually all types are available year round. However, in the summer and early fall, so-called green onions, with shiny, white bulbs and bright green tops, something like an overgrown scallion (which is what they are), are in some markets. They have a subtle fresh quality that I think makes them particularly nice in salads.

Onions come in all sizes and shapes, and in several colors. Look for firm, dry onions that feel heavy for their size. Avoid onions that feel soft or slippery, or that have any indication of mold or sprouting.

Store in a cool, dry, dark area. I have been told that it is best not to store near potatoes, or they will cause "eyes" to form on the potatoes. I have stopped, and the potatoes last longer.

The only way not to cry when peeling onions is to use sweet onions. I use large Spanish onions for all of my cooking, mainly due to laziness—they are easier to peel. The small yellow onion is more potent, and seems to cause everyone to tear. If you use those, work quickly, and expect to cry. I never have a problem with tears.

Scallions Scallions are immature onions. The variety that is grown in one area as a storage onion will be a scallion in another area. Look for clean, white bases with relatively firm roots, and straight, unblemished greens. Avoid scallions that feel slick, have limp roots or yellowing leaves, or show signs of bruising.

Store, unwrapped, in the vegetable drawer, and plan to use within a few days.

I am amazed when students ask which part of the scallion they should use. Use all that is available.

I start at the root end, and work my way up the green until it is no longer crisp and fresh. Unless a recipe stipulates using the white or green, I use both. I sometimes use the green in lieu of chives, even though the flavor is different.

Shallots For many people, these little darlings of haute cuisine are a little too precious. They wonder why they cannot just use an onion. You can, and you can substitute a scallion for a leek, but it is not the same. Shallots have a delicate flavor that enhances subtle foods superbly.

Look for firm, smooth heads without any sign of sprouting or shriveling. They should feel heavy for their size. Avoid cloves that feel soft.

Store in a cool, dry area unwrapped. Again, I keep mine in a basket. Unless the weather is very humid, they last for months.

Frozen

Frozen onions are sold whole or chopped and are acceptable in soups or stews, but they seem unnecessary, since fresh onions are always available.

Canned

Canned onions are not recommended.

Dried

Dried onion powder, garlic powder, garlic salt, and onion salt are unacceptable in fine cooking. They have a chemical aftertaste, and an aroma that is far removed from fresh.

When fresh vegetables were a problem, they could have had a use, but today they are unnecessary. The salts easily lead to oversalted and unappetizing foods.

Preparation

Chives

For some reason many writers recommend snipping chives with a pair of scissors. I have always found a sharp paring knife more than suitable for removing the leaves from the plant and cutting them to size. The recommendation for putting them in a measuring cup and snipping at them seems more difficult by far than making a few quick slices with a knife.

Garlic

To peel garlic easily, place the whole head on the counter and press it firmly in order to break the cloves off the base. With the flat side of a knife, slap the individual cloves to split the casing so that you can pick out the garlic. Make it a gentle tap to start. If you use more pressure, you will split the clove.

If you have several heads of garlic to peel, blanch the cloves in boiling water for 1 minute, drain, and refresh under cold water. Then cut the root end, and pinch the garlic out of its skin.

Cutting I do not like garlic presses. They are too difficult to clean and any leftover garlic can go rancid.

Mincing Place the garlic on the board and mince with a chef's knife until as fine as you wish. (A chef's trick: sprinkle a little salt over the garlic and mince the two together to help prevent the garlic from sticking to the blade.) There is an electric mini-chopper similar to a small food processor that does a wonderful job, if you do not mind washing it all the time. If you do not need the texture of tiny diced bits, smash the garlic with the side of the knife the same way you did to peel it, but with more force.

Onions

I am dismayed at how people peel and cut onions. It has always been such a simple procedure for me, and yet I find that so many people do it wrong.

Peeling Onions Cut the onion from root to stem. Place one half, cut side down, on a board and cut off a small section from each end. Peel off the thinnest layer of skin possible. Proceed with the second half (see page 3 for chopping, dicing, and slicing methods).

Using a Food Processor If used improperly, a food processor turns onions into a watery mush as opposed to neatly cut pieces.

Cut the onion into 1 inch cubes. Place the cubes in the processor and process with several on-off turns. Do not try to chop too much at one time, and do not leave the machine running. Prepare large amounts in batches. It is still much quicker than doing it by hand for most people. (The only exception to this method is if you must have onion rings. In that case, place the whole onion on a board and, holding it firmly in one hand, cut off the root end and then the stem end. Peel off the thinnest layer of skin.) To slice, pare a small slice off a rounded side, and place the onion on the board on the cut area. Slice into rounds. *This is the safest way to cut onion rings.* Cutting a rocking onion is an open invitation to cutting yourself!

Small White Onions They require special treatment. To peel, cut a small slice off both the root and stem ends and, with the point of a sharp knife, cut a cross in the root end. This protects them from coming apart during the cooking. Without it the center will burst from the onion. Blanch in boiling water for 5 minutes, drain, and refresh under cold water. The skins should slip off easily. The crisscross cut helps to keep the onion together during the cooking.

Shallots

Separate the cloves of shallots, and peel with a small paring knife. Cut into slices, or dice as indicated on page 4.

Cooking Methods

Onions are cooked using every method: boil, sauté, deep-fry, broil, roast, braise, steam, or cook in a microwave.

Boiling

Place the peeled onions in boiling salted water and simmer until tender—from 10 minutes to an hour depending on the size. They are most commonly served with a cream sauce.

Sautéing

Sauté in a little butter over low heat until tender.

Deep-Frying

Fried onion rings are a favorite. Fry them dipped in flour, batter, or in egg and crumbs.

Broiling

Place onion slices or small whole onions, brushed with oil, over a grill or under a broiler.

Roasting

Place whole or thickly sliced onions around a roast, or use whole garlic cloves, or shallots, and roast with the meat. The onions take about an hour, the garlic and shallots about 30 to 45 minutes.

Braising

Sauté the onions in some butter or oil until lightly colored, add a little wine and stock, cover, and braise until tender.

Steaming
Place the onions in a steamer over boiling water and steam until tender.

Microwaving
Place the onions in a covered container and cook for 4 to 6 minutes. Garlic needs long, slow cooking, and is not recommended for the microwave.

Quantity

Plan on 1½ pounds of onions for 6 persons. Or more easily, 1 medium or several smaller onions per person. With garlic, plan on a clove or two per person, unless you are serving whole heads, then one whole head a person.

Scallions, when served as a vegetable like leeks, require 1 bunch per person.

Shallots are not often served alone as a vegetable, but if serving roasted shallots, 4 to 6 cloves a person is sufficient.

Sauces
Onions are the base of dozens of sauces and take to other sauces as well. Serve with butter sauces, Hollandaise, cream sauces, tomato sauces, and serve cold with vinaigrette and mayonnaise.

Sauces

Onions and garlic not only get sauced, but are sauces in their own right. Garlic in particular is used to flavor a number of foods. Check the sauce chapter for those that are used often with other vegetables. Here are a few special sauces.

Aillade (Garlic Walnut Sauce for Shrimp)

½ cup chopped walnuts	¾ cup olive oil
3 garlic cloves, crushed	salt to taste
1 tablespoon lemon juice	2 tablespoons minced parsley

In a food processor, purée the walnuts, garlic, and lemon juice. With the machine running, add the olive oil. Correct the seasoning with salt, and add the parsley.

Serve at room temperature with cold shrimp, or serve with chèvre and toast.

Yield: 1½ cups

➤ Can be prepared several days ahead.

Rouille (*Garlic Red-pepper Sauce*)

This is usually swirled into fish soups, but it makes a wonderful replacement for mayonnaise, especially in fish salads. It is supposed to have some fire, so be generous with the Tabasco.

2 garlic cloves	¾ cup olive oil
2 red peppers, peeled	Tabasco sauce to taste
2 egg yolks	salt and pepper to taste

In a food processor, purée the garlic and red pepper. Add the egg yolks and, with the machine running, add the olive oil. Season with Tabasco, salt, and pepper.

Yield: 1½ cups

➤ Keeps 2 days, refrigerated.

NOTE: Other versions add ½ cup basil leaves, and in many areas they add ¾ cup fresh bread crumbs to give it more body and to stretch the budget.

Purée d 'Aulx (*Roasted Garlic Purée*)

In *Simple French Cooking*, Richard Olney wrote about this glorious product of Provence. Since then it has become almost a staple of many restaurants. Often the garlic is served whole, so each person can squeeze out his own.

6 heads garlic	sprigs of rosemary, thyme, or
1 or 2 tablespoons extra virgin	savory, optional
olive oil	

Preheat the oven to 400°F.

Peel off the outer skin of the heads of garlic, exposing the cloves, but leaving them attached to the base. If you have trouble, cut a circle around the top of the head and the outer leaves will pull off easily.

Place the garlic in a small casserole, or on a large sheet of foil. Drizzle with the oil, and place the herbs on top. Cover the casserole tightly, or wrap the foil around the garlic and twist to close. Place the foil on a baking sheet. Bake for 1 hour.

Yield: 6 servings

➤ Can be prepared ahead and reheated.

NOTE: To serve, cut off the top quarter of the head to expose the cloves in the skins. Give each guest a head of garlic, a small knife, and sliced French bread. They squeeze the head and spread the garlic on the bread. Serve with chèvre and additional extra virgin olive oil, if desired.

Use the garlic purée on vegetables, or mix it with butter or olive oil and pass it separately.

Lift the skin from the meat of a chicken, spread a thin layer of the purée over the meat, and bake or broil.

Toss the garlic with pasta and crumbled chèvre or Roquefort, and olive oil.

Roasted Garlic Cloves

Instead of roasting the whole head, break it into cloves and scatter the cloves around a roast as it cooks.

3 large heads garlic unpeeled

Preheat oven to 500°F.
Break garlic into cloves, and place in baking dish. Bake 25 minutes, and set aside for use as needed.

Yield: 6 servings

➤ Can be prepared ahead.

Variation:

Scatter unpeeled cloves in a skillet when sautéing chicken. Cook over low heat until the chicken is cooked and the garlic is browned. Serve the cloves, and let the diner press out the pulp with his fork.

Onion Soup

Everyone seems to have their favorite onion soup, or at least a firm idea as to what the perfect onion soup should be. These ideas often revert to a trip to Paris and a junket to Les Halles in the wee hours when somewhat inebriated. I am not opposed to "Les Nuits Blancs" as the French call these sessions, but I question one's critical abilities. I have never been a fan of food spilled over the sides of the container and burned to the edges. I find this sort of preparation messy and unappealing. While doing the research for my book, *The Book of Great Soups, Sandwiches and Breads*, I discovered a number of onion soups that are perhaps truer to the original than those blurry memories.

Gratinée Lyonnaise *(French Onion Soup from Lyon)*

Here is a version of the traditional soup with the cheese and bread topping that so many adore. The success of this soup depends on the very long, careful, slow cooking of the onions. Do not try to rush this. *Vive la différence!*

6 tablespoons butter
1½ pounds onions, thinly sliced
salt and pepper to taste
1½ quarts chicken or beef stock

1 loaf French bread, sliced and toasted
2 cups grated Gruyère cheese

In a heavy shallow pan, heat 3 tablespoons butter, and sweat the onions until wilted and very soft—about 15 minutes. Season with salt and pepper, cover, and cook over the lowest possible heat for 40 minutes or longer, until the onions just start to color. Remove the cover, and cook over medium heat, stirring, until the onions are caramelized and a deep golden brown. Be very careful that you do not burn the onions. Add the stock, and simmer for 30 minutes. Taste for seasoning.

Preheat the oven to 450°F.

Arrange the toast slices in layers, if necessary, in an ovenproof tureen, and pour the soup over the bread. Sprinkle generously with grated cheese, and dot with remaining 3 tablespoons of butter. Place the tureen on a baking sheet and bake until golden brown and bubbling hot. If desired, you can put under the broiler for a darker top.

Serve at once with the remaining cheese passed separately.

Yield: 6 servings

➤ The soup can be prepared the day before or frozen. Do the final baking just before serving.

Variations

Thourins, Tourins, or Torrins, from the Bordelais Region Use olive oil instead of butter, and add ½ cup of white wine to the soup with the stock. Use slices of rye bread instead of French bread, and only ⅔ cup of Gruyère. Prepare the soup as above, but layer a tureen with bread and cheese, pour on the soup, and let it stand for 5 minutes before serving.

Roquefort Use ½ to 1 cup of crumbled Roquefort in place of half the Gruyère. Add 1 or 2 tablespoons Cognac to the soup just before pouring into the tureen.

Ouilliat, Tourri, or Toulia
(Onion Soup from the Béarn)

½ cup olive oil	salt and pepper to taste
12 slices French bread	4 egg yolks
1 cup minced onion	½ pound Gruyère cheese,
½ cup flour	grated
2 quarts beef stock	⅓ cup Cognac or Armagnac

In a large skillet, sauté the bread in 4 tablespoons oil until golden. Drain on paper towels.

In a large kettle, pour the remaining oil, and any oil left in the skillet, and sauté the onions until they just start to turn golden. Sprinkle with flour, and cook, stirring, for 5 minutes, or until golden brown. Add 2 cups of stock, and bring to a boil, stirring. Add the remaining stock, and simmer, covered, for 30 minutes.

stock, and simmer, covered, for 30 minutes.

In a blender, food processor, or food mill, purée the soup and return to the kettle. Correct the seasoning with salt and pepper, and reheat.

In a soup tureen, whisk the egg yolks and half the cheese. Stir in the hot soup, 1 cup at a time, and top with the bread slices.

In a small saucepan, warm the Cognac and ignite. When the flames subside, pour into the soup, and stir. Sprinkle with the remaining cheese, and serve.

Yield: 6 servings

➤ The soup can be prepared ahead and frozen. Do not add the egg yolks and cheese until just before serving.

La Tourin Gascon à la Tomate
(Onion and Tomato Soup from Gasconny)

2 pounds onions, thinly sliced	salt and pepper to taste
3 tablespoons olive oil	5 cups water or chicken stock
8 garlic cloves, sliced	3 tablespoons Armagnac
2 pounds tomatoes, cubed	6 slices French bread, toasted
bouquet garni of parsley, thyme, and bay leaf	

In a kettle, sweat the onions and garlic in the oil until soft, but not brown. Add the tomatoes, bouquet garni, and water, and simmer for 45 minutes, stirring occasionally.

In a food mill, blender, or processor, purée the soup, and return to the kettle.

In a small saucepan, heat the Armagnac and ignite. When the flames subside, add to the soup.

Ladle the soup into bowls, and top with a slice of French bread.

Yield: 6 servings

➤ The soup can be prepared ahead and frozen.

White Wine Onion Soup

This is a personal favorite; the flavor is light, clean, and delicate, and it is quick to prepare and serve.

2 pounds onions, minced	½ cup grated Parmesan cheese
6 tablespoons butter	½ cup grated Gruyère cheese
4 cups chicken stock	¼ cup minced raw onion
1½ cups dry white wine	(optional)
salt and pepper to taste	¼ cup minced parsley
6 slices French bread, toasted	(optional)

Preheat the broiler.

In a large saucepan, sweat the onions in the butter until very soft, but not brown. Stir in the stock and wine, and simmer 20 minutes. Correct the seasoning with salt and pepper.

Place the toast slices on a baking sheet, and sprinkle with the Parmesan and Gruyère cheeses. Brown under the broiler.

Place the onion and parsley in small bowls. Serve the soup, and pass the croutons, onion, and parsley.

Yield: 6 servings

➤ Can be prepared ahead and frozen.

Zweibelcreme Suppe (Swiss Creamed Onion Soup)

6 slices whole-grain rye bread	3 cups milk
7 tablespoons butter	3 cups light cream
2 pounds thinly sliced onions	3 egg yolks
salt and pepper to taste	2 whole eggs
pinch of nutmeg	minced chives

Cut the bread into ¼ inch cubes. In a skillet, sauté the bread in the 4 tablespoons of butter until golden. Drain on paper toweling.

In a kettle, sweat the onions in the remaining butter until soft and just starting to color—about 30 minutes. Season with salt, pepper, and nutmeg. Stir in the milk and cream, and simmer 10 minutes, stirring occasionally.

In a bowl, beat the egg yolks and eggs until well-combined. Stir in 1 cup of hot soup to warm the eggs, and slowly stir the egg mixture into the soup over low heat. Cook over low heat until lightly thickened. Do not boil. Ladle into bowls, and sprinkle with the croutons and chives.

Yield: 8 servings

➤ The soup can be prepared ahead and frozen. Do not add the egg mixture until just before serving.

NOTE: Roggenbrot, a whole-grain rye bread, is suggested for this recipe. If you cannot locate it, you can use any fresh, firm-textured rye bread.

Wiltshire White Onion Soup

¼ cup butter	salt and pepper
2 pounds large white onions, thinly sliced	2 ounces Stilton cheese
	2 tablespoons butter
4 cups chicken stock	6 slices French bread, toasted
3 cups heavy cream	2 ounces cheddar, shredded
bouquet garni of thyme, bay leaf, and parsley	

Preheat the broiler.

In a saucepan over low heat, melt the butter, and cook the onions until soft but not brown—about 30 minutes.

Add the stock, and simmer 15 minutes.

Add the cream and bouquet garni, and simmer 20 minutes longer, stirring occasionally. Discard the bouquet garni.

Correct the seasoning with salt and pepper.

In a small bowl, cream the Stilton and butter, and spread evenly on the toast. Sprinkle with the cheddar.

Just before serving, broil the toasts until bubbling and starting to brown, and float on each bowl of soup.

Yield: 6 servings

➤ Can be prepared ahead and frozen.

Soupe à l'ail (Garlic Soup)

Garlic soups are favorites in many countries. The slow cooking creates a delicate, subtle flavor.

1 cup unpeeled garlic cloves	½ teaspoon salt
2 tablespoons butter	pinch of Cayenne pepper
¼ cup olive oil	nutmeg to taste
1 quart chicken stock	6 slices French bread, toasted
6 egg yolks	1 tablespoon minced parsley

In a saucepan of boiling water, blanch the garlic cloves for 1 minute. Drain, refresh under cold water, and pinch the skins. In a 3 quart casserole, sweat the garlic in the butter and 1 tablespoon of olive oil until soft, but not brown—about 15 minutes. Add the stock, and simmer 20 minutes.

In a bowl, beat the egg yolks until light in color and slightly thickened. Slowly beat in the remaining oil to make a mayonnaise-like mixture. Add 1 cup of the hot soup to the egg yolks, and mix well. Add to the hot soup in a slow, steady stream, and heat, but do not boil.

Strain the soup, forcing the garlic through the sieve, or purée in a blender. Return to the saucepan and heat gently. Correct the seasoning with salt, Cayenne, and nutmeg. Place the toast slices in the tureen, and pour over the soup. Sprinkle with the parsley, and serve.

Yield: 6 servings

➤ The soup mixture can be prepared several days ahead, or frozen, but do not add the egg yolks until shortly before serving.

Onion Spread

Serve this as an hors d'oeuvre on its own, or with a mild chèvre.

2 pounds onions, thinly sliced	1 tablespoon minced sage
½ teaspoon salt	Niçoise olives
6 tablespoons olive oil	1 loaf French bread, thinly
1 tablespoon anise-flavored	sliced, and toasted or
liqueur	sautéed in olive oil

In a large skillet, over very low heat, sweat the onion and salt in the oil, covered, until very soft—about 40 minutes. Remove the cover and cook, stirring, until the onions turn golden, taking care not to burn them. Stir in the liqueur and sage, and cook 10 minutes longer, stirring.

Serve warm or at room temperature, garnished with the olives and French bread slices.

Yield: 6 servings

➤ Can be prepared a day or two ahead and allowed to come to room temperature.

Oignons Frits (Fried Onions)

Fried onions are prepared with a batter coating (see page 8), or with egg and bread crumbs (see page 9). This, however, is the simplest, and I think the best way to make fried onion rings. Unless you are serving these as a garnish to a main course, expect to make a lot. They are addictive!

1 medium to large onion per	salt and pepper to taste
person	flour
milk	oil for deep-frying

Holding each onion firmly in one hand, cut off the root and stem ends. Cut a thin slice off one side of the onion to give it a sturdy base, and place it on a cutting board sliced side down. Again, holding the onion firmly in one hand, slice it into ¼ inch thick slices from each end. For the middle section, lay it flat on the board, and slice through it horizontally.

Poke the center of the onion out to make rings. (Onion rings do not have to be rings. If it is easier for you—and it is safer—cut the onion in half from root to stem and cut into slices.) Dip the slices in milk.

In a large bag, combine the salt, pepper, and flour, and add a handful of drained onions at a time. Shake vigorously, and turn into a sieve. Shake off any excess flour.

Heat the fat to 375°F. Fry a handful of onions at a time until they are golden brown. Drain on paper toweling, and sprinkle with salt.

Yield: 1 serving per person per onion

➤ Cannot be prepared ahead. The onions can be sliced several hours ahead and stored in a sealed container in ice water.

NOTE: These cannot be held after cooking. Plan on these for a party of close friends who will entertain you in the kitchen as you amaze them with this treat.

Perles Desirées (Glazed Pearl Onions)

This Provençal dish is served as part of an hors d'oeuvre platter, or as a side dish at dinner like a relish.

1½ pounds tiny white boiling onions (see Note)	2 teaspoons salt
	1 bay leaf
1½ cups peeled, seeded, and chopped tomatoes	¼ teaspoon fennel seeds
	⅛ teaspoon dried savory
½ cup golden raisins	⅛ teaspoon dried marjoram
2 tablespoons pine nuts	⅛ teaspoon dried oregano
1 cup tomato juice	⅛ teaspoon dried thyme
3 tablespoons lemon juice	⅛ teaspoon ground mace
2 tablespoons sugar	2 tablespoons olive oil
1 tablespoon white wine vinegar	

Peel the onions by blanching in boiling water for 3 minutes. Drain, refresh under cold water, and remove the skins. Cut a cross in the root end of each onion.

In a large skillet, simmer the onions, tomatoes, raisins, pine nuts, tomato juice, lemon juice, sugar, vinegar, salt, bay leaf, fennel seeds, savory, marjoram, oregano, thyme, and mace for 30 to 50 minutes, or until the onions are tender.

With a slotted spoon, remove the vegetables, raisins, pine nuts, and bay leaf; discard the bay leaf. Boil the juices until reduced to a thick syrup.

Return the vegetables, raisins, and pine nuts, and simmer, stirring often, until well-glazed—about 20 minutes longer. Correct the seasoning with salt and pepper. Cool to lukewarm and stir in the oil.

Yield: 6 servings

➤ Can be prepared a day or two ahead. Serve at room temperature.

NOTE: Use very small white onions, about the size of a marble. They can take less than 30 minutes to cook.

Sweet and Sour Glazed Onions

1½ pounds small white onions, peeled, and cross cut in root end	⅓ cup olive oil
	3 tablespoons sugar
	salt and pepper to taste
½ cup sherry vinegar	

In a large, non-corrosible, covered skillet, simmer the onions, vinegar, oil, sugar, salt, and pepper for about 25 minutes, or until the onions are tender. Remove the cover, and boil the liquid until syrupy.

Cool and store for 1 day for flavors to meld before serving. Serve at room temperature as an hors d'oeuvre with wooden skewers.

Yield: 6 servings

➤ Can be prepared 3 days before serving.

Cipolline d'Ivrea (Small Onions Ivrea Style)

In the early fall, Italian markets sell a brown-skinned small onion about the size of a walnut, called cipolline. If you can locate them, they are perfect in this recipe. If not, use any small white boiling onion.

1½ pounds cipolline, or small white onions, peeled and cross cut in the root end	4 tablespoons butter
	3 tablespoons olive oil
	1 bay leaf
⅔ cup beef, veal, or chicken stock	salt and pepper to taste
	⅔ cup dry white wine

In a skillet, simmer the onions with the stock, butter, olive oil, bay leaf, and a little salt until the liquid evaporates. Continue cooking the onions in the fat in the pan, shaking occasionally until golden brown. Add the wine, and simmer until it evaporates and the onions are tender.

Yield: 6 servings

➤ Can be prepared ahead and reheated, or served at room temperature.

Cipolle di Napoli (Braised Onions, Naples Style)

24 whole cloves	salt and pepper to taste
12 onions, 2 inches in diameter, peeled	sprig of thyme
	¼ cup dry Marsala
½ cup olive oil	1 tablespoon capers

Preheat the oven to 375°F.

Insert 2 cloves into each onion, and place in a single layer in a large casserole. Sprinkle with the olive oil, salt, and pepper. Bury the sprig of thyme in the onions.

Cover, and bake for 1 hour, or until the onions are soft but still hold their shape. Sprinkle with the Marsala, and bake, uncovered, until the Marsala evaporates, basting occasionally.

Arrange the onions on a serving platter. Discard the cloves, and sprinkle the capers on top.

Yield: 6 servings

➤ Can be prepared ahead and served at room temperature or reheated.

Oignons Rissolés *(Braised Onions)*

1½ pounds onions, minced   salt
3 tablespoons olive oil   pinch of sugar
3 tablespoons butter

In a large skillet, over low heat, cook the onions in the olive oil and butter until very soft and golden in color, stirring often. Do not let them brown. Season with salt and sugar.

Yield: 6 servings

➤ Can be prepared ahead and reheated.

NOTE: Use tiny whole onions if desired.

Gebackene Zweibeln *(Baked Whole Onions)*

6 medium onions, peeled   ¼ teaspoon sugar
1 cup beef stock   ⅛ teaspoon dried tarragon
⅓ cup Port or Madeira   ¼ teaspoon dried thyme
2 tablespoons butter   salt and pepper to taste
2 tablespoons minced parsley

Preheat the oven to 300°F.
Cut a thin slice from the stem end of each onion, and arrange them in a single layer in a casserole, root ends down. Pour over the stock and wine, and dot with butter. Sprinkle with parsley, sugar, tarragon, thyme, salt, and pepper.
Cover, and bake for 2 or 3 hours, or until tender. Reduce the liquid to a syrup.
Serve the onions basted with the syrup.

Yield: 6 servings

➤ Can be prepared ahead and reheated.

Baked Onions with Red Wine Vinegar

Use large onions, about 3 to 4 inches in diameter, for this, or use smaller onions and leave them whole.

3 yellow onions, quartered   salt and pepper
3 red onions quartered   6 tablespoons red wine vinegar
½ cup olive oil

Preheat the oven to 350°F.
In an ovenproof casserole, toss the onions with the olive oil, salt, and pepper until evenly coated. Cover the dish tightly, and bake for 30 minutes. Uncover, and bake 30 minutes longer, or until tender. Transfer onions to platter.
Add the vinegar to the pan, and stir up the browned bits until dissolved.

Yield: 6 servings

NOTE: Use a gratin pan or baking dish, and cover with foil, if you do not have a suitable casserole.

Braised Onion Slices

2½ tablespoons butter	6½ inch thick slices of onion
1 tablespoon brown sugar	¼ teaspoon dried thyme
salt and pepper to taste	1 tablespoon minced parsley

In a large, heavy skillet, melt the butter, brown sugar, and ¼ teaspoon of salt over low heat until bubbling. Add the onion slices in a single layer, cover, and cook over low heat until softened—about 10 minutes. Turn the onions, and season with thyme and pepper.

Cook, uncovered, turning once, until browned on both sides— about 5 minutes. Sprinkle with minced parsley.

Yield: 6 servings

➤ Can be prepared several hours ahead and reheated.

NOTE: It is vital to use low heat, or the sugar will burn before the onions are cooked. If the sugar is getting too dark, add 2 tablespoons of water to slow the browning.

Daube d'Oignons (Red-Wine Braised Onions)

2½ to 3 pounds Spanish onions, thinly sliced	1½ cups red wine
¼ cup butter	salt and pepper to taste
1 tablespoon sugar	1 teaspoon or more red-wine vinegar

In a heavy, covered, 4 quart saucepan, sweat the onions in the butter, stirring occasionally, over very low heat for 45 minutes. Uncover, increase heat to high, and cook, stirring, until glazed and golden brown—about 20 minutes. Sprinkle with sugar, and cook, stirring, 2 to 3 minutes until glazed. Turn the heat as low as possible, and add the wine.

Cook, stirring often, until onions are very soft and deep mahogany in color—about 1½ hours. Season with salt and pepper, and add vinegar to counteract sweetness.

Serve hot, lukewarm, or cold.

Yield: 6 servings

➤ Can be prepared the day before and reheated.

Confits d'Echalotes, d'Ail et de Petits Oignons
(Roasted Shallot, Garlic, and White Onions)

The vegetables should be roasted until they are as soft as jam. You can prepare this in a tightly sealed casserole, if you do not wish to serve each diner a single packet.

12 shallots	6 thyme sprigs
12 garlic cloves	6 tarragon sprigs
12 tiny white onions	½ teaspoon peppercorns
3 tablespoons clarified butter,	salt to taste
or olive oil	

Preheat the oven to 350°F. Cut 6 5 inch squares of foil, or parchment paper.

On each square place 2 shallots, 2 garlic cloves, 2 onions, ½ tablespoon butter, 1 thyme sprig, 1 tarragon sprig, a few peppercorns, and salt to taste. Pick up the corners of foil or paper, and twist together into a topknot. Bake for 40 minutes.

Yield: 6 servings

➤ Can be prepared for baking several hours before serving.

Gratin d'Oignons (Onion Gratin)

4 pounds onions, peeled and	nutmeg to taste
minced	3 tablespoons heavy cream
2 tablespoons butter	4 tablespoons grated Gruyère
2 tablespoons oil	cheese
salt and pepper to taste	1 tablespoon butter

Preheat the oven to 350°F.

In a large saucepan, simmer the onions in the butter and oil over low heat until soft—about 20 minutes—stirring often. The onions should not color. Season with salt, pepper, and nutmeg.

Stir in the cream, and pour the mixture into a buttered ovenproof dish. Sprinkle with cheese, dot with butter, and bake for 30 minutes, or until golden.

Yield: 6 servings

➤ Can be prepared for the final baking the day before.

Soubise (Onion Purée)

Serve this classic French purée on its own, or use as a filling for other vegetables, or spread it on toasts, sprinkle with Gruyère, and broil until golden to serve as an hors d'oeuvre.

½ cup butter	1 cup heavy cream
4 pounds onions, chopped	salt and pepper
1 cup rice	2 tablespoons minced parsley

Preheat the oven to 325°F. Place the butter in a covered casserole, and melt in the oven.

In a large kettle of boiling salted water, boil the onions and rice for 5 minutes, and drain. Turn into the casserole, and bake for 1 hour, stirring often. The onions should not color. When the onions are melting soft and the rice is fully cooked, purée in a processor or blender.

Stir in the cream, and season with salt and pepper. Bake, covered, for another 30 minutes, or until thick enough to hold its shape in a spoon. Stir in the parsley.

Yield: 6 servings

➤ Can be prepared ahead and can be frozen.

Variation:

For an onion casserole, do not purée the onions, but stir in 1 cup of grated Gruyère, the cream, parsley, salt, and pepper. Place in a buttered 9 by 13 baking dish, and bake uncovered for 30 minutes or until golden brown.

Grilled Onions with Raspberry Vinegar

3 Spanish onions, peeled, roots intact, and cut into 8 wedges
5 tablespoons raspberry vinegar

¼ cup olive oil
salt and pepper

Preheat the broiler, or a charcoal grill.

In a bowl, toss the onions with the vinegar, and marinate for 30 minutes. Drain the vinegar into a small bowl, and reserve. Add the oil, salt, and pepper to the bowl, and toss the onions to coat evenly.

Cover a baking sheet with foil. Drain the onions, reserving the vinegar, and arrange in a single layer. Or, if using charcoal, arrange in a wire basket in a single layer, and clamp shut. Broil until brown, but not charred—about 8 minutes per side.

Transfer to platter, and sprinkle with 1½ tablespoons reserved vinegar. Cool to room temperature.

Yield: 6 servings

➤ Can be prepared several hours ahead.

NOTE: You can cut the onion into ½ inch thick slices if that is easier.

Flavor the onions with crumbled thyme, tarragon, savory, or rosemary.

Use another vinegar of choice, such as balsamic, sherry, or black currant.

Stuffed Onions

Onions are a natural container for other ingredients. Many cultures have versions of stuffed onions in their repertoire. The process is simple, and though it does take a few minutes, the results are rewarding. If you use a large onion, it is possible to have a one-dish meal all in one vegetable. It is also a good way of stretching a small amount of meat.

Hollowing Onions for Stuffing

Cut off the stem end and leave the root end untouched. Peel the onion skin a layer at a time until you get to clear flesh.

In a large kettle of boiling water, parboil the onions for 10 minutes, drain, and run under cold water until cool enough to handle.

With a melon baller, scoop out the inside of the onion, starting at the center, and working to within two or three layers of the outer wall. Scoop down to but not through the base. (If the base should come out, place a small piece of onion in the bottom; the stuffing will hold it in place.) In most, but not all recipes, the inside of the onion is used in the filling. If it is not, save it to use in soups, or wherever you need chopped onions.

Oignons Farcis (Stuffed Onions with Rosemary)

Use these to accompany a roast.

6 medium onions, hollowed for stuffing	½ teaspoon minced rosemary
2 tablespoons olive oil	1 to 2 cups fresh bread crumbs
1 garlic clove, crushed	salt and pepper to taste
1 tablespoon minced parsley	1 cup beef or chicken stock

Preheat the oven to 350°F. Mince the centers that were removed from the whole onions.

In a skillet, sauté the centers in the oil with the garlic, parsley, and rosemary until soft, but not browned. Stir in enough bread crumbs to make a loose mixture, and sauté until slightly crisp. Correct the seasoning with salt and pepper, and stuff the onions.

Arrange the onions in a baking pan just large enough to hold them in a single layer. Pour in the stock, and bake for 30 minutes, or until the onions are tender, basting occasionally.

Yield: 6 servings

➤ Can be prepared ahead and reheated.

Potato Stuffed Onions

6 to 12 white onions, hollowed for stuffing	salt and pepper to taste
¾ pound peeled potatoes	nutmeg to taste
3 tablespoons heavy cream	2 tablespoons grated Parmesan cheese
2 tablespoons butter	

Preheat the oven to 400°F. Set the centers aside for another use. If the shells are not tender, cook in boiling salted water for 4 or 5 minutes longer.

In a saucepan of boiling salted water, cook the potatoes until tender. Put through a ricer, or mash, and beat in the cream, butter, salt, pepper, and nutmeg to taste. With a spoon, or a pastry bag fitted with a #8 plain tip, pipe the filling into the onion shells.

Place the onions in a baking dish, and sprinkle with the cheese. Bake until golden—about 15 minutes.

Yield: 6 servings

➤ Can be prepared for the final baking the day before.

NOTE: Plan on 1 to 2 onions per person, depending on the size. One 3 inch onion is suitable.

Mushroom and Zucchini Stuffed Onions

6 2½ inch onions, hollowed for stuffing	salt and pepper to taste
1 tablespoon olive oil	1 egg
½ pound zucchini, finely diced	½ cup chicken stock
2 ounces cèpes, shiitake, or other wild mushroom, minced	1 cup tomato sauce (see page 25)

Preheat the oven to 350°F. Mince the centers of the onions.

In a skillet, sauté the minced onion in the oil for 2 minutes. Add the onion shells, and sauté for 5 minutes. Add the mushrooms, and sauté until most of the liquid evaporates. Season with salt and pepper.

In a bowl, beat the egg, and fold in the vegetable mixture. Stuff the onions, and arrange in a baking dish. Add the stock, and bake covered for 20 minutes, or until tender. Remove the cover and bake for 10 minutes longer, or until the tops are browned. Serve the onions, and pass the tomato sauce.

Yield: 6 servings

➤ Can be baked ahead and reheated.

Oigons Farcis aux Duxelles (Mushroom Stuffed Onions)

6 onions, hollowed for stuffing	½ cup bread crumbs
2 tablespoons butter	3 tablespoons melted butter
¾ cup duxelles (see page 304)	1 cup chicken or beef stock
salt and pepper to taste	

Preheat the oven to 350°F. Mince the centers.

In a skillet, sauté the centers in the butter until soft, but not brown. Add the duxelles, and stir to combine. Correct the seasoning with salt and pepper. Fill the onions with the mixture, and sprinkle with the bread crumbs.

Drizzle the melted butter over the top, and arrange in a single layer in a baking dish. Pour in the stock, and bake for 30 minutes, or until tender.

Yield: 6 servings

➤ Can be prepared ahead and reheated.

Beef Stuffed Onions

6 Spanish onions, hollowed for stuffing	1 egg
	1 egg yolk
3 tablespoons butter	1 tablespoon Dijon mustard
¾ pound ground beef	2 teaspoons dried tarragon
salt and pepper to taste	2 tablespoons minced parsley
¼ cup fresh bread crumbs	½ cup beef stock

Preheat the oven to 350°F. Mince the centers of the onions.

In a skillet, sauté the onion in 1 tablespoon of butter until soft, but not brown.

In a bowl, mix the beef, egg, egg yolk, mustard, and tarragon. Stir in the onion, and season with salt and pepper. Fill the onions with the meat mixture.

In a bowl, mix the bread crumbs with the parsley, and sprinkle over the top of the onions. Place the onions in a baking dish in a single layer, and pour in the beef stock. Bake, uncovered, for 40 to 60 minutes, or until the onions are tender.

Yield: 6 servings

➤ Can be prepared ahead and reheated.

Onion Tarts

Onions, when cooked slowly, have a sweetness from the natural sugar that joins with pastry to make a perfect combination. In Alsace, Bavaria, and the bordering areas of Switzerland, onion tarts are found in almost every bakery. These low rimmed tarts, with their rich creamy onion fillings, are served as a simple luncheon or as the first course to a dinner. In Provence, the local pizza, pissaladière, is a fabulous combination of onions cooked until almost dissolved, spread over pastry, and topped with anchovies and olives. Americans love onions on their pizzas. In Canada they make a two crust onion pie. Onion tarts can raise everyone's spirits when palates flag.

Zweibletorte *(Onion Tart from Alsace)*

10 inch tart shell, baked blond   1 teaspoon salt
   (see page 551)   pinch of white pepper
1/4 cup butter   pinch of nutmeg
4 cups thinly sliced onions   2 eggs
1 tablespoon flour   1 cup half and half

Preheat the oven to 400°F. Bake the pastry until half-cooked. Lower oven to 375°F.

In a large skillet, melt the butter, add the onions, and cook until soft, but not brown. Stir in the flour, salt, pepper, and nutmeg.

In a bowl, whisk the eggs lightly, and stir in the half and half and the onion mixture. Pour into the shell, and bake until set—about 35 minutes.

Cool to lukewarm before serving.

Yield: 6 servings

➤ Can be baked and frozen.

Zewelwai Tarte à l'Oignon *(Swiss Onion Tart)*

9 inch tart shell, baked blond   salt to taste
   (see page 551)   pepper to taste
1½ pounds onions, thinly   nutmeg to taste
   sliced   3 egg yolks
4 tablespoons butter   3/4 cup heavy cream

Preheat the oven to 400°F.

In a skillet pan, melt the butter, and cook the onions until very soft and pale golden—about 30 minutes. Season with salt, pepper, and nutmeg. Stir in the egg yolks and the cream. Pour into the tart shell, and bake for about 30 minutes, or until just done.

Yield: 6 servings

➤ Can be baked and frozen.

Chèvre and Scallion Tart

1 10 inch tart shell, baked   1 pound chèvre cheese
   blond (see page 551)   1/4 cup heavy cream
1/4 cup thinly sliced scallions   2 eggs, lightly beaten
2 tablespoons butter   pepper to taste
1 pound cream cheese   1 scallion, thinly sliced

Preheat the oven to 375°F.

In a skillet, sauté the scallions in the butter until soft.

In a bowl, mix the cream cheese and the chèvre until smooth. Beat in the cream, eggs, and pepper, and fold in the sautéed scallions. Pour the mixture into the prepared pastry shell, and bake for 35 to 40 minutes, or until set. Let cool on a rack.

Serve garnished with the sliced scallion.

Yield: 6 servings

Canadian Onion Pie

Serve with roasted or grilled meat as both the starch and the vegetable for a meal.

pastry for a 2-crust pie   ½ teaspoon salt
5 cups thinly sliced onions   ½ teaspoon pepper
½ cup flour   ½ teaspoon dried thyme

Preheat the oven to 425°F.
Line a 9 inch pie plate with half of the pastry. Scatter the onions in the pastry, and sprinkle with the flour, salt, pepper, and thyme. Roll the remaining pastry and cover the filling. Crimp the edges and cut stem vents. Bake 1 hour.

Yield: 6 servings

➤ Can be prepared and frozen before or after baking.

NOTE: For a more attractive appearance, brush the top of tart with a glaze of milk, or an egg beaten with 1 tablespoon of milk before baking.

Pissaladière (Provençale Pizza)

2 pounds onions, thinly sliced   salt and pepper to taste
¼ cup olive oil   12 or more anchovy fillets
2 tomatoes, peeled, seeded,   12 or more pitted black olives
  and chopped   1 recipe pizza dough
3 garlic cloves, chopped

Preheat the oven to 450°F.
In a large covered skillet, sweat the onions in the olive oil, until very soft and pale gold—about 50 minutes. Stir in the tomatoes, garlic, salt, and pepper, and simmer until almost dry. Cool slightly.
Roll the pizza to fit an 11 by 15 inch jelly-roll pan. Spread the filling evenly over the dough. Make crisscross patterns of anchovies over the pizza, and fill the interstices with the olives. Bake 20 minutes, lower the heat to 350°F, and bake 20 minutes longer.
Serve at room temperature, cut into squares.

Yield: 6 or more servings

➤ Can be frozen after baking, but it is best prepared and served.

Cold Stuffed Onions

6 onions, hollowed for stuffing	salt and pepper to taste
6 tablespoons minced salted walnuts	½ bunch watercress, stems removed
6 stuffed olives, diced	1 cup vinaigrette
½ cup minced celery	
2 tablespoons minced green or red pepper	

Blanch the onions until tender. Mince the centers, and combine the walnuts, olives, celery, and peppers. Correct the seasoning with salt and pepper.

Fill the onions, and chill until ready to serve. Arrange the onions on a platter, surround with the watercress, and pass the vinaigrette.

Yield: 6 servings

➤ Can be prepared the day before.

Zwiebelsalat (Onion Salad)

5 cups thinly sliced red onions	2 tablespoons minced chives
salt and pepper to taste	½ teaspoon caraway seeds
⅓ cup olive oil	¼ teaspoon sugar
3 tablespoons red-wine vinegar	

In a large bowl, toss the onions with 1 tablespoon of salt, and cover with ice cubes. Let stand for 30 minutes.

In a bowl, whisk the oil, vinegar, 1 tablespoon of chives, ½ teaspoon of salt, caraway, sugar, and pepper to taste.

Drain the onions, discarding the ice. Add the dressing, and toss to coat. Let marinate at room temperature for 30 minutes. Sprinkle with the remaining chives.

Yield: 6 servings

➤ Can be prepared several hours before serving.

Marinated Onion Rings with Roquefort

½ cup olive oil	1 teaspoon salt
½ cup minced parsley	1 teaspoon sugar
¼ cup lemon juice	2 bunches watercress, stems removed
¼ cup minced dill	
1½ pounds thinly sliced onions	2 large tomatoes, ¼ inch slices
¼ pound Roquefort, crumbled	

Set aside 2 tablespoons of parsley and 1 teaspoon of dill.

In a large, covered container, combine the olive oil, parsley, lemon juice, and dill. Whisk until thickened, and add the onions, Roquefort, salt, and sugar.

Cover securely, and shake the container to coat the ingredients evenly. Refrigerate for 12 hours, shaking every hour.

Arrange a bed of watercress on a platter and top with the tomato slices. Fill the center with the onion salad, and sprinkle with the reserved parsley and dill.

Yield: 6 servings

➤ Best if eaten the same day.

Parsnips

*P*arsnips are a neglected vegetable. Most cooks have little knowledge of this tender, sweet vegetable other than as a flavoring for soup. Occasionally, people admit to liking a parsnip purée, but at the same time, I can remember when I was last *served* parsnip because it is so rare. Who really remembers the last time they ate carrots? Parsnips are not only delicious, they are quickly prepared and have great flavor. They do not need rich sauces, but they can be enhanced with herbed butters, or have their sweetness accented with horseradish. Deep-fried, they can stand on their own against potato chips.

Availability

Fresh
Parsnips first appear in the late fall, and are found through the winter. They sweeten in flavor after a frost, and can be left in the ground until spring.

Look for firm, plump roots that are not too large. Avoid large roots or those with cracked, shriveled, pithy, or decaying flesh.

Store in perforated plastic, or in the vegetable drawer, for 10 days to 3 weeks.

Frozen
Parsnips do not freeze well, unless puréed.

Canned
I do not believe parsnips are sold in cans.

Preparation

Peel with a vegetable peeler as with carrots. Cut in slices, roll cut (if small) in batons, julienne, or shred.

If the parsnips are particularly large, you may wish to remove the core. Cut the parsnip in half lengthwise and, starting at the stem end, pry out the core with a paring knife. In smaller parsnips, the core is edible.

Cooking Methods

Parsnips cook relatively quickly, and go from just barely done to over-done rapidly. Tend to them carefully toward the end of the cooking time.

Boiling
Cook in boiling salted water for 4 to 10 minutes, depending on the size.

Steaming
Cook over boiling water in a steamer until tender-crisp, about 8 to 15 minutes, depending on the cut.

Microwaving
Place in a covered container with 2 tablespoons of liquid and cook for 4 to 6 minutes.

Braising
Cook in flavored stock until just done.

Quantity

Allow 1½ pounds of parsnips for 6 persons. There is very little waste.

Sauces

Treat the same as carrots, Brussels sprouts, or turnips. Sauté in butter with an herbed flavoring, try spices, such as cinnamon or nutmeg, or seeds, such as poppy or caraway. Coat with cream sauces, or serve in combination with other vegetables, such as carrots and zucchini.

Sautéed Parsnips

Serve this simply, or augment the flavor with the variations.

1½ pounds parsnips, ¼ inch slices	3 tablespoons butter
	salt and pepper to taste

In a large skillet, sauté the parsnips in the butter until tender-crisp—about 8 minutes. If the parsnips are getting browner than you wish, but are not yet tender enough, cover and cook another minute or two until tender.

Yield: 6 servings

➤ Can be prepared ahead and reheated, but be careful not to overcook them.

Variations:

Season the turnips with ½ teaspoon ground cinnamon, or ⅛ teaspoon ground nutmeg, just before removing from the heat.

Add 2 teaspoons poppy or caraway seeds just before removing from the heat.

Add 1 tablespoon of curry powder to the butter when sautéing the parsnips.

Season with 1 teaspoon, or to taste, of allspice just before removing from the heat.

Add 1 cup of cream when almost done, and simmer until lightly thickened.

When the parsnips just start to brown, add 1 cup orange juice, and simmer 2 minutes. Add ¾ cup pomegranate seeds, and heat.

Sprinkle with minced chives, and season with salt.

Sautéed Parsnips and Leeks

1½ pounds leeks	grated zest of 2 lemons
1 pound parsnips, peeled	salt and pepper
½ cup butter	

Trim off the roots and the greens from the leeks, and cut the white to within one inch of the root end. Rinse the leek thoroughly in lukewarm water to remove the grit. Cut the white into ¼ inch strips. Cut the parsnips into ¼ inch strips the same length as the leeks.

In a skillet, melt the butter, and sauté the lemon for 30 seconds. Add the leeks and parsnips, and sauté for 1½ minutes. Cover the pan, and simmer until tender-crisp—about 5 minutes longer. Season with salt and pepper.

Yield: 6 servings

➤ Can be prepared ahead and reheated, but best if freshly prepared.

Sautéed Parsnips and Lettuce

1½ pounds parsnips, cut in julienne	1 tablespoon sugar
⅔ cup boiling water	¼ teaspoon minced ginger
3 tablespoons butter	salt and pepper
	2 cups shredded lettuce

In a saucepan, simmer the parsnips in the water, butter, sugar, ginger, salt, and pepper over moderate heat until tender.

Stir in the lettuce, and cook over high heat until the liquid evaporates. Correct the seasoning with salt and pepper

Yield: 6 servings

➤ Can be prepared ahead and reheated.

Sweet and Sour Parsnips

1½ pounds parsnips, thinly
   sliced
¼ cup melted butter
2 tablespoons minced parsley
2 tablespoons lemon juice

1 teaspoon brown sugar
½ teaspoon grated lemon rind
salt and pepper to taste
4 slices fried bacon, crumbled

In a skillet, sauté the parsnips in the butter over moderate heat for 10 minutes, or until tender. Stir in the parsley, lemon juice, sugar, lemon rind, salt, and pepper. Arrange in a serving dish, and sprinkle with the bacon.

Yield: 6 servings

➤ Can be prepared ahead and reheated.

Deviled Parsnips

1½ pounds parsnips, sliced
⅓ cup butter, melted
2 tablespoons wine vinegar
2 tablespoons brown sugar

1 tablespoon minced basil
1 teaspoon dry mustard
1 teaspoon minced chives
salt and pepper

In a skillet, sauté the parsnips in the butter until brown. Stir in the vinegar, sugar, basil, mustard, chives, salt, and pepper. Simmer until tender.

Yield: 6 servings

➤ Can be prepared ahead and reheated

Shredded Parsnips with Mustard

1 pound parsnips, shredded
3 tablespoons vegetable oil
½ cup chicken stock

salt to taste
2 teaspoons grainy mustard
2 tablespoons sour cream

In a skillet, simmer the oil, stock, and mustard for 1 minute. Add the parsnips, and season with salt and pepper. Cook stirring for 2 or 3 minutes, or until tender-crisp. Remove from the heat, and stir in the sour cream.

Yield: 6 servings

➤ Cannot be prepared ahead.

Parsnips with Rosemary

1½ pounds parsnips, cut into ½ inch slices
2 eggs
1 cup bread crumbs

½ teaspoon dried rosemary
salt and pepper to taste
¼ cup butter

In a saucepan of boiling salted water, boil the parsnips until just tender—about 7 minutes. Drain and pat dry.

Put the eggs into a bowl, and beat to combine.

Place the bread crumbs in a pie plate with the rosemary, salt, and pepper.

Dip the parsnips in the eggs, then in the crumbs, and sauté in the butter until golden.

Yield: 6 servings

➤ Can be prepared for frying several hours ahead.

Parsnips in Sour Cream

1½ pounds parsnips, cubed
1 cup sour cream

¼ teaspoon ground ginger
salt and pepper to taste

In a saucepan of boiling salted water, cook the parsnips until tender and drain. Mash. Beat in the sour cream, ginger, salt, and pepper.

Yield: 6 servings

➤ Can be prepared ahead and reheated.

Crisp-Fried Parsnips

1½ pounds parsnips
⅔ cup butter

salt and pepper to taste

Cut the parsnips into batons, and blanch in boiling salted water for 3 minutes. Drain, and refresh under cold water.

In a skillet, melt the butter, and fry the parsnips in a single layer until crisp and golden. Season with salt and pepper.

Yield: 6 servings

➤ Can be blanched the day before.

Deep-Fried Parsnips

If you prefer, blanch batons of parsnips until barely tender, and batter-coat before deep-frying.

1½ pounds parsnips in paper-thin slices.

oil for deep-frying
salt

Wash the parsnip slices, drain, and pat dry. In a large sauce pan, heat the oil to 375°F.

Fry the parsnips in batches until crisp and golden brown. Drain on paper toweling, and season with salt.

Yield: 6 servings

➤ If the slices are dry and thin, they will cook up like potato chips, and can be held for a day. If they are thicker, they are more like French-fried potatoes, and are best if served immediately.

Gratin du Panais *(Gratin of Parsnips)*

4 tablespoons butter	salt and pepper to taste
1½ pounds parsnips, ¼ inch thick slices	1½ cups medium cream
	1 cup grated Gruyère cheese

Preheat the oven to 350°F. Rub 1 tablespoon of butter in a 9 by 13 inch gratin pan.

Make layers of the parsnip slices, seasoning with salt and pepper, and dotting with butter. Pour on the cream, and sprinkle with the cheese. Bake until tender and golden brown—about 50 minutes.

Yield: 6 servings

➤ Can be prepared for baking several hours ahead. Best if eaten shortly after baking.

Parsnip Cakes

This Down-Maine recipe is a great way of using leftover parsnips, but try it with other mashed root vegetables as well.

3 cups cooked, mashed parsnips	¼ teaspoon pepper
1½ tablespoons butter	1 large egg
1½ tablespoons flour	2 cups cracker crumbs
1½ teaspoons salt	½ cup butter

In a bowl, mix the parsnips with the butter, flour, salt, pepper, and egg. Shape the mixture into 3 inch patties, and pat the cracker crumbs into all sides. In a large skillet, sauté the patties in the butter until golden brown.

Yield: 6 servings

➤ Can be prepared for sautéing about 1 hour before.

Grated Parsnip Salad

1½ pounds parsnips, shredded	1 cup vinaigrette
½ pound carrots, shredded	½ to 1 cup mayonnaise, sour
½ pound red cabbage	cream, or half of each
shredded	salt and pepper to taste
2 apples, peeled and grated	

In a large bowl, toss the parsnips, carrots, cabbage, and apples together. Add the vinaigrette, and toss to coat evenly. Let marinate for 1 hour. Fold in the mayonnaise, and correct the seasoning with salt and pepper.

Yield: 6 servings

➤ Can be prepared the day before. The longer the salad sits, the softer the texture.

Variations:

Add 2 tablespoons caraway seeds.
  Add ¼ cup Dijon mustard to the sauce.
  Add ½ cup raisins and ½ cup chopped walnuts or pecans.
  Add ¼ cup minced dill.

Peas

Peas, like corn, are best if cooked immediately after picking. The sugar starts to turn to starch as soon as the peas are picked. Unless you grow your own, or have access to a farm stand where they pick several times a day, you very probably have never tasted the glory of a freshly picked pea. Your next best bet is the fresh peas you buy in the supermarket. Unfortunately, even there, unless you are attentive, you may well miss the possibility of fresh peas. In recent years more peas are shipped from distant areas under less-than-perfect conditions. Peas like cool, relatively wet springs and dislike the heat. They appear for only a few short weeks in the early summer and then disappear. I recommend that you start to watch for them in late May, and buy them until they stop appearing, and then wait until next year. Those that come into market from great distances are usually woody and lack flavor. Snow peas and sugar snap peas have a longer season and store better, because the pea is secondary to the pod.

Peas are divided into two principal categories, the edible pod variety (snow peas and sugar snap peas), and the shelling variety. The shelling variety has a parchment-like lining on the pod which makes eating it unsatisfactory. Older shelled peas are not only sold fresh, but the maturer peas are dried and sold as split green peas, yellow peas, or chick peas. I have given the recipes for chick peas with dried beans on pages 000-000.

Snow peas and sugar snap peas have become restaurant favorites in recent years. They require little preparation, cook in seconds, have a bright-green color, and they taste good. How can you miss? Unfortunately, being on every plate has removed some of the treat that used to be involved in eating these delicious legumes. They are essential to many stir-fried dishes.

Fortunately, peas freeze well and, though not the same as fresh, they are reasonable, albeit not perfect, substitutes. Prepare the recipes listed below with frozen peas when necessary, but do make the effort to prepare them with fresh peas when they are in season.

Availability

Fresh
Available from January through July. Look for local garden-fresh peas. They should have shiny, bright-green, crisp, well-filled pods about 3

to 4 inches long. Avoid yellow, spotty, soft, or dull-colored pods. Store them in the refrigerator no more than a day or two.

Snow Peas Available year round, these were once a luxury vegetable, but their popularity has turned them into a common vegetable. Look for flat, shiny, crisp, bright-green pods with no sign of yellowing or dullness. Avoid soft or shriveled snow peas. Keep in a plastic bag for 1 to 2 days in the refrigerator.

Sugar Snap Peas A relatively new hybrid, these combine the best of edible pods and mature peas. They have a sweet flavor that is most appealing. Available in the late spring and early summer. Look for shiny, bright-green, crisp, well-filled pods, without any sign of yellowing or limpness. Keep in a plastic bag, refrigerated, for 1 to 2 days.

Frozen
Most of the fresh pea crop is frozen and found in the freezer case rather than the produce section. Though not as good as fresh, they are a reasonable substitute. Snow peas are sold frozen, but the delicate texture is destroyed in the blanching and freezing. Buy fresh, or select another recipe.

Sugar Snap Peas These freeze as well as shelled peas, but like them are not the same as fresh.

Canned Peas
The canning process turns peas into something else. The flavor and color have no relation to fresh peas.

Dried Peas
Dried peas are sold in the dried bean section of most markets. They are sold in boxes or plastic bags. Check the date on the container and be sure not to purchase peas over a year old. They will take longer to cook and may disintegrate in cooking.

Quantity

Peas
Because of the waste, plan on 3 pounds for 6 persons.

Snow Peas There is some waste, but because the pod is underdeveloped, people find these less filling than other peas. Plan on 2 pounds for 6 persons.

Sugar Snap Peas You will need about 1½ pounds for 6 persons.

Preparation

Fresh Peas

Press the flat side of the pod to split it open and push out the peas with your thumb. This is a slow, lazy type of activity. Sit on the porch watching the birds while you do this. Better still, let the children help. The point is that this is not a rush job, and you might as well use it as a relaxing experience rather than try to rush it along.

Edible Pods

Hold the pea in one hand, and pull the stem and attached string down the flat side of the pea. With snow peas and shelled peas, this is usually enough. With sugar snap peas, I take the tail end and pull the string down the rounded side.

Cooking Methods

The secret to cooking peas is to cook them quickly to retain their fresh taste and bright-green color.

Boiling

Cook shelled peas in boiling salted water until tender—about 5 to 15 minutes, depending on age. Plan to blanch snow peas and sugar snap peas for 2 to 5 minutes at the most.

Steaming

Steam sugar snap or snow peas over boiling water for 2 to 4 minutes. Steaming tends to turn the peas grey, and is not recommended.

Microwaving

Microwave 3 cups of peas in 3 tablespoons of liquid for about 6 to 8 minutes.

Braising

Braising with a little liquid, some butter, and seasonings is the preferred method of cooking peas, but not snow peas or sugar snap peas.

Sautéing

Sautéing, or stir-frying, are the preferred methods of cooking snow peas and sugar snap peas, and works with young peas.

Sauces

Peas are flavored with herbed butters, and served with cream. Select other sauces with care, because many overpower peas.

Pea, Pancetta, and Noodle Soup

Pancetta is an unsmoked Italian bacon. If necessary, substitute smoked bacon blanched for 2 minutes.

2 tablespoons butter
2 ounces pancetta, chopped
½ cup minced onion
3 tablespoons minced parsley
1 pound baby peas, shelled

1½ quarts chicken stock
¼ pound egg noodles (see Note)
salt and pepper
grated Parmesan cheese

In a skillet, heat the butter, and sauté the pancetta until browned. Add the onions and parsley, and sauté until soft, but not brown. Add the peas, and cook, stirring, for 2 minutes. Add the stock, and bring to a boil.

Add the noodles, and simmer until tender. Correct the seasoning with salt and pepper.

Serve with cheese on the side.

Yield: 6 servings

➤ This is best if it is made and served. If you try to hold it, the peas will overcook and the noodles will become mushy.

NOTE: Use any pasta shape you want, from ½-inch-wide egg noodles, such as tagliatelle, fettuccine, cappelini, or angel, to any small soup pasta, such as orzo, riso, ditalini, acine di pepe, or tiny bows or shells. If the pasta is fresh, it will only take a minute or two to cook, but dried pasta may need 10 minutes or longer, depending on the size. Add the peas after the pasta, if it will take more than 5 minutes to cook.

Risi e Bisi, Minestra di Riso e Piselli
(Rice and Peas in Broth)

In northern Italy, especially around Venice, Risi e Bisi is as common as spaghetti in southern Italy. Depending on how much liquid is added, it can be a soup, a rice course, or a vegetable to accompany meat or fish. In other parts of the country, it is clearly a thick soup (minestra).

¼ pound butter
2 tablespoons olive oil
4 pounds peas, shelled
½ cup minced onion
3 tablespoons minced parsley

2 ounces minced prosciutto
salt and pepper to taste
1 cup Arborio rice (see Note)
6 cups chicken stock
⅓ cup grated Parmesan cheese

In a large saucepan, cook the butter and oil, and add the peas, onion, parsley, prsociutto, salt, and pepper until the peas are half cooked—about 15 minutes. Add the rice, and stir to coat evenly. Add ½ cup stock, and cook, stirring, until the liquid evaporates.

Continue adding stock, ½ cup at a time, until the rice is tender, but the

center of the grains is still firm. Serve immediately, and pass the cheese.
If you want it soupier, add the remaining stock.

Yield: 6 servings

➤ Cannot be prepared ahead.

NOTE: Arborio rice is a short, fat-grained rice imported from Italy. You
can substitute long-grain rice.
Serve it as a first course, pasta, or a separate vegetable course.

Three-Color Delicious Soup

This is one of my favorite soups. The flavor is light, fresh, and delicious. Although it is a Chinese recipe, I often use it to introduce a
Western meal. The tomatoes should be about the size of the peas, and
the chicken dumplings only slightly larger.

½ large chicken breast,
  skinned and boned
1 egg white
1 tablespoon milk
salt to taste
6 cups chicken stock
salt

¾ cup cooked peas
1 tomato, peeled, seeded, and
  diced
3 tablespoons cornstarch
¼ cup water
2 egg whites

Cut the chicken into cubes, and purée in a processor with the egg
white, milk, and salt. Spoon into a pastry bag fitted with a #6 tube.
Bring the chicken stock to a boil, add the salt, peas, and tomatoes, and
immediately turn off the heat. Squeeze the chicken mixture into the
broth, cutting off small portions.
In a small bowl, stir the cornstarch and water together. Bring the
soup to a boil again, and stir in the cornstarch until lightly thickened.
Pour the soup into a tureen.
In a small bowl, beat the egg whites until frothy, and pour into the
hot soup in a slow, steady stream.
Serve.

Yield: 6 servings

➤ The soup can be prepared to the point of adding the egg whites
  ahead. In this case, do not add the peas until you are ready to reheat
  the soup.

Iced Pea and Curry Soup

1 onion, thinly sliced	1 tablespoon flour
¼ cup vegetable oil	2 cups chicken stock
2 teaspoons curry powder, or	pinch of nutmeg
to taste	pinch of mace
1 teaspoon salt	½ cup light cream
1½ teaspoons sugar	½ cup heavy cream
Cayenne pepper to taste	1 tablespoon minced chives
2 pounds shelled, or 2 10 ounce	3 ounces cooked chicken,
packages frozen peas	ham, or shrimp, diced
1½ cups water	

In a 2 quart saucepan, sauté the onion in the oil until golden. Add the curry powder, salt, sugar, and cayenne pepper to taste. Cook, stirring, over low heat until fragrant—about 5 minutes. Add the peas and ½ cup of water, and simmer until the peas are tender—about 15 minutes for fresh peas, and 7 minutes for frozen.

Stir in the flour, and cook 2 minutes. Add the chicken stock, remaining water, nutmeg, and mace, and simmer for 10 minutes. In a processor or blender, purée and strain through a sieve. Chill.

Stir in the light and heavy cream before serving, and garnish with the chives, chicken, ham, or shrimp.

Yield: 6 servings

➤ Can be prepared the day before, or frozen.

Cream of Snow Pea with Shrimp

½ cup butter	1 teaspoon minced mint
1½ pounds snow peas,	pinch of sugar
stringed	salt and pepper
4 cups chicken stock	¼ pound cooked shrimp
1 cup heavy cream	

In a saucepan, melt ¼ cup butter, and sauté the snow peas until tender—about 5 minutes. Add the stock, and simmer for 20 minutes.

In a blender, or through a food mill, purée the soup. If you use a processor, strain after puréeing to remove any hard bits of fiber. Return the soup to the saucepan, and bring to a simmer. Add the cream, mint, sugar, salt, and pepper.

Whisk in the remaining butter, and serve garnished with the shrimp.

Yield: 6 servings

➤ Can be prepared ahead and reheated. Can be frozen.

NOTE: If tiny shrimp (50 or more to a pound) are not available, buy 21 to 25's, and cut them into ½ inch dice. They should fit easily into a soup spoon.

If you do not want shrimp, garnish with a generous sprinkling of minced mint.

Purée Mongole Soup

This is a lovely, old-fashioned soup that was at one time very popular, and then disappeared from menus and mainly from books until the last few years. It is easy to prepare and an especially good way of using more mature peas.

4 or 5 large tomatoes, or 4
  cups canned Italian
  tomatoes, with juice
  reserved
2 cups green peas, cooked

2 cups chicken stock
salt and pepper to taste
1 cup heavy cream
⅓ cup chervil sprigs (optional)

In a food mill, purée the tomatoes and the peas, and put into saucepan. If you prefer to purée in a processor, strain through a sieve to remove the seeds and skins.

Add the stock, salt, and pepper. Bring to a boil, add the cream, and simmer for 20 minutes.

Serve garnished with the chervil sprigs, if desired.

Yield: 6 servings

➤ Can be prepared ahead and frozen.

Soupe aux Pois Canadienne (Canadian Yellow Pea Soup)

Green split pea soup is the norm, but this Canadian version, which has relatives in Scandinavia, is an interesting change.

1 pound dried whole yellow peas
2½ quarts water
½ pound salt pork, rinsed
2 cups chopped onions

½ cup diced carrot
salt and pepper to taste
½ teaspoon dried sage
minced parsley

Pick over the peas, and discard any stones or discolored peas.

In a large pot, bring the peas and the water to a boil, and cook 2 minutes. Turn off the heat, and let stand for 1 hour.

Cut the pork fat into ¼ inch dice, discarding the rind. In a skillet, fry the pork until golden, and drain on paper toweling. Discard the fat in the pan.

Return the peas to the heat, and add the fried pork, onions, carrots, 1 teaspoon of salt, and the sage. Simmer, partially covered, for 2½ hours, stirring often during the last half hour. If the soup is too thick, add water. Correct the seasoning with salt and pepper.

Serve garnished with the parsley.

Yield: 6 servings

➤ Can be prepared ahead and reheated.

Variations:
Use split yellow or green peas, if preferred.
Add 2 stalks of chopped celery with the carrots.
Add ½ pound diced ham just before serving and heat.

Cold Pea and Curry Soup

½ cup chopped onion	1½ cups water
¼ cup vegetable oil	1 tablespoon flour
2 teaspoons curry powder	2 cups chicken stock
salt	pinch of nutmeg
1½ teaspoons sugar	pinch of mace
Cayenne pepper, to taste	1 cup half and half cream
2 pounds peas, shelled, or 20	1 tablespoon minced chives
ounces frozen peas	

In a large saucepan, sauté the onion in the oil until golden. Add the curry powder, salt, sugar, and Cayenne pepper. Simmer 3 minutes. Add the peas and ½ cup water, cover, and simmer until the peas are tender—about 15 minutes for fresh peas, and 5 minutes for frozen. Stir in the flour, and cook 2 minutes. Add the chicken stock, remaining cup of water, nutmeg, and mace. Simmer 10 minutes.

In a processor or food mill, purée the soup, and strain to remove any skins. Chill. Stir in the cream, and serve garnished with the chives.

Yield: 6 servings

➤ Can be prepared a day or two before serving. Can be frozen.

Piselli con Prosciutto (Peas with Prosciutto)

Peas and ham are a natural combination, and almost every region of Italy has a version of peas with prosciutto.

This is the Roman version, but others use garlic, sometimes adding diced tomatoes, or mixing the dish with rice or pasta.

¼ cup minced onions	¼ cup chicken stock
¼ cup diced prosciutto (see	(approximately)
Note)	salt and pepper to taste
¼ cup butter	
3 pounds fresh peas, shelled	
(see Note)	

In a saucepan, sauté the onion and prosciutto in the butter until soft, but not brown. Add the peas and 2 tablespoons of stock, and season with salt and pepper.

Cover and cook over low heat for 10 minutes, or until the peas are tender. Add more stock, a tablespoon at a time, if it evaporates.

Yield: 6 servings

➤ Best if prepared just before serving.

NOTE: Use 2 10 ounce packages of frozen peas, if necessary, and cook for about 5 minutes.

Variations:
Florentine Use olive oil and 2 cloves of garlic instead of butter and onion.

Petit Pois è la Française (French Style Braised Peas)

This is one of the best ways of preparing peas.

2 tablespoons butter	½ teaspoon salt
6 tiny whole onions	3 pounds fresh peas, shelled
6 lettuce leaves, shredded	½ cup water
1 tablespoon sugar	1 tablespoon beurre manié
1 tablespoon minced parsley	(see glossary)
1 tablespoon minced chervil	

In a saucepan, place the butter, onions, lettuce, sugar, parsley, chervil, salt, peas, and water. Cover, and simmer for 15 minutes, or until the peas are just cooked. There should be about 2 or 3 tablespoons of liquid. If there is more, remove the peas and other ingredients with a slotted spoon, and reduce the liquid.

After the liquid is reduced, swirl in the beurre manie, ½ teaspoon at a time, until the mixture comes to a simmer. If necessary, return the peas to the pan and swirl until heated.

Yield: 6 servings

➤ Best if prepared just before serving.

NOTE: If using frozen peas, add the peas after the other ingredients have simmered for 10 minutes. Cook 5 to 7 minutes longer. You will not need more than ¼ cup of water.

Variation:
Add 1 to 2 tablespoons minced mint with the peas.

Petits Pois en Case (Fresh Peas in Shells)

Traditionally, the peas were served in pastry shells, but hollowed heated tomato, or fully cooked onion shells, make suitable containers.

Quick Cream of Pea Soup

Prepare this with fresh or frozen peas.

1 recipe Petit Pois à la Francaise (see previous recipe)	1 to 2 cups heavy cream salt and pepper to taste

In a processor or blender, purée the cooked peas and their juices. Strain through a fine sieve.

Return the pea purée to a saucepan, and add enough cream to thin to the desired consistency. Heat, and correct the seasoning with salt and pepper to taste.

Yield: 6 servings

Variations:

Substitute milk for the cream, or use half milk and half yogurt or sour cream.

Add just enough dry sherry so that there is only a suggestion of its presence.

Serve hot or cold.

Peas with Rosemary and Toasted Pine Nuts

½ cup chicken stock	3 tablespoons butter
2 scallions, sliced	⅓ cup pine nuts
½ teaspoon sugar	1 tablespoon minced rosemary
3 pounds peas, shelled	salt and pepper

In a saucepan, bring the stock, scallions, and sugar to a simmer. Add the peas, and simmer until tender—about 8 minutes. Drain and discard the liquid.

In a skillet, melt the butter, and sauté the pine nuts and rosemary until the pine nuts are golden. Add the peas and heat. Correct the seasoning with salt and pepper.

Yield: 6 servings

➤ The peas can be cooked several hours ahead.

Peas and Carrots

Peas and carrots are a perfect combination.

1 pound carrots, cut into batons	½ cup minced onion
salt and pepper to taste	salt
2 pounds peas, shelled	pinch of sugar
heart of a small lettuce	2 tablespoons butter

In a saucepan of boiling salted water, blanch the carrots for 4 minutes. Drain.

In the saucepan, place the peas, lettuce, onion, salt, sugar, and carrots. Dot with butter, cover, and simmer gently until the liquid from the vegetables evaporates. Correct the seasoning with salt and pepper.

Yield: 6 servings

➤ Best if prepared just before serving.

Tortino di Carote e Piselli *(Carrot and Pea Torte)*

This is not only a delicious vegetable, but is suitable for brunch or lunch, served with crusty rolls and a green salad.

⅓ cup olive oil	1 cup grated Parmesan cheese
5 cups shelled peas	3 tablespoons coarse bread crumbs
1 small onion, thinly sliced	5 tablespoons milk
salt and pepper to taste	1¼ cups chopped cooked carrots
8 eggs	

Preheat the oven to 325°F. Brush a 2 quart soufflé dish with olive oil.

In a saucepan, simmer the olive oil, ½ inch of water, peas, and onion, covered, for 15 minutes, or until the peas are tender. Drain, and season with salt and pepper.

In a bowl, combine the eggs and cheese. In another bowl, soak the bread in the milk, and squeeze out the excess. Blend into the egg mixture, and fold in the peas, onions, and carrots. Pour into the soufflé dish, and even the top.

Bake for 30 minutes, or until a knife inserted 1 inch from the edge comes out clean, and the top is nicely browned. Let stand 10 minutes before serving.

Yield: 6 servings

➤ Can be prepared for baking several hours ahead.

Sformato di Tagliatelle e Prosciutto
(Mold of Noodles and Prosciutto)

This is one pasta dish where making your own pasta can make a difference. The pasta should be very thin to keep this as light as possible. Use fettuccine if you do not have the time to make your own.

6 tablespoons butter	salt and pepper to taste
8 slices prosciutto	½ pound tagliatelle, or
½ cup mushrooms, sliced	fettuccine
½ cup tiny peas, parboiled	½ cup grated Parmesan cheese

Preheat the oven to 350°F. Butter a 7 inch soufflé dish with 1 tablespoon of butter. Place the narrower ends of the prosciutto in the center of the mold, and let the ends overlap the edges.

Melt 2 tablespoons of the butter in a skillet, and cook the mush-rooms and peas, covered, over high heat for 3 minutes. Set aside.

Cook the noodles in boiling salted water until just barely done. Drain. Immediately toss with 3 tablespoons butter, Parmesan, peas, and mushrooms, and mix gently. Pour into the prosciutto-lined mold. Fold the ends over the filling. Place in the oven for 5 to 6 minutes to heat through.

Remove from the oven and let stand for two minutes. Invert the mold onto a platter, and let stand for minute to let it settle. Remove the mold, and serve.

Yield: 6 servings

➤ The mold can be filled an hour before baking, but it is best if everything is done just before serving.

Chao Hsueh Tou (*Stir-Fried Snow Peas and Mushrooms*)

10 large Chinese mushrooms, soaked	¾ cup sliced bamboo shoots
3 tablespoons vegetable oil	1 tablespoon soy sauce
1½ pounds snow peas, stringed	¾ teaspoon sugar

Drain the mushrooms, reserving the liquid. Discard the stems, and cut the caps into large strips or quarters.

Heat a wok until hot, add the oil, and heat for 30 seconds. Stir in the mushrooms and bamboo shoots, and stir-fry for 2 minutes. Add the snow peas, soy sauce, and sugar, and stir-fry until coated. Add 2 table-spoons mushroom soaking water, and cook over high heat until the liquid evaporates.

Serve immediately.

Yield: 6 servings

➤ Cannot be prepared ahead.

Variations:
Add 1 tablespoon minced ginger before the mushrooms.
Add 1 tablespoon minced scallion before the mushrooms.
Use oyster sauce instead of the soy sauce.
Use sugar snap peas instead of snow peas.

Mange Toute et Champignons

The French, as always, have their version.

1 tablespoon minced shallot	1 pound snow peas, stringed
3 tablespoons butter	salt and pepper to taste
½ pound mushrooms, thinly sliced	½ cup heavy cream

In a large skillet, sauté the shallot in the butter until soft, but not brown. Add the mushrooms and cook until most of liquid evaporates. Add the snow peas and cook, stirring, for 1 minute, or until bright green. Season with salt and pepper. Add the cream, and cook over high heat until the sauce is thick enough to coat the snow peas.

Yield: 6 servings

➤ Cannot be prepared ahead.

Snow Pea and Corn Salad

1 pound snow peas, cut into ¼ inch diagonal slices	2 tablespoons balsamic vinegar
3 cups corn kernels	2 tablespoons chopped tarragon
1 shallot, minced	2 tablespoons chopped mint
2 tablespoons Dijon whole grain mustard	⅓ cup olive oil
	salt and pepper to taste

In a pot of boiling salted water, blanch the snow peas for 30 seconds. Drain, run under cold water, and drain again. In a bowl, mix the snow peas and corn.

In a small bowl, whisk the shallot, mustard, vinegar, tarragon, mint, olive oil, salt, and pepper until emulsified. Pour over the salad and toss gently.

Yield: 6 servings

➤ Can be prepared 2 or 3 hours before serving. If the snow peas marinate longer than that, they turn grey.

Peppers

Sweet, bell, and chile peppers, members of the *Capsicum frutescens* family, are native to the Americas and were introduced into Europe and other countries after 1500. They are a fruit that we eat as a vegetable, rather like tomatoes. Black pepper, a native of the Indian Archipelago, is now cultivated in most equatorial countries. The dried berries are used to make black or the less pungent white pepper, which is black pepper without the husk. It has been in use as a spice since the days of ancient Greece. In essence, we season food with black or white pepper berries and eat sweet peppers. This chapter is about bell or sweet peppers.

Sweet peppers ripen from green to red, yellow, or orange. The brighter the color, the sweeter the fruit. In most recipes the various colors are interchangeable. People who dislike the unripened green peppers often enjoy the ripe peppers. Chiles are varieties of sweet pepper eaten for the varying amounts of fire. Some people have a tolerance for these tasty torches that is astounding, while others find that being in the same room when they are cut can cause tearing, sneezing, and coughing. Read the preparation section to learn how to handle chiles.

There are are several types of peppers:

1. Bell peppers: Usually red or green, but there are varieties in all colors. Use for color and flavor. They are all sweet rather than fiery, with the red and other colors being sweeter than the green. The seeds can be hot. (Note: green chiles are generally hotter than red, because even they sweeten as they ripen.)

2. Poblano/Ancho: A large, dark-green, bell-shaped pepper, rarely seen in the fresh, red state, with a mild, deep, aromatic flavor. They are dried to a deep mahoganny color, and need to be soaked before using.

3. Anaheim, California, Chile Verde, Long Green, or Big Jim: These are different types of the same long, narrow, and slightly twisted chile, similar in appearance to the pepperoncini, but fatter. They range from mild to hot, depending on the growing conditions. Plan on them being semi-hot.

4. Pasilla: This is a long, brown pepper, which is usually sold dried. It is quite hot, and should be used with caution.

5. Pepperoncini or Italianelles: They are long, thin, twisted, and light-green, verging on yellow. They are mild in flavor, and can be used for stuffing or for pickling. Great in stir-fries.

6. Jalapeño: A small, two- to three-inches long, blunt-nosed, dark-green chili, often striated with tan lines. These can be very hot, and some people find them intolerable. Use sparingly. Avoid using the seeds, which can be quite hot.

7. Serrano: Similar to jalapeños, but longer and narrower. They are usually dark green, but can be found ripened to red. They are extremely hot. Use with discretion.

8. Cayenne: a small, narrow, fiery hot red pepper. Use with caution.

9. Pepin: A tiny, 1-inch long, fiery red pepper that turns brown when dried. Found in Asian markets. Use with great care.

All peppers contain capsaicin. The fiery substance in the ribs and seeds. In chiles, there is a lot more than in sweet peppers. To tame the fire, discard the seeds, and cut out the ribs. Some dishes are supposed to be hot—if you remove the hot peppers, the dish becomes insipid and uninteresting. If you do not like hot food, select another recipe, rather than ruining the dish. Leaving them out makes as much sense as making horseradish sauce without the horseradish.

Availability

Peppers are at their prime in July and August.

Fresh

Sweet Peppers Look for firm, thick-skinned peppers, with no sign of shriveling, dark spots, or dull color. The color can go from deep green to red orange, yellow, brown, or purple. They should feel heavy for their size. Store, unwrapped, in the refrigerator for a week or more. Plastic bags hasten rot.

Chiles Chiles range from large anchos to tiny pepins. The color ranges from green to bright red or orangy red, tending toward the brown. Generally speaking, green peppers are hotter than red. Red are riper and sweeter. Look for plump, glossy, crisp-looking chiles with no sign of shriveling or brown spots. Store in the vegetable drawer, unwrapped. Plastic bags hasten rot.

Frozen

Freezing peppers changes the texture, so frozen peppers should only be used in soups or casseroles. Do not use in place of fresh peppers.

Canned

Canned chiles come in varying degrees of heat. Sometimes the cans are labeled indicating whether they are hot or milk. When fire, and not texture, is required, they are acceptable.

Dried Chili Peppers

Cayenne pepper, red pepper flakes, and paprika are all dried peppers. Test the paprika first to make sure it is the right heat for the dish you are preparing. Most dishes use sweet paprika.

Quantity

Plan on 2 pounds of sweet peppers for 6 persons. The amount of chile pepper will depend on the amount of fire desired and the type and fieriness of the chile used. I strongly recommend that you follow the recipe, and then make additions to taste. Once they are added, you cannot remove them.

A pinch of cayenne is often called for in cream and other sauces in the same way as salt in desserts. It accents the flavor.

Preparation

Sweet Peppers
To Core Press your thumb on the stem of the pepper, and push into the vegetable. Twist the stem and remove. The stem and seeds will come out together. Or, cut down one side, and up the other into halves. Separate the halves, and lift out the seeds as a unit.

To Peel Pepper skin can be tough, and in many recipes the peppers should be peeled.

Broil the peppers, turning until all sides are evenly charred and the skin is blistered. Place the hot peppers into a paper bag and close. Let stand for 10 to 15 minutes, until the peppers are cool enough to handle. Remove the stems, and scrape off the papery skin. Scrape off any seeds.

An alternative method is to put the peppers into boiling water for 10 minutes until softened, and again seal in a bag until cool enough to handle. I find the broiling method gives the pepper flavor.

Chile Peppers
Chile peppers have a large amount of capsaicin, depending on the variety. This can burn sensitive areas of your skin, such as under your fingernails, and around the mouth, eyes, or other bodily openings. Some people are more sensitive than others. This is not an idle warning. Until you know how sensitive you are, use great care in working with hot peppers! The pain, though not damaging, can last for several hours.

Unless you are stuffing chile peppers, it is not necessary to peel them.

Place the peppers on a board, cut in half, and remove and discard the seeds and the ribs. Many people prefer to do this under cold running water to remove the capsaicin as it is released from the cut areas. Mince the peppers with a sharp knife, in a food processor, or a mini chopper, depending on the quantity. Wash the board, knife, or machine with hot soapy water to remove the capsaicin so it does not affect other foods.

Cooking Methods

Boiling
You can boil peppers, but the flavor is diminished.

Microwaving

Peppers will cook in a covered container to the tender-crisp soft stage in 8 to 10 minutes. This is another good method of precooking peppers before stuffing.

Sautéing

One of the best methods of cooking peppers. Cut into the desired size or shape and sauté in butter, olive oil, or even a small amount of chicken stock, in a non-stick skillet.

Grilling

Grilling or broiling peppers to char the skin not only makes them easy to peel (see above), but also enhances the flavor.

Baking

Bake peppers with just a bit of olive oil, salt, and pepper for a perfect, easy vegetable.

Stuffing

Every culture that uses peppers stuffs them. They are served hot, cold, and at room temperature. They can be stuffed with cheese, meat, fish, vegetables, or bread crumbs. Stuffed peppers can accompany a roast, or serve as a first course or vegetable course. They can be a main course for lunch, brunch, dinner, or supper.

Sauces

Peppers tend to marry well with slightly sharp flavors, such as vinegar or a sharp vinaigrette. Peppers have an oily quality that makes a squirt of lemon juice sufficient. They can also be sauced with cream, or cream sauces, but generally I prefer the clearer flavors of garlic and olive oil.

Shrimp and Red Pepper Bisque

Bisques are made from the shells of shrimp and lobster, and it is not uncommon to use the meat for another dish. This is an economical way of getting more shrimp for your money. See the note, below, about using the whole shrimp.

4 pounds shrimp in the shell	⅓ cup Cognac
3 tablespoons vegetable oil	4 sprigs thyme or 1 teaspoon
½ cup minced onion	dried thyme
½ cup minced carrot	1 bay leaf
½ cup minced celery	1½ cups heavy cream
¼ cup flour	4 red peppers, peeled
¼ cup tomato paste	salt and pepper to taste

Peel the shrimp, saving the shells, and set the shrimp aside for another use.

In a saucepan, heat the oil over high heat, and sauté ¾ of the shells until lightly browned. Add the onion, carrot, and celery, and cook, stirring occasionally, until soft, but not brown—about 10 minutes. Stir in the flour and tomato paste, and cook 1 minute.

Increase the heat, and whisk in the brandy, scraping up any browned bits, and simmer 3 minutes. Whisk in 7 cups water, the thyme, and the bay leaf, and bring to a boil, stirring frequently. Simmer for 45 minutes.

In another saucepan, simmer the remaining shells in the cream for 10 minutes. Strain, discarding the shells, and set the cream aside.

In a processor, purée the peppers, and set aside. Strain the soup, and return to the pan. Stir in the red pepper purée, and add the cream and shrimp mixture. Reheat, and correct seasoning with salt and pepper.

Yield: 6 servings

➤ Can be prepared ahead and frozen.

NOTE: You can save shrimp shells in the freezer to prepare the bisque at a later time. You will need about ¾ pound of shells.

If you wish to use the shrimp in the soup, add ¼ cup diced shrimp per serving.

Cold Pepper Soup

Select the color pepper of your choice. Red or yellow peppers are preferred, but the orange is also a good choice.

4 cups chicken stock
2 pounds roasted peppers, peeled and chopped
1½ cups peeled and diced potatoes
1 garlic clove, minced
¼ teaspoon dried marjoram
¼ teaspoon dried basil
¼ teaspoon dried savory
⅛ teaspoon dried oregano
1½ cups milk
¾ cup heavy cream

In a saucepan, simmer the chicken stock, peppers, potatoes, garlic, marjoram, basil, savory, and oregano for 30 minutes. Strain the soup, reserving the liquid and the vegetables.

In a blender or a processor, purée the solids and return to the soup, and stir in the milk and cream. Chill, and correct the seasoning with salt and pepper.

Yield: 6 servings

➤ Can be prepared the day before.

Pepperoni, Aglio, e Olio
(Sweet Peppers with Oil and Garlic)

2 pounds assorted peppers, cored	2 tablespoons thinly sliced garlic
½ cup olive oil	salt and pepper to taste

Cut away any veins, and cut the peppers into thin strips.

In a skillet, sauté the peppers in the oil over high heat for 4 minutes. Add the garlic, salt, and pepper, and cook, stirring, for 5 minutes longer.

Serve hot or at room temperature.

Yield: 6 servings

➤ Can be prepared the day before, but let it warm to room temperature before serving.

La Piperade (Pepper and Onion Garnish/Sauce)

In the Basque region, a common garnish to eggs, fish, and meats is the piperade—a sauté of peppers, onions, and tomatoes. It is a superb garnish for other foods, but grand enough to stand on its own as a vegetable.

1 pound green or red peppers, thinly sliced	4 cups peeled, seeded, and chopped tomatoes
¼ cup olive oil	1 tablespoon minced basil
2 cups finely sliced onions	1 teaspoon minced oregano
1 tablespoon minced garlic	salt and pepper to taste

In a skillet, sauté the peppers and onions in the oil until soft, but not brown. Add the garlic and cook for 1 minute. Add the tomatoes, basil, and oregano, and simmer until the moisture evaporates. Correct the seasoning with salt and pepper.

Yield: 6 servings as a garnish for omelettes, steak, or fish

➤ Can be prepared the day before and reheated.

Pepperoni Abbraciati
(Roasted Sweet Peppers with Garlic and Oil)

This is similar, but different from, the previous recipe, and indicates the difference between peeled and unpeeled peppers.

2 pounds assorted peppers, peeled and cut into strips	salt and pepper to taste
1 tablespoon thinly sliced garlic	3 tablespoons olive oil

In a small bowl, or ravier, arrange the peppers in layers with the garlic, salt, pepper, and olive oil. Cover, and refrigerate overnight. Let warm to room temperature before serving.

Yield: 6 servings

➤ Can be prepared ahead.

NOTE: In Italy, these would be left in a cool area instead of being refrigerated. If you refrigerate them, let them warm to room temperature for the best flavor.

Variation:
Instead of olive oil, sprinkle the peppers with vinegar to taste, and season with salt and pepper.

Serve the peppers with a vinaigrette flavored with marjoram and garnished with anchovies.

Prepare a vinaigrette with ¼ cup orange juice, 1 tablespoon Dijon mustard, 1 tablespoon grated orange rind, and ⅓ cup olive oil. Serve sprinkled with chopped, toasted hazelnuts and minced coriander.

Friggione (Sautéed Peppers, Onions, and Tomatoes)

2 tablespoons butter	1 pound pearl onions, thinly sliced
2 tablespoons olive oil	2 pounds tomatoes, peeled,
2 pounds green and red	seeded, and chopped
peppers, thinly sliced	salt and pepper to taste

In a large skillet, heat the butter and oil, and sauté the peppers and onions until the onions are soft—about 12 minutes. Add the tomatoes, cover, and simmer 10 minutes. Season with salt and pepper. Remove the cover, and cook over high heat until the liquid evaporates.

Serve hot or at room temperature.

Yield: 6 servings

➤ Can be prepared the day before and reheated.

Variation:
Add 2 garlic cloves, minced with the onions.
Use all olive oil.

Tian Rouge (Cold Red Pepper and Tomato Gratin)

Cold, here, really means at room temperature. This recipe, like so many others involving peppers, tastes best when allowed to cool to about 60 degrees.

Tian is a Provençale word for a gratin or flat casserole.

½ cup minced parsley	1½ pounds red peppers, peeled
⅓ cup minced basil	and cut into ½ inch strips
1 tablespoon dried thyme	salt and pepper to taste
3 tablespoons olive oil	1 tablespoon capers
6 large tomatoes, thickly sliced	2 tablespoons fresh bread crumbs

Preheat the oven to 400°F.

Mix the parsley, basil, and thyme together. Oil a gratin with 1 tablespoon of oil, and cover with a third of the tomato slices, sprinkle with ¼ of the herbs, and cover with a layer of half of the pepper strips.

Repeat, using up the ingredients. Sprinkle the top with the capers and bread crumbs, and drizzle with olive oil. Bake for 20 minutes, or until the tomatoes are tender.

Let cool to room temperature before serving.

Yield: 6 servings

➤ Can be prepared the day before and allowed to come to room temperature.

Gratin Froid à la Catalane (Cold Catalonian Gratin)

Cold in this instance means at room temperature, instead of piping hot, but this is as good—if not better—hot.

½ cup olive oil	3 tomatoes, ¼ inch slices
2 pounds Spanish onions, thinly sliced	1 teaspoon dried thyme
	½ cup fresh bread crumbs
2 pounds assorted sweet peppers, peeled and cut into thick strips	2 tablespoons minced parsley
	2 garlic cloves, minced
	1 can rolled anchovy fillets
salt and pepper to taste	(optional)

Preheat the broiler.

In a skillet, heat 3 tablespoons of oil and sauté the onions until soft, but not brown.

In a gratin, make a layer of peppers, cover with the onions, and season with salt and pepper.

Cover with the remaining peppers.

Arrange the tomatoes overlapping on top of the peppers, and season with salt, pepper, and thyme.

In the skillet, heat 3 more tablespoons of oil, sauté the bread crumbs, parsley, and garlic until pale-gold, and scatter over the tomatoes.

Drizzle the remaining oil over the crumbs.

Place under a broiler, and broil until browned and the tomatoes are heated, taking care not to burn the crumbs. If they start to brown too much, put on a lower shelf, or even in the oven, until the tomatoes are done.

Serve hot or at room temperature.

Garnish with the anchovies.

Yield: 6 servings

➤ Can be prepared the day before and allowed to come to room temperature.

Deep-Fried Peppers in Sesame Seeds

The sesame seeds give a crunchy texture, in addition to their nutty flavor.

½ cup flour
2 eggs, lightly beaten
salt and pepper to taste
½ cup untoasted sesame seeds

½ cup fresh bread crumbs
oil for frying
2 pounds large, thick skinned
  peppers, cut into ½ inch strips

On a plate, place the flour. In a bowl, mix the egg, salt, and pepper. On another plate, combine the sesame seeds and bread crumbs.

Heat the oil to 375°F. Dip the peppers in the flour, then in the egg, and next roll in the bread-crumb mixture. Let dry on a wire rack until ready to fry.

Fry the strips until golden. Drain on paper toweling, and serve immediately.

Yield: 6 servings

➤ Can be prepared for frying the day before.

Mousse des Poivrons Rouges Douces
(Sweet Red-Pepper Mousse)

vegetable oil
3 pounds red peppers, peeled
1½ cups chicken stock
2 packages unflavored gelatin
salt and pepper to taste
1 cup heavy cream
4 tomatoes, peeled, seeded,
  and chopped

⅓ cup minced onions
2 teaspoons minced garlic
2 tablespoons olive oil
1 tablespoon balsamic vinegar
¼ cup minced basil leaves
basil leaves for garnish

With a brush, lightly oil 6 ramekins.

In a saucepan, simmer the peppers in 1¼ cups chicken stock for 15 minutes, or until very soft. Drain, reserving the peppers and the liquid.

In a blender, purée the peppers, and set aside. Reduce the liquid to ½ cup.

In a small saucepan, soften the gelatin in the remaining ¼ cup stock, and heat over low heat, stirring until melted. Stir into the red pepper purée, and stir in the reduced liquid. Season with salt and pepper. Cool until the consistency of egg whites.

In a bowl, whip the cream to the soft-peak stage, and fold into the red-pepper mixture. Fill the prepared ramekins with the mousse, and smooth the top. Chill until set—about 4 hours.

In a bowl, mix the tomatoes, onions, garlic, olive oil, vinegar, and minced basil. Unmold the mousse on serving plates, and top with the tomato sauce.

Yield: 6 servings

➤ Can be prepared the day before.

Linguine with Pepper, Tomato, and Basil Sauce

½ cup minced onions
½ cup olive oil
4 garlic cloves, minced
3 pounds tomatoes, peeled,
  seeded, and chopped
¼ cup minced basil
2 teaspoons salt
¼ teaspoon pepper

1½ pounds red peppers,
  julienne
½ pound yellow peppers,
  julienne
2 tablespoons shredded basil
1½ pounds linguine
Basil, cut in julienne for
  garnish

In a large, heavy skillet, sweat the onions in ¼ cup of oil, stirring occasionally. Add half the garlic, and stir 30 seconds. Increase the heat to medium, and add the tomatoes, basil, salt, and pepper. Simmer until most of the liquid evaporates.

In another skillet, heat the remaining ¼ cup of oil, and sauté the peppers until the edges begin to brown, stirring occasionally. Add the remaining garlic, and stir in the shredded basil.

Cook the pasta in boiling salted water until just tender. Drain, and toss with the peppers. Transfer the pasta to a large bowl, and top with the tomato sauce. Garnish with the basil.

Yield: 6 servings

➤ Can be prepared the day before, but best when freshly made.

Orzo with Red Peppers and Pine Nuts

⅓ cup pine nuts
3 tablespoons olive oil
3 red peppers, diced
1½ cups orzo
salt to taste

pinch dry red pepper flakes
pepper
3 tablespoons minced chives
¾ cup peeled, seeded, and
  chopped tomato

In a skillet, sauté the pine nuts in the olive oil until golden. With a slotted spoon, remove the nuts to a sheet of paper towel. Add the peppers, and sauté until soft, but not brown.

Cook the Orzo in boiling salted water until tender. Drain, add to the peppers, and season with the salt and red pepper flakes. Heat. Fold in the chives and tomato.

Yield: 6 servings

➤ The peppers can be prepared several hours ahead. Do not cook the pasta and combine until just before serving.

Stuffed Peppers

Every country where peppers grow, the cooks stuff them. The stuffings can be as simple as rice mixed with a little cheese, or more elaborate combinations of meats, seasonings, cheeses, and other things. Almost anything you can stuff into another vegetable can be stuffed into a pepper.

Some recipes require that you peel the peppers before stuffing, but in most instances it is not necessary, so long as you add some stock, water, or tomato juice to the baking pan, and bake them until tender. As a rule, the stuffing is not affected by longer cooking. Other cooks suggest blanching the peppers in boiling water until tender, but I think this leaches out some of the flavor. The peppers can be stuffed from the top, or if they are large, cut in half and stuff the halves.

Serve stuffed peppers as a vegetable course, first course, or main course. Obviously, a large pepper suitable for a main course would be too much for an appetizer. Select the pepper size according to your use.

Töltött Paprika (Hungarian Stuffed Peppers)

1½ cups chicken stock	¼ pound Gruyère cheese,
½ cup white rice	grated
½ cup chopped onion	salt and pepper to taste
2 tablespoons oil	6 small or medium peppers,
¼ pound mushrooms chopped	roasted, peeled, and seeded
⅓ cup peas, cooked	

Preheat the oven to 400°F. Lightly oil a baking dish.

Bring stock to a boil, stir in the rice, cover, and simmer until the rice is tender and the liquid is absorbed—about 20 minutes.

In a skillet, cook the onion in the oil until soft, but not brown. Increase the heat, and sauté the mushrooms until the liquid evaporates. Stir in the peas and rice. Cool slightly. Stir the cheese into the filling, and season with salt and pepper.

Stuff the peppers, and place in the baking dish. Bake until hot—about 15 minutes.

Yield: 6 servings

➤ Can be prepared for baking the day before.

Poivrons Farcis au Riz (Rice-Stuffed Peppers)

3 tablespoons olive oil	2 cup cooked rice
½ cup minced onion	¼ pound grated Gruyère
¼ pound mushrooms, minced	cheese
1½ cups peeled, seeded, and	1 teaspoon paprika
chopped tomato	salt and pepper to taste
3 tablespoons butter	6 peppers, peeled and seeded
1 teaspoon Armagnac	

Preheat the oven to 400°F.

In a skillet, sauté the onion in the oil until soft, but not brown. Add the mushrooms, and cook until tender.

In another skillet, sauté the tomatoes in the butter until the juices evaporate. Stir in the Armagnac. Mix half the tomatoes with the mushrooms, and stir in the rice. Fold in half the cheese, the paprika, and the salt and pepper.

Stuff the peppers, and place in a baking dish. Spoon the remaining tomato over the peppers. Bake for 10 to 20 minutes, or until the peppers are hot.

Yield: 6 servings

➤ Can be prepared for baking the day before.

Pepperoni Ripiene (Cheese-Stuffed Peppers)

6 large peppers	1 teaspoon minced oregano
olive oil	2 hard cooked eggs, chopped
2 tablespoons butter	1 clove garlic, crushed
½ cup minced onions	4 large tomatoes, peeled,
⅓ cup rice	seeded, and chopped
⅔ cup hot stock or water	salt and pepper to taste
½ pound provola, diced	
4 tablespoons grated Parmesan	
cheese	

Preheat the oven to 375°F. Cut the caps off the peppers, and reserve. Remove the seeds and any thick ribs. Set aside.

In a saucepan, heat 2½ tablespoons oil with the butter, and sauté the onion until golden. Stir in the rice, and add the stock. Cover, and simmer until the rice is tender—about 15 minutes. Remove, and stir in the provola, Parmesan, oregano, and eggs.

Stuff the peppers, cover with their lids, and arrange upright in a shallow baking dish. Add ¼ inch of water, and bake for 45 minutes.

In a sauté pan, brown, but do not burn, the garlic in ¼ cup oil, and discard the garlic. Add the tomatoes, and season with salt and pepper. Cook over brisk heat for 10 minutes. Pour over the peppers, and bake 20 minutes longer, or until the peppers are soft.

Yield: 6 servings

➤ Can be prepared ahead and reheated, or served at room temperature.

Poivrons Farcis à la Niçoise (Stuffed Peppers Niçoise Style)

3 large red or green peppers, halved lengthwise and seeded	1 can anchovies, soaked in milk (see Note)
½ cup olive oil	½ teaspoon thyme
½ cup minced onion	¼ teaspoon rosemary
2 cups cooked rice	juice of 1 lemon
½ cup pitted black olives	pepper to taste
2 tablespoons drained capers	

Preheat the oven to 350°F. Brush 2 tablespoons of oil in a baking pan large enough to hold the peppers, cut side up, in a single layer.

In a skillet, in 1 tablespoon of oil, sauté the onions until soft, but not brown. Stir in the rice, olives, capers, anchovies, thyme, rosemary, lemon juice, pepper, and remaining olive oil. Mix well.

Stuff the peppers, and cover loosely with a sheet of foil. Bake for 45 to 60 minutes, or until the peppers are tender, basting with the pan juices occasionally. Add a little water if necessary.

Yield: 6 servings

➤ Can be prepared ahead and served hot or at room temperature.

NOTE: To soak the anchovies, place them in a bowl and add milk to cover. Let stand for 10 minutes, swish in the milk, and drain. The object is to remove some of the salt. You can omit this step if desired.

Use brine- or oil-cured imported black olives. Use an olive pitter to remove the pits. Canned olives are flavorless by comparison, and should not be used.

Pepperoni Imbottite (Stuffed Peppers)

2 tablespoons olive oil	1 egg
1 shallot, minced	1 ounce grated Romano
3 ounces pancetta, minced	¼ teaspoon oregano
7 anchovies, minced	¼ teaspoon marjoram
1½ cups bread crumbs	1 tablespoon minced parsley
1 clove garlic, minced	3 peppers, halved
⅓ cup cream	12 anchovy fillets

Preheat the oven to 350°F.

In a skillet, cook the shallot in the oil until soft, but not brown. Add the pancetta and anchovies, and cook until the anchovies dissolve. Add the bread crumbs and garlic, and cook until crumbs are lightly browned.

Stir in cream until absorbed. Transfer to a bowl and cool. Add the egg, cheese, oregano, marjoram, parsley, salt, and pepper.

Stuff the peppers, arrange on a baking dish, and brush with olive oil. Bake for 30 minutes, and top with anchovy fillets.

Yield: 6 servings

➤ Can be prepared ahead and reheated, or served at room temperature.

Variation:
Add ¼ cup shelled pistachio nuts, chopped, with the bread crumbs.
   Add ½ cup toasted pine nuts, and ¼ cup raisins or currants.
   Add ¼ cup capers and ¼ cup currants. Mince the anchovies, and stir them into the filling.

Poivrons Farcis à l'Italien
(Stuffed Peppers, Italian Style)

¼ cup olive oil	6 anchovy fillets, minced
4 tomatoes, peeled, seeded, and chopped	½ cup minced green olives
	2 tablespoons capers
2 garlic cloves, minced	1 tablespoon minced basil
2 tablespoons minced parsley	salt and pepper to taste
2 7½ ounce cans Italian tuna, drained, with oil reserved	6 peppers, seeded
	minced parsley
⅔ cup bread crumbs	

Preheat the oven to 350°F. Generously oil a baking dish.
   In a skillet, heat ¼ cup olive oil, and sauté the tomatoes, garlic, and parsley until the liquid evaporates. Stir in the tuna, bread crumbs, anchovies, olives, capers, basil, salt, and pepper, and cook 2 minutes longer.
   Stuff the peppers, and place in the baking dish. Drizzle with the oil from the tuna, and bake for 45 to 50 minutes, or until the peppers are tender. Cool to room temperature, and sprinkle with the minced parsley.

Yield: 6 servings

➤ Can be prepared the day before, but let come to room temperature before serving.

Variation:
Add ½ cup diced pepperoni with the tuna, or omit the tuna and use just the pepperoni, and drizzle with ¼ cup olive oil before baking.

Pepperoni Ripiene
(Stuffed Peppers with Meat and Rice)

½ cup cooked chopped veal,
chicken, or beef
½ cup cooked rice
½ cup bread crumbs
½ cup minced onion
3 anchovy fillets, minced
3 tablespoons olive oil
3 tablespoons grated Romano
cheese

1 tablespoon minced parsley
1 egg
salt and pepper to taste
6 peppers, seeded
⅓ cup olive oil
1 cup hot water
2 tablespoons tomato paste

Preheat the oven to 400°F.

In a bowl, mix the veal, rice, bread crumbs, onion, anchovy, 3 table-spoons olive oil, Romano, parsley, egg, salt, and pepper. Stuff the peppers, and arrange in a baking dish. Pour the remaining oil over the peppers.

In a bowl, whisk the water and tomato paste, and pour into the baking dish. Bake for 20 minutes, baste with the juices in the pan, and bake 20 minutes longer, or until tender.

Yield: 6 servings

➤ Can be prepared ahead and served hot or at room temperature.

Poivrons Verts Farcis (Stuffed Green Peppers)

6 green or red peppers, halved
and seeded
6 Italian sausages
1 cup minced onion
1 garlic clove, minced
1 tablespoon curry powder
salt and pepper to taste

1½ cups cooked rice
1 egg, lightly beaten
¼ cup chicken stock
2 tablespoons bread crumbs
2 tablespoons grated Parmesan
cheese
2 tablespoons olive oil

Preheat the oven to 400°F.

In a saucepan of boiling water, blanch the pepper for 1 minute. Drain and dry on paper toweling. Or, place the peppers on a baking sheet, and bake for 20 minutes.

Remove the skins from the sausages, put the meat into a skillet, and cook, stirring to break up any lumps, for 5 minutes. Add the onion, garlic, curry, salt, and pepper, and cook, stirring, for 8 minutes. Add the rice, egg, and stock, and mix well. Stuff the peppers.

In a small bowl, mix the bread crumbs and Parmesan, and sprinkle over the filling. Drizzle with the olive oil. Place in a baking dish, and bake for 45 minutes, or until the pepper is tender.

Yield: 6 servings

➤ Can be prepared ahead and reheated.

Chiles Rellenos (Batter-Fried Stuffed Chiles)

12 large green Poblano or   1/3 cup minced onions
green bell peppers, peeled   4 eggs, separated
12 pound sharp cheddar or   1/4 cup flour
Monterey Jack cheese, cut   3/4 teaspoon baking powder
into 3 inch batons   1/4 teaspoon salt

Slit the chiles along one side, and scrape out the seeds. In a bowl, mix the cheese and onions, and stuff the peppers with the mixture. Arrange the peppers on a plate, and chill for 1 hour.

In a bowl, beat the egg yolks until thick. Stir in the flour, baking powder, and salt, and mix well. In a clean bowl, with clean beaters, whip the egg white until stiff, and fold into the egg-yolk mixture.

Heat the oil to 375°F. Dip the chilies, one at a time, into the batter, and slide into the oil. Fry for 3 to 4 minutes, or until puffed and golden. Drain on paper toweling.

Yield: 6 servings

➤ The chiles can be prepared for frying the day before. Do not beat the egg whites and fold in until just before frying.

Shrimp and Scallion Dim Sum in Red Peppers

Serve these appetizers at a cocktail party, or as part of a Chinese dinner.

1/2 cup water chestnuts   1/4 teaspoon white pepper
2 scallions, 1 inch pieces   3 red peppers, quartered
2 teaspoons chopped ginger   lengthwise
1 pound shrimp   cornstarch
1 tablespoon dry sherry   1/2 cup soy sauce
2 teaspoons sugar   4 garlic cloves, minced
2 teaspoons sesame oil   2 tablespoons oil
1 teaspoon chili oil   1/4 cup water
1 teaspoon salt

In a processor, chop water chestnuts, scallions, and ginger with on-off turns. Add the shrimp, sherry, sugar, sesame oil, chili oil, salt, and pepper, and process until smooth.

Cut each pepper piece in half crosswise and dust insides with cornstarch. Spoon 1 tablespoon filling into each, and press lightly. In a bowl, mix the soy sauce and garlic, and set aside.

In an oiled skillet, over high heat, arrange the peppers filling side up. Lower the heat, cover, and cook 5 minutes. Add the water, cover, and steam until the filling is opaque—about 2 minutes longer.

Yield: 24 pieces

➤ Can be prepared ahead and reheated in a steamer.

Insalata di Fontina (Pepper and Fontina Salad)

6 yellow peppers, peeled and cut into strips	½ cup olive oil
½ pound Fontina cheese, diced	⅔ tablespoons cream
¼ cup green olives, pitted	1 teaspoon Dijon mustard
	salt and pepper to taste

Preheat the oven to 450°F.

In a bowl, combine the pepper strips, Fontina, and olives. In another small bowl, whisk the olive oil, cream, mustard, salt, and pepper. Toss with the peppers, and chill for 2 hours before serving.

Yield: 6 servings

➤ Can be prepared the day before.

Variation:

Use a variety of peppers.

Add ¼ cup sliced scallion, ½ cup diced celery, and 4 chopped anchovies. Dress with vinaigrette rather than the mustard cream dressing.

Red Pepper and Snow Pea Salad

3 red peppers, peeled and seeded	2 tablespoons red wine vinegar
¾ pound snow peas, stringed	1 tablespoon Dijon mustard
1 cup thinly sliced red onion	salt and pepper to taste
¼ cup olive oil	¼ cup minced parsley

Place the peppers in a bowl. In a pan of boiling salted water, blanch the snow peas for 2 minutes. Drain, refresh under cold water, and drain again. Add to the peppers with the onion.

In a small bowl, whisk the olive oil with the vinegar, mustard, salt, and pepper until emulsified. Pour over the salad, and toss gently. Sprinkle with the parsley.

Yield: 6 servings

➤ Can be prepared 2 hours before serving.

Red Pepper Relish

Serve this with broiled steak, lamb, swordfish, or mackerel.

3 red peppers, cored and chopped	2 teaspoons anchovy paste
¼ cup chopped basil	1 tablespoon balsamic vinegar
2½ tablespoons olive oil	salt and pepper to taste

In a processor, chop the peppers coarsely with the basil, olive oil, anchovy paste, and vinegar, using on-off turns.

Correct the seasoning with salt, pepper, and vinegar, if needed.

Yield: 6 servings

➤ Can be prepared the day before.

Potatoes

*P*otatoes are one of the favorite starches. We serve them regularly for breakfast, lunch, and dinner in every part of the menu, including breads, cakes, and cookies. They are not only appreciated, but loved.

The potato did not come to its current state of acceptance easily. It originated in South America, and when brought to Europe in the mid 1500's, it was looked upon as an oddity to be used for a floral decoration at best and as a poison at worst. But in time, Sir Walter Raleigh in England and Ireland, Antoine-August Parmentier in France, and Frederick the Great in Germany all promoted the potato. To this day, the name of Parmentier on a menu indicates potato as an ingredient. Frederick the Great almost force-fed potatoes to his subjects as an inexpensive way of feeding them.

Nutritionally, potatoes are relatively low in calories (it is what we do to them that raises the calorie level), high in carbohydrates and potassium, and low in sodium. They are good enough to be eaten without any additions, and they blend beautifully with many other foods, especially with garlic, onions, and tomatoes. Potatoes are particularly good with butter, olive oil, cream, milk, and cheese. In addition, you can use every cooking technique to prepare them. They can be chopped, diced, sliced, grated, shredded, minced, ground, puréed, and whipped, and can be shaped into cakes, patties, and logs.

For culinary purposes, potatoes are divided into two categories: waxy, low-starch boiling potatoes that hold their shape when boiled, such as new potatoes of any variety, and such specific varieties as red bliss and yellow Finn; and the floury, high-starch baking potatoes, such as many older potatoes, and specifically the Idaho russet. Unfortunately, the all-purpose potato has almost no good purpose. You *can* boil it, and you *can* bake it, but it is not a perfect boiling potato, nor is it a perfect baking potato. It will work for potato cakes and in gratins.

How do you know which to use? Easy! Use high-starch, dull-skinned Idaho, or baking, potatoes for baked, mashed, or french fried. Dry, floury potatoes tend to disintegrate when boiled. Use low-starch, shiny-skinned potatoes, such as red bliss, yellow Finn, or any new potato for boiling, gratins, and potato chips, where the potato must retain its shape. If you have no choice, use the all-purpose potato, which holds its shape when boiled and makes a good gratin potato, but is not as suitable for baking because the interior can become gummy, and the potato quality is heavier.

Availability

Potatoes are available year round.

Fresh

Baking Look for smooth, firm, dull-skinned potatoes in a long ovoid shape.

Boiling Look for smooth, firm, shiny-skinned potatoes with thin-looking skins. They can be round or oblong. Avoid potatoes with a lot of eyes, cracks, or any sign of softness or shriveling. With new potatoes, avoid those with signs of green at one end.

Store the potatoes in a cool, dry, dark area for a month or longer. Do not refrigerate.

If you discover a potato with any sign of rot, discard it, and pick over the remaining potatoes to make sure the rot has not spread.

Occasionally, you will find a potato that seems in perfect condition, but when you cut into it, it is rotted. Black rot is found usually in home grown potatoes, and is not detectable until the potato is cut. Discard it, and hope the others are fine. Commercially grown potatoes are treated to protect against disease, and are more resistant to disease.

Frozen

Potatoes become water when frozen, and freezing is not recommended unless they have been precooked. Commercial frozen potatoes are partially cooked—fried in most cases—before freezing. They are no rival for freshly-cooked, home-made fried potatoes. Convenient, yes, but you pay with a loss of flavor and quality.

Canned

Canned potatoes are only suitable in a dire emergency. They have a canned flavor and mediocre texture.

Preparation

To peel, or not to peel. There are certain lazy cooks who use nutrition as the excuse for their laziness. True, there are nutrients in the potato skin, and a baked potato with the skin is a heavenly treat. But dirty-gray mashed potatoes with flecks of skin are not appealing. When I roast, broil, or fry potatoes, I often leave the skin on, but when the dish is boiled, mashed, or served as a gratin I remove it. Just because you can leave the skin on does not mean that you should.

To Peel

See page 3 for instructions on peeling potatoes.

Once they are peeled, store the potatoes in a bowl of cold water until ready to cook them. If you are making potato cakes of sliced or shredded potato, do not let them sit in the water to long, or the starch will leach out and they will not hold together.

Quantity

Plan on at least 4 ounces per person, and 5 or 6 ounces is not too much for many people. I recommend 2 pounds of potatoes for 6 persons in most preparations.

Cooking Methods

Potatoes can be cooked by every cooking method. Remember to select waxy, firm, shiny coated potatoes for those recipes in which they should keep their shape, such as boiled, gratins, and potato chips; and floury, long, dull-coated potatoes for baked, mashed, or light french fries. You can use all-purpose potatoes in most recipes, but realize they will not be as light when baked, nor as firm when boiled.

Microwaving

Potatoes bake in 16 to 18 minutes, but the inside may be gummy instead of dry and light.

Boil in a covered container with ¼ cup of water for 8 to 12 minutes depending on the size.

Test the potatoes for doneness. The age, size, and power of your microwave all effect the cooking time. Start testing near the time when they should be done, and do not rely on an arbitrary period of time.

Remember, potatoes must be fully cooked, without any raw flavor.

Sauces

Potatoes are served without sauces more often than not. They do get served with flavored butters when sautéed or baked, and of course can be coated with a cheese sauce.

Soupe de l'Ubac *(Potato Soup from the Béarn)*

2 pounds potatoes, quartered	3 tablespoons butter
2 quarts water	¼ pound grated Gruyère
2 cups milk	cheese
1 veal bone (optional)	6 slices stale bread
salt and pepper to taste	

In a 3 quart saucepan, simmer the potatoes, water, milk, veal bone, salt, and pepper for 40 minutes. Discard the veal bone.

In a food processor, or through a food mill, purée the soup, and return to the saucepan. Simmer 10 minutes. In a heated tureen, put in the butter and cheese, and pour on the hot soup.

Serve garnished with the bread slices.

Yield: 6 servings

➤ Can be prepared ahead and frozen.

Potage Provençale
(Provençale Potato and Spinach Soup)

2 pounds potatoes, peeled and sliced	4 cups cold water
2 cups sliced onions	1 teaspoon salt
3 celery stalks, sliced	2 teaspoons white pepper
2 leeks, sliced	1 pound spinach, stripped
½ cup butter	½ cup light cream, scalded

In a 3 quart saucepan, simmer the potatoes, onions, celery, leeks, butter, water, salt, and pepper until the potatoes almost disintegrate. Add the spinach, and cook 2 minutes.

Force through a food mill, or purée in a processor, and return to the pan. Stir in the cream.

Yield: 6 servings

➤ Can be prepared the day before, or frozen.

NOTE: The soup is supposed to be thick, but if too thick, thin it with water or milk.

Shaker Potato and Leek Soup

1 quart water	3 slices lean bacon
6 medium boiling potatoes, unpeeled	2 cups milk
1½ teaspoons caraway seeds	1 teaspoon crumbled marjoram
1½ teaspoons salt	½ teaspoon paprika
3 leeks, chopped	⅛ teaspoon ground white pepper

In a casserole, bring the water to a boil, and cook the potatoes, caraway seeds, and salt for 20 minutes, or until the potatoes are almost done. Transfer the potatoes to a plate, and reserve the cooking liquid.

Peel the potatoes and chop finely. Stir into the cooking liquid along with the leeks, and simmer, partially covered, for 30 minutes. In a skillet, fry the bacon until crisp, drain and crumble.

Purée the soup through the coarsest blade of the food mill, and return to the casserole. Whisk in the milk, marjoram, paprika, and pepper. Correct seasoning with salt. Heat, whisking occasionally, and serve sprinkled with the bacon bits.

Yield: 6 servings

➤ Can be prepared ahead and frozen.

Soupe à la Bonne Femme or Vichysoisse
(Hot or Cold Potato Soup)

Soupe à la bonne femme is a standard of French cooking. Every housewife has a recipe for potato soup with leeks. In the winter it is served hot, and in summer, cold. Knowing this, Louis Diat, a French chef employed at the Ritz Carlton Hotel in New York a few years before World War I, decided to entice his customer's waning summer appetites with his mother's soup, strained and refined.

1½ cups diced leeks	2 cups hot milk
1 cup diced onion	1 tablespoon butter
1 tablespoon butter	1 tablespoons minced parsley
3 cups peeled, diced potatoes	2 cups light cream
4 cups hot water	1 cup heavy cream
2 teaspoons salt	¼ cup minced chives

In a 3 quart saucepan, sweat the leeks and onion in the butter until soft, but not brown. Add the potatoes, water, and salt, and simmer, covered, for 30 minutes, or until the potatoes almost disintegrate

Purée through a food mill, or in a processor. (For vichysoisse, strain the soup through a fine sieve if you use a food processor.)

For Soupe Bonne Femme Add the milk and butter, and heat. Serve garnished with the parsley.

For Vichysoisse Add the milk and light cream, and bring to a simmer.

Strain through a fine sieve, pressing through as much solid matter as possible. Refrigerate until cold, and strain again. Stir in the heavy cream, and refrigerate. Serve garnished with the chives.

Yield: 6 servings of Soupe Bonne Femme, and 8 servings of Vichysoisse

NOTE: The success of Vichysoisse depends on diligent straining. A superior velvety texture will be the result.

Boiled Potatoes

Select boiling potatoes, with waxy flesh and shiny, thin skins. If they are no bigger than a walnut, cook them whole, skins on. Cut off a narrow ribbon of skin around the middle of each potato so they do not split in the cooking, and also for a decorative effect. For larger potatoes, peel them or not, depending on the look you want, and cook them until tender and easily pierced with a sharp knife or kitchen fork. If you are unsure, remove one, cut it open and test it. Drain the potatoes, and toss with whatever sauce you are using. Tiny new potatoes are difficult to locate, so you may wish to prepare potato balls from larger potatoe.

You can steam the potatoes until just tender—about 15 minutes for walnut-sized potatoes, or cook in a covered container in a microwave for 6 to 10 minutes. Turn them often as they cook in the microwave, and test each one before removing. Microwave ovens can cook unevenly, leaving some overcooked while others are raw.

Parsleied Potatoes

2½ pounds new potatoes, or 6 large potatoes, cut into balls	½ cup butter
	3 tablespoons minced parsley
salt and pepper to taste	

In a large pot of boiling salted water, cook the potatoes until just done. Drain, and return to the pot. Add the butter, and cook, shaking the pan gently to coat the potatoes evenly. Season with salt, pepper, and parsley.

Yield: 6 servings

➤ These are best if made just before serving.

Variations:

Add 1 tablespoons lemon rind and 2 tablespoons lemon juice to the potatoes with the butter, and sprinkle with minced chives.

Add a sprig of mint to cooking water, and use 3 tablespoons of minced mint instead of the parsley.

Omit the parsley, and roll the potatoes in butter and toasted bread crumbs.

Use minced dill instead of parsley.

Use 1 tablespoon of caraway or poppy seeds instead of the parsley.

In a skillet, melt 2 tablespoons of butter, and sauté 2 pounds onions, minced with 2 teaspoons light brown sugar, until the onion is lightly caramelized. Stir in 2 teaspoons dried rosemary and the potatoes, and cook, stirring, until the potatoes are heated and glazed.

Stuffed New Potato Hors d'Oeuvre

One of the finest hors d'oeuvre is potatoes with caviar, but you can select fillings to suit almost any pocket.

2 pounds tiny new potatoes, or   1 cup sour cream
   slices (see below)   2 ounces caviar (see Note)

In a steamer, steam the potatoes until tender. With a melon baller,
scoop out the center of the potatoes and, if necessary, cut a small slice
off the bottom so they do not roll. Place a teaspoon of sour cream in
the openings, and top with a spoon of caviar.

Yield: 6 servings

➤ Cannot be prepared ahead.

NOTE: You can bake the potatoes, but I find steaming easier to manage
for large quantities.

   If the potatoes are larger, cut them into ½ inch slices, and scoop out
an indentation in one slice with a melon baller.

   Use the best caviar you can afford. Fresh salmon caviar is colorful and
good. Use it alone, or in combination with the more expensive beluga, os-
etra, or sevruga. Lumpfish roe has hard pellets and is not suitable.

Variations:

Caviar is expensive and, in some areas, hard to locate. Try some of
these toppings if its more convenient.

Bacon Fry ¼ pound bacon until crisp, and crumble. Put on top of
sour cream.

Chives Add ¼ cup minced chives to the sour cream, and garnish with
more minced chives.

Chicken Liver Sauté ½ pound chicken livers in 2 tablespoons butter
until medium. Drain and cool. Mince, and serve on top of the sour cream.

Dill Add minced dill to the sour cream, and top with dill sprigs.

Garlic Sauté 6 minced garlic cloves in 2 tablespoons olive oil until
golden. Drain the garlic, stir into the sour cream, and serve garnished
with parsley sprigs.

Salsa Fill the potatoes made with salsa (see page 26) and a touch of
sour cream, if desired. You can also top with some grated Monterey
Jack, and melt under a broiler.

Sausage Remove the skin from ½ pound Italian sausage, and sauté the meat in its own juices, crumbling as it cooks, until golden. Serve on top of sour cream.

Brunede Kartofler *(Danish Caramelized Potatoes)*

Sugar and potatoes may seem a strange combination, but the caramelizing gives this a marvelous flavor. Serve these with roasted goose, duck, or pork.

2 pounds small new potatoes   8 tablespoons butter, melted
½ cup sugar

In a large saucepan, cook the unpeeled potatoes in boiling water until tender. Let cool slightly, and peel.

In a skillet, melt the sugar over low heat, and cook until it is a light brown caramel. Stir in the butter, and as many potatoes as possible without crowding the pan. Shake the pan constantly to roll the potatoes and coat with the caramel. When the potatoes are hot, place in serving bowl with a slotted spoon, and finish with remaining potatoes.

Yield: 6 servings

➤ The potatoes can be cooked several hours ahead.

Potatoes, Shallots, and Cèpes

3 pounds boiling potatoes,   2 tablespoons olive oil
  cooked until tender   ½ cup minced shallots
1 cup dried cèpes or shiitake,   salt and pepper
  soaked   1 tablespoon minced chives
2 tablespoons butter

In a large saucepan, boil the potatoes in salted water until tender. Drain, peel, and cut the potatoes into ½ inch chunks.

In a skillet, melt the butter in the oil, and sauté the shallots until soft but not brown. Add the potatoes and mushrooms, and cook, stirring, until hot. Season with salt and pepper, and chives.

Yield: 6 servings

➤ The potatoes can be boiled the day before.

Potatoes with Garlic Sauce

3 garlic cloves, sliced   3 pounds small new potatoes
1¼ cups chicken stock   3 tablespoons butter
salt and pepper to taste   minced parsley

In a blender, purée the garlic in the chicken stock, and season with salt.

Put the potatoes into a skillet large enough to hold the potatoes in one layer, and pour on the garlic sauce. Cover, and simmer until tender—about 15 to 20 minutes. Add the butter, salt, pepper, and parsley.

Yield: 6 servings

➤ Can be prepared ahead and reheated.

Potatoes in Cream Sauce with Herbs

2 pounds potatoes	2 tablespoons minced scallions
salt and pepper to taste	pinched cayenne pepper
1½ cups milk	pinch grated nutmeg
¼ cup heavy cream	1 tablespoon minced parsley

In a large saucepan, boil the potatoes in salted water until tender. Drain. Peel the potatoes, and cut into 1 inch cubes.

In a casserole or saucepan, simmer the milk, cream, scallions, cayenne, nutmeg, and potatoes for 5 minutes, and sprinkle with parsley.

Yield: 6 servings

➤ The potatoes can be boiled the day before.

Variations:

Add the herbs of your choice: dill, tarragon, marjoram, savory, thyme, or the like.

Delmonico Potatoes

"Don't you just love Delmonico potatoes," say I. "No!" comes a resounding response from students. Those many years of buffets, banquets, and other catered events, with great containers of stodgy potatoes wallowing in some gluey cream sauce, have turned a treat into a regrettable experience. Made properly, Delmonico potatoes are not only good, but also delicious. A slice of ham, a roasted chicken breast, or just the potatoes and a green salad, can make a satisfying, delicious meal. They do take a few minutes to prepare, but with care they become a treat instead of an abomination.

4 pounds boiling potatoes, peeled and cut into ½ inch dice	1 cup bread crumbs
	¼ cup melted butter
2 cups Mornay sauce (see page 22)	

Preheat the oven to 350°F.

Cook the potatoes in boiling salted water until just tender, drain, and put into a bowl. Fold in the Mornay sauce, and pour into an ovenproof serving dish.

Toss the bread crumbs with the melted butter, sprinkle over the top of the potatoes, and bake for 20 minutes, or until golden.

Yield: 6 servings

➤ Can be prepared for the final baking the day before.

POTATOES

Creamed Potatoes

This is another old-fashioned recipe to serve with boiled, steamed, or grilled fish, or with meat.

2 pounds new potatoes, boiled
1 cup béchamel sauce (see page 21)
minced parsley

In a double boiler, heat the potatoes in the sauce until hot. Serve garnished with the parsley.

Yield: 6 servings

➤ Can be prepared for the final reheating the day before.

Papas con Aji (Potatoes in Hot Cream Sauce)

You can make this recipe as spicy or as mild as you wish by adding more or less green chili.

2 pounds potatoes boiled in their skins
1/2 cup minced onion
2 garlic cloves, crushed
1 green chili pepper, minced
1/4 cup olive oil
1 cup milk

1/2 cup crumbled goat cheese, such as feta
1 tablespoon minced parsley
salt and pepper to taste
minced chili pepper for garnish

Drain the potatoes, peel, and cut into 1/4-inch-thick slices.

In a skillet, sauté the onion, garlic, and chili in the olive oil, until the onion starts to brown. Add the milk and potatoes, and heat until hot. Sprinkle with the cheese, parsley, salt, pepper, and chili pepper.

Yield: 6 servings

➤ Can be prepared and reheated, but best when freshly made.

Pommes de Terre Normande (Potatoes, Normandy Style)

2 1/4 inch thick slices pork fat, about 4 inches square
2 tablespoons butter
1 medium onion, thinly sliced
2 leeks, thinly sliced

4 potatoes, peeled and thinly sliced
1 cup beef or chicken stock
salt and pepper to taste
minced parsley

In a saucepan of boiling water, blanch the pork fat for 5 minutes. Drain, and cut into julienne.

In a skillet, melt 1 tablespoon of butter, and sauté the pork until it starts to turn golden. Add the onions and leeks, and sauté until soft, but not brown. Add the potatoes and just enough stock to cover. Season with salt and pepper. Cover, and simmer until the potatoes are tender—about 8 minutes.

With a slotted spoon, lift the potatoes into a serving dish, and swirl in the remaining tablespoon of butter. Pour the sauce over the potatoes, and sprinkle with the parsley.

Yield: 6 servings

➤ Can be prepared ahead and reheated.

Blanquette de Pommes de Terre aux Poireaux
(Blanquette of Potatoes and Leeks)

3 leeks, minced	2 pounds potatoes, thinly sliced
3 tablespoons butter	salt and pepper to taste
1 tablespoon flour	bouquet garni
2 cups milk	minced chives

In a 3 quart saucepan, sweat the leeks in the butter until soft. Sprinkle with the flour, and cook, stirring, until the mixture starts to turn golden. Add the milk, stirring constantly, and bring to a boil. When the mixture has thickened, add the potatoes, salt, pepper, and the bouquet garni. Cover and simmer slowly until the potatoes are cooked tender—about 30 minutes.

Serve sprinkled with the chives.

Yield: 6 servings

➤ Can be prepared ahead and reheated.

NOTE: Bake in a 350°F oven for 45 minutes, if you are concerned about potatoes scorching.

Ragoût de Pommes de Terre Nîmoise
(Potato Ragoût Nîmes Style)

4 1½ inch onions, peeled	3 pounds new potatoes, peeled
4 whole cloves	2 tablespoons minced parsley
1 cup chicken or beef stock	1 teaspoon sugar
3 cups dry white wine	½ pound Canadian bacon, cut
1 bay leaf	into ½ inch cubes
¼ teaspoon dried rosemary	½ cup pitted ripe olives
¼ teaspoon dried thyme	
1½ pounds tomatoes, peeled,	
seeded, and chopped	

Cut three of the onions into quarters. Push the cloves into the remaining onion.

In a large casserole, simmer the onions, stock, wine, bay leaf, rosemary, and thyme for 10 minutes. Add the tomatoes, potatoes, parsley, and sugar, and simmer 10 minutes longer. Add the bacon, and simmer for 1 hour, uncovered, adding a little more wine if the vegetables become too dry. Add the olives, and remove and discard the bay leaf and the clove-studded onion.

Yield: 6 servings

➤ Can be prepared ahead and reheated.

Broiled Potatoes

The least common method of cooking potatoes, broiling or grilling brings out a unique flavor. Use baking potatoes. Be sure to watch the potatoes carefully, and be prepared to lower the potatoes from the broiler so they do not burn before they are cooked. Most recipes work best in ovens with top-of-the-oven broil units. If your broiler is only a few inches deep, choose another recipe, or plan to bake the potatoes in a 350°F oven until almost done, and then finish under the broiler.

Broiled Potatoes with Basil

⅓ cup oil	1½ teaspoons salt
3 or 4 baking potatoes, peeled	½ teaspoon pepper
and sliced	½ cup minced basil

Preheat the broiler.
Line a baking sheet with heavy-duty foil, and drizzle with 2 table-spoons oil. Arrange potatoe slices in the pan, overlapping as little as possible. Drizzle remaining oil over potatoes, and season with salt and pepper. Turn potatoes to coat.
Broil 5 or 6 inches from the heat until golden—about 12 minutes. Turn the potatoes, and broil 12 minutes longer, or until the other side is golden. Remove from oven, and sprinkle with basil. Toss lightly and serve.

Yield: 6 servings

➤ Cannot be prepared ahead.

Broiled Potato Slices with Parmesan

3 medium russet potatoes	¼ cup grated Parmesan cheese
salt and pepper to taste	¼ to ½ cup melted butter
paprika to taste	

Do not peel the potatoes. Cut into thin slices less than ⅛ inch thick, and drop into cold water.
When ready to prepare, drain the slices, and pour over 2 quarts of boiling water. Let stand for 5 minutes. Drain and dry the slices.
On a baking sheet, place the slices, just overlapping, in one layer, and season with salt, pepper, and paprika. Sprinkle with the cheese and the butter. Broil 12 inches from the heat until browned and crisp on top.

Yield: 6 servings

➤ Cannot be prepared ahead.

NOTE: This is a *Spa* recipe designed to give flavor and not have the appearance of being dietetic, therefore the amount of butter will vary depending on how diet-conscious you are.

A top-of-the-oven broiler is required to prepare these properly. If your broiler is only a few inches high, bake in a 375°F oven for 30 minutes.

Pommes de Terre Grillées (Broiled Potato Balls)

3 pounds russet potatoes,
  made into balls
½ cup butter
salt and pepper to taste

1 tablespoon minced dill
1 tablespoon minced chives
1 tablespoon minced parsley

Preheat the broiler.

Store the potatoes in cold water until ready to cook. Drain the potatoes, and pat dry.

Place a gratin, or baking dish large enough to hold the potatoes in one layer, under the broiler, with the butter, until melted. Add the potatoes, season with salt and pepper, and stir to coat evenly. Broil 6 inches from the heat, basting often, for about 20 minutes, or until the potatoes are tender and crusty golden brown.

In a small bowl, mix the dill, chives, and parsley, and sprinkle over the potatoes just before serving.

Yield: 6 servings

➤ Cannot be prepared ahead.

Variation:

Add 1 tablespoon minced garlic to the herb mixture.

Grilled Garlic Potatoes

6 potatoes, boiled or steamed
  until tender
2 eggs
1½ cups yogurt

½ cup olive oil
3 garlic cloves, minced
salt and pepper to taste
additional yogurt (if desired)

Slice the potatoes ½ inch thick, lengthwise, and arrange in a baking dish.

In a bowl, beat the eggs, yogurt, olive oil, garlic, salt, and pepper, and pour over the potatoes. Refrigerate for at least 12 hours.

Prepare a charcoal grill. Drain, reserving the marinade, and place in a grilling basket, or directly on the grill. Grill, turning often, and brushing with marinade until dark brown.

Serve with additional yogurt, if desired.

Yield: 6 servings

➤ Can be prepared for grilling the day before.

NOTE: You do not have to peel the potatoes.

Serve sprinkled with 2 tablespoons minced mint mixed with 2 tablespoons minced parsley. Add 1 clove minced garlic, if you want more garlic flavor.

Broilers do not give these the flavor they deserve. Save this recipe for the outdoor grill.

Pommes de Terre Grillées au Thyme
(Broiled Potatoes with Thyme)

6 potatoes, peeled and cut into 1 inch cubes	½ cup olive oil
	1 tablespoon minced thyme
1 cup chopped onion	salt and pepper to taste

Preheat the broiler.

In a baking dish large enough to hold the potatoes in one layer, mix the potatoes, onion, olive oil, thyme, salt, and pepper. Broil about 6 inches from the heat, turning often, until tender and golden-brown.

Yield: 6 servings

➤ Cannot be prepared ahead.

Sautéed Potatoes

Use low-starch boiling potatoes, and wash them to get rid of the excess starch. Many recipes suggest parboiling to make the final cooking easier and quicker. This also lets you prepare the recipe ahead. You can parboil the potatoes for any of the recipes here. There is a slight change in flavor, but the saving in last-minute activity may be worth it. Sauté raw potatoes over low heat, cook gently, stirring often, until the potatoes are tender, and then raise the heat to brown if needed.

Sautéed New Potatoes

24 small new potatoes	salt and pepper to taste
2 tablespoons olive oil	2 tablespoons minced chives

Cut a ribbon of skin from around the middle of each potato, and wash well.

In a skillet, heat the oil, add the potatoes, and cook over medium-low heat, shaking the pan occasionally, until the potatoes are tender and light golden-brown on all sides—about 25 minutes.

Season with salt, pepper, and chives.

Yield: 6 servings

➤ Cannot be prepared ahead.

NOTE: The potatoes must fit in one layer in the skillet. If necessary, use two skillets.

Variations:

The potatoes are peeled for most of the variations.

Pommes de Terre Rissolées The potatoes are cut into ¾ inch dice.

Pommes de Terre en Miettes The potatoes are cut into ¼ inch dice.

Pommes de Terre en Noisettes Cut potatoes with a melon-baller.

Pommes de Terre O'Brien Cut the potatoes into ½ inch dice, and add 1 cup diced red pepper when the potatoes start to turn golden.

Pommes de Terre Sablées Cook small new potatoes until golden all over. Add 2 tablespoons of fresh butter and ¼ cup fresh white bread crumbs, and sauté until the bread crumbs are crisp and golden.

Pommes de Terre Sautées à Cru *(Sautéed Raw Potatoes)*

2 pounds boiling potatoes, peeled and thinly sliced	6 tablespoons clarified butter
salt and pepper to taste	1 garlic clove, crushed
	3 tablespoons minced parsley

Wash the potato slices in cold water, and pat dry.

In a large skillet, heat the butter until hot, and add the potatoes. Cook over moderate heat until golden on the outside and soft in the center, stirring every five minutes. It should take about 20 minutes.

When the potatoes are done, turn into a serving bowl. In a small bowl, mix the garlic and parsley, and sprinkle over the potatoes.

Yield: 6 servings

➤ Cannot be prepared ahead.

Pommes de Terre au Citron *(Sautéed Potatoes with Lemon)*

2 pounds potatoes, thinly sliced	2 cloves garlic, crushed
¼ pound butter	½ teaspoon minced thyme
1 tablespoon olive oil	grated zest of ½ lemon
½ cup minced parsley	juice of ½ lemon
	salt and pepper to taste

Wash the potatoes in cold water, and pat dry.

In a large skillet, melt the butter in the olive oil, and cook the potatoes until golden.

Meanwhile, mince the parsley, garlic, thyme, and lemon rind together. Just before serving, add the herb mixture, mix to coat evenly, and let cook 1 minute.

Sprinkle with the lemon juice, and serve immediately.

Yield: 6 servings

➤ Cannot be prepared ahead.

Pommes de Terre à l'Ail *(Garlic Potatoes in Walnut Oil)*

6 tablespoons walnut oil	grated nutmeg to taste
2 pounds potatoes, thickly sliced	4 garlic cloves, chopped
	1½ cup minced celery
salt and pepper to taste	1 cup minced scallions

In a large skillet, heat the walnut oil. Wash the potato slices, and pat dry.

Cook the potatoes over very low heat until they are tender. Season with salt, pepper, and nutmeg. Cook, turning occasionally, until golden and cooked through. Add the garlic, parsley, and scallions, and cook, stirring occasionally, for 3 minutes.

Yield: 6 servings

➤ Cannot be prepared ahead.

Pommes de Terre Sautées Bonne Femme
(Sautéed Potatoes with Mushrooms)

2 pounds potatoes, ½ inch dice	2 tablespoons butter
3 tablespoons vegetable oil	½ cup minced onion
½ pound mushrooms, quartered	salt and pepper to taste
	2 tablespoons minced parsley

Rinse the potatoes, and pat dry.

In a large skillet, heat the oil over medium heat, and sauté the potatoes until they start to turn golden. Add the mushrooms, and cook, shaking the pan, for 2 minutes and until any liquid evaporates. Add the butter and onion, and cook until soft, but not brown. Season with salt, pepper, and parsley.

Yield: 6 servings

➤ Cannot be prepared ahead.

Pommes de Terre Rissolées Jeanette
(Sautéed Potatoes, with Garlic, Parsley, and Chives)

When this recipe originated, "nice" people did not eat garlic, but times have changed, and I serve the garlic.

2 pounds boiling potatoes, cut into 1 inch cubes	6 unpeeled garlic cloves
3 tablespoons lard	salt and pepper to taste
1 tablespoon peanut oil	1 tablespoon minced parsley
	1 tablespoon minced chives

Wash the potatoes, and pat dry.

In a large skillet, melt the lard in the oil, and add the garlic cloves and potatoes in one layer. Sauté over high heat until golden, shaking the pan to brown them on all sides. Season with salt, and cover the pan. Lower the heat, and cook 10 to 15 minutes longer, or until tender.

Remove the potatoes, and drain on paper toweling. Discard the garlic. Season with salt, and turn into a serving dish. Sprinkle with the parsley and chives.

Yield: 6 servings

➤ Cannot be prepared ahead.

La Truffado *(Sautéed Potatoes with Cantal Cheese)*

2 pounds potatoes, thinly sliced	1 garlic clove, minced
2 tablespoons butter	salt and pepper to taste
2 tablespoons peanut oil	2 ounces grated Tomme de
¼ cup minced bacon	Cantal (see Note)

Wash the potato slices, and pat dry.

In a large skillet, melt the butter in the oil, and add the potatoes, bacon, garlic, salt, and pepper. When it starts to sizzle, lower the heat, cover, and cook 15 minutes. Turn the potatoes, and cook until tender—about 1 more minute.

Sprinkle the cheese over the potatoes, and stir to combine. Cover and turn off the heat. When the cheese is melted (about 2 minutes), serve.

Yield: 6 servings

➤ Cannot be prepared ahead.

NOTE: If you cannot locate Tomme de Cantal, use Caerphilly, Port du Salut, or Gruyère cheese.

Pommes de Terre aux Truffles
(Sautéed Potatoes with Truffles)

This is a recipe for the very fortunate: those with access to fresh truffles, a recently cooked goose, and a fairly large pocketbook, or generous friends.

2 pounds boiling potatoes, thinly sliced	1 cup goose fat
	salt and pepper to taste
2 fresh truffles	

Wash the potatoes in cold water until the water runs clear. Drain, and pat dry. Peel the truffles, and dice the peels. Reserve. Dice one truffle, and thinly slice the second truffle, reserving them in separate containers.

In a large skillet, heat ½ cup goose fat, and stir in the potatoes to coat evenly. Cook for 2 minutes, lower the heat to medium, and add the diced truffles and peels. Cook, adding more fat as needed, until the potatoes are tender. Increase the heat, and cook until crisp and golden.

Drain the potatoes on toweling, and put on a serving platter. Garnish with the truffle slices, and season with salt and pepper.

Yield: 6 servings

➤ Cannot be prepared ahead.

NOTE: Canned black truffles do not have enough flavor to justify the cost. Canned white truffles have more flavor and are worth a go, but they are not the same as fresh black truffles.

You can use clarified butter instead of the goose fat, but the flavor will be a bit different.

Pommes de Terre au Romarin
(Sautéed Potatoes with Rosemary)

2 pounds boiling potatoes, peeled	salt and pepper to taste
6 tablespoons butter	2 teaspoons rosemary leaves, crushed

Put the potatoes into a pan of cold water, and bring to a boil. Drain, cut in half lengthwise, and then cut into ¼ inch slices.

In a skillet, heat the butter until foaming, and add the potatoes. Cook, shaking the pan, over moderate heat until golden and tender. Season with salt, pepper, and rosemary.

Yield: 6 servings

➤ The potatoes can be blanched several hours ahead. Do not slice until just before cooking.

Variations:

Sautéed Potatoes with Cumin Cut the potatoes into ½ inch slices and sauté in ½ cup olive oil. When golden, add 6 cloves, minced garlic, ¼ cup minced parsley, and 1 tablespoon ground cumin. Season with salt and pepper.

Patate alla Salvia e Parmigiano (Sautéed Potato with Sage and Parmesan) Cut the potatoes into wedges, and parboil until almost done. Drain and sauté in ½ cup butter and 2 teaspoons dried sage until the potatoes have absorbed all the butter. Add 1 cup grated Paremsan, and season with salt and pepper.

Pommes de Terre Sautées Clemenceau
(Sautéed Potatoes with Mushrooms and Peas)

2 pounds boiling potatoes, peeled and cut into 1 inch dice	¼ cup olive oil
½ pound mushrooms, thinly sliced	salt and pepper to taste
¼ cup butter	¾ cup cooked peas
	2 tablespoons minced parsley
	2 garlic cloves, minced

Cook the potatoes in boiling salted water for 5 minutes. Drain and pat dry.

In a skillet, sauté the mushrooms in two tablespoons of butter until browned. Set aside.

In a large skillet, sauté the potatoes in the oil until tender and brown. Season the potatoes with salt and pepper, and add the mushrooms, peas, and remaining butter, and sauté for 2 or 3 minutes, or until hot. Stir in the parsley and garlic.

Yield: 6 servings

➤ The potatoes can be boiled and the mushrooms sautéed several hours ahead. Do not do the final browning until just before serving.

Potato Pancakes and Cakes

Potato pancakes are individual cakes usually made with other ingredients, such as egg, and possibly a leavening. Potato cakes are one large cake that is cut into wedges. These are usually made with potatoes, a fat, and salt and pepper, although there are some more elaborate recipes.

Use Russet potatoes, because the high starch content holds the cake together. Do not cut the potatoes until just before cooking, or they will darken, and if you store them in water, the starch will leach out and the cake will not hold together.

Ideally, potato pancakes are served the minute they are cooked. If you are making potato pancakes for a crowd, you can make them ahead, freeze them, and reheat in a 350°F oven. They will be acceptable, if not perfect. Do not keep in a warm oven too long, because they dry out. Potato cakes must be served within minutes of cooking. If you try to hold them, the steam on the inside sogs up the crispy exterior.

Latkes (Potato Pancakes)

Latkes are a traditional food served during Chanukah, the Feast of Lights, in the Jewish Calendar. They are cooked in oil, to remind us that the lamp in the Temple burned without oil for 8 days and 8 nights.

2 large baking potatoes	1 egg, lightly beaten
¼ cup grated onion	4 tablespoons vegetable oil
½ teaspoon salt	1 cup applesauce (optional)
black pepper	1 cup sour cream (optional)
1 tablespoon matzo meal	

In a food processor, grate the potatoes, turn into a sieve, and press out excess liquid. Discard the liquid, and transfer the potatoes and onions to a large bowl. Season with salt and pepper. Stir in the matzo meal and egg until well combined.

In a large skillet over medium heat, heat the oil. Add the potatoes, and shape into 2½ inch pancakes, flattening slightly. Sauté until golden on both sides. Transfer to a paper-towel-lined baking sheet. If necessary, keep warm in a 250 °F oven.

Arrange pancakes on a platter, and serve with applesauce and/or sour cream.

Yield: 6 servings

➤ Best if prepared just before serving.

Variations:

Potato pancakes make a delicious hors d'oeuvre. Serve with traditional sour cream and applesauce, if you wish, or try some other toppings:

Sour cream and caviar.

Sour cream flavored with 1 teaspoon wasabi powder, and top with thin slices of fresh tuna, seared in a cast iron skillet until rare.

Sour cream and salsa (see page 26).

Slices of smoked salmon topped with sour cream and capers.

Applesauce alone or with sour cream.

Spiced Potato Pancakes Add 1 tablespoon of minced ginger, or 1 tablespoon minced jalapeño pepper, or a large pinch of Cayenne pepper to the mixture before cooking.

Potato Pancakes with Zucchini and Ham Add 1 cup grated zucchini and 1 cup minced ham to the potato mixture.

Other Recipes Check the index for pancakes made with potatoes and other vegetables.

Cheese Potato Crêpes

½ pound cream cheese, softened	2 tablespoons grated onion
3 tablespoons flour	1½ pounds potatoes, peeled and grated
2 eggs	sour cream
½ teaspoon salt	butter
pinch of Cayenne pepper	paprika
1¼ cups diced Gruyère cheese	

In a processor, cream the cream cheese, flour, eggs, salt, and Cayenne pepper. Turn into a bowl, and fold in the Gruyère and onion. Squeeze as much moisture as possible from the potatoes, and fold into the cheese. Add enough sour cream to make the mixture thin enough to spread—about ½ cup. In a skillet, sauté the crêpes in butter until crisp and golden-brown.

Serve the crêpes with sour cream and paprika.

Yield: 6 servings

➤ Cannot be prepared ahead.

Crêpes Vonnasiennes *(Potato Crêpes)*

The batter can be prepared well before these are cooked, because they are made from cooked potatoes. Sauté just before serving.

1½ pounds baking potatoes, boiled and peeled	¼ cup heavy cream
	¼ cup flour
2 cups milk	salt and pepper to taste
4 eggs	clarified butter

Grate the potatoes coarsely, and put into a bowl with the milk. In another bowl, mix the eggs, heavy cream, and flour, stir into the potatoes, and season with salt and pepper. Let stand 30 minutes.

In a skillet, heat a film of clarified butter, and use 1½ tablespoons of mixture to make a 3 inch crêpe. Cook over moderately high heat until the underside is browned, then turn and cook the other side.

Serve hot.

Yield: 6 servings

➤ Can be prepared for frying several hours ahead.

Potato Cakes

The potatoes are grated, minced, shredded, cut into batons, or sliced. After the cake is browned on one side, it is turned over to cook the other side. Chefs do this with a simple flick of the wrist. (It is easier than it would seem, but it does take practice. To get the motion, place a matchbook in a skillet, and practice with that.) The rest of us may give that some thought. A successful method is to place a flat lid or a baking sheet without sides (or use the bottom of a baking sheet with sides) on top of the skillet, and turn it over in one single fluid motion. Do not hesitate. Slide the cake back into the skillet.

A non-stick pan makes preparing potato cakes much easier. If you do not have one, consider seasoning the pan as you would for an omelet. Heat ¼ inch of unflavored vegetable oil in a skillet over the lowest possible heat until very hot—about 1 hour. Let cool. Save the oil for another use. Wipe the pan with paper toweling. Clarified butter also helps to prevent sticking. Cook slowly so the cake is fully cooked inside, and make sure the bottom is crusty and golden before turning. Cover the potatoes for the first half of the cooking. Remove the lid horizontally without tipping any moisture into the potatoes. Cook, uncovered, after the cake is turned.

Paillasson (Straw Potato Cake)

½ cup clarified butter   salt and pepper to taste
2 pounds potatoes, cut in
  julienne, or grated

In a large non-stick skillet, heat half the butter, and spread a layer of potatoes. Season with salt and pepper, and continue making layers, pressing firmly.

Cover, and cook over medium-low heat until golden brown on the bottom. When checking, be sure to remove the lid horizontally, and not to pour any of the moisture into the cake. Turn the cake over, and pour the remaining butter down the sides of the pan.

Shake the pan occasionally during cooking to keep it from sticking. The entire cooking time is about 30 minutes.

Yield: 6 servings

➤ Cannot be prepared ahead.

Variation:

Roesti Parboil the unpeeled potatoes for 10 minutes, or until about half-cooked. Drain, cool, peel, and then cut into long shreds.

Potato and Artichoke Pancake

2 cooked artichoke bottoms   4 tablespoons clarified butter
  (see page 35)   salt and pepper
4 potatoes, thinly sliced

Preheat the oven to 425°F.

In a skillet over medium heat, melt 2 tablespoons butter. Arrange half the potato slices in concentric circles in the skillet, shaking the skillet so potatoes do not stick. Season with salt and pepper. Cover with artichoke slices arranged in a concentric circles. Season with salt and pepper. Top with remaining potato slices, and season with salt and pepper.

Pour remaining butter over the top, and cover tightly. Cook over medium heat, shaking the pan occasionally, until browned on the bottom—about 30 minutes. Uncover, transfer to the oven, and bake until the potatoes are tender—about 20 to 25 minutes longer. Invert onto a platter, and serve cut into wedges.

Yield: 6 servings

NOTE: The potatoes can be kept in a bowl of cold water for several hours before cooking. Do not cook ahead.

Pommes de Terre Voisin
(Potato Cake with Gruyère Cheese)

½ cup butter	¾ cup grated Gruyère cheese
1½ pounds potatoes, peeled and minced	salt and pepper to taste

In a large skillet, heat half the butter, put in a layer of potatoes, and sprinkle with cheese, salt, and pepper. Continue making layers, ending with potatoes. Cover and cook, shaking the pan occasionally, until golden and crispy on the bottom—about 20 minutes.

Remove the lid horizontally, so the moisture does not drain into the cake, and turn the cake. Add the remaining butter down the sides of the pan, and cook, shaking the pan occasionally, until golden and crispy—about another 20 minutes.

Yield: 6 servings

➤ Cannot be prepared ahead.

Grapiau (Onion Potato Cheese Pancake)

This version does not require turning.

2 pounds potatoes, grated	pinch grated coriander
2 eggs, beaten	salt and pepper to taste
1 cup grated onion	4 tablespoons walnut oil
1 cup grated Gruyère	2 shallots, minced
2 tablespoons flour	2 tablespoons minced parsley
1 tablespoon Cognac	

In a large bowl, mix the potatoes, eggs, onion, Gruyère, flour, Cognac, coriander, salt, and pepper.

Heat the walnut oil in a 12 inch skillet, add the potato mixture, and spread it evenly. Cook the mixture for 15 minutes, then place 8 inches below the flame, and broil for 10 minutes. The pancakes should be very crunchy on both sides, with a moist center.

Sprinkle with shallots and parsley, and serve warm.

Yield: 6 servings

➤ Cannot be prepared ahead.

NOTE: If you use a smaller skillet, extend the cooking time, and cook over lower heat.

Pommes de Terre Sarladaise (Sautéed Potato Cake)

Saraladaise, in culinary terms, means the combination of potatoes and truffles. If you have one or two large truffles, chop them and cook with the potatoes.

3 tablespoons goose fat or lard	1½ tablespoons minced
2 pounds potatoes, thinly sliced	parsley
2 teaspoons minced garlic	salt and pepper to taste

In a 10 inch skillet, heat the fat. Add the potatoes, and cook over medium-high heat until browned. Cook, turning with a spatula to coat well and avoid sticking. Lower the heat, and press into a cake.

Cover, and cook 7 minutes. Remove the lid horizontally, and toss potatoes gently so that crisp bottom slices mix into the rest of the potatoes. Reshape the cake, cover, and cook 7 minutes longer, shaking the potatoes to prevent sticking.

Uncover, toss and reshape, and cover and cook 7 minutes longer. Remove the lid horizontally, spoon off any excess fat, and set aside. Turn the potatoes onto a flat lid or baking sheet, and slide back into the pan so the other side can crisp, over medium heat, uncovered. Slip onto a platter, and sprinkle with the garlic, parsley, salt, and pepper. Serve at once.

Yield: 6 servings

➤ Cannot be prepared ahead.

Truffade Dauphinaise (Potatoes Dauphinaise)

¼ pound bacon, diced	salt and pepper to taste
3 tablespoons olive oil	½ pound tomatoes, peeled,
2 pounds potatoes, thinly sliced	seeded, and diced

In a 10 inch skillet, sauté the bacon until golden. Add the oil, potatoes, salt, and pepper. Turn to coat evenly, flatten with a fork, and cook, covered, for 30 minutes.

Remove the lid horizontally, stir in the tomatoes, and press again into a flat cake. Raise the heat slightly and cook, shaking the pan occasionally, for another 10 minutes, or until golden on the bottom. Unmold onto a platter.

Yield: 6 servings

➤ Cannot be prepared ahead.

Mashed Potatoes

Perfect mashed potatoes are lump-free. They are mashed, or more correctly riced, and then beaten with butter, salt, pepper, and hot milk.

Some mothers consider potatoes perfectly mashed when there are still visible lumps. You may like them that way, but when you are cooking for others, perfectly smooth is the goal.

Mashing potatoes is such a simple process. Drain the potatoes, put them back in the pot and assault them with the potato masher, or put them into the processor and let it rip. Actually, the preparation requires a little more care and skill. A food processor should *never* be used because it makes the potatoes gluey. If you use a potato masher, diligently pound up and down until all the lumps are removed. This is more difficult than it would first seem. My mother, a woman who hated to cook, made wonderful mashed potatoes with a wire masher. She pounded up and down, and then finished with a number of circular motions to achieve smooth, light mashed potatoes. But that is a rare talent. I have spent hours with various designs of "potato mashers" trying to achieve the same result, and have had no luck. I prefer to use a ricer—a metal basket with holes in the bottom and sides. It is fitted with a plunger that forces the potatoes through the holes. Professionally, we use heavy-duty mixers with the beater blade. (If you choose to use a mixer, make sure that the motor of your machine is strong enough to do the job without burning out.) The drained, dried potatoes are put into the mixer and it is turned to medium. As soon as the potatoes are finely crumbled, we start adding the milk and other ingredients, and increase the speed to beat the potatoes until light and fluffy.

Once the potatoes are mashed or riced, add hot milk, a generous amount of butter, salt, and pepper. Other writers suggest adding eggs and heavy cream, but I do not see any advantage (other than building up the calorie level), unless the potatoes are to be shaped like duchess potatoes, when eggs will help them hold their form.

Pommes Purées ou Pommes Mousseline
(Puréed Potatoes or Whipped Potatoes)

Whatever you choose to call it, this is the basic recipe for perfect mashed potatoes.

2 pounds baking potatoes, unpeeled	¼ cup butter, or to taste
½ to ¾ cup hot milk	salt and pepper to taste

The potatoes can be boiled in their skins, or baked in a 400 °F oven until tender. (It is necessary to leave the skins on so that the interior will be dry.)

Peel the skins from the potatoes, and force the pulp through a ricer into a clean saucepan. Add the hot milk, whisking with a stiff wire whisk. Beat in the butter, salt, and pepper.

Yield: 6 servings

➤ Can be prepared several hours ahead and reheated in a double boiler, but they are best freshly mashed. Select one of the baked mashed potato recipes if you wish to prepare them ahead.

NOTE: You can boil peeled, boiling potatoes until tender, drain, and then return to the pan and heat to remove any excess moisture before mashing. This removes the surface moisture, but the potato is not as floury as a baking potato.

Variations:

Pommes de Terre Macaire Bake the potatoes, and purée the pulp. Beat in butter, salt, and pepper to taste, and pack into a buttered 1½-quart mold. Bake at 400°F for 1 hour, or until golden around the edges. Let stand outside the oven for 5 minutes, and unmold.

Pommes de Terre Byron Prepare the potatoes Macaire, and unmold onto a heatproof platter. Whip 2 tablespoons heavy cream until stiff and spread over the top of the potato. Broil until golden.

Garlic The garlic is supposed to be subtle and delicate—the sort of flavor that has guests asking why they are so good, rather than telling you that you added garlic! Add 1 or more cloves of garlic to the boiling water. When the potatoes are cooked, force the garlic through the ricer with the potatoes, and finish as above. If you are baking the potatoes, simmer the garlic cloves in the milk until tender. How much garlic? Anywhere from 1 clove to 2 heads for 6 persons. My preference is 1 clove per person.

Herbed Add 1 tablespoon of minced fresh mint, basil, or thyme with the butter.
Add 3 bay leaves to the boiling water, or simmer them in the milk.

With Roquefort Add a pinch of nutmeg, ¼ cup mixed fresh herbs—parsley, chives, thyme, rosemary, or tarragon—with the butter, and serve topped with ¼ pound Roquefort cheese, crumbled.

Vegetable Substitute ½ the amount of carrots, or turnips, for the potatoes, and mash together.

Wine Now this is fun and good! Use red wine instead of milk to mash the potatoes. Keep the lights low, because the color is mauve and not truly appealing, but the flavor is. White wine is nowhere near as good, but the color is more attractive.

Soufflé de Pommes de Terre *(Potato Soufflé)*

These are not the same as Pommes de Terre Soufflé, or souffléed potatoes (see page 427).

2 pounds potatoes, cooked and peeled	½ cup hot milk
	salt and pepper to taste
¼ cup butter	3 eggs, separated

Preheat the oven to 400°F. Butter a 1 quart soufflé dish.

Force the potatoes through a ricer, and beat in the butter, milk, salt,
and pepper. Beat in the egg yolks.

In a clean bowl, beat the egg whites until they hold firm peaks, but
are not dry. Fold into the potato mixture. Turn into the soufflé dish,
and smooth the top. Run your thumb around the inside edge of the
dish, pushing the potato toward the center. Bake for 30 minutes, or
until puffed and golden.

Yield: 6 servings

➤ Can be prepared for baking several hours ahead.

Variation:

Pommes de Terre Baden Prepare the potatoes as above, but add ½ cup
grated Cheddar cheese with the egg yolks. Reserve 1 cup of the potato
mixture, and fill the soufflé dish with the remainder. With a pastry bag fitted with a Number 5A open star tip, pipe a border around the outer edge.

Pommes de Terre Duchesse *(Duchess Potatoes)*

It is possible that you need to be of a certain age to remember Duchess
Potatoes. They have dipped into and out of popularity over the years.
When made with fresh potatoes, as opposed to packaged mixes, and
freshly cooked, they are a joy for the potato lover, and one way of preparing mashed potatoes ahead.

2 pounds potatoes, boiled and riced	pinch of nutmeg
	2 whole eggs
2 tablespoons butter	3 egg yolks
salt and pepper to taste	2 tablespoons milk

Preheat the broiler. Butter a baking sheet.

In a bowl, beat the riced potatoes until fluffy, and beat in the salt,
pepper, butter, and nutmeg. Add the whole eggs and 2 egg yolks, and
beat until well mixed.

Fit a 16 inch pastry bag with a number 5A open-star tube, and pipe
the mixture into 2½-inch-high rosettes onto the baking sheet.

In a small bowl, beat the egg yolk with the milk, and brush over the rosettes.

When ready to serve, brown under the broiler. If the potatoes have
cooled, it is better to bake them in a 400°F oven until heated, and then
brown under the broiler, if necessary.

Yield: 6 servings

➤ Can be prepared for reheating several hours ahead.

Variations:
Duchess of Chester Potatoes Add ½ cup grated sharp cheddar cheese, and shape into 3 inch cakes. Place on a buttered sheet, spread with the egg wash, and top with thin slices of sharp cheddar cheese. Bake at 400°F until the cheese melts and starts to brown.

Pommes de Terre Marquise Add ⅓ cup thick tomato purée to the potatoes, and shape into triangles, or cones. Brush with the egg wash, and broil, or bake, until brown.

Pommes de Terre Mont d'Or Boil the potatoes with an onion, and discard the onion. Prepare the duchess potato mixture, and place in an ovenproof serving dish in a tall mound. Sprinkle the top with 3 tablespoons grated Gruyère cheese, and bake at 400°F until piping hot and browned.

Aligot (Potato Cheese Purée)

This specialty of the Auvergne region.

2 pounds baking potatoes, peeled	3½ cups grated Tomme de
salt	Cantal or Gruyère
4 tablespoons butter	pepper
1 cup heavy cream	

Cut the potatoes into 2 or 3 even chunks, and simmer in a pot of boiling salted water until very tender. Drain, and return to the pot to dry out the excess moisture. Force through a ricer while still hot.

Return the potatoes to a heavy saucepan, and add the butter. Beat over a low fire until light and fluffy.

Still over the heat, beat in the cream and then the cheese, a handful at a time, and continue beating with a wooden spoon until the aligot forms long ribbons when it falls from the spoon. Add the pepper, and taste for seasoning.

Yield: 6 servings

➤ Cannot be prepared in advance.

NOTE: The potatoes are peeled before cooking, because they must remain hot during the entire process.

This is a recipe for the dining room performer. Bring the hot potatoes to the dining room and place in a chafing dish. Start beating in the butter and cream, and gradually beat in the cheese. As the cheese starts to melt, pick the mixture up and in long swirls, and return it to the pan. The mixture will stretch 2 to 3 feet when all the cheese is added. (You might want to practice on the family first.) Tomme de Cantal is a cheese with a similar density to Gruyère. Some writers suggest using port du salut in place of it. Do try to get the Cantal for the best flavor.

Hemel en Aarde *(Heaven and Earth)*

Both the Germans and the Swedes have a dish with this name. The Swedish version given here is made with potatoes and applesauce, and though it seem strange to the uninitiated, it is really very good. Serve it with roast goose or with pork.

¼ cup softened butter
1 pound hot mashed potatoes
2 cups unsweetened
 applesauce

2 tablespoons sugar
½ teaspoon ground nutmeg
salt and pepper to taste

Preheat the oven to 400°F.

Beat the butter into the potatoes, and then stir in the applesauce, sugar, nutmeg, salt, and pepper. Pack into a 1½ quart casserole, and lift the surface to peaks with the back of a spoon.

Bake until hot—about 30 minutes. If the top is not browned, put under a broiler to brown the peaks.

Yield: 6 servings

➤ Can be prepared for serving the day before.

Himmel und Erde *(Heaven and Earth)*

This German version has a little less heaven (apple) and a lot more earth (onions, potatoes, and turnips).

1 large onion, sliced
1 apple, peeled, cored, and
 chopped
¼ pound butter
½ cup minced parsley
1 pound potatoes, peeled and
 quartered

1 pound turnips, peeled and
 quartered
⅓ cup chicken stock
salt and pepper
1 tablespoon minced parsley

In a skillet, sweat the onion and apple in the butter over low heat until tender. Uncover, raise the heat, and cook until browned—about 5 minutes. In a processor, purée the onion mixture with the ½ cup parsley.

Meanwhile, cook the potatoes and turnips in boiling salted water until tender. Drain, and force through a ricer. Return to the saucepan, and beat in the onion mixture, chicken stock, salt, and pepper.

Serve sprinkled with the parsley.

Yield: 6 servings

➤ Can be prepared ahead and reheated.

La Purée à la Provençale (Potato Purée Provençale)

2 pounds potatoes, cooked and peeled	3 tomatoes, sliced olive oil
1 cup hot milk	3½ ounces anchovies in oil
¼ cup butter	20 black olives, pitted
1 egg yolk	salt and pepper

Preheat the oven to 450°F.

Rice the potatoes, and beat in the milk, butter, and egg yolk. Place in a gratin, and cover with tomato slices. Drizzle the slices with olive oil.

Arrange the anchovies and black olives over the tomatoes, and drizzle with more olive oil. Season with salt and pepper.

Bake for 15 minutes, or until the top is golden.

Yield: 6 servings

➤ Can be prepared ahead and baked just before serving.

Potato Filling

This Pennsylvania Dutch dish is served as a vegetable, but you can use it to stuff turkey, chicken, or goose.

10 tablespoons butter	½ cup minced onion
1½ pounds potatoes, peeled and quartered	4 or 5 slices white bread, cut into ¼ inch cubes
¼ cup milk	2 eggs, lightly beaten
½ teaspoon salt	¼ cup minced parsley
¼ teaspoon white pepper	

Preheat the oven to 350°F. Butter a 1 quart baking dish with 1 tablespoon of butter.

Cook the potatoes in boiling salted water until tender. Drain, purée the potatoes through a ricer, and beat in the milk, salt, and pepper.

In a skillet, sauté the onions in 8 tablespoons of butter until soft, but not brown. With a slotted spoon, remove the onions, and add to the potatoes. Add the bread cubes to the skillet, and cook, stirring, until crisp and lightly browned. Add the bread cubes, eggs, and parsley to the potatoes, and beat well.

Turn into the prepared baking dish, and smooth the top. Dot with the remaining butter. Bake for 35 minutes, or until golden-brown and crusty.

Yield: 6 servings

➤ Can be prepared for baking several hours ahead.

Polpettone di Patate e Formaggio
(Potato and Cheese Casserole)

If you like lumpy mashed potatoes, here is a dish that requires lumps to provide texture.

5 baking potatoes, unpeeled	1 cup cubed fontina cheese
½ cup plus 1 tablespoon butter	4 eggs, beaten
1 tablespoon plus 1 teaspoon olive oil	½ teaspoon salt
¼ cup flour	¼ cup bread crumbs
⅓ cup milk	¼ cup grated Parmesan cheese

Preheat the oven to 350°F.

Cook the potatoes in boiling salted water until tender. Drain, peel, and mash coarsely. In a large saucepan, heat ½ cup butter and 1 tablespoon olive oil.

Make a paste of the flour and milk, and add the cheese. Add to the pan, and cook, stirring, over medium heat until the cheese is melted. Add the potatoes, eggs, and salt. Mix well, and taste for seasoning.

Oil a casserole with the teaspoon of olive oil, and dust with 2 tablespoons bread crumbs. Place the potato/cheese mixture into the casserole, and smooth the top. Sprinkle with the Parmesan and the remaining 2 tablespoons bread crumbs, and dot the surface with the remaining tablespoon of butter. Bake for 20 minutes, or until the top is golden.

Yield: 6 servings

➤ Can be prepared for baking several hours ahead.

Entrée Renaissance

Serve this as a meal with a salad.

2 pounds baking potatoes	6 tablespoons butter
½ pound cooked ham, diced	½ cup heavy cream
4 eggs, lightly beaten	salt and pepper to taste

Preheat the oven to 400°F.

Butter a 1 quart mold. Bake the potatoes until tender. Lower the oven to 350°F. Force the potato pulp through a ricer, and beat in the ham, eggs, butter, cream, salt, and pepper.

Pack into the mold, and bake for 15 minutes, or until hot.

Yield: 6 servings

➤ Can be prepared for the final baking several hours ahead.

Potato and Spinach Pie

fine dry bread crumbs	3 eggs
4 pounds baking potatoes	2 tablespoons butter
2 ounces grated Parmesan cheese	2 teaspoons salt
3 cups Béchamel sauce	4 ounces mozzarella, finely diced
3 pounds spinach, cooked,	4 ounces Gruyère, diced
drained, and chopped	pepper

Preheat the oven to 375°F.

Butter a 12 by 8 by 2 inch baking dish, and sprinkle with the bread crumbs.

Boil potatoes until tender, then drain, peel, and rice. In a bowl, mix the potatoes, ½ cup Parmesan, eggs, butter, and salt. In another bowl, mix the remaining Parmesan, Béchamel, spinach, mozzarella, and Gruyère, and season with pepper.

Spread ⅔ of the potato in the bottom and sides of the prepared dish, covering completely. Spoon on the Béchamel-spinach mixture.

On a sheet of waxed paper or foil, pat the remaining potato into a 12 by 8 inch rectangle, and flip over onto the spinach mixture to cover it completely, sealing the edges. Bake for 45 minutes until hot and golden. Let stand 5 minutes before serving.

Yield: 6 servings

➤ Can be prepared for the final baking the day before.

Dumplings

Potato dumplings seem to imply a stodgy, heavy, and not very appealing dish. In fact, they can be quite light and truly satisfying. The Italians prepare *gnocchi di patate*, and the French are fond of *quenelles de pommes de terre*. Plan to make these, and serve them as a first, or even as a main course.

Gnocchi di Patate (Potato Gnocchi)

It may take a little practice to get these as light as you wish. The answer is not to overwork the dough. Shaping takes some practice, but once you get the knack, you will be amazed how quick and easy it is.

1¼ pounds baking potatoes,	1 cup flour
peeled and quartered	¼ teaspoon nutmeg
¼ cup softened butter	salt and pepper to taste
2 egg yolks	sauce (see Note)

In a saucepan of boiling salted water, cook the potatoes until tender, drain, and dry over medium heat. Force through a ricer, and beat in the butter. Let cool for 5 minutes.

Stir in the egg yolks, flour, nutmeg, salt, and pepper.

On a lightly floured board, shape a portion of the dough into a log about ½ inch in diameter. Cut the log into ½ inch sections.

Hold a dinner fork with the tines on a board at a slight angle. Place a piece of dough on the tines near the shaft, and flip a finger into the dough, letting it roll down the tines. The dough should have a curved, ridged back from the tines, and a slight hollow on the front from your finger. Do not force your finger against the dough; flick it down toward the board, and let the dough follow your finger.

Place the dough on a lightly floured baking sheet while you prepare the remainder. They can be prepared 6 hours or more before cooking.

In a large kettle of simmering salted water, cook the gnocchi, in batches, until they rise to the surface. With a slotted spoon, remove the gnocchi, and put into a buttered baking dish. Add sauce of your choice, and bake in a 400°F oven until hot.

Yield: 6 servings

➤ The gnocchi can be prepared several hours ahead, and baked just before serving.

NOTE: Remove the gnocchi as soon as they float to the surface, or they become heavy. They will collapse after they are removed.

Sauces

Sprinkle the gnocchi with ½ cup melted butter and 1 cup of grated Gruyère, Parmesan, or other grating cheese. Bake until hot and golden.

Add 1 to 2 cups of fresh tomato sauce to the baking dish, sprinkle with ½ cup grated Parmesan, and bake until hot and golden.

Coat with 2 cups Mornay sauce, and sprinkle with 1 cup grated Gruyère cheese. Bake until hot and golden.

Quenelles de Pommes de Terre (Potato Dumplings)

The French version uses the same mixture used for cream puffs to help lighten the dumplings. See Pommes Dauphine (page 429) for a deep-fried version of these.

1 pound potatoes, peeled	¾ cup plus 2 tablespoons flour
salt to taste	pinch of nutmeg
8 tablespoons butter	3 eggs

Cook potatoes in boiling salted water until tender—about 25 minutes. Drain, and put through a ricer.

In a saucepan, bring 1 cup water, ½ teaspoon salt, the butter, and nutmeg to a boil. Stir in the flour all at once, and cook until it forms a ball. Remove from the heat, and let stand for 5 minutes. Beat in the eggs one at a time. Beat in the riced potatoes.

Bring 4 quarts of water to a boil with 1 tablespoon of salt, and reduce heat to a simmer. Slip in the potato mixture in 2 teaspoon measures, or roll the dough on a lightly floured board into long ½ inch logs, and cut into 1 inch sections. Poach, in batches, for about 10 minutes, or until they float to the top. Remove with a slotted spoon, and put into a buttered baking dish.

Serve with the sauces listed for potato gnocchi, above.

Yield: 6 servings

➤ Can be prepared for the final baking several hours ahead.

Les Rambollets *(Potato Dumplings with Prunes)*

If you love potatoes and prunes, you will find these delicious and interesting. I like to serve them with baked ham or with smoked pork chops. They are a specialty of the Dauphiné region of western France.

12 potatoes	¼ pound prunes, pitted
2 eggs	2 onions, minced
⅓ cup flour	4 tablespoons butter
salt and pepper to taste	2 tablespoons oil

In a saucepan of boiling water, cook 4 potatoes in their skins until tender. Peel, and put through a ricer.

Peel and grate the remaining potatoes into a bowl, add the riced potatoes, eggs, flour, salt, and pepper, and mix well. Shape into balls, and stuff each ball with a prune. Press the edges of the dough around the prune to fully enclose it.

In a large kettle, poach the dumplings in simmering salted water for about 30 minutes. Meanwhile, sweat the onions in the butter and oil until tender.

When ready to serve, arrange the dumplings on a platter, and scatter the onion mixture over the top.

Yield: 6 servings

➤ Cannot be prepared ahead.

Deep-Frying

Use Russet potatoes; cut them into sticks, or batons ½ inch square by 3 inches long, or if you prefer, the ¼ inch julienne that is so popular at Macdonalds. You can shape them as chips, slices, gaufrettes, or waffled potatoes, or the truly tricky Souffléed Potatoes, where they are supposed to puff apart to look like oval balloons. For intrigue and fun, serve those in potato baskets, and perhaps surround them with fried potato balls. If you want more than just fried potatoes, make potato croquettes, or those heavenly little puffs called *pommes Dauphine*.

Pommes Frites *(French Fries)*

1 medium Idaho potato per person

oil for deep-frying (see Note)
salt to taste

Peel the potatoes, and keep in cold water until shortly before cooking. When almost ready to cook, cut the potatoes to size (see below), and dry well in toweling.

In a pan large enough to hold the potatoes, heat the oil to 375°F. Add the potatoes in batches, without crowding the pan, and fry until golden and crisp.

(A restaurant trick which produces crisper potatoes: When the potatoes barely begin to color, drain, and let cool. When ready to serve, heat the fat to 400°F, and fry until golden and crisp. This allows you to do most of the cooking before guests arrive.)

Drain on paper towels, and season with salt.

Serve immediately.

Yield: 1 serving

➤ Cannot be prepared ahead.

NOTE: Because of their size and shape, it is possible to fry potatoes in a skillet, rather than a deep pan. A large skillet gives far more surface area, and allows you to fry more potatoes at one time. Remember that the skillet should be no more than ⅓ full of oil before it is heated, and that the potatoes should float. Slide the potatoes, a few at a time, into the fat from the edge of the pan. Be sure to dry the potatoes. If they are wet, there will be a great frothing up of the oil, and it will spill over and possibly catch fire! When one batch is cooked, heat the oil to the correct temperature before adding the next batch.

French Fries Cut the potatoes into ½ inch square strips about 3 inches long. There are special cutters for this if you plan to make a lot.

Julienne or Matchstick Potatoes Cut the potatoes into ¼ inch square strips about 3 inches long. A mandoline, a special cutter, is used for these, or you can do it by hand.

Diced Cut French fries, and then cut across into ½ inch dice.

Gaufrettes or Waffle-Cut Potatoes You must have a ripple cutting knife. This is one of the blades on a mandoline. With the whole potato in one hand, make a first cut and discard it. Turn the potato at right angles and make the second cut. Keep turning the potato at right angle for each slice. The resulting slice should look like a waffle. It takes a few swipes to get the knack of this, but you will soon be able to slice enough for 6 persons in a very few minutes. Keep the potatoes covered with damp paper toweling until ready to fry, and plan to fry within 10 minutes.

Pont Neuf Slice the potatoes into ½ inch thick slices, and cut those into 1 inch wide by 3 inch long batons. These are served in stacks.

Balls Use a melon baller to make the potato balls.

Pommes Soufflés or Puffed Potato Ovals These are tricky, but fortunately the mistakes taste very good. Cut the whole potato into a large oval. Then cut the oval lengthwise into ⅛ inch thick slices. Soak the slices in iced water while preparing the remainder.

In a skillet, heat the fat to 275°F and fry in batches for 4 to 5 minutes, until they are limp, but not colored. Drain on paper toweling. When ready to serve, heat the oil to 400°F, and fry a few at a time. The second frying should cause the potatoes to puff apart and form crisp, hollow balloons. Drain and serve. If the potatoes are not "old" enough or thin enough, they will not puff, but will become large flat french fries.

Nids, Nests, or Baskets You need a bird's nest frying basket. This is made of two wire mesh baskets with long handles. Place julienned potatoes in the larger basket and shape up around the sides of the basket, leaving the center empty. Place the smaller basket on top of the potatoes, and clamp. Fry at 375°F until they start to turn golden. Gently twist the baskets apart. Tap the potato out of the frying basket, and return to the fat to finish cooking.

These take a little practice, but once cooked, the baskets of potatoes can be stored for a day or two. Reheat in a 350°F oven.

Potato Chips

For perfect potato chips, the need is to get rid of as much starch as possible, so they will be crisp.

6 baking potatoes, sliced wafer-thin	oil for frying salt

Soak the potato slices in cold water for 1 hour, changing the water every 20 minutes, and then rinse under cold running water until the water runs clear. Drain, and dry on toweling.

Preheat the oil to 350°F, and fry in batches until golden. Drain on paper toweling, and season with salt.

Yield: 6 servings

➤ Can be prepared ahead and stored in an airtight container.

Croquettes de Pomme de Terre (Potato Croquettes)

2 pounds potatoes, boiled, and riced or mashed	2 egg yolks flour
salt and pepper to taste	bread crumbs
3 whole eggs	oil for frying

In a bowl, mix the potatoes, salt, pepper, 2 whole eggs, and the egg yolks, and beat until fluffy. Sprinkle a pastry board with flour, roll 2 tablespoons of the mixture, and shape into balls or pears.

In a bowl, beat the remaining egg with a little salt. Place the bread crumbs in a pie plate. Roll the croquettes in the egg, and then in the bread crumbs. Let the croquettes stand on a wire rack for 20 minutes or longer.

Heat the oil to 375°F. Fry the croquettes until golden. Drain on paper toweling, and serve.

Yield: 6 servings

➤ Can be prepared for frying the day before, and kept uncovered in the refrigerator.

Variations:

There are many variations to potato croquettes. Try flavoring the potato mixture with a spice such as nutmeg, or sautéed minced garlic or onion.

Almond Croquettes Roll the croquettes in sliced blanched almonds instead of bread crumbs.

Patate Spinose (Potatoes Spinoza) Roll the croquettes in crumbled fidelini, or dried angel hair pasta.

Pommes de Terre Saint Florentin (Croquettes with Ham and Pasta) Add ¼ pound minced ham to the potato mixture. Shape into corks, and roll the croquettes in crumbled fidelini, or dried angel hair pasta.

Croccettini di Patate (Croquettes with Salami and Cheese) Add ¼ cup grated Parmesan, ¼ pound diced salami, and ¼ pound diced mozzarella to the potatoes before shaping.

Coccoli Di Patate (Croquettes with Pine Nuts and Marjoram) Add ¼ cup toasted chopped pine nuts and ⅛ teaspoon dried marjoram to the potatoes before shaping.

Croquettes Aux Fromage (Croquettes with Cheese) Add ½ cup grated Parmesan to the potatoes before shaping, and roll in a mixture of ½ cup of fresh bread crumbs and ½ cup grated Parmesan cheese.

Or, add 1 pound grated Gruyère to the potatoes and shape into corks before rolling in the bread crumbs.

Pommes de Terre Dauphine *(Potato Puffs)*

These are always a hit. Many restaurants serve these as their potato because they know they can never go wrong. They are simple to prepare, and although best if freshly cooked, you can hold them in a 300°F oven for 30 minutes or so until ready to serve.

½ cup water	1¼ pounds potatoes, cooked
¼ cup butter	and riced
1 teaspoons salt	¼ teaspoon ground nutmeg
½ cup flour	pinch of pepper
2 eggs	oil for deep-frying

In a saucepan, bring the water, butter, and salt to a full rolling boil. Add the flour all at once and, stirring constantly, cook until the mixture forms a ball and pulls away from the sides of the pan. It should start to film the bottom of the pan. The process takes about 2 minutes. Let cool for about 5 minutes.

Place the paste in a processor or a heavy-duty electric mixer. With the machine running, add the eggs, one at a time, and process until fully combined. Remove from the machine, and beat in the potatoes, nutmeg, and pepper.

Heat the oil to 375°F, and fry teaspoons of the mixture until puffed and golden brown.

Yield: 6 servings

➤ Can be prepared for frying several hours ahead.

NOTE: The dough is the same as used for cream puffs.

The dough will wait for 6 or more hours before cooking.

As the puffs fry, they constantly expand and puff open. Take care to let them open fully before removing them from the fat.

Pommes Lorette Shape with tablespoons or, with a pastry bag fitted with #8 plain tip, pipe one inch sections into the fat.

Pommes Chamonix *(Potato Puffs with Cheese)*

1 recipe Pomme de Terre	1 cup grated Gruyère cheese
Dauphine (see previous	oil for deep-frying
recipe)	

In a bowl, mix the Pomme de Terre Dauphine and cheese. Heat the oil to 375°F. Fry teaspoons of the mixture in the hot fat until puffed and golden.

Yield: 6 servings

➤ Can be prepared for frying several hours before.

Baked Potatoes

Use Idaho Russet potatoes with dull, dry-looking skins. Scrub with a brush to remove any soil, and place directly on the oven rack, or on a baking sheet. Rubbing the skins with oil makes the skins soft and wrapping in foil leads to soggy interiors. Cut a cross in the top of the potatoes to let the steam escape, and bake at 400°F for about 1 hour, depending on the size.

Press the cross to open, then cut, and serve with butter, or other accompaniments.

Variations:

Baked potatoes are also enhanced with other toppings.

Serve sour cream and minced chives on the side.

Sprinkle with toasted sesame seeds.

Serve with butter and poppy seeds.

Garnish with minced red and green pepper, and sprinkle with Parmesan cheese.

Select one of the flavored butters (see pages 13–16).

Oven Fries

Use this method to have fried potatoes with less fat.

5 Russet potatoes   salt to taste
½ cup clarified butter, melted

Preheat the oven to 375°F. Warm a baking sheet in the oven.

Cut potatoes into batons 3 inches long and 1 inch thick. It is not necessary to peel the potatoes. Rinse in cold water, and pat dry. In a bowl, mix the butter and potatoes to coat evenly.

Arrange the potatoes in a single layer, and bake for 20 minutes. Turn, and bake 20 minutes longer. Turn, and bake 15 minutes longer, and finally turn once more, and bake until browned—about 10 minutes more. Season with salt.

Yield: 6 servings

➤ Cannot be prepared ahead.

Variation:

Add 2 teaspoons of curry powder or paprika to the butter before stirring in the potatoes.

Hasselback Potatoes

These should look like a fan. To slice the potatoes without slicing all they way through, cut a thin slice off one side of the potato and put it on the board. Place a chopstick or a dowel on either side of the potato. Cut down to the stick.

6 baking potatoes	2 tablespoons shredded
¼ cup butter, melted	Gruyère cheese
½ cup heavy cream	

Preheat the oven to 325°F.

With a sharp knife, cut the potatoes into crosswise slices about ⅛ inch thick without cutting all the way. Place in ice water while cutting the remaining potatoes. Drain the potatoes, and place in a shallow baking pan. Brush with the butter, and bake until tender—about 1½ hours—basting occasionally with the cream and pan drippings.

Just before serving, sprinkle with cheese, and spoon over hot pan drippings.

Yield: 6 servings

➤ Cannot be prepared ahead.

Variations:

Swedish Roasted Potatoes with Dill Cut potatoes as above, and place on sheets of foil. Brush with butter, and sprinkle with salt and pepper and 2 tablespoons minced dill. Seal the foil around the potatoes, and bake at 400°F, or put over a charcoal fire until tender—about 50 minutes.

Garlic Potato Fans Cut the potatoes in half lengthwise, and rub all over with half a garlic clove. Cut into thin slices lengthwise, without cutting through one end. Place on a baking sheet, and press gently to fan slightly. Brush with melted butter, and bake at 375°F until golden and crisp—about 35 to 45 minutes. Serve, keeping shapes intact.

Garlic Roasted Potatoes

This is a garlic-and-potato-lovers' dream. The potatoes are crispy golden brown and permeated with garlic flavor. Serve the garlic pieces along with the potatoes.

6 Russet potatoes, peeled	¾ cup butter
2 heads garlic	salt and pepper to taste

Preheat oven to 375°F.

Cut the potatoes into quarters, and cook in boiling water for 5 minutes. Drain and pat dry. Break open the heads of garlic to separate the cloves without tearing the skin on the cloves.

In a large roasting pan, heat the butter in the oven. When melted, add the potatoes and garlic, and mix gently. Season with salt and pep-

per, and cook, turning often, for 50 minutes, or until golden
  Drain and serve.

Yield: 6 servings

➤ Can be prepared for baking several hours ahead.

NOTE: Plan on 1 clove of garlic for every piece of potato. The butter is
deliciously flavored, and can be used for garlic bread, or to sauté
chicken or fish.

Variation:
With Pancetta and Rosemary Omit the garlic, and add 6 ounces
thinly sliced pancetta, chopped, ½ cup olive oil, and 2 tablespoons
crumbled dried rosemary.

Pommes de Terre Fromagées (Cheese Roasted Potatoes)

2 pounds small new potatoes   3 tablespoons grated Gruyère
½ cup melted butter   cheese
3 tablespoons bread crumbs

  Preheat the oven to 350°F.
  In a saucepan of boiling salted water, cook the potatoes until almost
tender. Drain, place in a baking dish, and pour over the melted butter.
Sprinkle with the bread crumbs and cheese, and bake until golden,
turning often—about 25 minutes.

Yield: 6 servings

➤ Can be prepared for the final baking the day before.

Roasted Potatoes with Herbs

This is an exception to the rule about using older, floury potatoes for
baking. Use any small, shiny, thin-skinned potato for this recipe.

3 pounds small new potatoes   10 garlic cloves, peeled
¾ cup olive oil   2 bay leaves, crumbled
5 sprigs oregano   salt and pepper

  Preheat the oven to 400°F.
  In a baking dish, mix the potatoes, garlic, olive oil, oregano, bay
leaves, salt, and pepper. Stir to coat evenly.
  Bake, turning often, until the potatoes are golden brown and ten-
der—about 45 minutes.
  Discard the oregano and bay leaves.

Yield: 6 servings

➤ Cannot be prepared ahead.

Variations:

Add ⅓ cup lemon juice and 2 teaspoons grated lemon rind, omit the garlic and oregano, and insert 15 bay leaves among the potatoes.

Add 12 large peeled shallots and 2 teaspoons caraway seeds, and omit the garlic, oregano, and bay leaves.

Add ⅓ cup lemon juice, and sprinkle with minced mint when cooked. Omit the garlic, oregano, and bay leaves.

Tarte aux Pommes de Terres (Potato Pie)

2½ pounds waxy potatoes, peeled	3 tablespoons olive oil
5 garlic cloves	½ teaspoon salt
3 tablespoons butter	black pepper
	1 tablespoon minced parsley

Preheat the oven to 450°F.

In boiling salted water, boil the potatoes with 2 crushed garlic cloves until tender. Drain and cool. Slice ¼ inch thick.

In a 9 inch skillet, melt the butter in the olive oil, and sauté 2 more cloves of garlic, minced until golden. Discard the garlic pieces (if they remain in the pan, they will burn and become bitter).

In batches, sauté the potatoes over moderately high heat until lightly browned. Season with salt and pepper. Return all the slices to the skillet, and firmly press down.

Bake until potatoes are golden and crisp—about 20 to 25 minutes. Unmold the cake, and sprinkle with parsley and remaining clove of crushed garlic.

Yield: 6 servings

➤ Can be prepared for the final baking several hours ahead.

Gateau de Pommes de Terre (Baked Potato Cake)

2 pounds potatoes, peeled and minced	4 tablespoons butter
¼ cup vegetable oil	salt and pepper to taste

Preheat the oven to 450°F.

Heat the oil and 1 tablespoon of butter in a 1 quart soufflé dish in the oven until the butter is melted. Add the potatoes, and season with salt and pepper. Mix to coat evenly. Dot the top of the potatoes with the remaining butter.

Bake for 20 minutes, lower the heat to 300°F, and bake 20 minutes longer, or until tender. Let rest for 5 minutes, and unmold.

Yield: 6 servings

➤ Can be prepared for baking several hours before.

Pommes Anna *(Baked Potato Cake Anna)*

There is a special Pommes Anna pan, made of heavy copper with a lid that overlaps the bottom of the pan and comes down about 1 inch on the sides. Fortunately, a black cast-iron frying pan, or even a heavy 8 inch cake pan, will work.

½ cup clarified butter   salt and pepper to taste
2 pounds Russet potatoes,
   peeled and thinly sliced

Preheat the oven to 425°F.

Pour half of the butter into the Pommes Anna pan, cast-iron frying pan with a heatproof handle, or a heavy 8 inch cake pan. Place over high heat, and cook until the butter is very hot.

Arrange the potato slices in overlapping circles in one layer, season with salt and pepper, and continue making layers until the pan is filled.

The potatoes should mound over the top of the pan. Cover with foil, and put a heavy lid on top. The Pommes Anna pan lid is heavy enough, but if necessary, use a pie plate or smaller cake pan and a brick. Cook over moderately high heat for 15 minutes. Uncover, and bake for 30 minutes, or until the potatoes are crisp and brown around the edges.

With the Pommes Anna pan, you can leave the lid on and turn the cake upside down for the last 15 minutes. The cover is deep enough so any butter will not drain out, and heavy enough to brown the top of the cake.

Let the cake stand for 5 minutes. Run a knife around the edges and unmold.

Yield: 6 servings

➤ Can be prepared for baking several hours ahead.

Finnish Potato Dill Cake

½ cup butter, melted   1 teaspoon salt
3½ pounds baking potatoes,   1 tablespoon minced dill
   thinly sliced   dill sprigs

Preheat the oven to 325°F.

Pour 3 tablespoons butter in bottom of 10 inch deep-dish pie pan to coat bottom and sides. Overlap half the potatoes in layers in pan. Sprinkle with half the salt and dill. Layer in remaining potatoes. Drizzle the remaining butter over potatoes, and sprinkle with salt and minced dill. Cover with parchment and then foil, top with another pie pan, and weight with a brick.

Bake until the potatoes are tender—about 1¼ hours. Remove upper pie pan, and slide a thin spatula around the edge of the cake to loosen.

Turn onto platter. Garnish with dill sprigs.

Yield: 6 servings

➤ Cannot be prepared ahead.

Potato Cake with Rosemary

5 tablespoons butter	2 cups chopped onion
¼ cup toasted bread crumbs	1 tablespoon minced rosemary
4 large potatoes, thinly sliced	salt and pepper

Preheat oven to 325°F.

Butter a 9 inch pie plate with 2 tablespoons of butter, and sprinkle with half the bread crumbs.

Arrange a layer of potatoes in the pan, sprinkle with some onion and rosemary, and dot with butter.

Season with salt and pepper, and continue making layers, ending with potatoes.

Bake for 2 hours, or until tender.

Yield: 6 servings

➤ Should be baked and served. Can be served cold at a picnic.

Burgonyakéreg (Hungarian Potato Crust)

If you do not have barquettes, use custard cups.

1 pound potatoes, unpeeled	1 tablespoon minced parsley
2 eggs	salt and pepper to taste
2 tablespoons butter	

Preheat the oven to 375°F.

Boil the potatoes in water to cover until tender. Peel and rice the potatoes. Beat in the eggs, butter, parsley, salt, and pepper.

Butter small barquettes or other molds, and fill with the potato mixture. Bake for 10 minutes, or until the edges are golden brown. Unmold.

Yield: 6 servings

➤ Can be prepared for baking several hours before.

Gratin

Potatoes au gratin are called scalloped potatoes by New Englanders. Potatoes, usually sliced, are arranged in a flat baking dish and oversimmered in stock, milk, or cream. My mother's scalloped potatoes came to the table with curdled milk and a burned top. I liked them, but later, when I prepared Gratin Dauphinoise for the first time, I realized that there was a difference—like the difference between cream sauce made with yogurt and cornstarch, and one made with reduced cream.

The yogurt gives you the idea, but is more food as punishment than pleasure. Potatoes and cream are the base of many gratins, but others are made with stock, and still other ingredients can be added to the potatoes.

Preparing Ahead Gratins are best if served shortly after they are baked. If you wish to prepare ahead, place all of the ingredients in the baking dish several hours ahead, as long as there is enough liquid to cover them. Or, prepare the ingredients separately, and keep the potatoes in a bowl of cold water until you are ready to assemble and bake.

Pommes de Terre Boulangére
(Sliced Potatoes Baked in Stock)

It is only recently that French kitchens have had ovens. In past times, food that needed long, slow baking was assembled at home and then taken to the local bread baker (boulangér) early in the morning to be baked in the cooling ovens. At noon the homemakers would return to pick up their dinners—energy conservation in action!

1 tablespoon oil	3 cups thinly sliced onions
4 garlic cloves, thinly sliced	¼ teaspoon black pepper
2 bay leaves	2 pounds potatoes, peeled and
1 teaspoon minced thyme	thinly sliced
3 cups chicken stock	

Preheat the oven to 400°F. Have ready a deep 12 inch round baking dish or a 14 inch long baking dish.

In a skillet, heat the oil, and sauté the onion for 5 minutes, or until softened but not browned. Add the garlic, bay leaves, thyme, stock, and pepper, and bring to a boil.

Place the potatoes in the baking dish, and add the onion mixture, stirring to blend. Even the top, and place on a baking sheet to catch any drips.

Bake for about 1 hour, or until very tender and browned on the top. Let stand 20 minutes before serving.

Yield: 6 servings

➤ Best if served shortly after baking.

Basque Potatoes

8 bacon slices, diced	3 garlic cloves, crushed
3 pounds baking potatoes, ¼ inch thick slices	2 teaspoons minced thyme
	salt and pepper to taste
6 tomatoes, peeled, seeded, and quartered	½ cup medium-dry sherry
	½ cup butter, melted
2 cups sliced mushrooms	3 garlic cloves, melted
1½ cups pitted black olives, quartered	

Preheat the oven to 350°F.
In a heavy skillet, sauté the bacon over medium heat until almost crisp. Drain on paper towels.
In a 10 by 15 inch deep baking dish, arrange the potatoes, tomatoes, mushrooms, and olives in layers, sprinkling each layer with crushed garlic, thyme, salt, and pepper.
Cover with a sheet of foil, and bake 30 minutes. Combine the sherry, butter, and remaining garlic, and pour over the potatoes. Bake uncovered until potatoes are tender—40 to 45 minutes longer.

Yield: 6 servings

➤ Serve shortly after baking.

Gratin Savoyard

2 pounds potatoes, thinly sliced	1½ cups grated Gruyère cheese
1½ cups beef stock	¼ cup butter
	salt and pepper to taste

Preheat the oven to 350°F. Butter a large shallow gratin dish.
Arrange ¼ of the potatoes in the pan, and sprinkle with ¼ of the stock and the Gruyère cheese. Dot with the butter. Continue layering, ending with the cheese.
Bake for 1 hour, or until the potatoes are tender and the top is browned. If the top browns too quickly, place a sheet of foil on top.

Yield: 6 servings

➤ Can be prepared for baking several hours ahead, but the stock must cover the potatoes.

Variation:

Gratin de Bugey Substitute chicken stock for the beef stock, and rendered chicken fat for the butter.

Matahami Béarnaise

This is a version from the Béarn.

2 pounds potatoes, unpeeled	2 large onions, minced
½ pound lean salt pork, thinly sliced	2 garlic cloves, minced
	salt and pepper to taste

Preheat the oven to 325°F.
In a saucepan of boiling water, cook the potatoes for 15 minutes. Drain, peel, and slice thinly.
In a baking dish, layer the salt pork, potatoes, onions, and garlic. Season very lightly with salt and pepper to taste. Continue layering, ending with the salt pork.
Cover with a sheet of foil, and bake for 30 minutes. Remove the cover, and bake until tender.

Yield: 6 servings

➤ Best served within 30 minutes of baking.

Pommes de Terre en Daube *(Gratin of Potatoes)*

5 garlic cloves, crushed	3 or 4 bay leaves
2 cups water	⅓ cup olive oil
salt and pepper to taste	
2 pounds potatoes, thinly sliced	

Preheat the oven to 400°F.

In a saucepan, simmer the garlic in salted water for 15 minutes, covered. Drain, reserving both the garlic and the water. Purée the garlic, and return to the water (you can purée the garlic in a blender).

Rub the inside of a gratin with a little of the olive oil, and pack in the potatoes. Bury the bay leaves amid the potatoes, and pour the garlic water over the top. The water should cover the potatoes; add more water if needed.

Drizzle the oil over the top. Bake until tender—about 45 minutes.

Yield: 6 servings

➤ Serve shortly after baking.

Tortiere di Patate e Pomodori Pugliese *(Gratin of Potatoes, Mushrooms, and Tomatoes, Apulian Style)*

1½ cups hot water	¾ pound baking potatoes, thinly sliced
¾ ounce dried Porcini mushrooms	pepper to taste
¼ cup olive oil	¾ pound tomatoes, thinly sliced
½ pound mushrooms, thinly sliced	¼ cup grated Provolone cheese
1½ teaspoons salt	¼ cup grated Mozzarella cheese

Preheat the oven to 400°F.

In a bowl, combine the hot water and porcini mushrooms, and soak for 30 minutes. Squeeze mushrooms dry, and reserve ⅔ cup of the liquid. Chop the mushrooms.

In a skillet, sauté the sliced mushrooms in 2 tablespoons of olive oil until softened—about 5 minutes—and stir in the chopped porcini.

In a gratin, brush 1 tablespoon of oil, and arrange the potatoes in a layer. Add the soaking liquid, and season with salt and pepper.

Scatter the mushroom mixture over potatoes, and arrange the tomatoes on top. Drizzle with the remaining tablespoon of olive oil. Bake for 30 minutes, or until tender. Sprinkle with the cheeses, and bake until melted and golden.

Let rest for 10 minutes before serving.

Yield: 6 servings

➤ If desired, bake to the point of adding the cheese, and let cool. Add the cheese, and perform the final baking shortly before serving.

Variation:
Sprinkle the layers with 2 tablespoons minced basil and 1 teaspoon minced garlic.

Gratin Dauphinois I

1½ cups milk	salt and pepper to taste
1 clove garlic, crushed	nutmeg to taste
3 pounds potatoes, thinly	½ cup heavy cream
sliced	1½ cups grated Gruyère cheese

Preheat the oven to 375°F.
In a saucepan, scald the milk and garlic together, and let steep for 5 minutes. In a gratin pan, arrange the potatoes in layer.
Season the hot milk with the salt, pepper, and nutmeg. Stir in the cream. Pour the milk mixture over the potatoes, and sprinkle with the grated Gruyère. Bake for 45 minutes to 1 hour, or until tender and golden brown.

Yield: 6 servings

Gratin Dauphinois II

There are many versions of preparing this standard of French cookery.
Many cooks prefer to simmer the potatoes in milk to keep them as white as possible. Adding the garlic and bay leaf increases the flavor.

3 pounds waxy potatoes, thinly sliced	3 bay leaves
	pinch grated nutmeg
2 cups milk	pepper to taste
2 cups water	1 cup heavy cream
3 garlic cloves, minced	2 cups grated Gruyère cheese
¾ teaspoon salt	

Preheat the oven to 375°F.
Put potatoes into a saucepan with the milk, water, garlic, salt, and bay leaves. Bring to a boil, stirring occasionally. Lower the heat, and simmer gently, stirring occasionally until tender—about 5 to 10 minutes, depending on thickness.
With a slotted spoon, transfer half of the potatoes to a 13 by 9 inch baking dish, and season with nutmeg and pepper. Pour over half the cream, and sprinkle with half the cheese. Add the remaining potatoes,

and repeat with nutmeg, pepper, cream, and cheese. Bake for 1 hour, or until the top is crisp and golden.

Yield: 6 servings

Gratin of Potatoes and Scallions

3 pounds potatoes, thinly
  sliced
8 scallions, thinly sliced
¼ cup butter
1¼ cups heavy cream

1 cup milk
1 teaspoon salt
¼ teaspoon nutmeg
pepper to taste

Preheat the oven to 350°F.
In a large skillet, stir the potatoes and scallions in the butter, until coated. Add 1 cup cream, milk, salt, nutmeg, and pepper, and cook, stirring occasionally, over medium heat until the potatoes are almost tender.

Butter a gratin pan, and turn the potatoes into the dish, smoothing the top. Bake for 20 minutes, drizzle with the remaining cream, and bake 20 minutes longer, until the potatoes are tender and the top is browned.

Yield: 6 servings

➤ The initial cooking in the milk can be done several hours ahead, but bake shortly before serving.

Gratin Dauphinois aux Navets
(Creamy Potato and Turnip Gratin)

1½ quarts milk
1½ pounds potatoes, peeled
  and thinly sliced
1½ pounds turnips, peeled
  and thinly sliced

3 cups heavy cream
salt and pepper to taste
pinch of nutmeg
¾ cup grated Gruyère cheese
2 tablespoons butter

Preheat the oven to 350°F. Butter a large gratin or baking dish.
Put 3 cups of milk in each of 2 saucepans, and add the turnip slices to one and the potatoes to the other. Simmer 10 minutes, or until almost tender.

Drain the vegetables, and discard the milk. Return the potatoes to their saucepans.

In a third saucepan, reduce cream to 2½ cups. Divide between the potatoes and turnips, and season each with salt, pepper, and nutmeg. Simmer 10 minutes longer.

Spread ½ of potatoes on the bottom of a gratin and top with half the turnips. Repeat, and pour the cream over the vegetables. Sprinkle with cheese, dot with butter, and bake for 45 minutes, or until golden.

Yield: 8 servings

➤ Can be prepared for the final baking several hours ahead.

Garlic Scalloped Potatoes

1½ pounds baking potatoes, thinly sliced	⅓ cup flour
	3 tablespoons butter
1 large onion, thinly sliced	salt and pepper
6 cloves garlic, thinly sliced	1½ cups milk

Preheat the oven to 300°F. Butter a 9½ inch casserole or gratin. Put a third of the potatoes in the casserole. Scatter half the onion and garlic on top, and sprinkle with half the flour. Dot with 1 tablespoon of the butter. Season with ¼ teaspoon each of salt and pepper. Repeat with a second layer. Finish with the remaining potatoes, and pour over the milk. Dot with butter, and season to taste.

Bake for 1 hour, or until tender and golden on the top. If necessary, raise the heat to 375°F to brown the top, or glaze under the broiler.

Yield: 6 servings

Artichauts et Pommes de Terre au Gratin
(Artichokes and Potatoes au Gratin)

4 large artichokes	⅔ cup milk
2 lemons	⅔ cup heavy cream
½ cup minced onion	salt and pepper to taste
½ teaspoon minced garlic	¼ cup beef or chicken stock
3 tablespoons butter	1 bay leaf
2 baking potatoes, thinly sliced	

Preheat the oven to 350°F.

Trim the artichokes to make artichoke bottoms (see page 34). Rub the cut edges with half of a lemon. Poach the artichoke bottoms in water acidulated with the juice of 1 lemon until tender—about 3 to 6 minutes. Drain, and slice very thinly.

In a skillet, sauté the onion and garlic in 1½ tablespoons of butter until soft, but not brown.

Butter a gratin pan with the remaining butter. Scatter the onion in the bottom of the pan. Arrange overlapping rows of artichokes and potato slices.

In a bowl, combine ½ cup of cream, the milk, ½ teaspoon salt, ⅓ teaspoon pepper, the meat stock, and the bay leaf. Pour over the potatoes, and bake for 1 hour, or until tender.

Preheat the broiler. Fifteen minutes before serving, spoon the remaining cream over the potatoes, and put under a broiler until hot and golden brown.

Yield: 6 servings

➤ Prepare just before baking.

Gratin de Manigod

2 tablespoons butter	salt and pepper to taste
3 ounces slab bacon, cut into	2 eggs, lightly beaten
⅓ inch cubes	1½ cups milk
6 waxy potatoes, peeled and	2 garlic cloves, minced
grated	2 tablespoons minced parsley

Preheat the oven to 325°F. Butter a 1½ quart baking dish.
In a skillet, sauté the bacon until golden brown. Drain, and set aside.
Pile the potatoes into a colander, and rinse under cold running
water until the water runs clear. Pat the potatoes dry, and pile into a
bowl. Add the salt, pepper, eggs, milk, garlic, parsley, and bacon. Stir
into mix. Pour into the dish, and dot the top with 1 tablespoon of butter. Bake for 1 hour, or until the top is crisp and golden.

Yield: 6 servings

➤ The potatoes can be prepared about 30 minutes before baking.

La Râpée Morvandelle (Grated Potato and Cheese Gratin)

The walnut oil gives this preparation an elusive quality.

3 tablespoons butter or walnut oil	3 eggs
2 pounds potatoes	1½ cups grated Gruyère cheese
4 ounces cream cheese	1 tablespoon Cognac
½ cup heavy cream	salt and pepper to taste

Preheat the oven to 400°F. Spread the butter or walnut oil in a
gratin, and set aside.
Grate the potatoes, drain thoroughly, and squeeze gently. Pat dry.
Working quickly, mix the potatoes with the cheese, cream, eggs,
Gruyère, and Cognac. Season with salt and pepper. Spread the mixture
in the gratin, and bake for 45 minutes, or until golden brown and crisp
on the top.

Yield: 6 servings

➤ Bake as soon as assembled, and serve shortly after baking.

Gratin Râpée au Bleu de Bresse et Noisettes
(Grated Potato Casserole with Blue Cheese and Hazelnuts)

1 garlic clove	½ cup heavy cream
1 tablespoon of butter	salt and pepper to taste
½ pound Bleu de Bresse	2 pounds Idaho potatoes
cheese (see Note)	1 tablespoon butter
2 cups milk	½ cup chopped hazelnuts

Preheat the oven to 375°F. Rub the inside of a 14 by 9 inch gratin
or baking dish with the garlic clove. Reserve the remains of the clove.

In a processor, combine the reserved garlic, cheese, milk, and cream, and purée. Season with salt and pepper.

Working quickly, grate the potatoes, and put into a bowl. Toss with the milk mixture, and turn into the prepared pan. Smooth the top, and bake for 10 minutes. Lower the heat, and bake for 35 minutes.

In a skillet, melt the butter, and sauté the hazelnuts until golden. Pour over the potatoes, and bake until golden and the potatoes are tender.

Yield: 6 servings

➤ Cannot be prepared ahead.

NOTE: If Bleu de Bresse is not available, any rich, creamy blue cheese will serve, such as Danish blue, or even an uneven mixture of cream cheese and a sharp Roquefort.

Potato Salad

Potato salad, a year-round favorite, is often prepared with less attention than it deserves, resulting in a dish that is less than noteworthy. The current hysteria about handling vegetables has led many cooks to serve virtually raw potatoes for fear of overcooking, speckled messes of salad for fear of removing the skins, or potatoes smeared with a thick coating of mayonnaise to hide the potato skins.

The requirements for a superb potato salad are few and are easily achieved. Waxy potatoes boiled until just done, a full-flavored dressing based on a vinaigrette or mayonnaise, plus the judicious addition of a few seasonings, such as salt, pepper, onion, and an herb or two of choice, all mixed gently and served neither too hot nor too cold shows clearly why this dish is such a favorite.

Potatoes

As with any boiled potato dish, choose those that hold their shape, i.e., waxy, firm potatoes, such as red bliss, Yellow Finn, or any thin-skinned new potato.

Boil the potatoes in salted water until fully cooked and just tender. Drain and let cool.

For neat, clean pieces, boil the potatoes in their skins, and cool only enough to peel. Use a sharp knife that you rinse often to cut into slices or dice, and while still warm, toss with some vinaigrette or white wine, if desired.

If you want a dish with a softer look and texture, peel the potatoes before cooking, and chop coarsely while still hot. Sprinkle with some white wine or vinaigrette before they cool.

Dressing

Potato salads are dressed with vinaigrette or mayonnaise, or in some instances with both. Many cooks, and I am one, prefer to add some vinaigrette while the potatoes are still warm, because the potatoes absorb it better and the flavor is inside the potato instead of laying just on the surface. Even if the salad is to be coated with mayonnaise later, a small amount of vinaigrette greatly improves the flavor. On occasion I use white wine in place of vinaigrette, or add just a generous sprinkle of white wine and not bother with any vinaigrette at this stage.

Once the potatoes have cooled to room temperature, the remaining ingredients are added.

Seasonings

The standard seasonings for potato salad are onions (in one form or another), celery, and a dressing. You can add almost any vegetable you like and have a delicious salad, and some cooks like to add hard-cooked eggs or bits of diced ham, sausage, or even tuna fish. I like to add some diced anchovy.

Basic Potato Salad with Vinaigrette

This is sometimes called French potato salad.

3 pounds cooked boiling potatoes	¾ to 1 cup vinaigrette
¼ cup dry white wine, or chicken stock	¼ cup thinly sliced scallions
	¼ cup minced parsley

Peel the warm potatoes and slice or dice. Place in a bowl, and toss with white wine or chicken stock. Let stand 5 minutes. Add the vinaigrette, scallions, and parsley, and toss gently.

Place the salad in a serving bowl, and serve warm or at room temperature.

Yield: 6 servings

➤ Can be prepared the day before.

NOTE: In France this would be served while still hot to accompany poached sausage, or at room temperature as part of an *hors d'oeuvre variés* platter. The platter is a collection of vegetable salads, such as grated carrots, celery root with rémoulade sauce, and potato salad, and often accompanied by slices of pâté, salami, or pieces of smoked fish. Fish salads may also compose part of the platter. It is arguably the best possible lunch or summer dinner imaginable.

Variations:

You can leave the skins on red bliss potatoes.

Substitute minced onions, shallots, or sliced leeks for the scallions.

Add 1 clove crushed garlic to the vinaigrette.

Add 2 tablespoons or more to taste of a minced fresh herb, such as tarragon, chervil, thyme, marjoram, summer savory, or basil. Take care that the herb complements the potatoes and does not over power them.

Basic Potato Salad with Mayonnaise

Potato salad, like most so-called cold food, is best at room tempera- ture. If it is necessary to refrigerate it, let it sit at room temperature for 30 minutes to remove the refrigerator chill before serving it.

3 pounds boiled potatoes	¾ cup minced onion
¼ cup vinaigrette or white wine	1 cup minced green pepper
	2 tablespoons minced parsley
¾ cup minced celery	2 cups mayonnaise, or to taste

Peel the potatoes, and cut into slices or dice. Sprinkle with the vinaigrette while still warm, and let cool for at least 5 minutes.

Fold in the celery, onion, pepper, and parsley. Fold in enough may- onnaise to coat the salad ingredients evenly. Do not add too much mayonnaise.

Arrange the salad in a serving bowl, and pass mayonnaise on the side.

Yield: 6 servings

➤ Can be prepared the day before.

Variations:
You can leave the skin on red bliss potatoes.
Substitute red pepper for the green, or use both.
Add ½ cup peeled, seeded, and diced tomatoes just before serving.
Add 2 tablespoons minced Jalapeño chiles for zip.
Add 1 cup grated carrots.
Add 1 cup chopped watercress.
Add 1 cup chopped walnuts, or toasted slivered almonds.
Add 1 cup diced cooked asparagus just before serving.
Add 1 cup cooked broccoli florets just before serving.
Add ¼ cup or more of minced dill.
Add 2 tablespoons or to taste of minced tarragon, rosemary, thyme, marjoram, or summer savory.
Add 1 tablespoon, or to taste, of oregano.
Add 1 tablespoon, or to taste, of caraway, dill, or poppy seed.

Potato Salad with Basil and Pine Nuts

Few dishes have caught the imagination as fully as pesto, the Italian pasta sauce. It has been used to coat, and often to smother, almost every other food. Here it is used to enhance, and not overwhelm, a potato salad.

3 pounds boiled potatoes	⅓ cup toasted pine nuts
¼ cup white wine	¼ pound Parmesan cheese,
¾ cup vinaigrette	cut into paper-thin slices
2 tablespoons pesto sauce (see	(see Note)
page 27)	

Peel the potatoes, and cut into ½ inch dice. While still warm, sprinkle with the wine, toss gently, and let stand for 5 minutes.

In a bowl, mix the vinaigrette and pesto, and fold into the salad. Sprinkle with the pine nuts, and fold gently.

Arrange the salad in a serving bowl. Place the slices of Parmesan over the top of the salad.

Yield: 6 servings

➤ Can be prepared the day before.

NOTE: Using a cheese shaver, shave the Parmesan into paper-thin slices and arrange evenly over the salad.

New Potato and Pea Salad with Mint

2 cups mint leaves	½ teaspoon pepper
2 eggs	1½ cups oil
3 tablespoons white-wine	3 pounds boiled potatoes
vinegar	3 cups shelled peas, about 3
2 tablespoons Dijon mustard	pounds
1 teaspoons salt	salt and pepper to taste

To make the mint-flavored mayonnaise: In a processor, purée the mint, eggs, vinegar, mustard, salt, and pepper. With the machine running, slowly add the oil, and correct the seasoning. Set aside.

Peel the potatoes, cut into small dice, and place in a bowl.

Cook the peas in boiling salted water to cover until just done. Refresh under cold water, drain, and turn into the bowl with the potatoes. Fold in just enough mayonnaise to bind.

Arrange the salad in a serving bowl, and pass the remaining mayonnaise.

Yield: 6 servings

➤ Can be prepared the day before.

Variation:

To turn this into a main course, add 2 cups poached salmon broken into serving pieces, or use 2 cups diced ham.

Smoked Fish and Potato Salad

3 pounds boiled potatoes
¾ pound smoked fish, broken
   into bite-sized pieces
⅔ cup chopped walnuts
1 cup minced celery
⅓ cup minced scallions

1 cup mayonnaise
2 tablespoons lemon juice
¼ teaspoon Worcestershire
   sauce
Tabasco to taste
salt and pepper to taste

While the potatoes are still warm, peel, and cut into ¼ inch thick slices. Place in a bowl, and fold in the smoked fish, walnuts, celery, and scallions.

In another bowl, mix the mayonnaise, lemon juice, Worcestershire sauce, Tabasco, salt, and pepper together, and fold into the potato-fish mixture.

Arrange in a bowl.

Yield: 6 servings

➤ Can be prepared the day before.

NOTE: Use any smoked fish of your choice, such as salmon, blue fish, scallops, clams, oysters, or mussels—or for greater interest, an assortment of these.

Pumpkin

To most people, pumpkin is a Hallowe'en decoration, possibly a pie filling or, after a little thought, the base for a quickbread or a muffin—a sad comment for this most American of vegetables. South Americans do find more uses, but it is the European and African cooks who turn this vegetable into soups, serve it in stews, use it to fill pasta, and serve it as a vegetable course.

Availability

Fresh
Pumpkins are available from late September through late November. Ask for sugar or eating pumpkins, as opposed to carving pumpkins. The former are small and should weigh less than 7 pounds. Select pumpkins with firm rinds, and no spots or cracks. Store pumpkins in a dark cool place for 2 to 3 months.

Frozen
Puréed pumpkin freezes very nicely. Use it wherever pumpkin purée is needed.

Canned
Canned pumpkin is suitable when puréed pumpkin is needed.

Preparation

Cut off the top and bottom of the pumpkin, and set upright on the cutting board. With a large knife, cut down the sides of the pumpkin, cutting off sections of skin. Cut the pumpkin in half, and scoop out the seeds. You can toast the seeds (see page 453), to serve as a snack. If you wish to use the pumpkin as a container—it makes a spectacular soup tureen—cut out a top, about 1 inch in from the top edge. With a sharp metal spoon, scrape out the seeds and all the fibrous material. Brush the pumpkin with butter, and bake on a baking sheet at 400°F for 20 minutes, or until barely tender.

Prepare small pumpkins in the same way as acorn or butternut squash.

Cooking Methods

Boiling
Cook in boiling salted until just tender. Peel before or after boiling. Drain well.

Steaming
Steamed pumpkin uses less water, but takes longer to cook. Drain the pumpkin well before using.

Microwaving
Cook, covered, for about 8 minutes.

Quantity

Plan on about 4 pounds of whole pumpkin for 6 persons. You will lose about 50% in preparing a pumpkin.

Sauces

Serve plain pumpkin with one of the butter sauces. The pumpkin can also be sauced with Mornay and cream sauce. It is particularly good with ginger and jalapeños to perk up its bland flavor.

Puréed Pumpkin

Pumpkin is a watery vegetable and must be dried over medium heat or well drained after the initial boiling or steaming.

4 pound pumpkin

Cut off the top and bottom of the pumpkin, and peel. Cut into sections, and scrape out the seeds and any fibrous matter.

Steam the sections over boiling water until tender—about 25 minutes—or cook in boiling salted water about 20 minutes. Drain the pumpkin, and purée in a food processor or food mill.

Place the puréed pumpkin in a strainer lined with cheesecloth over a bowl, and let drain for at least 30 minutes. The drained pumpkin should be stiff enough to hold its shape in a spoon.

Yield: about 2 cups

➤ Can be frozen.

Soupe de Potiron *(Pumpkin Soup)*

3 pounds pumpkin, peeled, seeded, and cut into 1 inch cubes	⅛ teaspoon ground cloves
	¼ cup butter
	white pepper to taste
1 teaspoon salt	6 slices French bread sautéed
2 cups milk	in butter (croûtes)
⅛ teaspoon nutmeg	

In a large pot, simmer the pumpkin with 6 cups of salted water, covered, until very tender—about 25 minutes. Drain the pumpkin, and purée in a food processor. Put back into the pot, and add the milk, nutmeg, cloves, butter, and pepper, and bring to a simmer.
Serve garnished with the croûtes.

Yield: 6 servings

➤ Can be prepared ahead and reheated.

NOTE: Substitute 1½ cups canned or frozen pumpkin, if desired.

Puréed de Potiron *(Cream of Pumpkin Soup)*

1½ pounds pumpkin, peeled and cut up	¼ cup chopped sorrel (optional)
½ cup sliced potatoes	¼ cup chopped spinach
5 cups water	¼ cup chopped leeks
salt and pepper to taste	¼ cup cooked rice
4 cups heavy cream	2 tablespoons cooked peas
⅔ cup butter	1 tablespoon minced parsley
2 tablespoons butter	

In a 3 quart saucepan, simmer the pumpkin and potatoes in the salted water until tender. Purée in a food processor or food mill, reserving the cooking liquid.
Clean the casserole, and add the purée, cooking liquid, cream, and ⅔ cup butter. Heat.
In a skillet, melt the 2 tablespoons butter, and sweat the sorrel, spinach, and leeks until tender. Stir into the soup along with the rice, peas, and parsley. Correct the seasoning with salt and pepper.

Yield: 6 servings

➤ Can be frozen.

Potiron à la Parmesan (Pumpkin with Parmesan Cheese)

Add just enough salt, nutmeg, and cinnamon to enhance the pumpkin without overpowering its delicate flavor. Start with a tiny pinch, and continue adding more until you just begin to sense the flavors.

4 pounds pumpkin, peeled	nutmeg to taste
½ cup clarified butter	cinnamon to taste
salt to taste	½ cup grated Parmesan cheese

Preheat the oven to 400°F.

Cut the pumpkin into 1 inch chunks, and blanch in boiling salted water until tender, but still firm. Drain, and pat dry.

In a skillet, heat the butter, and toss the pumpkin with salt, nutmeg, and cinnamon until lightly colored. Place in an ovenproof serving dish, and sprinkle with the cheese. Bake for 10 minutes, or until the cheese is browned.

Yield: 6 servings

➤ Can be prepared for the final baking several hours ahead.

Gratin de Potiron (Pumpkin Gratin)

4 pounds pumpkin, peeled and cut into 2 inch cubes	pinch of nutmeg
salt and pepper to taste	½ cup heavy cream
2 tablespoons butter	1 cup grated Gruyère cheese
2 cups onion, chopped	2 tablespoons fresh bread crumbs
12 thick slices bacon	

Preheat the oven to 375°F.

In a pot of boiling salted water, cook the pumpkin until just barely tender, and drain in a colander.

In a skillet, sauté the onions in the butter until soft, and remove to a bowl. Add the bacon, and fry until crisp.

Place the drained pumpkin cubes in a gratin, and sprinkle with the onion, bacon, nutmeg, cream, cheese, and bread crumbs. Bake for 30 minutes, or until golden.

Yield: 6 servings

➤ Can be prepared for baking several hours ahead.

Gratin de Potiron Provençale
(Baked Pumpkin with Garlic)

4 pounds pumpkin, peeled, seeded, and cut into ½ inch cubes	½ cup olive oil
	10 to 12 cloves garlic, minced
	¼ cup minced parsley
⅓ cup flour	salt and pepper to taste

Preheat the oven to 325°F.

In a bowl, toss the pumpkin cubes with the flour until evenly coated. Oil a gratin, and add the pumpkin. Sprinkle with the garlic and parsley. Season with salt and pepper, and drizzle the remaining oil over the top. Bake for 2 hours, or until the top is a rich, dark brown.

Yield: 6 servings

➤ Can be prepared for baking several hours ahead.

Stracci (Soup with Pumpkin Ravioli)

This recipe makes about 70 ravioli, which is more than you need. Freeze the remainder. Serve with melted butter, and ground walnuts or sautéed wild mushrooms.

3½ cups flour, sifted	1 teaspoon sage leaves, chopped
1 teaspoon salt	2 tablespoons grated Parmesan
3 eggs	cheese
1 tablespoon olive oil	grated nutmeg to taste
½ cup plus 2 tablespoons	salt and pepper to taste
warm water	6 cups simmering chicken stock
1½ cups pumpkin purée	1½ tablespoons minced
1 cup walnuts, chopped	parsley

In a processor, mix the the flour, salt, eggs, and 1 tablespoon olive oil. With the machine running, slowly add the water, and let the machine run for 2 minutes.

Place the dough on a lightly floured board, cover, and let rest for 30 minutes.

Pumpkin Filling In a bowl, mix the pumpkin, walnuts, sage, bread crumbs, Parmesan, nutmeg, and salt and pepper. Set aside.

In a pasta machine, roll the dough as thinly as possible.

Place teaspoons of the filling along one side of the dough, brush the dough with water, fold the unfilled side over the filling, and press to seal. Store on a lightly floured baking sheet until ready to serve.

Poach the ravioli in the stock until just done—about 3 minutes.

Yield: 6 servings

➤ The ravioli can be frozen and cooked later.

Variation:

Fill the dough with this filling for a change: In a bowl, mix 1 cup canned pumpkin, 1 egg, 6 amaretto cookies finely crushed, 1 cup grated Parmesan cheese, pinch of nutmeg, and salt and pepper to taste.

Fried Pumpkin, or Sweet Potato Chips, with Cayenne and Coriander

2 pound wedge pumpkin, peeled and seeded, or 2 or 3 large sweet potatoes	¾ cup flour
	½ teaspoon salt
	¾ teaspoon Cayenne pepper
2 cups oil for frying	¼ cup minced coriander
1 cup milk	

Cut the pumpkin into ⅛ inch thick slices, and cut the slices into 1 by ½ inch rectangles. Heat the oil to 370°F.

Pour milk into a large bowl. In a pie plate, mix the flour, salt, and ¼ teaspoon Cayenne.

Dip potato slices into milk, dredge in the flour, and shake off the excess. Fry in batches in the hot oil, stirring gently, until golden—about 3 to 5 minutes. Sprinkle with the remaining Cayenne.

Place the coriander in a strainer, and fry for 5 seconds. Drain, and sprinkle over the pumpkin chips.

Yield: 6 servings

➤ Cannot be prepared ahead.

Toasted Pumpkin Seeds

2 cups pumpkin seeds, unwashed	2 tablespoons vegetable oil
	salt to taste

Preheat the oven to 250°F.

In a bowl, mix the seeds, oil, and salt. Place seeds in a single layer in a baking sheet, and bake for 1¼ hours, or until dried and golden.

Yield: 2 cups

➤ Can be prepared several days ahead and stored in an airtight container.

Radish

The familiar, round or oval, rather spicy red radish is found in most markets. The milder white, black, or purple radishes are more often found in Asian markets. The Chinese, Japanese, and Koreans consume gargantuan quantities of daikon (white radish) as pickled or preserved vegetables in soups or stir-fries, or grated for salads. They are carved into boats, or birds, or cut into lacy veils as garnishes. The black radishes, which are less common, are similar to the white radish once peeled.

Availability

Fresh
Available year round. Look for firm smooth roots, with fresh green leaves, if they are still attached. Avoid spongy, dried, cracked, or black spotted radishes, as well as those with wilted or yellowed leaves. Remove the leaves, and store in a plastic bag in the refrigerator for 2 to 3 weeks. Look for medium-sized red radishes. Daikon are often quite large, and relatively firm. If they are limp, firm up by soaking in cold water.

Frozen
Do not freeze.

Canned
Radish is canned only after pickling.

Preparation

Red Radishes
Cut off all but ¼ inch of stem, wash, and remove any hairy roots. Serve cold. If cooking, cut off roots and stems, and slice. Peeling is not necessary.

White Radishes *(Daikon)*
Peel the radish like a carrot. Cut into slices, dice, julienne, shred, or grate. If very small, a light scrubbing will suffice.

Black Radishes
Prepare the same as white radish.

Cooking Methods

Steaming
Place over boiling water, and steam until tender—about 10 minutes.

Microwaving
Cook in a covered container with 1 tablespoon water for about 4 minutes.

Sautéing
Toss sliced radishes in hot butter for about 6 minutes, or until tender-crisp.

Quantity

Plan on ¾ to 1 pound of red radishes per person.

Sauces

Sauté with flavored butters, or toss with poppy seeds, caraway seeds, or toasted sesame seeds. Serve in cream sauce, or as a salad with vinaigrette.

Radishes with Butter

The most popular method of serving red radishes in Europe is as a sandwich.

1 pound red radishes	¼ pound butter
Sliced French or dark rye bread	coarse salt

Slice or mince the radishes as finely or as coarsely as you wish.

Spread the bread lavishly with butter, and arrange the slices, or sprinkle a pile of radishes on top. Sprinkle with salt.

Yield: 6 servings

➤ Can be prepared an hour before serving.

Sautéed Radishes in Cream

1 pound sliced radishes	salt and pepper to taste
2 tablespoons butter	1 cup heavy cream
1 teaspoon dill seed	

In a large skillet, sauté the radish slices in the butter until well-coated. Add the dill seed, and season with salt and pepper.

Sauté until tender-crisp. Add the cream, and boil over high heat until thick enough to coat the back of a spoon.

Yield: 6 servings

➤ Can be prepared and reheated, but best if prepared just before serving.

Radish Salad

For most of us, the principal method of using radishes is in salad. Add sliced or diced radishes to potato, green bean, or corn salads for pungency. But try radishes as a salad on their own.

Radish Sesame Salad

1 pound red radishes, thinly sliced	1 tablespoon Japanese soy sauce (Tamari will do)
3 tablespoons rice vinegar	1 teaspoon Asian sesame oil
1 tablespoon sugar	2 tablespoons toasted sesame seeds

In a bowl, mix the radishes, vinegar, sugar, soy sauce, and sesame oil. Cover and refrigerate for 6 hours, stirring occasionally.

Just before serving, fold in the sesame seeds.

Yield: 6 servings

➤ Can be prepared the day before.

Radish Fans

Select oval radishes rather than rounds for these. Use them as a garnish or as part of an hors d'oeuvre platter.

24 radishes	1 teaspoon salt
1 tablespoon sugar	

Wash the radishes, and remove all but a bit of stem. Place on a board, and cut paper-thin slices from the root to the stem, without cutting through the stem end. Put into a bowl with the salt and sugar, and toss well. Marinate for at least 6 hours, turning often. Discard the liquid.

Yield: 6 servings

➤ Can be prepared the day before.

Orange and Radish Salad

1 pound radishes or daikon, grated	2 tablespoons lemon juice
2 tablespoons sugar	2 tablespoons orange juice
2 oranges, peeled, segmented, and seeded	salt to taste
	pinch of cinnamon

Place the grated radish in a clean towel, and squeeze out the liquid. Place in a serving dish, and sprinkle with the sugar, lemon juice, orange juice, and salt. Toss gently, and refrigerate for 1 hour. Drain off the liquid, and fold in the oranges. Arrange in a serving dish, and dust with cinnamon.

Yield: 6 servings

➤ Can be prepared 6 hours ahead.

Salsify

Salsify and scorzonera are members of the same family. Salsify, often called oyster plant, has a long, pale-colored root similar to a turnip. Scorzonera, or black salsify, and sometimes sold as oyster plant, has a brownish-black skin and a long skinny root that looks something like a pencil. Both vegetables are uncommon, and appear rarely in most markets. Check Italian and French markets in the fall. The roots are somewhat delicate and will "bleed" if mishandled, so they are not a popular commercial crop.

Although the oyster flavor is enhanced with cooking, there are people who insist that the flavor suggests coconut or artichokes. Use salsify in the same way you use Jerusalem artichoke.

Availabilty

Fresh
From mid July through early November. They can be wintered over in the ground in some regions, and can appear in the early spring. Look for medium-sized firm clean roots without any sign of softness or shriveling. They do not store well. Keep in a plastic bag, uncleaned, for no more than two days.

Frozen
Salsify loses texture in freezing, and is not sold frozen.

Canned
Canned salsify can be used for salsify purée, but it is too soft for other preparations.

Preparation

Peel like a carrot, and cut into 2 or 3 inch lengths. Salsify, like cardoons and several other vegetables, turns dark when exposed to the air. Put it into a bowl of acidulated water as soon as it is peeled, and use a stainless-steel knife to cut it.

Cooking Methods

The cooking time for salsify or scorzonera depends on the thickness of the root. A large salsify can take as long as 45 minutes to become tender.

Boiling
Boil in a *blanc* until tender, about 10 to 15 minutes.

Steaming
Because the vegetable turns dark, steaming is not recommended.

Microwaving
Cook in a covered container with the water on the roots for 6 to 7 minutes.

Braising
Sauté the drained salsify in butter until coated, add ½ to 1 cup of chicken or beef stock, and simmer until tender. Drain, and reduce the liquid to a glaze. Swirl in 1 tablespoon butter and 1 tablespoon minced parsley.

Quantity

Plan on 2 pounds for 6 persons.

Sauces

Once boiled, salsify can be tossed with flavored butters, sauced with Hollandaise or vinaigrette, or coated with Mornay and made into a gratin. It can also be cooked alla trifolati or alla parmigiana. Serve with sauces that will enhance, not overpower, its delicate flavor.

Salsifis Sautés (Sautéed Salsify)

2 pounds salsify, peeled and
   soaked in acidulated water
3 tablespoons butter

salt and pepper to taste
1 tablespoon minced parsley

In a large skillet, sauté the drained salsify in the butter until golden brown and tender. Season with salt and pepper, and sprinkle with the parsley.

Yield: 6 servings

➤ Cannot be prepared ahead.

Variations:

Provençale Add 1 tablespoon minced garlic with the parsley.

À la Crème Add ½ to ¾ cup heavy cream when tender, and simmer until thick enough to coat the back of a spoon. Sprinkle with parsley.

Salasifis au Menthe Normande
(Minted Salsify Normandy Style)

2 pounds salsify, peeled and cooked *à blanc*	½ cup thinly sliced onions
	1 tablespoon minced mint
¼ cup butter	salt and pepper to taste

In a large skillet, sauté the salsify in the butter until browned on all sides. Add the onions, and sauté until soft, but not brown.

Sprinkle with the mint, and correct the seasoning with salt and pepper.

Yield: 6 servings

➤ Can be precooked the day before.

Beignets de Salsifis *(Salsify Fritters)*

2 pounds salsify, peeled and soaked in acidulated water *blanc* (see page 6)	3 tablespoons lemon juice
	1 tablespoon minced parsley
	fritter batter (see page 8)
6 tablespoons olive oil	oil for deep-frying

In a large saucepan, cook the drained salsify in the *blanc* until tender. Drain.

In a bowl, mix the oil, lemon juice, and parsley until emulsified, and add the salsify. Marinate for at least 15 minutes.

Heat the oil to 375°F.

When ready to serve, drain the salsify, dip in the fritter batter, and fry until golden.

Yield: 6 servings

➤ Can be prepared for frying several hours ahead.

Spinach

Spinach is the *bête noire* of many cooks. There is all that grit that seems impossible to remove at times. The stems have to be stripped from each leaf, and finally, you have to cook a mountain of it to feed a few people. The grit is easily removed by sloshing the spinach in a sink of lukewarm water until the grit sinks. With fresh garden spinach, this may require two or three washings, or even more. Store-bought spinach may be clean, but the smart cook always gives it another washing just in case. Stripping the stems from the leaves is idiot work for which there is no quick solution. Relax, take a deep breath, and start. You must strip each leaf, or end up with stems in the spinach. Spinach has a lot of water, so the natural shrinking does mean you have to prepare a lot to feed a few people, but the superb flavor is worth the effort.

Availability

Fresh
Spinach, though best in the spring, is available year round. Try to buy loose spinach so you can pick out the tender young leaves with delicate stems. Look for dark green, flat, or curly leaves with a bouncy texture. Avoid wilted, yellowed, or blackened leaves, and if possible, those with thick, woody stems.

Frozen
Spinach freezes well, but unfortunately most packagers leave on the stems, and the result is too fibrous. If necessary, use it when puréed or finely minced spinach is needed. Otherwise the result will be less palatable.

Canned
Canned spinach is overprocessed, and the flavor is not appealing.

Preparation

Washing
Fill a sink with *lukewarm* water. The lukewarm water relaxes the leaves so the grit is not trapped in the crevices. Slosh the leaves in the

water several times, and lift into a colander, letting the water drain into the sink. Repeat until no more grit is in the sink. Locally grown produce may require numerous washings, but even packaged spinach should be washed to remove any grit that would destroy the final dish.

Stripping the Stems
Fold the sides of each leaf together, exposing the back rib. Grasp the end of the stem, and strip towards the tip of the leaf, removing it and the fibrous strings. There is no shortcut.

Cutting
Grasp a fistful of spinach at a time and place on a cutting board, holding it securely. Cut across into strips. It is not necessary to be precise.

Cooking Methods

Aluminum and cast iron can give a metallic flavor to spinach. Do not use unless the surface is coated.

Boiling
There are two methods of boiling spinach: Heat several quarts of salted water to a full rolling boil, add the spinach, and boil for 2 to 3 minutes, until wilted. Drain, run under cold water, and press out the excess moisture. The second method, and the one I use most often: Place the spinach in a large pot with the water on its leaves, cover, and cook over high heat for 2 to 3 minutes, stirring occasionally, until wilted. Drain, run under cold water, and press out the excess moisture.

Steaming
Place the spinach leaves in a steamer over boiling water, and steam for 4 to 5 minutes, or until wilted. Run under cold water, and squeeze out the excess moisture.

Microwaving
Place ½ pound spinach in a covered container, and cook for 3 minutes. Drain, run under cold water, and squeeze out the excess moisture. If you need more than ½ pound, repeat the process, rather than trying to double the amount, for evenly cooked spinach.

Sautéing
In a skillet, cook drained shredded spinach in butter until wilted. Raise the heat, and cook until the moisture evaporates.

Quantity

Spinach shrinks dramatically. Plan on at least 3 if not 4 pounds for 6 persons.

Sauces

Serve spinach with butter, Hollandaise, or cream sauces.

Use in combination with mushrooms, eggs, and chicken. Sauce raw spinach with vinaigrette.

Cold Cream of Spinach Soup with Prosciutto and Peppered Croutons

1½ tablespoons oil	1 tablespoon lemon juice
½ cup thinly sliced onion	6 slices French bread sautéed
1 pound spinach, stripped	in olive oil
4 cups chicken stock	¾ cup shredded prosciutto
salt and pepper to taste	ham
1 cup heavy cream	

In a large saucepan, sauté the onion in the oil until soft, but not brown. Add the spinach, and cook, stirring, until wilted. Add the stock, salt, and pepper, and simmer for 5 minutes.

In a processor, purée the soup, and transfer to a bowl. Stir in the cream and lemon juice, and chill. Correct seasoning with lemon juice, salt, and pepper.

Serve with sautéed bread and prosciutto.

Yield: 6 servings

➤ Can be prepared the day before, or frozen.

Spinacci alla Piemontese (Spinach Piedmont Style)

3 pounds spinach, stripped	6 anchovy fillets, minced
and boiled	1 clove garlic, minced
½ cup butter	1 cup croûtons, sautéed in
salt and pepper to taste	olive oil

Drain the spinach, squeeze out the excess moisture, and chop coarsely. In a skillet, heat the butter until it begins to brown.

Add the spinach, salt, pepper, anchovies, and garlic. Cook, stirring, over low heat until hot.

Serve garnished with croûtons.

Yield: 6 servings

➤ The spinach can be prepared for the final cooking several hours ahead.

Variations:

Spinacci alla Milanese (Spinach Milan Style) Add ⅓ cup toasted pine nuts, and omit the croûtons.

Add ⅓ cup raisins with the pine nuts, and omit the croûtons.

Shaker Style Add ¼ cup minced scallions, ½ teaspoon dried rosemary, and 1 tablespoon minced parsley.

Add ½ cup chopped toasted pecans, ¼ cup orange juice, and 1 orange cut into sections with membranes removed.

Spinach and Pears

This is an adaptation of a Michel Guérard dietetic recipe for creamed
spinach.

3 pounds spinach, stripped,   2 teaspoons lemon juice
   boiled, and drained   salt and pepper to taste
2 ripe pears, peeled and seeded   ½ cup heavy cream (optional)

Squeeze the moisture from the spinach, and put into a processor
with the pear. Purée, adding the lemon juice, salt, and pepper. If you
are not watching your diet, add the cream. Return to the saucepan,
and reheat.

Yield: 6 servings

➤ Can be prepared ahead and reheated.

NOTE: The flavor is extraordinary, and particularly good with
poached or broiled salmon.

Spinach with Madeira

3 pounds spinach, stripped   ⅓ cup Madeira
   and boiled   ¼ cup heavy cream
1 cup chopped mushrooms   1 teaspoon salt
¼ cup butter   ¼ teaspoon nutmeg
1 tablespoon flour   ⅓ cup crumbled crisp bacon

Drain the spinach, run under cold water, and press out the moisture.
Chop coarsely.

In a skillet, sauté the mushrooms in the butter until the moisture
evaporates. Sprinkle with flour, and cook, stirring, for 1 minute. Stir in
the Madeira and cream, and cook until lightly thickened. Correct the
seasoning with salt and nutmeg.

Place in a serving dish, and sprinkle with the bacon.

Yield: 6 servings

➤ Can be prepared ahead and reheated.

Spanakorizo (*Spinach and Rice*)

This Greek dish is a buffet favorite.

1 cup minced onion	3 cups chicken stock, or water
¼ cup olive oil	1½ cups rice
1 teaspoon tomato paste	½ cup minced mint
1 pound spinach, stripped and chopped	salt and pepper to taste

In a saucepan, sauté the onion in the olive oil until soft but not brown. Stir in the tomato paste and spinach, and cook, stirring, until the spinach is wilted. Add the chicken stock, and and bring to a boil. Stir in the rice, mint, salt, and pepper, and simmer, covered, until the rice is cooked—about 18 minutes.

Yield: 6 servings

➤ Can be prepared a half hour before serving.

Gnocchi Verdi-Strozzapretti-Rabaton
(*Green Gnocchi, Choke a Priest, Spinach and Cheese Sausages*)

These are just a few of the names assigned to this wonderful recipe. Although a specialty of Florence, these are found in many areas of Italy.

1 pound spinach, stripped	1½ cups grated Parmesan cheese
½ cup boiling salted water	
1¼ cups ricotta cheese, drained	salt and pepper to taste
	1 cup flour
2 eggs	¼ cup butter, melted

In a saucepan, cook the spinach in the boiling salted water until wilted. Drain, run under cold water, and press out the excess moisture. Chop finely, but do not purée, and press out the remaining moisture.

In a bowl, mix the spinach, ricotta, eggs, and ½ cup grated cheese. Season with salt and pepper. If the gnocchi is soft, chill for an hour before proceeding.

Flour your hands, and shape the mixture into small sausages, balls, or eggs, and set on a lightly floured baking sheet.

When ready to cook, bring a large pot of salted water to a simmer, and poach the gnocchi until they rise to the surface. With a slotted spoon, remove the gnocchi and drain on a towel.

Preheat the oven to 400°F.

Brush a gratin pan with butter, and arrange the gnocchi in one layer. Sprinkle with the remaining butter and Parmesan. Bake until heated and the cheese has just melted—about 5 minutes.

Yield: 6 servings

➤ Can be prepared for baking the day before.

Raviolle aux Herbes
(Gnocchi with Spinach and Beet Greens)

This specialty of Savoy is more a gnocchi than a ravioli, but whatever
you call it, it is different and delicious.

1 pound spinach, stripped and minced	2 eggs
1 pound beet leaves, stripped and minced	salt and pepper to taste
	1 tablespoon butter
1 tomato, peeled, seeded, and minced	1 cup milk
	½ cup heavy cream
¼ cup flour	¼ pound Gruyère, grated

Preheat the oven to 375°F.

Chop both greens very finely without puréeing them. In a bowl, mix
the greens with the tomatoes, flour, and eggs, and correct the seasoning with salt and pepper. With floured hands, shape the mixture into
small sausages.

In a large pan of simmering salted water, poach the gnocchi until
they rise to the surface—about 10 minutes. Drain well.

Butter a gratin pan, and place the gnocchi in the pan. In a bowl, mix
the milk and cream, pour over the gnocchi, and sprinkle with the
cheese. Bake for 20 minutes, or until golden.

Yield: 6 servings

➤ Can be prepared for baking several hours ahead.

Épinards et Champignons Gratinés
(Spinach and Mushroom Gratin)

4 pounds spinach, stripped and wilted	½ pound mushrooms, thinly sliced
½ cup butter	2½ cups grated Gruyère cheese
salt and pepper to taste	

Preheat the oven to 425°F.

Drain the spinach, run under cold water, and press out the excess
moisture. In a skillet, sauté the spinach in ¼ cup butter until the moisture evaporates. Season with salt and pepper, remove, and set aside. In
the same skillet, sauté the mushrooms in ¼ cup butter until the liquid
evaporates, and season with salt and pepper.

Stir in the spinach and 1¼ cups of grated cheese. Place in a gratin,
and sprinkle with the remaining cheese. Bake until browned—about
15 minutes.

Yield: 6 servings

➤ Can be prepared for baking the day before.

Variation:

Substitute 2 pounds of lettuce for 2 pounds of spinach, omit the

Gruyère, and cover the top of the gratin with ½ cup Mornay sauce made with Parmesan cheese.

Sformata di Spinaci (Spinach Mold)

5 tablespoons butter	3 tablespoons flour
2 tablespoons dry bread crumbs	1 cup milk
3 tablespoon minced onion	3 eggs, separated
1 10 ounce package frozen spinach, thawed	¼ cup grated Parmesan cheese
	salt and pepper to taste

Preheat the oven to 325°F. Butter a 1 quart mold, and dust with the bread crumbs. Set aside.

In a small skillet, sauté the onion in 2 tablespoons of butter until soft, but not brown.

Squeeze the spinach dry, and mince. Add the spinach to the onion, and cook, stirring, until the moisture evaporates.

In a saucepan, melt the remaining 2 tablespoons of butter, and stir in the flour. Cook, stirring, for 2 minutes, add the milk, and cook, stirring, until the sauce comes to a boil and thickens. Remove from the heat, and beat in the egg yolks, one at a time. Stir in the spinach mixture and the grated cheese. Correct the seasoning with salt and pepper.

Beat the egg whites until stiff but not dry, and fold into the spinach mixture. Turn into the prepared mold, and cover with foil. Place the mold into a baking pan filled with 1 inch of hot water, and bake for about 1 hour, or until the top is firm to the touch. Run a knife around the edge, and unmold onto a serving platter.

Yield: 6 servings

➤ Can be prepared for baking an hour ahead.

Timables aux Épinards (Spinach Custards)

2 pounds spinach, stripped and wilted	½ clove crushed garlic
3 eggs	½ teaspoon nutmeg
1 egg yolk	salt and pepper to taste
¼ cup grated onions	2 cups milk
	¼ cup grated Parmesan cheese

Preheat the oven to 350°F. Oil 6 timbales or custard cups. Drain the spinach, and press out the excess moisture. Mince finely. In a bowl, mix the spinach, eggs, egg yolk, onion, garlic, nutmeg, salt, and pepper. Stir in the milk and Parmesan cheese.

Fill the timbales, and place in a baking pan with 1 inch of hot water. Bake for 35 minutes, or until a knife inserted into the center comes out clean. Let stand 2 minutes, run a knife around the edge, and unmold.

Yield: 6 servings

➤ Can be prepared for baking several hours ahead.

Spinach Salad

There are many versions of spinach salads, but they are really no different from any other green salad. Wash the leaves well in lukewarm water, drain, wrap in paper toweling, and crisp in the refrigerator for an hour. When ready to serve, toss the spinach with vinaigrette and serve. Garnish the salad with croutons, sliced mushrooms, sliced onions, radishes, grated carrots, bean sprouts, or any other favorite salad ingredient. Or, choose another dressing, but remember the dressing should enhance, not overwhelm, the other ingredients.

Spinach Salad with Creamy Dressing

½ cup mayonnaise
⅓ cup buttermilk
1 teaspoon bacon drippings
1 teaspoon white-wine vinegar
1 garlic clove, minced
salt and pepper to taste
6 cups spinach, stemmed

½ red onion, thinly sliced
½ pound mushrooms, thinly
  sliced
¼ pound crisp bacon,
  crumbled
1 cup croûtons

In a small bowl, mix the mayonnaise, buttermilk, bacon drippings, wine vinegar, garlic cloves, salt, and pepper. Chill.

In a large bowl, mix the spinach, onions, mushrooms, dressing, bacon, and croûtons. Toss gently.

Yield: 6 servings

Wilted Spinach and Egg Salad

Wilted salads are a favorite of middle-European countries. They are a pleasant change.

1½ pounds cleaned spinach,
  torn into bite-sized pieces
3 hard cooked eggs, finely
  diced
2 tablespoons diced onion
2 tablespoons olive oil
1 tablespoon red or white
  wine vinegar

1 tablespoon chicken stock
1 teaspoon salt
½ teaspoon pepper
pinch of curry powder
6 slices bacon, fried until crisp
  and crumbled

In a salad bowl, mix the spinach, eggs, and onion. In a saucepan, heat the oil, vinegar, chicken stock, salt, pepper, and curry to a simmer.

Just before serving, pour the hot dressing over the salad, and toss. Add the bacon, and toss again.

Yield: 6 servings

➤ Cannot be prepared in advance.

Squash

As with so many other vegetables, the many varieties of squash can be treated in the same manner. The principal varieties are summer and winter, with their various children. Summer squashes—yellow, crookneck, straight, pattypan, and zucchini—are best when picked small. They should not be any longer than 8 inches, or in the case of pattypan, 4 inches in diameter. These squashes become watery and flavorless as they mature. No friendly gardener is a friend when he gives you one of those giant zucchini. Toss it in the compost heap, or cut out the center and use it as a flower container. Winter squashes, on the other hand, must be mature before they are picked. They should be left on the vine long enough for the skin to harden and for the weather to have cooled at night to bring out the sugar. Their size has nothing to do with the final product. Huge squash are as good as babies.

Availabilty

Fresh
One variety or another of both summer and winter squashes is always in the market. The prime season for summer squashes is from May to September, and winter squashes are prime from late September through January, depending on where they are harvested. Winter squashes store well and are available almost year round, and summer squashes are shipped from other regions.

Summer, Yellow, Straight, or Crookneck Select small, no longer than 8 inches, for the best flavor and tenderness, with a pale-yellow color and a firm, smooth, or slightly pebbled shiny skin. Avoid those larger than 8 inches with bright yellow or heavily pebbled skins. Also avoid soft, flabby squashes with blemished skin or wrinkled ends.

Pattypan, Cymlings Look for flat, scalloped squash that are less than 4 inches in diameter, with white, pale-green, or yellow-green skins with a smooth shiny surface that feel heavy for their size. Avoid light-feeling, larger squash with dull, shriveled, or damaged skin.

Zucchini Select small to medium zucchini—no longer than 8 inches—with smooth, plump, shiny, dark-green skins. Avoid large, dull, or yellowish skinned squash, and those with blemishes, soft flesh, or wrinkled ends.

Winter Squashes

Acorn Select dark, dull-green acorn squash, with only a touch of orange, that feel heavy for their size. Avoid shiny-skinned squashes that are more than half orange, as well as those that feel light, are cracked, or have soft spots.

Butternut Look for squashes with smooth, tan skins, about 10 to 11 inches long, that feel heavy for their size. Avoid those with green-tinted skins, or that feel light for their size or have soft spots.

Chayote, Mirilton, Christophene, or Vegetable Pear Look for lime-green color and firm flesh, and avoid those that are pale, or have soft or spongy flesh.

Hubbard, Turban This is a large group of squashes that comes in many colors. The skin can be dark green, bluish gray, or bright orange. They can have tapered ends or be rounded, but the skin should be hard and have a bumpy surface with even color. They should be heavy for their size. Avoid those that are light for their size, or have cracked or spotted skins.

Spaghetti Select oval, creamy-white or pale-yellow squashes with a hard skin, and that feel heavy for their size. Avoid lightweight squashes, and those with cracks or soft spots.

Storage

Store summer squashes, unwrapped, for no more than 4 days in the refrigerator.

Chayote should be stored like summer squash, but it will keep for two to three months.

Store winter squashes in a cool, dark, dry, well-ventilated area for one to two months. Do not refrigerate.

Frozen

Summer squash loses texture when frozen, and should only be frozen after it is cooked.

Winter squash, once puréed, freezes very well, and can be used in most preparations for puréed squash.

Canned

Summer squashes is not sold in cans.

Canned winter squash is suitable when puréed squash is required.

Preparation

Summer squash is usually served unpeeled. Some cooks use the back of a knife to scrape the small fibers from the skin of zucchini and others prefer to peel it, but the skin, if the squash is young, is edible. Pattypans are often hollowed and stuffed.

Chop, dice, slice, mince, or grate for the various recipes. Peel winter squashes, with the exception of Acorn squash, which is usually eaten from the shell. Cut off both ends. Cut the squash in half lengthwise or into sections, and use a sharp paring knife to peel off the skin. With hard-skinned squashes, this can take some effort. Many cooks prefer to peel the squash after it is cooked.

Cook whole, halved, cut into chunks, or puréed.

Summer squashes have a high water content, and some recipes call for salting and draining to remove the excess water. Rinse the salted squash under cold running water, and press out the excess moisture (do not wring it out, just press out the excess). Or, run the whole squash under cold water and store until ready to use. You can avoid this step, but the texture will be much better if you make the effort. Refrigerate the squash for several hours until ready to cook.

Cooking Methods

Boiling
Boiling is the least satisfactory method of cooking squashes (with the exception of spaghetti squash), because it drains off much of the subtle flavor.

Steaming
Steam both summer and winter squashes. It will take as little as 6 to 8 minutes for cut-up summer squashes to as long as an hour for a whole spaghetti squash. Steam the squash with or without its skin.

Microwaving
Cook 1 pound of summer squash in a covered dish with 2 to 3 tablespoons of water, and cook for 4 to 6 minutes. Place winter squashes, except for spaghetti squash, cut up on a plate, and cover. Cook from 8 to 15 minutes until tender, checking often. Cook whole spaghetti squash uncovered for about 15 minutes. A knife should pierce the shell easily.

Sautéing
One of the best methods of cooking summer squashes is to sauté them with a little butter or oil alone, and possibly a favorite herb.

Quantity

Plan on 1½ to 2 pounds of summer squash for 6 persons. The water content makes it easy to consume a little extra and not notice.

Winter squash can have a lot of waste. Plan on 2½ to 3 pounds of winter squash for 6 persons. If the squash is cut up, peeled, and seeded, 1½ pounds should provide for 6.

Sauces

Serve squash with simple sauces such as herbed butters, fresh tomato sauce, or in combination with other summer vegetables. Alla trifolati, or alla parmigiana bring out the flavors delightfully. Combine winter squashes with other winter vegetables, such as sweet potatoes and rutabagas, or toss with walnuts, almonds, or pecans. Serve in casseroles with Mornay or Béchamel sauce.

Recipes for pumpkin and winter squashes are interchangeable.

Zucchini in Agrodolce (Sweet and Sour Zucchini)

1 garlic clove, crushed	2½ tablespoons wine vinegar
2½ tablespoons olive oil	3 tablespoons pine nuts
2 pounds zucchini or summer squash, cut in batons	3 tablespoons yellow raisins
	4 anchovy fillets, minced

In a skillet, sauté the garlic in the oil until golden, and discard. Add the zucchini, cover, and cook for 5 minutes. Add the vinegar and 2½ tablespoons of water, and simmer 10 minutes.

Stir in the pine nuts, raisins, and anchovies, and stir gently. Simmer 2 minutes.

Serve at room temperature.

Yield: 6 servings

➤ Can be prepared ahead.

Courgettes Râpées (Grated Zucchini)

The way a vegetable is cut can affect the flavor. Serve this grated zucchini in the middle of zucchini season for a change of texture and flavor.

2½ pounds zucchini, grated	2 tablespoons minced shallot
salt and pepper to taste	2 to 3 tablespoons butter

In a colander, toss the zucchini with 1 teaspoon of salt per pound, and let drain for 30 minutes. Rinse under cold water to remove the excess salt, and gently squeeze out the excess moisture.

In a skillet, sauté the shallots in the butter until soft, but not brown.

Raise the heat, and sauté the zucchini until tender-crisp—about 5 more minutes. Correct the seasoning with salt and pepper.

Yield: 6 servings

➤ Can be prepared for the final cooking several hours in advance.

Variations:

Use grated summer squash in place of, or along with, the zucchini. Add julienned red pepper for color.

Add 2 pounds stripped, shredded spinach with the zucchini.

Add 1 clove crushed garlic with the shallot.

Add ½ cup heavy cream after 4 minutes of cooking.

Add 1 tablespoon curry powder with the cream.

Add 1 cup peeled, seeded, and chopped tomatoes to the shallots, and cook until the liquid evaporates.

Add ½ pound sliced mushrooms to the shallots, and cook until the liquid evaporates.

Zucchini in Red Wine

2 pounds small zucchini, ½ inch slices
½ cup minced onion
¼ cup olive oil
3 tablespoons butter

⅔ cup red wine
salt and pepper to taste
lemon juice to taste
minced parsley for garnish

In a skillet, sauté the zucchini and onion in the olive oil and butter for 5 minutes, stirring frequently. Add the wine, season with salt and pepper, and simmer 5 minutes, or until most of the liquid evaporates. Season with lemon juice and more oil, if desired.

Serve hot or cold, garnished with the parsley.

Yield: 6 servings

➤ Can be prepared ahead.

Courgettes à la Pierrette (Zucchini with Cointreau)

1½ pounds small zucchini, peeled and thinly sliced
3 tablespoons Cointreau, or other orange-flavored liqueur

¼ cup flour
¼ cup clarified butter
2 tablespoons minced tarragon

Sprinkle the zucchini with the Cointreau and then with the flour.

In a skillet, sauté the floured zucchini in the butter until golden and tender. Sprinkle with the tarragon.

Serve hot or cold.

Yield: 6 servings

➤ Can be prepared ahead.

Pattypan Squash with Tomatoes

1 garlic clove, minced
2 shallots, minced
2 tablespoons butter
6 small pattypan squashes, quartered and sliced

1 cup peeled, seeded, and chopped tomatoes
salt and pepper to taste

In a skillet, sauté the garlic and shallots in the butter until soft, but not brown. Add the squash slices, and sauté until they soften—about 3 minutes. Add the tomatoes, and stir to coat. Cook until heated, and correct the seasoning with salt and pepper.

Yield: 6 servings

➤ Can be cooked ahead, but best if prepared just before serving.

Zucchini all 'Aglio e Pomodoro
(Zucchini with Garlic and Tomatoes)

½ medium onion, sliced
⅔ cup olive oil
1 large garlic clove, crushed
⅔ cup drained canned tomatoes, chopped

2 tablespoons minced parsley
2 pounds zucchini or summer squash, thickly sliced
¼ cup shredded basil
salt and pepper to taste

Preheat the oven to 350°F.

In an ovenproof skillet, sauté the onion in the oil until soft, but not brown. Add the garlic, and sauté until it colors lightly. Stir in the tomatoes and parsley, and simmer for 15 minutes.

Add the zucchini, basil, salt, and pepper, and cook until tender—about 20 minutes.

Place the skillet in the oven, and bake for 5 minutes, or until the zucchini liquid evaporates.

Yield: 6 servings

➤ Can be prepared ahead and reheated.

Summer Squash, Corn, and Tomatoes

This is a type of succotash without the usual beans, but you can add 1 cup of lima beans if desired.

1 pound summer squash, ½ inch dice
2 tablespoons butter
salt and pepper to taste
1 bunch scallions, ½ inch lengths

kernels from 3 ears of corn
3 tomatoes, peeled, 1 inch cubes
1 tablespoon minced parsley

In a skillet, sauté the squash in the butter for 2 minutes. Season with salt and pepper. Add the scallions, cover, and cook for 1 minute. Add the corn and tomatoes, cover, and cook 5 minutes, stirring occasionally. Correct the seasoning with salt and pepper. Serve sprinkled with parsley.

Yield: 6 servings

➤ Can be prepared ahead and reheated, but best if served immediately.

Courgettes à l'Endaye
(Zucchini with Apples and Tomatoes)

2 pounds zucchini, sliced	2 cups tomatoes, peeled,
½ cup butter	seeded, and chopped
2 cups chopped onions	salt and pepper
2 apples, peeled, cored, and	minced parsley
cubed	

In a large saucepan of boiling salted water, blanch the zucchini for 30 seconds, drain, and set aside.

In a skillet, melt ¼ cup butter, and cook the onions, stirring, for 1 minute. Add the apples, and stir until coated with the butter. Add the tomatoes, and stir to combine.

In a skillet, melt the remaining ¼ cup of butter, and sauté the zucchini for 2 minutes, until well coated. Season with salt and pepper.

Stir in the apple mixture with the parsley, and simmer 10 minutes, or until the zucchini is tender and the flavors have amalgamated. Correct the seasoning with salt and pepper.

Yield: 6 servings

➤ Can be prepared ahead and reheated.

Orzo with Zucchini and Mint

Serve this simple, delicious dish as a hot vegetable, or cold as a salad.

¾ cup orzo	2 tablespoons minced mint
2 to 6 ounces zucchini,	2 tablespoons olive oil
coarsely chopped	salt and pepper to taste

In 1 quart of boiling salted water, cook the orzo until just tender—about 8 to 10 minutes. Add the zucchini, and cook until barely tender—about 1 minute. Drain and transfer to a bowl. Mix in the mint, olive oil, and salt and pepper.

Serve hot or at room temperature.

Yield: 6 servings

➤ Can be prepared several hours ahead and served at room temperature.

NOTE: Orzo is a rice-shaped pasta, but any tiny pasta is suitable. If the orzo must wait, taste before serving, and correct the seasoning with mint, olive oil, salt, and pepper.

Zucchini alla Farfalle
(Summer Squash with Butterfly-Shaped Pasta)

⅓ cup olive oil
1½ pounds zucchini or summer
   squash, cut into batons
1 cup minced onion
1 garlic clove, minced
⅔ cup heavy cream

1 pound farfalle, cooked al
   dente
½ cup grated Parmesan cheese
salt and pepper to taste
grated Parmesan cheese

In a large skillet, heat the oil, and sauté the zucchini in batches until golden. Transfer to a bowl with a slotted spoon. Add the onion, and sauté until golden. Add the garlic, and cook until it starts to color. Add the cream, and reduce by half. Stir in the cooked farfalle, zucchini, and ½ cup Parmesan. Season with salt and pepper, toss to coat evenly, and heat.

Serve with additional cheese on the side.

Yield: 6 servings

➤ Cannot be prepared ahead.

Fusilli alla Pappone
(Fusilli with Zucchini and Basil Sauce)

1 pound zucchini, cut into ¼
   inch thick batons
½ cup olive oil
6 tablespoons butter
1 teaspoon flour, dissolved in
   ⅓ cup milk

salt and pepper to taste
¼ cup shredded basil
1 egg yolk
½ cup grated cheese
1 pound fusilli

In a skillet, sauté the zucchini, in batches, in the oil until golden. Drain and set aside.

In a saucepan, melt 3 tablespoons of butter, stir in the milk and flour, and cook until thickened and smooth. Stir in the zucchini, and season with salt, pepper, and basil. Remove from the heat, and stir in the remaining 3 tablespoons of butter, the egg yolk, and the cheese.

Cook the fusilli in boiling salted water until tender, and drain. Pour the salve over the pasta and serve.

Yield: 6 servings

➤ The sauce can be prepared 1 or 2 hours ahead.

Kolokithopeta *(Baked Zucchini)*

2 pounds zucchini, scraped	¾ cup olive oil
1 cup sliced onion	1 cup water
1 cup minced parsley	1 tablespoon flour
salt and pepper to taste	paprika (optional)

Preheat the oven to 350°F.

Slice the zucchini lengthwise, ¼ inch thick. In a baking dish, arrange the zucchini and onion in alternate layers. Sprinkle with parsley, salt, and pepper to taste. Pour on the olive oil and water, and sprinkle with flour. Bake for about 40 minutes, or until tender. Sprinkle with paprika just before serving.

Serve hot or cold.

Yield: 6 servings

➤ Can be prepared ahead.

Courgettes aux Amandes *(Zucchini Nut Casserole)*

2 pounds zucchini, sliced and steamed until tender	salt and pepper to taste
	½ cup chopped almonds, pecans, or walnuts
3 slices white bread	¼ cup bread crumbs
½ cup milk	butter
1 egg	

Preheat the oven to 350°F. Butter a 1 quart casserole.

Drain the zucchini, and chop coarsely. In a bowl, soak the bread in the milk for 5 minutes, and mash. Mix in the zucchini, eggs, salt, pepper, and almonds. Turn into the casserole, and sprinkle with the bread crumbs. Dot with the butter. Bake for 30 minutes, or until the top is browned.

Yield: 6 servings

➤ Can be prepared for baking the day before.

Zucchini and Tomato Gratin

2 pounds small zucchini	1 tablespoon olive oil
2 tomatoes, peeled and thinly sliced	salt and pepper to taste
	1 tablespoon grated Parmesan cheese
¼ cup minced onion	
2 tablespoons minced parsley	

Preheat the oven to 325°F. Butter a 1½ quart gratin.

In a large saucepan, parboil the zucchini until tender-crisp. Cut into ¼ inch slices, and place in overlapping slices in the gratin. Top with overlapping slices of tomato, and sprinkle with the onion, parsley, olive oil, salt, pepper, and Parmesan.

Bake for 10 to 15 minutes, or until heated and the top starts to brown.

Yield: 6 servings

➤ Can be prepared for the final baking the day before.

Tortino Tricolore (Three-Colored Gratin)

This recipe, like so many other Italian recipes, is in the color of the Italian flag.

2 pounds zucchini, thinly sliced	¾ pound tomatoes, peeled, and thinly sliced
2½ tablespoons butter	oregano to taste
1 tablespoon olive oil	salt and pepper to taste
½ pound mozzarella, thinly sliced	3 tablespoons grated bread crumbs
2 ounces sliced Parmesan cheese	2 ounces grated Parmesan cheese

Preheat the oven to 375°F.

In a skillet, sauté the zucchini in 1 tablespoon of butter and the olive oil until tender—about 15 minutes.

Butter a gratin dish, put half the zucchini in the bottom, and cover with half the mozzarella and Parmesan slices. Layer the tomatoes on top, and season with salt, pepper, and oregano. Cover with the remaining mozzarella, Parmesan, and zucchini slices.

In a bowl, mix the grated bread crumbs and Parmesan. Sprinkle on top, and dot with remaining butter. Bake until bubbling hot and golden—about 20 minutes.

Yield: 6 servings

➤ Can be prepared for baking the day before.

Timballo di Zucchini alla Pizzaiola
(Baked Zucchini with Mozzarella)

This recipe uses almost the same ingredients as the previous one, but results in a different flavor.

3 pounds zucchini, thinly sliced	¾ pound tomatoes, peeled and chopped
salt	¼ cup minced basil
½ cup olive oil, or more if needed	½ pound mozzarella cheese, sliced
4 teaspoons tomato paste	4 anchovy fillets, halved lengthwise
½ cup minced onion	pepper

Preheat the oven to 375°F.

Sprinkle the zucchini with the salt, and let drain for 1 hour. Wipe dry.

In a skillet, sauté the zucchini in the oil until golden, and drain on paper toweling. In a small bowl, dilute the tomato paste with 2 table-spoons of warm water.

In a small skillet, heat 2½ tablespoons of oil (from cooking the zuc-chini if any is left), and sauté the onion until soft, but not brown. Stir in the tomato paste, tomatoes, and basil, and boil for 10 minutes, or until thickened, slightly.

Brush a gratin with some olive oil, and add the zucchini slices. Spread the tomato sauce over the top, and cover with the sliced cheese. Arrange the anchovies in a pattern, and season with pepper. Bake for 30 minutes, or until the cheese melts and begins to brown.

Yield: 6 servings

➤ Can be prepared ahead and reheated.

Gratin of Zucchini à la Bordelaise

3 tablespoons butter	1 egg yolk
¼ cup bread crumbs	½ cup grated Parmesan cheese
2 pounds zucchini, cut into ½ inch slices	¼ teaspoon pepper
	1 tablespoon olive oil
salt and pepper to taste	2 tablespoons minced parsley
1 cup light cream	2 garlic cloves, minced
3 eggs	1 tablespoon minced shallot

Preheat the oven to 350°F. Using 1 tablespoon, butter a 2 quart oval gratin dish, and sprinkle with 2 tablespoons bread crumbs.

Place zucchini in a colander, sprinkle with salt, and let drain 30 minutes. Dry on paper toweling.

In a skillet, melt 2 tablespoons butter, and sauté zucchini in batches until lightly browned. Drain on paper toweling.

In a bowl, mix the cream, eggs, egg yolk, ¼ cup Parmesan, salt, and pepper. Add the zucchini, and mix well. Add the zucchini mixture and bake for 14 to 18 minutes, or until almost set.

In a dry skillet, heat the remaining 2 tablespoons bread crumbs, parsley, garlic, and shallot until fragrant—about 1 minute. Sprinkle over the top of the gratin, and bake for 5 minutes longer. Sprinkle the remaining ¼ cup Parmesan over the top and broil until nicely browned—about a minute.

Yield: 6 servings

➤ Can be prepared for baking the day before.

Stuffed Zucchini

There are two methods of stuffing zucchini or yellow squash: Select squash that are at least 1½ inches in diameter, and cut off both ends. Using a special zucchini corer, or an apple corer, make a hollow tube.

Or, cut the squash in half lengthwise, and scoop out the center to make boats. Pattypan squash are hollowed by cutting a slice off the stem end and scooping out the center.

Zucchini Ripiene (Stuffed Zucchini)

This recipe is a specialty of Liguria.

½ ounce dried mushrooms
12 small zucchini
salt and pepper to taste
1 slice white bread, soaked in
   ¼ cup milk

2 eggs, beaten
1 teaspoon oregano
½ tablespoon grated Parmesan
   cheese
½ cup olive oil

Preheat the oven to 375°F.

Soak the mushrooms in warm water for 30 minutes, squeeze dry, and chop. Cook the zucchini in boiling salted water for 10 minutes, and drain.

Using a zucchini or apple corer, scoop out the flesh through the stem end to make a hollow tube. Reserve, and mince the pulp from the zucchini.

Squeeze the bread dry, and put into a bowl with the zucchini pulp, mushrooms, eggs, salt and pepper, oregano, and Parmesan cheese. Mix well. Stuff the zucchini shells with the mixture.

In a large skillet or flame-proof gratin, sauté the zucchini in the oil until browned. Lower the heat, cover, and cook 20 minutes longer, or until tender. Or, bake for about 30 minutes.

Yield: 6 servings

➤ Can be prepared ahead and reheated, or served at room temperature.

Zucchini Boats with Herbed Stuffing

6 larger zucchini
2 tablespoon olive oil
1½ cups chopped onions
1 tablespoon chopped garlic
½ cup minced scallions
4 cups bread cubes
1 cup milk
½ cup minced marjoram,
   savory, thyme, tarragon, or
   basil

½ cup grated Parmesan cheese
Cayenne pepper to taste
2 eggs
salt and pepper to taste
olive oil (optional)
herb sprigs (optional)
red wine vinegar (optional)

Preheat the oven to 375°F.

Trim the ends from the zucchini, and cut in half lengthwise. Scoop our seeds and some of the flesh to make shells. Chop the pulp coarsely.

In a skillet, heat 2 tablespoons of oil, and sauté the onions until golden. Add the garlic, scallions, and reserved flesh, and sauté, stirring occasionally, until soft. Set aside.

Add the bread to the milk, and mix until most of the milk has been absorbed. Beat the mixture to make a paste, and stir in the herbs, Parmesan, Cayenne, eggs, ½ teaspoon salt, and pepper. Add the sautéed zucchini mixture.

Arrange the hollowed zucchini in a roasting pan, and season with salt. Mound the stuffing in the zucchini. Bake for 30 minutes, and brown under the broiler, if needed.

Serve hot, sprinkled with additional olive oil and herbs. For a tangier taste, sprinkle with vinegar.

Yield: 6 servings

➤ Can be prepared ahead and reheated.

Zucchini e Pepperoni (Zucchini Stuffed with Peppers)

6 small zucchini	1 clove garlic, crushed
salt to taste	2 or 3 sprigs basil
olive oil	6 anchovy fillets
2 yellow peppers, peeled and cut into julienne	12 slices Cacciocavallo cheese
5 large ripe tomatoes, peeled, seeded, and chopped	

Preheat the oven to 350°F.

Trim ends of zucchini, cut in half lengthwise, and scoop out some of the pulp and discard. Blanch the halves in boiling salted water for 2 minutes. Drain.

Brush a baking dish with olive oil, and arrange the halves in it. Cut the peppers in long, thin strips.

In a saucepan, heat 1 tablespoon of oil, and sauté the garlic, basil, and tomatoes seasoned with salt over high heat for 20 minutes. Cut the anchovy fillets in half lengthwise.

Put a spoonful of tomato mixture in each zucchini half, and add a few strips of pepper, a slice of cheese, and a piece of anchovy. Sprinkle with olive oil, and bake for 15 minutes or until the cheese is melted and the zucchini are slightly browned. Serve at room temperature.

Yield: 6 servings

➤ Can be prepared ahead.

Courgettes Farcis (Stuffed Zucchini)

6 medium zucchini, cut in half lengthwise	¼ pound ground pork, or veal
¼ cup olive oil	¾ cup bread crumbs
¾ cup minced onion	1 egg
1 garlic clove, minced	salt and pepper to taste
½ teaspoon hot pepper flakes	¼ cup grated Parmesan cheese
	¼ cup chicken stock

Preheat the oven to 400°F. Lightly oil a baking dish large enough to hold the zucchini in one layer, and set aside.

In a pot of boiling water, simmer the zucchini for 1 minute. Drain, and scoop out the center of each shell. Put the shells in the baking dish, and chop the pulp.

In a skillet, heat 1 tablespoon of oil, and sauté the onion and garlic until soft, but not brown. Stir in the zucchini pulp, hot pepper flakes, pork, and ½ cup of bread crumbs. Cook, stirring, until heated. Stir in the egg, salt, pepper, and 2 tablespoons of grated Parmesan. Mound into the zucchini, and sprinkle with the remaining bread crumbs and Parmesan. Drizzle on the remaining oil.

Pour the chicken stock into the bottom of the dish, and bake for 30 minutes, or until the zucchini are tender.

Yield: 6 servings

➤ Can be prepared ahead and reheated.

Variations:
Add 2 tablespoons minced parsley and 3 tablespoons minced dill to the pork.

Use sausage (casings removed) instead of the pork, and season with 1 teaspoon dried marjoram, ½ teaspoon dried oregano, and ⅛ teaspoon allspice.

Omit the pork, and add 2½ ounces chopped anchovies, 3 ounces pitted chopped Alfonso olives, 2 tablespoons capers, and 2 tablespoons minced parsley.

Barchette di Zucchini Ripiene Al Forno
(Baked Stuffed Zucchini Boats)

6 medium zucchini, cut in half lengthwise	1 cup Bechamél sauce
salt and pepper to taste	1 egg
3 tablespoons butter	¼ cup grated Parmesan cheese
1 tablespoon minced onion	pinch of nutmeg
½ cup minced ham	¼ cup bread crumbs

Preheat the oven to 400°F. Butter a baking dish large enough to hold the zucchini.

With a melon baller, scoop out the inside of the zucchini shells, and chop half the pulp. Discard the remaining pulp. Blanch the zucchini shells in boiling salted water until half cooked—about 5 minutes. Drain, and arrange in the baking dish.

In a skillet, melt 2 tablespoons of butter, and sauté the onion and ham with the reserved zucchini pulp until the pulp is creamy and starts to turn golden. Remove the mixture from the skillet with a slotted spoon, letting the cooking oil drain back into the pan.

Stir the pulp into the Bechamél, and add the egg and Parmesan. Correct the seasoning with nutmeg, salt, and pepper.

Fill the zucchini shells with the ham mixture, and sprinkle with the bread crumbs. Bake for 20 minutes, or until golden and crusty.

Yield: 6 servings

➤ Can be prepared for baking the day before.

Timbale de Courgettes et Épinards
(Zucchini and Spinach Molds)

Prepare as one large mold or as individual servings.

1 pound zucchini, grated	⅓ cup grated Gruyère cheese
salt and pepper to taste	¾ cup medium cream
1 pound spinach, wilted and minced	6 eggs, well beaten
1 cup minced onion	3 tablespoons butter
¼ cup butter	½ cup fresh bread crumbs
⅓ cup grated Parmesan cheese	3 tablespoons minced parsley

Preheat the oven to 375°F.

Line the bottom of a charlotte mold or 6 individual ramekins with buttered waxed paper, and butter the sides.

Sprinkle the zucchini with 1 teaspoon of salt, and drain in a colander for 30 minutes. Squeeze out the excess moisture. Squeeze the excess moisture from the spinach.

In a skillet, sauté the onions in the butter until soft, but not brown. Add the zucchini and spinach, and cook, stirring, until the water evaporates. Correct the seasoning with salt and pepper.

In a large bowl, stir the zucchini mixture, Parmesan, Gruyère, cream, and eggs until well combined. Pour into the prepared molds, place in a baking pan, and add 1 inch of hot water. Bake until a knife inserted halfway between the center and the edge comes out clean—about 40 minutes for the charlotte and 18 minutes for the ramekins. Remove from the water bath, and let stand for 5 minutes. Unmold onto a serving plate.

In a skillet, melt the remaining butter, and sauté the bread crumbs until golden and crisp. Stir in the parsley, and pour over the top of the the timbales.

Yield: 6 servings

➤ Can be prepared for baking several hours ahead.

Winter Squash

Winter squash is not often given its due. It stores well, and for many that makes it a staple that is served as a purée, often sweetened with brown sugar, maple syrup, or molasses, and various spices, until almost a dessert. Acorn squash is usually halved and filled with a sweet stuffing. In fact it deserves better treatment than that. Try using some of the stuffings for zucchini and summer squash in acorn squash for a start. Serve thin sections for a raw vegetable platter. Grate the flesh of butternut squash, and sauté in butter with garlic, similar to grated zucchini, and add to soups and stews as you would potatoes.

Chayotes, christophenes, and mirlitons are different names for the same pear-shaped squash with a corrugated skin. It is popular in the southern United States, particularly Louisiana, and in the Caribbean. It can be served boiled, but more often is used to hold a savory filling. The squash itself tastes more like a summer squash, and has a non-assertive flavor.

Spaghetti squash is an oddity that caught the imaginations of food editors a few years ago. The whole squash is boiled until a knife pierces the center easily. Cut the squash in half and use a fork to pull apart the strands of flesh. The strands have a slightly crisp quality and very little flavor. The only similarity between this and spaghetti is that it is long and stringy. Most pasta sauces overwhelm the squash, and its own earthy taste mixes poorly with most other flavors. Serve it as an oddity tossed with melted butter, minced coriander, and peeled, seeded, and diced fresh tomato. Try it with peanut-flavored sauces used in Asian noodle recipes.

La Courge au Gratin (Gratin of Squash)

4 pounds butternut or hubbard squash, peeled and seeded	2 eggs
¼ pound butter	salt and pepper to taste
¾ cup milk	nutmeg to taste
	½ cup bread crumbs

Preheat the oven to 400°F.

Cook the squash in boiling salted water until just tender—about 20 minutes. Drain the squash in a sieve, and press to remove the excess moisture. Place the squash in a bowl, and break it up with a fork, working in 6 tablespoons of butter and the milk. Beat in an egg and an egg yolk. Season with salt, pepper, and nutmeg.

In a small bowl, beat the egg white until stiff, and fold into the mixture. Sprinkle with the bread crumbs, and dot with the remaining butter. Bake for 10 minutes, or until just set.

Yield: 6 servings

Baked Mashed Stuffed Acorn Squash

3 acorn squash, cut in half and seeds discarded	salt and pepper to taste
6 teaspoons butter	¼ cup light cream
	¼ teaspoon ground nutmeg

Preheat the oven to 400°F.

Put a teaspoon of butter into each acorn half, and season with salt and pepper. Arrange the halves, cut side up, in a shallow baking dish, and add 1 inch of hot water. Bake for 50 minutes, or until the squash are tender.

Pour the butter from the squash into a processor, and holding each squash in a towel or pot holder, scoop the pulp into the processor, without damaging the shells. Purée. With the machine running, add the cream and nutmeg. Correct the seasoning with salt and pepper.

Mound into the shells, lightly. Bake 20 minutes, or until golden brown.

Yield: 6 servings

➤ Can be prepared the day before for the final baking.

Maple Syrup Baked Acorn Squash

3 acorn squash, halved and seeds discarded	3 tablespoons maple syrup
6 tablespoons butter	salt and pepper to taste

Preheat the oven to 375°F.

Arrange the squash in a baking dish, hollow side up. Put 1 tablespoon of butter and 2 teaspoons of maple syrup in each squash. Season with salt and pepper.

Pour 1 inch of boiling water into the baking dish, and bake for 1 hour, or until tender.

Yield: 5 servings

➤ Can be prepared for baking several hours ahead.

Variations:

Fill cavity with a mixture of 1 cup grated carrot, ½ cup grated apple, 2 tablespoons raisins, 2 tablespoons melted butter, and salt and pepper.

Add butter to the cavity, and season with a mixture of 1 teaspoon cinnamon, ¼ teaspoon nutmeg, ¼ teaspoon all spice, and 1 cup brown sugar.

Add a teaspoon of butter to each cavity, and season with salt and pepper. Serve with sour cream, mixed with minced scallions to taste.

Add ¼ cup maple syrup, 1 tablespoon dry bread crumbs, and ½ cup chopped walnuts or pecans.

Shelada del Garas *(Zucchini Salad)*

1½ pounds zucchini, cut into
    1 inch cubes
1 garlic clove, minced
1 teaspoon salt

⅓ cup olive oil
3 tablespoons lemon juice
1 teaspoon paprika
½ teaspoon ground cumin

In a saucepan with water to cover, simmer the zucchini, garlic, and salt until the zucchini is tender—about 10 minutes. Drain, rinse under cold water, and drain again.

In a salad bowl, mix the zucchini with the oil, lemon juice, paprika, and cumin. Chill.

Yield: 6 servings

➤ Can be prepared the day before.

Minted Zucchini and Corn Salad

3 tablespoons olive oil
2 pounds zucchini, batons
1 onion, minced
1 garlic clove, minced
2 tablespoons wine vinegar

1 teaspoon oregano
3 tablespoons minced mint
¾ cup corn kernels
salt and pepper
mint sprigs for garnish

In a skillet, heat 1 tablespoon of olive oil, and sauté ⅓ of the zucchini until lightly browned. Transfer to a bowl, and continue with the remaining zucchini and oil. Add the onion, and sauté until soft, but not brown. Stir in the garlic, and cook until soft. Stir in the vinegar and oregano, and cook for 2 minutes.

Pour the hot vinegar over the zucchini, and stir in the mint. Cool. Cook the corn, if necessary, and add to the zucchini.

Correct the seasoning with salt, pepper, and vinegar.

Serve garnished with mint sprigs.

Yield: 6 servings

➤ Can be prepared the day before.

NOTE: Use fresh, frozen, or canned corn.

Zucchini Mousse

1 pound zucchini, thinly sliced
1 cup thinly sliced onion
¼ cup butter
½ teaspoon salt
1½ teaspoons curry powder
pinch of cayenne pepper

2 envelopes unflavored gelatin
½ cup cold chicken stock
2 cups chicken stock
1 cup heavy cream, whipped
3 tablespoons minced scallions

Oil a 1½ quart mold. Set aside 12 slices of zucchini for a garnish. In a skillet, sauté the zucchini and onion in the butter until soft. Stir in the curry powder and Cayenne, and cook 1 minute longer. Drain. Coarsely chop 1 cup of the mixture, and set aside.

In a blender, purée the remaining with 2 cups chicken stock.

In a small saucepan, soften the gelatin in the ½ cup cold chicken stock, and heat over low heat until dissolved. Stir into the zucchini mixture, and chill until cold, but not set.

Fold in the heavy cream, scallions, and the chopped zucchini, and pour into the mold. Chill until set—about 5 hours. Unmold onto a serving platter, and garnish with the reserved zucchini slices.

Yield: 6 servings

➤ Can be prepared the day before.

Sweet Potatoes

Sweet potatoes, the yellow or deep-orange colored vegetable that in some areas is called a yam or a Louisiana yam, should not be confused with the yellow African yam, which is usually sold in Latin American markets. The sweet potato is not related to the true yam, or to the true potato, but is the root of a vine related to the morning glory. The flesh is nutritious, and is a wonderful change from the more common white or Irish potato. In fact, it may be used in many of the same ways as the Irish potato, but because it lacks much of the starch found in Irish potatoes, it is not used in recipes where the potatoes are supposed to stick together, such as potatoes Anna and potato baskets. You can make wonderful French fries from sweet potatoes, and they can be cooked with garlic, cream, and cheese to make gratins, or mashed dishes. Try a sweet potato salad at your next picnic for a change. Prepare it in the same manner as regular potato salad, taking particular care not to overcook the potatoes.

Most of the preparations for sweet potatoes come from the South, and there is a tendency to "gussy" them up with a lot of sweeteners. Quantities of marshmallows, brown sugar, molasses, and the like are often poured over the top, and in the process the delicate flavor of the potato is obliterated. I suggest using discretion and at most a small amount of sweetener for this already sweet vegetable. In fact, one of the best ways of adding some sweetness is to use a fruit, such as apple, pear, peach, or apricot, or another sweet tasting vegetable, such as carrot or turnip.

Availability

Fresh
Harvested in the late fall in the North, sweet potatoes are in the markets year round. Look for relatively smooth, dull-looking, dry potatoes with tapering at both ends. The skin can be white, yellow, orange, purple, or brown. The flesh can be pale yellow to deep orange. Avoid potatoes with bruises, blemishes, or any cracks. Store in a cool, dark area, but not in the refrigerator. Sweet potatoes rot readily unless kept dry,

so it is best not to refrigerate. They will keep for several weeks in a cool dry area.

Frozen
Puréed sweet potatoes are sold frozen. Also, some brands come sweetened, but are not recommended.

Canned
Sweet potatoes are canned as a purée or in chunks in brine or syrup. They are not recommended.

Preparation

Treat the same as regular potatoes.

Cooking Methods

Boiling
Peel and cook in boiling salted water until tender—about 15 to 20 minutes.

Steaming
Steam over boiling water until tender—about 20 to 25 minutes.

Microwaving
Bake in their skins for about 8 minutes, turning once or twice.
    Cook cut up potatoes in a covered container for about 5 minutes, turning at least once.

Baking
Bake the same as Irish potatoes.

Quantity

Because of the rich-tasting quality of sweet potatoes, people tend to eat less than Irish potatoes. Plan on about 1½ pounds for 6 persons.

Sauces

There is a tendency to sauce sweet potatoes with sweet sauces and overwhelm the potato. Use sauces with a suggestion of sweetness—a small amount of honey, brown sugar, or the like, to enhance rather than over-power. Save the marshmallows for the next Boy Scout jamboree.

Mashed Sweet Potatoes and Carrots

Sweet potatoes can be mashed in a processor without becoming gluey—unlike Irish potatoes.

1 pound sweet potatoes, peeled and sliced	4 to 6 tablespoons heavy cream
	2 tablespoons butter
4 carrots, peeled and sliced	salt to taste

In boiling salted water, cook the potatoes and carrots until tender. In a processor, purée the potatoes and carrots with the cream, butter, and salt.

Yield: 6 servings

➤ Can be prepared ahead and reheated.

Variations:

Omit the carrots, and add 2 peeled and cored apples to the processor. Season with ¼ teaspoon cinnamon and ⅛ teaspoon nutmeg for more zest.

Omit carrots, and add 2 peeled and cored pears to the processor.

Sweet Potatoes Brûlées

6 sweet potatoes, peeled	1 cup boiled chestnuts, chopped
6 tablespoons butter	½ cup molasses
salt and pepper to taste	¼ cup brandy, heated

Preheat the oven to 375°F.

In a saucepan, boil the potatoes until tender, drain, and force through a ricer, or purée in a processor. Stir in 3 tablespoons of butter, and season with salt and pepper.

Spread the potatoes in a gratin, and sprinkle the chestnuts on top. Pour the molasses over, and dot with the remaining butter. Bake for 30 minutes, or until the top is bubbly and brown. Pour the brandy over, and serve.

Yield: 6 servings

➤ Can be prepared for the final heating the day before.

Sweet Potato Puffs

1 pound sweet potatoes, peeled and cubed	pinch of salt
½ cup milk	½ cup flour
¼ cup butter	2 eggs
pinch of sugar	oil for deep-frying

Cut the potatoes into cubes, and steam or boil until tender. Purée in a processor. Set aside.

In a small saucepan, bring the milk, butter, sugar, and salt to a full rolling boil. Add the flour all at once, and beat over medium heat, until the mixture forms a ball and pulls away from the sides of the pan. You will see a film of dough on the bottom of the pan. Let cool 5 minutes.

Put the dough into a processor with 2 eggs, and process until shiny, smooth, and stiff enough to hold its shape in a spoon. Beat in the sweet potato purée.

Heat the oil to 375°F. When ready to serve, drop teaspoonfuls of dough into the hot fat, and fry until golden and crisp. Drain on paper toweling, and sprinkle with salt. Serve immediately.

Yield: 6 servings

➤ The mixture can be prepared for frying several hours ahead.

Baked Sweet Potatoes with Honey-Mint-Butter Roccos

This is a perfect example of seasoning a sweet potato without overpowering it. The idea is from Rocco's restaurant in Boston. I have found that other butters, flavored with apricot purée or other fruits, combine beautifully with sweet potatoes.

¼ pound butter	salt and pepper
1½ teaspoons honey	6 medium sweet potatoes
½ teaspoon minced mint	

Preheat the oven to 450°F.

In a bowl, cream the butter, and beat in the honey and mint. Season with salt and pepper. Set aside.

Cut a cross in the top of each potato, and bake until tender—about 1 hour. Open potatoes, and serve with the butter.

Yield: 6 servings.

➤ The butter can be prepared several days ahead and even frozen.

Lemon Sweet Potatoes

6 medium sweet potatoes, peeled and cut into 1 inch slices	2 lemons
	3 tablespoons butter

Preheat the oven to 350°F.

In a large pot of boiling water, cook the potatoes until just barely done. Drain and cool. Quarter the cooked slices.

Scrub the lemons, cut in half, and squeeze the juice from two halves. Cut the remaining halves into thin slices.

Lightly butter a large gratin pan, add the potatoes and lemon slices, and sprinkle with the lemon juice. Dot with the butter. Bake for 30 minutes, stirring once or twice, until the potatoes are fully cooked and nicely glazed with lemon.

Yield: 6 servings

➤ Can be prepared for baking the day before.

Candied Sweet Potatoes

1 cup sugar	¼ cup orange juice
1 teaspoon ground cinnamon	1 lemon, thinly sliced
½ teaspoon ground nutmeg	¼ pound butter
6 sweet potatoes, peeled and cut into ½ inch thick slices	

Preheat the oven to 350°F.

In a small bowl, mix the sugar, orange juice, cinnamon, and nutmeg. Arrange the potatoes in layers in a baking dish, sprinkling each layer with the sugar mixture, lemon slices, and bits of butter. Bake uncovered for 1¼ hours, or until tender, basting often.

Yield: 6 servings

➤ Can be baked ahead and reheated, but best if freshly prepared.

Sweet Potatoes, Apples, and Chestnuts

6 sweet potatoes, unpeeled	1 cup maple syrup
6 apples, peeled, cored, and cut into ¼ inch thick slices	¼ teaspoon cinnamon
	pinch of nutmeg
1½ cups boiled, peeled chestnuts	¼ cup butter

Preheat the oven to 350°F.

Cook the potatoes in boiling water until barely tender. Peel, and cut into ¼ inch thick slices.

Overlap the potato and apple slices in a buttered baking dish, and cover with the chestnuts. Pour the syrup over, and sprinkle with the cinnamon and nutmeg. Dot with the butter. Bake for 45 minutes, basting several times, or until the potatoes are tender and glazed.

Yield: 6 servings

➤ Can be prepared ahead and reheated.

Salmon Sweet Potato and Red Pepper Chowder

Cut the onions, peppers, tomatoes, potatoes, and fish to the same ½ inch dice.

2 tablespoons butter	1 pound boneless salmon cut
1 cup diced onions	into ½ inch pieces
2 shallots, minced	1 clove garlic, minced
1 red pepper, diced	4 cups clam juice, or fish stock
6 plum tomatoes, peeled and	1 cup water
diced	3 sweet potatoes, ½ inch dice
chives	1 teaspoon minced thyme
salt and pepper to taste	3 scallions, minced

In a casserole, heat the butter, and cook the onions and shallots until soft, but not brown. Add the red pepper, tomatoes, and garlic, and cook, stirring occasionally, for 5 minutes, or until the tomatoes are soft. Add the clam juice, water, potatoes, thyme, chives, and black pepper, and simmer for 15 minutes, or until the potatoes are tender, but still retain their shape. Add the salmon, and simmer 1 to 2 minutes, or until the salmon is just cooked.

Serve garnished with the scallions.

Yield: 6 servings

➤ The soup is best freshly prepared.

Swiss Chard

Swiss chard is called chard, white chard, beet chard, or strawberry spinach, and the French call it Bette, Blette, or Poirée à carde, for example. Whatever the name, it is an under-appreciated vegetable. Although very popular in France (especially around Lyon) and in Italy, it has a very limited audience in the United States. Perhaps this is because most markets sell over-large chard with large, tough stems. Or, more likely it is because cooks do not know how to handle it. It is almost waste-free, because both the leaves and the stems are edible, but unless very young, the leaves must be stripped from the stems, and the stems need to be peeled of their strings in a similar fashion as celery. Serve the leaves like spinach on their own, or cook the stems separately, and serve the two at the same meal.

Availability

Fresh
Seldom available out of season. Look for chard from early fall through the first frost. Select chard with firm white or reddish stalks that show no signs of flabbiness or wilting. Store the leaves for no more than 3 days in a plastic bag in the refrigerator. The stripped stalks will keep for up to 10 days, refrigerated.

There is a slight difference in taste between red and white chard; interchange them according to availability.

Frozen
Freezing destroys the texture of the stalks, but the leaves freeze like spinach.

Canned
Swiss chard is not usually canned.

Preparation

Preparing chard is the same as spinach (see page 462), but on a larger scale. Hold the leaf in one hand with the back rib exposed, and pull the rib toward the leaf to separate the two. Chop the leaves as you would spinach. To remove the strings from the stalk, break off the end of the stalk, and gently pull it toward the leaf end as you would with celery (see page 172). Cut the stalks on the diagonal into sections.

Cooking Methods

Chard stems, like many other vegetables, turn dark in cooking. To prevent this, blanch them *à blanc* (see page 6) to keep the stems white. This is not necessary with the red-stemmed chard.

Boiling
Boil the leaves in salted water until tender—about 6 minutes. It is best to blanch the stalks in a *blanc*.

Steaming
Steam the leaves until wilted and tender—about 8 minutes—but it is best not to steam the stems, to keep them from turning dark.

Microwaving
Cook the leaves for 6 to 8 minutes, or until wilted, in just the water remaining from washing the leaves. The stalks tend to turn dark in a microwave.

Quantity

Plan on 2 pounds of chard for 6 persons, or 1½ pounds of leaves or stems.

Sauces

Sauce the same as spinach, or cook like other greens. Béchamel and Mornay sauce seem especially suited to chard. They can be dressed in vinaigrette and served hot or cold.

Substitute chard in recipes calling for spinach or other greens, and substitute chard stems in recipes calling for asparagus, or even green beans.

Sautéed Swiss Chard

2 pounds chard, stripped, stems cut into 1 inch sections	*blanc* (see page 6) 3 tablespoons butter salt and pepper

Set aside the leaves for another use, or see Note.

Simmer the stems in the *blanc* until almost tender—about 5 minutes. Drain well.

In a large skillet, heat the butter, and sauté the chard until heated and coated with butter. Season with salt and pepper.

Yield: 6 servings

➤ The stems can be prepared for the final sautéing the day before.

NOTE: If you wish to use the leaves, remove the cooked stems from the skillet with a slotted spoon and put in a warm serving dish. Shred the leaves, and sauté in the fat left in the pan until wilted and tender—about 3 to 4 minutes.

Variations:

Add a large pinch of savory or dill to the butter.

Add ½ cup heavy cream after 2 minutes, and simmer until it has thickened and the chard is tender.

Prepare the chard with cream, place in a gratin, sprinkle with ¾ cup grated Gruyère or Parmesan cheese, and bake at 375°F until golden.

Sauté 1 cup of shallots until soft, add the blanched stems and leaves of chard and stir in 1 tablespoon of grated lemon peel and nutmeg to taste. Serve sprinkled with 2 tablespoons minced parsley.

Sauté a clove of garlic, minced, in 3 tablespoons of olive oil until golden. Add the chard and cook until tender.

Season with salt and pepper.

Blettes à la Hollandaise (Chard with Hollandaise Sauce)

2 pounds chard, leaves stripped and set aside *blanc* (see page 6)	1 cup Hollandaise sauce (see page 19)

Cut the chard stems into even lengths about 3 inches long.

In a sauce pan, bring the *blanc* to a boil, add the stems, and cook until barely tender. Drain well, and place on a warm serving platter. Spoon a ribbon of Hollandaise over the top, and pass the remainder.

Yield: 6 servings

➤ Cannot be prepared ahead.

Chard Swiss Style

Prepare this with spinach or other greens if you prefer.

3 tablespoons olive oil	4 eggs
½ cup fresh bread crumbs	3 leeks, minced
3 slices bread, crumbled	⅔ cup minced celery leaves
⅓ cup milk	½ cup grated Gruyère cheese
1 ounce dried porcini	⅓ cup minced parsley, or chives
mushrooms	1 garlic clove, minced
2 pounds chard, blanched and	salt and pepper to taste
drained	grated nutmeg to taste

Preheat the oven to 350°F. Spread 2 tablespoons of oil in a 2 quart baking dish. Mix the bread crumbs with 1 tablespoon of oil, and set aside.

In a large bowl, soak the crumbled bread in the milk. In another small bowl, soak the mushrooms in hot water until soft—about 10 minutes—squeeze dry, and mince.

When the bread has absorbed the milk, mix in the mushrooms, chard, eggs, leeks, celery leaves, Gruyère, parsley, garlic, salt, pepper, and nutmeg. Mix well, and turn into the prepared baking dish. Sprinkle the crumbs over the top. Bake for 30 minutes, or until it has set and the top is browned.

Yield: 6 servings

➤ Can be prepared for baking several hours ahead.

Braised Swiss Chard with Shallots

2 pound green Swiss chard	1 tablespoon grated lemon peel
5 tablespoons butter	nutmeg
1 cup thinly sliced shallots	salt and pepper
2 tablespoons olive oil	2 tablespoons minced parsley

Separate stalks from leaves. Slice stalks into 1 inch pieces, and cut leaves into 1 inch ribbons.

Blanch stalks in boiling salted water for 3 minutes and add the leaves. Cook 2 minutes longer. Drain, refresh, and squeeze out excess moisture.

In a large skillet, melt butter, and cook shallots until they start to turn golden. Add the oil, and increase heat. Add the chard, and stir until liquid is absorbed. Stir in lemon peel, nutmeg, salt, and pepper.

Serve topped with parsley.

Yield: 6 to 8 servings

Tomatoes

*I*t is a tragedy that the quality of America's most popular vegetable is far too often the least acceptable. More poor-quality tomatoes are foisted off on the public than any other vegetable. No wonder one of the first crops of every home gardener are tomatoes. We all yearn for those memories of fresh, garden-ripe, sweet, bright-red, juicy fruits of the vine. What we get, except for a few short weeks in the summer (if we are lucky), are hard balls that come in various colors from pale green to perfect tomato red and are pulpy and virtually tasteless. No industry does more for the canned tomato packer than the fresh tomato grower. The wise cook often succumbs to using canned tomatoes because they taste far better than the flavorless bullets sold in most markets most of the time. Harsh words, but it is time we all refused to purchase those poor facsimiles of the real thing.

It is amazing that Mexico can ship good, if not perfect, tomatoes in mid winter, but growers in the United States still insist upon picking the tomatoes green, and then insisting they have been "vine-ripened," or that other euphemism: "vine-matured." Ripe tomatoes are red, unless they are of the yellow variety. They give to pressure, they are not hard, and if they have ripened on the vine, they have flavor!

Tomatoes are a very American vegetable. Originally cultivated in Mexico and Peru, they went to Europe in the 1600's, where they were first prized as an ornamental plant. Partially because of their relation to the nightshade family, they have at times been considered poisonous, but fortunately no one believes that nonsense anymore. Although tomatoes are one of the largest crops, most of the production goes into cans as juice, whole tomatoes, purée, sauce, or paste. As Americans, we put tomatoes in one form or another with almost everything. They are something that tastes good and are good for you! Consider the tomato's low caloric content (that is good), and how much high-calorie ketchup is used to drown otherwise decent food (that is bad). It is ironic.

During tomato season, fill up on tomatoes in their simplest form. Eat them like an apple seasoned with salt, or if garden-warm, with a sprinkle of sugar, as we did as children. Slice them and pour on the best olive oil you can afford, and a scatter salt, pepper, and maybe an herb such as basil—or more interestingly, perhaps, marjoram, oregano, thyme, or savory. Use dill, allspice, curry, or most of the other contents of the spice shelf. Tomatoes seem to work with almost everything. Once the season is over, leave the fresh tomatoes on the shelf. For most cooked dishes, canned tomatoes are superior by far.

Availability

Fresh
Good fresh tomatoes are available from late July through early October, depending on your location. Underripe tomatoes (that never ripen) are available year round. Look for firm, plump, red tomatoes that feel heavy for their size. Avoid any pale-colored, soft, bruised, cracked, moldy, or broken-skinned tomatoes. Store fresh tomatoes at room temperature until ripe. If necessary, store them in a brown paper bag to let the ethylene, the natural ripening gas, ripen the tomato. Never refrigerate, unless you are trying to hold an overripe tomato. Refrigeration not only slows the ripening process, but also changes the flavor.

Frozen
Tomatoes are not sold frozen, because freezing destroys their texture. Of course, you can freeze home-made tomato purée, or tomato sauce, for future use.

Canned
Out-of-season canned tomatoes are often to be preferred over fresh. Try several brands to find a brand that pleases you. Use it in every recipe that calls for cooked tomatoes (except for stuffed tomatoes). The flavor will be far better. If you have a need for texture, add some fresh tomatoes as a filler.

Sun-Dried
In recent years, an Italian specialty, sun-dried tomatoes, have become very popular. The tomatoes are laid in the sun, or more often in drying ovens, and dried until the moisture evaporates and they become leathery with a deep mahogany-red color. The tomatoes are stored dried, or often put into containers of olive oil to preserve them. They have an intense flavor that is quite different from fresh tomatoes. They combine particularly well with goat cheese and, of course, with olive oil and wild mushrooms. Use them in chicken dishes, or in pasta.

Preparation

Truly fresh tomatoes need only be eaten. However, there are occasions and uses when slicing, dicing, peeling, and/or seeding are not only recommended, but are mandatory. Peel the skins, which can be tough (and can toughen in cooking), when they would be in the way, such as in sauces, or for a more refined salad.

To peel tomatoes Place the tomatoes, cored or not, in a pot of boiling water to cover for 10 to 50 seconds, depending on ripeness. Plunge into cold water, and use the edge of a paring knife and your thumb to pull off the skin.

Tomato Seeds The seeds, which toughen in cooking, should be removed to avoid the gritty quality, but more important—for me, at least—to get rid of the jelly that holds them in place. In plum tomatoes, with their thick walls of flesh, this is not as important as other varieties, where there is more jelly than meat. It saves cooking time and provides for a fresher flavor.

To Remove the Seeds Cut the tomato, peeled or not, in half horizontally to expose the seeds, rather than from stem to blossom end, because then you will only expose one section of the seeds. Hold each half in your hand, cut side out, over a sink, and snap your wrist downward. The seeds and jelly should fall out. If necessary, use your index finger to scoop any stubborn seeds. If a few seeds remain, do not worry. The object is to get rid of most of the seeds and the jelly.

Cooking Methods

Tomatoes are cooked with most of the cooking methods, although not all are satisfactory. Boiled or stewed tomatoes were a feature of my childhood which I am happy to forget. Steaming also does little for tomatoes. However, sautéed tomato slices are wonderful. I have never understood the fascination with sautéed cherry tomatoes, herbed or not. Biting into one of those generally means a shower of juice over self and friends, usually accompanied by a burnt tongue. I feel that cherry tomatoes are suitable raw—only. Tomatoes, grilled on the barbecue, used in sauces, baked with herbs, in combination with other vegetables, or in a gratin—these are all superb cooking methods. Finally, tomatoes make a perfect container for other ingredients, such as spinach, purée, or a myriad of other fillings.

Quantity

In theory it is easy: plan on a tomato per person. In fact, because some tomatoes are large (and sometimes *very* large), you may want to serve only half, or even a quarter per person or, if the tomatoes are particularly small, you may prefer to plan on 2. Generally, 2 pounds will serve 6 persons.

Sauces

Tomatoes *are* the sauce in many instances. They combine particularly well with vinaigrette and many of its variations. Other than herbed butters, most of the classic sauces are not used with tomatoes alone.

Gazpacho (Cold Tomato Soup with Assorted Vegetables)

There are many versions of gazpacho; this is my favorite.

3 cups peeled, seeded, and chopped tomatoes, or 3 cups tomato juice
1½ cups cubed white toast
3 tablespoons olive oil
1 to 4 garlic cloves, crushed
1 tablespoon salt
1½ teaspoons ground cumin
3 cups cold water
2 to 4 tablespoons vinegar

black pepper, to taste
Cayenne pepper, to taste
3 ice cubes
2 to 3 cups sautéed croûtons
2 peppers, diced
2 celery stalks, diced
1 cucumber, seeded and diced
1 onion, diced
2 tomatoes, peeled, seeded, and diced

In a processor, purée the tomatoes, bread, olive oil, garlic, salt, and cumin. Pour into a bowl, and add the cold water, vinegar, black pepper, and cayenne pepper, to taste. Add vinegar to taste and ice cubes, stir well, and chill.

In separate bowls, arrange the croûtons, peppers, celery, cucumber, onion, and remaining tomatoes.

Serve the soup, and pass the croutons and vegetables.

Yield: 6 servings.

➤ Prepare the soup up to 3 days before serving or freeze if desired. The vegetables should be prepared only a few hours before serving.

Pomodori al Forno (Oven-Baked Tomatoes)

6 ripe tomatoes, halved
3 tablespoons minced parsley
2 teaspoons minced garlic

salt and pepper to taste
6 tablespoons olive oil

Preheat the oven to 325°F.

In a flameproof casserole, arrange tomatoes, cut side up, in one layer. Crowd them if need be. Sprinkle with parsley, garlic, salt, and pepper. Add enough oil to come ¼ inch up the side of the pan. Cook on top of the stove, over medium heat, until tender—about 15 minutes.

When soft, baste with the oil, transfer to the next-to-the-highest rack of the oven, and bake about 1 hour, basting often, until the tomatoes shrink to little more than half their size.

Transfer the tomatoes to a platter, leaving the oil behind. Use the oil for pasta sauces on another occasion.

Yield: 6 servings

➤ Can be prepared ahead and reheated, or served at room temperature.

Tomates Grillées (Grilled Tomatoes)

Basil is the most common herb for tomatoes, but try savory, rosemary, or thyme for a change.

3 large beefsteak tomatoes, halved	salt and pepper to taste
1 tablespoon minced basil, or other herb	3 tablespoons butter, or olive oil

Preheat the broiler.

Sprinkle the cut side of the tomatoes with basil, salt, and pepper, and dot with butter or drizzle with olive oil. Broil until cooked through and lightly browned.

Yield: 6 servings

➤ Can be prepared for grilling several hours ahead.

Variation:

Sprinkle a crushed garlic clove on the tomatoes.

Sprinkle the tomatoes with minced hot peppers.

Sautéed Tomato Slices

Use only firm tomatoes.

3 large tomatoes cut into ½ inch thick slices	¼ cup butter or olive oil
	salt and pepper to taste

In a large skillet, sauté the tomatoes in the butter until just lightly colored. Season with salt and pepper.

Yield: 6 servings

➤ Cannot be prepared ahead.

Notes: Do not cook too long, or the tomatoes will disintegrate.

Variations:

Sprinkle the tomatoes with minced onion, garlic, or herbs, just before they are done.

Green Tomatoes

At the end of the growing season, most gardeners end up with a quantity of green tomatoes. Cut them into thick slices and coat lightly with corn meal, flour, or bread crumbs, and sauté until lightly browned on both sides.

Add ⅓ cup grated Parmesan or sap sago cheese to the corn meal before coating the tomatoes.

Tomates à la Tomate *(Tomatoes with Tomato Garnish)*

10 tomatoes	salt and pepper to taste
3 tablespoons butter	3 tablespoons vegetable oil
1 cup minced onion	1 cup heavy cream
1 garlic clove, minced	
bouquet garni of thyme,	
parsley, and bay leaf	

Preheat the oven to 375°F.

Peel, seed, and chop 5 tomatoes. Cut the remaining 5 in half.

In a skillet, sauté the onion and garlic in 2 tablespoons of butter until soft, but not brown. Add the chopped tomato, garlic, and bouquet garni. Simmer, covered, for 25 minutes, or until thickened. Remove and discard the bouquet garni. Whisk in the remaining tablespoon of butter. Season with salt and pepper.

In a skillet, sauté the tomato halves in the vegetable oil, cut side down, for 3 minutes. Turn over, and bake for 10 minutes. Remove the tomato halves to a serving platter, and pour the oil from the skillet, without cleaning.

Return the tomato halves, and add the cream. Simmer until lightly thickened. Place the tomato halves back on the platter, nappe with the cream, and surround with the chopped tomato mixture.

Yield: 6 servings

➤ Can be prepared ahead and reheated.

Pasta Sauces

One of the most common uses of tomatoes, fresh or canned, is in pasta sauces. For many people, tomato sauce means tomatoes cooked for hours, or even days. Fortunately, this is not only not necessary, but more often than not leads to a heavy sauce with an overcooked flavor. The best tomato sauces are made in a matter of a minutes rather than hours, and many superb sauces require no cooking at all.

La Pasta di Casamicciola *("Donkey House" Pasta)*

There are many versions of uncooked tomato sauces. This is the first one I discovered, and one of the best. These sauces are best served with small pastas, such as shells, cavatelli, or butterflies, rather than long thin pastas like spaghetti.

1 pound tomatoes, peeled, seeded, and chopped	lemon juice to taste
½ cup olive oil	salt and pepper to taste
1 tablespoon minced basil	1 pound pasta

In a bowl, mix the tomatoes, olive oil, basil, and enough lemon juice to give a slightly tart flavor. Some tomatoes are tart enough without the lemon juice. Let stand for 20 minutes before serving.

Cook the pasta until al dente, drain, and add to the sauce. Toss and serve immediately. This is not usually served with grated cheese.

Yield: 6 servings

➤ The tomato mixture can be prepared several hours ahead.

Variations:

Add 2 thinly sliced garlic cloves and ½ cup oil-cured black olives, pitted and chopped.

Add 2 tablespoons capers, drained, 8 ounces of Mozzarella, diced, and ¼ cup grated Parmesan cheese.

Add 2 red peppers, chopped, and 4 ounces diced taleggio.

Add 2 garlic cloves, crushed, 1 small hot chili, minced, ½ cup chopped fresh basil, ½ cup grated Parmesan cheese, and ½ pound shredded fontina cheese.

Sugo di Pomodor Fresco
(Fresh Tomato Sauce with Pancetta)

This sauce is ready literally in minutes, and has a fresh, clean taste.

½ cup olive oil	salt and pepper to taste
½ cup sliced onion	1 large red or green pepper, thinly sliced
2 garlic cloves, crushed	2 tablespoons minced mint
3 thin slices pancetta, diced	
2 pounds tomatoes, peeled and seeded	

In a skillet, heat the oil, and sauté the onion and garlic, discarding the garlic as it begins to brown.

In a processor, purée the tomatoes, and add to the skillet along with the pancetta. Season with salt and pepper, and add the fresh pepper and mint.

Simmer, partially covered, for 30 minutes, or until lightly thickened.

Yield: 6 servings

➤ Can be prepared ahead and frozen.

Simple Tomato Sauce

¼ cup minced onions
1 garlic clove, minced
6 tablespoons butter
1 pound plum tomatoes, cubed
½ teaspoon thyme

1 bay leaf
salt and pepper to taste
dash Tabasco sauce
grated Parmesan cheese

In a saucepan, sauté the onion and garlic in 2 tablespoons butter until soft. Add the tomatoes, thyme, bay leaf, salt, and pepper, and simmer 20 minutes.

Discard the bay leaf, and purée the sauce in a blender. Add the remaining butter, and strain. Taste for seasoning, adding Tabasco, if desired.

Serve cheese separately.

Yield: 6 servings

➤ Can be prepared ahead and frozen.

NOTE: Out of season, use canned plum tomatoes, drained of any water juices.

Spaghettini alla Carretiera *(Spaghetti Carter's Style)*

Another simple, quick sauce, prepared with canned tomatoes. There are a number of sauces whose names indicate the need for a quick meal. The busy carter who has only a chance for a quick bite, between loads, or the busy "street walker" who has but a minute or two between clients—hers usually has hot pepper added for some spice.

2 cups drained canned tomatoes
1 cup loosely packed basil
  leaves, chopped
5 large garlic cloves, crushed

⅓ cup olive oil
salt and pepper to taste
1 pound spaghettini

In a saucepan, simmer the tomatoes, basil, garlic, olive oil, salt, and pepper, uncovered, over medium high heat until lightly thickened—about 15 minutes. Correct the seasoning with salt and pepper.

Cook the pasta until al dente, drain, and toss with the sauce. Grated cheese may be passed.

Yield: 6 servings

➤ Can be prepared ahead and frozen, but the point of this sauce is that it is so quick, you can always make it fresh.

Variation:

Alla Puttanesca ("Streetwalker's Sauce") Add 2 tablespoons capers, 12 pitted black olives, 1 hot chili pepper, 1 teaspoon minced oregano instead of the basil, and 1 small can of chopped anchovies.

Sugo di Pomodori e Panna (Tomato Cream Sauce)

Cream is a relatively recent addition to Italian tomato sauces. It gives the sauce a smoothness and finesse usually associated more with French cookery.

¼ pound butter	salt and pepper to taste
3 tablespoons minced onion	¼ teaspoon sugar (optional)
3 tablespoons minced carrot	½ cup heavy cream
3 tablespoons minced celery	
2½ cups canned Italian tomatoes	

In a saucepan, simmer the butter, onion, carrot, celery, tomatoes, salt, and sugar until lightly thickened—about 45 minutes to 1 hour. Purée in a blender or processor, and strain off the seeds.

Return to the saucepan, and bring to a simmer. Stir in the cream. Correct the seasoning with salt and pepper.

Yield: 6 servings

➤ Can be prepared ahead and frozen.

Stuffed Tomatoes

Tomatoes are a natural container for other foods. You can be as creative as you are capable in making fillings for tomatoes and, because of their low caloric content, you can do it with a clear conscience. Certainly there are some classic fillings, such as bread crumbs and garlic for *Tomates Provençales* or *Tomates Florentines*, but there are many other possibilities.

Tomates Provençales (Stuffed Tomatoes Provence Style)

Make these with crumbs made from fresh bread for a lighter dish.

6 tomatoes, halved	2 teaspoons minced parsley
3 tablespoons melted butter	1 teaspoon minced fresh basil
1 garlic clove, crushed	1 cup fresh bread crumbs
salt and pepper to taste	

Preheat the oven to 450°F.

Gently squeeze the seeds out of the tomato halves, and use a spoon to remove the pulp. Chop the pulp.

In a skillet, melt the butter, and sauté the tomato pulp with the garlic until softened. Stir in the salt, pepper, parsley, and basil, and sauté for

1 minute longer. Stir in the bread crumbs, and correct the seasoning with salt and pepper.

Fill the tomato shells loosely, and put into a baking dish. Bake for 10 to 15 minutes, until heated.

Yield: 6 servings

➤ Can be prepared for baking the day before.

Pomodori Ripiene (Stuffed Tomatoes, Italian Style)

6 tomatoes, cut in half horizontally	1 garlic clove, minced
⅓ cup soft bread crumbs	2 egg yolks, or 1 whole egg
¼ cup milk	¼ cup grated Parmesan cheese
2 tablespoons minced parsley	salt and pepper to taste
	½ cup olive oil

Preheat the oven to 375°F.

Press the seeds out of the tomatoes, and discard. With a teaspoon, scoop out the pulp and chop.

In a medium bowl, soak the bread crumbs in the milk. Add the tomato pulp, parsley, and garlic. Stir in the egg yolks and cheese, and season with salt and pepper to taste.

Rub some of the olive oil in a baking dish, arrange the tomatoes on top, and drizzle with the remaining olive oil. Bake for 30 minutes or until cooked, but they should still retain their shape.

Yield: 6 servings

Tomates Florentines
(Stuffed Tomatoes Florentine Style, with Spinach)

6 tomatoes, halved horizontally	salt and pepper to taste
salt and pepper to taste	nutmeg to taste
1 tablespoon butter	½ cup heavy cream
1 teaspoon flour	grated Parmesan cheese
2 pounds spinach, stripped and wilted	

Preheat the oven to 350°F.

With a teaspoon, scoop out the pulp and seeds of the tomatoes. Arrange the tomatoes in a baking dish in a single layer.

Drain the spinach, squeezing out the excess moisture. Mince or purée in a processor or blender.

In a large skillet, melt the butter, stir in the the flour, and cook until the roux starts to turn golden. Stir in the spinach, and cook until the mixture is quite dry. Season with salt, pepper, and nutmeg. Add the cream, and cook until thickened.

Fill the shells with the spinach, and sprinkle with the Parmesan cheese. Bake for 20 minutes or until hot, but the shells should retain their shape.

Yield: 6 servings

➤ Can be prepared for baking the day before.

Tomatoes with Grated Zucchini

6 tomatoes, halved
　horizontally
salt and pepper to taste
1 pound grated zucchini,
　cooked (see page 470)

2 tablespoons grated Parmesan
　cheese

Preheat the oven to 375°F.
With a teaspoon, scoop the seeds and pulp from the tomatoes.
Season the shells with salt and pepper, and drain, upside down, for 10 minutes. Arrange in baking dish in a single layer.
Prepare the zucchini, and stuff the tomato shells. Sprinkle with the Parmesan, and bake for 10 minutes or until heated and the tomatoes are just cooked.

Yield: 6 servings

➤ Can be prepared for the final baking the day before.

Pomodori alla Veneziana (Stuffed Tomatoes Venetian Style)

6 firm tomatoes, peeled and
　halved
½ cup minced onion
2 tablespoons olive oil
1 garlic clove, crushed
1 tablespoon minced parsley
⅓ cup minced mushrooms

4 anchovies, chopped
salt and pepper to taste
12 oysters
3 tablespoons chicken stock
few drops lemon juice
½ cup bread crumbs

Preheat the oven to 375°F.
With a teaspoon, scoop the pulp and seeds from the tomatoes. Arrange the shells in a buttered baking dish in a single layer.
In a saucepan, sauté the onion in the olive oil until golden. Add the garlic, parsley, mushrooms, anchovies, salt, and pepper, and simmer 5 minutes. Add the oysters and stock, and cook until the edges of the oysters begin to curl.
Fill the tomatoes with the mixture, and sprinkle with a few drops of lemon juice and the bread crumbs. Bake for 10 minutes, or until crumbs just begin to brown.

Yield: 6 servings

➤ Can be prepared for baking several hours ahead.

Tomates Printanières
(Tomatoes Stuffed with Spring Vegetables)

6 tomatoes, halved
  horizontally
salt and pepper to taste
6 tablespoons butter
2 tablespoons water
1 teaspoon sugar

1½ pounds fresh peas, shelled
¾ cup minced ham
1 teaspoon flour
1 tablespoon minced parsley
2 teaspoons minced mint

Preheat the oven to 350°F.

Sprinkle the tomato shells with salt, and turn upside down to drain. In a small saucepan, melt the butter, and add the water, sugar, and peas, and cook, covered, for 8 to 10 minutes, or until the peas are just done. With a slotted spoon, remove the peas.

Reduce the liquid to 2 tablespoons, and stir in the ham. Add the peas, and sprinkle with flour. Cook, stirring, until the mixture becomes creamy. Correct the seasoning with salt and pepper. Stir in the parsley and mint.

Fill the tomato shells. Bake for 10 minutes or until heated.

Yield: 6 servings

➤ Can be prepared for the final baking several hours ahead.

Tomatoes à la Hussarde
(Tomatoes with Ham and Mushrooms)

6 tomatoes halved horizontally
salt and pepper to taste
½ cup minced onions
2 tablespoons butter
½ cup soft bread crumbs

1 cup minced ham
1½ cups minced mushrooms
2 tablespoons minced parsley
1 tablespoon butter

Preheat the oven to 350°F.

With a teaspoon, scoop the seeds and pulp from the tomatoes. Season the shells with salt and pepper, and turn upside down to drain.

In a skillet, sauté the onion in the butter until soft, but not brown. Stir in the bread crumbs, and cook 1 minute. Add the ham, mushrooms, parsley, salt, and pepper, and cook 3 minutes longer.

Arrange the tomatoes in a baking dish, and fill with the mixture. Dot with the butter. Bake for 30 minutes, or until the tomatoes are cooked.

Yield: 6 servings

➤ Can be prepared for the final baking several hours ahead.

Pomodori del Ghiottone *(Glutton's Tomatoes)*

The Italians seem to have a fondness for descriptive names for various dishes: Whore's Pasta, Choke a Priest Gnocchi, and the like!

6 tomatoes, halved horizontally	½ teaspoon crushed garlic
1¼ teaspoons salt	½ pound mushrooms, minced
½ teaspoon pepper	¼ pound ham, minced
2½ tablespoons olive oil	4 eggs
5 tablespoons butter	3 tablespoons bread crumbs

Preheat the oven to 350°F.

With a spoon, scoop the pulp and seeds from the tomatoes, and season with salt and pepper. Turn upside down to drain. In a saucepan, heat 1 tablespoon of olive oil and 2 tablespoons of butter.

Sauté the garlic, mushrooms, ¼ teaspoon salt, and ¼ teaspoon pepper until most of the liquid evaporates. Add the ham, and heat.

Sprinkle the tomato shells with 1½ tablespoons olive oil, arrange in a baking dish, and bake for 10 minutes. Meanwhile, in a bowl, beat the eggs.

In a skillet, melt 1 tablespoon of butter, and brush against the sides of the pan. Add the eggs, and cook over medium-low heat until thick and creamy.

Stir the mushrooms into the eggs, and fill the tomato halves. Sprinkle with bread crumbs, and dot with butter. Bake 5 minutes longer or until the tops are golden.

Yield: 6 servings

➤ Cannot be prepared ahead.

Sausage Stuffed Tomatoes

6 tomatoes, halved horizontally	¼ cup chicken stock (optional)
salt and pepper to taste	2 teaspoons red-wine vinegar
½ teaspoon olive oil	1 cup cooked rice
1 tablespoon butter	2 tablespoons minced parsley
¼ cup minced onion	1 tablespoon minced basil
1 garlic clove, crushed	3 tablespoons pine nuts
3 Italian sausages, peeled and chopped	¼ cup grated Parmesan cheese
	1 egg, lightly beaten

Preheat the oven to 375°F.

With a spoon, scoop out the pulp and seeds from the tomatoes, and chop the pulp. Season the shells with salt and pepper, and turn upside down to drain.

In a skillet, heat the oil and butter, and sauté the onion and garlic until soft, but not brown. Add the sausage meat, and cook, stirring, until no longer pink. Add the tomato pulp and chicken stock, and simmer until the liquid evaporates. Sprinkle with vinegar, and stir in the rice, parsley, basil, pine nuts, half the Parmesan, and the egg.

Fill the tomatoes, and arrange in a baking dish. Sprinkle with the remaining cheese, and bake for 30 minutes.

Yield: 6 servings

➤ Can be prepared for the final baking several hours ahead.

Tomates à l'Antiboise (Tomatoes Stuffed Antibes Style)

6 tomatoes, halved horizontally	1 tablespoon minced parsley
salt and pepper to taste	1 tablespoon minced tarragon
⅓ cup olive oil	1 tablespoon minced chervil
2 tablespoons vinegar	¾ cup mayonnaise
3 hard-cooked eggs, minced	1 tablespoon anchovy paste
1 cup tuna, drained	6 lemon slices
1 tablespoon capers	6 parsley sprigs

With a teaspoon, scoop the seeds and pulp from the tomatoes. Sprinkle the inside of each shell with salt, pepper, 1 tablespoon of oil, and 1 teaspoon of vinegar. Marinate for 2 hours. Pour the marinade into a small bowl.

In a bowl, mix the hard-cooked eggs, tuna, capers, parsley, tarragon, and chervil together. Stir in the mayonnaise and anchovy paste.

Fill each tomato with the mixture, and arrange on a serving dish. Top each with a slice of lemon and a spring of parsley. Sprinkle the reserved marinade over the top.

Yield: 6 servings

➤ Can be prepared several hours ahead.

Tomatoes Dubarry (Califlower-Filled Tomatoes)

6 small tomatoes	½ to ¾ cup mayonnaise
salt and pepper to taste	parsley sprigs
1 small head cauliflower	

Cut a slice off the stem end of the tomatoes, and scoop out the insides. Season the shells with salt and pepper, and turn upside down to drain on paper toweling.

Break the cauliflower into florets, and cook in boiling salted water until tender. Drain, and refresh under cold water.

Place 1 teaspoon of mayonnaise in the bottom of each tomato shell, and fill with cooled cauliflower florets. Sprinkle with pepper, and nappe with mayonnaise. Garnish with parsley sprigs.

Yield: 6 servings

➤ Can be prepared the day before.

Tomates Farcies aux Concombres
(Tomatoes Stuffed with Cucumbers)

6 tomatoes   ½ to ¾ cup sauce vinaigrette
salt and pepper to taste
1 or 2 medium cucumbers,
   peeled, seeded, and chopped

Cut off the top third of each tomato, and scoop out the insides. Season the shells with salt and pepper, and turn upside down to drain on paper toweling.

Mix the cucumber with vinaigrette to coat, and fill the tomatoes. Pass remaining vinaigrette.

Yield: 6 servings

➤ Can be prepared 2 hours before serving.

Tomatoes Andalusian Style

6 medium tomatoes   1½ cups cooked rice
salt and pepper to taste   mayonnaise
3 tablespoons minced onion   thin green-pepper strips, or
⅓ cup minced green pepper   cutouts
2 tablespoons olive oil

Cut off the top third of each tomato, and scoop out the insides. Season the shells with salt and pepper, and turn upside down to drain on paper toweling.

In a small skillet, sauté the onion and the pepper in the oil until soft, but not brown. Stir into the rice, and add enough mayonnaise to bind. Correct the seasoning with salt and pepper.

Fill the tomatoes, and garnish the tops with green pepper strips or cutouts.

Yield: 6 servings

➤ Can be prepared the day before.

NOTE: To make cutouts, cut the flesh from the pepper in thin sections. Use truffle cutters to cut out fancy designs, or use a paring knife to cut diamonds, leaf shapes, and the like.

Tomates à la Russe
(Tomatoes Stuffed with Russian Vegetables)

For a fuller description of vegetables à la Russe, see page 524.

6 small tomatoes	1 teaspoon lemon juice
1½ cups cold, diced mixed	1 teaspoon minced onion
cooked vegetables (carrots,	¼ to ⅓ cup mayonnaise
peas, celery, potatoes, green	green pepper strips
beans, turnips, and the like)	shredded lettuce

Cut off the top third of each tomato, and scoop out the insides. Season the shells with salt and pepper, and turn upside down to drain on paper toweling.

In a bowl, mix the vegetables, lemon juice, onion, and enough mayonnaise to bind. Correct the seasoning with salt and pepper.

Fill the tomatoes, and garnish with the green pepper strips. Serve on a bed of shredded lettuce, with the top of each tomato set off-center.

Yield: 6 servings

➤ Can be prepared several hours before serving.

Tomatoes Gervais

6 medium tomatoes	salt and pepper to taste
6 ounces Petit Suisse cheese	½ cup vinaigrette
3 or 4 tablespoons cream	bunch of watercress
2 tablespoons minced chives	

Cut off the top third of each tomato, and scoop out the insides. Season the shells with salt and pepper, and turn upside down to drain on paper toweling.

In a bowl, cream the cheese, and add enough cream to make a smooth, light mixture. Season with salt, pepper, and 1 tablespoon of chives. Place the mixture in a pastry bag fitted with a #5 open star tip, and pipe a swirl of cheese into each tomato.

Spoon some vinaigrette over the top, and garnish with the watercress. Coat with remaining vinaigrette just before serving.

Yield: 6 servings

➤ Can be prepared 2 or 3 hours before serving.

Insalata Siciliana (Sicilian Tomato Salad)

6 tomatoes	4 teaspoons capers
salt and pepper to taste	2½ tablespoons cooked peas
¼ pound mushrooms in oil	1 cup cooked cannellini beans
¼ pound Italian-style pickles	1 cup mayonnaise
25 olives, pitted	

Cut off the top third of each tomato, and scoop out the insides. Season the shells with salt and pepper, and turn upside down to drain on paper toweling.

Mince the mushrooms, pickles, and olives, and put into a bowl with the capers, peas, and beans. Bind with the mayonnaise, and correct the seasoning with salt and pepper.

Fill the tomato shells with the mixture. Arrange any extra filling on a platter, and surround with the tomatoes.

Yield: 6 servings

➤ Can be prepared several hours before serving.

Tomatoes with Lobster and Eggs

This is a truly beautiful and delicious luncheon dish.

6 large tomatoes, peeled	1½ tablespoons tomato paste
1 1 pound lobster, boiled and shelled	¼ cup Pernod
	6 soft-cooked or poached eggs
1½ cups mayonnaise	1 tablespoon minced parsley
2 cloves garlic, crushed	1 tablespoon capers

Cut off the top third of each tomato, and scoop out the insides. Season the shells with salt and pepper, and turn upside down to drain on paper toweling. Slice the meat from the lobster tail and claws.

In a bowl, mix the mayonnaise, garlic, tomato paste, any tomalley and coral from the lobster, and the Pernod. Correct the seasoning with salt and pepper.

Place an egg in the bottom of each tomato shell, and garnish with lobster pieces. Coat lightly with the sauce, and pass the remainder. Sprinkle the top with parsley and capers.

Yield: 6 servings

➤ Can be prepared 2 or 3 hours before serving, but should be served at room temperature.

NOTE: For soft-cooked eggs, cook the egg, in its shell, in almost boiling water, for 6 to 8 minutes. Drain, rinse under cold water, and peel very gently to avoid breaking the egg. Poached eggs are easier. Prepare the eggs the day before if you prefer, and store in a bowl of cold water in the refrigerator.

Coppa di Pomoddoro all Capricciose
(Capricious Stuffed Tomatoes)

3 large tomatoes, halved	salt and pepper to taste
¾ cup Arborio rice, cooked	¾ cup grated Parmesan cheese
3 slices prosciutto, julienne	½ teaspoon minced parsley
2 tablespoons olive oil	

Cut off the top third of each tomato, and scoop out the insides. Season the shells with salt and pepper, and turn upside down to drain on paper toweling.

In a bowl, mix the rice, ham, oil, salt, pepper, cheese, and parsley. Fill the tomatoes and serve cold.

Yield: 6 servings

➤ Can be prepared the day before.

Tomato Salad

Although fresh ripe tomatoes are delicious when added to salads, they all-too-often are hard, flavorless wedges, dropped on top of iceberg lettuce for the "house" salad. Tomatoes, especially when fresh and in their prime, deserve better. Use them as containers, as in the recipes above, or as an uncooked sauce for pasta (see page 25). Or just slice them and season accordingly.

Sliced Tomato Salad

6 tomatoes, thinly sliced	salt and pepper to taste
½ cup extra virgin olive oil	

Arrange the tomatoes on a serving platter. Drizzle the oil over the top, and season with salt and pepper.

Yield: 6 servings

➤ Prepare no more than 20 minutes before serving.

NOTE: That is arguably the simplest tomato salad. Some would say that sprinkling the slices with salt or sugar alone is even simpler.

Variations:
Add an herb of choice to the oil: tarragon, thyme, savory, marjoram, basil, parsley, or the like.

Add a vinaigrette instead of just oil.

Add herbs to the vinaigrette.

Alternate slices of fresh Mozzarella cheese (not the presliced packaged kind, but the water-packed, Mozzarella di Bufalo, if possible). Dress with oil or vinaigrette.

Alternate the tomatoes with slices of chevre, dress with oil or vinaigrette and perhaps sprinkle with chopped sun dried tomatoes.

Sprinkle the tomatoes with shredded Genoa salami or prosciutto, and dress with oil or vinaigrette.

Sprinkle the tomatoes with minced black olives, or olives, chopped anchovies, and minced basil, if you wish, and dress with oil or vinaigrette.

Dress the tomatoes with a mayonnaise thinned with light cream or sour cream.

Add minced dill to sour cream to dress.

Add crumbled blue cheese to sour cream or thinned mayonnaise.

Alternate tomato slices with thin slices of onion, and dress with vinaigrette, thinned mayonnaise, or sour cream.

Dress with mustard-cream sauce.

Dress with sour cream mixed with horseradish and lemon juice, and season with black pepper.

Dress the tomato slices with honey, and sprinkle liberally with black pepper.

Shelada del Felfla *(Tomato and Sweet Pepper Salad)*

3 large green peppers, peeled, seeded, and chopped	3 tablespoons lemon juice
	3 tablespoons olive oil
3 tomatoes, peeled, seeded, and chopped	½ teaspoon ground cumin
	salt and pepper to taste
1 cup minced parsley	

In a bowl, mix the peppers, tomatoes, parsley, lemon juice, olive oil, and cumin. Mix well, and correct the seasoning with salt and pepper. Refrigerate until cold.

Yield: 6 servings

➤ Can be prepared up to 12 hours before serving.

Tomato Aspic

Gelatin salads, or congealed salads, as they are called in the South, are seldom served any more. In some cases this is a blessing. We are no longer assaulted with marshmallows and canned fruit cocktail afloat in sickly sweet fruit flavored gelatin mixed with ginger ale. However, in abandoning the truly awful, we have also lost some wonderful dishes. A perfectly flavored aspic is a delight, and a tomato aspic makes a cool, refreshing accompaniment to many other foods.

3½ cups tomato juice
4 stalks celery with leaves
3 tablespoons minced onion
2 tablespoons lemon juice
1 bay leaf
1½ teaspoons sugar
1 teaspoon salt
½ teaspoon paprika

2 tablespoons gelatin
1 cup cold water
1 cup minced celery
1 cup minced tomatoes
3 tablespoons minced onions
lettuce leaves
mayonnaise flavored with basil

In a saucepan, simmer the tomato juice, celery stalks, onion, lemon juice, bay leaf, sugar, salt, and paprika for 30 minutes. Strain.

In a small bowl, soften the gelatin in the cold water and stir into the hot juice. Add water, if needed, to make 4 cups.

Chill until just beginning to set. Stir in the minced celery, tomatoes, and onions, and pour into a 6 cup mold, rinsed in cold water. Refrigerate until set. Unmold and serve with mayonnaise.

Yield: 6 servings

➤ Can be prepared the day before.

NOTE: Do not prepare more than 1 day ahead, or it will become rubbery.

For the mayonnaise, add 1 or 2 tablespoons minced basil to 1 cup of mayonnaise. The aspic is the featured flavor, not the basil.

Tomato Jam

For the lucky person who has a garden with too many tomatoes, or for those who love jams, try this old-fashioned recipe.

2¼ pounds ripe tomatoes,
    peeled, seeded, and chopped
¼ cup lemon juice

1½ teaspoons grated lemon rind
6 cups sugar
1 bottle pectin

In a saucepan, simmer the tomatoes for 10 minutes. Measure 3 cups into a clean saucepan, and add lemon rind, juice, and sugar. Mix well.

Bring to a full rolling boil, and boil hard for 1 minute. Remove from the heat, and immediately stir in the pectin. Return to the heat, and stir and skim by turns for 5 minutes. Place in sterilized jelly glasses and seal.

Yield: Six 8 ounce jars

➤ Store in a cool dark place for up to a year.

Sun-Dried Tomatoes

Sun-dried tomatoes are treated differently than regular tomatoes. If they are not packed in oil, rehydrate them by soaking in boiling water to cover until supple—about 10 minutes. Drain and coat with olive oil, and let stand for at least 30 minutes. Sun-dried tomatoes that are packed in oil need only be drained. Use the oil to sauté veal or chicken cutlets, or in a pasta sauce.

Sun-Dried Tomato and Chèvre Toasts

6 slices French bread, toasted on one side	1 teaspoon crushed rosemary
6 slices chèvre cheese	6 sun-dried tomatoes
	2 tablespoons olive oil

Preheat the oven to 400°F.

Arrange the bread slices on a baking sheet, uncooked side up. Cover with a slice of chèvre, sprinkle with the rosemary, and cover with a slice of tomato.

Drizzle the olive oil over the top. Heat in the oven until the cheese is hot and begins to melt.

Yield: 6 servings

➤ Can be prepared for the final baking several hours ahead.

NOTE: Serve these as an hors d'oeuvre, or in lieu of a cheese course, with a green salad.

Fettuccine with Sun-Dried Tomatoes and Wild Mushrooms

¼ cup minced shallots	2 cups heavy cream
¼ cup butter	salt and pepper to taste
½ pound fresh wild mushrooms, quartered	1 pound fettuccine
6 sun-dried tomatoes, julienne	2 or 3 scallions, sliced

In a skillet, sauté the shallots in the butter until soft, but not brown. Add the mushrooms and tomatoes, and cook, stirring, for 3 minutes. Add the cream, and season with salt and pepper. Boil over high heat until reduced to a sauce—about 10 minutes.

Cook the fettuccini in boiling salted water until al dente. Drain, and toss with sauce. Garnish with scallions.

Yield: 6 servings

➤ The sauce can be prepared several hours before serving.

Fettuccine with Sausage, Summer Savory, and Sun-Dried Tomatoes

2 tablespoons summer savory
  leaves, minced
6 tablespoons softened butter
½ pound Italian sausage,
  peeled and minced
2 garlic cloves, minced

½ cup chicken stock
8 sun-dried tomatoes, chopped
salt and pepper to taste
1 pound fettuccine
2 ounces chèvre, diced

In a bowl, mix the savory and butter, and shape into a log 1 inch in diameter. Wrap in waxed paper, and chill.

In a skillet, cook the sausage over medium heat until it loses its pink color. Stir in the garlic, and cook for 1 minute, until softened. Add the chicken stock and tomatoes, and simmer for 5 minutes. Stir in 3 tablespoons of the savory butter, and set the mixture aside.

Cook the pasta in boiling salted water until al dente. Drain, and toss with the sauce and the remaining 3 tablespoons of butter. Correct the seasoning with salt and pepper. Add the chèvre, toss quickly, and serve.

Yield: 6 servings

➤ The sauce can be prepared ahead and reheated.

Chèvre and Sun-Dried Tomato Salad

2 cups crumbled Montrachet
  or other goat cheese
6 sun-dried tomatoes, ½ inch
  dice
2 tablespoons capers
2 tablespoons vinegar

2 teaspoons Dijon mustard
¼ cup olive oil
salt and pepper to taste
salad greens, such as romaine,
  arugula, escarole, chicory,
  or radicchio

In a bowl, toss the Montrachet, tomatoes, and capers together gently. In another bowl, whisk the vinegar, mustard, olive oil, and salt and pepper until emulsified.

Place a mixture of greens in a salad bowl. Add the cheese mixture, and toss lightly. Rewhisk the dressing, pour over the salad, and toss again.

Serve immediately.

Yield: 6 servings

➤ The dressing and lettuces may be prepared ahead, but do not toss until just before serving.

Turnips

Rare is the person who wakes up with a craving for turnips. Though many of us like this delightful vegetable, many others have no idea of what a turnip is. Probably it is because they have never had a delicate purple-top turnip, and assume that it is the same as a rutabaga—and they have only had those when over-large and overcooked.

Turnips, sometimes called purple tops, are small white balls with a purple colored cloak. Once peeled, the root is white and the flavor, when young, is quite delicate. As it gets older and larger, the pulp can become woody and the flavor almost tasteless. Rutabagas, or Swedes as they are sometimes called, are believed to be a cross between the turnip and the cabbage. They were first grown in Scandinavia in the early 1700's. They are two or three times the size of turnips, and have a yellow orange flesh and a purple cloak as well. (There is another version of turnip grown in New England, called the Cape Cod Turnip. It is the size of a rutabaga, but has a green cloak over a white body. The flavor is half-way between the purple top and rutabaga.) Both vegetables are prized as food for the indigent and as cattle-fodder in much of Europe. The Asians also prepare various turnips, particularly in szechuwan preserved vegetables, and as an ingredient in Korean *kim chee.*

Turnips and Rutabagas are members of the cabbage family, which in turn is a member of the larger mustard family. In fact they are treated in many of the same ways as other cabbage-family members, such as cauliflower and broccoli, and the leaves are treated as mustard greens or kale, other family members.

Availability

Fresh
Rutabagas are in the markets year round. Turnips appear in the spring and again in the fall, but not usually in the summer months.

Turnips Look for small- to medium-firm, with smooth white roots, free of blemishes and any sign of wrinkling. If they have leaves, the leaves should be crisp, without any signs of yellowing or wilting.

Rutabagas Look for rutabagas about the size of a grapefruit that feel heavy for their size, and are without signs of cracking or other blemishes. They are often waxed to prevent dehydration.

Frozen
Turnips and rutabagas freeze poorly unless turned into a purée.

Canned
Not usually sold in cans.

Preparation

Turnips and rutabagas are usually peeled before cooking. Peel turnips the same as a potato. Store in a bowl of cold water until ready to cook.

Rutabagas are more work to peel. Cut off both ends, and stand the rutabaga on one end. With a sharp knife, cut down the sides to remove the skin. Cut into sections to cook.

Both vegetables can be cut into slices, dice, ovals, or can be shredded.

They can be eaten raw in crudite's, or shredded for salad like celery root or grated carrot. In fact, mix them with those vegetables for a grated vegetable salad.

Cooking Methods

Both vegetables can be prepared by most cooking methods.

Boiling
Place in boiling salted water and cook until tender—about 15 to 25 minutes.

Steaming
Steam over boiling salted water until tender.

Microwaving
Cook in a covered container with 1 or 2 tablespoons of water. Allow 4 minutes for turnips, and 8 to 12 minutes for rutabaga.

Braising
This is one of the best methods for cooking these vegetables.

Baking
Cut into 1 inch sections, brush with butter, and bake at 350°F for about 35 to 40 minutes for turnips and up to an hour for rutabagas.

Roasting
Add turnips to the same pan as the roast about 40 minutes before the roast is done, but add rutabagas about an hour before. (If the vegetable is not done and the meat is, remove the meat to a platter, and let it rest while the turnip finishes cooking. It should only be another few minutes.)

Quantity

Plan on 1½ pounds of turnip or rutabaga for 6 servings.

Sauces

Dress boiled or steamed turnips with plain or herbed butter, or season the butter with spices such as cinnamon or allspice. Add poppy or toasted sesame seeds. Serve with Béchamel or Mornay sauce to make a gratin.

Braised Turnip or Rutabaga

1½ pounds turnip or rutabaga, cut into 1 inch pieces	1 cup chicken stock
5 tablespoons butter	salt and pepper to taste
½ cup minced onion	2 tablespoons minced parsley

In a large skillet, sauté the turnip in the 3 tablespoons butter until it starts to brown. Add the onion, and cook until soft, but not brown. Add the chicken stock, and season with salt and pepper.

Cover, and simmer until the turnip is done. Remove the turnip, and reduce the liquid to ¼ cup. Whisk in the remaining butter, and add to turnip. Stir to coat, place in a serving dish, and sprinkle with the parsley.

Yield: 6 servings

➤ Can be prepared ahead except for adding the final amount of butter.

Variations:
Add 1 tablespoon minced savory with the chicken stock.
Add 1 tablespoon minced rosemary with the chicken stock.
Use cream instead of chicken stock.

Curried Turnips

3 tablespoons butter	1 teaspoon salt
1 cup thinly sliced onion	½ teaspoon pepper
1 teaspoon ground thyme	3 tablespoons yogurt
1 teaspoon ground marjoram	2 pounds white turnips,
1 teaspoon turmeric	peeled 1 inch cubes
½ teaspoon ground ginger	1 teaspoon curry powder

In a skillet, sauté the onion, thyme, and marjoram until the onion is soft and golden. Add the turmeric, ginger, salt, and pepper, and cook, stirring, for 3 minutes. Add the yogurt, and simmer 3 minutes longer. Add the turnips, and cook, covered, for 5 minutes, stirring occasionally.

Lower the heat, and simmer, covered, for 25 to 30 minutes, stirring occasionally, until almost tender. Stir in the curry powder, and cook until tender. If necessary, add water to prevent sticking.

Yield: 6 servings

➤ Can be prepared ahead and reheated.

Turnips in Orange Sauce

2 pounds turnips, cut into ½	2 tablespoons brown sugar
inch cubes	¼ teaspoon ginger
salt and pepper to taste	3 tablespoons butter
½ cup orange juice	1 cup orange sections

Preheat the oven to 350°F.

In a saucepan of boiling salted water, cook the turnips until tender. Drain.

In a processor, purée the turnips, and add salt and pepper to taste, orange juice, brown sugar, ginger, and butter.

Turn into a 1 quart baking dish, and decorate with orange sections. Bake for 20 minutes, or until hot.

Yield: 6 servings

➤ Can be prepared for the final baking the day before.

Turnip Purée with Sautéed Shallots

1½ pounds turnips or	salt and pepper to taste
rutabagas, 2 inch dice	6 tablespoons butter
1 baking potato, peeled and	½ cup heavy cream
halved	6 shallots, thinly sliced
1 onion, peeled and halved	

Preheat the oven to 350°F.

In a covered baking dish, place the turnip, potato, and onion, and season with salt and pepper. Add 3 tablespoons of butter, cover, and bake for 45 minutes, or until the vegetables are tender.

In a processor, purée the vegetables with the butter from the pan, and beat in the cream. Correct the seasoning with salt and pepper. Turn into a serving dish.

Meanwhile, in a skillet, melt the remaining 3 tablespoons of butter, and sauté the shallot slices for about 20 minutes over medium heat, stirring occasionally, until crisp and golden.

Sprinkle the shallots over the turnips, and serve.

Yield: 6 servings

➤ To prepare ahead, cook the turnips and the shallots. Arrange in a baking dish, and reheat in a 350°F oven until hot.

Turnip and Pear Purée

1½ pounds turnips, peeled and quartered	1 tablespoon lemon juice
1 to 1½ pears, peeled, cored, and quartered	1 tablespoon butter
	salt and pepper to taste

In a saucepan, cook the turnips in salted water to cover until tender—about 15 to 20 minutes. Drain and keep warm.

In another saucepan, cook the pears and lemon juice, covered, over low heat until soft. In a processor, purée the turnips, pears, butter, salt, and pepper.

Yield: 6 servings

➤ Can be prepared ahead and reheated.

Variations:

Use an apple instead of a pear, add to the purée, and season with a few gratings of nutmeg. Use rutabaga in either recipe.

Navets Anna (Turnips Anna)

These are prepared in the same fashion as Potatoes Anna.

1½ pounds turnips, peeled and thinly sliced	5 tablespoons butter
	salt and pepper to taste

Preheat the oven to 400°F.

In a skillet, heat 4 tablespoons butter, and cook the turnip, stirring until limp and transparent—about 10 minutes. Season with salt and pepper.

Butter a potatoes anna pan, or a 9 inch cake pan, and arrange the turnip in concentric circles. Bake for 15 minutes, cover with a lid, and bake 15 minutes longer.

Remove the cover, and bake for another 30 minutes. Let stand for 5 minutes, and then unmold onto a serving platter.

Yield: 6 servings

➤ Can be prepared for the final baking the day before.

Shredded Sautéed Turnip

Follow the instructions for grated zucchini sauté (see page 473). It is not necessary to salt the turnip.

Turnip Salad

1 pound turnips, cut in julienne	2 tablespoons minced parsley
½ cup vinaigrette	1 tablespoon minced chives
¾ pound thinly sliced radishes	1 hard-cooked egg, separated and sieved

In a bowl, mix the turnips with the vinaigrette, and refrigerate for 2 hours.

When ready to serve, drain the turnips, and arrange in a platter. Add the radishes to the marinade, and arrange around the turnips. Sprinkle the parsley, chives, and eggs over the top.

Yield: 6 servings

➤ Can be prepared the day before.

Mixed Vegetables

*M*any of the finest vegetable dishes are combinations of several vegetables. Some vegetables combine perfectly with one another to create a third flavor, while other vegetable combinations maintain distinct flavors rather than meld into a third flavor. Ratatouille, for instance, has a complexity of flavors that is not eggplant, tomato, zucchini, and the rest, but all of those melded into a composite. It is similar to mixing red and green to get brown, or red and yellow to get orange. Other foods, though thoroughly mixed, evolve as separate flavors. When I first read of Michel Guérard's Spinach with Pears (see page 462), I assumed that the result would be a third flavor, and yet my mind could not conceive of what that might be. When I prepared the dish, I found that there was no third flavor. You taste pears and you taste spinach, separately but at the same time. It is rather like making a stripe of red along side a stripe of yellow without overlapping.

There are many vegetable combinations, and indeed they can fill volumes. I have placed combinations of vegetables in which one vegetable dominates in the chapter on that dominant vegetable. In this chapter you will find vegetable combinations where they all are equally important. Here are the recipes for the large vegetable casseroles that can serve many, and can also serve as a main course—the sort of dish to take to the church supper, or feed to the family when all your recipes seem dull, or when you frankly have a need to clean out the vegetable bins. Read these recipes with an eye to making substitutions to suit your needs and the supply of ingredients on hand.

A few suggestions for creating casseroles of this sort: Generally, vegetables of a season blend well. For instance, the summer fruits of the harvest, such as eggplant, tomatoes, and zucchini, all mix well, and can be mixed in various combinations. Adding chopped turnip seems intrusive—edible, but not ideal. At the same time, a marriage of root vegetable, such as turnips, potatoes, carrots, and celery root, all work beautifully together, while tomatoes and zucchini would seem out of place here. Generally, the foods should be of similar shape when cut. Mixing uncut green beans and peas does not work very well, although if you cut the green beans to the size of the peas, and mix them with diced carrots, potatoes, and possibly turnips, and toss them with mayonnaise, you have Salade Russe, a classic dish for the cold buffet.

Perhaps it is needless to say that the colors should blend, and you must use some care with vegetables that bleed like beets. The Salade Russe mentioned above can be made with beets, but then the salad turns a rather brilliant pink. I prefer to put the diced beets around a mound of the salad to serve as a collar.

Minestrone alla Genovese (Genoese Vegetable Soup)

Minestra is a soup, and a minestrone is a big soup. There is no single recipe for Minestrone; every region has its own version. The requirements are beans, a fat (which can be olive oil, bacon, lard, or other pork fat), aromatics such as onion, carrot, and garlic, and some fresh vegetables. These can include anything that is in season. Then you need a thickening agent, which is usually pasta, but can be rice or even toasted bread. Many, but not all, are finished with a dollop of Pesto (see page 27) and grated cheese.

1⅓ cups dried white beans	2 cups peeled and chopped
6 to 7 pints water	tomatoes
salt to taste	1 tablespoon minced marjoram
1 cup thinly sliced onion	½ pound maccheroncini rigati
1 cup diced celery	(see Note)
½ cup sliced carrot	5 teaspoons pesto (see page 27)
½ cup olive oil	4 tablespoons grated percorino
1½ cups sliced zucchini	sardo cheese
1½ cups diced potatoes	

In a bowl, soak the beans in 6 pints of water overnight.

In a large kettle, cook the beans in the soaking liquid for 1 hour, without salt. Add the salt, onion, celery, carrot, and 5 tablespoons of oil, and simmer for 1 hour. Add the zucchini, potatoes, tomatoes, and marjoram, and simmer 30 minutes longer. Add the maccheroncini and, as soon as it is tender, stir in the pesto, remaining oil, and cheese.

Yield: Serves 6 to 8

➤ Can be prepared ahead and reheated.

NOTE: Maccheroncini rigati is a long-ridged pasta which should be broken into 1 inch sections before adding to the soup. If it is not available, any small pasta can be used. Pecorino sardo is a sharp-tasting grating cheese which is stronger than regular pecorino. If it is not available, substitute pecorino Romano, or even Parmesan. If desired, add any fresh vegetable in season. Italian favorites are leeks, pumpkin, cabbage, summer squash, zucchini, dried or fresh mushrooms, peas, and/or eggplants.

Kesakeitto *(Finnish Summer Vegetable)*

1½ cups diced carrots	2 tablespoons butter
¾ cup green peas	2 tablespoons flour
1 cup cauliflower florets	1 cup milk
½ cup diced new potatoes	1 egg yolk
½ cup diced string beans	¼ cup heavy cream
4 small radishes, halved	½ pound shrimp, cooked,
2 teaspoons salt	peeled, and deveined
¼ pound spinach finely	¼ teaspoon white pepper
chopped	2 tablespoons minced dill

In a large pot, place the carrots, peas, cauliflowers, potatoes, string beans, and radishes, and cover with cold water. Add the salt, and boil, uncovered, until almost tender—about 8 minutes. Add the spinach, and cook 5 minutes. Remove from the heat, strain off the liquid, and reserve separately.

In the pot, melt 2 tablespoons butter, stir in the flour, and cook, stirring, until it begins to turn golden. Add the reserved vegetable stock, and bring to a boil. Add the milk, and return to a simmer.

In a bowl, mix the egg yolk and cream, and whisk 1 cup of hot soup into the mixture to warm it.

Return these to the soup, and bring it almost to a boil. Add the vegetables, and heat until hot. Add the shrimp, and heat. Correct the seasoning with salt and pepper. Sprinkle with dill.

Yield: 8 servings

➤ Can be prepared and reheated. Be careful not to boil the soup after adding the egg mixture.

Soupe Printanière *(Spring Vegetable Soup)*

1½ quarts chicken stock	½ head romaine, shredded
⅔ pound green peas, shelled	pinch of sugar
(1/4 pound shelled)	salt and pepper to taste
3 leeks, thinly sliced	6 sautéed croûtons
3 ribs celery, thinly sliced	

In a medium-sized saucepan, bring the stock to a boil, and add the peas, leeks, celery, lettuce, and sugar. Season with salt and pepper, and simmer, uncovered, for 15 minutes.

Serve with croûtons.

Yield: 6 servings

➤ Best if prepared just before serving.

Potage Printanière *(Spring Garden Soup)*

A soup can be thick or thin, however, a potage is always thicker, but in this case not heavier.

3 leeks, minced
½ cup minced onion
2 tablespoons butter
2 potatoes, thinly sliced
½ cup thinly sliced carrots
salt and pepper to taste

1½ cups hot water
¼ cup rice
10 stalks asparagus, cut in 1
   inch pieces
½ pound spinach, chopped
1 cup light cream

In a 3 quart casserole, sauté the leeks and onions in the butter until soft, but not brown, stirring occasionally. Add the potatoes, carrots, salt, and hot water to the casserole, and simmer, covered, for 15 minutes. Add the rice, and simmer 10 minutes. Add the asparagus, and simmer 5 minutes longer. Add the spinach, and return to a simmer.

Stir in the cream, and heat until hot. Correct the seasoning with salt and pepper.

Yield: 6 servings

➤ Can be reheated, but best if freshly made.

Maple-Glazed Carrots, Parsnips, and Turnips

½ pound carrots, cut in batons
½ pound parsnips, cut in
   batons
½ pound rutabaga, cut in
   batons

4 tablespoons butter
1 tablespoon lemon juice
1 tablespoon maple syrup
¼ teaspoon cinnamon
salt and pepper to taste

In a large pot, bring salted water to a boil.

Cook the carrots until tender-crisp, and remove with a slotted spoon. Add the parsnips to the water, cook until tender-crisp, and remove with a slotted spoon. Add the turnips, cook until tender, and drain. Add the butter to the pan, and melt. Stir in the lemon juice, maple syrup, cinnamon, salt, and pepper, and stir gently to coat evenly.

Heat until hot.

Yield: 6 servings

➤ Can be prepared for the final heating the day before.

Sautéed or Stir-Fried Vegetables

Until recently, stir-fried vegetables have been held in a certain awe. They connoted Chinese or Asian cooking, and perhaps the unknown. In fact, many cultures prepare assorted vegetables and cook them quickly in a small amount of fat. Here are a number of suggestions that should expand your repertoire. Substitute a similar vegetable if one is missing, or add or delete some according to what you have on hand, or to your favorites.

Sautéed Shredded Vegetables

Shredding vegetables changes the taste, and can make an ordinary vegetable extraordinary!

3 tablespoons butter	2 zucchini, shredded
3 large shallots, minced	2 summer squash, shredded
4 carrots, shredded	salt and pepper to taste

In a large skillet, melt the butter, and sauté the shallot until soft, but not brown. Add the shredded vegetables, and cook, tossing, until just tender—about 4 to 5 minutes. Correct the seasoning with salt and pepper.

Yield: 6 servings

➤ The vegetables can be shredded several hours ahead. Do not cook until just before serving.

Mixed Vegetable Sauté

2 teaspoons vegetable oil	2 celery stalks, julienne
½ cup chopped pecans	1 red pepper, julienne
salt and pepper to taste	2 zucchini, julienne
9 tablespoons olive oil	5 garlic cloves, minced
1 eggplant, julienne	2 tablespoons minced oregano
2 leeks, julienne	2 tablespoons minced parsley

In a skillet, sauté the pecans in 2 teaspoons of oil with salt to taste, until lightly browned. Set aside.

In a large skillet, heat 3 tablespoons oil, and sauté the eggplant until just tender. Transfer to a bowl, and season lightly with salt.

Heat 4 tablespoons of oil, and sauté the leeks and celery until softened. Add the red pepper, season with salt and pepper, and cook until almost tender. Add the zucchini and eggplant, and cook, stirring, until the zucchini is tender-crisp. Turn onto a platter, and keep warm.

Heat remaining tablespoon of olive oil, and sauté the garlic until soft, but not brown. Add the oregano and parsley, and pour over the vegetables. Toss gently, and taste for seasoning. Garnish with pecans.

Yield: 6 servings

➤ Can be prepared ahead and served at room temperature.

Herbed Carrots and Green Beans

1 garlic clove, crushed	1 teaspoon minced rosemary
4 tablespoons butter	¼ teaspoon salt
¾ pound green beans, 2 inch	¼ teaspoon pepper
pieces	3 anchovy fillets, mashed
6 carrots, in 2 inch batons	grated zest of 1 lemon
3 tablespoons minced parsley	2 teaspoons lemon juice
2 teaspoons minced marjoram	

In a skillet, sauté the garlic in the butter over low heat until lightly colored—about 2 minutes.

Add the beans, carrots, parsley, marjoram, rosemary, salt, and pepper, and stir. Cover tightly, and cook, shaking the pan occasionally, until just tender—10 to 12 minutes. If necessary, add 1 or 2 tablespoons of water to prevent sticking. Add the anchovies, lemon zest, and lemon juice. Cook, tossing, for 2 minutes.

Serve hot or at room temperature.

Yield: 6 servings

➤ Can be prepared several hours ahead.

Fagiolini con Zucchini e Patate
(Green Beans with Zucchini and Potatoes)

1 cup thinly sliced onion	4 cups green beans
3 tablespoons olive oil	2 cups zucchini in ½ inch
2 cups ripe tomatoes, chopped	thick slices
3 tablespoons minced basil	salt and pepper to taste
3 potatoes, cut into ¼ inch	minced parsley, to taste (optional)
thick slices	

In a skillet, sauté the onion in the oil until golden. Add the tomatoes and basil, cover, and simmer for 5 minutes, stirring occasionally. Add the potatoes, beans, and zucchini. Season with salt and pepper.

Cover, and cook over moderate heat, stirring occasionally, until the potatoes are tender. Garnish with minced parsley, if desired.

Yield: 6 servings

➤ Can be prepared ahead and served at room temperature, or reheated.

Funghi a Funghetto Genovese
(Mushrooms with Eggplant and Zucchini, Genoa Style)

Actually, the title translates more as Mushrooms and Large Mushrooms.

1 eggplant, ½ inch dice	1½ teaspoons oregano
salt and pepper to taste	¼ cup olive oil
¾ pounce dried porcini	2 zucchini, ½ inch slices
mushrooms	½ pound mushrooms, thinly
1 cup hot water	sliced
1 garlic clove	lemon juice to taste
1 tablespoon minced parsley	

Sprinkle the eggplant with 2 teaspoons salt, and let drain in a colander for 30 minutes.

In a small bowl, soak the porcini in the hot water for 20 minutes. Drain, reserving ½ cup liquid, rinse the porcini under cold water, squeeze dry, and chop coarsely.

Mince the garlic clove, parsley, and oregano together. Set aside. Rinse the eggplant under cold running water, and pat dry.

In a skillet, heat half the oil over high heat, and sauté the eggplant until browned on all sides. Add the zucchini, and sauté until tender, adding more oil if needed.

Heat the remaining half of the oil in a second skillet, and sauté the mushrooms until the liquid has evaporated. Add the porcini and the reserved soaking liquid, and cook, uncovered, until the liquid evaporates. Combine the mushrooms and eggplant, and correct the seasoning with salt and pepper. Simmer together for 5 minutes.

Turn into a serving dish, and sprinkle with the garlic mixture. Add lemon juice to taste.

Yield: 6 servings

➤ Can be prepared ahead and reheated.

Ching Tsao Su Tsai
(Stir-Fried Mixed Chinese Vegetables)

The Chinese are masters at cooking a few vegetables together quickly to retain all their freshness and flavor. There are other examples in other chapters, where one vegetable seems to predominate.

3 tablespoons oil	½ cup sliced bamboo shoots
6 Chinese mushrooms, soaked	24 snow peas, stringed
1 tablespoon minced scallion	½ teaspoon sugar
2 cups sliced celery cabbage	1 teaspoon salt
½ cup sliced water chestnuts	

Heat a wok over high heat until very hot, add the oil, and heat until almost smoking. Stir-fry the mushrooms and scallion in the oil for a few seconds. Add the cabbage, and stir-fry for 1 minute. Then add the water chestnuts, bamboo shoots, and snow peas. Add 1 tablespoon of water, cover, and cook for 1 minute. Stir in the sugar and salt.

Yield: 6 servings

➤ Cannot be prepared in advance.

Gratin of Ratatouille

Ratatouille is a perfect marriage of flavors.

4 tablespoons olive oil	½ cup peeled, seeded, and
1 cup thinly sliced onions	chopped tomatoes
1 cup thinly sliced green	2 tablespoons minced parsley
pepper	1 tablespoon minced basil
1½ cups diced eggplant	2 teaspoons minced marjoram
1½ cups ½ inch thick slices	1 garlic clove, minced
zucchini	salt and pepper to taste

In a large skillet, sauté the onions in the oil until soft, but not brown. Add the peppers and eggplants, and cook 5 minutes, stirring often. Add the zucchini and tomatoes, and simmer gently for 30 minutes.

Stir in the parsley, basil, marjoram, garlic, salt, and pepper, and simmer 15 to 20 minutes longer until the vegetables are amalgamated.

Yield: 6 servings

➤ Can be prepared ahead and reheated.

NOTE: Because of the number of vegetables, it is difficult to make ratatouille in a small quantity. However, you can serve it hot or cold, as a vegetable, a dip for hors d'oeuvre, a salad, a filling for crepes or cocktail puffs, or a base for eggs. Leftovers should not be a problem. It can also be frozen.

Variations:

Volumes could be written on how to prepare ratatouille. Some cooks prefer all the vegetables to retain their shape, so they sauté each one separately, combine in a casserole, and simmer for 20 minutes, or until heated and the flavors are melded.

None of the vegetables listed above should be omitted, but feel free to add summer squash, and red or yellow peppers. You can add more garlic, and use thyme instead of marjoram, or just a large amount of basil.

A final note: It is often better the next day.

Caponata

Caponata amounts to the Italian version of Ratatouille—similar but different.

1½ pounds eggplant, unpeeled, cut into 1 inch cubes	½ cup chopped pitted green olives
salt and pepper to taste	1 pound can of Italian Plum tomatoes, drained
½ cup olive oil	¼ cup capers
2 cups chopped onions	2 tablespoons toasted pine nuts
1 cup chopped celery	2 tablespoons wine vinegar

Sprinkle the eggplant with salt, and let drain for 30 minutes. Rinse under cold water, and pat dry with paper towels.

In a large skillet, heat the oil until hot, and sauté the eggplant until softened and browned. With a slotted spoon, remove the eggplant and set aside. Add the onions, celery, olives, and tomatoes, and cook until the celery is tender-crisp and the tomatoes are slightly thickened.

Return the eggplant to the pan along with the capers, pine nuts, and vinegar, and simmer for 10 minutes. Correct the seasoning with salt and pepper.

Serve hot or cold.

Yield: 6 servings

➤ Can be prepared ahead and frozen.

NOTE: Caponata can be served as a vegetable course, or as a spread on French or Italian bread as an hors d'oeuvre.

Verdura alla Romana (Roman Vegetables)

This vegetable medley can be served hot, but more often is served cold as part of an antipasto platter.

½ cup olive oil	2 red peppers, 1 inch dice
4 small zucchini, ¼ inch slices	2 garlic cloves, sliced
1 small head cauliflower, florets	2 bay leaves
1 small eggplant, 2 inch cubes	¾ teaspoons salt
2 stalks celery, 1 inch sections	¼ teaspoon pepper
¼ pound green beans, 1 inch pieces	½ cup tomato purée
4 small carrots, batons	¼ cup dry white wine
12 small mushrooms, whole	¼ cup white-wine vinegar
12 small white onions, whole	2 tablespoons sugar
1 large green pepper, 1 inch dice	12 Spanish olives
	lemon juice to taste

In a large casserole, over medium heat, heat the oil. Add the zucchini, cauliflower, eggplant, celery, green beans, carrots, mushrooms, onions, green pepper, red peppers, garlic cloves, bay leaves, salt, and pepper.

Cook, covered, for 8 minutes, stir, and taste. They should be tender-crisp. If necessary, cook another 4 to 5 minutes.

In a bowl, mix the tomato purée, wine, vinegar, and sugar, and stir into the vegetable mixture. Add the olives, cover, and simmer, covered, until the vegetables are tender but not mushy—about 10 minutes longer.

Serve hot, or cool and serve at room temperature. Season with lemon juice, if desired.

Yield: 6 generous servings

➤ Can be prepared ahead and served at room temperature or reheated.

Smeazza *(Vegetable Casserole from Ticino)*

6 leeks, chopped	1 tablespoon flour
6 tablespoons butter	1 tablespoon cornmeal
1 pound spinach, cooked and chopped	1 teaspoon salt
	½ teaspoon pepper
1 pound Swiss chard leaves, cooked and chopped	¼ pound grated Gruyère or Italian fontina cheese
3 eggs, beaten	

Preheat the oven to 350°F.

In a small skillet, sauté the leeks in 2 tablespoons butter until soft, but not brown. Mix in the spinach and chard, and cook until the moisture evaporates.

In a bowl, mix the eggs, flour, cornmeal, salt, and pepper. Stir in the vegetables and cheese, and turn into a 1½ quart baking dish. Dot with the remaining butter.

Bake until a knife inserted halfway between the edge and the center comes out clean—about 25 minutes.

Yield: 6 servings

➤ Can be prepared for baking several hours ahead.

La Ghiotta *(Abruzzi Vegetable Casserole)*

A ghiotta is a dripping pan, and the masculine form of the word means gluttonous. This dish is good enough to lead to gluttony.

½ cup minced carrot	olive oil
½ cup minced celery	3 cups thinly sliced onion
2 tablespoons minced parsley	3 cups thinly sliced red pepper
1 garlic clove, minced	3 cups thinly sliced potatoes
½ teaspoon oregano	3 cups thinly sliced zucchini
salt and pepper	¼ cup olive oil

Preheat the oven to 350°F. Oil a 2 quart baking dish.

In a bowl, mix the carrot, celery, parsley, garlic, oregano, salt, and pepper (see Note).

In the casserole, make a layer of onions, sprinkle with some of the carrot mixture and some olive oil, add a layer of red peppers, and sprinkle with more carrot mixture and olive oil. Continue with the potatoes and zucchini, sprinkling with the carrot mixture and olive oil each time.

Drizzle more oil over the top. Bake until tender—45 to 60 minutes. Drain off excess oil, and serve warm.

Yield: 6 servings

➤ Can be prepared ahead and reheated.

NOTE: The carrot, celery, and parsley mixture is called a *soffrito*, and many cooks believe that the flavor is different and better if the ingredients are chopped together. In Italy this is done with a *mezzaluna*, a half-moon-shaped chopper. A processor does the job just as well, and much faster.

Braised Spring Vegetables

The small amount of sugar is used to caramelize the vegetables and add color as well as flavor; the result is not sweet.

3 tablespoons butter	4 lettuce leaves, shredded
1½ cups diced carrots	2 tablespoons minced parsley
1 tablespoon sugar	2 tablespoons minced chervil
1 cup diced turnips	salt and pepper to taste
1 cup tiny white onions	1 tablespoon *beurre manié*
2 cups fresh or frozen peas	(see glossary)
1 cup chicken stock	

In a skillet, melt 1 tablespoon of butter, and sauté the carrots until well-coated with butter. Add 1 teaspoon of sugar, and cook, shaking the pan, until the sugar caramelizes and turns a rich golden-brown. Remove to a saucepan.

Repeat the same cooking method with turnips and onions, using the remaining butter and sugar, and add all of this to the saucepan. Add the peas, chicken stock, lettuce, parsley, chervil, salt, and pepper, and cover.

Simmer for about 12 to 15 minutes, or until just done. Stir enough of the *beurre manié* into the simmering liquid to thicken the liquid.

Yield: 6 servings

➤ Can be prepared ahead and reheated.

Legumes d'Hiver au Mornay
(Winter Vegetables with Mornay Sauce)

½ pound cooked beets, diced
½ pound cooked turnips, diced
½ pound cooked parsnips, diced

1½ cups Mornay sauce
¼ cup grated Gruyère cheese

Preheat the oven to 350°F.

In a gratin pan, mix the beets, turnips, and parsnips with 1 cup Mornay sauce to coat evenly. Level the vegetables in the pan, pour over the remaining Mornay sauce, and sprinkle with the Gruyère. Bake until bubbly and golden brown—about 20 minutes.

Yield: 6 servings

➤ Can be prepared for baking several hours ahead.

Mediterranean Vegetable Platter

Serve this colorful platter at a buffet.

6 small zucchini
6 very small eggplant
48 tomato slices
salt and pepper to taste
olive oil
6 thin slices Gruyère cheese

3 tomatoes
½ cup cooked peas
1 cup cooked rice
2 tablespoons minced onion
1 teaspoon oregano

Preheat the oven to 350°F.

Cut 4 slits into each zucchini and each eggplant from the bottom toward the stem. Arrange the eggplant and zucchini in separate baking dishes. Insert a tomato slice into each slit, and season with salt and pepper. Drizzle with olive oil. Bake the eggplant for 20 to 25 minutes, or until tender, and the zucchini for 10 to 15 minutes.

Meanwhile, cut the tomatoes in half horizontally, and remove the centers. Dice ½ cup of the centers, sprinkle the insides of the shells with salt and pepper, and turn upside down to drain.

In a bowl, mix the chopped tomatoes, peas, rice, onion, and oregano with salt and pepper to taste. Stuff the tomato shells with the mixture, and place in a baking dish. Bake the tomatoes for 10 to 15 minutes, or until hot.

On a serving platter, arrange the stuffed tomatoes in the center, and surround with spokes of zucchini and eggplant.

Yield: 6 servings

➤ Can be prepared for baking the day before.

Stuffed Vegetables

Many vegetables make natural and attractive containers. Here are a couple of suggestions for stuffing them, but in other chapters individual vegetables receive a similar treatment. Use your favorite filling in one or more vegetables to serve as a luncheon, brunch, light supper, or as an assortment for a buffet.

Baked Stuffed Tomatoes with Eggplant and Zucchini

6 tomatoes	¼ teaspoon sugar
salt and pepper to taste	1 garlic clove, minced
3 tablespoons olive oil	¼ cup minced basil
¾ cup minced zucchini	¼ cup minced parsley
⅔ cup minced eggplant	2 tablespoons bread crumbs
½ cup minced onion	2 teaspoons red-wine vinegar
¼ cup minced green pepper	

Preheat the oven to 350°F.

Slice top quarter from the top of each tomato, and trim out the stem. Chop the top. Scoop out the insides to make a shell. Season the shells with ¼ teaspoon salt, and drain on paper towels.

In a skillet, cook the zucchini, eggplant, onion, green pepper, sugar, and chopped tomato until softened—about 5 minutes. Add the garlic, and cook 1 minute longer. Stir in the basil, parsley, bread crumbs, and vinegar. Correct the seasoning with salt and pepper.

Fill the tomato shells, and place in a baking dish. Bake 20 minutes, or until tomatoes are tender.

Serve hot or cold.

Yield: 6 servings

➤ Can be prepared ahead.

Farcis à la Niçoise (Stuffed Vegetables Niçoise Style)

These make a marvelous buffet display that allows guests to select their favorites. Use small vegetables, or if necessary cut them into smaller portions after baking.

3 tablespoons olive oil	½ cup chopped lean salt pork
3 small eggplants, halved	3 cups cooked rice
3 peppers, halved	1 cup minced parsley
6 onions, peeled	2 teaspoons thyme
3 small cucumbers, peeled	2 garlic cloves, crushed
3 small zucchini	salt and pepper to taste
6 small tomatoes	2 eggs
½ cup chopped onion	½ cup grated Parmesan or
2 cups chopped beef, lamb, or	Gruyère cheese
ham	½ cup fresh bread crumbs

Preheat the oven to 350°F.

Lightly oil the eggplants and peppers, and place on a baking sheet. Bake for 10 minutes. Raise the heat to 375°F.

Cut the eggplants in half, scoop out the pulp, and chop. Place pulp in a bowl. Cut the peppers in half, and remove and discard the seeds. Set aside.

In a large pot of salted water, blanch the onions, cucumbers, and zucchini for 15 minutes. Drain. Cut the onions in half, and scoop out all but 3 layers of skin. Chop the centers, and add to the eggplant pulp. Cut the zucchini and cucumbers in half, and scoop out and discard the seeds.

Cut a lid from the tomatoes, and scoop out the centers. Chop the centers, and add to the bowl.

In a skillet, heat 2 tablespoons of oil, and sauté the ½ cup of chopped onion until soft, but not brown. Add the vegetable pulp, beef, salt pork, rice, parsley, thyme, garlic, salt, and pepper, and cook, stirring, for 15 minutes or until the vegetables are soft. Remove from the heat, and stir in the eggs. Correct the seasoning with salt and pepper.

Stuff the vegetables with the meat mixture, and place in a baking pan. Sprinkle with the bread crumbs and Parmesan cheese. Bake for 1 hour, or until the vegetables are tender.

Yield: 6 servings

➤ Can be prepared ahead and reheated or served at room temperature.

Stuffed Vegetables Armenian Style

2 tomatoes	salt and pepper
2 red peppers	⅔ pound ground beef
2 green peppers	⅔ pound ground lamb
4 zucchini	¼ cup minced parsley
1 Savoy cabbage	½ teaspoon Cayenne pepper
1½ tablespoons olive oil	parsley stems
3 onions, minced	¼ cup lemon juice
½ cup rice	
3 tomatoes, peeled, seeded, and chopped	

Cut a slice from the top of each tomato, and scoop out the insides. Discard seeds and reserve pulp.

Cut a slice from the top of each pepper, and discard the seeds and ribs.

Halve the zucchini crosswise and, using a zucchini or apple corer, hollow out the center. Cut the cabbage leaves from the core, and trim any tough stems.

In a skillet, cook the rice in the oil with 1½ teaspoons salt until golden. Stir in the onion, and cook until it begins to soften. Add the chopped tomatoes and reserved pulp, and cook, stirring often until the juices are reduced—about 5 minutes. Cool.

Add the beef, lamb, 3 tablespoons parsley, Cayenne pepper, and 1½ teaspoons salt. Mix well.

Stuff the hollowed tomatoes, peppers, and zucchini, and put on lids. Wrap the remaining stuffing in the cabbage leaves, and roll up.

Line the bottom of a large casserole with the parsley stems and remaining cabbage. Add the lemon juice, 1 cup water, and about ¾ teaspoon salt.

Arrange the peppers cut side up in pot, with zucchini on their sides placed together. Arrange the tomatoes and cabbage on top of peppers, and put a small dish on top of the vegetables. Simmer over low heat until done—about 30 minutes.

Add the remaining tablespoon of minced parsley to the broth, and serve on the side.

Yield: 6 or more servings

➤ Can be prepared ahead and reheated.

Chartreuse of Vegetables

Centuries ago, the Carthusian monks, who created the liqueur Chartreuse, at La Grande Chartreuse Convent near Grenoble, also created this vegetarian entrée. Over the years, the term came to mean a molded dish with meat, game birds, or poultry as well. In more recent years, the dish has reverted to its vegetarian origins.

The first recipe requires some effort and patience to arrange the vegetables, but the second recipe is a quickly assembled copy, not as striking, but as good.

Chartreuse de Légumes *(Vegetable Chartreuse)*

butter	1 cup Brussels sprouts
1 cup thinly sliced zucchini	½ head cauliflower
2 cups carrot batons	1 cup cooked peas
2 cups string beans	4 cups mashed potatoes
1 cup thinly sliced summer squash	¼ cup clarified butter

Preheat the oven to 350°F. Using fresh butter, butter a container well. Use a 2 quart soufflé dish or round steel bowl.

In a kettle, bring salted water to a full rolling boil, and cook each vegetable, except the mashed potatoes, until tender-crisp. Remove with a slotted spoon, and refresh in cold water before adding the next vegetable. Place the vegetables in separate bowls, spooning and refreshing each in cold water.

Place a Brussels sprout in the center bottom of the bowl, surround with a ring of slightly overlapping slices of summer squash, and surround the squash with a ring of overlapping zucchini slices. Surround the zucchini with cauliflower florets, and then a row of peas at the outer edge of the soufflé dish. Arrange the carrot sticks alternating, upright, around the outer edge of the dish. Pack the mashed potatoes into the center.

In the steel bowl, you can set the carrots and beans at an angle, and can separate rows with strips of beans or carrots laid horizontally.

Pour the clarified butter over all. Bake until heated, about 30 minutes, if all the ingredients are cold. Let stand 5 minutes, then unmold onto a serving platter.

Yield: 6 servings

➤ Can be prepared the day before and baked just before serving.

NOTE: Use other colorful vegetables, if you prefer, and arrange them as pleasingly as you can. Arrange the vegetables in wedges from the bottom of the bowl up the sides, separating each section with strips of carrots, for instance. Cut the carrots into long diagonals, rather than batons.

Quick Chartreuse of Spring Vegetables

4 cups mashed potatoes
1 cup puréed carrots
1 cup cooked peas
1/4 cup minced scallion
1 teaspoon dried tarragon
salt and pepper to taste

1/3 cup melted butter
1 pound cooked asparagus cut
  into 3 inch sections
1/2 cooked cauliflower in florets
parsley sprigs (optional)

In a large saucepan, mix the potatoes, carrots, peas, scallion, tarragon, salt, and pepper, and heat, stirring until hot. Heat the butter in a large skillet, and heat the asparagus and cauliflower.

On a heated serving platter, make a mound of potatoes, shaping them into a tall cone. Starting at the top, arrange the asparagus against the side of the cone, and repeat with a second row if necessary. Arrange the cauliflower around the base like a ruff, and garnish with the parsley, if desired.

Yield: 6 servings

➤ The vegetables can be prepared ahead, but do not heat and assemble until ready to serve.

Terrines and Timbales

Vegetable terrines and timbales have been in the répertoire for many many years, and periodically resurface as something new. With the advent of the food processor, these preparations became a favorite of many chefs. The recipes here are just a few examples of the possibilities. You can make something as simple as one or two purées mixed with a little cream and some egg, and baked in individual timbales or custard cups, or more elaborate preparations with several purées and perhaps whole spears of asparagus, carrot strips or other vegetables blanched until tender to create loaves that look like a mosaic when cut.

Le Far de Poitou *(Vegetable Terrine From Poitou)*

A *far* is a type of pudding found in areas on the west coast of France, especially in Brittany, Poitou, and the Vendée. Some, the *Far Bréton*, are specifically desserts, while others are vegetable-flavored custards such as this.

1 pound cabbage, quartered and
   cooked until tender-crisp
1½ pounds leeks, blanched
   until tender
2 pounds stripped spinach,
   cooked until tender
½ pound lean slab bacon, ¼
   inch dice
1 cup minced onion

butter
salt and pepper to taste
pinch of nutmeg
4 eggs
1 cup heavy cream
Sauce Aurore (see below)
3 tablespoons grated Gruyère
   cheese

Preheat the oven to 375°F. Butter a 1½ quart loaf pan, line with waxed paper, and butter the paper.

Drain the cabbage, leek, and spinach, and chop coarsely. Press out the excess moisture.

In a saucepan of boiling water, blanch the bacon for 10 minutes. Drain, and render the fat in a large skillet until it is golden-brown. Remove with a slotted spoon, and drain on paper toweling. In the fat in the pan, sauté the onion until golden, adding a little butter, if needed. Add the vegetables, and cook, stirring, until the liquid evaporates. Season with salt, pepper, and nutmeg.

In a large bowl, beat the eggs and cream, add the sautéed bacon and vegetables, and mix well. Correct the seasoning with salt and pepper. Turn into the prepared pan, and cover with waxed paper.

Place in a water bath, and bake until a knife inserted in the center comes out clean—about 1 hour. Remove from the water bath, and let stand for 10 minutes.

Preheat the broiler. Unmold onto a heatproof platter, and blot up any liquid. Pour half the sauce over the top, sprinkle with the grated Gruyère, and brown under the broiler. Pass the remaining sauce separately.

Yield: 6 servings

➤ Can be prepared for baking several hours ahead.

Sauce Aurore

Originally, Sauce Aurore was a tomato-flavored béchamel sauce. This contemporary version has a lighter texture.

1 cup heavy cream   1 cup coulis of tomatoes
                                     (see Note)

In a saucepan, heat the cream and coulis until hot but not boiling.

Yield: 2 cups

➤ Can be prepared ahead and reheated.

NOTE: For the coulis, cook 2 cups of peeled, seeded and diced tomatoes in 1 tablespoon of butter over high heat until water evaporates.

Gourmandise de Legumes *(Vegetable Timbales)*

2 turnips, cooked until tender   1 egg
2 carrots, cooked until tender   2 egg yolks
1 bunch broccoli florets,   1 tablespoon lemon juice
   cooked until tender   pinch of grated nutmeg
1 pound mushrooms, minced   salt and pepper to taste
1 tablespoon butter   Hollandaise sauce
1 cup heavy cream

Preheat the oven to 350°F. Butter 6½ cup timbale molds or custard cups.

In a processor, purée the turnip, carrot, and broccoli separately, and measure 1 cup of each into separate bowls. Discard the remainder, or save for another use.

In a skillet, sauté the mushrooms in the butter until all the moisture has evaporated and the mushrooms are dry.

In a bowl, mix the cream, egg, egg yolks, lemon juice, and nutmeg. Add 2 tablespoons of the mixture to each purée, and correct the seasoning with salt and pepper.

Fill each mold ¼ full of turnip, then carrot, broccoli, and mushroom, smoothing each layer. Place the molds in a water bath, and cover with foil. Bake until a knife inserted in the center comes out clean— about 20 minutes. Unmold onto serving plates, and nappe with the sauce.

Yield: 6 servings

➤ Can be prepared for baking several hours ahead.

Terrine de Lègumes, Froide *(Cold Vegetable Terrine)*

½ pound green beans, cooked
   and refreshed
10 ounces shelled peas,
   cooked and refreshed
10 ounces small carrots,
   cooked and refreshed
10 ounce package frozen
   artichoke hearts, cooked
   and refreshed

1 pound skinless, boneless
   chicken breast
2 egg whites
1 cup heavy cream
salt and pepper to taste
12 large spinach leaves,
   steamed
uncooked tomato sauce (see
   page 24)

Preheat the oven to 350°F. Butter a 9 by 5 by 3 inch loaf pan, and line the inside of the pan with parchment or waxed paper. Butter the paper.

Prepare all of the vegetables, and set aside to cool, separately.

In a processor, purée the chicken breast and, with the motor running, add the egg whites. Stop, and scrape down the sides. With the machine running, slowly add the cream until fully incorporated. Correct the seasoning with salt and pepper.

Line the prepared mold with spinach leaves, reserving the remainder. Spread a thin layer of chicken over the spinach leaves, top with the beans in an even layer, spread on a layer of chicken, and cover with the peas. Add another layer of chicken, and arrange a layer of carrots, another layer of chicken, and then the artichokes. Finish with a layer of chicken. Cover with the remaining spinach leaves.

Cover with buttered parchment or waxed paper, and place in a water bath. Bake until a knife inserted in the center comes out clean— about 30 minutes. Cool, and chill overnight. Unmold onto a platter, and surround with the tomato sauce.

Yield: 6 servings

Finnish Vegetable Pie

1½ cups flour
2 teaspoons baking powder
1 teaspoon salt
½ cup butter
1 cup sour cream
7 tablespoons butter
2 cups shredded carrot
1 cup shredded parsnip
½ cup sliced scallion
2 garlic cloves, minced
5 cups shredded cabbage

2 cups shredded Gruyère cheese
1½ cups cooked rice
¼ cup minced parsley
¼ cup heavy cream
1 teaspoon salt
1 teaspoon dried oregano,
   crumbled
pinch of grated nutmeg
pinch of ground allspice
1 egg, beaten with 2
   tablespoons milk

Preheat the oven to 400°F. Butter a 10 inch pie plate.

In a bowl, mix the flour, baking powder, and salt. Cut in the butter until the mixture resembles coarse meal. Stir in the sour cream, and shape into a flat cake. Wrap in waxed paper, and refrigerate.

In a skillet, melt 3 tablespoons butter, and cook the carrot, parsnip, scallion, and garlic, stirring, for 5 minutes. Add the cabbage, and stir until wilted—about 12 minutes longer. Turn into a bowl, cool to room temperature, and blend in the cheese, rice, parsley, cream, salt, oregano, nutmeg, and allspice.

On a lightly floured surface, roll ¾ of the dough into a 12 inch circle. Fit into the pie plate, trim, and form an edge. Spoon in the filling, and dot with the remaining butter.

Roll remaining dough into an 11 inch rectangle, and cut into ½ inch strips. Brush the edge of the pie with the egg glaze, and arrange the strips as a lattice top. Brush the strips with the remaining glaze. Bake until browned—about 45 minutes.

Yield: 6 servings

➤ Can be prepared ahead and served at room temperature or cold.

Pasta alla Primavera
(Spaghetti with Spring Garden Vegetables)

This is a deceptively simple recipe. In order to be perfect, it takes great care and attention. Fortunately, it is worth the effort.

1 bunch broccoli florets, cooked and refreshed
2 small zucchini, cut into batons, cooked, and refreshed
4 asparagus spears, cut in thirds, cooked, and refreshed
1½ cups green beans, 1 inch lengths, cooked and refreshed
½ cup peas, cooked and refreshed
¾ cup pea pods, cooked and refreshed
1 tablespoon oil
2 cups thinly sliced mushrooms
salt and pepper to taste

1 teaspoon minced chili pepper
¼ cup minced parsley
6 tablespoons olive oil
1 teaspoon minced garlic
3 cups tomatoes, 1 inch cubes
¼ cup minced basil
1 pound spaghetti, or other pasta (see Note)
4 tablespoons butter
2 tablespoons chicken stock
½ cup heavy cream
⅔ cup grated Parmesan cheese
⅓ cup toasted pine nuts

Trim the broccoli into florets, cook in boiling salted water until just done, drain, and refresh under cold water. In a bowl, combine the broccoli, zucchini, asparagus, green beans, peas, and pea pods.

In a skillet, sauté the mushrooms in the oil until the liquid evaporates. Season with salt and pepper. Add to the bowl of vegetables. Add the chilies and parsley.

In a saucepan, heat 3 tablespoons of olive oil, and sauté ½ teaspoon garlic and the tomatoes over medium heat, stirring gently, in order not to break up the tomatoes. Stir in the basil, and set aside.

In a large skillet, heat the remaining 3 tablespoons of oil, ½ teaspoon of garlic, and the vegetable mixture. Cook, stirring, until heated. Cook the pasta until al dente, and drain well.

In a large casserole, melt the butter, and add the chicken stock, the cream, and the cheese, and cook, stirring, until smooth. Stir in the spaghetti, and toss to blend. Add half the vegetables and the liquid from the tomatoes, toss gently, and add the remaining vegetables. If the mixture seems dry, add another ¼ cup of cream. Add the pine nuts, toss again, and serve topped with the remaining tomato sauce.

Yield: 6 servings

➤ The various components of this recipe can be prepared ahead, but do not assemble until just before serving.

NOTE: The success of this recipe depends on the proper cooking of the vegetables. They must be cooked until tender, but not mushy. It is as bad to undercook as to overcook. Ideally, the vegetables and the pasta should be almost of the same consistency.

Although the original recipe calls for spaghetti, I prefer to make it with pastas that are of a similar size and shape to the vegetables so you can enjoy the flavors together. I suggest using small shells, cavatelli, rotini, and the like.

Salsa alla Giardiniera *(Garden Sauce)*

½ cup chopped parsley	3 tablespoons olive oil
2 garlic cloves, chopped	1 cup finely chopped cabbage
2 onions, chopped	4 tomatoes, peeled, seeded,
6 slices prosciutto, chopped	and diced
4 radishes, chopped	2 small zucchini, diced
2 carrots, chopped	1 cup chicken stock
1 leek, chopped	salt and pepper to taste
½ cup basil leaves	1 pound pasta
3 tablespoons butter	grated Parmesan cheese

In a processor, chop the parsley, garlic, onions, prosciutto, radishes, carrots, leek, and basil until finely minced to make a *soffrito*.

In a large kettle, heat the butter and oil, and sauté the *soffrito* until the vegetables are soft, but not brown. Stir in the cabbage, tomatoes, zucchini, and chicken stock. Season with salt and pepper, cover, and simmer for 20 minutes.

Cook the pasta in boiling salted water until done. Toss with the sauce, and serve with the grated cheese on the side.

Yield: 6 servings

➤ The sauce can be prepared ahead and frozen.

Composed Salads

Simple salads are a collection of greens with a dressing. Composed salads are a combination of vegetables, sometimes including greens, with a dressing. They are more of a complete meal than simple salads, and are usually served on buffets or even as the main course for a light meal.

Salade Macédoine (Mixed Vegetable Salad)

This is sometimes called Salade Russe, even though the original had the addition of mushrooms, truffles, lobster, tongue, ham, and capers among the other ingredients.

The success of the recipe is to have all of the ingredients the same size.

1 cup cooked green beans, ½ inch pieces	1½ cups cooked diced potatoes
1 cup cooked diced carrots	2 artichoke bottoms, diced
½ cup cooked diced turnips	½ cup mayonnaise, or to taste
½ cup cooked peas	salt and pepper to taste

In a bowl, mix the beans, carrots, turnips, peas, potatoes, and artichokes with enough mayonnaise to bind. Correct the seasoning with salt and pepper.

Yield: 6 servings

➤ Can be prepared the day before.

NOTE: Add 1 tablespoon of gelatin softened in 2 tablespoons of cold water, and melted over low heat, to 1 cup of mayonnaise if you wish to mold the salad.

The salad can be served in a bowl with lettuce leaves, packed into molds, or used as a bed for sliced chicken breasts, cold poached eggs, or cold fish.

Salmagundi Salad

3 cups ½ inch cubes of cooked beef, chicken, veal, or lamb	1 cup peas
1 cup ½ inch diced, cooked potatoes	1 cup ½ inch sections green beans
1 cup ½ inch diced, cooked carrots	1 cup vinaigrette with tarragon
1 cup ½ inch diced cooked eggplant	hearts of lettuce
	anchovy fillets

In a large bowl, mix the beef, potatoes, carrots, eggplant, peas, beans, and vinaigrette, and fold in the vinaigrette. Marinate for 1 hour. Drain, and mix with the mayonnaise to bind.

Serve on the hearts of lettuce, and garnish with the anchovies.

Yield: 6 servings

➤ Can be prepared the day before.

Salade Marguérite (Marguerite Salad)

2 cups ½ inch diced, cooked potatoes	1 cup asparagus tips
1 cup small florets of cauliflower	⅔ cup vinaigrette
	salt and pepper to taste
	mayonnaise
1 cup ½ inch diced green beans	3 hard-cooked eggs, separated

Put each vegetable in a separate bowl, and mix with the vinaigrette. Marinate for 1 hour. Correct the seasoning with salt and pepper.

In a bowl, mix all of the vegetables together, and arrange in a serving bowl. Spread a thin layer of mayonnaise over the surface.

Make a large daisy for the center and smaller daisies for the edges with strips of egg whites. Sieve the yolks, and sprinkle in the center of the flowers.

Yield: 6 servings

➤ Can be prepared several hours ahead.

Salade Carmen

2 cups diced raw cucumbers	½ teaspoon minced garlic
2 cups diced cooked carrots	1 teaspoon lemon juice
2 cups cooked green beans, ½ inch sections	¼ teaspoon sugar
	½ cup vegetable oil
2 cups diced cooked beets	¼ cup olive oil
2 cups diced, peeled, and seeded tomatoes	salt and pepper to taste
	2 cups chopped hard-cooked eggs
1 egg yolk	
2 tablespoons tarragon vinegar	4 small bunches watercress
2 tablespoons sour cream	

Arrange the cucumbers, carrots, beans, beets, and tomatoes in separate bowls.

In a processor, beat the egg yolk and vinegar and, with the machine running, add the sour cream, garlic, lemon juice, and sugar. Slowly add the vegetable oil and olive oil. Correct the seasoning with salt and pepper.

Fold a little dressing into each vegetable. Place the vegetables in pie-shaped sections on a large platter. Garnish the center with the chopped egg, and place the watercress around the outer edge.

Yield: 6 servings

➤ Do not prepare more than 2 hours ahead.

Brazilian Salad

3 cups ½ inch diced cooked
potatoes
1 bunch cooked broccoli, in
florets
1 cup ½ inch sections cooked
green beans
1 cup ½ inch diced cooked
zucchini
1 small cooked cauliflower in
florets

1 cup ½ inch diced cooked
carrots
1 cup cooked peas
1 cup ½ inch diced hearts of
palm
2 cups ½ inch dice celery
1 cup diced scallions
2 cups mayonnaise

In a bowl, mix the potatoes, broccoli, beans, zucchini, cauliflower, carrots, peas, hearts of palm, celery, and scallions with enough mayonnaise to bind. Arrange in a salad bowl, and pass mayonnaise on the side if desired.

Yield: 8 to 10 servings

➤ Can be prepared several hours ahead.

Insalata alla Carnica (Salad Carnica Style)

¾ pound thinly sliced
mushrooms
4 stalks celery, thinly sliced
1 small cauliflower, in florets
1 green pepper, thinly sliced
4 radishes, thinly sliced

1 small cucumber, peeled and
thinly sliced
½ cup olive oil
¼ cup red wine vinegar
1 tablespoon minced parsley
salt and pepper to taste

In a bowl, mix the mushrooms, celery, cauliflower, peppers, radishes, and cucumbers.

In a small bowl, whisk the olive oil, vinegar, parsley, salt, and pepper. Pour over the vegetables, and toss gently. Let marinate for at least 1 hour.

Yield: 6 servings

➤ Can be prepared the day before.

Salade Krisciunas

Many years ago, my friend and student, Valentina Krisciunas, gave me this recipe for a Lithuanian salad.

3 cups diced cooked beets
1 cup cooked peas
1 cup diced cooked carrots
½ cup minced onion

1 cup sour cream
½ teaspoon ground coriander
salt and pepper to taste

In a bowl, mix the beets, peas, carrots, and onions.

In a small bowl, mix the sour cream, coriander, salt, and pepper. Fold the sauce into the vegetables, and turn into a serving bowl.

Yield: 6 servings

➤ Can be prepared the day before.

Salade Niçoise *(Salad Nice Style)*

There are many versions of this salad, some of which have many more ingredients. In effect, it is an arrangement of several salads garnished with tuna and hard-cooked eggs.

2 cups diced cold cooked potatoes	3 tomatoes, quartered 3 hard-cooked eggs, quartered

2 cups cold cooked green
   beans in 1 inch pieces
	6 ounce can tuna, broken into
	   chunks

½ cup vinaigrette	½ cup pitted ripe olives
salt and pepper to taste	6 to 12 anchovies
clove of garlic	

In separate bowls, dress the potatoes and beans with the vinaigrette, and season with salt and pepper.

Rub the inside of a salad bowl with the garlic, and arrange the potatoes and beans in the bowl. Decorate with the tomatoes and eggs. Place the tuna in the center, and garnish with the olives and anchovies.

Yield: 6 servings

➤ Can be prepared several hours before serving.

NOTE: Green beans, potatoes, and tuna are the only requirements for this salad. Add some of the following for variety:

2 cups sliced green or red pepper, marinated in vinaigrette.

1 cup green peas, marinated in vinaigrette.

1 cup grated carrots, marinated in vinaigrette.

1 cup grated celery root, marinated in vinaigrette.

Garnish with ¼ pound slivered salami.

1-2 cups broccoli or cauliflower, marinated in vinaigrette.

½ pound thinly sliced, or tiny button, mushrooms, marinated in vinaigrette.

Arrange the salad on a bed of mixed greens such as romaine, radicchio, Belgian endive, or the like. I prefer heartier greens for this substantial salad, rather than the butter lettuces.

Carrot, Turnip, and Leek Salad with Mustard Mayonnaise

¾ pound carrots, julienne	1 tablespoon minced dill
¾ pound turnips, julienne	salt and pepper to taste
2 large leeks, julienne	mustard mayonnaise
⅔ cup minced parsley	lettuce
1 teaspoon lemon juice	

In a bowl, mix the carrots, turnips, leeks, parsley, lemon juice, dill, salt, and pepper, and enough mayonnaise to bind. Cover, and chill overnight.

When ready to serve, arrange the lettuce on a platter, and place the salad on top, leaving the liquid in the bottom of the bowl. If desired, add more mayonnaise to moisten.

Yield: 6 servings

➤ Can be prepared the day before.

Tunisian Salad

2 cups peeled, seeded, and chopped tomatoes	1 cup peeled, cored, and diced green apple
1 cup chopped onion	3 tablespoons wine vinegar
1 cup chopped green pepper	⅔ cup olive oil
1 cup chopped red pepper	¼ cup minced mint or 2
2 teaspoons minced jalapeño pepper	tablespoons dried mint, rubbed
	salt and pepper to taste

In a bowl, mix the tomatoes, onion, green pepper, red pepper, chili pepper, and apple.

In another bowl, whisk the vinegar, oil, mint, salt, and pepper together, and fold into the salad. Let marinate for at least 30 minutes.

Yield: 6 servings

➤ Can be prepared 2 or 3 hours before serving.

Czech Mushroom, Cauliflower, and Carrot Salad

1 tablespoon vinegar	1 head cauliflower, cut into florets, cooked, and drained
¼ teaspoon allspice	
1 tablespoon sugar	1½ cups diced carrots
1 small bay leaf	½ cup sour cream
½ pound mushrooms, thinly sliced	2 tablespoons minced parsley
	1 teaspoon Dijon mustard

In a saucepan, bring ½ cup water, vinegar, allspice, sugar, and bay leaf to a boil. Add the mushrooms, and simmer for 5 minutes. Drain, and put into a bowl with the cauliflower and carrots.

In another bowl, mix the sour cream, parsley, and mustard, and fold into the vegetables. Chill.

Yield: 6 servings

➤ Can be prepared the day before.

Glossary

No cook worth his salt would consider preparing a recipe without tasting. Taste is always subjective, and is necessarily open to adjustment. Professional chefs taste food, keeping in mind whether they like a lot or a little salt, for example, and seek a mid-range. They add enough to bring out the flavor of the dish without making it too salty. Some chefs know that their preference for certain flavors makes them heavy-handed when preparing for their own pleasure, and thus they avoid inflicting their likes on others. The fact that they like handfuls of garlic does not mean that they use a lot when cooking for others. You, too, should learn to think of your guests before yourself.

You should always use the care of the professional, and prepare food as it is supposed to be and not as it might suit your personal preferences. This does not mean that you cannot make changes and adjustments, but it does mean that you must consider the tastes of all of your guests. I *always* follow a new recipe exactly as it is written. Then I taste it for the final seasoning. I consider the salty, spicey, sweet, sour, and bitter qualities, and adjust the seasonings accordingly. If it is a new recipe, how do I know what it is supposed to taste like? I do not, but by making the recipe as written the first time I will learn, and then be free to make adjustments. The first time I correct it only for salt and pepper. There should be enough salt so the food is not dull and listless in flavor. On the other hand, food with too much salt is inedible. The dish must interest my palate. If I am satisfied, I can only assume my audience will be. (Yes, on occasion a new recipe has been less than expected—to the point where changing seasonings is not the answer. Bad recipes get discarded immediately.) The next time I prepare the recipe I may choose to adjust it according to my own likes and to the comments from guests. I might decide that changing an ingredient is in order, or that enhancing the sharpness with lemon or a little more cayenne pepper is appropriate. These adjustments are always made with the idea of improving and refining the basic recipe without losing its integrity. If I prepare *szechuan eggplant*, which is supposed to have a fiery sauce, I add all the pepper, knowing it is supposed to be that hot. If I do not want a dish with that much fire, then I choose another recipe, rather than remove the very soul of the recipe.

The hundreds of recipes in this book come from many countries, with ingredients from many cultures. What is a familiar food to one can seem exotic and strange to another. In many instances the right ingredient is critical to the outcome of a particular recipe; however, in many others it is not vital, and often substitutions are more than acceptable. Sometimes a substitution may be the basis of a new, and possibly even better, recipe. How do you know whether and what to substitute? If there is a known substitution, I have tried to give such information. If there is none listed, assume that the recipe needs the specific ingredient, and choose another recipe rather than try to make a substitution.

All cooks bring a certain understanding about ingredients to their cooking, based on their experience. Horseradish to one cook means only freshly grated, while another automatically reaches for a bottle of prepared. I have found that the difference between the two is a bit more zest with the fresh, but not enough of a difference to make an adjustment in the recipe itself. Therefore, when I write horseradish, the cook can decide whether to use fresh or prepared. Some reviewers have raised questions about ingredients that I consider common knowledge, and have helped me to realize that knowledge is common only within the same experience. Therefore, to help the readers I am providing a list of ingredients—some common, some not—to help you in the preparation of these recipes.

Because many of the recipes are of Asian origin, they may require a trip to an Asian market, but some of these are readily available and can be found in supermarkets across the country. Generally, these ingredients have a lengthy shelf life, so you do not have to be concerned about leftovers.

Anise, Star
The stars are a soft brown color, and have eight points and a strong anise flavor. They are sold dry in Asian groceries and in many supermarkets in the gourmet foods section. Keep in a tightly covered container indefinitely.

Baked Blond
Line an unbaked pie shell with foil and weight with pie weights, dried beans, or rice and bake at 400°F for about 10 minutes. The edges of the shell should stand on their own; if they are not firm enough, bake a few minutes longer. Remove the weights and foil and continue to bake the shell until pale blond.

Bamboo Shoots
Sold canned in either thin slices, or large chunks, in most supermarkets. Asian markets sometimes sell them fresh, but for these recipes the canned are suitable. For dim sum the size is not important, because

they are chopped before using in the recipes. They keep indefinitely unopened. Once opened, store in the refrigerator covered with water for 2 to 4 days. Leftovers can be frozen.

Beans, Black; Salted; Fermented
These are sold in small plastic bags in Asian markets. They can have any or all of the names listed above. If tightly covered, they keep indefinitely on a pantry shelf.

Bean Curd
Comes in blocks that usually weigh about 1 pound, or larger. Bean curd comes in soft, medium, and firm. For most of the recipes, the medium is suitable. If another density is required, it is listed in the recipe. Sold in most supermarkets, as well as in Asian markets and health food stores. The bean curd comes packed in water. Keep covered with fresh water, and change the water every other day. It will keep about 1 week.

Bean Paste, Sweet or Hot
Bean paste is sold hot (sometimes called szechuan), or sweet. It comes in small cans or jars. Once opened, store it in a covered container in the refrigerator. It will keep for 6 months or longer.

Bread Crumbs
In almost every instance, fresh bread crumbs are preferred to dried. When liquid is mixed into dried bread crumbs, they become sodden and heavy. Fresh bread crumbs become moist, but remain light. To make fresh bread crumbs, remove the crusts from day old bread and pulverize in a processor or blender. If you wish to make ahead and store, keep in the freezer; they will become moldy quickly in a refrigerator or on a pantry shelf.

Buerre Manie
In a bowl, mix 1 tablespoon of butter with 1½ tablespoons of flour to form a paste. Stir into simmering liquid in pea-sized pieces, until lightly thickened.

Butter
The recipes have been tested with unsalted butter. However, salted butter should not be a problem in any of the recipes, because you always add salt to taste. If a specific quantity of salt is mentioned, use about ⅓ less if you use salted butter, and then taste for seasoning.

Chestnuts, Peeling
To peel fresh chestnuts, cut a cross on the flat side of the chestnut and simmer in boiling water, or roast in a 400°F oven for 10 minutes. Cool and peel off the shell. This is a tedious task and sometimes it is easier to use dried chestnuts. These are found in Italian markets. Let soak in cold water overnight to reconstitute and then cook as directed in the recipe until tender.

Chestnuts, Water

These small, round roots are used as much for texture as for taste. They are sold fresh or canned. For these recipes the canned are suitable. Fresh water chestnuts are available in Asian markets, but the canned are found in most grocery stores. The fresh keep about 1 week, refrigerated. Peel before using.

Chili Oil, Hot Oil

This hot oil is usually sold in small bottles with a shaker top. You can prepare your own by heating 1 cup of peanut oil to 370°F and adding 6 tablespoons of Cayenne pepper. Sold in many supermarkets and all Asian markets. Keeps indefinitely on the pantry shelf.

Chili Paste with Garlic

This is a fiery hot-pepper relish. It is used sparingly in some Asian recipes, and should perhaps be served with a warning. It is found in Asian markets and some specialty markets. Once opened, it can be kept in the pantry in a tightly sealed container indefinitely.

Cloud Ears

Asian cookery uses many forms of fungus in cooking. Cloud ears are one form. They are also called wood ears, silver ears, dried fungus, tree fungus, and brown fungus. They are sold dried, in plastic bags. They vary greatly, from tiny bits to about 1½ inches. To use them, they are soaked in hot water until soft—about 30 minutes. They increase dramatically after soaking. A teaspoon of dried tiny cloud ears can expand to ¼ cup. They are sold in Asian markets, and there is no substitute. They keep indefinitely.

Coconut

Some of the recipes call for grated coconut. Of course you can purchase fresh coconuts and grate the meat yourself, but such labor is not necessary. Most supermarkets now sell grated, unsweetened coconut. It is important to use unsweetened coconut. Sweetened coconut would change the dish drastically. The grated coconut will keep for several months in a tightly sealed container, and can be frozen.

Coconut Milk

Coconut milk or cream is sold in some supermarkets. Again, be sure to purchase it unsweetened. The cans keep indefinitely. If opened they will keep in the refrigerator for several days, and can be frozen.

Corn

A number of recipes call for corn kernels. I have not found a major difference in flavor using fresh corn, canned corn, or frozen corn. Generally, I use an unsalted canned corn packed in a small amount of water. If fresh is preferred, I have tried to indicate that in the recipe.

Creole Mustard

Some fancy food stores outside of Louisiana carry this flavorful and spicy product. If you cannot locate a brand, create an acceptable substitute by adding 1 tablespoon of Creole Seasoning (see below) to each cup of Dijon or brown mustard.

Creole Seasoning

There are commercial preparations for creole seasoning available in many markets, however, the seasoning is not stocked in every region.

Creole Seasoning Mix

To prepare your own:

¼ cup salt	¾ teaspoon granulated onion
1 tablespoon granulated garlic	¼ teaspoon cayenne pepper
1 tablespoon pepper	¼ teaspoon dried thyme
1 tablespoon paprika	¼ teaspoon dried oregano

In a small container, mix the ingredients.

➤ The mixture will keep 6 months in a tightly sealed container.

Curry Paste

There is a difference between curry powder and curry paste. The paste generally has a more intense, but not necessarily hotter, taste than the powder. The paste is usually sold in small cans, but sometimes in small foil packages. The packages are more convenient to use. They can be stored in the pantry indefinitely. Once a can has been opened, the unused portion should be put into a clean, small jar, and kept tightly sealed in the refrigerator. It will last about 6 months. Curry powder can be used as a substitute.

Curry Powder

Curry powders are found in most supermarkets. They vary in flavor, intensity, and heat from packager to packager. Buy the smallest container possible of different brands to select the one that pleases you most, or have several on hand to vary the flavor of your curried dishes. It is wisest to buy curry in small quantities and replace it often because, like most dried spices, it loses its flavor fairly quickly. Plan to replace it every 6 months. Keep in a tightly covered container in a cool, dark place.

Eggs

The recipes have been tested with large eggs. However, on occasion I have prepared the recipes with medium or extra large eggs, and not found a major difference. In those few instances where the size of the egg is critical, I have specified the size.

Five-Spice Powder

A mixture of peppercorns, star anise, fennel seeds, cinnamon, and powdered cloves. Some brands list more than 5 spices, and label it as Spice Powder. I have not found a major difference in flavor. It is available in small packages in Asian markets. Once opened, store it in a tightly covered container. It loses its potency within 6 months. Allspice can be used as a poor substitute.

Garam Masala

A blend of seasonings ground together and used in Indian dishes. Available in some Indian markets. Keeps indefinitely in a tightly closed container.

Garam Masala

1 tablespoon whole cumin seeds	½ cinnamon stock
1 tablespoon whole coriander seeds	1½ tablespoons black peppercorns
1 tablespoon whole cardamom seeds	½ teaspoon whole cloves

In a non-stick skillet, toast the spices until fragrant and lightly colored—about 3 minutes. Cool, and grind in a mortar and pestle or a spice mill. Transfer to a jar with an airtight lid. Store for up to 3 months.

Yield: ¼ cup

Gingeroot

Fresh gingeroot is mandatory for most Chinese and many of the Asian recipes. To use, pare off the skin, and mince or slice. If fresh is not available, well-rinsed preserved ginger can be used. It is available in most supermarkets, as well as Asian markets. It keeps several weeks in pantry or refrigerator. The ginger can be kept using other methods. For example, peel it, put it into a container, and cover it with sherry. The sherry can be used as the wine in many Asian dishes. Or, freeze the ginger, and grate off the amount needed when ready to use. One other method is to put the ginger into a container of damp sand. The theory is that it will continue to sprout new growths.

Herbs

Fresh herbs are used in the recipes unless dried are specified. You can almost always substitute one for another using the following ratio: use 3 times as much fresh as dried. Certain herbs, however, change their flavor completely when dried, and have little or no relation to the fresh herb.

Basil
Fresh basil is almost as popular as parsley. Its distinct flavor makes it vastly preferable to dried. It is available in many areas year round. It is easily grown; the least efficient gardener—given a sunny window and a little care—will produce a thriving plant.

Coriander
Also called Chinese parsley, or *cilantro* in Spanish, this herb has become a true favorite in the last several years. The strong musky flavor of the fresh is irreplaceable. Some writers have suggested flat leaf parsley as a substitute and, although they look similar, there is no relation in regard to the flavor. Fortunately, with popularity there has come availability, and many markets carry it as a common food item. The dried herb is ground root or seed and, although the aroma is similar, the flavor is not the same. Unless dried is specified, fresh is necessary.

Hoisin Sauce
A thick, dark-brown paste with a pungent, sweet flavor, made from mashed soy beans, salt, sugar, garlic, and sometimes pumpkin. It is used as a marinade for roasted meats, and as a dipping sauce, alone or combined with other ingredients. Sold in cans or jars. It is available in the specialty foods section of some supermarkets and Asian markets. It keeps indefinitely in a tightly covered container.

Ketjap Manis *(Indonesian Sweet Soy Sauce)*
The name of American ketchup originates from the Malaysian ketjap. The original version was made from fermented fish brine. Ketjap manis is an Indonesian sweet soy sauce with spices. It is used in sauces. Keeps indefinitely in the pantry, and can be found in some specialty and Asian markets.

Mascarpone
This is is the Italian version of cream cheese, and has an extraordinary richness and flavor. It is really more like very thick, heavy cream than cheese. It is found in cheese shops and other specialty stores. Once opened, it will keep a week or longer in the refrigerator. Check the expiration date. If it is not available, cream cheese, softened and then thinned with heavy cream until almost thin enough to pour, is an acceptable substitute.

Mushrooms, Dried
The recipes that call for dried mushrooms are usually of Asian origin, and the various Asian mushrooms are suitable. There are European

and American dried mushrooms, but they are not suitable substitutes for their Asian kin.

Mushrooms, Asian Dried
These vary in quality and cost. The best are thick and bulbous, and have relatively tightly shaped caps with a striated surface. The mushrooms can be very costly, but it is not necessary to buy the most expensive ones. Soak the mushrooms in warm water for 10 to 30 minutes until softened. Cut out the mushroom stems and discard. You may use the strained soaking water to flavor soups, or in place of the liquid in some recipes. Available in many supermarkets and all Asian markets. Keep indefinitely in a cool dry place.

Some of the recipes call for other forms of fungus, such as cloud ears (see above).

Mustard, Chinese
There is no mystery to Chinese mustard. It is dry mustard powder sold in every market, mixed with a liquid. Use cold beer, white wine, or water to mix with the mustard powder. Let stand ten minutes. Loses strength within 2–3 hours.

Nam Pla *(Thai Fish Sauce)*
A fish sauce made from salted fish and used in lieu of salt in many Thai dishes. It keeps indefinitely in the pantry. It is available in some specialty food shops as well as Asian Groceries. You can substitute Nuoc Mam from Vietnam.

Nuoc Mam *(Vietnamese Fish Sauce)*
This is the equivalent of salt to Western cooking and soy sauce to Japanese or Chinese cookery. It is prepared from fresh anchovies and salt layered in wooden barrels and allowed to ferment for several months. The fish sauce of Vietnam is preferred and Philippine or Chinese fish sauce is not an acceptable substitute. Nam Pla from Thailand may be substituted. Keeps indefinitely in the pantry.

Noodles
Although there is some question about the Asians having invented noodles, there is none about the extraordinary variety they use in their cuisine. They make noodles made from bean threads, rice, or flour. The particular recipes specify which noodles to buy. Follow the recipes to learn how to use these, and then feel free to interchange the noodles for different effects.

Egg noodles, won ton wrappers, egg roll wrappers, and some rice noodles are sold in many supermarkets. Asian markets carry these noodle products. The fresh noodles keep several days in the refrigerator. Dried noodles keep indefinitely in the pantry. The Japanese also use noodles. The forms found here are a dried, flat, long, buckwheat noodle called soba; a wheat and water noodle (that looks something like linguine) called udon (these can be interchanged with soba). They are sold in Asian markets.

Oyster Sauce

This rich-tasting, thick, brown sauce is used as a flavoring. It is sold in bottles, and is found in many supermarkets and Asian markets. Keeps indefinitely in the refrigerator.

Olive Oil

In recent years the prevalence of information on various olive oils has turned an everyday commodity into a fad of cult status. In the past the good cook bought a good-quality olive oil for general use and an extra virgin oil for salads. Today, if one believes the hype, you need not only have several different brands, but also you must spend a fortune on each one. That, of course, is not true. The well-stocked kitchen needs a good all-purpose pure olive oil for cooking, and an extra virgin olive oil for drizzling over salads or marinated vegetables. Select the oils that suit you. Some oils are so fruity that they overpower the very foods they are supposed to enhance.

Sambal Oelek

A hot pepper relish from Indonesia. This is a fiery hot sauce that should be used sparingly. It is only fair to warn guests when serving this, unless they know about its potency. It is sold in jars in Asian markets, and keeps indefinitely on the shelf. Chili paste with garlic is an acceptable substitute.

Sesame Oil

Asian and Middle-Eastern countries both have sesame oils, but they are very different. The Asian version extracted from roasted sesame seeds has a full-flavored nutty aroma and taste.

The Middle-Eastern, and the cold-pressed sesame oil found in health food stores, are bland cooking oils that can be substituted for any other bland oil. They are not recommended for use in any of the recipes in this book.

The Asian sesame oil is an exciting ingredient in many of the recipes in this book. It is usually added toward the end of the recipe, and not used as a cooking oil. It smokes at a low temperature, which can result in an overpowering taste. It can be found in the foreign foods section of many supermarkets and, of course, in most Asian markets. There is no major difference in the oil from the different Asian countries and, unlike the case with soy sauce, Japanese sesame oil is suitable for Chinese recipes and vice versa. In a cool, dark place it will keep indefinitely.

Sesame Paste *(Middle Eastern and Asian)*
Again there is a major difference between sesame paste from the Middle East, called tahini, and sesame paste from Asia. The Asian variety is made from toasted sesame seeds, and is a dark-golden color similar to peanut butter. It has a fragrant, toasted-nut aroma and flavor. The Middle Eastern tahini is relatively bland. It is important not to substitute one for the other. In this book, Middle Eastern sesame paste is referred to as Tahini, and Asian sesame paste as sesame paste. Both versions keep indefinitely, stored in the refrigerator in tightly covered containers. Be sure to mix the paste and oil together before using.

Soy Sauce
There is an enormous difference in flavor from one type of soy sauce to another. The recipes in this book call for Chinese light, or thin, soy sauce unless specified differently. Some of the recipes use dark, or thick, soy. Domestic soy sauce has a completely different flavor, and is not suitable. So-called "Lite Soy" or low-sodium soy is not recommended. If there is a salt problem, it is better to select another recipe. Japanese soy sauce has a very different flavor from Chinese. Tamari is an aged Japanese soy sauce. Neither is recommended for these recipes unless specified. Soy sauces of different types are found in all supermarkets. Do take the trouble to get the right soy for the dish. Soy sauce keeps indefinitely in the pantry.

Szechuan Peppercorns
On occasion these are also called anise pepper. They have a reddish-brown color, and are more pungent than black pepper. Often they are toasted in a dry skillet until fragrant before they are ground into a powder. Use a mortar and pestle or a spice grinder to grind them. They will keep in a tightly sealed container for 6 months or longer. The whole peppercorns are available in many gourmet shops, as well as Asian groceries.

Tahini
This is a bland sesame paste made from untoasted sesame seeds. It is used commonly in Middle-Eastern cookery. It is different from the paste used in Asian Cookery (see above). Store in the pantry until opened. Stir well before using, and store in the refrigerator after opening. Keeps indefinitely.

Tapioca Flour

Also called Tapioca Starch. Made from Cassava-like regular tapioca. It is used in some dim sum. It is sold in small bags in Asian markets, and will keep indefinitely on the pantry shelf. There is no substitute for Tapioca flour. However, because it is usually made into a dim sum wrapper, you can substitute won ton wrappers.

Vegetable Oil

Vegetable oils can be made from a variety of products—cottonseed oil, rape seed oil, soybean oil, peanut oil, or corn oil—for example. Select any one that has a light, almost non-existent flavor. I find it most convenient and economical to buy the oil in gallon containers, and then transfer it to smaller containers for everyday use. This provides a steady supply and the cost savings is considerable. The oil will last at least 6 months in a cool dry place.

Vinegar

There are literally dozens of different vinegars on the market. You may often change a recipe, or enhance it, by selecting a flavored vinegar, but make sure that it is suitable for the recipe.

Red-Wine Vinegar

Also called red vinegar. You may use any red-wine vinegar. Balsamic or sherry vinegar can also be substituted in most instances.

White Vinegar

Refers to distilled white vinegar.

White-Wine Vinegar

Refers to vinegar made with white wine. Many white-wine vinegars are flavored with herbs. For most recipes they should be unflavored, unless specified to the contrary.

Rice Vinegar

Is used in Asian recipes for sushi rice and for many dipping sauces. It is available in Asian markets, and many supermarkets. You can substitute distilled white vinegar.

Wheat Starch

A wheat flour with the gluten removed. It is used in dim sum pastry. There is no substitute; if it is not available use a different wrapper for the dim sum. Available in Asian markets, and keeps indefinitely.

Wine

Some years ago, Craig Claiborne stated two rules for using wine in recipes. They are as valid today as when he wrote them originally. The first rule says, if it does not say sweet use dry. Dry white, dry red—and you have covered most of your cooking bases. The second rule says, if you will not drink it, do not use it. In other words—if it is not good enough to drink, it is not suitable in cooking, especially in any recipe where it might be reduced and the flavor strengthened.

Index